16th Conference of the Association for Machine Translation in the Americas (AMTA 2024)

Volume 1: Research Papers

Chicago, Illinois, USA
28 September – 2 October 2024

Editors:

Akiko Eriguchi
Rebecca Knowles
Shivali Goel
Jay Marciano

ISBN: 979-8-3313-0482-9

Printed from e-media with permission by:

Curran Associates, Inc.
57 Morehouse Lane
Red Hook, NY 12571

Some format issues inherent in the e-media version may also appear in this print version.

Association for Computational Linguistics
209 N. Eighth Street
Stroudsburg, Pennsylvania 18360

Phone: 1-570-476-8006
Fax: 1-570-476-0860

acl@aclweb.org

Additional copies of this publication are available from:

Curran Associates, Inc.
57 Morehouse Lane
Red Hook, NY 12571 USA
Phone: 845-758-0400
Fax: 845-758-2633
Email: curran@proceedings.com
Web: www.proceedings.com

AMTA 2024 CHICAGO

The 16th Conference of the Association for Machine Translation in the Americas

www.conference.amtaweb.org

Volume 1: Research Papers

Editors:
Akiko Eriguchi and Rebecca Knowles (Research Track Co-chairs); Shivali Goel (Publications Chair); Jay Marciano (General Conference Chair)

Welcome to the 16th conference of the Association for Machine Translation in the Americas – AMTA 2024!

Dear MT & AI Colleagues and Friends,

For this year's conference of the Association for Machine Translation in the Americas – AMTA 2024 – we come together in person in metropolitan Chicago, at the Renaissance Schaumburg Convention Center Hotel, and online in our virtual conference application.

2024 marks the 30th anniversary of the first AMTA conference, held in Columbia, Maryland, in October 1994, and 70 years since the first public demonstration of machine translation in New York City, a project involving IBM and Georgetown University.

By today's standards, the demonstration was stunningly limited: a mere 250 words translated from Russian to English in about 60 mostly short and highly repetitive sentences. Each sentence had to be typed into a device that created a machine-readable punch card. Each card was then fed individually into a room-sized IBM 701 mainframe, hardware that cost $500,000 at the time (the equivalent of $5.8 million today!).

Infamously, the experimenters predicted that usable Machine Translation in "important functional areas of several languages" could be "an accomplished fact" within five or maybe even only three years, a wildly inaccurate underestimation of the complexity of the challenge.

But to their credit, the experimenters also recognized that they had taken but baby steps, comparing their accomplishment to the Wright brothers' 1903 flight at Kitty Hawk, a single-passenger, 12-second, 36-meter hop in a heavier-than-air vehicle along the beach in North Carolina that hardly hinted at the fact that safe transoceanic passenger flights would be commercially available just 36 years later, nor that in less than the 70 years that have passed since the first demonstration of MT, mankind would fly to the moon, land on it, walk around, and fly back to Earth.[1]

It is mind-boggling to consider how much has changed in our field since these events and yet how much the fundamental need for facilitating multilingual communication with technology remains. Here we are now, not even one full human lifetime from the 1954 demonstration and not quite two years since the general availability of generative AI tools, and the very words "machine translation" sound almost quaint in the tidal wave of news about large language models. But let's not forget that transformer models, the cornerstone of the boom in generative AI, are a direct result of advances in machine translation.

So, this is an appropriate time for all of us who work on or with MT or generative AI to recognize the giants on whose shoulders we stand and to ask ourselves what more needs to be done before we have reached the NLP equivalent of the moon.

In the spirit of honoring those who have contributed to the development of MT before us, it is with great sadness and lasting gratitude that I report the passing of Muriel Vasconcellos, founding president of AMTA (1991-1996), president of IAMT (1997-1999), and IAMT Award of Honor recipient

---

[1]Machine translation: from real users to research: 16th Conference of the Association for Machine Translation in the Americas, AMTA 2004, Washington, DC, September 28 – October 2, 2004; ed. Robert E.Frederking and Kathryn B.Taylor (Berlin: Springer Verlag, 2004); pp. 102-114

(1999), on September 14, 2024 at the age of 91, a few short months after she wrote her contribution to this volume. Computational linguist and ATA-certified English to Portuguese translator, Muriel earned a PhD in linguistics from Georgetown University and was centrally instrumental in the introduction of machine translation at the Pan American Health Organization/World Health Organization. Her passion for facilitating open and collegial communication among MT researchers, developers, and users is still and will remain a defining characteristic of AMTA.

We are pleased once again with the number and quality of submissions to our conference, which reflect great progress in MT, not only in the scope of supporting ever more languages and in improving and assessing output quality, but also in the use of large language models either as translation systems in and of themselves or, as you will see in many of the papers and presentations this year, in augmenting machine translation systems with additional processing via LLMs.

A unique aspect of AMTA conferences is that they bring together users and practitioners from across the MT spectrum of academia, industry, and government so that R&D personnel can learn from those who are using the technology and vice versa. And this year we are doubling down on this aspect by organizing sessions not by whether works come from researchers, users and providers, or government representatives, but instead by topic area so that our various constituents have even more opportunity to see how much their interests intersect and enjoy more direct contact.

Another novelty this year is the first ever AMTA Best Thesis Award, a tradition that we borrowed from our sister organization EAMT. We congratulate its first winner, Dr. Eleftheria Briakou, for her thesis "Detecting Fine-Grained Semantic Divergences to Improve Translation Understanding Across Languages," an abstract of which is included in this volume.

As with all our conferences, AMTA 2024 would simply not have been possible without the selfless work of so many people on the AMTA board and organizing committee, all of whom are volunteers. I express my heartfelt thanks, respect, and admiration to each of them. They include:

Janice Campbell, AMTA Secretary, Local Arrangements

Alex Yanishevsky, AMTA Vice President, Conference Online Platform

David Bishop, AMTA Treasurer

Akiko Eriguchi, Peer-review Track and Best Thesis Award organizer

Rebecca Knowles, Peer-review Track and Best Thesis Award organizer

Cecilia Yalangozian, Workshops and Tutorials, Presentations Track

Georg Kirchner, Workshops and Tutorials

Konstantin Savenkov, Presentations Track

Marianna Martindale, Presentations Track

Kelly Ko, Webmaster

Derick Fajardo, Communications and Marketing

Lara Daly, Sponsorships

Shivali Goel, Publications

Steve Richardson, AMTA Councilor

Alon Lavie, AMTA Consultant

Finally, I express my gratitude to our sponsors, whose support has helped us to mitigate the added cost of the hybrid format. Our Leader Level sponsors include Systran by ChapsVision and Apptek. Our Exhibitor-level sponsors include Star and Intento, and our Media and Marketing sponsor is Slator. Many of these participating companies will provide demonstrations of their systems and software during our Technology Exhibition sessions, and we hope that our attendees will take advantage of this opportunity to see the latest commercial offerings and advancements in the world of MT.

Again, welcome to AMTA 2024! I look forward to seeing many of you in person in Chicago and to interacting with many others online.

Jay Marciano

AMTA President and AMTA 2024 General Conference Chair

Statements on 30 Years of AMTA Conferences by Former Presidents of the Association for Machine Translation in the Americas

Former presidents of AMTA were invited to take part in a panel discussion at AMTA 2024 to mark the 30th anniversary of the first AMTA conference, held in Columbia, Maryland in early October 1994. Those who were not able to make it in person to the event were invited to submit a written statement about their presidency.

The first contribution, by the inaugural president of AMTA, Dr. Muriel Vasconcellos, provides an account of the founding of the Association. The other pieces (by our second president, Dr. Eduard Hovy, our third president, Dr. Elliott Macklovitch, and our fifth and seventh president, Dr. Mike Dillinger), recount major events in MT research and development during their terms of office and offer their current view of the future of machine translation.

The Founding of AMTA

By Muriel Vasconcellos, AMTA President (1991–1996)

The first conversation on the founding a machine translation association took place at a dinner table. If memory serves me, it was in Hakone, Japan, in 1989, at a meeting convened by Dr. Makoto Nagao. Dr. Nagao had called the meeting of about 400 Japanese participants and had invited a few international speakers. At the table were Dr. Nagao, a Japanese computer scientist; Veronica Lawson, a patent translator from London, England; and myself, then head of the machine translation project at the Pan American Health Organization.

When the topic of a machine translation association came up, Veronica said she had been thinking of such an association for a long time. As we continued talking, we pointed out the differences between projects in Asia, Europe, and the Americas (Canada and the United States), with different emphasis on research, commercial development, and operational applications. At that time, Japan had done research and had initiated a few projects. Europe was mainly into research. In the Americas, especially in Canada and the United States, academic research was overshadowed by commercial and governmental operations. The IBM MARK II Russian-English System, installed at the Wright-Patterson Air Force Base in 1964, has been said to be the first production application of MT. Later it was replaced by SYSTRAN. MÉTEO, inaugurated in 1977, was designed for broadcasting weather reports. LOGOS, founded in 1970, was also a player, but did not then have a significant commercial imprint.

Taking into account the different characteristics as well as the physical distances between these geographical areas, we proposed three regions: Asia-Pacific, Europe, and the Americas. That discussion led to the formation of a local MT association in each of them.

The Asia-Pacific Association for Machine Translation (AAMT) got started under the presidency of Dr. Nagao. The preparations for founding a European association were led by Margaret (Maghi) King.

Steps were also being taken to found the Association for Machine Translation in the Americas (AMTA). Its organizing meeting took place in 1992 at an international machine translation meeting in Washington, D.C., at the Mayflower Hotel. To my surprise, I was elected president. Roberta Merchant was elected treasurer. Without her ongoing support, our history might have been much different.

AMTA was incorporated under the laws of the District of Columbia in 1994. I quickly realized that the association would exist only on paper unless I organized an encounter. Our first general meeting with speakers took place on October 5-8, 1994, in Columbia, Maryland.

I am so pleased that AMTA is alive and doing well thirty years later!

Some thoughts from the Presidency of 1996–2000

By Eduard Hovy, AMTA President (1996–2000)

I was the second President, having the honor of following Muriel, and it was during this time that the Statistics Wars in MT really hit home in MT. Up to the early 1990s MT technology had been strictly 'symbolic', meaning not using machine learning. The introduction of Statistical MT (SMT) by the IBM Candide team around 1989 and its rapid adoption in the research MT community was viewed initially with bemusement, then puzzlement, and then alarm by the commercial MT community. Starting in the mid-1990s, though, it was clear that SMT was not just a research fad but was here to stay, and when Franz Och left my group at ISI to head the Google MT team all the MT companies started making plans for how to respond. So, the second half of the 1990s saw a significant change in the nature of the research papers of the conference, followed by a slower change in the style of the commercial demos. Little changed for the third leg of the AMTA tripod, the translators: to them, it was not clear whether the still-not-perfect SMT results were more useful than the highly optimized commercial MT outputs, though the general cross-domain promise of SMT was attractive. The famous Great Debate in Montreal in 1992 with reversed affinities, in which Graeme Hirst and Ron Kaplan argued *for* SMT while Ken Church and Geoffrey Sampson argued *against*, lives on in the memories of those who were present.

After its creation and first conference in 1994, AMTA continued to grow steadily, averaging around 120 members by 2000 (this no doubt seems small by today's standards!). The 1998 conference near Philadelphia and 1999 Summit in Singapore were high points, as were the conferences in Santiago de Compostela and in New Orleans a few years later.

It is great to see now that AMTA continues to flourish. I would have liked to be present! I send everyone greetings.

The challenges faced during my presidency

By Elliott Macklovitch, AMTA President (2000–2004)

MT can be used for various purposes. Our concern in Canada and at the RALI (my former research group) has predominantly been with high-quality translation fit for publication or widespread dissemination, as opposed to information gathering or gisting, where lower quality may be acceptable.

Although the transition from rule-based MT to statistical MT was well underway during the period of my presidency, the broad MT user base at the time was very modest. Moses, an open-source toolkit for developing SMT systems, was available during those years, but it was far too complicated for the great majority of potential end users and largely remained a research vehicle. Moreover, the quality of the translations produced by the SMT systems that were developed back then left much to be desired (particularly the fluency) and demanded extensive post-editing – work that most translators did not relish. This is why our group at the RALI invested in the development of various translators' aids, alongside parallel efforts to advance the state of the art in fully automatic MT.

What I thought the future of MT would be back then

Based on the technology that was available at the time, and judging from the modest gains that researchers were able to achieve – half a BLEU point here, half a point there – I was not overly optimistic that MT would ever be able to achieve widespread acceptance or use.

The advent of neural MT some ten years later and the impressive improvement in translation quality that it ushered in caught me very much by surprise.

What I now think the future of MT will be

Allow me to reformulate the question: "Has the problem of MT finally been solved?" To which I would answer: From a strictly scientific point of view, yes it has, to a very large extent.

Now if I may qualify: The problem posed by translation is not like a problem in mathematics, where there is only one correct solution. In translation, most source sentences admit of several acceptable target equivalents. In a large majority of cases, the output produced by today's NMT and GenAI systems does fall within the set of acceptable target-language equivalents. This is not to say that these machine-generated translations cannot be improved by human posteditors; very often, they can. But the age-old problem of automatically generating a grammatically correct target-language equivalent that conveys the essential meaning of the source-language sentence has by and large been resolved – although this is only true for the handful of "major languages" for which a training corpus of sufficient size and quality is available.

In the not-so-distant future, GenAI-based machine translation will become increasingly dominant, largely displacing dedicated NMT systems. And machine translation will increasingly infiltrate our day-to-day lives, to the point that people will no longer be aware of this astounding technological accomplishment.

MT: Then, Now, and Next

By Mike Dillinger, AMTA President (2006–2008, 2012–2014)

My first term as AMTA President, from 2006 to 2008, culminated in the conference at a small hotel a couple of blocks from the beach in Waikiki. The location turned out to be a good choice: although a few people moaned that they wouldn't be able to get funding for what was obviously a free vacation, we ended up attracting far more people than usual from Asia and Europe – about doubling attendance over the mean of previous meetings. So, we actually finished in the black.

Our key goal at the time was to showcase applications of MT as a strategy to increase interest and, hopefully, membership. As a result, the program jumped from around 10% presentations on applications in industry and government to more than 50%, which is why we titled the proceedings *MT at Work*. I remember spending quite a bit of time coaching authors of the User presentations to provide more details, and particularly numbers, to communicate better with the Researchers. That usually led to more informative and more interesting presentations across the board.

In fact, 2008 was the first time we had similarly sized tracks for MT Users (partnering with LISA and the DIA) and MT Researchers. Users were pleased to see so many more use cases, and many researchers found themselves jumping over to hear more about the challenges that applications brought to the fore. And we had a solid Student Research Workshop, as well, so there was a lot going on. We also took the time to build bridges with the American Translators' Association leadership, starting a collaboration that lasted for several years – despite a few unnecessarily adversarial presentations in the beginning from their side and included lots of very well attended presentations from our side at their conferences.

The core value that AMTA brought to the table at the time was diversity: diversity of applications, diversity of perspectives, and diversity of approaches. Even the Research track was by no means a series of reports on tweaks to the same approach: phrase-based statistical MT predominated but there were hybrid approaches, work on building targeted corpora or lexica, and of course on evaluation. The Board of Directors at the time recognized this diversity as the key differentiator of AMTA and we worked very hard to cultivate it.

My take is that the overall mood was very much one of enriching statistical approaches with qualitative linguistic information rather than fighting about which of the two approaches one *had* to choose. People were still scratching their heads about how to bring semantics in at scale, and of course there was no inkling of the maelstrom that transformer-based MT would end up creating. If there were heated, drag-down, knock-out arguments in the corridors, I didn't hear about them. I did hear, though, about people sneaking off to surf and swim between sessions. The venue, I think, contributed significantly to a mellower, much more collaborative meeting.

After Laurie Gerber, who also served as AMTA president from 2004 to 2006, sweet-talked me into joining the AMTA Board of Directors so many years ago, I ended up spending more than ten years in one or another leadership role at AMTA, including as President again from 2012 to 2014 for the Vancouver conference. I was lucky enough to study or work directly with many of the early pioneers of MT – from Paul Garvin and David Hays to Bud Scott and Hiroshi Uchida – and through AMTA, I got to collaborate with the next generations, as well. What a privilege it's been to participate in the field for so long!

As for where MT is headed, I'm totally biased: I've always thought that our job isn't done until we can incorporate meaning and knowledge at scale. Data-driven MT continues to yield very powerful, highly scalable tools like LLMs and to open new investments and applications. But there's still a lot left for us to do to serve a wider range of users and use cases well. Next-gen Knowledge-driven MT will likely leverage knowledge graphs and hypergraphs to take these startling advances to the next level: translation systems that can check their own coherence and accuracy while querying human expertise as needed. That will always be necessary – until someone can fix the crappy source texts that we so often must deal with!

Inaugural Edition of the AMTA Best Thesis Award

For the first edition of the AMTA Best Thesis Award, we had a very strong slate of eligible candidates and theses, resulting in a difficult decision to choose a single Best Thesis Award winner. Each thesis was assessed by multiple reviewers for its relevance to the field of machine translation, the past, current, and potential future impact of the thesis work on the field, and how challenging the thesis's core problem was. To ensure fairness in this single-blind process, reviewers were assigned to avoid institutional or other COIs, and where necessary, members of the board recused themselves.

A committee appointed by the AMTA Board, consisting of Akiko Eriguchi, Alon Lavie, and Rebecca Knowles, oversaw the process, summarized the reviews, deliberated and ultimately submitted a recommendation for the selected winner to the full AMTA Board for approval.

We are pleased to announce that the 2024 AMTA Best Thesis Award is awarded to:

Dr. Eleftheria Briakou

for her thesis entitled "*Detecting Fine-Grained Semantic Divergences to Improve Translation Understanding Across Languages*" (University of Maryland, College Park, USA).

This thesis provides a novel take on challenges in the field of machine translation, focusing on subtle meaning differences in translation, how to detect these meaning differences automatically, the impact they have on machine translation systems, how to mitigate this impact, and more, exploring the topic in both depth and breadth. The Proceedings include a short summary of the thesis's main contributions, and we encourage interested readers to explore the full thesis in greater depth. Dr. Briakou will present her work at the 2024 AMTA conference and will receive a prize of $1000 USD along with a free AMTA membership and waived registration costs.

We thank the following reviewers for their work on this process:

Akiko Eriguchi (Microsoft)
Alon Lavie (Phrase)
Chi-kiu Lo (National Research Council Canada)
Jay Marciano (AMTA)
Kevin Duh (Johns Hopkins University)
Konstantin Savenkov (Intento, Inc.)
Marine Carpuat (University of Maryland)
Michel Simard (National Research Council Canada)
Philipp Koehn (Johns Hopkins University)
Rebecca Knowles (National Research Council Canada)
Stephen Richardson (Brigham Young University)

We also thank the European Association for Machine Translation, especially Helena Moniz and Carolina Scarton, for sharing their expertise from the long-running Anthony C Clarke EAMT Best Thesis Award, which served as inspiration for the new AMTA Best Thesis Award.

Introduction to the Research Papers Volume

As the Association for Machine Translation in the Americas marks 30 years since the first AMTA conference in 1994, we present a program of research that explores longstanding challenges in the field, experiments with novel approaches to machine translation, and brings new perspectives to the conversation.

The Research Papers volume of the AMTA 2024 Proceedings includes 20 research and position papers as well as the abstract for the 2024 AMTA Best Thesis Award. Among these papers, we see a new rise in interest in large language models, with more than a third of the papers focusing on this topic. We also see interest in multimodal and multilingual translation, moving beyond text-only translation or translation between only two languages. There are also several papers focusing on topics like terminology and low-resource translation. Reflecting the broad range of interests represented in the AMTA research community, we see papers from perspectives rooted in academia, industry, government, and more.

Given the overlap with the Presentations track in terms of many of these topics, we look forward to another fruitful conference that brings together a wide variety of perspectives on the past, present, and future of MT research.

We thank the many reviewers, emergency reviewers, the AMTA organizing committee, and the past research chairs for their assistance in helping us to bring together this program of papers.

Sincerely,

Akiko Eriguchi and Rebecca Knowles

Research Directors, 2024

Program Committee (Peer-Reviewed Track)

Adam Poliak (Johns Hopkins University)
Akihiro Tamura (Doshisha University)
Akiko Eriguchi (Microsoft)
Alina Karakanta (Leiden University Centre for Linguistics)
Atsushi Fujita (NICT, Japan)
Atul Ojha (National University of Ireland Galway)
Bing Zhao (SRI International)
Chao-Hong Liu (ADAPT Centre, Dublin City University)
Christophe Servan (LISN-CNRS)
Colin Cherry (Google)
Delaney Lothian (National Research Council Canada)
Elizabeth Marshman (University of Ottawa)
Evgeny Matusov (AppTek)
Flammie Pirinen (UiT–Norgga árktalaš universitehta)
François YVON (CNRS)
Gabriel Bernier-Colborne (National Research Council Canada)
Haiyue Song (NICT)
Hajime Tsukada (Toyohashi University of Technology)
Harcharan Kabbay (World Wide Technology)
Hideya Mino (NHK)
Jasper Kyle Catapang (Money Forward)
Javad Pourmostafa Roshan Sharami (Tilburg University)
Jeremy Gwinnup (Air Force Research Laboratory)
Katsuhito Sudoh (Nara Women's University)
Kenji Imamura (National Institute of Information and Communications Technology (NICT))
Kevin Duh (Johns Hopkins University)
Koichiro Watanabe (The University of Tokyo)
Makoto Morishita (NTT)
Marcello Federico (Amazon)
Mengzhe GENG (The Chinese University of Hong Kong)
Michel Simard (National Research Council Canada)
Muyun Yang (Harbin Institute of Technology)
Nathaniel Oco (Philippines)
Ohnmar Htun (Rakuten Asia Pte.Ltd.)
Patrick Simianer (Lilt)
Philipp Koehn (Johns Hopkins University)
Raj Dabre (NICT)
Rebecca Knowles (National Research Council Canada)
Rico Sennrich (University of Zurich)
Roman Grundkiewicz (Microsoft Research)
Samuel Larkin (National Research Council Canada)
Santanu Pal
Stephen Richardson (Brigham Young University)
Sweta Agrawal (Instituto de Telecomunicações)
Takashi Ninomiya (Ehime University)
Taro Watanabe (Nara Institute of Science and Technology)
Tetsuji Nakagawa (Google Japan G.K.)
Thamme Gowda (Microsoft)
Tomek Korybski (University of Surrey)
Toshiaki Nakazawa (The University of Tokyo)
Valentin Malykh (Moscow Institute of Physics and Technology)
Xiaolin Wang (National Institute of Information and Communications Technology)
Xinyi Wang (Carnegie Mellon University)
Xuan Zhang (Johns Hopkins University)

Content

Detecting Fine-Grained Semantic Divergences to Improve Translation Understanding Across Languages

Eleftheria Briakou
Department of Computer Science, University of Maryland, College Park, MD
ebriakou@umd.com

Abstract

In this thesis, we focus on detecting fine-grained semantic divergences—*subtle meaning differences in sentences that overlap in content*—to improve machine and human translation understanding.

EN ... *The Maple Leaf Forever served for many years as a Canadian national anthem...*
FR ... *The Maple Leaf Forever (en) qui est un chant patriotique pro canadien...*
... *The Maple Leaf Forever which is a Canadian patriotic song...*

1 Introduction

A widespread hypothesis adopted by machine translation research is that a source text and its (human) translation—*or* parallel text—are equivalent in meaning. In principle, this hypothesis drives the way we think about our models when designing our training losses and our evaluation metrics and protocols. Yet when humans translate, they make lexical decisions influenced by cultural and situational aspects of language that break the hypothesis of meaning equivalence in nuanced ways (Hirst, 1995; Zhai et al., 2019). Consider the English and French sentences above drawn from WikiMatrix (Schwenk et al., 2021), a corpus that is routinely used to train translation systems and is perceived as highly parallel. While they share important content, highlighted words convey meaning missing from the other language (i.e., *served for many years*) or content reflecting fine-grained semantic divergences between concepts that, although related, are not equivalent (i.e., *national anthem* vs. *patriotic song*).

Regardless of why such subtle divergences exist in parallel texts, we hypothesize that they matter for machine translation systems—as they yield challenging training samples—and for humans—who might benefit from a nuanced understanding of the source. Thus, in this line of work, we argue that quantifying fine-grained divergences is crucial to **improve both *machine* and *human* translation understanding across languages**.

In what follows, we start by introducing methods for detecting fine-grained divergences in the wild (Briakou and Carpuat, 2020). As we will see, such methods lay the foundation for studying their connection to machine translation models (Briakou and Carpuat, 2021, 2022; Briakou et al., 2022) and human evaluations pipelines (Briakou et al., 2023).

2 Detecting Fine-grained Divergences

In our first piece of work, we start our exploration by asking: ***How frequent are semantic divergences in parallel texts?*** Our goal is to address challenges in detection of fine-grained divergences within bitexts in two settings: *human annotation* and *automatic prediction* (Briakou and Carpuat, 2020).

Starting with human annotation, we contribute the Rationalized English-French Semantic Divergences corpus, based on a novel divergence annotation protocol that exploits rationales to improve annotator agreement. Annotations on the collected dataset reveal that semantic divergences are surprisingly frequent, comprising 40% of samples in a corpus consisting of Wikipedia-mined translations, and are perceived as highly parallel.

After establishing that divergences exist, we explore computational methods for detecting them at scale, crucially, without assuming access to gold supervision. To that end, we introduce a contrastive loss designed to make a multilingual language model sensitive to subtle cross-lingual differences between linguistically motivated synthetic samples. Despite being trained only on synthetic samples, we show that our model detects fine-grained divergences accurately, outperforming a strong sentence-level similarity model (Schwenk and Douze, 2017).

3 Improving Machine Translation

Equipped with the tools that allow us to study divergences at scale we now ask: ***How do fine-grained divergences impact Neural Machine Translation?*** We contribute a controlled empirical analysis on several aspect of NMT models that are exposed to different types and amounts of divergences at training time. Our findings reveal that small divergences hurt translation accuracy and confidence of NMT models, and crucially are one of the root causes that lead to neural text degeneration, i.e., translation outputs that are incoherent or get stuck in repetitive loops (Briakou and Carpuat, 2021).

Drawing from those findings, a natural question arises: ***How can we mitigate the negative impact of divergences on* NMT*?*** To this aim, we explore two orthogonal strategies. Our first strategy intervenes in the training assumption of translation equivalence in parallel texts and aims to model divergences explicitly. Drawing from our prior work on automatically detecting divergences, we propose a divergent-aware framework—DIV-FACTORIZED—that incorporates token-level divergence signals into NMT training (Briakou and Carpuat, 2021).

Our second strategy proposes an orthogonal mitigation direction: instead of altering training to model divergences closely, we aim to automatically re-write divergent samples to yield more equivalent translations. In this direction, we introduce two approaches to solve this problem in the lack of supervised data. Our first approach—EQUIV SEMDIV—relies on synthetic translations, i.e., translations generated by MT, that selectively replace divergent references under a semantic equivalence condition (Briakou and Carpuat, 2022). Our extensive evaluations on both intrinsic and extrinsic tasks for two medium-resource languages show that this approach is capable of revising divergences in parallel texts, given synthetic translations of sufficient quality. In our subsequent work, we address this problem in low-resource conditions via introducing—BITEXTEDIT—an editing-based model that, given a parallel text, edits one of the two references to generate a refined version of the original as necessary. Our editing model is trained solely on synthetic supervision via leveraging recent advances in bitext mining based on massively multilingual sentence embeddings (Artetxe and Schwenk, 2019) and is shown to utilize divergences more effectively in heterogeneous data scenarios (Briakou et al., 2022).

4 Assisting Humans to Detect Translation Differences in Meaning

After exploring how detecting semantic divergences helps us improve machine translation understanding, we finally turn to analyze ways of assisting *humans* in understanding and detecting translation differences. Although detecting divergences in parallel texts as a binary classification task, i.e., equivalence vs. divergence, is found to be sufficient for augmenting and improving NMT, we hypothesize that other task framings that shed more light on the nature of divergences are needed to improve human translation understanding. In this direction, our last piece of work asks: ***How can we explain semantic divergences in a human-interpretable fashion?***

To that end, we equip divergence detectors with the ability to indicate not just *whether* divergences exist but also tell us *where* the translation differences reside (Briakou et al., 2023). Drawing on social science studies, we introduce a method to extract contrastive phrasal highlights that explain the predictions of our divergent detectors by explicitly modeling the relationships between the contrasted texts. We contribute evidence that contrastive phrasal highlights match human-provided rationales of divergence better than standard highlighting approaches, and more importantly, they assist bilingual speakers in annotating fine-grained divergences, easing the need to ask for human rationales. Finally, we show that contrastive highlights could help humans detect critical errors due to local mistranslations in machine-translated texts.

References

Artetxe, M. and Schwenk, H. (2019). Massively multilingual sentence embeddings for zero-shot cross-lingual transfer and beyond. *Transactions of the Association for Computational Linguistics*, 7:597–610.

Briakou, E. and Carpuat, M. (2020). Detecting Fine-Grained Cross-Lingual Semantic Divergences without Supervision by Learning to Rank. In Webber, B., Cohn, T., He, Y., and Liu, Y., editors, *Proceedings of the 2020 Conference on Empirical Methods in Natural Language Processing (EMNLP)*, pages 1563–1580, Online. Association for Computational Linguistics.

Briakou, E. and Carpuat, M. (2021). Beyond noise: Mitigating the impact of fine-grained semantic divergences on neural machine translation. In Zong, C., Xia, F., Li, W., and Navigli, R., editors, *Proceedings of the 59th Annual Meeting of the Association for Computational Linguistics and the 11th International Joint Conference on Natural Language Processing (Volume 1: Long Papers)*, pages 7236–7249, Online. Association for Computational Linguistics.

Briakou, E. and Carpuat, M. (2022). Can synthetic translations improve bitext quality? In Muresan, S., Nakov, P., and Villavicencio, A., editors, *Proceedings of the 60th Annual Meeting of the Association for Computational Linguistics (Volume 1: Long Papers)*, pages 4753–4766, Dublin, Ireland. Association for Computational Linguistics.

Briakou, E., Goyal, N., and Carpuat, M. (2023). Explaining with contrastive phrasal highlighting: A case study in assisting humans to detect translation differences. In Bouamor, H., Pino, J., and Bali, K., editors, *Proceedings of the 2023 Conference on Empirical Methods in Natural Language Processing*, pages 11220–11237, Singapore. Association for Computational Linguistics.

Briakou, E., Wang, S., Zettlemoyer, L., and Ghazvininejad, M. (2022). BitextEdit: Automatic bitext editing for improved low-resource machine translation. In Carpuat, M., de Marneffe, M.-C., and Meza Ruiz, I. V., editors, *Findings of the Association for Computational Linguistics: NAACL 2022*, pages 1469–1485, Seattle, United States. Association for Computational Linguistics.

Hirst, G. (1995). Near-synonymy and the structure of lexical knowledge. In *AAAI Symposium on Rep- resentation and Acquisition of Lexical Knowledge: Polysemy, Ambiguity, and Generativity. pages 51– 56.*, pages 51–56.

Schwenk, H., Chaudhary, V., Sun, S., Gong, H., and Guzmán, F. (2021). WikiMatrix: Mining 135M parallel sentences in 1620 language pairs from Wikipedia. In Merlo, P., Tiedemann, J., and Tsarfaty, R., editors, *Proceedings of the 16th Conference of the European Chapter of the Association for Computational Linguistics: Main Volume*, pages 1351–1361, Online. Association for Computational Linguistics.

Schwenk, H. and Douze, M. (2017). Learning joint multilingual sentence representations with neural machine translation. In Blunsom, P., Bordes, A., Cho, K., Cohen, S., Dyer, C., Grefenstette, E., Hermann, K. M., Rimell, L., Weston, J., and Yih, S., editors, *Proceedings of the 2nd Workshop on Representation Learning for NLP*, pages 157–167, Vancouver, Canada. Association for Computational Linguistics.

Zhai, Y., Safari, P., Illouz, G., Allauzen, A., and Vilnat, A. (2019). Towards recognizing phrase translation processes: Experiments on english-french. *CoRR*, abs/1904.12213.

Leveraging LLMs for MT in Crisis Scenarios: a blueprint for low-resource languages

Séamus Lankford seamus.lankford@adaptcentre.ie
ADAPT Centre, Department of Computer Science, Munster Technological University, Cork, T12P928, Ireland.
Andy Way andy.way@adaptcentre.ie
ADAPT Centre, School of Computing, Dublin City University, Dublin, D09DXA0, Ireland.

Abstract

In an evolving landscape of crisis communication, the need for robust and adaptable Machine Translation (MT) systems is more pressing than ever, particularly for low-resource languages. This study presents a comprehensive exploration of leveraging Large Language Models (LLMs) and Multilingual LLMs (MLLMs) to enhance MT capabilities in such scenarios. By focusing on the unique challenges posed by crisis situations where speed, accuracy, and the ability to handle a wide range of languages are paramount, this research outlines a novel approach that combines the cutting-edge capabilities of LLMs with fine-tuning techniques and community-driven corpus development strategies. At the core of this study is the development and empirical evaluation of MT systems tailored for two low-resource language pairs, illustrating the process from initial model selection and fine-tuning through to deployment. Bespoke systems are developed and modelled on the recent Covid-19 pandemic. The research highlights the importance of community involvement in creating highly specialised, crisis-specific datasets and compares custom GPTs with NLLB-adapted MLLM models. It identifies fine-tuned MLLM models as offering superior performance compared with their LLM counterparts. A scalable and replicable model for rapid MT system development in crisis scenarios is outlined. Our approach enhances the field of humanitarian technology by offering a blueprint for developing multilingual communication systems during emergencies.

1 Credits

This work was supported by ADAPT, which is funded under the SFI Research Centres Programme (Grant 13/RC/2016) and is co-funded by the European Regional Development Fund. The research was also funded by the Munster Technological University in Cork, Ireland.

2 Introduction

The excitement surrounding LLMs stems from their potential to revolutionise many fields, from language translation (Costa-jussà et al., 2022) and content generation (Brown et al., 2020) to chatbots[1] and virtual assistants. Way (2024) observes that from the very outset, machine translation (MT) capability has been overhyped at each paradigm shift over the past 75 years, but with their ability to 'understand' language and generate complex responses, LLMs do appear capable of enhancing human communication and productivity in ways that were unimaginable with previous approaches, especially given that LLMs are not restricted to text-based use-cases, and can be used in creative applications such as generating music[2] or art.

When building LLMs, the focus is on designing and training the model architecture. This involves selecting the appropriate neural network architecture and hyperparameters, as well as deciding on the training data and optimisation techniques to

[1] https://chatgpt.com
[2] https://soundraw.io

use.

Tuning an MLLM or LLM, in contrast, involves adjusting the parameters of a pre-trained model to improve its performance on a specific task. In neural networks such as MLLMs, the weights and biases are parameters that the network adjusts through training to minimise a cost function. This is performed by training the model on a task-specific dataset and adjusting the model's hyperparameters to optimise its performance. Tuning an MLLM can be a challenging task, as the model is often very complex and the training process can take a long time, but Lankford et al. (2023a) offer an open-source solution to fine-tuning pre-built MLLMs, with a particular focus on low-resource language pairs, thus overcoming much of this complexity. In contrast to predictions of their imminent demise (van der Meer, 2021), Way (2024) predicts that tools such as adaptMLLM will instead allow translators to gain a competitive edge, by building and tuning their own models with their own high-quality data, "while retaining full control over the process, leading to self-empowerment and an improved sense of well-being".

Given their potential, this paper investigates whether tools such as adaptMLLM can be used to rapidly build good-quality MLLM-based MT systems for deployment in crisis scenarios, where speed of development is crucial, but not at the expense of quality altogether. These deployments are contrasted with the development of custom GPTs and fine-tuned LLMs. For two language pairs and four language directions, each featuring a minority language, we present and evaluate a pipeline that we hope can be used as a blueprint for rapid deployment in crisis scenarios to improve multilingual communication.

3 Background

Way et al. (2020) observe that there "have been alarmingly few attempts to provide automatic translation services for use in crisis scenarios". To the best of our knowledge, the first was Microsoft's effort (Lewis, 2010) to build Haitian Creole systems following the devastating earthquake in 2010, as the title makes clear "from scratch in 4 days, 17 hours, & 30 minutes". Estimated casualties ranged from 100,000 to over 300,000 deaths, with around a third of all citizens affected in some way or other by the earthquake measuring 7.0 on the Richter scale. The main issues for the Microsoft team were a complete lack of knowledge of the language (grammatical structure, encoding, orthography etc), and no data at all to train high-quality statistical MT engines. However, the team quickly identified some available resources (the Bible is available in most languages), and a small number of native speakers to help with translation and, especially, validation of the MT output generated. Eventually, around 150,000 segments of training data were collected to build the system, which obtained a BLEU (Papineni et al., 2002) score of almost 30 for Creole to English, and 18.3 for English to Creole, sufficiently high (especially for the into-English direction) for the system to be deployed for use by relief workers in the field.

This remarkable effort led to the writing of a cookbook for MT in crisis scenarios (Lewis et al., 2011), so that the lessons learned from the exercise could be put into practice when other crises arose, as they do all too commonly, regrettably. Importantly, Lewis et al. (2011) note that "If done right, MT can dramatically increase the speed by which relief can be provided". In any such scenario, translation is almost always needed, and despite its importance, it is often overlooked.

In response to the need for better preparation for translation readiness in crises, Sharon O'Brien coordinated the Interact project[3] featuring partners from academia, industry, as well as NGOs. Federici et al. (2019) provide a set of recommendations within that project which apply mainly to human translation provision in crisis scenarios.

3.1 Multilingual Language Models—NLLB

MT has become a significant area of research with the aim of eliminating language barriers worldwide. However, the current focus is limited to a small number of languages, neglecting the vast majority of low-resource languages. In an effort to address this issue, the No Language Left Behind (NLLB) initiative was launched to try to overcome the challenges of using MT for low-resource language translation by developing datasets and models that bridge the performance gap between low- and high-resource languages. The NLLB team has also created architectural and training enhancements tailored to sup-

[3]https://sites.google.com/view/crisistranslation/home

port MT for low-resource languages. Their work is open source,[4] and many of their models serve as baselines for fine-tuning with adaptMLLM (Lankford et al., 2023a).[5] While projects like this are undoubtedly a step in the right direction, Ignat et al. (2023) observe that "state-of-the-art MT models such as NLLB-200 … still perform poorly on many low-resource languages, such as African languages" (p.3), so much work remains to be done.

3.2 Large Language Models

The increasing availability of large datasets provides the raw material for LLM training (Radford et al., 2019; Conneau et al., 2020; Winata et al., 2021), enabling performance improvement on a wide variety of NLP tasks.

LLMs have the potential to improve the use of technology across a wide range of domains, including medicine, education and computational linguistics. In education, LLMs may be used for personalised student learning experiences (Kasneci et al., 2023), while in the medical domain, analysing large amounts of medical files can assist doctors in treating patients (Iftikhar et al., 2023). Of particular interest to our research is the manner in which LLMs can be used within the realm of NLP, more specifically in the field of MT, and we now provide details of some of the main candidates in this space.

3.2.1 GPT-4

The primary distinction between GPT-3.5 and GPT-4[6] is that while the former is a text-to-text model, the latter is more of a data-to-text model, exhibiting the ability to perform tasks that its predecessor could not. For example, GPT-4 is capable of processing visual input as part of a prompt, such as images or web pages, and can even generate text that explains the humour in memes. Consequently, GPT-4 can be classified as a "multimodal model". Furthermore, GPT-4 has a longer memory than its previous versions, with a short-term memory closer to 64,000 words, enabling it to maintain coherence during extended interactions. GPT-4 also enables users to select different personalities for the model's responses.

The number of parameters utilised in the training of GPT-4 has not been disclosed by OpenAI; however, other sources, such as AX Semantics,[7] have estimated the number to be around 100 trillion, with such a large model costing around $100 million to build. AX Semantics maintains that such a number makes the language model (LM) more akin to the functioning of the human brain with respect to language and logic.

3.2.2 Gemini

Gemini[8] comes in three versions tailored for varying levels of complexity and application: Gemini Ultra for the most demanding tasks, Gemini Pro for a broad range of activities, and Gemini Nano for on-device applications. The Ultra variant, in particular, has demonstrated SOTA performance, outperforming human benchmarks in massive multitask language understanding (MMLU) across a suite of 57 subjects. Team (2024) documents the performance of Gemini on the "Machine Translation from One Book (MTOB)" benchmark (Tanzer et al., 2023), essentially how good a model is at learning a language from almost no resources. For an evaluation of Gemini 1.5 Pro on the FLORES-200 benchmark (Costa-jussà et al., 2022) against Google Translate, GPT-3.5 and GPT-4, and other systems, see Akter et al. (2023) (p.12).

3.2.3 CoPilot

Microsoft has introduced Microsoft 365 Copilot,[9] a generative AI tool designed to enhance workplace productivity and creativity. Copilot integrates LLMs with user data from Microsoft Graph and Microsoft 365 apps, to allow users to utilise natural language commands across familiar Microsoft 365 applications such as Word, Excel and PowerPoint.

Central to this announcement is the launch of Business Chat, which synergies with the LLM, Microsoft 365 apps, and user data to generate outputs such as status updates from natural language prompts, drawing from various data sources like emails, meetings, and documents. This ensures that users remain in control, enabling them to adjust or

[4] https://github.com/facebookresearch/fairseq/tree/nllb
[5] https://github.com/adaptNMT/adaptMLLM
[6] https://openai.com/product/gpt-4
[7] https://en.ax-semantics.com
[8] https://gemini.google.com
[9] https://copilot.microsoft.com

refine the outputs as needed.

4 Datasets

4.1 Language Pairs

To benchmark the translation performance of adaptMLLM in fine-tuning MLLMs for low-resource languages, we had to choose suitable language pairs for which appropriate datasets existed. The English-to-Irish (EN↔GA) and English-to-Marathi (EN↔MR) language pairs were selected since they fulfilled the criteria of low-resource languages, and data was freely available from shared tasks featuring these language pairs in crisis scenarios. Therefore, these language pairs were very suitable for evaluating our proposed pipeline for rapidly generating high-quality translations in crisis situations by fine-tuning MLLMs.

Irish is the first official language of the Republic of Ireland, and is also recognised as a minority language in Northern Ireland. Irish is an official language of the European Union and a recognised minority language in Northern Ireland with an ISO code of "GA".[10]

The dominant language spoken in India's Maharashtra state is Marathi, with an ISO code of "MR". It has over 83 million speakers, and it is a member of the Indo-Aryan language family. Despite being spoken by a significant number of people, Marathi is considered to be relatively under-resourced when compared to other languages used in the region.

4.2 Shared Task Datasets

To benchmark the performance of our adaptMLLM-trained models, datasets from the LoResMT2021 shared task (Ojha et al., 2021) were used, since the shared task focused on low-resource languages including both EN↔GA and EN↔MR in the specific domain of translation of COVID-related data.

The datasets from the shared task provided 502 Irish and 500 Marathi validation sentences whereas 250 (GA→EN), 500 (EN→GA), and 500 (EN↔MR) sentences were made available in the test datasets. Training data consisted of 20,933 lines of parallel data for the EN↔MR language pair and 13,171 lines of parallel data were used to train the EN↔GA models. A detailed breakdown of all resources is available in Ojha et al. (2021).

[10]https://www.iso.org

5 Approach

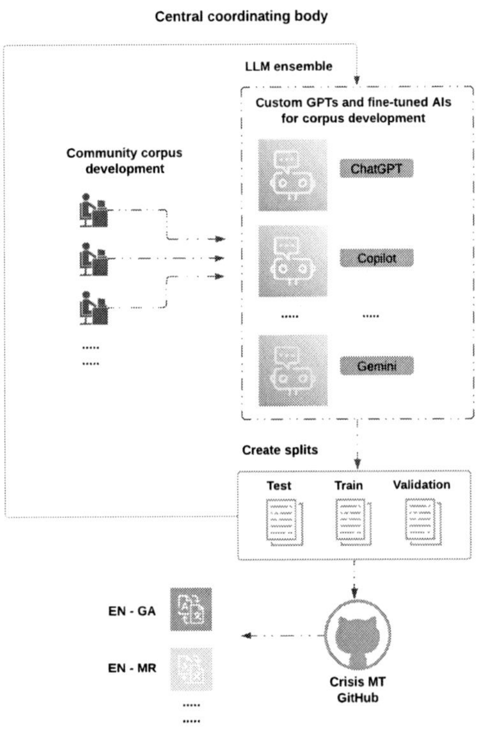

Figure 1: Community corpus development using custom GPTs from a range of foundation models.

Our approach to enhancing MT in crisis situations involves three key elements. Initially, a custom GPT would be created on the ChatGPT platform immediately after a crisis, enabling users to contribute to a specialised knowledge base with new terms relevant to the crisis, effectively crowd sourcing a dataset for crisis-specific language pairs. With this approach both in-domain corpora and simple first iteration models are developed in real time by disparate users entering source and reference translations. Within the custom GPT interface on ChatGPT the functionality also exists to upload relevant documents which adds to the knowledge base of custom GPTs. Another interesting feature of ChatGPT is its ability to publicly share custom GPTs by sharing links. In this manner, it is trivial to develop corpora by implementing a simple link-sharing strategy that invites community-wide, expert-only or an ensemble of contributions.

As the crisis evolves, these corpora are then used to develop more accurate MT models with new weights tailored to the specific language needs of the crisis by fine-tuning OpenAI models, or other LLM foundation models.

Finally, a bespoke model could be created using an open-source tool like adaptMLLM, fine-tuned with a custom dataset developed during the crisis. Such a phased approach allows for a rapid initial response and progressively more tailored MT solutions as the crisis unfolds, leveraging community input and specialised training to improve translation accuracy in critical situations.

Of course, a major consideration when designing an MT system in crisis scenarios is the availability of suitable parallel corpora which contain new terminology associated with the unfolding crisis. However, it is precisely at these times when the production of such datasets presents the greatest challenge.

Figure 1 presents a structured approach to developing language corpora with community involvement, using customised LMs, and preparing the data for MT projects which are shared on GitHub. A central coordinating body (such as ACL,[11] AMTA,[12] EAMT[13] or an equally invested stakeholder) could oversee the process working in conjunction with relevant industry partners and other stakeholders.

There are two parallel streams in this process, the first of which entails a community corpus development effort, involving multiple contributors, using a collaborative, crowdsourced approach. In this phase, selected users and language experts interact with LLMs on an *ad hoc* basis by presenting text in the source language and providing the translation in the target language. In this manner, an in-domain parallel dataset relevant specifically to the particular crisis is rapidly developed for the chosen language pair.

The second stream, LLM ensemble, incorporates several elements: models from ChatGPT, Copilot, Gemini and other foundation models. The corpus creation process is carried out by simply exporting and concatenating the conversation histories from each of the customised LLMs. Duplicate entries created in the corpus development stage are removed and the corpus is split into three datasets: "Test", "Train", and "Validation". The training dataset is used to fine-tune a pre-trained (M)LLM to create a bespoke in-domain crisis MT model. The validation dataset is also used as part of this fine-tuning process before the test set is used to evaluate the performance of the MT system using standard BLEU, TER (Snover et al., 2006) and ChrF (Popović, 2015) metrics.

Finally, the output of the process feeds into a crisis MT GitHub which is the central repository for the development of MT systems for multiple language pairs. Models and datasets developed as part of this process would be shared on GitHub for open-source collaboration and distribution.

A Colab notebook has been developed to help with this process and we have made it publicly available as part of this paper's GitHub which is freely available for download.[14] A Gradio-based web app is incorporated within this notebook which facilitates the involvement of non-technical users in corpus creation. This is our first implementation of such a notebook for aiding crisis MT corpus development and as an open-source tool, improvements and contributions from the community are welcomed.

[11] https://acl.org

[12] https://amtaweb.org

[13] https://eamt.org

[14] https://github.com/adaptNMT/crisisMT/blob/main/communitycorpus.ipynb

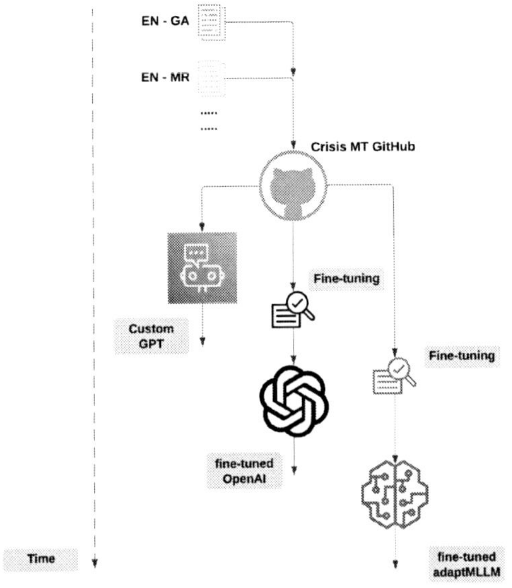

Figure 2: Model development process.

The elements of model development required to manage MT in a crisis are highlighted in Figure 2. All models use the outputs from the corpus development process. In the initial phase of the crisis, a custom GPT is created from the crowd-sourced corpus development. At this point, a parallel track is in progress where a fine-tuned LLM, such as a pre-trained OpenAI model, is developed and made available at a later date. Our approach proposes a third parallel track which develops a fine-tuned MLLM-specific model using a tool such as adaptMLLM. Fine-tuning an open-source MLLM using adaptMLLM has been shown to empirically deliver the highest translation performance (see Section 6). Subsequent phases of model development would also benefit from the availability of a significantly expanded crisis-relevant corpus via the ongoing crowd-sourcing effort. The links to the custom GPTs developed for both language pairs have been open-sourced.[15]

6 Empirical Evaluation

After outlining the details of our approach, the quality of the models developed is evaluated by training models for the EN↔GA and the EN↔MR language pairs.

6.1 Infrastructure and Hyperparameters

All MLLM models were trained by fine-tuning a 3.3B parameter NLLB pre-trained model using the adaptMLLM application with a Google Colab Pro+ subscription. The DeepSpeed library enables our models to be loaded across both GPU and system memory, thus reducing the required compute resources. The optimal hyperparameters used for developing models for both language pairs are the same as those identified by Lankford et al. (2023a).

Both the custom GPT models and the baseline models used the GPT-4 model under a standard ChatGPT subscription. The OpenAI fine-tuned models were developed using a pay-as-you-go plan. In fine-tuning the OpenAI models, GPT-3.5-turbo-0125 was the chosen pre-trained model since GPT-4 was unavailable for fine-tuning. Default parameters were kept and the number of epochs was set to auto. For inference on these models, a temperature setting of 0.5 was chosen to ensure a more deterministic output which aligns with the requirements for translation models.

6.2 Results: Automatic Evaluation

To determine the quality of our translations, automated metrics were employed. For comparison with previous results, the performance of our new models was measured using three automatic evaluation metrics: BLEU, TER, and ChrF. We report case-insensitive BLEU scores at the corpus level. Note that BLEU and ChrF are precision-based metrics, so higher scores are better, whereas TER is an error-based metric so lower scores indicate better translation quality. All models, notebooks and translations generated as part of our experiments are freely available for download.[15]

6.2.1 Translation in the EN↔GA Directions

The experimental results in the EN↔GA directions are summarised in Tables 2 - 3 and are compared with the baseline highest scores from the LoResMT2021 Shared Task.[16]

The highest-performing EN→GA system in the LoResMT2021 Shared Task was submitted by ADAPT (Lankford et al., 2021). The model was developed with an in-house application, adapt-

[15]https://github.com/adaptNMT/crisisMT
[16]https://machinetranslate.org/loresmt-2021

NMT (Lankford et al., 2023b) using a Transformer (Vaswani et al., 2017) architecture. It performed well across all key translation metrics (BLEU: 36.0, TER: 0.531 and ChrF3: 0.6).

By fine-tuning the NLLB MLLM, using the parameters outlined in Table 1, a significant improvement in translation performance was achieved. The adaptMLLM EN→GA en2ga system, shown in Table 2, achieves a BLEU score of 41.2, which is 5.2 BLEU points higher (14% relative improvement) than the score of the winning system in 2021.

Both the custom GPT-4 and GPT-4 baseline models performed well compared to the GPT-3 models. However, there was a significant differential when compared to the adaptMLLM fine-tuned NLLB models which recorded an increase of 8.4 BLEU points which corresponds to a relative improvement of 25%. In a crisis scenario, a GPT-4 baseline model would be available in real-time. A custom GPT could be available within a matter of minutes once a relevant training corpus is uploaded to the GPT's knowledge base. Such approaches would be suitable for assisting translators in the immediate aftermath of a crisis and would help in issuing bilingual press releases. However, more detailed documentation would greatly benefit from the improved translation quality of a bespoke fine-tuned adaptMLLM solution.

For translation in the GA→EN direction, illustrated in Table 3, the best-performing model for the LoResMT2021 Shared Task was developed by IIITT with a BLEU score of 34.6, a TER score of 0.586 and ChrF3 score of 0.6. Accordingly, this serves as the baseline score by which we can benchmark our GA→EN MLLM model, developed by fine-tuning a 3.3B parameter NLLB using adaptMLLM. Similar to the results achieved in the EN→GA direction, significant improvement in translation performance was observed using this new method. The performance of the adaptMLLM model offers an improvement across all metrics with a BLEU score of 75.1, a TER of 0.385 and a ChrF3 result of 0.71. In particular, the 117% relative improvement in BLEU score against the IIITT system is very significant.

The results from our GA→EN experiments reinforce the findings derived from translating in the EN→GA direction. The custom and baseline GPT-4 models immediately deliver a translation system with good quality BLEU scores of 53 points. However, a higher-quality translation system with a 21.2 BLEU score improvement can delivered in a matter of hours once a fine-tuned adaptMLLM NLLB sytem is put in place. The exact length of time for system development is dependent on the quality of the underlying training infrastructure and also, more importantly, on how rapidly the training corpus can be assembled.

6.2.2 Translation in the EN↔MR Directions

The experimental results from the LoResMT2021 Shared Task in the EN↔MR directions are summarised in Tables 4 and 5, and are compared with adaptMLLM. For the shared task, the highest-performing EN→MR system was submitted by the IIITT team. Their model used a Transformer architecture and achieved a BLEU score of 34.6, a TER of 0.586, and ChrF3 of 0.61.

Again the approach taken by adaptMLLM in fine-tuning a 3.3.B parameter NLLB MLLM yielded the best performance compared with other systems entered for the shared task. The EN→MR adaptMLLM en2mr system achieves the highest BLEU score of 26.4, a 2.2 point improvement (9% relative) compared with IIITT, the winning team in the EN→MR shared task.

The MLLM-based system, trained using adaptMLLM, is also compared with GPT-4 and GPT-3.5 LLM-based systems. For the purposes of our experiments, the best-performing LLM used a custom GPT-4 model which recorded a BLEU score of 19.0 points in the EN→MR direction. This was only a marginal improvement on the baseline GPT-4 model with a BLEU score of 18.5 points. Critically, however, this solution could be delivered in real time which makes such a model a potential starting point for an immediate crisis response. A relative improvement of 42% and 7.9 BLEU points is available once sufficient time is given to developing the fine-tuned MLLM model.

For translation in the MR→EN direction, the best-performing model for the LoResMT2021 Shared Task was developed by oneNLP-IIITT with a BLEU score of 31.3, a TER of 0.58 and ChrF3 of 0.646. This serves as the baseline against which our MR→EN model, developed using adaptMLLM, can be benchmarked. The performance of the adaptMLLM model offers a significant improvement across all metrics with a BLEU score of 52.6, a TER of 0.409 and a ChrF3 of 0.704. Again this represents a

Hyperparameter	Values
Epochs	1, 3, **5**
Batch size	8, 12, **16**
Gradient steps	2, 4, **8**
Learning rate	$1{\times}10^{-5}$, $\mathbf{3{\times}10^{-5}}$, $9{\times}10^{-5}$
Weight decay	0.01, **0.1**, 1, 2
Mixed precision	False, **True**

Table 1: HPO with optimal hyperparameters highlighted in bold

System	BLEU	TER	ChrF3
adaptMLLM	41.2	0.51	0.48
adaptNMT	36.0	0.531	0.60
custom GPT-4	32.8	0.553	0.594
GPT-4 baseline	31.1	0.564	0.584
adaptMLLM-base	29.7	0.595	0.559
fine-tuned GPT-3.5	22.7	0.701	0.488
GPT-3.5 baseline	20.0	0.712	0.475

Table 2: EN→GA

System	BLEU	TER	ChrF3
adaptMLLM	75.1	0.385	0.71
GPT-4 baseline	53.9	0.365	0.754
custom GPT-4	53.2	0.37	0.747
fine-tuned GPT-3.5	50.2	41.9	0.713
adaptMLLM-base	47.8	0.442	0.692
GPT-3.5 baseline	41.6	51.2	0.668
IIITT	34.6	0.586	0.61

Table 3: GA→EN

System	BLEU	TER	ChrF3
adaptMLLM	26.4	0.56	0.608
IIITT	24.2	0.59	0.597
adaptMLLM-base	19.8	0.656	0.57
custom GPT-4	19.0	0.678	0.528
GPT-4 baseline	18.5	0.689	0.527
fine-tuned GPT-3.5	9.9	0.894	0.442
GPT-3.5 baseline	6.7	1.06	0.392

Table 4: EN→MR

System	BLEU	TER	ChrF3
adaptMLLM	52.6	0.409	0.704
adaptMLLM-base	42.7	0.506	0.639
custom GPT-4	38.8	0.539	0.626
GPT-4 baseline	38.6	0.546	0.617
oneNLP-IIITH	31.3	0.58	0.646
GPT-3.5 baseline	27.9	0.688	0.568
fine-tuned GPT-3.5	27.6	0.716	0.501

Table 5: MR→EN

very strong relative improvement of 68% in BLEU compared with the winning team from the shared task.

The best-performing MLLM-based system in the MR→EN direction is also compared with our LLM-based systems. The highest-performing LLM used a custom GPT-4 model which recorded a BLEU score of 38.8 points. This was only a marginal improvement on the baseline GPT-4 model with a BLEU score of 38.6 points. As previously noted, the GPT4 baseline solutions can be delivered in real time which makes this model the ideal starting point for an immediate crisis response. A relative improvement of 36% and 14 BLEU points is available once sufficient time is given to developing the fine-tuned MLLM model.

7 Discussion

A significant finding of this research is the demonstrated capability to substantially improve translation quality for low-resource languages through fine-tuning with crisis-specific datasets. The adaptability and speed of deployment offered by LLMs and MLLMs hold the promise of making such rapid response a standard practice in future crises, ensuring that linguistic barriers do not impede vital aid and information flow.

However, this potential comes with its share of challenges, particularly concerning the assembly and quality of training datasets. This study's proposed solution, leveraging community input through custom GPTs to crowd-source and refine translation data, presents a scalable model for corpus development in crisis scenarios. Looking ahead, this research lays the groundwork for expanding the application of LLMs and MLLMs beyond MT to address a wider range of NLP challenges in crisis situations. The blueprint provided for rapid MT system deployment in emergencies, emphasising community involvement and model fine-tuning, offers valuable insights for future endeavours aiming to harness AI for humanitarian purposes.

8 Conclusion

In this paper, we outlined how the advent of LLMs has transformed our ability to rapidly develop MT systems for low-resource languages in crisis scenarios. A system for rapid corpus development was presented which adopts a collaborative approach, emphasising community involvement and open-source methodologies.

The appropriate response to developing MT systems at different phases of a crisis were highlighted. Using the recent Covid pandemic as a reference crisis, MT systems were developed using custom GPTs, fine-tuned models from OpenAI and fine-tuned MLLM models. We demonstrated that a custom GPT delivers a functioning MT system rapidly whereas a fine-tuned MLLM delivers a higher-quality solution given a longer time horizon.

By highlighting how a fine-tuned MLLM can provide SOTA accuracy during a crisis, our work demonstrates how LLMs and MLLMs can provide more inclusive communication. Language barriers in crisis communication will be diminished with the help of this approach which in turn helps minority communities in times of real need.

Our paper introduces a pipeline which is applicable to a broader range of NLP problems. As part of future work, the methodologies and insights derived from our research could extend beyond the scope of MT to other domains within NLP. Consequently, a versatile framework for addressing a variety of language processing challenges in crisis scenarios has been put forth in this study.

Limitations of study

The proprietary nature of MLLMs and LLMs such as NLLB and GPT-4, which do not disclose the specifics of their training datasets presents a problem. When fine-tuning these models for specific tasks, there is a risk of overlapping data that cannot be easily identified or removed. This limitation underscores a broader issue within the field of NLP and MT research, where the exact composition of training data in SOTA models often remains opaque.

References

Akter, S. N., Yu, Z., Muhamed, A., Ou, T., Bäuerle, A., Cabrera, A. A., Dholakia, K., Xiong, C., and Neubig, G. (2023). An in-depth look at gemini's language abilities. eprint arXiv:2312.11444.

Brown, T., Mann, B., Ryder, N., Subbiah, M., Kaplan, J., Dhariwal, P., Neelakantan, A., Shyam, P., Sastry, G., and Askell, A. (2020). Language models are few-shot learners. In *Proceedings of the 34th Conference on Neural Information Processing Systems (NeurIPS 2020)*, volume 33, pages 1877–1901, Vancouver, BC, Canada.

Conneau, A., Khandelwal, K., Goyal, N., Chaudhary, V., Wenzek, G., Guzmán, F., Grave, E., Ott, M., Zettlemoyer, L., and Stoyanov, V. (2020). Unsupervised cross-lingual representation learning at scale. In *Proceedings of the 58th Annual Meeting of the Association for Computational Linguistics*, pages 8440–8451, Online.

Costa-jussà, M., Cross, J., Çelebi, O., Elbayad, M., Heafield, K., Heffernan, K., Kalbassi, E., Lam, J., Licht, D., and Maillard, J. (2022). No language left behind: Scaling human-centered machine translation. arXiv.

Federici, F., O'Brien, S., Cadwell, P., Marlowe, J., Gerber, B., and Davis, O. (2019). International network in crisis translation—recommendations on policies. 11p.

Iftikhar, L., Iftikhar, M., and Hanif, M. (2023). Docgpt: Impact of chatgpt-3 on health services as a virtual doctor. *EC Paediatr.*, 12:45–55.

Ignat, O., Jin, Z., Abzaliev, A., Biester, L., Castro, S., Deng, N., Gao, X., Gunal, A., He, J., Kazemi, A., Khalifa, M., Koh, N., Lee, A., Liu, S., Min, D., Mori, S., Nwatu, J., Perez-Rosas, V., Shen, S., Wang, Z., Wu, W., and Mihalcea, R. (2023). A phd student's perspective on research in nlp in the era of very large language models. eprint arXiv:2305.12544.

Kasneci, E., Sessler, K., Küchemann, S., Bannert, M., Dementieva, D., Fischer, F., Gasser, U., Groh, G., Günnemann, S., and Hüllermeier, E. (2023). Chatgpt for good? on opportunities and challenges of large language models for education. *Learn. Individ. Differ.*, 103:102274.

Lankford, S., Afli, H., and Way, A. (2021). Machine translation in the covid domain: An english-irish case study for loresmt 2021. In *Proceedings of the 4th Workshop on Technologies for MT of Low Resource Languages (LoResMT2021)*, pages 144–150, Virtual.

Lankford, S., Afli, H., and Way, A. (2023a). adaptmllm: Fine-tuning multilingual language models on low-resource languages with integrated llm playgrounds. *Information*, 14:638.

Lankford, S., Afli, H., and Way, A. (2023b). adaptnmt: An open-source, language-agnostic development environment for neural machine translation. *Lang. Resour. Eval.*, 57:1671–1696.

Lewis, W. (2010). Haitian creole: How to build and ship an mt engine from scratch in 4 days, 17 hours, & 30 minutes. In *EAMT-2010: Proceedings of the 14th Annual Conference of the European Association for Machine Translation*, St. Raphael, France. 6p.

Lewis, W., Munro, R., and Vogel, S. (2011). Crisis mt: Developing a cookbook for mt in crisis situations. In *Proceedings of the Sixth Workshop on Statistical Machine Translation*, page 501–511.

Ojha, A., Liu, C., Kann, K., Ortega, J., Shatam, S., and Fransen, T. (2021). Findings of the loresmt 2021 shared task on covid and sign language for low-resource languages. In *Proceedings of the 4th Workshop on Technologies for MT of Low Resource Languages (LoResMT2021)*, pages 114–123, Virtual.

Papineni, K., Roukos, S., Ward, T., and Zhu, W. (2002). Bleu: A method for automatic evaluation of machine translation. In *Proceedings of the 40th annual meeting of the Association for Computational Linguistics*, pages 311–318, Philadelphia, PA, USA.

Popović, M. (2015). chrf: character n-gram f-score for automatic mt evaluation. In *Proceedings of the Tenth Workshop on Statistical Machine Translation*, pages 392–395, Lisboa, Portugal.

Radford, A., Wu, J., Child, R., Luan, D., Amodei, D., and Sutskever, I. (2019). Language models are unsupervised multitask learners. OpenAI Blog.

Snover, M., Dorr, B., Schwartz, R., Micciulla, L., and Makhoul, J. (2006). A study of translation edit rate with targeted human annotation. In *Proceedings of the 7th Conference of the Association for Machine Translation in the Americas: Technical Papers*, Cambridge, MA, USA. Citeseer. Forest Grove, OR, USA.

Tanzer, G., Suzgun, M., Visser, E., Jurafsky, D., and Melas-Kyriazi, L. (2023). A benchmark for learning to translate a new language from one grammar book. eprint arXiv:2309.16575.

Team, G. (2024). Gemini 1.5: Unlocking multimodal understanding across millions of tokens of context. Google blog.

van der Meer, J. (2021). Translation economics of the 2020s: A journey into the future of the translation industry in eight episodes. *Multilingual Magazine*. July/Aug 2021.

Vaswani, A., Shazeer, N., Parmar, N., Uszkoreit, J., Jones, L., Gomez, A., Kaiser, L., and Polosukhin, I. (2017). Attention is all you need. In *Proceedings of the 31st International Conference on Neural Information Processing Systems*, pages 6000–6010, Long Beach, CA, USA.

Way, A. (2024). *What does the Future hold for Translation Technologies in Society?* Routledge, Abingdon, Oxon, UK. In S. Baumgarten and M. Tieber (eds.) Routledge Handbook of Translation Technology and Society, forthcoming.

Way, A., Haque, R., Xie, G., Gaspari, F., Popovic, M., and Poncelas, P. (2020). Rapid development of competitive translation engines for access to multilingual covid-19 information. *Informatics*, 7(2):21.

Winata, G., Madotto, A., Lin, Z., Liu, R., Yosinski, J., and Fung, P. (2021). Language models are few-shot multilingual learners. In *Proceedings of the 1st Workshop on Multilingual Representation Learning*, pages 1–15, Punta Cana, Dominican Republic.

Adding multimodal capabilities to a text-only translation model

Vipin Vijayan vipin255@gmail.com
Braeden Bowen bowen_braeden@bah.com
Scott Grigsby grigsby_scott@bah.com
PAR Government Systems Corporation, Dayton, OH*

Timothy Anderson timothy.anderson.20@us.af.mil
Jeremy Gwinnup jeremy.gwinnup.1@us.af.mil
Air Force Research Laboratory 711HPW/RHWTE, Dayton, OH

Abstract

While most current work in multimodal machine translation (MMT) uses the Multi30k dataset for training and evaluation, we find that the resulting models overfit to the Multi30k dataset to an extreme degree. Consequently, these models perform very badly when evaluated against typical text-only testing sets such as the newstest datasets.

In order to perform well on both Multi30k and typical text-only datasets, we use a performant text-only machine translation (MT) model as the starting point of our MMT model. We add vision-text adapter layers connected via gating mechanisms to the MT model, and incrementally transform the MT model into an MMT model by 1) pre-training using vision-based masking of the source text and 2) fine-tuning on Multi30k.

We achieve a state-of-the-art performance on the Multi30k 2016 en-de test set of 46.5 BLEU4 score and 0.61 CoMMuTE score via this approach while retaining the performance of the original text-only MT model against the newstest dataset.

1 Introduction

The task of multimodal machine translation (MMT) is to automatically translate text while using additional modalities (e.g., image, video, audio) to aid in translation. Prior work has shown that MMT can use contextually relevant images to aid in translation of sentences that contain ambiguities or missing textual information (Caglayan et al., 2019; Wu et al., 2021). For example, the noun "bank" is ambiguous and contextually dependent in English ("financial institution" or "river edge") but unambiguous in French ("*banque*" or "*rive*"). The hypothesis that these ambiguities or missing information can be resolved with contextually relevant images is persuasive.

Much work in MMT (Yao and Wan, 2020; Yin et al., 2020; Wu et al., 2021; Li et al., 2022) focus on the Multi30k dataset (Elliott et al., 2016), a dataset comprising 30,014 image captions and corresponding translations in different languages.

However, compared to the domain of text-only translation where MT models are trained using millions of examples, the Multi30k dataset is an extremely small dataset. Consequently, the MMT models will naturally overfit to the Multi30k dataset and perform poorly against testing sets that text-only translation models are typically evaluated against (Section 4).

Text-only machine translation is a much larger domain than multimodal machine translation and many strong models have been developed in the field (Kocmi et al., 2022). Thus, using a pre-trained text-only model as a starting point for MMT is a promis-

* Now doing business as Booz Allen Hamilton Corporation.

ing approach to advance the state of MMT. To demonstrate this, we incrementally transform a text-only MT model into an MMT model, resulting in state-of-the-art performance against the Multi30k dataset while retaining the performance of the pre-trained model against text-only test sets.

We use a pre-trained Transformer-based translation model as our starting point. We evolve this text-only translation model into an MMT model using adapters (Houlsby et al., 2019) and gating mechanisms such that the model learns how to use visual information while preserving its original translation performance. We do this by 1) combining a strong pre-trained translation model and a pre-trained vision-language model to create an MMT model, 2) pre-training the MMT model on a dataset of captions augmented with informed visual grounding and machine generated translations along with a dataset collated from a text-only MT dataset, and 3) fine-tuning against the Multi30k dataset.

Using this model architecture and training process, we achieve high performance against the Multi30k test sets while retaining high performance against text-only testing sets (Table 1).

2 Related Works

2.1 Adapting pre-trained models for MMT

Caglayan et al. (2021) converted a translation language model into a vision-based translation language model by pre-training using Conceptual Captions (Sharma et al., 2018), translating English captions to German using a translation model, and fine-tuning using Multi30k.

Futeral et al. (2023) also proposed a model that adapts a language model into an MMT model by simultaneously training against the MMT objective using the Multi30k dataset and the visually-conditioned masked language modeling objective using the Conceptual Captions dataset. While they used a visual-conditioned masked language modeling object, we use the much simpler training process of directly optimizing the output using cross-entropy loss. Furthermore, while they randomly choose words for visual grounding, we choose vision-based words selected using an object detection method for our masking.

2.2 Masking for visual grounding

Masking words for visual grounding is a common approach employed by such works as Wu et al. (2021), Ive et al. (2019), Caglayan et al. (2019), Wang and Xiong (2021). We cover a subset of these works.

Ive et al. (2019) masked specific words (ambiguous, inaccurate, and gender-neutral words) in the English source text to force the MMT models to use the visual information to generate target texts. They show that the additional visual context was helpful in text generation.

Caglayan et al. (2019) performed masking based on color deprivation, whole entity masking, and progressive masking on source texts. However, they found that training based on masking results in performance degradation on the Multi30k testing sets, which indicates that the vision information was not being fully utilized by their models.

Wang and Xiong (2021) performed masking of source text based on Flickr30k-Entities (Plummer et al., 2016) that were vision related and used a multi-task object to train their MMT model, where they optimized for object-masking loss in addition to the text generation.

2.3 Gating mechanism for MMT

Similar to our work, Wu et al. (2021), Zhang et al. (2020), Lin et al. (2020) and Yin et al. (2020) use a trainable gating mechanism in the context of MMT to control the fusion between vision and text. However, our work uses two gating parameters each for the six adapter layers that we add, totaling 12 gating parameters, which is considerably fewer than in their work, which uses two trainable gating matrices of size 2048×512 and $T \times 512$ where T is the number of input text tokens. Furthermore, while the average of the gating parameters used by Wu et al. (2021) tended towards 0.0 (consequently weighing vision information lower) as more training is done, we show in this work how the use of vision-based masking allows the training of our gating mechanism to use more of the vision information.

3 Methods

We take a similar approach that Alayrac et al. (2022) used to create their generative vision-language model, Flamingo, while adapting their approach for the MMT task.

Flamingo is a generative decoder-only vision-language model created by combining a pre-trained generative language model and a pre-trained vision model, where vision and text interactions are modeled by via gated vision-text cross-attention layers inserted before each decoder layer. Then, the model is incrementally converted from using only text information to using both vision and text information by freezing the pre-trained portions of the model. The gating values are set to 0.0 at the beginning of training in order that the vision-language model initially performs equivalently to the language model, and as training progresses the gating values diverge from 0 via back-propagation and consequence learns to use vision information gradually.

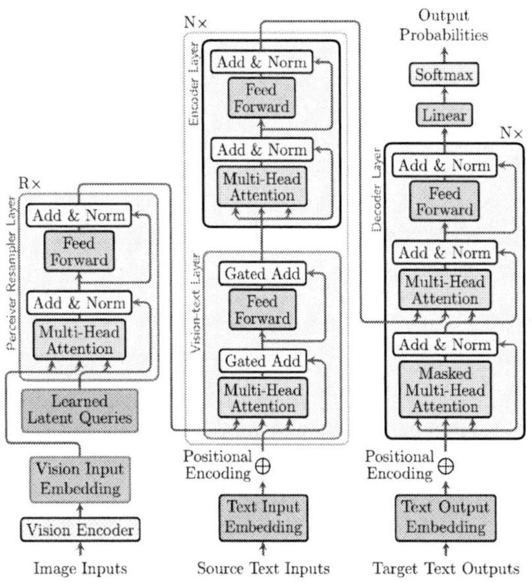

Figure 1: Multimodal translation architecture, where multimodal components are incorporated into the Transformer translation model introduced by Vaswani et al. (2017). The parameters in the model bordered by red are initialized randomly and updated for training, while the parameters in the pre-trained vision encoder and the pre-trained Transformer translation model bordered by black are frozen. The gating parameters in the vision-text layers are updated using back-propagation, allowing us to smoothly transition from a text-only translation model into a multimodal translation model.

Analogously, we start from a pre-trained Transformer-based text-only MT model and a pre-trained vision model to create an MMT model by inserting a vision-text cross-attention layer before each encoder layer. Using trainable gating parameters, we incrementally convert the model from using only text information to using both vision and text information to perform translation. We call our model GRAM (Gating and Residual Adapter-based Model).

While trainable gating parameters have been used in previous work for MMT (Wu et al., 2021; Zhang et al., 2020; Lin et al., 2020; Yin et al., 2020), our work is unique in the much lower number of gating parameters and in that it allows for the smooth transition of the model from performing as an MT model to performing as an MMT model.

Both the Flamingo model and our model were trained using the next-token prediction task, as is typical for text-only machine translation. Unlike Flamingo, which is a decoder-only model, our model is an encoder-decoder model. We inserted the vision-text layers before each of the encoder layers only, as we found it to perform better than inserting vision-text layers before the decoder layers only or before both the encoder and decoder layers (Appendix D.1). Aside from the perceiver resampler module and the gated vision-text cross attention layers used in Flamingo model, which we use to convert our model from an MT model to an MMT model, our GRAM model follows the original text-only Transformer MT model's hyper-parameters, layers, and training objectives as closely as possible.

3.1 GRAM model architecture

We start with a pre-trained Transformer translation model introduced by Vaswani et al. (2017) and add lightweight multimodal components (Figure 1). We use a pre-trained vision encoder, CLIP, to encode the input images (Section 3.1.1). We then link the vision encodings to the Transformer translation model using two components, the perceiver resampler (Section 3.1.2) and the vision-text layers (Section 3.1.3). The vision encodings, which can come from an arbitrary number of images, are converted into a fixed number of vision tokens using the perceiver resampler. Then, interactions between the vision tokens and the text embeddings are modeled using the vision-text cross-attention layers. The vision-text layers are incorporated into the Transformer layers by interleaving the vision-text layers and the original self-attention layers of the Transformer encoder.

In more detail, given an input sequence of text tokens $\boldsymbol{t} = (t_1, \ldots, t_n)$ and images $\boldsymbol{I} = (I_1, \ldots, I_l)$ where n and l may vary depending on the number of input text tokens and images, the output token sequence is generated auto-regressively as follows.

The vision encoder maps the images $\boldsymbol{I}$ into vision encodings $\boldsymbol{v} = (v_1, \ldots, v_l)$ where $v_i \in \boldsymbol{R}^e$ and e is the size of the image encodings. The vision input embedding layer maps the vision encodings $\boldsymbol{v}$ into vision embeddings $\boldsymbol{w} = (w_1, \ldots, w_l)$ where $w_i \in \boldsymbol{R}^d$ and d is the size of the text and image embeddings. The text input embedding layer maps the text tokens $\boldsymbol{t}$ to text embeddings $\boldsymbol{x} = (x_1, \ldots, x_n)$ where $x_i \in \boldsymbol{R}^d$. The perceiver resampler remaps the variable number of image embeddings to a constant number of vision tokens $\boldsymbol{p} = (p_1, \ldots, p_r)$ where $p_i \in \boldsymbol{R}^d$, using the r learned latent queries.

Then, the encoder, consisting of a sequence of interleaved vision-text cross-attention layers and encoder layers, maps the text embeddings $\boldsymbol{x}$ and vision tokens $\boldsymbol{p}$ into a sequence of representations $\boldsymbol{z} = (z_1, \ldots, z_n)$ where $z_i \in \boldsymbol{R}^d$. Given $\boldsymbol{z}$, the decoder generates the output probabilities for the next output token in an auto-regressive manner, thus producing the output token sequence, $y_1, \ldots, y_m$.

3.1.1 Vision encoder

We use a pre-trained vision-language model, CLIP (Radford et al., 2021), to encode the input images. CLIP was trained on 400 million image-text pairs using a contrastive image-text approach. The vision encodings produced by CLIP contain rich semantic information relevant to vision-language tasks, and it has been shown to perform well on a wide variety of these tasks. We use the vision encoder in CLIP's best performing ViT-L/14@336px model, which outputs vector encodings of length 768.

3.1.2 Perceiver resampler

The perceiver resampler, used for the Flamingo model, receives a variable number of vision embeddings and outputs a fixed number of vision tokens. This concept was initially used to map a large number of inputs to a fixed number of tokens (Jaegle et al., 2021) and for object detection, where each of the visual tokens corresponds to an object class (Carion et al., 2020).

Given the vision embeddings $\boldsymbol{w}$, let $\boldsymbol{\lambda} = (\lambda_1, \ldots, \lambda_r)$ be the learned latent queries, and let **MHA** and **FF** be the multi-head attention layer and the feed forward layer, respectively. Then, the first perceiver resampler layer **PR** is $\mathbf{PR}(\boldsymbol{\lambda}, \boldsymbol{w}) = \boldsymbol{\lambda}' + \mathbf{FF}(\boldsymbol{\lambda}')$ where $\boldsymbol{\lambda}' = \boldsymbol{\lambda} + \mathbf{MHA}(K{=}[\boldsymbol{w}, \boldsymbol{\lambda}], V{=}[\boldsymbol{w}, \boldsymbol{\lambda}], Q{=}\boldsymbol{\lambda})$ and $[\boldsymbol{w}, \boldsymbol{\lambda}]$ is the concatenation of the two vectors. Then, the perceiver resampler layers continue with $\boldsymbol{\lambda}{\leftarrow}\mathbf{PR}(\boldsymbol{\lambda}, \boldsymbol{w})$ for R layers. The vision tokens $\boldsymbol{p}{\leftarrow}\boldsymbol{\lambda}$ are outputted by the final perceiver resampler layer.

3.1.3 Vision-text layer

Similar to the Flamingo model, in order to smoothly train our MMT model to ensure it behaves at the beginning of training like the pre-trained MT model and behaves at the end of training like an MMT model, we insert vision-text cross-attention layers before each of the original Transformer encoder layers and we use a gating mechanism for each of the vision-text layers.

Given the vision tokens $\boldsymbol{p}$ output by the perceiver resampler and the input text embeddings $\boldsymbol{x}$, let g_a and g_f be the learnable gating parameters for the multi-head attention layer **MHA** and the feed forward layer **FF** respectively, with $\gamma_a = \tanh(g_a)$, $\gamma_f = \tanh(g_f)$. Then, the first gated cross-attention layer **GCA** is $\mathbf{GCA}(\boldsymbol{x}, \boldsymbol{\lambda}) = \boldsymbol{x}' + \gamma_f \, \mathbf{FF}(\boldsymbol{x}')$ where $\boldsymbol{x}' = \boldsymbol{x} + \gamma_a \, \mathbf{MHA}(K{=}\boldsymbol{p}, V{=}\boldsymbol{p}, Q{=}\boldsymbol{x})$. The gated cross-attention layers then continue with $\boldsymbol{x}{\leftarrow}\mathbf{E}(\mathbf{GCA}(\boldsymbol{x}, \boldsymbol{\lambda}))$ for N layers where **E** is the original Transformer encoder layer following the cross-attention layer.

Gating parameters are set to 0.0 at the start of training and so it passes the text embeddings $\boldsymbol{x}$ through without modification. As training continues and as more vision information is used, $|g_a|$ and $|g_f|$ increases via back-propagation; consequently $|\gamma_a| = |\tanh(g_a)|$ and $|\gamma_f| = |\tanh(g_f)|$ approaches 1.0, since the tanh function maps the gating parameters g_a and g_f to be between -1.0 and 1.0

Since the gating parameters initially start at 0.0, vision information is ignored and the model performs as well as the text-only Transformer. During the training process the gating parameters are updated to gradually incorporate vision information for the multimodal translation task. The gating parameters can be seen as a proxy for how much vision information is used by the model.

3.1.4 Model hyper-parameters

During training, only the multimodal components are updated, while the vision encoder and the rest of the parameters in the text-only Transformer are kept frozen. For the vision encoder, we use pre-trained weights from the CLIP vision encoder model and ignore CLIP's text encoder model[1]. For the text-only translation components, we use weights from the pre-trained MT model from FAIR's WMT19 submission[2]. Since our model uses FAIR's WMT19 MT model, we use the same byte-pair encoding (BPE) and vocabulary used by the MT model. Since the text-only portion of the model is frozen, training is relatively fast, typically 3 batches/sec using two Nvidia V100 GPUs where each batch contains 3,584 tokens.

Since we use the FAIR's WMT19 text-only Transformer as the starting point, we use those hyperparameters for our additional layers unless otherwise specified. For the perceiver resampler, we use two layers, i.e., $R = 2$, as was done for Flamingo. For both the perceiver resampler and the vision-text cross attention layers, we use the same parameters as in the text-only Transformer model, except for the number of attention heads being 16 and the intermediate feed-forward layer size being 4,096. The number of parameters are detailed in Appendix A).

3.2 Training

Beginning with the pre-trained text-only translation model, we add vision embedding layers and gated adapter layers that to the translation model to create a multimodal translation model (Section 3.1). Then, setting the initial gating values to 0.0, which allows our MMT model to perform equivalently to the MT model, we freeze the text-only parameters and train the additional vision-text parameters. We first pre-train the vision-text parameters of our model (Section 3.2.1) and then fine-tune the vision-text parameters using the Multi30k dataset (Section 3.2.2). During training, the gating value diverge from 0.0 as more vision information gets used by the model.

3.2.1 Pre-training

The intent of the pre-training step is to force the model to use contextually relevant image information by masking vision related words in the source sentence while performing the translation task. We pre-train our model on a dataset collated using vision-based masking of source sentences that we call the CR dataset.

First, we translate 2,878,999 of the English captions in the Conceptual Captions (CC) dataset (Sharma et al., 2018) that had images available to German using FAIR's WMT19 translation model, and then perform vision-based masking on the English captions.

For vision-based masking, we create a list of vision related phrases, or topic phrases, by using the VinVL object detector (Zhang et al., 2021) against the CC images. VinVL is able to detect 1,848 object classes and 524 attribute classes, resulting in a much richer possible vocabulary than other object detectors. With relatively high thresholds of 0.8 for object classes and 0.7 for attribute classes, we create a list of 7,494 "`attribute object`" combinations, such as "red car".

Then, for each English-German sentence pair, we search for topic phrases in the English sentence. For each topic phrase we find, we replaced it with the <unk> token (as we are restricted to using tokens present in the pre-trained FAIR WMT19 model, the <unk> token is the closest available token to a mask token). This results in an MMT dataset of 2,663,331 (masked source text, target text, image) triplets.

In addition, we also concatenate to the CR dataset 2,878,999 (<unk>, target text, image) triplets created from each of the captions in the CC dataset to further force the usage of vision information to generate text.

Furthermore, so that the model does not overfit to inputs that always contain image information while still maintaining the capacity to translate complex sentences, we concatenate to the CR dataset 1,183,301 (source text, target text, ∅) triplets created from the RAPID 2019 (Kocmi et al., 2022) dataset.

We train our GRAM model using the typical cross-entropy loss for machine translation. The optimization details for the pre-training step are described in Appendix C.1.

3.2.2 Training against Multi30k

Fine-tuning. We use the same vision-based masking described in Section 3.2.1 for the source sentences in the Multi30k training set, which resulted in 29,000 masked source text, target text, and image triplets. We refer to this resulting dataset as M30k. Since the Multi30k dataset contains only 29,000 examples, fine-tuning after the above pre-training step resulted in much better performance compared to directly

[1] See https://github.com/openai/CLIP to download weights.

[2] The weights are from the transformer.wmt19.de-en single model located in the pytorch/fairseq torch hub. See https://github.com/facebookresearch/fairseq for details.

training against the M30k dataset (Section 4).

Note that we train our model using a concatenation of the Multi30k training set with images and the Multi30k training set without images. This is to account for evaluation artifacts where the model performance when given both text and image input is higher than model performance with only text input, but the result is only due to the model overfitting on training data that only has (source text, target text, image) triplets and no examples of (source text, target text, ∅) triplets. We also explore fine-tuning of three other dataset variations including the original unmasked Multi30k dataset, which we discuss in Appendix E. The optimization details are described in Appendix C.2.

Direct training. We also directly training using the above described Multi30k dataset without the pre-training step for comparison. Due to its small size, we also explored directly training against the Multi30k dataset using smaller perceiver resampler and vision-text layers, and found performance to be similar (Appendix D.2). Thus, we show performance results using the same model sizes.

4 Results and Discussion

We use the evaluation framework proposed by Vijayan et al. (2024), where they argued that MMT models should be evaluated by measuring both 1) their use of visual information to aid in the translation task and 2) their ability to translate complex sentences as is done for text-only machine translation.

We evaluate model performances against 1) the CoMMuTE (Futeral et al., 2023) test set, 2) the Multi30k (Elliott et al., 2016) test sets, and 3) the WMT news translation task (Kocmi et al., 2022) test sets (newstest) using CoMMuTE score and BLEU4 calculated using SacreBLEU (Post, 2018).

The main evaluation results are shown in Table 1 and two examples from the CoMMuTE test dataset are shown in Figure 2. The label FAIR-WMT19 shows our model's performance before our training process, i.e., the original text-only Transformer's performance. M_{CR} is our GRAM model pre-trained on the CR dataset (Section 3.2.1). $M_{\text{CR,M30k}}$ is our model pre-trained on CR and fine-tuned on Multi30k (Section 3.2.2). M_{M30k} is our model trained on Multi30k without the pre-training step (Section 3.2.2). We compare against the Gated Fusion and RMMT models (Wu et al., 2021), which are both trained solely on the Multi30k dataset, as well as the reported performance of VGAMT (Futeral et al., 2023), which was introduced along with the CoMMuTE test set.

Label	CoMMuTE	Multi30k		newstest	
		2016	2017	2019	2020
	Score	BLEU4			
Multimodal inputs					
M_{CR}	0.57	39.2	36.8		
$M_{\text{CR,M30k}}$	**0.61**	46.5	**43.6**		
M_{M30k}	0.50	45.9	42.7		
Gated Fusion	0.50	42.0	33.6		
VGAMT	0.59	43.3	38.3		
Text inputs only					
FAIR-WMT19	0.50	40.7	37.7	40.6	**36.2**
M_{CR}	0.50	40.2	37.8	40.6	35.4
$M_{\text{CR,M30k}}$	0.50	46.4	42.9	**42.7**	**36.2**
M_{M30k}	0.50	45.9	42.8	36.1	26.8
RMMT	0.50	41.5	33.0	1.3	0.8
Non-matching inputs					
M_{CR}	0.51	39.0	36.7	42.1	35.6
$M_{\text{CR,M30k}}$	0.51	**46.6**	43.2	42.0	**36.2**
M_{M30k}	0.50	45.9	42.8	36.1	26.8
Gated Fusion	0.50	42.0	33.6	1.3	0.6

Table 1: Performance results for English to German (en-de) translations. The label FAIR-WMT19 shows our model's performance before our training process, i.e., the original text-only Transformer's performance. M_{CR} is our model pre-trained on the CR dataset; $M_{\text{CR,M30k}}$ is our model pre-trained on CR and fine-tuned on Multi30k; M_{M30k} is our model trained on Multi30k without the pre-training step; Gated Fusion and RMMT are our evaluations of the models published by Wu et al. (2021); VGAMT is the reported performance of the model published by Futeral et al. (2023). "Text inputs only" shows performance of when only the source text is given. "Multimodal inputs" shows the performances when both source text and image is used as input. "Non-matching inputs" shows performance when source text along with a random image is used as input.

4.1 Pre-training using vision-based masking

Since we begin with a performant MT model, we expect that our model will retain the high text-only performance of the MT model while transforming into an MMT model. In order to ensure this, we followed the work by Alayrac et al. (2022), where they incrementally transformed a language model into a vision-language model which retaining text-only performance, both in terms of the design of our model architecture and our training process (Section 3).

Figure 2: Examples from the CoMMuTE test dataset of our model (the $M_{\text{CR,M30k}}$ model from Table 1) resolving ambiguous input text when given contextual images. The ambiguous words in the input sentences and the resolved ambiguities in the output and reference sentences are in *italics*.

Similar to Alayrac et al. (2022), we found that a pre-training step is necessary to successfully transform the model without performance loss. When we pre-train our model and then fine-tune against the Multi30k dataset, this results in state-of-the-art performance against the Multi30k test sets and CoMMuTE score (Table 1, label $M_{\text{CR,M30k}}$), as well as little to no degradation of performance against the newstest datasets.

However, when we train against the Multi30k dataset without pre-training, we achieve good performance in the Multi30k test sets but only 0.5 for the CoMMuTE score (Table 1, M_{M30k}), which indicates that image information is not being used by the model, and degraded performance on the newstest datasets (e.g., 36.2 BLEU4 on newstest2020 for the text-only FAIR-WMT19 model compared to 26.8 BLEU4 for M_{M30k}).

While our pre-training step does degrade performance slightly on the newstest datasets compared to the original text-only Transformer (e.g., 36.2 BLEU4 on newstest2020 for the text-only FAIR-WMT19 model compared to 35.4 BLEU4 for the M_{CR} model), we note that our pre-training process is relatively rudimentary (Section 3.2.1) while FAIR-WMT19 is a model that was fine-tuned specifically for the news translation task using the news commentary dataset (Ng et al., 2019). Interestingly, and contrary to expectations, fine-tuning on the Multi30k dataset after pre-training improves performance against the newstest2019 and newstest2020 datasets, which might indicate that the FAIR-WMT19 model is overfitted to the news commentary dataset.

4.2 Training against Multi30k without pre-training

Due to the small size of the Multi30k training set, it is expected that models trained against Multi30k without pre-training would perform badly against testing sets such as the newstest datasets. For comparison, in the text-only translation domain, MT models such as FAIR-WMT19 are trained on millions of examples and then evaluated against the newstest dataset. We evaluated the Gated Fusion and RMMT MMT models, introduced by Wu et al. (2021) and trained solely on Multi30k, against the newstest datasets. As expected, there is a drastic drop in performance when the models are evaluated against the newstest datasets (Table 1).

For the Gated Fusion model, we evaluate by associating random images to the source text and evaluate against the newstest datasets. Since the associated images are not necessarily related to the source text, this can be considered non-matching evaluation. For the RMMT model, which takes as input only the source text, and uses the source text to perform image retrieval for the translation task, we simply use the source text to evaluate against the newstest datasets. As shown in Table 1, while the models perform well against the Multi30k test sets, they perform very badly against the newstest datasets.

In contrast, since our model uses a performant text-only MT model as the starting point, our model performs well when given non-matching inputs while still having high performance against CoMMuTE and the Multi30k testsets.

4.3 Text-only translations in Multi30k

One point to note when evaluating against the Multi30k test sets is that most of its captions do not require the image in order to be correctly translated due to the captions being unambiguous. Specifically, Futeral et al. (2023) analyzed the Multi30k Test2016 and Test2017 and showed that only 2.1% and 2.0%, respectively, of the examples in the test sets have ambiguous source sentences that can be resolved using the associated images. Thus, we expect that correct translations can be achieved with the text alone without the associated images for the vast majority of the remaining examples. Fitting our expectations, we see that state-of-the-art performance on the Multi30k test sets can be achieved without making use of image information at all (Table 1, "Text inputs only" rows).

Since high performance can be achieved on the Multi30k test sets without the use of contextual images, it is important that an evaluation framework such as the CoMMuTE evaluation framework that can confirm that visual information is being used to aid in the translation task should always be used in conjunction with the Multi30k test sets when evaluating MMT models.

4.4 Gating parameters

As in the Flamingo model, our model uses gating parameters to transform from a model that uses only text information to a model that uses both vision and text information to produce outputs. The gating parameters, explained in Section 3.1, can be viewed as how much the model weighs the image information compared to the text information. Since the g_f can potentially solely use text information in the training set, the g_a values should be interpreted as the main proxies that indicate how much image information influences the output of the model.

Gating parameters have been used previously for MMT, with Wu et al. (2021) having explored in detail how gating parameters that weighed vision and text information are affected in MMT models. For their model, as training progressed, the average value gating parameters tended towards 0.0, indicating that their model learned to not use image information as training progressed.

In contrast, our gating parameters did not trend towards 0.0 as training progressed (Figure 3), primarily due to the pre-training approach that we employ (as indicated by the difference in the progress of the gating values in pre-training vs. direct training in Figure 3). However, unlike in the Flamingo model, where the maximum of the attention gating values $|\gamma_a| = |\tanh g_a|$ reaches around 0.8 towards the end of training, and the maximum of the feed-forward gating values $|\gamma_f| = |\tanh g_f|$ reaches 0.95, our gating values reach 0.035 for $|\gamma_a|$ and 0.2 for $|\gamma_f|$. This suggests that image information is not necessarily as important for the multimodal translation task compared to the Flamingo model, which can perform a wide variety of tasks including visual question answering. On the other hand, improvements in the training datasets and processes may increase the gating values to be closer to that of the Flamingo model.

5 Conclusion

Text-only machine translation is a much larger domain than multimodal machine translation and many strong models have been developed in the field. The approach of transforming a language model into a vision-language model was successful demonstrated via Flamingo, and thus have a high probability of working well in the similar task of machine translation. Following this idea, we designed an MMT model that began as a performant text-only MT model and incrementally transformed it into a MMT model by 1) pre-training using informed vision-based masking of the source text and 2) fine-tuning on Multi30k. We achieved a state-of-the-art performance on the Multi30k 2016 test set of 46.5 BLEU4 score via this approach while retaining high performance against CoMMuTE and the newstest datasets. There are many approaches for improving our model including the training process, where the pre-training dataset can be improved using more text-only datasets or augmenting text-only datasets using image retrieval, and model architecture, where techniques such as VMLM can be used to further enforce the use of image information in the model.

Acknowledgements

Thanks to AFRL SCREAM Lab and AFRL 711HPW/RHWTE for their help in this project. **Funding:** This work was supported by the AIM-MIER project via Infoscitex Corporation (IST) and Air Force Research Laboratory (AFRL) under Air Force contract FA8650-20-D-6207.

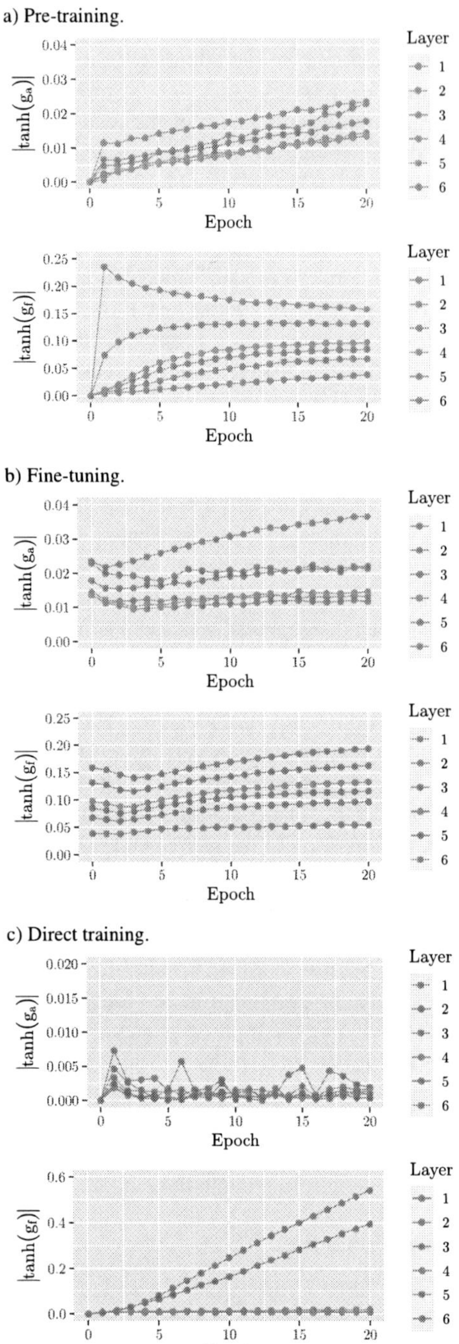

Figure 3: Gating values during a) pre-training over the CR dataset, b) fine-tuning over the Multi30k dataset, and c) directly training on the Multi30k dataset. Layer 1 is the vision-text adapter layer that is closest to the input. Note that some of the gating values overlap in some of the plots.

References

Alayrac, J.-B., Donahue, J., Luc, P., Miech, A., Barr, I., Hasson, Y., Lenc, K., Mensch, A., Millican, K., Reynolds, M., Ring, R., Rutherford, E., Cabi, S., Han, T., Gong, Z., Samangooei, S., Monteiro, M., Menick, J., Borgeaud, S., Brock, A., Nematzadeh, A., Sharifzadeh, S., Binkowski, M., Barreira, R., Vinyals, O., Zisserman, A., and Simonyan, K. (2022). Flamingo: a Visual Language Model for Few-Shot Learning.

Caglayan, O., Kuyu, M., Amac, M. S., Madhyastha, P., Erdem, E., Erdem, A., and Specia, L. (2021). Cross-lingual visual pre-training for multimodal machine translation. In Merlo, P., Tiedemann, J., and Tsarfaty, R., editors, *Proceedings of the 16th Conference of the European Chapter of the Association for Computational Linguistics: Main Volume*, pages 1317–1324, Online. Association for Computational Linguistics.

Caglayan, O., Madhyastha, P., Specia, L., and Barrault, L. (2019). Probing the Need for Visual Context in Multimodal Machine Translation. In *Proceedings of the 2019 Conference of the North American Chapter of the Association for Computational Linguistics: Human Language Technologies, Volume 1 (Long and Short Papers)*, pages 4159–4170, Minneapolis, Minnesota. Association for Computational Linguistics.

Carion, N., Massa, F., Synnaeve, G., Usunier, N., Kirillov, A., and Zagoruyko, S. (2020). End-to-end object detection with transformers. In *Computer Vision – ECCV 2020: 16th European Conference, Glasgow, UK, August 23–28, 2020, Proceedings, Part I*, page 213–229, Berlin, Heidelberg. Springer-Verlag.

Elliott, D., Frank, S., Sima'an, K., and Specia, L. (2016). Multi30K: Multilingual English-German Image Descriptions. In *Proceedings of the 5th Workshop on Vision and Language*, pages 70–74. Association for Computational Linguistics. event-place: Berlin, Germany.

Futeral, M., Schmid, C., Laptev, I., Sagot, B., and Bawden, R. (2023). Tackling ambiguity with images: Improved multimodal machine translation and contrastive evaluation. In Rogers, A., Boyd-Graber, J., and Okazaki, N., editors, *Proceedings of the 61st Annual Meeting of the Association for Computational Linguistics (Volume 1: Long Papers)*, pages 5394–5413, Toronto, Canada. Association for Computational Linguistics.

Houlsby, N., Giurgiu, A., Jastrzebski, S., Morrone, B., De Laroussilhe, Q., Gesmundo, A., Attariyan, M., and Gelly, S. (2019). Parameter-Efficient Transfer Learning for NLP. In Chaudhuri, K. and Salakhutdinov, R., editors, *Proceedings of the 36th International Conference on Machine Learning*, volume 97 of *Proceedings of Machine Learning Research*, pages 2790–2799. PMLR.

Ive, J., Madhyastha, P., and Specia, L. (2019). Distilling translations with visual awareness. In Korhonen, A., Traum, D., and Màrquez, L., editors, *Proceedings of the 57th Annual Meeting of the Association for Computational Linguistics*, pages 6525–6538, Florence, Italy. Association for Computational Linguistics.

Jaegle, A., Gimeno, F., Brock, A., Vinyals, O., Zisserman, A., and Carreira, J. (2021). Perceiver: General Perception with Iterative Attention. In Meila, M. and Zhang, T., editors, *Proceedings of the 38th International Conference on Machine Learning*, volume 139 of *Proceedings of Machine Learning Research*, pages 4651–4664. PMLR.

Kocmi, T., Bawden, R., Bojar, O., Dvorkovich, A., Federmann, C., Fishel, M., Gowda, T., Graham, Y., Grundkiewicz, R., Haddow, B., Knowles, R., Koehn, P., Monz, C., Morishita, M., Nagata, M., Nakazawa, T., Novák, M., Popel, M., and Popović, M. (2022). Findings of the 2022 conference on machine translation (WMT22). In Koehn, P., Barrault, L., Bojar, O., Bougares, F., Chatterjee, R., Costa-jussà, M. R., Federmann,

C., Fishel, M., Fraser, A., Freitag, M., Graham, Y., Grundkiewicz, R., Guzman, P., Haddow, B., Huck, M., Jimeno Yepes, A., Kocmi, T., Martins, A., Morishita, M., Monz, C., Nagata, M., Nakazawa, T., Negri, M., Névéol, A., Neves, M., Popel, M., Turchi, M., and Zampieri, M., editors, *Proceedings of the Seventh Conference on Machine Translation (WMT)*, pages 1–45, Abu Dhabi, United Arab Emirates (Hybrid). Association for Computational Linguistics.

Li, Y., Panda, R., Kim, Y., Chen, C., Feris, R., Cox, D., and Vasconcelos, N. (2022). Valhalla: Visual hallucination for machine translation. In *2022 IEEE/CVF Conference on Computer Vision and Pattern Recognition (CVPR)*, pages 5206–5216, Los Alamitos, CA, USA. IEEE Computer Society.

Lin, H., Meng, F., Su, J., Yin, Y., Yang, Z., Ge, Y., Zhou, J., and Luo, J. (2020). Dynamic Context-guided Capsule Network for Multimodal Machine Translation. *Proceedings of the 28th ACM International Conference on Multimedia*. ISBN: 9781450379885 Publisher: ACM.

Ng, N., Yee, K., Baevski, A., Ott, M., Auli, M., and Edunov, S. (2019). Facebook FAIR's WMT19 news translation task submission. In Bojar, O., Chatterjee, R., Federmann, C., Fishel, M., Graham, Y., Haddow, B., Huck, M., Yepes, A. J., Koehn, P., Martins, A., Monz, C., Negri, M., Névéol, A., Neves, M., Post, M., Turchi, M., and Verspoor, K., editors, *Proceedings of the Fourth Conference on Machine Translation (Volume 2: Shared Task Papers, Day 1)*, pages 314–319, Florence, Italy. Association for Computational Linguistics.

Ott, M., Edunov, S., Baevski, A., Fan, A., Gross, S., Ng, N., Grangier, D., and Auli, M. (2019). fairseq: A Fast, Extensible Toolkit for Sequence Modeling. In *Proceedings of NAACL-HLT 2019: Demonstrations*.

Plummer, B. A., Wang, L., Cervantes, C. M., Caicedo, J. C., Hockenmaier, J., and Lazebnik, S. (2016). Flickr30k Entities: Collecting Region-to-Phrase Correspondences for Richer Image-to-Sentence Models. *International Journal of Computer Vision*, 123:74 – 93.

Post, M. (2018). A call for clarity in reporting BLEU scores. In *Proceedings of the Third Conference on Machine Translation: Research Papers*, pages 186–191, Belgium, Brussels. Association for Computational Linguistics.

Radford, A., Kim, J. W., Hallacy, C., Ramesh, A., Goh, G., Agarwal, S., Sastry, G., Askell, A., Mishkin, P., Clark, J., Krueger, G., and Sutskever, I. (2021). Learning Transferable Visual Models From Natural Language Supervision. In Meila, M. and Zhang, T., editors, *Proceedings of the 38th International Conference on Machine Learning*, volume 139 of *Proceedings of Machine Learning Research*, pages 8748–8763. PMLR.

Sharma, P., Ding, N., Goodman, S., and Soricut, R. (2018). Conceptual Captions: A Cleaned, Hypernymed, Image Alt-text Dataset For Automatic Image Captioning. In *Proceedings of the 56th Annual Meeting of the Association for Computational Linguistics (Volume 1: Long Papers)*, pages 2556–2565, Melbourne, Australia. Association for Computational Linguistics.

Vaswani, A., Shazeer, N., Parmar, N., Uszkoreit, J., Jones, L., Gomez, A. N., Kaiser, L. u., and Polosukhin, I. (2017). Attention is all you need. In Guyon, I., Luxburg, U. V., Bengio, S., Wallach, H., Fergus, R., Vishwanathan, S., and Garnett, R., editors, *Advances in Neural Information Processing Systems*, volume 30. Curran Associates, Inc.

Vijayan, V., Bowen, B., Grigsby, S., Anderson, T., and Gwinnup, J. (2024). The case for evaluating multimodal translation models on text datasets. *arXiv:2403.03014 [cs.CL]*.

Wang, D. and Xiong, D. (2021). Efficient Object-Level Visual Context Modeling for Multimodal Machine Translation: Masking Irrelevant Objects Helps Grounding. *Proceedings of the AAAI Conference on Artificial Intelligence*, 35(4):2720–2728.

Wu, Z., Kong, L., Bi, W., Li, X., and Kao, B. (2021). Good for misconceived reasons: An empirical revisiting on the need for visual context in multimodal machine translation. In Zong, C., Xia, F., Li, W., and Navigli, R., editors, *Proceedings of the 59th Annual Meeting of the Association for Computational Linguistics and the 11th International Joint Conference on Natural Language Processing (Volume 1: Long Papers)*, pages 6153–6166, Online. Association for Computational Linguistics.

Yao, S. and Wan, X. (2020). Multimodal Transformer for Multimodal Machine Translation. In *Proceedings of the 58th Annual Meeting of the Association for Computational Linguistics*, pages 4346–4350, Online. Association for Computational Linguistics.

Yin, Y., Meng, F., Su, J., Zhou, C., Yang, Z., Zhou, J., and Luo, J. (2020). A Novel Graph-based Multi-modal Fusion Encoder for Neural Machine Translation. In *Proceedings of the 58th Annual Meeting of the Association for Computational Linguistics*, pages 3025–3035, Online. Association for Computational Linguistics.

Zhang, P., Li, X., Hu, X., Yang, J., Zhang, L., Wang, L., Choi, Y., and Gao, J. (2021). VinVL: Revisiting Visual Representations in Vision-Language Models. In *Proceedings of the IEEE/CVF Conference on Computer Vision and Pattern Recognition (CVPR)*, pages 5579–5588. _eprint: 2101.00529.

Zhang, Z., Chen, K., Wang, R., Utiyama, M., Sumita, E., Li, Z., and Zhao, H. (2020). Neural Machine Translation with Universal Visual Representation. In *International Conference on Learning Representations*.

A Number of parameters in the GRAM model

The number of parameters in the original text-only Transformer is 269,746,176. While there are also 304,293,888 parameters in the ViT-L/14@336px CLIP vision encoder model that we use, the vision encoder is not used during training since we cache the image encodings to file. We add 68,051,980 parameters via the perceiver resampler and the six vision-text layers, which are that parameters that we optimize over. Thus, the entire model contains 337,798,156 parameters. If we include the vision encoder as well, then the entire model contains 642,092,044 parameters.

B Datasets

Dataset	Only text	With image	Total
CR	1,183,301	5,542,330	7,725,631
M30k	29,000	29,000	58,000

Table 2: Training datasets used in this work. CR is the augmented Conceptual Captions and RAPID2019 datasets described in Section 3.2.1 that we use for pre-training. M30k is the augmented Multi30k dataset used for fine-tuning and is described in Section 3.2.2. "Only text" is the number of examples in the dataset with no associated image. "With image" is the number of examples with one or more associated images. "Total" is the total number of examples in the dataset.

C Optimization details

C.1 Pre-training

We use the same optimization hyper-parameters as FAIR's WMT19 model (Ng et al., 2019) with Fairseq (Ott et al., 2019) as the training and evaluation framework. For pre-training, we use the Adam optimizer with $\beta_1 = 0.9, \beta_2 = 0.98$, with a warm-up phase of 4,000 steps where we linearly increase the learning rate from 10^{-7} to 0.0007. Each training batch contains 3,584 source/target tokens and we train for 20 epochs. We use the checkpoint from the last epoch for fine-tuning.

C.2 Training against Multi30k

Fine-tuning. When we perform fine-tuning, we lower the learning rate to 0.0002 and train for 20 epochs. Since the Multi30k dataset is small, we use a warm-up phase of 240 steps where we linearly increase the learning rate from 10^{-7} to 0.0002. We select the checkpoint that performs best against the Multi30k validation set with respect to BLEU4 score.

Direct training. When we directly train, we set the learning rate to 0.0007 and train for 20 epochs using a warm-up phase of 240 steps.

D Model variations

D.1 Where to insert the vision-text adapter layers

For the GRAM model, vision-text cross-attention adapter layers can be added before each of the layers in the Transformer model. Since we modify an encoder-decoder Transformer in order to transform it from an MT model to an MMT model, there are three options for where we add the vision-text layers. One is to insert the vision-text layers before each layer in the Transformer encoder (M_{CR}). Second is to insert the vision-text layers before each layer in the Transformer decoder (DO_{CR}). Third is to insert the vision-text layers before each layer in both the Transformer encoder and decoder (ED_{CR}).

We compare the performance of the three options, the results which are in Table 3. We selected the M_{CR} for fine-tuning since the CoMMuTE score was 0.57 compared to CoMMuTE score of 0.55 for DO_{CR} and 0.52 for ED_{CR}.

D.2 Smaller model variations when directly training against Multi30k

We also explored smaller models when directly training against Multi30k due to the small size of the dataset. For the first smaller model, we set the number of attention heads to 8 and intermediate feed-forward layer size to 2,048 of the vision-text cross-attention layers (S_{M30k_o} and S_{M30k}). For the second smaller model, we set the number of attention heads to 4 and intermediate feed-forward layer size to 1,024 of the vision-text cross-attention layers (T_{M30k_o} and T_{M30k}). As shown in Table 4, we found performance to be similar.

Label	PT	FT	CoMMuTE		Multi30k				newstest	
					2016	2017	coco	2018	2019	2020
			Score	BLEU4						
				Multimodal inputs						
M_{CR}	CR		0.57	35.08	39.17	36.79	31.45	35.72		
DO_{CR}	CR		0.55	32.59	41.16	37.54	33.46	36.64		
ED_{CR}	CR		0.52	34.14	39.56	37.45	31.34	35.94		
				Text inputs only						
FAIR-WMT19			0.50	32.63	40.66	37.70	33.97	36.45	40.62	36.20
M_{CR}	CR		0.50	31.98	40.22	37.75	32.81	36.41	40.56	35.35
DO_{CR}	CR		0.50	30.01	40.85	37.19	33.36	35.84	38.36	33.79
ED_{CR}	CR		0.50	30.61	40.03	37.80	32.34	36.11	40.18	34.15
				Non-matching inputs						
M_{CR}	CR		0.51	30.37	39.01	36.73	32.10	35.35	42.09	35.62
DO_{CR}	CR		0.50	33.07	41.02	37.72	33.54	36.59	42.17	36.20
ED_{CR}	CR		0.50	34.02	39.67	37.44	31.19	35.74	40.84	34.95

Table 3: Performance results of our model under various pre-training and fine-tuning conditions for English to German (en-de) translations. The label FAIR-WMT19 shows our model's performance before our training process, i.e., the original text-only Transformer's performance. M_{CR} is our model pre-trained on the CR dataset. DO_{CR} and ED_{CR} are variations where the vision-text layers are inserted before the decoder layers only (DO_{CR}) and inserted before both the encoder and decoder layers (ED_{CR}), while the M_{CR} model is the variation where the vision-text layers are inserted before the encoder layers only. "Text inputs only" shows the performances of our model when only the source text is given and a zero vector is given as the vision encoding. "Multimodal inputs" shows the performances of our model when both source text and image is used as input. The model is evaluated against the CoMMuTE (Futeral et al., 2023) testing set, the Multi30k (Elliott et al., 2016) sets, and the newstest (Kocmi et al., 2022) testing sets using BLEU4, calculated using SacreBLEU (Post, 2018). Both CoMMuTE score and BLEU4 scores against the CoMMuTE test dataset are shown for completeness; since the CoMMuTE sentences are very short, the BLEU4 score for CoMMuTE should be weighed lightly. PT indicates pre-training and FT indicates fine-tuning. The datasets used for pre-training and fine-tuning are described in Table 2.

E Dataset variations

We explore four variations of our model where we fine-tune against four datasets: M30k$_o$, M30k, M30k$_o$/ncv14, and M30k/ncv14 (Table 6). The results are shown in Table 6.

M30k$_o$ is the original Multi30k dataset. However, we train our model using a concatenation of the Multi30k training set with images and the Multi30k training set without images. This is to account for evaluation artifacts where the model performance when given both text and image input is higher than model performance with only text input, but the result is only due to the model overfitting on training data that only has (source text, target text, image) triplets and no examples of (source text, target text, ∅) triplets.

M30k is the Multi30k dataset with vision-based masking of the source sentences as done in Section 3.2.1. For each (source text, target text, image), we search for topic phrases (see Section 3.2.1) in the source sentence and replace each instance of the topic phrase with the <unk> token. We also concatenate the original Multi30k dataset with the (source text, target text, image(s)) triplets and the Multi30k dataset with images removed (source text, target text, ∅) to this.

M30k$_o$/ncv14 and M30k/ncv14 are the concatenation of M30k$_o$ and M30k, respectively, to the news commentary v14 dataset. The news commentary v14, a news translation dataset comprising X sentence pairs, has been used by Ng et al. (2019) in their

Label	PT	FT	CoMMuTE		Multi30k				newstest	
					2016	2017	coco	2018	2019	2020
			Score				BLEU4			
					Multimodal inputs					
M_{M30k_o}	M30k$_o$		0.50	31.99	45.52	42.20	37.51	39.30		
M_{M30k}	M30k		0.50	27.12	45.93	42.76	37.64	38.82		
S_{M30k_o}	M30k$_o$		0.50	33.61	46.41	42.29	37.83	39.71		
S_{M30k}	M30k		0.50	29.70	46.09	41.61	38.58	38.98		
T_{M30k_o}	M30k$_o$		0.50	33.06	46.74	42.44	38.06	39.32		
T_{M30k}	M30k		0.50	27.12	45.93	42.76	37.64	38.82		
					Text inputs only					
M_{M30k_o}	M30k$_o$		0.50	31.99	45.52	42.20	37.51	39.30	37.77	28.30
M_{M30k}	M30k		0.50	27.12	45.93	42.76	37.64	38.82	36.09	26.81
S_{M30k_o}	M30k$_o$		0.50	33.61	46.41	42.29	37.83	39.71	37.75	27.59
S_{M30k}	M30k		0.50	29.70	46.09	41.61	38.58	38.98	36.71	27.89
T_{M30k_o}	M30k$_o$		0.50	33.06	46.74	42.44	38.06	39.32	37.09	28.12
T_{M30k}	M30k		0.50	29.38	46.21	42.20	38.08	38.88	37.37	28.21
					Non-matching inputs					
M_{M30k_o}	M30k$_o$		0.50	31.99	45.52	42.20	37.51	39.30	37.77	28.30
M_{M30k}	M30k		0.50	27.12	45.93	42.76	37.64	38.82	36.09	26.81
S_{M30k_o}	M30k$_o$		0.50	33.61	46.41	42.29	37.83	39.71	37.75	27.59
S_{M30k}	M30k		0.50	29.70	46.09	41.61	38.58	38.98	36.71	27.89
T_{M30k_o}	M30k$_o$		0.50	33.06	46.74	42.44	38.06	39.32	37.09	28.12
T_{M30k}	M30k		0.50	29.38	46.21	42.20	38.08	38.88	37.37	28.21

Table 4: Performance results of our model under various pre-training and fine-tuning conditions for English to German (en-de) translations. The label FAIR-WMT19 shows our model's performance before our training process, i.e., the original text-only Transformer's performance. M_{CR} is our model pre-trained on the CR dataset; $M_{\text{CR,M30k}}$ is our model pre-trained on CR and fine-tuned on Multi30k; M_{M30k} is our model trained on Multi30k without the pre-training step. S_{M30k} and T_{M30k} are smaller variations of the M_{M30k} model. The datasets used for pre-training and fine-tuning are described in Table 2.

fine-tuning step in order to perform well against the newstest testing sets.

Optimization details for the dataset variants. When we perform fine-tuning, we lower the learning rate to 0.0002 and train for 20 epochs. Since the Multi30k dataset is small, for M30k$_o$ and M30k we use a warm-up phase of 240 steps where we linearly increase the learning rate from 10^{-7} to 0.0002. We select the checkpoint that performs best against the Multi30k validation set with respect to BLEU4 score. For M30k$_o$/ncv14 and M30k/ncv14, we use a warm-up phase of 1200 steps where we linearly increase the learning rate from 10^{-7} to 0.0002. We create a validation set from the concatenation of the WMT19 validation set and the Multi30k validation set and select the checkpoint that performs best against the validation set with respect to BLEU4 score.

E.1 Simultaneously fine-tuning Multi30k and a text-only dataset

Since the pre-training step does degrade performance on the newstest datasets (e.g., 36.2 BLEU4 on newstest2020 for the text-only FAIR-WMT19 model compared to 35.4 BLEU4 for the M_{CR} model), and fine-tuning against Multi30k alone only slightly improves this performance, we explore how to fine-tune our model such that we preserve the performance on the Multi30k test sets and improve the performance on the newstest datasets.

Ng et al. (2019) used the news commentary dataset (Kocmi et al., 2022), a news translation dataset, as the final fine-tuning step in order to improve performance against the newstest datasets. Similarly, we perform fine-tuning on a concatenation of the Multi30k and news commentary v14 dataset, which resulted in improvements in both the newstest datasets and the Multi30k test sets (e.g., 35.4 BLEU4 on newstest2020 for the M_{CR} model compared to 36.2 BLEU4 for the $M_{\text{CR,M30k/ncv14}}$ model).

E.2 Fine-tuning without vision-based masking of source text

Since most of the captions in Multi30k do not require the image in order to be correctly translated due to the captions being unambiguous (Futeral et al., 2023), MMT models tend to ignore visual information during the training process (Caglayan et al., 2019; Wu et al., 2021). We are able to quantitatively see this when directly training against the original Multi30k dataset (for M_{M30k_o}, the CoMMuTE score is 0.5).

So we ask ourselves how we may preserve CoMMuTE performance along with newstest and Multi30k test performances. Since vision-based masking of source sentences was used to improve performance during the pre-training stage, we explore whether it can improve performance during the fine-tuning stage as well.

Thus, we create the M30k and the M30k/ncv14 datasets as described above. The M30k contains masked source sentences from the Multi30k dataset and the M30k/ncv14 dataset is a concatenation of the M30k and the text-only news commentary v14 datasets. We see that fine-tuning using these datasets preserve the CoMMuTE score much better than when not using informed masking (Table 6) while only slightly decreasing BLEU4 scores.

Label	PT	FT	CoMMuTE		Multi30k				newstest	
					2016	2017	coco	2018	2019	2020
			Score				BLEU4			
			Multimodal inputs							
M_{CR}	CR		0.57	35.08	39.17	36.79	31.45	35.72		
$M_{\text{CR,M30k}_o}$	CR	M30k$_o$	0.58	33.03	47.11	43.75	39.48	40.94		
$M_{\text{CR,M30k}}$	CR	M30k	0.61	35.03	46.50	43.57	39.10	40.40		
$M_{\text{CR,M30k}_o\text{/ncv14}}$	CR	M30k$_o$/ncv14	0.58	33.99	47.38	42.95	39.83	40.92		
$M_{\text{CR,M30k/ncv14}}$	CR	M30k/ncv14	0.63	34.88	46.57	43.58	39.78	41.03		
M_{M30k_o}	M30k$_o$		0.50	31.99	45.52	42.20	37.51	39.30		
M_{M30k}	M30k		0.50	27.12	45.93	42.76	37.64	38.82		
			Text inputs only							
FAIR-WMT19			0.50	32.63	40.66	37.70	33.97	36.45	40.62	36.20
M_{CR}	CR		0.50	31.98	40.22	37.75	32.81	36.41	40.56	35.35
$M_{\text{CR,M30k}_o}$	CR	M30k$_o$	0.50	31.25	47.10	43.08	38.48	40.82	42.64	36.00
$M_{\text{CR,M30k}}$	CR	M30k	0.50	32.11	46.43	42.88	37.88	40.35	42.66	36.22
$M_{\text{CR,M30k}_o\text{/ncv14}}$	CR	M30k$_o$/ncv14	0.50	31.17	47.40	43.30	38.86	40.70	41.80	36.44
$M_{\text{CR,M30k/ncv14}}$	CR	M30k/ncv14	0.50	32.95	46.65	43.06	38.95	40.73	41.86	36.46
M_{M30k_o}	M30k$_o$		0.50	31.99	45.52	42.20	37.51	39.30	37.77	28.30
M_{M30k}	M30k		0.50	27.12	45.93	42.76	37.64	38.82	36.09	26.81
			Non-matching inputs							
M_{CR}	CR		0.51	30.37	39.01	36.73	32.10	35.35	42.09	35.62
$M_{\text{CR,M30k}_o}$	CR	M30k$_o$	0.52	32.17	47.08	42.97	38.55	41.12	42.31	36.12
$M_{\text{CR,M30k}}$	CR	M30k	0.51	31.22	46.56	43.19	37.94	40.75	42.04	36.18
$M_{\text{CR,M30k}_o\text{/ncv14}}$	CR	M30k$_o$/ncv14	0.50	29.39	47.24	43.44	39.48	41.11	41.82	36.52
$M_{\text{CR,M30k/ncv14}}$	CR	M30k/ncv14	0.51	31.69	46.37	43.06	38.90	40.72	41.78	36.27
M_{M30k_o}	M30k$_o$		0.50	31.99	45.52	42.20	37.51	39.30	37.77	28.30
M_{M30k}	M30k		0.50	27.12	45.93	42.76	37.64	38.82	36.09	26.81

Table 6: Performance results of our model under various pre-training and fine-tuning conditions for English to German (en-de) translations. The label FAIR-WMT19 shows our model's performance before our training process, i.e., the original text-only Transformer's performance. M_{CR} is our model pre-trained on the CR dataset; $M_{\text{CR,M30k}}$ is our model pre-trained on CR and fine-tuned on Multi30k; M_{M30k} is our model trained on Multi30k without the pre-training step. The datasets used for pre-training and fine-tuning are described in Table 2.

Detecting concrete visual tokens for multimodal machine translation

Braeden Bowen bowen_braeden@bah.com
Vipin Vijayan vipin255@gmail.com
Scott Grigsby grigsby_scott@bah.com
PAR Government Systems Corporation, Dayton, OH*

Timothy Anderson timothy.anderson.20@us.af.mil
Jeremy Gwinnup jeremy.gwinnup.1@us.af.mil
Air Force Research Laboratory 711HPW/RHWTE, Dayton, OH

Abstract

The challenge of visual grounding and masking in multimodal machine translation (MMT) systems has encouraged varying approaches to the detection and selection of visually-grounded text tokens for masking. We introduce new methods for the detection of visually and contextually relevant (concrete) tokens from source sentences, including detection with natural language processing (NLP), detection with object detection, and a joint detection-verification technique. We also introduce new methods for selection of detected tokens, including shortest n tokens, longest n tokens, and *all* detected concrete tokens. We utilize the GRAM MMT architecture to train models against synthetically collated multimodal datasets of source images with masked sentences, showing performance improvements and improved usage of visual context during translation tasks over the baseline model.

1 Introduction

The challenge of multimodal machine translation (MMT) is to design a system that automatically translates text from one language to another while utilizing other modalities (e.g., image, video, audio) as inputs to assist in translation (Caglayan et al., 2016).

Prior work has shown that translation ambiguities and missing textual information can be supplied by contextually-relevant images, aiding in multilingual translation (Lala and Specia, 2018; Caglayan et al., 2019; Wu et al., 2021). For example, the noun "bank" is ambiguous and contextually dependent in English ("financial institution" or "river edge") but unambiguous in French ("*banque*" or "*rive*") (Futeral et al., 2023). The hypothesis for MMT research is that these translation ambiguities can be resolved with the inclusion of image context.

In practice, not every sentence has semantic ambiguities, missing information, or relevant visual context; it is therefore beneficial to ensure that ambiguous text is visually and contextually relevant to an associated image (Zhou et al., 2018).

To enforce reliance on image context for translation tasks, some MMT models mask tokens from text inputs (Caglayan et al., 2019; Sato et al., 2023). While most early masking iterations randomly selected tokens for masking, more recent efforts have sought to mask tokens based on contextual relevance to a given image (Tan and Bansal, 2020), increasing the usefulness of the image in resolving ambiguity. Still, those methods tend to ignore deterministic selection of relevant tokens, opting to randomly select from a pool of viable tokens.

While these approaches have displayed performance improvements over text-only and random

* Now doing business as Booz Allen Hamilton Corporation.

masking models, these methods generally do not take into account the relevance of a masked token. Therefore, we hypothesize that more intentional selection and masking of **concrete** (i.e., visually and contextually relevant) text tokens will improve visual grounding and increase model usage of multimodal context.

In order to select visually and contextually relevant tokens, we explore a combination of natural language processing (NLP) techniques and object detection models and examine deterministic methods for token selection from the set of available detections.

Using these techniques, we collate multimodal datasets based on the Multi30k dataset (Elliott et al., 2016); the resulting datasets are triplets of source sentences with masked concrete tokens, unmasked target sentences, and associated images.

When masking concrete text tokens from source sentences, we find improvements in both usage of visual information in translation and in performance on evaluation challenges, including CoMMuTE scores of up to 0.67 and BLEU scores of up to 46.2.

2 Related Works

2.1 Masking for Visual Grounding

In a text-only modality, Devlin et al. (2019) randomly masked text tokens during pre-training of a bidirectional transformer encoder-decoder and found performance improvements against other text-only models.

Zhou et al. (2018) utilized jointly-encoded unmasked text and image embeddings to visually ground entire source sentences to images. Using a visual-text attention mechanism on the embeddings, they extracted words that shared semantic context with the images.

Ive et al. (2019) combined these approaches, randomly *and* manually masking ambiguous and gender-neutral words from source texts to force their MMT model to utilize visual information on evaluation tasks. This work showed that the model was able to use image context to recover from missing, inaccurate, or ambiguous textual context.

Caglayan et al. (2019) used image descriptions from the Flicker30k-Entities dataset (Plummer et al., 2015) to dynamically mask "visually depictable entities" and color descriptors from source sentences, but noted a degradation in performance on the Multi30k test sets (Elliott et al., 2016). In contrast, Wang and Xiong (2021) found that masking *irrelevant* objects improved performance on MMT evaluation tasks, suggesting that state-of-the-art MMT models are ineffectively utilizing visual information.

A meta-analysis by Wu et al. (2021) found that many reported improvements in MMT performance are the result of regularization effects, not model interpolation of multimodal features; similarly, Zhuang et al. (2023) found that while visual grounding can improve performance in word learning, these improvements are only marginal. However, they also found that training sets with less textual information and fewer direct co-occurrences of visual words more effectively utilize visual information, suggesting that the relationship between text and image context is still viable.

2.2 Token Selection for Visual Grounding

In practice, many sentences have more than one visually grounded token; in these cases, available tokens must be dynamically selected for masking. The standard method is to randomly select viable tokens (Devlin et al., 2019); however, recent work in masked language modeling (MLM) has shown that informed selection of masked tokens may improve performance (Sato et al., 2023).

Other work has given consideration to the length of source segments in text masking (Xiao et al., 2023) and to the number of tokens selected (Joshi et al., 2020), but little work has been done to select tokens deterministically (e.g., by token length).

3 Approach

We perform improved visual grounding by detecting concrete tokens in source sentences. We explore three detection techniques to identify concrete text tokens (Section 3.1) and four selection techniques to appropriately select the identified concrete text tokens (Section 3.2.1). We then collate permutations of synthetic MMT datasets by masking the selected concrete tokens from source sentences and aligning each sentence with its original dataset image pair. We then train an MMT model (Section 3.3) on these datasets, expanding on work by Vijayan et al. (2024) and Caglayan et al. (2019).

SRC: A girl in sunglasses walks by a red car.
DT1: *girl, red car, sunglasses, girl*
DT2: *sunglasses, A girl*
DT3: *girl, red car, **sunglasses**, girl*
MSK: A girl in <unk> walks by a red car.

SRC: Young boy kicks a red and white soccer ball on a grassy field.
DT1: *field, young boy, ball, young, white soccer ball, boy, grassy field*
DT2: *soccer, field, young boy, grassy field, young, boy, white soccer ball, ball*
DT3: *field, young boy, ball, young, **white soccer ball**, boy, grassy field*
MSK: Young boy kicks a red and <unk> <unk> <unk> on a grassy field.

SRC: A construction worker fits metal pipes together.
DT1: *construction worker, worker, pipes*
DT2: *construction worker, worker, construction, pipes*
DT3: ***construction worker**, worker, pipes*
MSK: A <unk> <unk> fits metal pipes together.

Figure 1: Multi30k source pairs (image, **SRC**) with results from each detection technique (**DT**) and an example masked source text (**MSK**). **DT1** represents the *NLTK* technique; **DT2** represents the *MDETR Detection* technique; **DT3** represents the *Joint Detection* technique. The masked sentence **MSK** represents a possible masked sentence based on the bold tokens in the **DT3** detections.

3.1 Detection of Concrete Tokens

As Caglayan et al. (2019) found, masking visually relevant objects from a source text can force the model to utilize image context to fill in the artificially-created gap in lexical/semantic understanding. We hypothesize that for a given text-image pair, the masking of text tokens that are directly relevant to the image (i.e., "concrete" tokens), will improve visual grounding, increasing model correlation of image inputs during downstream translation tasks.

We present three techniques for detection of concrete tokens: NLP with NLTK (Section 3.1.1), object detection with MDETR (Section 3.1.2), and joint NLTK/MDETR detection and grounding (Section 3.1.3). While techniques one and two respectively use text and image context, method three uses contextual information from both modalities to make decisions about which text tokens are concrete.

3.1.1 Detection with NLTK

The first concrete token detection approach is to parse sentences for nouns and noun phrases that are likely to represent visual context. By masking tokens that are critical to comprehension and translation of the text, we can encourage the model to learn with visual context.

The Natural Language Toolkit (NLTK) (Loper and Bird, 2002) includes the WordNet corpus (Fellbaum and Miller, 1998), an English-language lexical database that provides structured relationships between cognitive synonyms ("*synsets*") for nouns, verbs, adjectives, and adverbs. Specifically, WordNet defines a directed acyclic graph (DAG) for each of these parts of speech (POS), containing synonyms, troponyms, antonyms, and meronyms (Figure 2). Critically, these relational graphs establish affiliations between English words, their definitions, and their related parent categories (i.e., "hypernyms").

Starting with specific synonyms and troponyms (e.g., "`sedan`", "`hatchback`", "`SUV`") and traversing the DAG upwards, WordNet collapses definitions and synsets into their associated hypernym classes (e.g., "`car`", "`vehicle`") until it reaches a root hypernym (e.g., "`physical_entity`", "`entity`"). Using recursive graph traversal, we can select any node in the DAG and parse its hypernyms upward until we reach either a root hypernym or a parent hypernym on which we can base an estimate of the root hypernym (e.g., "object" generally maps to "physical_entity").

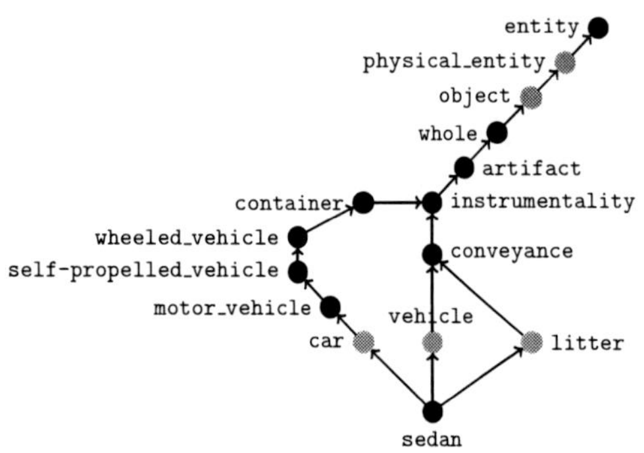

Figure 2: An example hypernym graph. The original token, sedan, its three synset entries (labeled in blue), and its associated concrete hypernyms (labeled in red).

Concrete Hypernyms	Abstract Hypernyms
physical_entity	abstract_entity
physical_object	abstraction
stuff	
object	
person	
unit	
whole	

Table 1: Labeled WordNet (Fellbaum and Miller, 1998) hypernyms. A token is classified as concrete or abstract if any of the above hypernyms are in its DAG.

Given that there exists only a small cluster of root and high-level parent hypernyms for nouns in WordNet, we can classify the hypernym DAG of any noun or noun phrase as "**concrete**" or "**abstract**" based on these high-level hypernyms (Table 1).

While this method provides a simple concrete/abstract classifier for text tokens, it introduces additional complications. Although most DAG nodes have multiple child hyponyms (e.g., "car" may have "sedan" and "hatchback"), some have multiple cognitive synonyms, as English words often have multiple equally likely definitions. For a given node, each of its "definitions" will appear as an entry into its synset; for example, the English noun "link" has nine values in its WordNet synset, ranging from "*URL*" to "*channel for communication*" to "*element of a chain*." These varied definitions may branch to different root hypernyms, impacting the classification based on which definition is chosen (Table 1).

To compensate, we consider each entry in a word's synset and extract a ratio of concrete/abstract definitions, which more comprehensively projects a token's likelihood of being concrete. We perform recursive graph traversal for each entry and retain the percent of concrete entries as a "concreteness score." To then classify the original word as abstract or concrete, we establish a threshold of 33% likelihood and only accept words above that concreteness score.

3.1.2 Detection with MDETR

While the NLTK approach can quickly and efficiently select concrete tokens from a sentence, it incorrectly assumes that every concrete token in the sentence is relevant to its associated image. Contextually linking an irrelevant concrete token to a given image could negatively impact model performance, especially if the token has high commonality in a dataset. As a second approach to concrete token detection, we utilize an object detection model to select concrete tokens. Rather than relying solely on the text processing for detection, we inspect the image itself for object classes relevant to the text.

For this approach, we use MDETR (Kamath et al., 2021), an end-to-end object detection model. Rather than relying exclusively on pre-defined object classes, MDETR uses NLP techniques alongside a pre-trained detection model (Carion et al., 2020) to perform object detection and image classification based on the input tokens. Given a text-image pair (Figure 3), the model assigns each text token an object classification, confidence score, and bounding box. To maximize the number of detectable tokens, we pass an entire Multi30k sentence into the MDETR model and filter out detections with low confidence scores, retaining only the tokens with a high confidence of correlation to the image. While Kamath et al. (2021) filter all outputs with confidence less than 0.7, we filter at 0.85; after analyzing performance at threshold increments between 0.5 and 0.95, we found that this threshold ensured the most balanced object confidence.

SRC: Cooking hot peppers in the cold winter!

DT2: *"cooking hot peppers in the cold winter"*

DT3: *"pepper"*

Figure 3: Multi30k source pair (image, **SRC**) with results from the MDETR (**DT2**, top image) and Joint (**DT3**, bottom image) detection techniques. MDETR query strings, bounding boxes, and confidence scores are shown. In this example, supplying the entire source sentence as text input to the MDETR object detection model incorrectly identifies the peppers being cooked, while querying only the word *"pepper"* increases the model's confidence and more closely identifies the region containing the query.

3.1.3 Detection with Joint Visual Grounding

While the MDETR technique is less likely than the NLTK technique to improperly select text tokens as visually-grounded, the pre-trained MDETR model will always attempt to assign a bounding box to some text token, often resulting in outputs with high confidence but incorrect alignment. In practice, providing extended textual context (i.e., entire captions or sentences) further exacerbates this problem (Figure 3).

Therefore, we are left with two techniques with contrasting weaknesses: NLTK ignores image context, and MDETR misinterprets textual context. To mitigate these issues, we present a conjoined detection technique that "verifies" the presence of NLTK-detected concrete tokens within an image using MDETR, ensuring that concrete tokens are visually grounded in the image.

Like the MDETR technique, the joint technique parses text-image pairs (unlike the NLTK technique, which is image-agnostic). The source sentence is first processed by the NLTK technique, which returns the noun and noun phrase tokens that met or surpassed the concrete threshold. Each of those tokens is paired with a copy of the source image and passed into the MDETR technique, which performs object detection and filters out all tokens whose resulting confidence is below the confidence threshold. This simultaneously reduces the probability of incorrect alignment by the object detection model and ensures that text tokens are visually grounded, resulting in a set of linguistically concrete and visually-grounded text tokens with high probability of relevance to the source image. Masking these explicitly-relevant tokens will force model reliance on image context.

3.2 Synthetic Dataset Collation

Because most current work in MMT focuses on the Multi30k dataset (Elliott et al., 2016), an image-caption dataset consisting of 30,014 images with English sentences and corresponding multilingual translations, we collate synthetic datasets of masked sentence-image pairs from Multi30k.

We use each detection technique (Section 3.1) to detect concrete tokens and align them to their original dataset image. From these masked sentence-image pairs, we collate a series of MMT datasets in which a maximum of two concrete tokens are masked from each sentence and associated with the relevant image from the original dataset, resulting in training and validation sets that are at most twice as large as the original Multi30k sets.

3.2.1 Token Selection Techniques

During the dataset collation process, a single sentence may have $n > 2$ available concrete tokens; in this case, additional consideration must be given to which tokens are selected for inclusion in the dataset. The standard method has generally been to randomly select from the available tokens (Devlin et al., 2019), but recent work in masked language modeling (MLM) has shown that more informed selection of masked tokens may actually improve performance (Sato et al., 2023).

To examine this, we implement two deterministic token selection techniques, selecting the n **longest** and **shortest** tokens (by number of characters) respectively for each sentence. We compare these techniques to a **random** selection of n tokens and an **unrestricted** selection which ignores the n=2 normalization and accepts all available concrete tokens.

3.3 GRAM Model

As the basis for our multimodal translation architecture, we utilize the GRAM architecture (Vijayan et al., 2024). GRAM modifies the FAIR WMT19 (Ng et al., 2019) text-only model, an encoder/decoder-based transformer architecture (Vaswani et al., 2017), by adding additional multimodal components to create an MMT model.

To process text input, GRAM uses the same byte-pair encoding (BPE) and vocabulary dictionary as the FAIR WMT19 model (Ng et al., 2019). Masked sentences are BPE-encoded and fed as standard text inputs to the MMT model. We mask by replacing each token with an `<unk>` token, as that token is the closest to a mask token available in the FAIR WMT19 model (Ng et al., 2019). Our method expands on prior work by Tang et al. (2022) and Wu et al. (2021) while increasing the requirements for a token to be visually grounded to an image.

To process image input, the GRAM model uses CLIP, a pre-trained text-only translation model alongside a pre-trained vision encoder, a perceiver resampler, and vision-text cross-attention layers (Radford et al., 2021). While the original GRAM paper utilizes the `ViT-L/14@336px` CLIP model, we noted better results within our evaluation framework when using the `RN50x4` CLIP model; we present those results below (Section 4.2). This vision encoder converts input images into image embeddings, enabling the perceiver resampler to convert those embeddings into a fixed number of vision tokens. Vision tokens and corresponding text embeddings are interleaved into vision-text cross-attention layers within the transformer encoder, creating mappings from both the text and the image embeddings onto a sequence of joint representations. Finally, the transformer decoder ingests this sequence and outputs probabilities for the next output text token in the target sequence.

The number of parameters in the original text-only Transformer is 269,746,176; the number of parameters in the RN50x4 CLIP vision encoder is 101,520,396, for a total of 371,266,572 parameters in our GRAM model. Additionally, our GRAM perceiver resampler contains 87,137,080 parameters.

4 Results and Discussion

4.1 Experimental Framework

We train the GRAM models on unique permutations of synthetically collated datasets representing each combination of detection (**NLTK**, **MDETR**, **Joint**) (Section 3.1) and selection (**unrestricted**, **restricted-long**, **restricted-short**, **restricted-random**) (Section 3.2.1) techniques. We compare the resulting trained versions to the GRAM model trained on a unmasked dataset of original sentences.

Most current work in MMT focuses on the Multi30k dataset; because of its prevalence in other MMT works, we utilize the Multi30k dataset for collation of our training datasets. We then evaluate the GRAM models on the Multi30k 2016, 2017, and COCO test sets using BLEU4 scores.

We also evaluate the GRAM model with an additional metric, Contrastive Multilingual Multimodal Translation Evaluation (CoMMuTE). Futeral et al. (2023) proposed the CoMMuTE dataset to evaluate both performance on translation tasks and usage of visual information by MMT models. In the ensemble CoMMuTE evaluation, the model is given two images, a lexically or semantically ambiguous English sentence, and a target language translation that resolves the ambiguity according to one of the two images. The task involves determining which of the two images the sentence pairs best match. The evaluation is made using the perplexity of the model output, and the resulting CoMMuTE score is calculated using the model's determination of accuracy across 100 text-image pairs.

Detection	Selection	Score			
		CoMMuTE	Multi30k BLEU4 (en-de)		
			2016	2017	COCO
Futeral et al. (2023)		*0.59*	*43.3*	*38.3*	*35.7*
Vijayan et al. (2024)		*0.61*	***46.5***	***43.6***	*39.1*
Unmasked		0.5	45.0	42.0	38.2
NLTK	Unrestricted	0.55	45.7	41.9	**39.2**
NLTK	Restricted-Longest	0.62	46.0	42.5	37.8
NLTK	Restricted-Shortest	0.63	46.0	42.0	37.9
NLTK	Restricted-Random	**0.67**	46.2	41.4	37.8
MDETR	Unrestricted	0.56	46.0	42.4	38.4
MDETR	Restricted-Longest	0.63	45.7	41.7	38.0
MDETR	Restricted-Shortest	0.63	45.0	41.2	36.9
MDETR	Restricted-Random	0.63	45.6	42.2	37.6
Joint	Unrestricted	0.52	45.5	42.4	38.9
Joint	Restricted-Longest	0.63	45.8	42.6	38.8
Joint	Restricted-Shortest	0.61	45.4	42.0	37.9
Joint	Restricted-Random	0.61	45.5	42.4	37.5

Table 2: Selected performance results of our model against the CoMMuTE and Multi30k test sets. The best result by column is indicated in **bold**; the best result for each detection technique is underlined. Results as reported by GRAM (Vijayan et al., 2024) and VGAMT (Futeral et al., 2023) are included for reference.

Detection	Concrete %	Unique Detections
NLTK	99.51	5,393
MDETR	99.92	6,674
Joint	99.49	4,761

Table 3: Unique concrete token detections and percent of Multi30k sentences with detected tokens by detection technique.

4.2 Results

We review the performance of the model variants trained using the synthetic Multi30k datasets (Section 3.2) on the above evaluation metrics. We train 13 variants, consisting of one unmasked baseline and 12 models representing each combination of detection (Section 3.1) and selection (Section 3.2.1) techniques.

4.3 Detection Results

We introduced three distinct methods for detection of concrete text tokens: the NLTK technique (Section 3.1.1), which parses nouns and noun phrases from sentences, the MDETR technique (Section 3.1.2), which inputs sentences as queries to an object detection model, and the Joint technique (Section 3.1.3). Each technique generates the same output structure: multimodal datasets of sentences masked concrete tokens and matching images. We hypothesize that masking concrete tokens with these techniques will improve performance on evaluation metrics. We further hypothesize that the Joint technique will be more selective with its detections than its component NLTK and MDETR techniques, and will thus utilize image context more efficiently and critically.

We found that all three techniques consistently extracted relevant tokens from the text: each technique extracted concrete tokens from over 99% of Multi30k sentences (Table 3). The MDETR detection technique was the most successful, extracting 23.8% and 40.2% more unique concrete tokens than the NLTK and Joint techniques, respectively. This resulted in the MDETR technique masking the highest concentration of original Multi30k sentences (114 and 120 sentences more than NLTK and Joint, respectively).

Increased rates of detection did not correlate with better performance, though. All tested models outperformed the unmasked (baseline) dataset in CoMMuTE and BLEU scores, but in contrast to our hypothesis the NLTK technique outperformed both the MDETR and Joint techniques both in CoMMuTE and BLEU score (Table 2). The Joint technique, which we hypothesized would improve on its component techniques, consistently underperformed against the others. This is especially true in the `Joint Unrestricted` model, which only improved its CoMMuTE score by 0.02 and its BLEU score 0.5 over the baseline. We suggest that the Joint technique was actually hindered by its strict selection process, leading to a much smaller pool of objects to mask from. Conversely, the MDETR technique tended to over-select longer, rarely-used, or irrelevant tokens (Figure 3), contributing to the larger masking percentages but the lower overall performance. The success of the NLTK technique over the others was its "middle ground" approach, classifying concrete tokens more liberally than the Joint technique but more consistently than the MDETR technique.

23% of tested models underperformed the original GRAM model (Vijayan et al., 2024) on CoMMuTE metrics, 15.4% performed identically, and the remaining 53.8% outperformed. All tested models underperformed the original GRAM model in Multi30k 2016/2017 BLEU metrics. One model (`NLTK Unrestricted`) outperformed the original GRAM model in the Multi30k COCO metric, but the improvement is well within a margin for normalization effects. We suggest that the performance disparity between models in these Multi30k BLEU metrics is due to dataset size: the original GRAM model was pre-trained trained on the Conceptual Captions dataset (Sharma et al., 2018) of $2,878,999$ text-image pairs, resulting in synthetic datasets nearly 100 times larger than those used here. Despite this, the majority of models outperformed GRAM in CoMMuTE metrics, achieving scores of up to 0.67.

In general, we also note an inverse relationship between CoMMuTE and BLEU performance: that is, when CoMMuTE scores increase, BLEU scores tend to decrease. For example, the `MDETR Unrestricted` model notched the highest average BLEU score across all three Multi30k metrics, but had the second-lowest CoMMuTE score.

4.4 Selection Results

Critical to the synthetic dataset collation system is the process of selecting concrete tokens for masking. Prior efforts have generally selected tokens at random (Ive et al., 2019); we introduced three additional techniques (Section 3.2.1), longest-token selection, shortest-token selection, and unrestricted selection, and test each against a baseline of randomly-selected concrete tokens. We hypothesize that the presented token selection techniques will outperform the baseline of random selection; specifically, we hypothesize that longest-token and unrestricted selection will encourage additional usage of visual context and thus improve CoMMuTE score, and that shortest-token selection will minimize the number of token predictions required by the model (Section 3.3) and thus improve BLEU score.

We found that while all tested selection techniques (Section 3.2.1) outperformed the unmasked baseline, comparative performance between techniques are less conclusive. When paired with the NLTK detection technique, the random selection technique outperformed the others in CoMMuTE and Multi30k 2016 BLEU scores. When paired with the MDETR metric, none of the restricted selection techniques had any impact on CoMMuTE score. When paired with the Joint detection technique, the longest-token selection technique improved CoMMuTE and Multi30k 2016/2017 BLEU scores.

Contrary to our hypothesis, the deterministic token selection techniques did not consistently outperform the random selection technique. The most consistent results were with the unrestricted selection technique, which significantly degraded CoMMuTE performance but tended to improve BLEU performance (especially in the COCO BLEU metric, where it outperformed all other tested models). Shortest-token selection also tended to follow these patterns of performance degradation, but not as substantially: its NLTK and Joint detection variants performed identically on the Multi30k 2017 and COCO BLEU metrics and performed near the bottom of results for the CoMMuTE and 2016 BLEU metrics across all three detection techniques.

Each of these findings runs counter to our hypotheses in this area, suggesting that token selection at this scale has less impact on model performance than we expected; in fact, random or pseudo-random token selection of the identified concrete tokens may actually improve performance over deterministic methods.

4.5 Future Work

Given the high percentage of visually-grounded tokens in the Multi30k training set, future work should consider the techniques against both larger MMT datasets and MMT datasets with lower concentrations of visually-grounded tokens (e.g., Conceptual Captions). Similarly, future work should consider synthetically collated datasets that combine elements of multiple multimodal datasets (e.g., images from Conceptual Captions, sentences from Multi30k), including synthetic datasets created from text-only datasets.

Additionally, future work should compare baseline scores for tokens selected completely at random to more accurately gauge the efficacy of object token selection.

Finally, future work should consider a more deterministic way to classify the concreteness of a token with NLP, including selection of definitions based on contextual awareness.

5 Conclusion

The continued challenge of visual grounding and masking in MMT systems has encouraged varying approaches to the detection and selection of visually-grounded text tokens for masking (Caglayan et al., 2019; Wu et al., 2021).

We introduced three new techniques for detection of concrete tokens from source sentences: detection with natural language processing (NLP), detection with object detection, and joint NLP/object detection. We also introduced deterministic methods for the selection of detected tokens, including longest and shortest n tokens.

Finally, we utilized the GRAM MMT architecture (Vijayan et al., 2024) to train models against synthetically collated datasets of masked sentences and associated images. We showed performance improvement over the baseline models and elevated usage of visual context during translation tasks.

Acknowledgements

Thanks to AFRL SCREAM Lab and AFRL 711HPW/RHWTE for their help in this project. **Funding:** This work was supported by the AIM-MIER project via Infoscitex Corporation (IST) and Air Force Research Laboratory (AFRL) under Air Force contract FA8650-20-D-6207.

References

Caglayan, O., Aransa, W., Wang, Y., Masana, M., García-Martínez, M., Bougares, F., Barrault, L., and van de Weijer, J. (2016). Does multimodality help human and machine for translation and image captioning? In *Proceedings of the First Conference on Machine Translation: Volume 2, Shared Task Papers*. Association for Computational Linguistics.

Caglayan, O., Madhyastha, P., Specia, L., and Barrault, L. (2019). Probing the need for visual context in multimodal machine translation. In *Proceedings of the 2019 Conference of the North American Chapter of the Association for Computational Linguistics: Human Language Technologies, Volume 1 (Long and Short Papers)*, pages 4159–4170, Minneapolis, Minnesota. Association for Computational Linguistics.

Carion, N., Massa, F., Synnaeve, G., Usunier, N., Kirillov, A., and Zagoruyko, S. (2020). End-to-end object detection with transformers.

Devlin, J., Chang, M.-W., Lee, K., and Toutanova, K. (2019). BERT: Pre-training of deep bidirectional transformers for language understanding. In *Proceedings of the 2019 Conference of the North American Chapter of the Association for Computational Linguistics: Human Language Technologies, Volume 1 (Long and Short Papers)*, pages 4171–4186, Minneapolis, Minnesota. Association for Computational Linguistics.

Elliott, D., Frank, S., Sima'an, K., and Specia, L. (2016). Multi30k: Multilingual english-german image descriptions.

Fellbaum, C. and Miller, G. A. (1998). *WordNet: An Electronic Lexical Database*. The MIT Press.

Futeral, M., Schmid, C., Laptev, I., Sagot, B., and Bawden, R. (2023). Tackling ambiguity with images:

Opinions, interpretations, conclusions, and recommendations are those of the authors and are not necessarily endorsed by the United States Government. Cleared for public release on 12 Feb 2024. Originator reference number RH-24-125351. Case number AFRL-2024-0803.

Improved multimodal machine translation and contrastive evaluation. In Rogers, A., Boyd-Graber, J., and Okazaki, N., editors, *Proceedings of the 61st Annual Meeting of the ACL (Volume 1: Long Papers)*, pages 5394–5413, Toronto, Canada. Association for Computational Linguistics.

Ive, J., Madhyastha, P., and Specia, L. (2019). Distilling Translations with Visual Awareness. *ArXiv*, abs/1906.07701.

Joshi, M., Chen, D., Liu, Y., Weld, D. S., Zettlemoyer, L., and Levy, O. (2020). SpanBERT: Improving Pre-training by Representing and Predicting Spans. *Transactions of the Association for Computational Linguistics*, 8:64–77.

Kamath, A., Singh, M., LeCun, Y., Synnaeve, G., Misra, I., and Carion, N. (2021). Mdetr – modulated detection for end-to-end multi-modal understanding.

Lala, C. and Specia, L. (2018). Multimodal lexical translation. In *Proceedings of the Eleventh International Conference on Language Resources and Evaluation (LREC 2018)*, Miyazaki, Japan. European Language Resources Association (ELRA).

Loper, E. and Bird, S. (2002). NLTK: The natural language toolkit. *Proceedings of the ACL Workshop on Effective Tools and Methodologies for Teaching Natural Language Processing and Computational Linguistics*.

Ng, N., Yee, K., Baevski, A., Ott, M., Auli, M., and Edunov, S. (2019). Facebook FAIR's WMT19 News Translation Task Submission.

Plummer, B. A., Wang, L., Cervantes, C. M., Caicedo, J. C., Hockenmaier, J., and Lazebnik, S. (2015). Flickr30k entities: Collecting region-to-phrase correspondences for richer image-to-sentence models. In *2015 IEEE International Conference on Computer Vision (ICCV)*, pages 2641–2649.

Radford, A., Kim, J. W., Hallacy, C., Ramesh, A., Goh, G., Agarwal, S., Sastry, G., Askell, A., Mishkin, P., Clark, J., Krueger, G., and Sutskever, I. (2021). Learning Transferable Visual Models From Natural Language Supervision. In Meila, M. and Zhang, T., editors, *Proceedings of the 38th International Conference on Machine Learning*, volume 139 of *Proceedings of Machine Learning Research*, pages 8748–8763. PMLR.

Sato, J., Caseli, H., and Specia, L. (2023). Choosing what to mask: More informed masking for multimodal machine translation. In *Proceedings of the 61st Annual Meeting of the Association for Computational Linguistics (Volume 4: Student Research Workshop)*, pages 244–253, Toronto, Canada. Association for Computational Linguistics.

Sharma, P., Ding, N., Goodman, S., and Soricut, R. (2018). Conceptual captions: A cleaned, hypernymed, image alt-text dataset for automatic image captioning. In *Proceedings of the 56th Annual Meeting of the Association for Computational Linguistics (Volume 1: Long Papers)*, pages 2556–2565, Melbourne, Australia. Association for Computational Linguistics.

Tan, H. and Bansal, M. (2020). Vokenization: Improving language understanding with contextualized, visual-grounded supervision.

Tang, Z., Zhang, X., Long, Z., and Fu, X. (2022). Multimodal neural machine translation with search engine based image retrieval. In *Proceedings of the 9th Workshop on Asian Translation*, pages 89–98, Gyeongju, Republic of Korea. International Conference on Computational Linguistics.

Vaswani, A., Shazeer, N., Parmar, N., Uszkoreit, J., Jones, L., Gomez, A. N., Kaiser, L., and Polosukhin, I. (2017). Attention is all you need.

Vijayan, V., Bowen, B., Grigsby, S., Anderson, T., and Gwinnup, J. (2024). Adding multimodal capabilities to a text-only translation model. *arXiv:2403.03045 [cs.CL]*.

Wang, D. and Xiong, D. (2021). Efficient Object-Level Visual Context Modeling for Multimodal Machine Translation: Masking Irrelevant Objects Helps Grounding. *Proceedings of the AAAI Conference on Artificial Intelligence*, 35(4):2720–2728.

Wu, Z., Kong, L., Bi, W., Li, X., and Kao, B. (2021). Good for misconceived reasons: An empirical revisiting on the need for visual context in multimodal machine translation.

Xiao, Y., Xu, R., Wu, L., Li, J., Qin, T., Liu, Y.-T., and Zhang, M. (2023). Amom: Adaptive masking over masking for conditional masked language model.

Zhou, M., Cheng, R., Lee, Y. J., and Yu, Z. (2018). A visual attention grounding neural model for multimodal machine translation.

Zhuang, C., Fedorenko, E., and Andreas, J. (2023). Visual grounding helps learn word meanings in low-data regimes.

Predicting Anchored Text from Translation Memories for Machine Translation Using Deep Learning Methods

Richard Yue
Northeastern University, San Jose, CA
yue.r@northeastern.edu

John E. Ortega
Institute for Experiential AI, Northeastern University, Boston, MA
j.ortega@northeastern.edu

Abstract

Translation memories (TMs) are the backbone for professional translation tools called computer-aided translation (CAT) tools. In order to perform a translation using a CAT tool, a translator uses the TM to gather translations similar to the desired segment to translate (s'). Many CAT tools offer a fuzzy-match algorithm to locate segments (s) in the TM that are close in distance to s'. After locating two similar segments, the CAT tool will present parallel segments (s, t) that contain one segment in the source language along with its translation in the target language. Additionally, CAT tools contain fuzzy-match repair (FMR) techniques that will automatically use the parallel segments from the TM to create new TM entries containing a modified version of the original with the idea in mind that it will be the translation of s'. Most FMR techniques use machine translation as a way of "repairing" those words that have to be modified. In this article, we show that for a large part of those words which are *anchored*, we can use other techniques that are based on machine learning approaches such as Word2Vec. BERT, and even ChatGPT. Specifically, we show that for anchored words that follow the continuous bag-of-words (CBOW) paradigm, Word2Vec, BERT, and GPT-4 can be used to achieve similar and, for some cases, better results than neural machine translation for translating anchored words from French to English.

1 Introduction

Professional translators use computer-aided translation (CAT) tools (Bowker, 2002) to translate text from one language called the source language (SL) to a target language (TL). Most CAT tools have an option known as *fuzzy-match repair* (FMR) (Kranias and Samiotou, 2004; Hewavitharana et al., 2005; Dandapat et al., 2011; Ortega et al., 2016; Bulté et al., 2018; Tezcan et al., 2021), which is backed by a parallel translation memory (TM) that contains sentences (called segments) in the SL and TL. Each pair, or unit, of parallel segments in the TM is known as a *translation unit* (TU). A TU contains a source segment (s) along with a target segment (t). When a professional translator attempts to translate a segment in the SL (denoted as s') a fuzzy-match lookup is performed using a word-based Levenshtein distance (Levenshtein, 1966) between s' and s where a 100% match means that the words from s' are identical to the words in s. It is often the case that a professional translator uses matches from FMR to only translate a few words (called sub-segments) from the entire segment. In this article, we focus on improving those cases where there exists only one word to translate, known as an *anchored* word, whose position is in between two words that are already captured. In our studies, the anchored word is a common case that professional translators often use. We experiment with four techniques to translate the anchored word: (1) Neural Machine Translation, (2) a BERT-based (Sanh et al., 2019) implementation, (3) Word2Vec (Mikolov et al., 2013) and (4) OpenAI GPT-4 prompting (Achiam et al., 2023).

The prediction of an anchored word has been presented in many contexts and can be considered the main objective of a language model. Several models based on attention allow a weight to be assigned to certain words within a context window so that surrounding words that strongly influence the overall context can have a greater impact on the prediction made. This could potentially be used in order to improve predictions made for anchored text by taking longer contexts into account than the surrounding words. We discuss this approach in the context of generative models, where such systems could be harnessed to generate highly accurate predictions.

The rest of this article is structured as follows. The next section discusses related work by accentuating the differences between FMR based on MT and anchored-word prediction. Section 3 then presents the BERT, Word2Vec, and GPT-4 approaches used for translating anchored words. In Section 4, we describe the corpus and configurations used for our experiments whose results are reflected in Section 5, followed by concluding remarks in Section 6.

2 Related Work

For the majority of FMR approaches, MT is used to translate mismatches, regardless if they are anchored words or not. Generally, MT techniques for FMR are focused on the decoding process where statistical-based systems (Biçici and Dymetman, 2008; Simard and Isabelle, 2009; Zhechev and Genabith, 2010; Koehn and Senellart, 2010; Li et al., 2016; Liu et al., 2019) or neural-based systems (Ortega et al., 2014, 2016; Gu et al., 2018; Bulté et al., 2018; Bulte and Tezcan, 2019) are used in such a manner to "repair" either the MT system or the mismatched sub-segments between s' and s. This article is focused on repairing the mismatched sub-segments in specific situations where sub-segments of s are common in s' with the exception of one word (e.g. s='the **brown** dog' and s'='the **red** dog').

Previous work (Ortega et al., 2016; Bulté et al., 2018) can be considered identical to this article as it uses FMR to first find mismatches between s' and s and then translates the missing words with different MT systems. However, their system uses context around *all* mismatches where we only consider mismatches with anchored words, similar to Kranias and Samiotou (2004). While other techniques (Hewavitharana et al., 2005; Dandapat et al., 2011) are based on probabilistic MT models or employ different algorithms for aligning s' and s, we use a word-based edit distance (Levenshtein, 1966; Wagner and Fischer, 1974) that marks the mismatched sub-segments and discards non-anchored words.

Tezcan and Bulté (2022) investigate a wide range of automatic quality estimation (QE) metrics in order to assess what effect integrating fuzzy matches can have on a number of aspects of translation quality, in addition to performing manual MT error analysis. They further evaluate what influence fuzzy matches have on a translation and how further quality improvements can be made by quantitative analyses that focus on the specific characteristics of a retrieved fuzzy match. Neural Fuzzy Repair (NFR) outperforms baselines in all automated evaluation metrics. There was not a discernable difference between NFR and Neural Machine Translation (NMT) error in manual evaluation, but different error profiles emerged in this study, highlighting some of the strengths and weaknesses of each method. Namely, NFR produced more errors in the category of "semantically unrelated", whereas the baseline NMT system produced more errors in the categories of "word sense" and "multi-word expression". The NFR system made more accuracy errors, but producing fluent output was its strong suit. Meanwhile, in terms of lexical choices, NMT produced more "non-existing/foreign" errors, which was not an issue for NFR. The baseline system performed better on grammar and syntax. Our study differs in that it focuses specifically on anchored text and on leveraging the strengths of language models in next word prediction in order to fill in single-word gaps.

Esplà-Gomis et al. (2011) attempt to improve CAT via the TM using pre-computed word alignments between source and target TUs in the TM. When a user is translating s' with a fuzzy match score greater than or equal to 60%, the proposed system marks the words that need to change as well as those that must remain the same in order to obtain t'. Alignments are obtained from GIZA++ (Brown et al., 1993; Vogel et al., 1996) and take both a statistical and syntactic approach to detecting where changes need to occur. The experiments offer insight into how human decisions to keep/change text during translation can be integrated into FMR. Our approach differs in that we specifically locate anchored text and, following that, continue on to a prediction step, providing the content needed to perform fuzzy match repair in the translation step.

İrsoy et al. (2020) compare performance of pre-trained word embeddings in use in language models such as BERT with continuous bag of words (CBOW) embeddings trained with Word2Vec. The authors claim that, while BERT embeddings are useful and effective, they often offer only marginal gains as compared to Word2Vec embeddings trained using Gensim (Řehřek et al., 2011). The latter are much less computationally expensive to obtain; 768-dimensional vectors were trained in one epoch in 1.61 days on a 16-CPU machine. CBOW embeddings are trained by using surrounding context to predict a center word. While training via CBOW has often shown inferior performance to training via skipgram (SG), this paper shows that with a proper implementation, performance of CBOW embeddings can be on par with SG. Our work puts the CBOW prediction objective to good use, harnessing it to predict anchored text in source language segments.

3 Methodology

Neural MT systems have been shown by previous work (Bulte and Tezcan, 2019) to be the state-of-the-art for FMR. In this article, we experiment on the one hand with word-based language models that are trained using context around a word, like those that use the continuous bag of words (CBOW) model (Mikolov et al., 2013) (Word2Vec) or masked language modeling (Sanh et al., 2019) (BERT). On the other hand, it is our belief also that generative language modeling techniques may be a good candidate for accomplishing this task. To explore this avenue, we also compare output from these models with predictions obtained from prompting GPT-4 and find it to be competitive with the other methods. An example of a source sentence and the output from each method is provided in Table 1 with predicted (or reference) word in bold. In our experiment, the two language modeling techniques as well as the generative approach are compared against machine translation and measured using character rate and accuracy against sets of anchored words from the test set. A prediction or translation was deemed correct when the center word from a tri-gram of anchored words was correctly found. In the following sub-sections, we discuss each approach. In Section 4 we provide further details about the corpora and configuration.

3.1 Machine Translation

We train the neural MT system with Open-NMT (Klein et al., 2020) using the default transformer configuration. In order to get a wider range of difference with the MT system, we translate using two methods: (1) the translation of the s'_{en} segment to t^*_{fr} then translation from t^*_{fr} to s^*_{en}; and, (2) the translation of the three-word sub-segment only (i.e. the anchored tri-gram with the center word to be translated) from $s'_{trigram-en}$ to $t^*_{trigram-fr}$ then translation from $t^*_{trigram-fr}$ to $s^*_{trigram-en}$. For both methods, correctly translated center words from tri-grams were counted in the overall evaluation. Predictions by the other two methods were scored similarly. Further details on parameters and configuration are found in Section 4.2.

3.2 Word2Vec

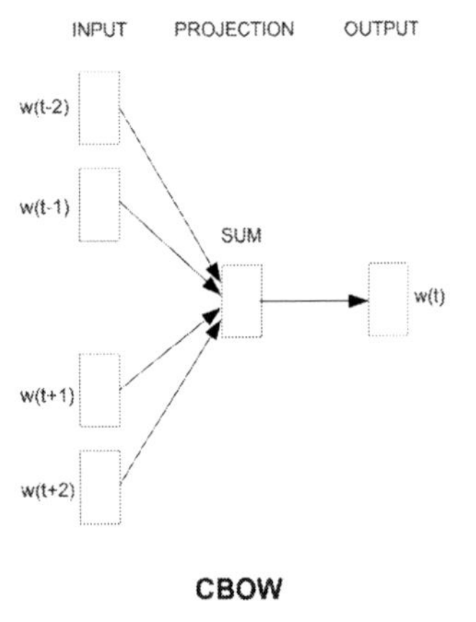

Figure 1: An illustration of predicting a word given the context around it (denoted as *anchored words in this article)*, called Continuos Bag of Words (CBOW) by Mikolov et al. (2013).

We used a pre-trained language model (PLM) for experimentation with Word2Vec (Mikolov et al.,

[1]We use the pre-trained word news vectors from Google found here:https://github.com/mmihaltz/word2vec-GoogleNews-vectors?tab=readme-ov-file.

Method	Output
Original French	"Afin d'évaluer si l'établissement identifie toutes les situations qui doivent être considérées comme des défauts, conformément à l'article 178, paragraphes 1 à 5, du règlement (UE) no 575/2013..."
Reference Translation	"In order to assess whether the institution identifies all situations which are to be considered defaults in accordance with Article 178 (1) to (5) of Regulation (EU) No 575/2013..."
Reference tri-gram	assess **whether** the
BERT	assess **whether** the
Word2Vec	assess **commission** the
MT	assess **obligatory** the
GPT-4	assess **and** the

Table 1: Anchored tri-gram reference and predictions (predicted word in bold)

2013).[1] The hope is that through the use of a PLM we can capture context in several different domains, specifically the corpus that we use which is parliamentary in nature.

The PLM weights from Word2Vec were used as a manner to predict anchored words due to the fact that the training method for them is based on a CBOW model. CBOW was selected because, as shown in Figure 1, its training objective most closely resembles the task we are trying to accomplish—the prediction of a word surrounded by anchored text (one word on the left and one word on the right).

As a first step, the PLM was downloaded and experimented as-is in its out-of-the-box state which consists of 300 dimensions and a default vocabulary. Then, in order to fine-tune the model, we adapted it to our parliamentary corpus. After the fine-tuning of the model, anchored tri-grams were extracted from s' and used as input to the PLM where the center word is used for prediction and the left and right "anchors" are used as input one-hot encoded embeddings, similar to the training exercise from Mikolov et al. (2013). Further details on parameters and configuration are found in Section 4.3.

3.3 BERT

Models based on the BERT (Kenton and Toutanova, 2019) algorithm are used frequently in modern times. They use an attention mechanism (Vaswani et al., 2017) and are known to be capable of capturing information better than previous implementations such as Word2vec. Therefore, in order to compare both algorithms to MT for predicting anchored words, we experiment with DistilBERT (Sanh et al., 2019), a BERT-based model that uses masked language modeling that in theory captures more parameters than the Word2Vec CBOW model.

Similar to the Word2Vec method, we fine-tune our DistilBERT model on the parliamentary corpus with a masked language modeling objective. We chose the masked language modeling objective as it is the most similar objective to CBOW. Further details on parameters and configuration are found in Section 4.4.

3.4 GPT-4

We experiment with prompting GPT-4 to predict anchored text using a temperature of 0 and the following prompt: *"You are an expert lexicographer and natural language processing assistant. Additionally, you are highly specialized in parliamentary proceedings. Given a trigram I provide with a '?' character in the center word, I need you to predict the '?' character with the most likely single-word token. Please return one predicted token without any text except the predicted token in your response. Do not provide the surrounding text or any additional information. Do not include the text 'predicting', 'predict', 'prediction', 'predicted' 'the predicted token is' or 'The predicted token is' in your response. Do not include any extra characters such as apostrophes, commas, colons, or semicolons in your re-*

sponse. Do not include any newline characters in your response.".

4 Experimental Settings

4.1 Corpus

The corpus consists of 393,371 SL-TL pairs of European parliamentary proceedings, a freely available translation memory (Steinberger et al., 2012) obtained from the European Commission DGT-Translation Memory repository.[2] The corpus is divided randomly with a random state of 42. We divide the corpus up into 70% train, 20% dev, and 10% test sets as shown in in Table 2.

4.2 Machine Translation

As mentioned previously, we use the Open-NMT (Klein et al., 2020) framework to build our French to English (FR–EN) and English to French (EN–FR) MT system. The system is based on a transformer architecture model with the following hyperparameters: A maximum sequence length of 500, an early stopping parameter of 4, 7,800 train steps, 1,000 validation steps, a bucket size of 262,144, a batch size of 4,096, and a validation batch size of 2,048. The optimizer is an Adam (beta2 of 0.998) optimizer with with fp16 activated, a learning rate of 2, noam decay, label smoothing of 0.1, a hidden size of 512, word vector size of 512, 8 attention heads, a dropout of 0.1, and an attention dropout of 0.1. The choice of parameter selection is inspired by previous work from Yasmin Moslem.[3]

In order to verify that the NMT system is on-par with the latest MT systems for FR–EN and EN–FR, we first test the system in both directions on the test set. During test, we achieved a BLEU score of 55.84 for FR–EN and 62.60 for EN-FR. Nonetheless, as we show in Section 5, the translation of anchored words as measured by character rate and accuracy was not remarkable.

4.3 Word2Vec

The CBOW algorithm for Word2vec is a well-known algorithm performed as a way of capturing semantics via a language model (Mikolov et al., 2013). We describe our Word2Vec CBOW implemenation. Before fine-tuning, the Word2Vec model has 300 dimensions with a window size of 2 and a minimum word count of 1. Additionally, predefined vocabulary is used in the Google News Vectors that contains billions of words. The model is fine-tuned with our training set which is tokenized using the NLTK RegexpTokenizer[4]. The embeddings created from the training set use lockf at 1.0 and a window size of 3, similar to Zarrar Shehzad.[5]

4.4 BERT

Our BERT model is based on a PLM called DistilBERT[6]. (Sanh et al., 2019) We train DistilBERT using the HuggingFace PyTorch Trainer with 10 training epochs, a learning rate of 2e-5, weight decay of 0.01, and FP16 mixed precision set to true. Hyperparameters are inspired by HuggingFace.[7]

4.5 GPT-4

GPT-4 was prompted using the gpt-4-turbo variant and queried repetitively through the OpenAI API. Due to newline mismatches that occurred during batch processing, we opted to run an API call for every line in the dataset.

5 Results

In this section, we compare the results obtained from running four approaches for predicting the anchored word: (1) Neural Machine Translation (NMT) (2) Word2Vec (3) BERT and (4) GPT-4. NMT is divided into the two approaches mentioned in Section 3.1 (sentence-level and tri-grams). Accuracy measurements are performed and reported for all holes[8]. Additionally, we report on character matches for each approach after dividing the segments into fuzzy-match thresholds, common practice for FMR work (see (Ortega et al., 2016; Bulte and Tezcan,

[2] https://joint-research-centre.ec.europa.eu/language-technology-resources/dgt-translation-memory_en
[3] https://github.com/ymoslem/OpenNMT-Tutorial
[4] https://www.nltk.org/_modules/nltk/tokenize/regexp.html
[5] https://czarrar.github.io/Gensim-Word2Vec/
[6] https://github.com/huggingface/transformers/tree/main/examples/research_projects/distillation
[7] https://huggingface.co/learn/nlp-course/en/chapter7/3
[8] A hole is a span of a tri-gram where the center word is predicted.

Data set	Segment Size
Train	275,317
Development	77,877
Test	40,117
Total	393,371

Table 2: Experimental sets from the European Commission DGT Translation memory used for creating and evaluating the three approaches.

	60–69%	70–79%	80–89%	90–100%
BERT	**8.97**	**9.61**	**7.98**	**7.87**
GPT	4.82	5.58	3.85	2.74
W2V	3.39	3.46	2.89	3.02
NMT-1	0.15	0.14	0.28	0.19
NMT-2	3.75	4.36	4.16	6.35

Table 3: Accuracy scores for various fuzzy-match threshold on five deep-learning approaches.

2019)).

First, we report on character match rates for the three approaches. Character match is defined as the number of characters in the output token that correspond to characters in the desired string. In Figure 2, we report the average character match for GPT-4, BERT, Word2Vec, NMT-1 (segment-level MT) and NMT-2 (tri-gram MT). We observe a marked improvement in average character match with language modeling approaches (BERT and Word2Vec) and GPT-4 performs competitively in most cases. BERT outperforms all approaches across all fuzzy-match thresholds. From an MT standpoint, the secondary approach (called NMT-2 in Figure 2) outperforms the primary approach; it appears that in our experiments the translation of anchored tri-grams is better than translating the entire segment.

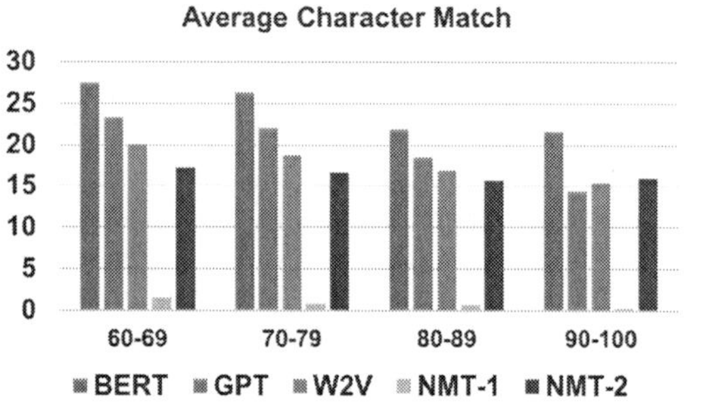

Figure 2: Average character match (y-axis) by fuzzy-match rate percentage (x-axis) by segment of the four experimental approaches: BERT, GPT, Word2Vec, Neural Machine Translation 1 and Neural Machine Translation 2 systems for different segment-level fuzzy-match thresholds.

Additionally, we measured the accuracy for the three approaches in order to better understand the hole span coverage. For accuracy, we measure only if prediction was correct or not; we do not take into account other predictions like blank, extra words, or others. To this end, we present accuracy scores in Table 3.

In our experiments, we notice that the NMT systems perform better on stop words and digits such as the phrase: "beyond **90** ghz". Both the BERT and NMT systems were found to perform well in those situations. However, the MT system oftentimes did not replace one word only—in several cases it aggregated several words more. BERT performed well on average when compared with the other approaches. GPT remains competitive on all fuzzy match ranges except 90–100.

6 Conclusion

In this article, we have illustrated that via the use of a language model, predicting anchored words performed better in our experiments. The BERT model outperforms other approaches including neural machine translation (with two approaches) when measured via character match and tri-gram anchored word coverage.

We also demonstrate how generative models might be prompted to aid in predicting anchored text. It is our belief that this work could assist CAT tools backed by TMs and MT systems.

References

Achiam, J., Adler, S., Agarwal, S., Ahmad, L., Akkaya, I., Aleman, F. L., Almeida, D., Altenschmidt, J., Altman, S., Anadkat, S., et al. (2023). Gpt-4 technical report. *arXiv preprint arXiv:2303.08774*.

Biçici, E. and Dymetman, M. (2008). Dynamic translation memory: Using statistical machine translation to improve translation memory fuzzy matches. *Computational Linguistics and Intelligent Text Processing*, pages 454–465.

Bowker, L. (2002). *Computer-aided translation technology: a practical introduction.* University of Ottawa Press.

Brown, P. F., Della Pietra, S. A., Della Pietra, V. J., and Mercer, R. L. (1993). The mathematics of statistical machine translation: Parameter estimation. *Computational Linguistics*, 19(2):263–311.

Bulte, B. and Tezcan, A. (2019). Neural fuzzy repair: Integrating fuzzy matches into neural machine translation. In *Proceedings of the 57th Annual Meeting of the Association for Computational Linguistics*, pages 1800–1809, Florence, Italy.

Bulté, B., Vanallemeersch, T., and Vandeghinste, V. (2018). M3TRA: integrating TM and MT for professional translators. In *Proceedings of the 21st Annual Conference of the European Association for Machine Translation*, pages 69–78, Alacant, Spain.

Dandapat, S., Morrissey, S., Way, A., and Forcada, M. L. (2011). Using example-based MT to support statistical MT when translating homogeneous data in a resource-poor setting. In *Proceedings of the 15th Annual Conference of the European Association for Machine Translation*, pages 201–208, Leuven, Belgium.

Esplà-Gomis, M., Sánchez-Martínez, F., and Forcada, M. L. (2011). Using word alignments to assist computer-aided translation users by marking which target-side words to change or keep unedited. In *European Association for Machine Translation Conferences/Workshops*.

Gu, J., Wang, Y., Cho, K., and Li, V. O. (2018). Search engine guided neural machine translation. In *Proceedings of the 32 AAAI Conference on Artificial Intelligence*, pages 5133–5140, New Orleans, USA.

Hewavitharana, S., Vogel, S., and Waibel, A. (2005). Augmenting a statistical translation system with a translation memory. In *Proceedings of the 10th Annual Conference of the European Association for Machine Translation*, pages 126–132, Budapest, Hungary.

İrsoy, O., Benton, A., and Stratos, K. (2020). Corrected cbow performs as well as skip-gram. *arXiv preprint arXiv:2012.15332*.

Kenton, J. D. M.-W. C. and Toutanova, L. K. (2019). Bert: Pre-training of deep bidirectional transformers for language understanding. In *Proceedings of NAACL-HLT*, pages 4171–4186.

Klein, G., Hernandez, F., Nguyen, V., and Senellart, J. (2020). The opennmt neural machine translation toolkit: 2020 edition. In *Proceedings of the 14th Conference of the Association for Machine Translation in the Americas (Volume 1: Research Track)*, pages 102–109.

Koehn, P. and Senellart, J. (2010). Convergence of translation memory and statistical machine translation. In *Proceedings of AMTA Workshop on MT Research and the Translation Industry*, pages 21–31, Denver, USA.

Kranias, L. and Samiotou, A. (2004). Automatic translation memory fuzzy match post-editing: a step beyond traditional TM/MT integration. In *Proceedings of the Fourth International Conference on Language Resources and Evaluation*, pages 331–334, Lisbon, Portugal.

Levenshtein, V. (1966). Binary codes capable of correcting deletions, insertions and reversals. *Soviet Physics Doklady.*, 10(8):707–710.

Li, L., Parra Escartín, C., and Liu, Q. (2016). Combining translation memories and syntax-based SMT. *Baltic Journal of Modern Computing*, 4:165–177.

Liu, Y., Wang, K., Zong, C., and Su, K.-Y. (2019). A unified framework and models for integrating translation memory into phrase-based statistical machine translation. *Computer Speech & Language*, 54:176–206.

Mikolov, T., Chen, K., Corrado, G., and Dean, J. (2013). Efficient estimation of word representations in vector space. *arXiv preprint arXiv:1301.3781*.

Ortega, J. E., Sánchez-Martínez, F., and Forcada, M. L. (2014). Using any machine translation source for fuzzy-match repair in a computer-aided translation setting. In *Proceedings of the 11th Biennial Conference of the Association for Machine Translation in the Americas (AMTA 2014, vol. 1: MT Rsearchers)*, pages 42–53, Vancouver, BC, Canada.

Ortega, J. E., Sánchez-Martínez, F., and Forcada, M. L. (2016). Fuzzy-match repair using black-box machine translation systems: what can be expected? In *Proceedings of the 12th Biennial Conference of the Association for Machine Translation in the Americas (AMTA 2016, vol. 1: MT Researchers' Track)*, pages 27–39, Austin, USA.

Řehřek, R., Sojka, P., et al. (2011). Gensim—statistical semantics in python. *Retrieved from genism. org*.

Sanh, V., Debut, L., Chaumond, J., and Wolf, T. (2019). Distilbert, a distilled version of bert: smaller, faster, cheaper and lighter. *arXiv preprint arXiv:1910.01108*.

Simard, M. and Isabelle, P. (2009). Phrase-based machine translation in a computer-assisted translation environment. In *Proceeding of the 12th Machine Translation Summit (MT Summit XII)*, pages 120–127, Quebec, Canada.

Steinberger, R., Eisele, A., Klocek, S., Pilos, S., and Schlüter, P. (2012). DGT-TM: A freely available translation memory in 22 languages. In Calzolari, N., Choukri, K., Declerck, T., Doğan, M. U., Maegaard, B., Mariani, J., Moreno, A., Odijk, J., and Piperidis, S., editors, *Proceedings of the Eighth International Conference on Language Resources and Evaluation (LREC'12)*, pages 454–459, Istanbul, Turkey. European Language Resources Association (ELRA).

Tezcan, A. and Bulté, B. (2022). Evaluating the impact of integrating similar translations into neural machine translation. *Inf.*, 13:19.

Tezcan, A., Bulté, B., and Vanroy, B. (2021). Towards a better integration of fuzzy matches in neural machine translation through data augmentation. In *Informatics*, volume 8, page 7. MDPI.

Vaswani, A., Shazeer, N., Parmar, N., Uszkoreit, J., Jones, L., Gomez, A. N., Kaiser, Ł., and Polosukhin, I. (2017). Attention is all you need. *Advances in neural information processing systems*, 30.

Vogel, S., Ney, H., and Tillmann, C. (1996). HMM-based word alignment in statistical translation. pages 836–841, Copenhagen.

Wagner, R. A. and Fischer, M. J. (1974). The string-to-string correction problem. *Journal of the Association for Computing Machinery*, 21(1):168–173.

Zhechev, V. and Genabith, J. V. (2010). Seeding statistical machine translation with translation memory output through tree-based structural alignment. In *Proceedings of SSST-4 - 4th Workshop on Syntax and Structure in Statistical Translation*, pages 43–49, Dublin, Ireland.

On Translating Technical Terminology: A Translation Workflow for Machine-Translated Acronyms

Richard Yue
Northeastern University, San Jose, CA
yue.r@northeastern.edu

John E. Ortega
Institute for Experiential AI, Northeastern University, Boston, MA
j.ortega@northeastern.edu

Kenneth Ward Church
Institute for Experiential AI, Northeastern University, Boston, MA
k.church@northeastern.edu

Abstract

The typical workflow for a professional translator to translate a document from its source language (SL) to a target language (TL) is not always focused on what many language models in natural language processing (NLP) do – predict the next word in a series of words. While high-resource languages like English and French are reported to achieve near human parity using common metrics for measurement such as BLEU and COMET, we find that an important step is being missed: the translation of technical terms, specifically acronyms. Some state-of-the art machine translation systems like Google Translate which are publicly available can be erroneous when dealing with acronyms – as much as 50% in our findings. This article addresses acronym disambiguation for MT systems by proposing an additional step to the SL–TL (FR–EN) translation workflow where we first offer a new acronym corpus for public consumption and then experiment with a search-based thresholding algorithm that achieves nearly 10% increase when compared to Google Translate and OpusMT.

1 Introduction

With the myriad of artificial intelligence tools available for professional translators, it can be hard for translators to select solutions that address their core needs. Ideally, translation approaches based on machine learning techniques should improve translator proficiency and achieve higher overall quality. One such approach focuses on *technical terminology* (TT) where domain-specific terms in the form of acronyms in a source language (SL) must be translated into their target language (TL) counterpart.

TT is considered important to translators as it is one of the main sources of error a professional translator might encounter on a daily basis. The importance of TT is further displayed by the latest machine translation (MT) workshops (Semenov et al., 2023; Molchanov et al., 2021; Hasler et al., 2018) that stress the importance of correctly addressing terminology issues—including correctness of technical terms. While modern MT systems do not seem to focus on acronym and term disambiguation[1], workshops like the "Machine Translation using Terminologies" workshop[2] (Jon et al., 2021) clearly state that they focus on both translation accuracy and consistency. Since the dominant metric used (BLEU) for most MT approaches does not center so much on terminology expansion with acronyms and other mechanisms, we present in this article a novel method that hones in specifically on the day-to-day work in terminology that a professional translator may encounter, which has not been

[1] MT research generally use metrics such as BLEU (Papineni et al., 2002) or COMET (Rei et al., 2020).

[2] `https://www.statmt.org/wmt21/terminology-task.html`

addressed by most of the recent literature.

In this article, we present two main novelties that are based on the translation of acronyms: (1) the introduction of a new corpus made publicly available for others to use and (2) a fact-checking step that is used to verify the combination of a technical term and its acronym (long form (LF) and short form (SF)). We do this for several published articles in the TL, which is English. We aim to show that acronym disambiguation can improve term error rate by reducing the risk of default MT models that generally do not have an acronym approach. Our claim is that translators can use this method as a novel verification step in the normal translation pipeline. We also believe that other automated work such as generative MT may be able to include this step as a mechanism for evaluation.

To that end, we present the following sequence. First, we introduce relevant work in Section 2. Second, we describe our motivation and high-level proposal methodology in Section 3. We then cover the details of our corpus creation in Section 4.4. Afterwards, we show the results of our SF/LF method in Section 5 and finally we conclude our work in Section 6.

2 Related Work

In the WMT 2023 Shared Task on Machine Translation with Terminologies, Semenov et al. (2023) emphasize the effectiveness of incorporating terminology dictionaries and respecting domain-specific terminology constraints. The authors also distinguish terminology incorporation from general MT methods.

Post et al. (2019) explore the use of masking to properly isolate and translate specific named entities such as terminology spans. Their findings show that masking solves some problems, but relies entirely on the masks being properly aligned.

Ghazvininejad et al. (2023) propose a method for translating rare words such as technical terminology. The method, called DiPMT, is a prompting technique that provides an LLM with multiple translation choices from a dictionary as well as hints about their meaning for a subset of input words. It outperforms baselines for low resource and out-of-domain MT. The authors also extract bilingual dictionaries from the training data to assist in this process. Doing so allows for fine-grained control over the use of domain-specific terminology.

Anastasopoulos et al. (2021) stress the importance of taking terminology into account in neural MT and propose metrics to measure MT output consistency with regard to domain constraints. Dagan and Church (1994) propose a system to identify technical terms in a source text as well as their translations. The system uses part-of-speech tagging and word alignment techniques to assist translators during the translation process. Smadja et al. (1996) address the issue of translating collocations in a variety of domains.

Grefenstette (1999) offers an example-based method for dealing with terminology problems in translation as well as other NLP tasks. The method proposed uses search to find the most statistically likely translation of an entire noun phrase. Lee and Kim (2002) provide a knowledge-based approach to translation that includes using word-sense disambiguation to semantically derive the meaning of a word before seeking a target translation corresponding to that meaning.

Skadiņš et al. (2013) demonstrate the use of a cloud-based terminology search system that fully integrates with statistical methods to address the need for domain-specific terms and their integration into neural MT systems. Meanwhile, Bosca et al. (2014) stress the importance of term verification and consistency in the translation process and propose using external terminological databases to assist in fact checking and correcting domain-specific terminology.

3 Background and Motivation

In order to better understand how ineffective acronym disambiguation may be for translators, we investigate the performance of LFs and their SF acronyms within the realm of commercial MT systems. We perform this necessary step in order to confirm our hypothesis that: **acronym disambiguation in the current state-of-the-art French MT systems is not being addressed properly**. In Table 1, we provide a specific agreement comparison that uses a widely-used commercial MT system – Google translate[3]. For both cases (LFs and SFs) agreement is between 54% and 63%, giving way to a high amount of room for improvement. We illustrate

[3]https://translate.google.com/

Type of Term	Agreement
Long Forms (LFs)	62.1%
Short Forms (SFs)	54.3%

Table 1: Google Translate agreement for long- and short-form acronyms.

Input French	Output English	
	Google	**Gold**
indice	engine	motricity
moteur	index	index
fréquence	cardiac	heart
cardiaque	frequency	rate
roue	polar	claw
polaire	wheel	pole

Table 2: Erroneous Google Translate examples on long forms (LFs).

Input French	Output English	
	Google	**Gold**
AOMI	PAAD	PAD
DE	DE	EE
ICMI	CIMI	CLI

Table 3: Erroneous Google Translate examples on short forms (SFs).

this with further analysis in Tables 2 (long forms) and 3 (short forms).

As a way of mitigating the room for improvement, we propose the following novel method for MT that decomposes translation into four high-level steps by taking into account that Google Translate is more successful on LFs than SFs. For other MT systems, this may not be the case; we focus solely on Google Translate here as the oracle for our experiment.

1. Use Google Translate to translate each LF from French (FR) to English (EN).
2. Extract the LF from Google Translate's EN pair output (using a simple split command).
3. Generate several SF hypotheses using the extracted LF from Step 2.
4. Use a search technique to verify and evaluate certainty of hypotheses.

To better describe Steps 1 through 4, we provide the following in-depth description. A term such as "acide désoxyribonucléique **(adn)**" would first be translated in Step 1 from French to English as "deoxyribonucleic acid **(dna)**". We then extract the English LF (deoxyribonucleic acid) and SF (dna) for use in the next steps. Step 3 consists of the use of AB3P[4] (Sohn et al., 2008; Church and Liu, 2021), an acronym tool that provides LFs in English created by the United States government and contains acronyms from crawls of PubMed[5] and arXiv[6]. If a sufficient number of documents is not found that contain the English LF and SF together, we then generate a list of acronym hypotheses translations from the translated LF. Each hypothesis is generated using a fine-tuned version of the Scibert (Beltagy et al., 2019) model described in section 4.

Step 4 consists of the verification process, also known as "Fact Checking". Typically, the translation process for technical terms involves a significant component of researching the meaning of

[4]https://github.com/ncbi-nlp/Ab3P
[5]https://pubmed.ncbi.nlm.nih.gov/
[6]https://arxiv.org

a source language term, identifying multiple target language candidate terms, and finally, proceeding through the n-best list in order and seeking out the use of a chosen term in context in similar target language texts, written by experts in the field in question.[7] According to Bowker (2021), professional translation term verification is done on the basis of observed frequency in a corpus; if enough experts use the selected term in context, it is considered to be valid. Domain expertise from professional translation trade unions such as the ATA[8] point to two or three sources being sufficient to substantiate use of a given term. We replicate that process using the search method below.

We implement a Boolean retrieval system that contains acronyms extracted from AB3P output on a crawl of arXiv and Pubmed along with the long forms they map to and source paper ID. If a sufficient number of sources have been found to employ the desired term-acronym pair (in the form *cardiopulmonary resuscitation (CPR)*), term validation is deemed to be successful and the term pair is returned to the user alongside the list of sources for verification. This re-appropriates the term verification method employed by professional translation agencies in the field (and facilitates verification by a reviewer, who may need to fact check term sources at a later stage).

The translation of acronyms is further complicated by non-English languages opting to adopt a better known English acronym alongside a translation of the term. The French translation for "large language model" (grand modèle de langue) is condensed using the English acronym "LLM," even though the acronym does not correspond to the first letters of each word. Despite this limitation, our search step allows for the verification of such cases, as the pairing of term and acronym is likely to occur in the literature if they have found consensus in the field. Thus, verification would succeed and the disambiguation step would not be performed. Furthermore, fine tuning on corpora such as Pubmed was foregone due to the non-compositionality of many technical terms; boolean search ensures that the term is verified as a fixed unit.

While an exact match (e.g. 'RCP' to 'CPR') is the objective of our system, it is important to note that for evaluating the system we distinguish between *agreement* (an exact match) and *verification* (verified by a search) as noted:

Agreement – The candidate SF is an exact match with the gold SF.

Verification – The candidate SF was found near the LF in at least two published papers in the target language (English).

4 Experimental Settings

4.1 Translation Models

For **Google Translate**, experiments were performed using the Google API[9] as available to the public on October 14, 2023. For **Opus MT**, the vanilla model was used without any fine tuning. The French-to-English language variant from Hugging Face[10] was downloaded for this purpose.

4.2 Baselines

We compare the inclusion of our method against several baselines that are executed with and without our proposed step. Our experiments are performed on the acronym corpus that we created and allow for public consumption. Our first set of experiments focuses on three main baseline approaches found in Table 5 that we call: (1) *Identity*, (2) *Reverse*, and (3) *Google/Opus*[11]. The Identity baseline is the most straightforward experiment which is when the English SF output is **equal to** the French SF input (e.g. ADN in French is equal to ADN in English). The Reverse baseline is when the English SF output is the **reverse** of the French SF input (e.g. ADN in French is equal to NDA in English). The Google/Opus baseline takes the LF and SF in French and outputs an SF in English.

4.3 Hypothesis Generation

For the disambiguation of acronyms, we use a SciBERT (Beltagy et al., 2019) model that is fine-tuned on 1.8M term-acronym pairs in the target language (English) with these parameters: Adam as the optimizer, an initial learning rate of 2e-5, 1,000 warmup

[7] https://www.technitrad.com/how-to-perform-terminology-research/

[8] https://www.atanet.org/growing-your-career/terminology-management-what-you-should-know/

[9] https://cloud.google.com/translate

[10] https://huggingface.co/Helsinki-NLP/opus-mt-fr-en

[11] We use the OpusMT system for an extra comparison https://huggingface.co/Helsinki-NLP/opus-mt-fr-en

Input: LF ([MASK])	Gold SF
cardiopulmonary resuscitation ([MASK])	CPR
deoxyribonucleic acid ([MASK])	DNA
Organization of the Petroleum Exporting Countries ([MASK])	OPEC

Table 4: Training data for SF candidate generation.

Baseline	Input	Output
Identity	ADN	ADN
Reverse	ADN	NDA
Google/Opus	acide désoxyribonucléique (ADN)	DNA

Table 5: Examples of our three baseline methods.

steps, and a weight decay of 0.01. We use data downloaded from arXiv[12] and then processed by AB3P for fine-tuning as shown in Table 4. The final model accepts input in the form: "LF ([MASK])" and outputs an n-best list of SF candidates.

4.4 Acronym Corpus

A new test set[13] (called the **acronym corpus** here) has been created for evaluating machine translation systems on acronyms. The test set consists of 437 LF-SF pairs obtained from a corpus of 13,500 abstracts crawled from HAL[14], a repository of French academic papers, many of which are from medicine and science. The pairings contain an LF and SF for each term in both French (source) and English (target). Examples were selected such that no offensive content or personal information was to be included.

The HAL repository provides abstracts in both French and English. These abstracts contain many technical terms. An example of an abstract is "[...] 42/194 patients (21%) did not want **cardiopulmonary resuscitation (CPR)** and 15/36 (41%) did not prefer intensive care unit (ICU) admission [...]." When the abstract introduces an acronym, the gold labels in the test set specify the long form (LF) and the short form (SF) in both French and English. An example of the acronym translation task is to input a French LF such as **réanimation cardiopulmonaire** and its corresponding SF, in this case **RCP**. The output should be the correct translation of the SF: **CPR**.

5 Results

We compare the baselines first in Table 6. We provide both agreement and verification for consistency purposes, which show that verification is generally much lower than agreement for all systems.

When compared, our proposed technique, which includes search and verification, achieves 9.9% improvement (43.9%) for agreement and 17.8% improvement (32.7%) for verification compared to the baseline when using the OpusMT system. Google translate scores are also markedly higher, with 8.3% improvement (**62.6%**) and 13.6% (**42.8%**), respectively. It is clear that through the use of our proposed system, the acronym resolution is much higher for both agreement and verification.

Additionally, we illustrate the comparisons in more detail from a precision and recall perspective in Table 7 for all experimental systems. Our experiments show that through the use of our proposed step which uses agreement and verification, professional translators that use the Annotated Corpus will have more success using our system. Precision is presented here as the portion of agreed terms that are

[12] https://info.arxiv.org/help/bulk_data/index.html
[13] https://github.com/rtotheich/acronym_corpus/tree/main
[14] https://theses.hal.science/?lang=en

Method	Agreement	Verified
Identity Baseline	21.5%	0.06%
Reverse Baseline	28.5%	14.6%
Opus Baseline	34%	14.9%
Google Baseline	54.3%	29.2%
Gold Labels	100%	42%

Table 6: Agreement and verification for the baseline experiments on the *Acronym Corpus*.

Method	Precision	Recall
Identity Baseline	0.28	0.06
Reverse Baseline	0.51	0.15
Opus Baseline	0.43	0.15
Google Baseline	0.54	0.29
Gold Labels	0.42	0.42
Proposed (Opus)	0.75	0.33
Proposed (Google)	**0.68**	**0.43**

Table 7: Precision and recall comparisons for all experimental systems.

verified and recall as the portion of verified terms.

6 Conclusion

Professional translators must be well versed in the source and target languages that they are translating. Translating technical terminology can be so important that it has been compared to the job of a terminologist (Cabré, 2010). Quality translations will take into account several units of measurement such as fluency, adequacy, and more. However, it has been the case in the past that, more often than not, terminology, specifically the translation of acronyms, is not included as a major improvement to a translator's pipeline. Domain-specific standards (GHENŢULESCU, 2015), nonetheless, have been set such that verification of terminology like acronyms is considered an important step in translation.

Translators and AI practitioners could benefit highly from the use of a system like the one presented in this article. We believe that our corpus and findings provide sufficient evidence and materials to reproduce a benefit to warrant future work on the topic.

7 Limitations

The results of applying our method may not transfer to languages that are very different from English in orthography (e.g., Chinese, Japanese) and/or morphology. The working languages of the authors being French and English, hand curating a corpus was limited to these only. Our solution also may not scale to longer texts; the method is based on working with term-acronym pairs and working on a full text would require a pre-processing step to identify term pairs as well as inference time for each acronym. Training a model for this task also requires access to GPU resources.

8 Ethics Statement

In line with the concept of professional translator ethics presented by Lambert (2020), it is of paramount importance to guard against translations that "represent their source texts in unfair ways." This refers to unfaithful translations that do not correctly transfer the true meaning in the source language, a prime example being incorrect or unverifiable terminology. Our system upholds this doctrine of translation ethics and adheres to ethics policies outlined by the translation community.

References

Anastasopoulos, A., Besacier, L., Cross, J., Gallé, M., Koehn, P., Nikoulina, V., et al. (2021). On the evaluation of machine translation for terminology consistency. *arXiv preprint arXiv:2106.11891.*

Beltagy, I., Lo, K., and Cohan, A. (2019). Scibert: A pretrained language model for scientific text. In *Proceedings of the 2019 Conference on Empirical Methods in Natural Language Processing and the 9th International Joint Conference on Natural Language Processing (EMNLP-IJCNLP)*, pages 3615–3620.

Bosca, A., Nikoulina, V., and Dymetman, M. (2014). A lightweight terminology verification service for external machine translation engines. In *Proceedings of the Demonstrations at the 14th Conference of the European Chapter of the Association for Computational Linguistics*, pages 49–52.

Bowker, L. (2021). Machine translation literacy instruction for non-translators: A comparison of five delivery formats. In *Proceedings of the Translation and Interpreting Technology Online Conference*, pages 25–36.

Cabré, M. T. (2010). Terminology and translation. *Handbook of translation studies*, 1:356–365.

Church, K. and Liu, B. (2021). Acronyms and opportunities for improving deep nets. *Frontiers in Artificial Intelligence*, 4:732381.

Dagan, I. and Church, K. (1994). Termight: Identifying and translating technical terminology. In *Fourth Conference on Applied Natural Language Processing*, pages 34–40.

Ghazvininejad, M., Gonen, H., and Zettlemoyer, L. (2023). Dictionary-based phrase-level prompting of large language models for machine translation. *arXiv preprint arXiv:2302.07856.*

GHENŢULESCU, L. R. (2015). The importance of terminology for translation studies. *In the Beginning Was the Word". On the Linguistic Matter of Which the World Is Built. Bucureşti: Ars Docendi*, pages 54–61.

Grefenstette, G. (1999). The world wide web as a resource for example-based machine translation tasks. In *Proceedings of Translating and the Computer 21.*

Hasler, E., De Gispert, A., Iglesias, G., and Byrne, B. (2018). Neural machine translation decoding with terminology constraints. *arXiv preprint arXiv:1805.03750.*

Jon, J., Novák, M., Aires, J. P., Variš, D., and Bojar, O. (2021). Cuni systems for wmt21: Terminology translation shared task. *arXiv preprint arXiv:2109.09350.*

Lambert, J. (2020). Professional translator ethics. *The Routledge Handbook of Translation and Ethics Routledge*, pages 165–179.

Lee, H. A. and Kim, G. C. (2002). Translation selection through source word sense disambiguation and target word selection. In *COLING 2002: The 19th International Conference on Computational Linguistics.*

Molchanov, A., Kovalenko, V., and Bykov, F. (2021). Promt systems for wmt21 terminology translation task. In *Proceedings of the Sixth Conference on Machine Translation*, pages 835–841.

Papineni, K., Roukos, S., Ward, T., and Zhu, W.-J. (2002). BLEU: a method for automatic evaluation of machine translation. In *Proceedings of the 40th annual meeting of the Association for Computational Linguistics*, pages 311–318.

Post, M., Ding, S., Martindale, M., and Wu, W. (2019). An exploration of placeholding in neural machine translation. In *Proceedings of Machine Translation Summit XVII: Research Track*, pages 182–192.

Rei, R., Stewart, C., Farinha, A. C., and Lavie, A. (2020). Comet: A neural framework for mt evaluation. *arXiv preprint arXiv:2009.09025.*

Semenov, K., Zouhar, V., Kocmi, T., Zhang, D., Zhou, W., and Jiang, Y. E. (2023). Findings of the wmt 2023 shared task on machine translation with terminologies. In *Proceedings of the Eight Conference on Machine Translation (WMT).* Association for Computational Linguistics.

Skadiņš, R., Pinnis, M., Gornostay, T., and Vasiļjevs, A. (2013). Application of online terminology services in statistical machine translation. In *Proceedings of Machine Translation Summit XIV: Posters.*

Smadja, F., McKeown, K. R., and Hatzivassiloglou, V. (1996). Translating collocations for bilingual lexicons: A statistical approach. *Computational Linguistics*, 22(1):1–38.

Sohn, S., Comeau, D. C., Kim, W., and Wilbur, W. J. (2008). Abbreviation definition identification based on automatic precision estimates. *BMC bioinformatics*, 9(1):1–10.

Exploring the Advantages and Challenges of a Concept-Guided Approach in Large Language Model Aided Machine Translation: Integrating Generative AI And Human-like Cognition

Ming Qian mqian@cra.com
Human-Centered AI, Charles River Analytics, Cambridge, MA 02138, USA

Chuiqing Kong chuiqingkong@gmail.com
Linguist, San Mateo, CA 94403, USA

Abstract

Humans outperform large language models (LLMs) on sophisticated tasks because human cognition involves a range of cognitive functions and their dynamic interactions. This study explores how integrating human cognition through concept-guided instruction and few-shot teaching in the prompt can guide LLMs to improve translation outcomes. We first demonstrate that for simple and widely used concepts, concept-guided prompting approaches offer significant benefits. We then test prompt engineering with Chinese-to-English translation examples, using hypothetical spaces—generated by GPT4—to estimate the complexity of various concepts and Likert scores—generated by human experts—to evaluate the translation performance. Our findings show that LLM translation performance declines as concept complexity increases. We also identify additional challenges: LLMs struggle with continuity in explaining and practicing sophisticated concepts due to the lack of human-like cognitive functions, such as cognitive dissonance. Additionally, LLMs lack a graceful speed-accuracy tradeoff because they do not possess the dynamic information processing, response strategies, and performance assessment that humans do. However, LLMs can mitigate some of these challenges by using Chain-of-Thought (CoT) reasoning, which is especially effective for problems requiring consistent, well-structured reasoning steps. Despite this, LLMs can only represent the effects of complex human cognitive functions through (often) fragmented linguistic descriptions, whereas humans excel at understanding critical and broader contexts and the interconnections between cognitive aspects.

1 Introduction

Humans possess superior capabilities compared to large language models (LLMs) because human cognition emcompasses a range of mental functions: language processing, perception, attention, memory, reasoning, problem-solving, planning, decision-making, and executing actions. According to triadic cognition theory (Cook 2018), dual process theory (Chaiken 1999; Daniel 2017), embodied cognition (Shapiro 2014), and cognitive psychology (Neisser 2014), human cognition arises from the dynamic interaction of these functions, yielding a more nuanced, multifaceted understanding of real-world contexts than a simplistic and static computational model.

Recent advancements in large language models (LLMs) have shown that while these models still do not match the full breadth of human cognition, they are making significant strides in specific areas such as machine translation (Fan 2020 and Zhu 2023). Unlike traditional machine translation (MT) tools such as Google Translate and DeepL, which rely solely on the source language text, LLMs possess the ability to follow instructions and can even learn from bilingual training examples provided within the prompt. This capability allows LLMs to provide context-sensitive translations with improved performance, making them as a more adaptable and user-friendly option to traditional methods (Qian and Kong, 2024A and 2024B).

Concepts serve as a common entity used across multiple cognitive functions, both in human minds and large language models. John McCarthy's insight, "To understand natural language is to understand the concepts in the language, not just the words," (McCarthy 2007) captures the fundamental cognitive principle that language is a tool for conveying and manipulating concepts, and true understanding requires engaging with those underlying mental constructs rather than simply processing linguistic symbols.

One important approach to guide the LLM-based translation outcome is to provide concept definitions and examples through prompt engineering. In section 2, by experimenting with many examples associated with common sense concepts (e.g., systems of measurement such as the metric system and the imperial system) and cross-cultural conceptualization, we show that, given proper prompts in the form of pre-editing analysis, concept-guided translation prompt instruction, and post-editing revision, LLMs can successfully reflect the relevant concepts in the translation outcome.

On the other hand, for more sophisticated translation concepts, we want to test whether performance of the concept-guided approach degrades as the concepts become more complex. In section 3, we test prompt-engineering-based implementations of multiple translation-related concepts using Chinese-to-English translation examples. By using hypothetical spaces to represent the complexity levels of various concepts, we verify that LLMs' translation performance degrades as concept complexity level increases. Also in section 3, we identify and analyze several challenges faced by the concept-guided approach: LLMs lack continuity to explain and practice sophisticated concepts; and compared with humans, LLMs lack graceful speed-accuracy tradeoff. These challenges stem from the fundamental differences between LLMs and human cognition. As artificial systems designed solely for generating text, LLMs' internal processes do not mimic or engage the complex cognitive functions and dynamic interactions typical of the human brain. Consequently, these limitations in simulating human-like cognition contribute to the observed deficiencies.

Nevertheless, LLMs have been shown to exhibit human-like cognitive functions such as reasoning patterns (Lampinen 2024; Hagendorff 2023). Section 4 demonstrates that LLMs can use Chain-of-Thought (CoT) reasoning (Wei 2022) to overcome some challenges and enhance the performance. This is particularly effective for sub-problems that benefit from well-formed, consistent reasoning steps, ultimately leading to the correct conclusion. However, while humans use multiple cognitive functions to solve complex problems, LLMs can only project this complexity, often in fragmented form, as linguistic descriptions. Again, these broader perspectives and interconnections are critical strengths of the complex cognitive functions and dynamic interactions typical of the human brain.

Section 5 concludes our findings.

2 Advantages of Concept-guided Pre-editing Analysis, Translation Instruction, and Post-editing Revision

The role of concepts across multiple cognitive functions is multifaceted and central to human cognition: facilitating reasoning and generalization (William 2010), guiding decision-making by providing a framework for understanding and categorizing new information (Snowden 2007), integrating multiple features and dimensions of information (Villani 2019) to support flexible cognition (Ionescu 2006, Johnsson 2021), bridging episodic and semantic memory (Morton 2013), and creating functionally unitary representations that can be accessed and used across different cognitive tasks (Mahon 2009).

In this section, we showcase several examples where concept-guided prompting has significant advantage by using LLM-based pre-analyses, translation instructions and post-editing revisions.

2.1 LLMs Leverage Pre-editing Style Analysis as Translation Instructions

LLMs can generate style analysis reports for narratives. Table 1 presents an example using GPT4 to analyze an English narrative's style. In (Qian 2023), we compared these results with analyses by two human professional translators on the same text.

GPT4's analysis was not only more comprehensive and accurate but also faster than human analysts. Subsequently, a GPT4 prompt could use this pre-editing style analysis as a guide. For example, the prompt might be: "Translate the following text from English to Chinese, incorporating applicable styles such as humor, self-deprecation, conversational tone, vivid descriptions, casual language and slang, honesty, anecdotal use, exaggeration for effect, direct address, and rhetorical questions." Using pre-editing auto-analysis as a translation style guide can significantly improve upon current methods that do not support style instruction.

User (Prompt)
Please read the story at https://www.thecut.com/2020/03/book-excerpt-samantha-irbys-wow-no-thank-you.html **and derive a list of the author's writing style.**
ChatGPT (Used Link Reader)
Based on the excerpt from Samantha Irby's essay collection "Wow, No Thank You.", here are some characteristics of her writing style:
1. Humorous and Self-deprecating: Irby often uses humor and self-deprecation to engage her readers. She makes fun of herself and her situations, which adds a light-hearted tone.
2. Conversational Tone: Her writing style is conversational, feeling personal and relatable.
3. Vivid Descriptions: Irby uses vivid and detailed descriptions to paint a clear picture of her experiences. This helps to immerse the reader in her stories.
4. Casual Language: She uses casual language, slang, and colloquialisms, which contributes to the conversational/informal tone.
5. Honesty and Authenticity: Irby's writing is characterized by its honesty and authenticity. She doesn't shy away from discussing personal and sometimes uncomfortable topics.
6. Anecdotes: She uses anecdotes to illustrate points and make writing more relatable.
7. Exaggeration for Effect: Irby often uses exaggeration to emphasize her points.
8. Direct Address: She frequently addresses the reader directly, which helps to establish a connection between her and the reader.
9. Use of Rhetorical Questions: Irby often uses rhetorical questions to engage the reader.
10. ...

Table 1: GPT4 analyzed the discourse-level writing style, with human-identified entries highlighted in bold (more details on this example can be found in Qian 2023).

2.2 LLMs Utilize Concept-guided Prompts to Guide Translation and Post-editing

Concepts are crucial in human cognition, allowing us to mentally group similar objects, events, and ideas. Unlike traditional machine translation and editing methods, which focus on sentence-by-sentence and word-by-word changes, an LLM-based approach can leverage various concepts to guide translations and revisions more effectively.

For example, Table 2 illustrates how a GPT-4 prompt describes converting units of measure from the imperial system to the international system of units (SI) to enhance machine translation revisions. This allows for converting multiple types (such as inches, pounds, and gallons to meters, kilograms, and liters) across multiple sentences in a single instruction. This method represents a significant improvement, demonstrating that concept-guided instructions are major advancements over traditional approaches.

User (Prompt)
Translate the following text segment from English to Chinese:
Original English: ...
ChatGPT
The Chinese translation is:
...他的身高是 5 英尺 10 英寸 (His height is 5 feet and 10 inches)...
User (Prompt)
Revise the translation to reflect the following concepts:
"convert the units of measure to the international system of units (SI)"
ChatGPT
The Revised Chinese translation is:
... 他的身高是 1.78 米 (His height is 1.78 meters)...

Table 2: GPT-4 prompt uses concept descriptions to automatically revise machine translation results, such as converting units from inches to meters.

Table 3 showcases an instance where GPT4 introduces a cultural difference issue in the prompt and guides a revision effort to address the issue. In such situations, human translators might only be able to fix one issue at a time. However, we can leverage concept-guided translation memory that can identify similar text segments based on concept similarity so that (conceptually) similar sentences can be processed in similar fashion (Qian and Kong, 2024B).

User (Prompt)
Translate the following text segment from English to Chinese:

Original English: The last time I wore a Halloween mascot was in the second-grade costume parade at Lincoln Elementary School in 1986 (go dolphins).
The Chinese translation is:
ChatGPT
上一次我穿万圣节服装是在1986年林肯小学的二年级服装游行中（加油， 海豚）。
User (Prompt)
Keep in mind that "dolphins" in this context refer to the school mascot. **Since most Chinese schools do not have mascot, please modify the translation to make the meaning more clear to Chinese audience.**
ChatGPT
上一次我穿万圣节服装是在1986年林肯小学的二年级服装游行中(加油，林肯小学的吉祥物海豚）。

Table 3: GPT4 Instructed translation revision: to reflect a cultural difference (most Chinese schools do not have mascot), GPT4 revision provides further elaboration ("林肯小学的吉祥物"—Lincoln elementary school's mascot) in front of the word "海豚".

2.3 Summary

For simple and straightforward concepts, concept-guided approaches, supported by prompt-engineering using LLMs, show significant benefits.

In the next section, we evaluate translation concepts with various complexities to evaluate the challenges faced by the concept-guided approaches.

3 Challenges Faced by the Concept-guided Approach

In this section, we test Chinese-to-English translation concepts with varying levels of difficulty. We found that while LLMs perform well with simple and straightforward concepts, they encounter significant challenges when handling more sophisticated concepts (Qian and Kong 2024A, Qian and Kong 2024B).

3.1 LLMs' Performance Declines with Increasing Concept Complexity

In cognitive linguistics and mental spaces theory, a hypothetical space is a dynamically constructed partial and temporary conceptual domain used during thinking and speaking (Nolan, 2001). These mental spaces facilitate the representation of complex scenarios, counterfactuals, and hypothetical situations.

Two translation concepts are compared for illustration:

"Subject omission" describes a linguistic phenomenon where a language permits the omission of subject if they can be inferred pragmatically or grammatically.

"Changing subject selection" involves choosing a different subject than the original one in the source language to enhance readability and fluency in the target language.

Applying concept 2 generally requires a larger hypothetical space than concept 1, as it often involves selecting from multiple possible subjects—nouns, noun phrases, or clauses—making it more complex.

We had used GPT4 to analyze the hypothetical space of ten translation concepts: (1) The term "pro-drop" describes a linguistic feature where a language permits the omission of subjects (and occasionally other pronouns) if they can be inferred pragmatically or grammatically. (2) The linguistic term "dislocation" describes the occurrence where the placement of words or phrases within a sentence varies considerably between two languages. (3) The concept of implicit conjunctions and the use of linking or transition words in Chinese contrasts with English. Chinese frequently omits conjunctions that are essential in English. (4) The practice of amalgamating clauses and brief sentences in Chinese to form an extended English sentence is noteworthy. (5) Deverbalization, a key concept in translation studies related to abstract meaning from the source language to effectively convey the intended message in the target language, becomes especially pertinent when translating between languages with markedly different structures, such as from Chinese to English. (6) Eliminating redundancy is a common practice in translating Chinese, enhances the readability and clarity of the target text. (7) Changing subject selection involves selecting a different subject than the one in the source text to enhance the readability and fluency of the English translation. (8) Changing perspective in the context of translating from Chinese to English involves altering the viewpoint or approach when converting text from one language to the other. (9) Changing parts of speech is essential to faithfully convey the meaning of the original while ensuring adherence to English expressions, regardless of the corresponding parts of speech in Chinese. (10) Cultural translation aims to retain the intended meaning of a culturally sensitive message while considering cultural differences, in order to avoid confusion that may result from a direct translation.

GPT4 was used to generate a normalized score (ranged between 0 and 1) towards each concept in terms of the hypothetical spaces. A detailed concept description plus three examples prepared by human experts are provided in the prompt to set up the context for evaluation. Table 4 shows an example on deverbalization and the related complexity evaluation results generated by GPT4; The detailed GPT prompt and GPT-generated hypothetical space evaluation on all ten translation concepts are listed in Appendix 1.

User (Prompt)

Deverbalization is a concept in translation studies, particularly relevant in the context of translating between languages with significantly different structures, such as Chinese to English. The core idea of deverbalization is to move away from a direct, word-for-word translation, which often leads to awkward or inaccurate results due to the differences in grammar, syntax, and cultural contexts. …

…

Three examples are listed below to illustrate the Chinese-to-English translation reflecting the concept above:

Chinese: 过去带动高增长的主要是高投资，而高投资主要是三大需求来源，出口、基础建设、房地产。

English: The key driver of rapid growth has been investment, which is needed in three areas/goes to three areas, export, infrastructure, and real estate.

Chinese: 本土化人才了解中国市场上的需求和消费者的心理。

English: Local talents understand the market needs in China and know what customers want.

Chinese: 中国现在很多地区复工率很高。

English: Many areas in China have reopened their economies.

Evaluating the size of the "hypothetical space" for each of these translation concepts **involves considering the range of interpretations, adaptations, and choices a translator might need to navigate when applying these concepts from Chinese to English. This hypothetical space represents the complexity and variability inherent in each concept, indicating the level of creativity, cultural understanding, and linguistic expertise required.** Here's a rating for each concept, on a scale from 0 (minimal complexity) to 100 (maximum complexity), reflecting the size of their hypothetical spaces:

ChatGPT

Deverbalization (80/100): This concept requires deep understanding of both source and target languages, along with the ability to abstract and reconceptualize ideas in culturally appropriate ways. It involves a significant hypothetical space due to the need for creative interpretation and expression.

Changing Subject Selection (70/100): Adapting the subject for better readability and fluency can involve moderate to high complexity, especially when ensuring that the shift does not alter the intended meaning of the original text.

…

Table 4: GPT4 prompt and hypothetical space evaluation scores for the ten concepts (detailed prompt and GPT4-generated evaluation results are listed in Appendix 1).

Machine translation evaluation employed human experts to assign 5-point Likert scores to GPT-4's English-to-Chinese translation outcomes of ten concepts. The scale scores used were; Strongly Disagree = -2; Disagree = -1; Neither Agree nor Disagree=0; Agree=1; Strongly Agree = 2. The experiment used a dataset of 40 English-Chinese sentence pairs, with four pairs per concept (detailed in Appendix 2). Using 1-in-4 leave-one-out cross-validation, the GPT-4 model was given three Chinese-English sentence pairs (as few-shot training examples) and the concept definition in the prompt, and then generated the English translation for the fourth pair's Chinese sentence. This process was repeated to produce four distinct translations for each Chinese sentence, all of which were subject to human evaluation.

Figure 1 displays human-generated Likert scores for concept-guided machine translations (top plot) and GPT-4-generated scores for hypothetical space complexity (bottom plot). Generally, GPT-4 translation performance declines as the complexity of the concepts increases, indicating that LLMs struggle with more sophisticated concepts involving larger hypothetical spaces. An exception is the "cultural translation" concept, which, unlike others focused on syntax and semantics, falls into a unique category. This suggests that GPT-4's complexity scores for hypothetical space may not accurately reflect challenges in cultural translation.

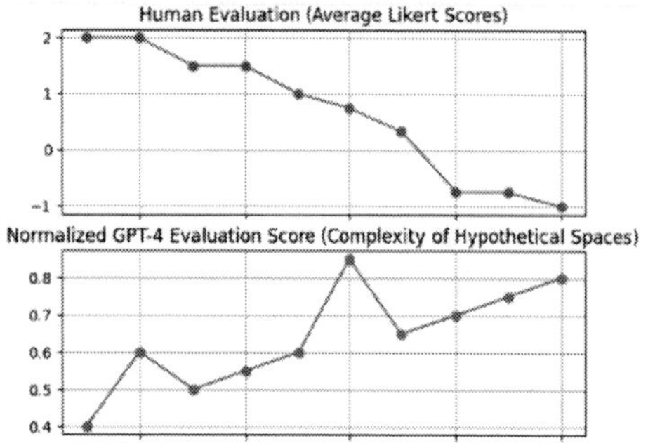

Figure 1: As GPT4's hypothetical space evaluation scores increase (normalized from 0 to 1), its performance (Likert Scores generated by human evaluators) degrades. The X-axis lists ten concepts, from left to right: eliminating redundancy, prodrop, implicit conjunction and linking, combining clauses and short sentences, dislocation, cultural translation, changing part of speech, subject selection, perspective, and deverbalization.

3.2 LLMs Lack Continuity

The "continuity" of AI models, particularly LLMs, refers to their ability to maintain coherent memory, reasoning, and contextual understanding over time. The lack of continuity in LLM models is a significant challenge that raises concerns about their ability to achieve human-like intelligence and self-awareness (Lieberman, 2024).

Table 5 presents an example where GPT4 contradicts itself. The concept under focus is "Pro-drop" that refers to the grammatical feature where subjects/pronouns are omitted if their meaning can be inferred from context. In the example, GPT4 shows that it has epistemological knowledge about the concept. In addition, with the help of the definition and few-shot examples, GPT4 identifies that the concept should be applied and states that the subject is missing in the original Chinese text, yet it identifies a subject in its direct translation and retains this subject in the final translation, where it also claims to add a subject absent from the Chinese version. This example highlights the inconsistencies and logical flaws of large language models (LLMs) when dealing with complex concepts.

User (Prompt) What is the concept of "Pro-drop" in the context of Chinese-to-English translation? ChatGPT The concept of "Pro-drop" (short for pronoun dropping) refers to the grammatical feature in certain languages where pronouns that are syntactically expected can be omitted if their meaning is understood from context. This characteristic is particularly relevant in the context of translating from Chinese to English because Chinese is a Pro-drop language, whereas English generally is not. In Chinese, speakers often omit subjects and sometimes objects when these are clear from the context or previously mentioned in the discourse…
User (Prompt) The concept of "pro-drop" refers to the ability of a language to omit subjects (and sometimes other pro-nouns) when they are pragmatically or grammatically inferable. Chinese is a pro-drop language, meaning that subjects can be and often are omitted when they are un-derstood from context. In contrast, English is a "non pro-drop" language, meaning that subjects are almost always explicitly stated, as English need the presence of subjects for clarity and grammatical correctness. Three examples are listed below to illustrate the Chinese-to-English translation reflecting the concept above: Chinese: 对传统那些没有比较优势和竞争优势产业，继续给予必要保证。 English: Traditional industries without comparative advantage and competitiveness should be given the support.

Chinese： 要重视发挥家庭、学校和社区作用，帮助儿童抵御恐怖极端思想侵蚀。
English: Attention should be paid to the roles of families, schools, and communities in preventing children from being influenced by extreme terrorism.
Chinese: 需要货币政策传导机制来保证资金流动到位。
English: We need transmission mechanism of monetary policy to ensure the availability of capital flows.
If you are an expert-level translator, do you think we should apply the same concept on the following Chinese text segment?
Chinese: 各地积极性高涨。
Please give a score between 0 and 100 (0 means the concept definitely should not be applied on translating the sentence while 100 means that the concept definitely should be applied on translating the sentence.
If the score is above 75, what should be the proper translation reflecting the concept. Please generate a proper English translation reflecting the concept.
ChatGPT
The Chinese sentence "各地积极性高涨" can be translated while considering the pro-drop concept. This sentence, when directly translated, means "Enthusiasm is high everywhere." In a non pro-drop language like English, it's necessary to specify the subject for clarity. However, in this Chinese sentence, the subject is dropped because it's understood from the context.
In this case, I would give a score of around 85, indicating that the pro-drop concept should be applied in translation. The English translation, reflecting this concept and the inherent meaning of the sentence, could be:
"Enthusiasm is high in all regions."
Here, the subject "enthusiasm" is explicitly stated to maintain clarity in English, which is a non pro-drop language. The translation captures the essence of the original Chinese sentence while adhering to the syntactic requirements of English.

Table 5: GPT-4 "understands" the “pro-drop” concept; with the help of concept definition and few-shot examples, it identifies that the concept should be applied (a subject needs to be added for English) but it contradicts itself by keeping the same subject.

Cognitive dissonance, a psychological theory proposed by Leon Festinger (Festinger 1962), suggests that individuals experience discomfort when holding conflicting beliefs, attitudes, or behaviors. This discomfort, known as dissonance, drives individuals to seek consistency between their beliefs and actions to reduce the associated stress. Cognitive dissonance involves several cognitive functions: detecting discrepancies (attention and memory), experiencing physiological arousal and discomfort (emotion regulation), perception and confirmation (perception), and rationalization and justification (decision making).

LLMs are powerful tools for generating text and understanding language, but they lack the ability to leverage human cognitive functions, such as cognitive dissonance, to maintain consistency.

3.3 LLMs Lack Graceful Speed-Accuracy Tradeoff

The speed-accuracy tradeoff, as described in (Heltz, 2014), refers to the intricate relationship between an individual's preference for responding slowly with fewer errors versus responding quickly with more errors.

Compared to humans, LLMs were found unable to manage the speed-accuracy tradeoff as effectively (Goodman, 2024). In the context of translation, we tested multiple concepts and had similar findings. Table 6 presents a case study where GPT-4 was taught the concept of "changing subject selection"—selecting a subject different from the one in the source text (e.g., Chinese) to improve the readability and fluency of the target language (e.g., English) translation—using an instruction followed by three examples. In theory, any noun, noun phrase, or noun clause can serve as the subject in English. However, the training examples emphasized the initial possessive noun phrases in Chinese, consistently selecting the possessor noun as the English subject. Most human translators, upon reviewing these examples, would likely choose the possessor noun (迁移-migration) as the subject in their English translation. In contrast, GPT-4 failed to make this choice. Unlike humans, who can make a well-judged speed-accuracy tradeoff based on a few examples, LLMs' performance appears less adept and sometimes even seems irrational or confused.

User (Prompt)

For Chinese-to-English translation, changing subject selection involves selecting a subject different from the one in the source text to improve the readability and fluency of the English translation.

Below are three examples:

1. 技术的进步极大地改变了我们的生活方式。(direct translation: The advancement of **technology** has greatly changed our way of life.)

English translation: **Technology** have greatly advanced to change our way of life.

2. 老年人本身的免疫功能就相对于年轻人要弱一些。(direction translation: The immune function of the **elderly** is weaker than that of the young.)

English translation: Unlike younger people, **the elderly** have weaker immune systems.

3. 未来20年气候变化的威胁将超过恐怖主义。(direct translation: The threat of **climate change** will be more than terrorism in the next 20 years.)

English: In the next two decades, **climate change** will pose a greater threat than terrorism.

… Please generate a proper Chinese-to-English translation, and a proper English translation reflecting the concept and the few-shot examples :

Chinese: 迁移的流向和形式也都发生了很大的变化。(direct translation: The patterns and forms of **migration** have also undergone great changes.)

ChatGPT

English: The patterns and forms of migration have undergone significant changes.

Table 6: GPT-4 shows less graceful speed-accuracy tradeoff by not following the patterns illustrated by the three teaching examples.

Human's ability to have graceful speed-accuracy tradeoff is supported by several cognitive functions such as information processing dynamics (involving perception, attention, memory, and problem-solving), response strategy (decision making), and performance assessment (metacognition).

LLMs are powerful tools for generating text and understanding language, but they lack the ability to leverage human cognitive functions to achieve graceful speed-accuracy tradeoff.

3.4 Summary

This section highlights three challenges in the concept-guided approach: (1) LLMs' performance declines as the complexity of the required conceptual space increases; (2) LLMs struggle with continuity in explaining and practicing advanced concepts; and (3) LLMs lack the ability of graceful speed-accuracy tradeoff. The challenges stem from the absence of comprehensive human-like cognitive functions in LLMs.

4 Chain-of-Thought (CoT) Reasoning Provides a Structured Way for LLMs to Support Sophisticated Concepts

In this section, we explore methods to address the limitations identified previously. We focus on Chain-of-Thought (CoT) reasoning prompting as a solution and evaluate the pros and cons of this approach.

4.1 CoT Demonstrates Detailed Reasoning Steps

Reasoning is a fundamental cognitive function that involves drawing conclusions, solving problems, and making decisions and encompasses various cognitive functions. Chain-of-thought (CoT) prompting can improve the performance of large language models (LLMs) on complex reasoning tasks (Wei 2022). The key idea behind CoT is to provide the LLM with examples that demonstrate step-by-step reasoning (intermediate reasoning steps) towards the final results, rather than just giving the final answer directly. This guides the LLM to construct a logical pathway from the original input to the final solution, rather than relying solely on its internal knowledge base which may have gaps or biases.

Compared to simple prompting without step-by-step reasoning, CoT prompting proves itself as effective solutions to complex translation concepts. Below are some examples in which CoT prompting shows significant benefits.

4.2 CoT Addresses the Issue of Lacking Continuity

Although fully implementing human-like cognitive dissonance is challenging, the linguistic part of its rationalization and justification component can be implemented through CoT reasoning to address the issue of continuity.

Table 7 shows that CoT prompting solves the "lack of continuity" example we described in section 3.2 and Table 5 related to the "Pro-drop". An additional reasoning step is added to reflect the omitted subject in each teaching examples, and during the generation phase, GPT4 is able to infer the omitted subject for the test example and generate the correct translation outcome that reflects the "pro-drop" concept correctly.

User (Prompt)
The concept of "pro-drop" refers to the ability of a language to omit subjects (and sometimes other pronouns) when they are pragmatically or grammatically inferable. Chinese is a pro-drop language, meaning that subjects can be and often are omitted when they are understood from context. In contrast, English is a "non pro-drop" language, meaning that subjects are almost always explicitly stated, as English need the presence of subjects for clarity and grammatical correctness.
Three examples are listed below to illustrate the Chinese-to-English translation reflecting the concept above:
Original Chinese: 对传统那些没有比较优势和竞争优势产业，继续给予必要保证。
Omitted subject: 传统产业 (traditional Industries)
English Translation: Traditional industries without comparative advantage and competitiveness should be given the support.
Original Chinese：要重视发挥家庭、学校和社区作用，帮助儿童抵御恐怖极端思想侵蚀。
Omitted subject: 注意力（attention or extra attention）
English： Attention should be paid to the roles of families, schools, and communities in preventing children from being influenced by extreme terrorism.
Original Chinese: 需要货币政策传导机制来保证资金流动到位。
Omitted subject: 我们（we）or 中央银行（central bank）
English: We need transmission mechanism of monetary policy to ensure the availability of capital flows.
If you are an expert-level translator, do you think we should apply the same concept on the following Chinese text segment?
Chinese: 各地积极性高涨。
Please give a score between 0 and 100 (0 means the concept definitely should not be applied on translating the sentence while 100 means that the concept definitely should be applied on translating the sentence.
If the score is above 75, what should be the omitted subject and the proper translation reflecting the concept.
Please generate a proper English translation reflecting the concept.
ChatGPT
I would score this 90. The concept of "pro-drop" should indeed be applied here as the subject is contextually inferable.
Omitted subject: 各地人民 (People in various regions)
Proper Translation: "People in various regions are highly enthusiastic."

Table 7: By incorporating an additional CoT reasoning step, GPT4 addresses the issue of lacking continuity.

4.3 CoT Addresses the Issue of Lacking Speed-Accuracy Tradeoff

Although fully implementing human-like speed-accuracy tradeoff is challenging, the linguistic part of its information processing and response strategy components can be implemented through CoT reasoning to address the issue of continuity.

Table 8 shows that CoT prompting solves the "lacking speed-accuracy tradeoff" example we described in section 3.3 and Table 6 related to the "subject changing". In each teaching example, multiple reasoning steps are added to reflect the direct translation, the subject phrase, and the alternative subject selection using the possessor noun in the subject phrase. Then during the generation phase, GPT4 is able to infer the same reasoning steps for the test example and have human-like speed-accuracy tradeoff and generate the corresponding translation outcome.

User (Prompt)
For Chinese-to-English translation, changing subject selection involves selecting a subject different from the one in the source text to improve the readability and fluency of the English translation.
Below are three examples:
1. Original Chinese: 技术的进步极大地改变了我们的生活方式。
Direct translation: The advancement of technology has greatly changed our way of life.
The subject phrase: The progress of technology
English translation with alternative subject selection using the possessor noun in the subject phrase: Technology have greatly advanced to change our way of life.
2. Original Chinese: 老年人本身的免疫功能就相对于年轻人要弱一些。
Direction translation: The immune function of the elderly is weaker than that of the young.
The subject phrase: The immune function of the elderly

English translation with alternative subject selection using the possessor noun in the subject phrase:
Unlike younger people, the elderly have weaker immune systems.
3. Original Chinese: 未来 20 年气候变化的威胁将超过恐怖主义。
Direct translation: The threat of climate change will be more than terrorism in the next 20 years.
The subject phrase: The threat of climate change
English translation with alternative subject selection using the possessor noun in the subject phrase: In the next two decades, climate change will pose a greater threat than terrorism.
Please follow the same pattern to translate the following Chinese sentence:
Original Chinese: 迁移的流向和形式也都发生了很大的变化。
ChatGPT
The sentence "迁移的流向和形式也都发生了很大的变化" directly translates to "The directions and forms of migration have also undergone significant changes." Here, the subject phrase is "The directions and forms of migration."

Applying the pattern of using the possessor noun as the subject, the translation would be: "Migration has changed significantly in its directions and forms."

Table 8: GPT4 achieves a more effective speed-accuracy tradeoff through the application of Chain of Thought (CoT) reasoning, as demonstrated by three illustrative teaching examples. In each teaching example, multiple reasoning steps are added to reflect the direct translation, the subject phrase, and the alternative subject selection using the possessor noun in the subject phrase. Then during the generation phase, GPT4 can infer the same reasoning steps and generate the correct result.

4.4 Summary

We show that LLMs can use Chain-of-Thought (CoT) reasoning to overcome some challenges and enhance the performance of the concept-guided approach. This is particularly effective for problems that benefit from well-formed, consistent reasoning steps, ultimately leading to the correct conclusion.

On the other hand, while humans use multiple cognitive functions to solve complex problems, LLMs can only model this complexity, often in fragmented form, as linguistic description. This approach may work for some challenges but falls short for others. It demands unrealistic expectations to predefine linguistic solution steps and risks overlooking the broader context and interconnections between cognitive aspects—areas where human cognition excels.

5 Conclusion

Humans outperform large language models (LLMs) because human cognition involves a range of cognitive functions and their dynamic interaction. This study explores how integrating human cognition through concept-guided instruction and few-shot teaching can guide LLMs to improve translation outcomes. We first demonstrate that for simple and widely used concepts, concept-guided approaches offer significant benefits. We then tested prompt engineering with Chinese-to-English translation examples, using GPT-4 to estimate the complexity of various concepts and human experts to evaluate translation outcomes' quality. Our preliminary findings show that LLM translation performance declines as concept complexity increases.

We also identify several challenges in the concept-guided approach: LLMs struggle with continuity in explaining and practicing sophisticated concepts due to the lack of human-like cognitive functions, such as cognitive dissonance. Additionally, LLMs lack a graceful speed-accuracy tradeoff because they do not possess the cognitive functions such as dynamic information processing, response strategies, and performance assessment that humans do.

However, LLMs can mitigate some of these challenges by using Chain-of-Thought (CoT) reasoning, which is especially effective for problems requiring consistent, well-structured reasoning steps. Despite this, LLMs can only model cognitive complexity as fragmented linguistic descriptions, unlike humans, who excel at understanding broader contexts and interconnections between cognitive aspects. This limitation makes it unrealistic to expect LLMs to effectively define solution steps automatically, a task that humans can accomplish by naturally considering critical context.

The findings from this preliminary study on the English-to-Chinese language pair indicate that further research is necessary to validate the key results.

References

Bao, CY. (2022). Class notes on Chinese-to-English translation, "Advanced Translation and Interpretation" course, Translation and Interpretation Program, Middlebury Institute of International Studies

Chaiken, S., & Trope, Y. (Eds.). (1999). *Dual-process theories in social psychology*. Guilford Press.

Cook, N. D. (2018). The triadic roots of human cognition: "Mind" is the ability to go beyond dyadic associations. *Frontiers in Psychology*, *9*, 1060.

Daniel, K. (2017). *Thinking, fast and slow*.

Fan, A. (2020). Introducing the first AI model that translates 100 languages without relying on English. Meta. Accessed 28th April 2024. https://about. fb. com/news/2020/10/first-multilingual-machine-translation-model.

Fenton, K. (2024). *Psy 210-002: Introduction to Psychology.* Openstax Pressbook.

Festinger, L. (1962). Cognitive dissonance. Scientific American, 207(4), 93-106.

Goodman, Noah (2024). Reasoning in Human and Machine Intelligence. Keynote Presentation, AAAI Spring Symposium on Empowering Machine Learning and Large Language Models with Domain and Commonsense Knowledge, Palo Alto, CA, USA.

Hagendorff, T., Fabi, S., & Kosinski, M. (2023). Human-like intuitive behavior and reasoning biases emerged in large language models but disappeared in ChatG PT. *Nature Computational Science*, *3*(10), 833-838.

Harris, C. L. (2006). Language and cognition. Encyclopedia of cognitive science, 10(0470018860), s00559.

Heitz, R. P. (2014). The speed-accuracy tradeoff: history, physiology, methodology, and behavior. Frontiers in neuroscience, 8, 86875.

Ionescu, M., & Ralescu, A. (2006, July). Multidimensional Conceptual Spaces for Summarization. In *2006 IEEE International Conference on Fuzzy Systems* (pp. 560-565). IEEE.

Johnsson, L. (2021). Multidimensional property supplementation: A method for discovering and describing emergent qualities of concepts in grounded theory research. Qualitative Health Research, 31(1), 184-200.

Lampinen, A. K., Dasgupta, I., Chan, S. C., Sheahan, H. R., Creswell, A., Kumaran, D., ... & Hill, F. (2024). Language models, like humans, show content effects on reasoning tasks. *PNAS nexus*, *3*(7).

Lazzara, J. (2020). *Chapter 7 Psy 2E: Thinking, Language, and Problem Solving*. Openstax Pressbook.

Lieberman, Henry (2024). The Next Grand Challenge for AI: Making Better Mistakes. Keynote Presentation, AAAI Spring Symposium on Empowering Machine Learning and Large Language Models with Domain and Commonsense Knowledge, Palo Alto, CA, USA.

Mahon, B. Z., & Caramazza, A. (2009). Concepts and categories: a cognitive neuropsychological perspective. Annual review of psychology, 60(1), 27-51.

Morton, N. W. (2013). Interactions between episodic and semantic memory. Technical report, Vanderbilt Computational Memory Lab.

McCarthy, J. (2007). *What is artificial intelligence.*

Neisser, U. (2014). *Cognitive Psychology: Classic Edition. Psychology Press.*

Perlovsky, L. (2011). Language and cognition interaction neural mechanisms. *Computational Intelligence and Neuroscience*: 1-13.

Qian, M., Wu, HQ., Yang, L., and Wan, A. (2023). Augmented Machine Translation Enabled by GPT4: Performance Evaluation on Human-Machine Teaming Approaches. In *Proceedings of the First Workshop on NLP Tools and Resources for Translation and Interpreting Applications*. pages 20–31, Varna, Bulgaria.

Qian, M., Kong, CQ. (2024A). Exploring the Gap: The Challenge of Achieving Human-like Generalization for Concept-based Translation Instruction Using Large Language Models. *Symposium on Human-Like Learning. AAAI 2024 Spring Symposium Series,* Stanford University. Palo Alto, USA.

Qian, M., Kong, CQ. (2024B). Enabling Human-centered Machine Translation Using Concept-based Large Language Model Prompting and Translation Memory, In *Proceedings of 4th International Conference on Artificial Intelligence in HCI (AI-HCI), Part of HCI International Conference*, Washington DC, USA.

Shapiro, L. A., & Spaulding, S. (Eds.). (2014). The Routledge handbook of embodied cognition.

Snowden, D. J., & Boone, M. E. (2007). A leader's framework for decision making. *Harvard business review*, *85*(11), 68.

Villani, C., Lugli, L., Liuzza, M. T., & Borghi, A. M. (2019). Varieties of abstract concepts and their multiple dimensions. Language and Cognition, 11(3), 403-430.

Wei, J., Wang, X., Schuurmans, D., Bosma, M., Xia, F., Chi, E., ... & Zhou, D. (2022). Chain-of-thought prompting elicits reasoning in large language models. Advances in neural information processing systems, 35, 24824-24837.

Williams, J. J., & Lombrozo, T. (2010). The role of explanation in discovery and generalization: Evidence from category learning. *Cognitive science*, *34*(5), 776-806.

Zhu, W., Liu, H., Dong, Q., Xu, J., Huang, S., Kong, L., ... & Li, L. (2023). Multilingual machine translation with large language models: Empirical results and analysis. arXiv preprint arXiv:2304.04675.

Appendix 1: Complexity Evaluation on the Ten Translation Concepts Using Hypothetical Spaces

Below are the GPT-4 analyses on the hypothetical spaces (complexity), the black/regular font words are the prompt and red/italicized font words are the generated outcomes by the GPT4.

Below are definitions and few-shot examples of ten concepts related to Chinese-to-English Translation:

1. Deverbalization is a concept in translation studies, par-ticularly relevant in the context of translating between languages with significantly different structures, such as Chinese to English. The core idea of deverbalizatio is to move away from a direct, word-for-word translation, which often leads to awkward or inaccurate results due to the differences in grammar, syntax, and cultural contexts. Instead, the translator interprets the meaning of the source text at a deeper, more abstract level, and then re-expresses this meaning in the target language.

Three examples are listed below to illustrate the Chinese-to-English translation reflecting the concept above：

Chinese: 过去带动高增长的主要是高投资，而高投资主要是三大需求来源，出口、基础建设、房地产。

English: The key driver of rapid growth has been investment, which is needed in three areas/goes to three areas, export, infrastructure, and real estate.

Chinese: 本土化人才了解中国市场上的需求和消费者的心理。

English: Local talents understand the market needs in China and know what customers want.

Chinese: 中国现在很多地区复工率很高。

English: Many areas in China have reopened their economies.

2. For Chinese-to-English translation, changing subject selection involves selecting a subject different from the one in the source text to improve the readability and fluency of the English translation.

Three examples are listed below to illustrate the Chinese-to-English translation reflecting the concept above：

Chinese: 资源环境约束边界临近，最典型的例子就是雾霾。

English: Resources and environment almost reach the limit with smog being the biggest concern.

Chinese: 老年人本身的免疫功能就相对于年轻人要弱一些。

English: Unlike younger people, the elderly have weaker immune systems.

Chinese: 迁移的流向和形式也都发生了很大的变化。

English: Migration was happening in different directions and ways.

3. The concept of "pro-drop" refers to the ability of a language to omit subjects (and sometimes other pro-nouns) when they are pragmatically or grammatically inferable. Chinese is a pro-drop language, meaning that subjects can be and often are omitted when they are understood from context. In contrast, English is a "non pro-drop" language, meaning that subjects are almost always explicitly stated, as English need the presence of subjects for clarity and grammatical correctness.

Three examples are listed below to illustrate the Chinese-to-English translation reflecting the concept above:

Chinese: 各地积极性高涨。

English: There is a lot of discussion and enthusiasm on this issue.

Chinese：要重视发挥家庭、学校和社区作用，帮助儿童抵御恐怖极端思想侵蚀。

English: Attention should be paid to the roles of families, schools, and communities in preventing children from being influenced by extreme terrorism.

Chinese: 对传统那些没有比较优势和竞争优势产业，继续给予必要保证。

English: Traditional industries without comparative advantage and competitiveness should be given the support.

4. Changing the perspective in the context of Chinese-to-English translation refers to adapting the viewpoint or approach when translating text from Chinese into English. This concept is crucial due to significant differences be-tween the two languages in terms of grammar, syntax, idiomatic expressions, and cultural contexts.

Three examples are listed below to illustrate the Chinese-to-English translation reflecting the concept above：

Chinese: 中国经济已经触底，中速增长平台初步确定，将来会逐步进入中速增长期，也就是由高速增长阶段转向高质量发展阶段。

English: China's economy has touched the bottom. It is set for medium-speed growth, which will last for a period of time. There will be more focus on quality instead of speed.

Chinese: 随着经济发展，可能是不同时期有不同热门的行业。

English: Along with economic development, sectors could become popular at different times.

Chinese: 本地化产生了多语言的需求。

English: Location involves translation into multiple languages.

5. For Chinese-to-English translation, Changing parts of speech is to faithfully convey the meaning of the original at the same time accords with English means of expression irrespective of the part of speech of a word in Chinese.

Three examples are listed below to illustrate the Chinese-to-English translation reflecting the concept above：

Chinese: 存货、出口和生产性投资逐步进入回升期，将对基础设施投资减速形成对冲。

English: Investments in inventory, export, and manufacturing are bouncing back, offsetting the decline in infrastructure investment.

Chinese: 我是研究农村经济开始的。

English: I started my career as a researcher in rural economy.

Chinese: 委员们提出了许多很有操作性、针对性的意见建议。

English: Members of the committee have made a number of suggestions that are specific and easy to implement.

6. The linguistic concept dislocation refers to the phenomenon where the positioning of words or phrases in a sentence differs significantly between two languages. This can pose challenges in translation, particularly between languages with distinct syntactic structures, like Chinese and English.

Chinese: 常态化防控和应急处置放松了要求。

English: The requirements for daily prevention and control, as well as emergency response, have been relaxed.

Chinese: GDP比重，非典时期才影响26%，这(次)是占到74%。

English: 26% of the GDP was affected during the SARS outbreak. But this time, the proportion is 74%.

Chinese: 我知道这个目标目前在国际上是很多国家所没有制定的。

English: I'm aware that many countries around the world have not yet set this goal.

7. The concept of implicit conjunctions and linking/transition words for Chinese-to-English translation: Chinese often omits conjunctions that would be necessary in English. This is because Chinese relies heavily on context and the inherent logic of the sentence structure. For instance, two

clauses might be placed side by side without a conjunction, yet a native Chinese speaker would understand their relationship based on the context. That usually is not the case for English.

Three examples are listed below to illustrate the Chinese-to-English translation reflecting the concept above：

Chinese: 学校决定精简机构，减少系科。

English: The school decided to streamline the administration by reducing the number of departments.

Chinese: 比如，欧洲老龄化程度高、死亡率高。

English: For instance, the death rate in Europe is very high due to a large aging population.

Chinese: 提炼出中国智慧，总结出中国方案。

English: Draw some lessons so that we can come up with Chinese wisdoms and solutions.

8. The concept of combining clauses and short sentences in Chinese to create a longer English sentence. English allows for complex sentences with multiple clauses, often linked by conjunctions, which can express detailed nuances and conditions. Chinese, on the other hand, favors brevity and conciseness.

Three examples are listed below to illustrate the Chinese-to-English translation reflecting the concept above：

Chinese: 跨国公司的生产经营是在本土，但是它的经营生产战略是全球化的。

English: Multinational corporations are based in their home countries but with global operations and strategies.

Chinese: 本轮疫情呈现出多地暴发、波及范围广、确诊人数多等特点。

English: Recently, the pandemic took place in many locations with extensive scale and cases.

Chinese: 俄罗斯的改革比中国晚起步10年左右，但他们的金融抑制指数已经到了0.4，时间跨度更短、下降速度更快。

English: Russia started its reform 10 years later than China, but it has already reached a financial repression index of 0.4 in a shorter period of time and at a faster pace.

9. Eliminating redundancy is a common practice for Chinese-to-English because redundancy is commonly seen in the Chinese language. Although some redundancies may serve as emphasis, many could be eliminated without compromising the intended meaning. Removing unnecessary repetition during translation could improve the readability and clarity of the target text.

Three examples are listed below to illustrate the Chinese-to-English translation reflecting the concept above：

Chinese: 全世界气候变化的原因来看，大概主要就是有两个原因。

English: Climate change has two factors.

Chinese: 水电是包含在可再生能源当中的，世界各国都把水电作为可再生能源的一部分。

English: Hydropower is considered a source of renewable energy by all countries.

Chinese: 从需求侧来讲，中国经济过去长时间的高增长，主要是高投资在支撑，而高投资主要有三大需求在支撑，也就是基础设施建设、房地产和出口。

English: On the demand side, the driver of China's economic growth has long been high investment required in three key areas: infrastructure, real estate, and exports.

10. Cultural translation aims to show the cultural differences while respecting the source culture as well.

Chinese: 有"歇歇脚、缓一缓"的心态。

English: Some people tend to let down their guard.

Chinese: 美联储把利率降到零，弹药全部用完。

English: There isn't much space as the Fed has lowered interest rate to zero.

Chinese: 我要是不来，那也是非常遗憾的。我这次来，即使被打得鼻青脸肿也在所不惜。

English: I would regret it if I didn't come, so I'm here today no matter what happens.

These concepts (constrained by both definitions and examples) have different levels of complexity when they are applied. Can you provide a rating evaluation (minimum 0 and maximum 100) in terms of the size of typical "hypothetical spaces" that need to be considered when the concepts are applied?

Evaluating the size of the "hypothetical space" for each of these translation concepts involves considering the range of interpretations, adaptations, and choices a translator might need to navigate when applying these concepts from Chinese to English. This hypothetical space represents the complexity and variability inherent in each concept, indicating the level of creativity, cultural understanding, and linguistic expertise required. Here's a rating for each concept, on a scale from 0 (minimal complexity) to 100 (maximum complexity), reflecting the size of their hypothetical spaces:

Deverbalization (80/100): This concept requires deep understanding of both source and target languages, along with the ability to abstract and reconceptualize ideas in culturally appropriate ways. It involves a significant hypothetical space due to the need for creative interpretation and expression.

Changing Subject Selection (70/100): Adapting the subject for better readability and fluency can involve moderate to high complexity, especially when ensuring that the shift does not alter the intended meaning of the original text.

Pro-drop (60/100): Translating from a pro-drop language like Chinese to a non-pro-drop language like English requires careful addition of explicit subjects without making the text feel redundant or altering its meaning, presenting a moderate hypothetical space.

Changing the Perspective (75/100): Adapting the viewpoint requires a strong grasp of cultural and contextual nuances as well as linguistic fluency. The hypothetical space is large because it involves rethinking and sometimes reimagining the original message from a different angle.

Changing Parts of Speech (65/100): This task involves creatively maintaining the original's meaning while changing the grammatical structure, which can be complex due to the flexibility required in reconceptualizing the message.

Dislocation (60/100): Addressing syntactic differences involves understanding the functional and positional flexibility of elements in both languages. The hypothetical space is moderate, as it often has clear-cut rules but also requires attention to readability and flow.

Implicit Conjunctions and Linking (50/100): While the concept itself may seem straightforward, applying it effectively requires a nuanced understanding of how ideas are connected in English, presenting a moderate hypothetical space.

Combining Clauses and Short Sentences (55/100): This concept requires skill in creating complex sentences that are still clear and coherent, involving a moderate level of complexity in the hypothetical space due to the need to balance detail with readability.

Eliminating Redundancy (40/100): While often technical, this task requires less creative interpretation than others, presenting a smaller hypothetical space. The challenge lies in discerning which redundancies are stylistic versus those adding unnecessary repetition.

Cultural Translation (85/100): This concept encompasses a vast hypothetical space due to the need to convey cultural nuances and contexts accurately and respectfully, requiring deep cultural knowledge and sensitivity.

These ratings reflect the relative complexity and breadth of choices translators must navigate within each concept, acknowledging that individual translation tasks might present unique challenges that could affect these evaluations.

Table 9: Hypothetical spaces (complexity) Analyses for the ten translation concepts using GPT-4.

Appendix 2: English-Chinese sentence pairs (four pairs per concept) used for 1-in-4 leave-one-out cross-validation evaluation

Below is a dataset of 40 English-Chinese sentence pairs (four pairs per concept) that was used for 1-in-4 leave-one-out cross-validation evaluation of GPT-4 generated translation.

Pro-drop

Chinese: 各地积极性高涨。

English: There is a lot of discussion and enthusiasm on this issue.

Chinese：要重视发挥家庭、学校和社区作用，帮助儿童抵御恐怖极端思想侵蚀。English: Attention should be paid to the roles of families, schools, and communities in preventing children from being influenced by extreme terrorism.

Chinese: 对传统那些没有比较优势和竞争优势产业，继续给予必要保证。

English: Traditional industries without comparative advantage and competitiveness should be given the support.

Chinese: 需要货币政策传导机制来保证资金流动到位。

English: We need transmission mechanism of monetary policy to ensure the availability of capital flows.

Dislocation

Chinese: 常态化防控和应急处置放松了要求。

English: The requirements for daily prevention and control, as well as emergency response, have been relaxed.

Chinese: GDP比重，非典时期才影响26%，这(次)是占到74%。

English: 26% of the GDP was affected during the SARS outbreak. But this time, the proportion is 74%.

Chinese: 我知道这个目标目前在国际上是很多国家所没有制定的。

English: I'm aware that many countries around the world have not yet set this goal.

Chinese: 当地语言以前中国公司不太注重。

English: Chinese companies didn't pay enough attention to local languages.

Implicit conjunctions and linking/transition words

Chinese: 学校决定精简机构，减少系科。

English: The school decided to streamline the administration by reducing the number of departments.

Chinese: 比如，欧洲老龄化程度高、死亡率高。

English: For instance, the death rate in Europe is very high due to a large aging population.

Chinese: 提炼出中国智慧，总结出中国方案。

English: Draw some lessons so that we can come up with Chinese wisdoms and solutions.

Chinese: 本地化是跨国公司进驻中国，打通语言通道的关键。

English: Localization is an im-portant tool to break the language barrier as they enter the Chinese market.

Combining clauses and short sentences in Chinese to create a longer English sentence

Chinese: 跨国公司的生产经营是在本土，但是它的经营生产战略是全球化的。

English: Multinational corporations are based in their home countries but with global operations and strategies.

Chinese: 本轮疫情呈现出多地暴发、波及范围广、确诊人数多等特点。

English: Recently, the pandemic took place in many locations with extensive scale and cases.

Chinese: 俄罗斯的改革比中国晚起步10年左右，但他们的金融抑制指数已经到了0.4，时间跨度更短、下降速度更快。

English: Russia started its reform 10 years later than China, but it has already reached a financial repression index of 0.4 in a shorter period of time and at a faster pace.

Chinese: 说到可再生能源，首先是可再生，就说明它是资源量非常大的，可以永续利用，同时它的污染很小、分布很广。
English: Speaking of renewable energy, the word "renewable" suggests that these energy sources are abundant, sustainable, and widely distributed with very little pollution.

Deverbalization
Chinese: 过去带动高增长的主要是高投资，而高投资主要是三大需求来源，出口、基础建设、房地产。
English: The key driver of rapid growth has been investment, which is needed in three areas/goes to three areas, export, infrastructure, and real estate.
Chinese: 本土化人才了解中国市场上的需求和消费者的心理。
English: Local talents understand the market needs in China and know what customers want.
Chinese: 中国现在很多地区复工率很高。
English: Many areas in China have reopened their economies.
Chinese: 中国对外开放的步伐也在不断加快，我们要向外商提供更开放、更透明的、更有力的投资环境。
English: As China further opens up to the outside world, we should pro-vide a more open, transparent, and helpful investment environment.

Eliminating redundancy
Chinese: 全世界气候变化的原因来看，大概主要就是有两个原因。
English: Climate change has two factors.
Chinese: 水电是包含在可再生能源当中的，世界各国都把水电作为可再生能源的一部分。
English: Hydropower is considered a source of renewable energy by all countries.
Chinese: 从需求侧来讲，中国经济过去长时间的高增长，主要是高投资在支撑，而高投资主要有三大需求在支撑，也就是基础设施建设、房地产和出口。
English: On the demand side, the driver of China's economic growth has long been high investment required in three key areas: infrastructure, real estate, and exports.
Chinese: 我们需要的是强劲的反弹，所以需要10倍的努力来推动反弹。
English: We need to achieve a robust rebound through ten times of effort.

Changing subject selection
Chinese: 资源环境约束边界临近，最典型的例子就是雾霾。
English: Resources and environ-ment almost reach the limit with smog being the biggest concern.
Chinese: 老年人本身的免疫功能就相对于年轻人要弱一些。
English: Unlike younger people, the elderly have weaker immune sys-tems.
Chinese: 迁移的流向和形式也都发生了很大的变化。
English: Migration was happening in different directions and ways.
Chinese: 未来20年气候变化的威胁将超过恐怖主义。
English: In the next two decades, climate change will pose a greater threat than terrorism.

Changing the perspective
Chinese: 中国经济已经触底，中速增长平台初步确定，将来会逐步进入中速增长期，也就是由高速增长阶段转向高质量发展阶段。
English: China's economy has touched the bottom. It is set for medium-speed growth, which will last for a period of time. There will be more focus on quality instead of speed.
Chinese: 随着经济发展，可能是不同时期有不同热门的行业。
English: Along with economic development, sectors could become popular at different times.
Chinese: 本地化产生了多语言的需求。
English: Location involves translation into multiple languages.
Chinese: 大多数国家对创业投资都是采取一种比较鼓励的政策。
English: Many countries have policies that encourage venture capital investment.

Changing Parts of Speech
Chinese: 存货、出口和生产性投资逐步进入回升期，将对基础设施投资减速形成对冲。
English: Investments in inventory, export, and manufacturing are bouncing back, offsetting the decline in infrastructure investment.
Chinese: 我是研究农村经济开始的。
English: I started my career as a researcher in rural economy.
Chinese: 委员们提出了许多很有操作性、针对性的意见建议。
English: Members of the committee have made a number of suggestions that are specific and easy to implement.

Chinese: 城镇化就是阶段性的，到了一定阶段一定会减速。 English: Urbanization takes place in different stages. It will slow down at a certain stage.
Cultural translation Chinese: 有“歇歇脚、缓一缓”的心态。 English: Some people tend to let down their guard. Chinese: 美联储把利率降到零，弹药全部用完。 English: There isn't much space as the Fed has lowered interest rate to zero. Chinese: 我要是不来，那也是非常遗憾的。我这次来，即使被打得鼻青脸肿也在所不惜。 English: I would regret it if I didn't come, so I'm here today no matter what happens. Chinese: “大干快上”本身没有错，关键是干什么、上什么。

Table 10: A dataset of 40 English-Chinese sentence pairs (four pairs per concept) was used for 1-in-4 leave-one-out cross-validation evaluation.

How Effective is Synthetic Data and Instruction Fine-tuning for Translation with Markup using LLMs?

Raj Dabre NICT, Japan raj.dabre@nict.go.jp
Haiyue Song NICT, Japan haiyue.song@nict.go.jp
Miriam Exel SAP, Germany miriam.exel@sap.com
Bianka Buschbeck SAP, Germany bianka.buschbeck@sap.com
Johannes Eschbach-Dymanus SAP, Germany johannes.eschbach-dymanus@sap.com
Hideki Tanaka NICT, Japan hideki.tanaka@nict.go.jp

Abstract

Recent works have shown that prompting large language models (LLMs) is effective for translation with markup where LLMs can simultaneously transfer markup tags while ensuring that the content, both inside and outside tag pairs is correctly translated. However, these works assume the existence of high-quality parallel sentences with markup for prompting, which may not always be available. Furthermore, the impact of instruction fine-tuning (IFT) in this setting is unknown. In this paper, we provide a study, the first of its kind, focusing on the effectiveness of synthetically created markup data and IFT for translation with markup using LLMs. We focus on translation from English to five European languages, German, French, Dutch, Finnish and Russian, where we show that regardless of few-shot prompting or IFT, synthetic data created via word alignments, while leading to inferior markup transfer compared to using original data with markups, does not negatively impact the translation quality. Furthermore, IFT mainly impacts the translation quality compared to few-shot prompting and has slightly better markup transfer capabilities than the latter. We hope our work will help practitioners make effective decisions on modeling choices for LLM based translation with markup.

1 Introduction

While a significant majority of machine translation (MT) research has been conducted on translating plain sentences from one language to another, much of the web and proprietary or business documents requiring translation come in structured formats like HTML pages or Microsoft Office files containing markup. Therefore, practical MT systems should be adept not only at translating plain sentences but also sentences with markup (see Figure 1 for an example), where the task is to translate content in the source language while simultaneously ensuring that markup tags wrap the appropriate content in the target language. Until the advent of deep learning, the most commonly used approach for handling markup was the detag-and-project approach (Hanneman and Dinu, 2020a), which is not end-to-end and is prone to error compounding from individual components such as the MT system, word-aligner and projection algorithms. Therefore, using end-to-end neural networks for translation with markup (Cho et al., 2014) makes a more attractive solution.

Recently, researchers have shown that transformer (Vaswani et al., 2017) based large language models (LLMs) (Brown et al., 2020) can seamlessly translate sentences with markup despite not explicitly being trained to do so (Buschbeck et al., 2022; Dabre et al., 2023). They show that few-shot prompting (Brown et al., 2020) enables LLMs to transfer markup tags when translating from source to target languages. Surprisingly, despite being general purpose, their markup transfer capabilities approach, if not surpass, highly optimized models

English	Click <uicontrol>Prepayment</uicontrol>.
German	Klicken Sie <uicontrol>Vorauszahlung</uicontrol>.
French	Cliquez <uicontrol>Prépaiement</uicontrol>
Japanese	<uicontrol>前払</uicontrol>をクリックします。

Figure 1: Examples with inline markup, inspired by (Buschbeck et al., 2022).

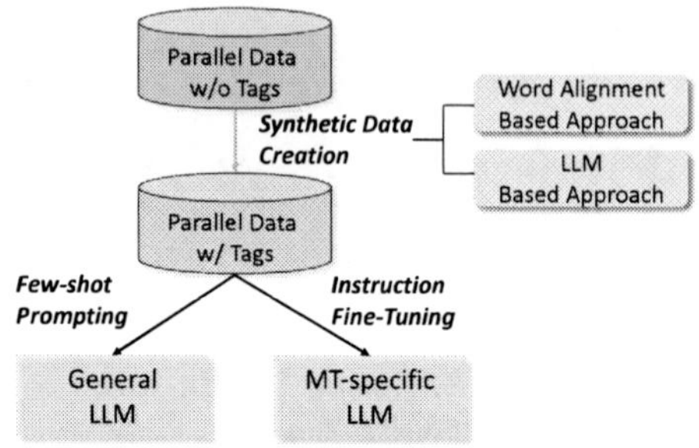

Figure 2: Our framework.

trained specifically for this purpose. However, they assume the existence of high-quality parallel corpora with markup when prompting, and this kind of data may not always be available. Furthermore, while they utilize pre-existing generic instruction fine-tuned (IFT) models, they do not IFT their own MT models, the effectiveness of which remains unknown. In this paper, we fill this gap via a two-pronged exploration on the effectiveness of synthetic data and IFT for translation with markup.

We take the case of translation from English to five European languages, German, French, Dutch, Finnish and Russian, and first establish the efficacy of zero- and few-shot prompting on a popular open-source LLM, namely BLOOM (Le Scao et al., 2022). Following this, we explore approaches for synthetically creating parallel data with markup to understand its efficacy for prompting. We further deepen our investigation by performing IFT of BLOOM with both clean and synthetic data and attempt to discern settings in which synthetic data can be useful. We show that regardless of few-shot prompting or IFT, synthetic data created via word alignments leads to slightly inferior markup transfer compared to high-quality human-curated data; however, it does not negatively impact the translation quality. Furthermore, somewhat surprisingly, we find that IFT itself mainly improves the translation quality compared to few-shot prompting and has only slightly better markup transfer capabilities than the latter. We hope our findings will act as guidelines for practitioners to make effective decisions on modeling choices for translation with markup.

2 Related Work

Our work focuses on machine translation with markup, LLMs and synthetic data.

2.1 MT Model Based Approaches

Detag-and-project is a prevalent technique for translating sentences with markup comprising two steps: 1) stripping tags from the source sentence and translating the plain text, and 2) reinserting tags into the translations. Joanis et al. (2013) utilize a Statistical Machine Translation (SMT) model to translate sentences with markup using a set of tag reinsertion rules in the *project* phase. Similarly, researchers compared various strategies for handling markup using SMT techniques and found that involving complex rules achieves the highest tag projection accuracy (Müller, 2017). More recent works use NMT as the translation model and apply a translation management system to handle the document structure (Hanneman and Dinu, 2020b).
End-to-end approach becomes possible with NMT models. They are often enhanced with data augmentation strategies to optimize the large number of parameters. Synthetic data can be created by inserting tags into corresponding fragments in the source and target plain text parallel sentences (Hanneman and Dinu, 2020b). However, aligned phrases are identified through an exhaustive search, which is computationally expensive. To address this, researchers use efficient word alignments for tag augmentation during the *project* phase (Ryu et al., 2022).

2.2 LLM Based Approaches

LLMs such as GPT-3 (Brown et al., 2020), BLOOM (Le Scao et al., 2022), BLOOMZ (Muennighoff et al., 2022), XGLM (Lin et al., 2022) and Llama-2 (Touvron et al., 2023) with few-shot in-context-learning (Brown et al., 2020) are well known for their ability to tackle diverse tasks owing to having seen vast amounts of data. Due to their flexibility, LLMs can be directly applied to the structured document translation task without further fine-tuning (Dabre et al., 2023). They apply retrieval-augmented (Lewis et al., 2020) few-shot prompting, which assumes the training set contains numerous parallel sentences with markup in hand. However, for most translation directions, there is usually no dataset with markups available. To this end, we propose to generate synthetic data. Furthermore, rather than prompting, we apply IFT, which our experiments show can achieve higher performance.

2.3 Datasets

Datasets are crucial in advancing structured text (usually with markup) translation. Hashimoto et al. (2019a) create a high-quality multilingual dataset comprising structured web pages designed for the documentation domain translation. Likewise, Buschbeck et al. (2022) develop a multilingual and multi-way evaluation dataset for structured document translation, focusing on Asian languages but only providing evaluation sets.

3 Methodology

Figure 2 presents an overview of the methodology followed in this paper: few-shot prompting in Section 3.1, instruction fine-tuning (IFT) in Section 3.2, and our methods for creating synthetic parallel data with markup in Section 3.3.

3.1 Few-shot Prompting

For our experiments, we use the N-shot approach, selecting N translation pairs (S_i, T_i) from an example pool to prompt the LLM. Like Dabre et al. (2023), unless (plain) data without markup is used, we use structure-aware prompting, where we use examples containing markup tags for test sentences with tags, and examples without markup tags for test sentences without tags. The specific template is in Appendix A.1.

3.2 Instruction Fine-tuning (IFT)

IFT is simply fine-tuning a pre-trained LLM with parallel data to enable it to translate from a source language to a target language without needing to provide demonstrations (or shots). The specific template is in Appendix A.3. As is common practice (Wei et al., 2022), we only consider the loss computed on the completion part of the sequence.

3.3 Synthetic Data Creation

We consider two approaches for synthetic data creation: using word alignment and LLMs.

Word Alignment Based Approach

The overview of the word alignment based approach is shown in Figure 3 and we call the resultant data Alignment-Synthetic-Tagged (AST). This approach involves the following steps:

1. Obtain word alignments for a parallel corpus without markup.

2. Randomly sample a phrase of a *maximum size* from the source sentence.

3. Use the word alignments with the min-max algorithm[1] (Zenkel et al., 2021) to identify the aligned phrase in the target sentence.

4. Uniformly[2] sample a tag from a pre-defined set.

5. Wrap both the source and target sentence phrases with the sampled markup tag.

Our approach is mainly motivated by the detag-and-project methods (Hanneman and Dinu, 2020b) and the idea of grouping words into phrases in phrase-based SMT (Och, 1999), and the results of data augmentation (Ryu et al., 2022). However, ours is more efficient than the one by Hanneman and Dinu (2020a), which relied on a more computationally expensive approach by exhaustively covering multiple phrase spans and translations via MT to identify high-quality aligned phrases.

LLM Based Approach

Random sampling in the word-alignment-based approach often results in *unnatural* phrases.[3] To this end, we propose utilizing LLMs to select *natural* phrases for inserting markup, as shown in Figure 4.

[1] If we have the source phrase $s_i...s_N$, word alignments $A = \{i : j\}$, then the aligned target words are $L = \cup_{x=i}^{N} A(x)$ and the aligned target phrase is $t_{min(L)}...t_{max(L)}$.

[2] Although it might seem unnatural to consider all tags appearing with the same probability, in practice there is no way to know the tag distribution in a realistic setting so we make no assumptions and rely on uniform sampling of tags.

[3] Unnatural means that those phrases are unlikely to be surrounded by tags in the real structured data, resulting in the mismatch of the distribution of training data and test data.

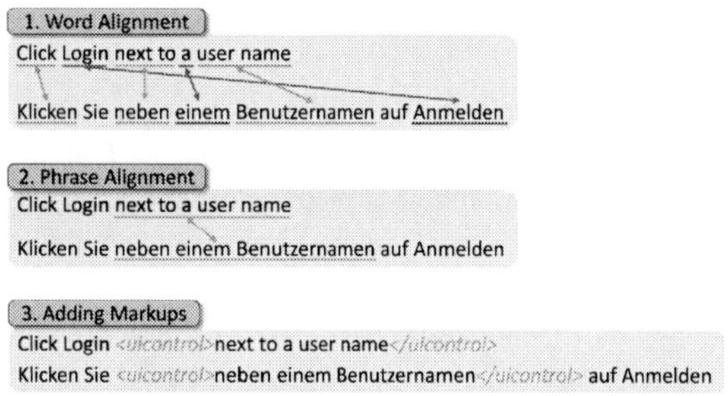

Figure 3: The overview of the word-alignment-based synthetic data creation method. It generates word alignments in the first stage, samples a phrase in the second stage, and inserts a randomly sampled tag pair in the final stage.

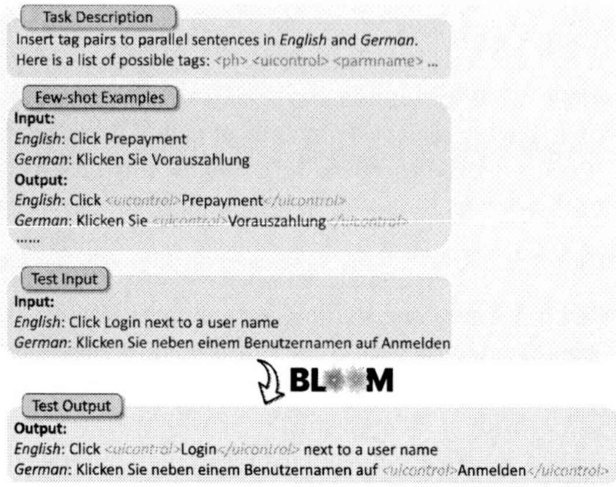

Figure 4: The overview of the LLM-based synthetic data creation method. We prompt the LLM with few-shot examples, and the model directly generates parallel sentences with tag pairs.

We called the resultant data as LLM-Synthetic-Tagged (LST). We prompt the LLMs (BLOOM 7B in our experiments) with few-shot examples, and the model takes source and target sentences without markup as input and outputs source and target sentences with markup. The hand-crafted and fixed *5-shot* examples (prompt in Appendix A.2) show how a sentence pair without markup can be transformed into a pair with markup.

4 Experimental Settings

This section describes datasets, implementation details, and various settings for analysis.

4.1 Datasets and Languages

We consider the Salesforce Localization Dataset (Hashimoto et al., 2019b) which spans English and seven languages, out of which we choose five European target languages, namely, German, French, Dutch, Finnish and Russian. The data for each language pair consists of approximately high-quality 100k training, 2k development and 2k testing high-quality sentence pairs of which 26% of the pairs *naturally* contain markup. We use the development set of 2,000 sentence pairs as the test set because the test set is hidden. Furthermore, since LLM IFT is computationally expensive, and our objective is to study the efficacy of synthetic data and IFT, we choose a subset of the training data for our experiments. Specifically, we choose the first 2,000 sentence pairs for development (instead of the official development set), and the next 20,000 sentence pairs for few-shot prompting or IFT. We create a version of the 20,000 pairs by removing all markup information and call this *Plain* data, whereas the corresponding version with 26% of the sentences naturally containing (high-quality/gold) markup is called *Clean* data.

Synthetic Data Settings

When creating synthetic sentence pairs with markup using word alignment (Alignment-Synthetic-Tagged or *AST*), we experiment with maximum source (English) spans of size 4 and 6 tokens, where we randomly choose one source phrase whose token length is less or equal to this number.[4] For synthetic data created with LLMs (LLM-Synthetic-Tagged or *LST*), we cannot control maximum spans and leave it to the model to wrap phrases with markup tags as it sees fit. We prompt the model with 5 manually constructed shots, which are fixed for each language pair. For the decoding algorithm, we applied greedy search with a temperature of 0. As for the percentage of sentence pairs with markup tags in the training data, we experiment with 1%, 2%, 5%, 15% and 26% of examples with synthetic markup where 26% is analogous to the amount of *naturally*

[4]The aligned target spans may be longer or shorter, but this is not something that can be controlled.

occurring markup in *Clean* data. For LST, due to reasons explained in Section 5.3, we were only able to generate a maximum of 24% and 14% tagged data with synthetic markup only for English-German and English-Russian, respectively. For these pairs, henceforth 26% actually implies 24% and 14% respectively. Unless explicitly mentioned, we use the data containing 26% pairs with markup for AST and LST when experimenting with prompting and IFT.

4.2 Implementation, Training, and Evaluation

We implement the code for creating synthetic data and prompting in Python. For word alignment, we used FastAlign[5] (Dyer et al., 2013) with default settings for forward, reverse, and we symmetrize alignments with grow-diag-final-and. We use open-instruct[6] (Wang et al., 2023) for IFT. We use the 7.1 billion parameter variant[7] of the BLOOM model (Le Scao et al., 2022). We choose this model over more recent ones like Llama (Touvron et al., 2023) since the latter is not explicitly suited for non-English generation.[8] Due to our low-resource setting, we use LoRA (Hu et al., 2021) for fine-tuning, with a rank of 4 and an alpha of 8, and a LoRA dropout of 0.05. We use a total batch size of 32 with gradient accumulation. We train for a maximum of 4 epochs, evaluate every epoch, and choose the checkpoint corresponding to the lowest loss.[9] Our experiments are performed on 40GB A100 GPUs. For decoding the test sets, we perform greedy decoding.

For evaluation, while Hashimoto et al. (2019b) propose XML-BLEU, we consider XML-chrF as a measure of overall translation quality, including both, *content as well as markup transfer quality*. They use multi-bleu,[10] however, since Post (2018) have shown that using multi-bleu is not reliable, we switch to sacrebleu[11] and following recent trends, chrF scores (Popović, 2015) to report XML-chrF. Additionally, just as Hashimoto et al. (2019b) do, we report XML-Structure-Match, henceforth XML-Match, as a measure of *purely* the markup transfer capabilities, with details explained in Appendix B.

4.3 Prompting Settings

For few-shot prompting on the test set, we use 0-, 1- and 4-shot prompting when the base BLOOM model is used. After performing IFT, we only use 0-shot prompting. The 1- and 4-shot prompting examples are chosen randomly. We perform three runs and report the mean scores.

5 Results

We structure the results in two major sections: the first focusing on synthetic data and using it for prompting, and the second focusing on IFT along with synthetic data.

5.1 Synthetic Data for Prompting

Table 1 gives the results for 0-, 1- and 4-shot prompting with plain, clean and synthetic data. Perhaps the most surprising result is that 0-shot prompting has very high XML-Match indicating that the markup structure is almost always correctly transferred from source to target language. However, the XML-chrF scores are rather low, except for English to French, indicating that while the LLM can transfer markup, it cannot translate content well. Increasing the number of shots has a marked improvement on the XML-chrF scores. On the other hand, the XML-Match scores do not vary much regardless of the data used for prompting.

Although Dabre et al. (2023) used different metrics for evaluation, their *tag* metric is analogous to XML-Match and they always reported very low scores for the same. Note that they focused on Japanese, Chinese and Korean, which are **a.** Not well-supported in BLOOM and **b.** are linguistically distant from English. On the other hand, we focus on European languages which are better supported in BLOOM and are linguistically closer to English. This results in the following finding:

[5]https://github.com/clab/fast_align

[6]https://github.com/allenai/open-instruct/

[7]https://huggingface.co/bigscience/bloom-7b1

[8]While these models are known to be able to generate in non-English models, our main goal is not obtaining SOTA results but to study how LLMs behave in the context of synthetic data in conjunction with IFT. Therefore, we rely on BLOOM in our experiments.

[9]This is different from typical MT experiments where early stopping is done on the downstream metric itself. Since this is expensive for LLMs, we rely on loss, which can be computed non-autoregressively.

[10]https://github.com/moses-smt/mosesdecoder/blob/master/scripts/generic/multi-bleu.perl

[11]https://github.com/mjpost/sacrebleu

Prompting Data Type	XML-chrF en→de	en→fi	en→fr	en→nl	en→ru	Avg.	XML-Match en→de	en→fi	en→fr	en→nl	en→ru	Avg.
						0-shot						
Baseline	33.6	18.3	54.3	33.3	24.1	32.7	96.5	**95.6**	95.3	95.3	**94.4**	**95.4**
						1-shot						
Plain	39.0	17.2	58.6	38.6	30.9	36.9	96.2	89.9	96.4	95.8	94.1	94.5
Clean	39.5	17.6	59.0	38.6	30.9	37.1	96.3	90.0	96.0	95.6	94.0	94.4
AST-4	39.3	17.7	58.6	38.8	30.8	37.0	96.1	90.5	96.2	95.6	93.3	94.3
AST-6	39.4	17.6	58.2	38.8	30.6	36.9	96.2	90.3	95.9	95.6	92.9	94.2
LST	39.5	17.2	58.4	38.7	30.9	36.9	95.8	88.4	95.7	95.5	92.6	93.6
						4-shot						
Plain	**41.5**	**19.3**	61.3	40.7	**32.9**	**39.1**	**96.9**	90.9	**96.8**	**96.1**	94.1	95.0
Clean	41.1	18.9	**61.5**	40.7	**32.9**	39.0	96.1	89.7	96.6	93.4	94.3	94.1
AST-4	41.0	18.9	61.2	**40.9**	32.1	38.8	95.9	89.6	96.5	**96.1**	92.3	94.1
AST-6	40.9	19.0	61.4	40.7	32.3	38.9	96.0	90.0	96.7	95.8	92.6	94.2
LST	41.3	18.0	60.7	40.3	32.3	38.5	96.0	86.6	96.3	95.4	92.6	93.4

Table 1: XML-chrF and XML-Match of different types of data for few-shot prompting. Best results in each direction are **bolded**. **Plain** refers to data w/o markup, and **Clean** means markup data created by humans from the dataset.

Prompting Data Type	XML-chrF en→de	en→fi	en→fr	en→nl	en→ru	Avg.	XML-Match en→de	en→fi	en→fr	en→nl	en→ru	Avg.
						Reference: Prompting Results						
Plain 4-shot	41.5	19.3	61.3	40.7	32.9	39.1	96.9	90.9	96.8	96.1	94.1	95.0
						Instruction Fine-Tuning Results						
Plain	57.5	46.5	72.1	59.4	45.4	56.2	94.0	95.2	96.7	95.0	88.5	93.9
Clean	**60.1**	**47.9**	**75.3**	**60.7**	**50.0**	**58.8**	**97.2**	**96.8**	**98.7**	**96.4**	**95.4**	**96.9**
AST-4	58.5	46.3	72.7	59.3	47.5	56.9	96.2	95.0	96.6	95.4	93.5	95.3
LST	55.9	44.9	73.6	59.2	46.4	56.0	91.8	92.1	97.0	94.8	89.6	93.1

Table 2: XML-chrF and XML-Match of different types of data for instruction fine-tuning. Best results are **bolded**. **Plain** refers to data w/o markup, and **Clean** means markup data created by humans from the dataset.

Finding 1: *Base LLMs are fairly good at markup transfer of well-supported languages, and demonstrations (or shots) mainly affect the content translation quality.*

5.1.1 Does Synthetic Data Even Matter for Prompting?

Comparing the 1- and 4-shot results in Table 1, it is clear that there is no notable difference in performance between using examples with (Clean, AST, LST) and without (Plain) markup for translating sentences with markup. Among synthetic data (AST-4, AST-6 and LST), the approach for synthetic data does not matter. This leads to the following finding:

Finding 2: *The LLM likely sees markup tags as tokens to be transferred from source to target and does not distinguish them from regular words/tokens, and it uses shots only to know how to translate.*

5.2 Synthetic Data for Instruction Fine-Tuning

Having shown the impact of various types of data with and without markup for prompting, we now show results for using the aforementioned data for instruction fine-tuning. Table 2 shows the fine-tuning results, and in-context-learning results as a reference, where we prompt the LLM with 5-shot translation samples in the target domain without markup.

Different from few-shot prompting, the impact of different types of data is visible. While fine-tuning using data without markup (Plain) significantly improves XML-chrF, the markup transfer itself (XML-match) is negatively affected. In fact, few-shot prompting does better. Since we want our model to translate as well as transfer markup, fine-tuning on data without markup is not viable. On the other hand, fine-tuning with human-created data (Clean) not only has better markup transfer but also

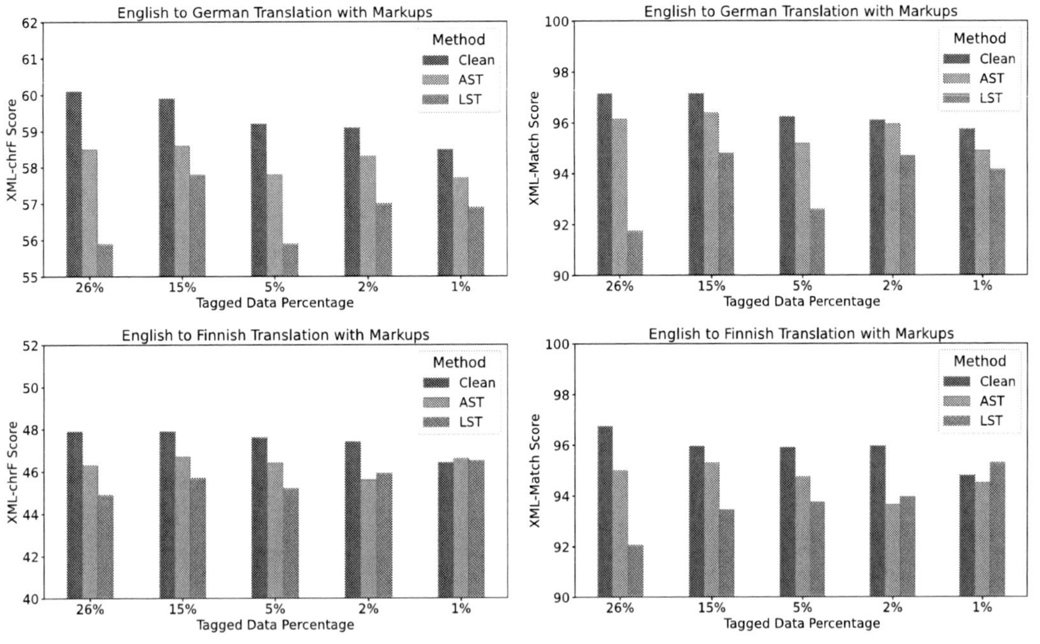

Figure 5: Results of IFT using varying percentages of data with markup. We show XML-chrF (left figure) scores and XML-Match scores (right figure) of randomly choosing X percentage of pairs with markup from the original data (Clean), and data generated by our AST (with max span of 4) and LST approaches. X ranges from natural max, that is the markup data percentage in Clean of 26%, to 15%, 5%, 2% and 1%.

has better content translation quality, mostly indicated by the significant increase in chrF by about 5 points. However, it's not always possible to have human created data with markup, but in this case synthetic data appears to be useful. Comparing AST-4,[12] and Clean, we see that while the former is expectedly slightly inferior to the latter, the gap is rather small. Although we expected LST to be better than AST, its performance was disappointing. Our analysis in the following subsection will shed some light on this. Our finding is:

Finding 3: *IFT requires high-quality data with markup for the best performance, however synthetically generated data is certainly a viable option.*

5.2.1 Does Synthetic Data Quantity Matter?

Previously, we did not focus on the ratio of data without and with markup and created as much synthetic data as was present in the human created version. However, it is not clear what the optimal ratio is. To this end, we explore varying markup data ratios in the training set. Figure 5 shows the result for English to German and Finnish. Here, we have 3 important observations: a. Clean data is almost always better than synthetic data, but the gap keeps diminishing as the amount of markup data drops. b. Even having 1% data with markup is still better than having no data with markup. c. LST is inferior to AST in most settings. We put the full table of five language pairs in Appendix C. The finding is:

Finding 4: *High-quality markup data is always useful at any scale even if it forms 1% of the overall IFT data, however synthetic data generated using alignment is a viable alternative at all scales.*

5.3 Evaluation of Synthetic Data

We briefly evaluate synthetic data to understand its quality. Consider the following Clean, AST and

[12] In our preliminary experiments for IFT, we did not notice any difference between AST-4 and AST-6, so we only report results for AST-4.

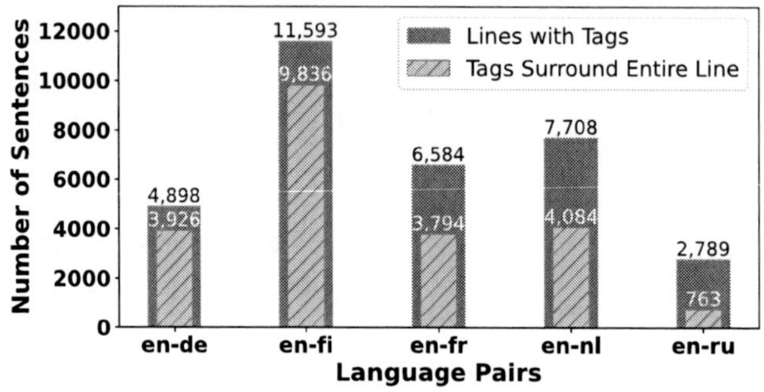

Figure 6: Maximum number of sentence pairs with tags, out of 20,000, that could be generated using LST. Of this, we select pairs corresponding to a maximum of 26% of the training/prompting data. We also show the number of pairs with tags surrounding entire sentences (tags only at the beginning and the end).

LST variations of the same English-German pair:

Clean (En): From Setup, enter <userinput>Salesforce Classic Configurations</userinput> in the <parmname>Quick Find</parmname> box, then select <uicontrol>Salesforce Classic Configurations</uicontrol>.

Clean (De): Geben Sie unter "Setup" im Feld <userinput>Schnellsuche</userinput> den Text <parmname>Konfigurationen für Salesforce Classic</parmname> ein und wählen Sie dann <uicontrol>Konfigurationen für Salesforce Classic</uicontrol> aus.

AST (En): From Setup, enter <uinolabel>Salesforce Classic Configurations in the Quick Find</uinolabel> box, then select Salesforce Classic Configurations.

AST (De): Geben Sie unter "Setup" im Feld <uinolabel>Schnellsuche den Text Konfigurationen für Salesforce Classic ein</uinolabel> und wählen Sie dann Konfigurationen für Salesforce Classic aus.

LST (En): From Setup, enter <uicontrol>Salesforce Classic Configurations</uicontrol> in the Quick Find box, then select <uicontrol>Salesforce Classic Configurations</uicontrol>.

LST (De): Geben Sie unter "Setup" im Feld Schnellsuche den Text <uicontrol>Konfigurationen für Salesforce Classic</uicontrol> ein und wählen Sie dann <uicontrol>Konfigurationen für Salesforce Classic</uicontrol> aus.

It is clear that LST data is more similar to Clean data in which shorter phrases corresponding to keywords are wrapped with tags, whereas AST covers a longer phrase. Although not evident in this example, AST can tag unnatural phrases and given discrepancies compared to Clean data, it makes sense that models trained with AST data will always underperform those trained with Clean data. However, the confounding factor is why models trained on LST data are worse than on AST, despite LST data looking similar to Clean data. We found that LST tends to wrap entire sentences with tags more often than AST, with examples in Appendix D.

As shown in Figure 6, many of the LST examples are with tag pairs surrounding the entire sentence. For English to German, of 4,898 LST tagged examples, 3,926 are entire sentences. Whereas in the AST data, out of 5,235 tagged examples, only 460 are entire sentences. For reference, in Clean, out of 5,235 tagged sentences, only 60 are entire sentences. This large proportion of entire tagged sentences appears to have a larger impact than having non-keyword or unnatural phrases. For the sentences with tags but not surrounding the entire sentence, the average number of words surrounded by one tag pair is approximately 2 for all languages which is reasonable. Furthermore, despite our best efforts, we could not compel BLOOM to generate the desired number of tagged sentences. Finally, there is a significant variation in the number of sentences with tags across different language pairs, which contributes to the variation in MT performance, implying the need for future study.

6 Conclusion

In this paper, we have studied the effectiveness of synthetic data and instruction fine-tuning for translation with markup. We observed that an LLM without few-shot prompting or IFT already has impressive markup transfer capabilities, but suffers from low translation ability in the document domain. Although few-shot prompting can help improve translation quality, IFT is more effective, while also improving markup transfer capabilities regardless of whether high-quality or synthetic data was used. In the future, we would like to explore more controllable and scalable ways to generate synthetic data and eliminate the need for human curated data.

References

Brown, T., Mann, B., Ryder, N., Subbiah, M., Kaplan, J. D., Dhariwal, P., Neelakantan, A., Shyam, P., Sastry, G., Askell, A., Agarwal, S., Herbert-Voss, A., Krueger, G., Henighan, T., Child, R., Ramesh, A., Ziegler, D., Wu, J., Winter, C., Hesse, C., Chen, M., Sigler, E., Litwin, M., Gray, S., Chess, B., Clark, J., Berner, C., McCandlish, S., Radford, A., Sutskever, I., and Amodei, D. (2020). Language models are few-shot learners. In Larochelle, H., Ranzato, M., Hadsell, R., Balcan, M., and Lin, H., editors, *Advances in Neural Information Processing Systems*, volume 33, pages 1877–1901. Curran Associates, Inc.

Buschbeck, B., Dabre, R., Exel, M., Huck, M., Huy, P., Rubino, R., and Tanaka, H. (2022). A multilingual multiway evaluation data set for structured document translation of Asian languages. In He, Y., Ji, H., Li, S., Liu, Y., and Chang, C.-H., editors, *Findings of the Association for Computational Linguistics: AACL-IJCNLP 2022*, pages 237–245, Online only. Association for Computational Linguistics.

Cho, K., van Merrienboer, B., Bahdanau, D., and Bengio, Y. (2014). On the properties of neural machine translation: Encoder–decoder approaches. In *Proceedings of SSST-8, Eighth Workshop on Syntax, Semantics and Structure in Statistical Translation*, pages 103–111, Doha, Qatar. Association for Computational Linguistics.

Dabre, R., Buschbeck, B., Exel, M., and Tanaka, H. (2023). A study on the effectiveness of large language models for translation with markup. In Utiyama, M. and Wang, R., editors, *Proceedings of Machine Translation Summit XIX, Vol. 1: Research Track*, pages 148–159, Macau SAR, China. Asia-Pacific Association for Machine Translation.

Dyer, C., Chahuneau, V., and Smith, N. A. (2013). A simple, fast, and effective reparameterization of IBM model 2. In Vanderwende, L., Daumé III, H., and Kirchhoff, K., editors, *Proceedings of the 2013 Conference of the North American Chapter of the Association for Computational Linguistics: Human Language Technologies*, pages 644–648, Atlanta, Georgia. Association for Computational Linguistics.

Hanneman, G. and Dinu, G. (2020a). How should markup tags be translated? In *Proceedings of the Fifth Conference on Machine Translation*, pages 1160–1173.

Hanneman, G. and Dinu, G. (2020b). How should markup tags be translated? In Barrault, L., Bojar, O., Bougares, F., Chatterjee, R., Costa-jussà, M. R., Federmann, C., Fishel, M., Fraser, A., Graham, Y., Guzman, P., Haddow, B., Huck, M., Yepes, A. J., Koehn, P., Martins, A., Morishita, M., Monz, C., Nagata, M., Nakazawa, T., and Negri, M., editors, *Proceedings of the Fifth Conference on Machine Translation*, pages 1160–1173, Online. Association for Computational Linguistics.

Hashimoto, K., Buschiazzo, R., Bradbury, J., Marshall, T., Socher, R., and Xiong, C. (2019a). A high-quality multilingual dataset for structured documentation translation. In Bojar, O., Chatterjee, R., Federmann, C., Fishel, M., Graham, Y., Haddow, B., Huck, M., Yepes, A. J., Koehn, P., Martins, A., Monz, C., Negri, M., Névéol, A., Neves, M., Post, M., Turchi, M., and Verspoor, K., editors, *Proceedings of the Fourth Conference on Machine Translation (Volume 1: Research Papers)*, pages 116–127, Florence, Italy. Association for Computational Linguistics.

Hashimoto, K., Buschiazzo, R., Bradbury, J., Marshall, T., Socher, R., and Xiong, C. (2019b). A high-quality multilingual dataset for structured documentation translation. In *Proceedings of the Fourth Conference on Machine Translation (Volume 1: Research Papers)*, pages 116–127.

Hu, E. J., Shen, Y., Wallis, P., Allen-Zhu, Z., Li, Y., Wang, S., Wang, L., and Chen, W. (2021). Lora: Low-rank adaptation of large language models.

Joanis, E., Stewart, D., Larkin, S., and Kuhn, R. (2013). Transferring markup tags in statistical machine translation: a two-stream approach. In O'Brien, S., Simard, M., and Specia, L., editors, *Proceedings of the 2nd Workshop on Post-editing Technology and Practice*, Nice, France.

Le Scao, T., Fan, A., Akiki, C., Pavlick, E., Ilić, S., Hesslow, D., Castagné, R., Luccioni, A. S., Yvon, F., Gallé, M., et al. (2022). BLOOM: A 176b-parameter open-access multilingual language model. *arXiv preprint arXiv:2211.05100*.

Lewis, P., Perez, E., Piktus, A., Petroni, F., Karpukhin, V., Goyal, N., Küttler, H., Lewis, M., Yih, W.-t., Rocktäschel, T., et al. (2020). Retrieval-augmented generation for knowledge-intensive nlp tasks. *Advances in Neural Information Processing Systems*, 33:9459–9474.

Lin, X. V., Mihaylov, T., Artetxe, M., Wang, T., Chen, S., Simig, D., Ott, M., Goyal, N., Bhosale, S., Du, J., Pasunuru, R., Shleifer, S., Koura, P. S., Chaudhary, V., O'Horo, B., Wang, J., Zettlemoyer, L., Kozareva, Z., Diab, M., Stoyanov, V., and Li, X. (2022). Few-shot learning with multilingual generative language models. In Goldberg, Y., Kozareva, Z., and Zhang, Y., editors, *Proceedings of the 2022 Conference on Empirical Methods in Natural Language Processing*, pages 9019–9052, Abu Dhabi, United Arab Emirates. Association for Computational Linguistics.

Muennighoff, N., Wang, T., Sutawika, L., Roberts, A., Biderman, S., Scao, T. L., Bari, M. S., Shen, S., Yong, Z.-X., Schoelkopf, H., et al. (2022). Crosslingual generalization through multitask finetuning. *arXiv preprint arXiv:2211.01786*.

Müller, M. (2017). Treatment of markup in statistical machine translation. In Webber, B., Popescu-Belis, A., and Tiedemann, J., editors, *Proceedings of the Third Workshop on Discourse in Machine Translation*, pages 36–46, Copenhagen, Denmark. Association for Computational Linguistics.

Och, F. J. (1999). An efficient method for determining bilingual word classes. In Thompson, H. S. and Lascarides, A., editors, *Ninth Conference of the European Chapter of the Association for Computational Linguistics*, pages 71–76, Bergen, Norway. Association for Computational Linguistics.

Popović, M. (2015). chrF: character n-gram F-score for automatic MT evaluation. In Bojar, O., Chatterjee, R., Federmann, C., Haddow, B., Hokamp, C., Huck, M., Logacheva, V., and Pecina, P., editors, *Proceedings of the Tenth Workshop on Statistical Machine Translation*, pages 392–395, Lisbon, Portugal. Association for Computational Linguistics.

Post, M. (2018). A call for clarity in reporting BLEU scores. In *Proceedings of the Third Conference on Machine Translation: Research Papers*, pages 186–191.

Rei, R., Stewart, C., Farinha, A. C., and Lavie, A. (2020). COMET: A neural framework for MT evaluation. In *Proceedings of the 2020 Conference on Empirical Methods in Natural Language Processing (EMNLP)*, pages 2685–2702.

Ryu, Y., Choi, Y., and Kim, S. (2022). Data augmentation for inline tag-aware neural machine translation. In Koehn, P., Barrault, L., Bojar, O., Bougares, F., Chatterjee, R., Costa-jussà, M. R., Federmann, C., Fishel, M., Fraser, A., Freitag, M., Graham, Y., Grundkiewicz, R., Guzman, P., Haddow, B., Huck, M., Jimeno Yepes, A., Kocmi, T., Martins, A., Morishita, M., Monz, C., Nagata, M., Nakazawa, T., Negri, M., Névéol, A., Neves, M., Popel, M., Turchi, M., and Zampieri, M., editors, *Proceedings of the Seventh Conference on Machine Translation (WMT)*, pages 886–894, Abu Dhabi, United Arab Emirates (Hybrid). Association for Computational Linguistics.

Touvron, H., Lavril, T., Izacard, G., Martinet, X., Lachaux, M.-A., Lacroix, T., Rozière, B., Goyal, N., Hambro, E., Azhar, F., et al. (2023). Llama: Open and efficient foundation language models. *arXiv preprint arXiv:2302.13971*.

Vaswani, A., Shazeer, N., Parmar, N., Uszkoreit, J., Jones, L., Gomez, A. N., Kaiser, Ł., and Polosukhin, I. (2017). Attention is all you need. *Advances in neural information processing systems*, 30.

Wang, Y., Ivison, H., Dasigi, P., Hessel, J., Khot, T., Chandu, K. R., Wadden, D., MacMillan, K., Smith, N. A., Beltagy, I., and Hajishirzi, H. (2023). How far can camels go? exploring the state of instruction tuning on open resources.

Wei, J., Bosma, M., Zhao, V., Guu, K., Yu, A. W., Lester, B., Du, N., Dai, A. M., and Le, Q. V. (2022). Finetuned language models are zero-shot learners. In *International Conference on Learning Representations*.

Zenkel, T., Wuebker, J., and DeNero, J. (2021). Automatic bilingual markup transfer. In *Findings of the Association for Computational Linguistics: EMNLP 2021*, pages 3524–3533.

Limitation

One limitation of this work is that we only used BLOOM-7B1, thus the performance of different LLM families such as Llama-3 or Gemma, or LLMs with different amounts of parameters such as BLOOM-560M or Llama-3 70B, is not verified. It is possible that larger language models can have higher markup transfer capability, have higher translation capability on data in structured document domain, generate better synthetic data, and are more controllable.

A Prompting Details

A.1 Few-shot prompting for MT

The prompting template is as follows:

Translate the following sentence from E to F. The translation should be in F and no other language.
E: [S_1]
F: [T_1]
...
E: [S_N]
F: [T_N]
E: [S_t]
F:

In the template above, E is the source language, F is the target language, and S_t is the test example for which we want to obtain a translation. Note that in the template, each source and target language sentence is wrapped in opening and closing square brackets ([,]). After the model produces outputs, we remove the prompted prefix and retain the first segment produced by the model within the [and] brackets as the model's translation.

A.2 Few-shot prompting for synthetic data creation

This section formats the prompt, and the real prompt with five demonstrations is shown in Table 4.
Insert tag pairs to parallel sentences in E and F. Here is a list of possible tags: <ph> <uicontrol> <parmname> <b> <codeph> <xref> <userinput> <varname> <filepath> <i> <li> <systemoutput> <term> <title> <p> <note> <cite> <indexterm> <fn> <u>.
Input:
E: S_i
F: T_i
Output:
E: S'_i
F: T'_i
...
Input:
E: S_t
F: T_t
Output:

In the template above, E is the source and F is the target language. (S_i, T_i) is parallel sentences without markup and (S'_i, T'_i) is parallel sentences with markup. (S_t, T_t) is the test example which contains parallel sentences without markup. After generating the parallel sentences, we post-process the output to extract S'_t and T'_t, and verify whether there are tags in both of them and whether the detagged version of them equal to S_t and T_t. We only use the outputs that passed these verification processes.

A.3 IFT prompt template

The data format fed to the LLM for IFT is as follows:

Translate the following sentence from E to F. The translation should be in F and no other language.
E: [S]
F: [T]

Here, [T] consists of the completion and everything before it is the prompt.

B Details of Evaluation Metrics.

We explain the calculation details of XML-Match and XML-chrF metrics. We first use `etree` to extract the XML structure of the output and reference. The XML-Match is the percentage of outputs that have exactly the same XML structures as their references. If the XML structures of an output and its reference match, then the translation and reference are split by the XML tags and we evaluate the chrF score by comparing each split segment. If the structures do not match, the chrF score is counted as zero to penalize the irrelevant outputs. We leave COMET score reporting (Rei et al., 2020) for the future.

C Full Results of IFT using Varying Percentages of Tagged Data

We present the results of instruction fine-tuning using varying percentages of data with markup for all five language pairs in Figure 7. As per the explanation in Section 5.3 and Appendix D, we were unable to control the amount of sentence pairs with synthetic markup for LST. Corresponding to Clean which naturally has 26% data with markup and AST where we can generate the exactly 26% of pairs with markup, LST was unable to generate more than 24% pairs with markup for English-German. For English-Russian, a maximum of 14% pairs with markup could be generated. Since we have no control over this, for English-German, the scores corresponding to 26% synthetic markup pairs using LST are actually scores for 24% synthetic markup pairs using LST. For English-Russian, the scores corresponding to 26% as well as 15% synthetic markup pairs using LST are actually scores for 14% synthetic markup pairs using LST.

Comparing different methods, we found that clean data is almost always better than synthetic data, and LST is inferior to AST in all directions except English→French, where LST showed higher performance even than clean data using 26% of tagged data. This may be because, for French, there is a large number of *normal* tagged sentences (not tags surrounding the entire sentence). For English→Dutch, which also has a large number of normal tagged sentences, the XML-chrF scores are better than AST using 15% and 2% of tagged data. However, for language pairs where LST generates low-quality tagged data, such as English→German, the final performance is also low. Compared to LST, AST is more stable where the gap between Clean data is small (or comparable) for all language directions. Furthermore, we observed that AST performed better than Clean using 1% tagged in English→German and English→Dutch directions, and the gap with using 26% tagged data is small. This shows that we can achieve high-quality transfer learning by AST with a tiny amount of noisy data.

D LLM is not Always Controllable.

LLM-based (to be specific, *BLOOM7B1-based*) synthetic data creation is not stable because it does not always generate output with tags even if we always prompt the model to do so. In fact, English-German and English-Russian were especially hard. For English-German we were unable to generate more than approximately 24% and for English-Russian more than approximately 14% sentences with markup. What's worse, it simply added tags at the beginning and the end of one sentence in many cases. We show examples in Table 3 and statistics in Figure 6, from which we can observe that for English-Finnish, English-French, and English-Dutch, a large percentage of the tagged data are not helpful with tag pairs only at the beginning and the end. In the future, we will explore larger LLMs such as Llama-3-70B-Instruct, which may generate more natural tagged sentence pairs.

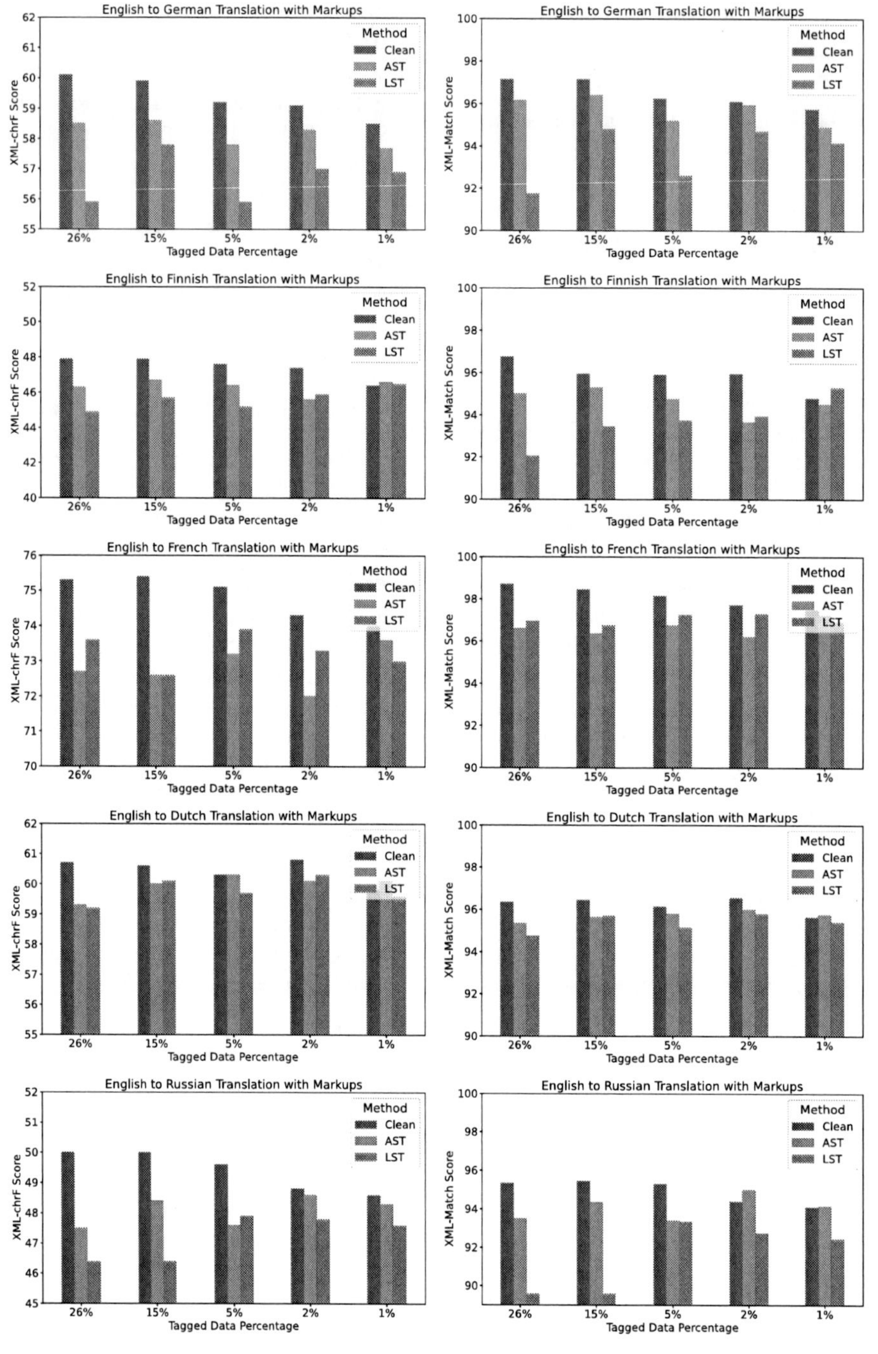

Figure 7: Results of IFT using varying percentages of data with markup for all five language pairs. We show XML-chrF (left column) scores and XML-Match scores (right column) of randomly sampling X percentage of tagged data from the original data (Clean), and data generated by our AST (with max span of 4) and LST approaches. X ranges from natural max, that is the tagged data percentage in Clean of 26%, to 15%, 5%, 2% and 1%.

English:	<xref>Size of the work items in the queue based on its routing configuration.</xref>
German:	<xref>Die Größe der Arbeitselemente in der Warteschlange basierend auf ihrer Weiterleitungskonfiguration.</xref>
English:	<codeph>Only included if you choose to import campaigns data to Sales Analytics through the configuration wizard.</codeph>
Finnish:	<codeph>Sisällytetään vain, jos päätät tuoda kampanjadataa Sales Analyticsiin ohjatun määritystoiminnon kautta.</codeph>
English:	<ph>Support for macros is different in Salesforce Classic and Lightning Experience.</ph>
French:	<ph>La prise en charge des macros diffère entre Salesforce Classic et Lightning Experience.</ph>
English:	<parmname>Ability to manage all case comments</parmname>
Dutch:	<parmname>Mogelijkheid tot beheer van alle caseopmerkingen</parmname>
English:	<userinput>Running user does not have permission to access report type.</userinput>
Russian:	<userinput>Текущий пользователь не имеет права доступа к типу отчета.</userinput>

Table 3: Examples of sentence pairs with tags that only appear at the beginning and the end outputted by BLOOM.

Insert tag pairs to parallel sentences in English and German.
Here is a list of possible tags:
<ph> <uiontrol> <parmname> <b> <codeph> <xref> <userinput> <varname> <filepath> <i> <li> <systemoutput> <term> <title> <p> <note> <cite> <indexterm> <fn> <u>

Input:
English: For more information, see Using the Agent Console List View.
German: Weitere Informationen finden Sie unter Verwenden der Listenansicht der Agentenkonsole.
Output:
English: For more information, see <xref><ph>Using the <ph>Agent Console</ph> List View</ph></xref>.
German: Weitere Informationen finden Sie unter <xref><ph>Verwenden der Listenansicht der <ph>Agentenkonsole</ph></ph></xref>.

Input:
English: In the Folders pane on the Reports tab, select Opportunity Reports.
German: Wählen Sie im Fenster Ordner auf der Registerkarte "Berichte" die Option Opportunity-Berichte.
Output:
English: In the <parmname>Folders</parmname> pane on the Reports tab, select <uicontrol>Opportunity Reports</uicontrol>.
German: Wählen Sie im Fenster <parmname>Ordner</parmname> auf der Registerkarte "Berichte" die Option <uicontrol>Opportunity-Berichte</uicontrol>.

Input:
English: Measure – Choose a measure for the metric chart
German: Maßeinheit: Wählen Sie eine Maßeinheit für das metrische Diagramm aus
Output:
English: <b>Measure</b> – Choose a measure for the metric chart
German: <b>Maßeinheit</b>: Wählen Sie eine Maßeinheit für das metrische Diagramm aus

---

Input:
English: On your profile page, click Update under your photo (or Add Photo if you haven't added a photo yet), then select Show in communities with publicly accessible pages.
German: Klicken Sie auf Ihrer Profilseite unter Ihrem Foto auf Aktualisieren (bzw. auf Foto hinzufügen, wenn Sie noch kein Foto hinzugefügt haben) und wählen Sie dann die Option In Communities mit öffentlich zugänglichen Seiten anzeigen.
Output:
English: On your profile page, click <uicontrol>Update</uicontrol> under your photo (or <uicontrol>Add Photo</uicontrol> if you haven't added a photo yet), then select <parmname>Show in communities with publicly accessible pages</parmname>.
German: Klicken Sie auf Ihrer Profilseite unter Ihrem Foto auf <uicontrol>Aktualisieren</uicontrol> (bzw. auf <uicontrol>Foto hinzufügen</uicontrol>, wenn Sie noch kein Foto hinzugefügt haben) und wählen Sie dann die Option <parmname>In Communities mit öffentlich zugänglichen Seiten anzeigen</parmname>.

Input:
English: Salesforce supports the open-standard cross-domain identity management SCIM specification 1.1, and provides a few extensions to the spec so you can edit and manage user properties using the REST API.
German: Salesforce unterstützt die Open-Standard-SCIM-Spezifikation 1.1 (System for Cross-domain Identity Management) und stellt einige Erweiterungen für die Spezifikation bereit, sodass Sie Benutzereigenschaften mit der REST-API bearbeiten und verwalten können.
Output:
English: <ph>Salesforce</ph> supports the open-standard cross-domain identity management SCIM specification 1.1, and provides a few extensions to the spec so you can edit and manage user properties using the <ph>REST API</ph>.
German: <ph>Salesforce</ph> unterstützt die Open-Standard-SCIM-Spezifikation 1.1 (System for Cross-domain Identity Management) und stellt einige Erweiterungen für die Spezifikation bereit, sodass Sie Benutzereigenschaften mit der <ph>REST-API</ph> bearbeiten und verwalten können.

Input:
English: ${English Sentence}
German: ${German Sentence}

Table 4: The full prompt for LLM to generate tagged sentences in English and German.

Guiding In-Context Learning of LLMs through Quality Estimation for Machine Translation

Javad Pourmostafa Roshan Sharami j.pourmostafa@tilburguniversity.edu
Dimitar Shterionov d.shterionov@tilburguniversity.edu
Pieter Spronck p.spronck@tilburguniversity.edu
Department of Cognitive Science and Artificial Intelligence, Tilburg University

Abstract

The quality of output from large language models (LLMs), particularly in machine translation (MT), is closely tied to the quality of in-context examples (ICEs) provided along with the query, i.e., the text to translate. The effectiveness of these ICEs is influenced by various factors, such as the domain of the source text, the order in which the ICEs are presented, the number of these examples, and the prompt templates used. Naturally, selecting the most impactful ICEs depends on understanding how these affect the resulting translation quality, which ultimately relies on translation references or human judgment. This paper presents a novel methodology for in-context learning (ICL) that relies on a search algorithm guided by domain-specific quality estimation (QE). Leveraging the XGLM model, our methodology estimates the resulting translation quality without the need for translation references, selecting effective ICEs for MT to maximize translation quality. Our results demonstrate significant improvements over existing ICL methods and higher translation performance compared to fine-tuning a pre-trained language model (PLM), specifically mBART-50.

1 Introduction

Pre-trained large language models (LLMs) quickly gained popularity (and continue to do so) due to their performance on a large set of natural language processing (NLP) tasks, including machine translation (MT) (Zhu et al., 2023; Xu et al., 2024). However, the accuracy of their outputs is significantly influenced by the quality of the *in-context* examples (ICEs) provided to them (Jiang et al., 2020; Alves et al., 2023).[1] If these examples do not align well with the specific task and source domain, the LLMs' outputs can be inaccurate. Therefore, there is a critical need to develop (better) methods for selecting appropriate examples that match the task and source domain being translated. These methods collectively fall under the umbrella of in-context learning (ICL) (Liu et al., 2022).

Traditionally, creating ICEs for MT involves either random selection (Sia and Duh, 2023) or using a strategy such as maximizing an evaluation metric like BLEU, to choose examples that improve the metric (Agrawal et al., 2023). The former was initially used for its simplicity and ease of implementation. However, relying on randomness can lead to inconsistent results and pose significant computational costs (Lu et al., 2022). Recent state-of-the-art (SOTA) ICL approaches focus on retrieving training examples that are closely relevant to the context of source sentences of test sets using unsupervised retrievers, such as BM25 (Robertson and Zaragoza, 2009). Recent studies have also shown that a range of factors, such as order (Lu et al., 2022), template (Jiang et al., 2020), domain, and number of ICEs, significantly impact the performance (Agrawal et al., 2023; Raunak et al., 2023a).

Naturally, the most effective ICEs for a given source text are the ones that would impact the resulting translation quality, which would ultimately de-

[1] For simplicity, we sometimes refer to it as "example(s)" throughout this paper.

pend on translation references or human judgment. In MT, quality estimation (QE) has become a standard approach for evaluating an MT system's output without relying on reference translations Blain et al. (2023). Recently, Lee (2020), Ye and Li (2023), and Sharami et al. (2023) showed the effectiveness of domain-specific QE when it comes to domain-specific MT (in contrast to the ineffectiveness of generic QE). Building on this and to address the aforementioned challenges, our work proposes to leverage domain-specific QE to assist in the selection of ICEs, with the goal of determining the suboptimal number and combination of ICEs to maximize MT quality, all without reference translations. As QE would assess the impact of different ICE combinations and sequences, we hypothesize that this integration has the potential to not only improve translation performance but also reduce processing time, as QE could result in smaller sets of ICEs, which would reduce the inference times (Petrov et al., 2023). This is particularly crucial considering the limited number of ICEs that can be fed into LLMs (Agrawal et al., 2023). Therefore, our study aims to investigate the feasibility of selecting ICEs on a per-source basis. Specifically, we aim to answer the following research question (RQ): *How effective are domain-specific QE models in determining ICEs for translation tasks in an LLM?*

Our proposed ICL methodology for MT combines an unsupervised retriever to select ICEs with QE to assess their impact on the translation quality, determining which ICE combination to include. Instead of feeding all selected examples, we only select examples whose QE points to maximizing the LLM translation quality.

Our findings on German-English translations demonstrate that our proposed approach outperforms the current SOTA ICL methods for MT as well as a fine-tuned mBART-50 (Tang et al., 2020).

2 ICL Using Quality Estimation for MT

To utilize LLMs for effective MT, as noted in Section 1, what is needed is a set of examples to provide the context (and thus guide or steer the LLM toward a correct, context-specific translation) — that is, a set of ICEs — and what is further important is the number of ICEs and their combination.[2] Ultimately, what is required is that the ICEs provide context that is neither too specific nor too broad and can effectively boost the translation. Our goal with this work is to develop a methodology that optimizes both these aspects in order to deliver high-quality MT. Our methodology for identifying effective ICEs involves two key components: (1) an unsupervised retriever that locates examples closely related to the sentence to be translated and (2) a search algorithm that uses QE to select a combination of examples that leads to the improvement of translation quality, i.e., aiming to maximize the BLEU score.

2.1 Unsupervised Retriever Ranking

We employ the *BM25* ranking algorithm (Trotman et al., 2014) due to the effective utilization of unsupervised retriever methods demonstrated in previous research, such as (Agrawal et al., 2023). BM25 sorts training pairs (source text and their translations) based on their relevance to a given query, i.e. the sentence to be translated. Subsequently, we select the top K sentence pairs ranked by the algorithm, where K is a hyperparameter that controls the number of pairs to be fed into the search algorithm.

2.2 Search Algorithm Coupled with QE

Our search algorithm comprises three main phases: *Selection, Translation*, and *Estimation*. During the Selection phase, the algorithm selects the highest-ranked training example from the initial ICEs provided by the unsupervised retriever ranking method (out of K ICEs). This selected example is then concatenated with the previously selected ICEs. In the first iteration, no ICEs have been selected before. In the Translation phase, the selected ICE is translated by the model. In the Estimation phase, the LLM output (translated text) and the original source text are inputted into the domain-specific QE model to estimate the quality of the translation. Our proposed methodology relies on sentence-level QE.

Next, the selected ICE, together with its estimated quality and the LLM translation output, are appended to an intermediate list. To track the highest quality obtained thus far, the algorithm sorts the list in descending order based on the estimated quality. To avoid duplication, the selected ICE is removed before the next iteration. This iterative process continues until the best-estimated translation quality no longer improves within the specified pa-

[2]The question of the order of examples is not specifically discussed in this paper but is left for future work.

tience threshold. Alternatively, the process terminates once all K ICEs have been selected.

This methodology allows for the systematic selection of ICEs that improve translation quality compared to previous ICL methodologies while efficiently managing the computational resources required for the search process. This efficiency is achieved by integrating early stopping conditions with predetermined patience. Notably, we do not explore permutations of initial ICEs, as doing so would require a large number of attempts, leading to high computational costs during the search process.[3]

3 Experiments Setup

We conducted four main experiments to test the effectiveness of our methodology. Three of these experiments compare our methodology to existing ICL ones in different settings, or *Modes*. The fourth experiment compares our methodology to a fine-tuned mBART-50, aiming to assess which method is preferred (with respect to obtaining better translations).

It is important to note that we do not fine-tune the LLM. The process of building the QE model used in our experiments is detailed in Section 3.2.

3.1 Search Algorithm

We conducted experiments using the search algorithm outlined in Section 2.2 across three operational modes:

Mode 1: This mode uses QE with ICEs ordered by BM25 to assess the effectiveness of combining BM25 and QE in the proposed ICL methodology.

Mode 2: This mode investigates the impact of ordering ICEs by n-gram overlap, particularly unigrams, alongside QE, on the proposed methodology. Given the success of ordering ICEs based on their n-gram overlap match with the source, as demonstrated in (Agrawal et al., 2023), we assess how this ordering, based on ICEs' n-gram overlap with the source text, influences the translation quality. This involves reordering ICEs according to their n-gram overlap, which is calculated using the NLTK word tokenizer. Higher overlap matches prioritize ICEs in the list and feed them into LLMs earlier.

Mode 3: Instead of relying on QE, in this mode, we compute the BLUE score on the existing **test set**. This approach is not a realistic case, but it is the most favorable scenario, and we use it as the highest bound to compare with Mode 1.

The search algorithm generates up to 16 candidates. In each mode, we conducted experiments using three early stopping patience values (3, 8, and 16), determining the maximum number of ICEs (K) generated. We included Patience 16, which implies no early stopping, to evaluate the model's performance with the maximum ICEs. Additionally, the search process halts if the estimated label reaches or exceeds 100, preventing further evaluations.

3.2 Quality Estimation

Following (Ranasinghe et al., 2020; Lee, 2020; Sharami et al., 2023), we develop a domain-specific QE model. First, we trained a QE model using out-of-domain (OOD) data (as detailed in Section 3.2.1) to ensure generalizability; and second, we fine-tuned the model using the training set described in Section 3.4 to provide domain-specific QE model and address domain mismatch, which is critical (Koehn and Knowles, 2017).

In our experiments, we used BLEU as the quality label because our study focused on translation performance rather than post-editing effort, which is typically evaluated using (H)TER (Specia and Farzindar, 2010). We employed the "MonoTransQuest" architecture from the TransQuest framework (Ranasinghe et al., 2020), known for its success in prior QE studies. However, instead of employing softmax computation, we directly utilized logits to estimate the quality labels. This strategy saves computation time, as softmax computation can be resource-intensive (Ruder, 2016).

3.2.1 QE data

We utilized the German-English "EuroPat" dataset, accessed through Opus (Tiedemann, 2012), to develop our generic QE model. We chose this dataset because it provides ample data samples, ensuring broad coverage of vocabulary — a critical aspect in developing generic models.

However, as MT datasets like EuroPat typically consist of pairs of source and translated text, it was necessary to synthetically create post-editing text

[3] A pseudocode outlining the search methodology can be found in Algorithm 1 in the Appendix. The phases of translating a source text of a test set using our methodology are depicted in Figure 2.

(since the QE data creation process requires a triplet input: source text, machine-translated text, and post-edited text). To accomplish this, we used a pre-trained multilingual MT model, namely mBART-50 that supported the language pair used in our experiment. This involves translating 1M randomly chosen source texts from EuroPat. Afterward, the resulting translations were considered as machine-translated text, with the corresponding reference translations acting as post-edited text.

Using SacreBLEU, we calculated the BLEU score, comparing the translated text with its corresponding post-edited text. This approach, which has been demonstrated to be effective in QE (Negri et al., 2018; Lee, 2020; Sharami et al., 2023), enabled us to use the source and (machine-) translated text as input and the BLEU score as the target value for the QE model. For building domain-specific QE, we utilized the training set detailed in Section 3.4 and applied the aforementioned approach to synthetically generate BLEU scores for the entire dataset.

3.3 Multilingual Large Language Model

For our experiments and hypothesis validation, we used XGLM (Lin et al., 2022). This choice stems from the outstanding performance of the model in the MT field. This also ensures a fair comparison of our proposed methodology with previous research, such as (Agrawal et al., 2023), which introduced SOTA approaches in ICL for MT.

We used the 7.5 billion-parameter XGLM implementation and tokenizer by Hugging Face[4], consistent with previous research. We employed a template from Lin et al. (2022) to maximize translation performance. $< /s >$ serves as the ICE separator in this template. "BLANK" denotes an empty string within the template.

$$\{\text{source text}_1\} = \{\text{target text}_1\} < /s >$$
$$\{\text{source text}_2\} = \{\text{target text}_2\} < /s >$$
$$\ldots = \ldots < /s >$$
$$\{\text{source text}_n\} = \text{BLANK}$$

3.4 Dataset and Evaluation Metrics

We used a dataset comprising German-to-English translation pairs within the IT domain, sourced from (Aharoni and Goldberg, 2020). This dataset was chosen due to the challenges that MT systems and LLMs face when translating out-of-domain contexts, particularly in specialized fields, as noted in previous studies (Koehn and Knowles, 2017; Agrawal et al., 2023). The specialized and constrained nature of the IT domain provided an ideal setting for evaluating our methodology's performance under these conditions.

The dataset utilized in this study consisted of approximately 222k training sentences, 2k development sentences, and 2k test sentences. To assess the translation effectiveness of the models, we employed metrics such as BLEU from SacreBLEU (Post, 2018) and COMET (Rei et al., 2020).

3.5 Number of ICEs

We use between 1 and 16 ICEs. These may originate either from a random approach or from an advanced (guided) selection. To keep these separated in our analysis, we designate two different counts – p and q. This choice and naming convention is grounded by previous research exploring the impact of varying ICE numbers. While our study explicitly caps the upper limit of q at 16, values spanning from 1 to 16 remain feasible options — unlike the fixed value in the compared systems.

3.6 Compared Systems

We conducted a comparative analysis with methods from previous studies; *random* and *task-level sampling*, *BM25*, *R-BM25*, and *fine-tuned mBART-50*.

Random: We conducted three random trials, generating random numbers based on parameter p. These numbers, ranging from 1 to the size of the training set, selected corresponding translation pairs. To create the prompt[5], in addition to the training examples (i.e., ICEs), we need the source side intended for translation. We utilize the source from the development set, in contrast to the advanced methods in ICL, where the source text from the test set is typically employed. The reason for selecting the development set over the test set in this approach is that development sets are generally from the same distribution, domain, and context as the test set. This similarity increases the likelihood that the examples in the development set will better match the content and context of the test set, thereby enhancing the rel-

[4]https://huggingface.co/docs/transformers/model_doc/xglm

[5]In the literature, the term "prompt" is frequently used interchangeably with "ICE"

evance and effectiveness of the prompts.

The generated prompt is inputted into the LLM for translation. Then, the BLEU score of the development set is computed. The random number that produces the highest score among the trials is selected, and the training examples linked to this number are concatenated with the test set's source text.

Task-level: Based on the work of Agrawal et al. (2023), the task-level approach is similar to the random approach but differs in the number of trials used. We employ 100 trials for the task-level approach, a significantly higher number than the random approach. The reason for using more trials is to generate a greater variety of ICEs, aiming to enhance the performance of LLMs in the translation task. However, this results in longer execution times compared to the random approach.

BM25: Using the Moses Tokenizer (Koehn et al., 2007), we first tokenize the training set's source samples. Then, a BM25 model is created for the tokenized corpus by employing the *BM25Okapi* implementation within the *rank_bm25* package.[6]

Next, the test set is tokenized using the tokenized source. The algorithm then searches for similar training samples based on BM25 criteria, selecting the top q matches for the model. This methodology utilizes the test set as opposed to random and task-level approaches using the development set.

Re-rank BM25 (R-BM25): BM25 aims to find translation examples with the highest n-gram overlap with the source sentence (Luo et al., 2023). However, since retrieved examples score independently, top matches may lack coverage of all source n-grams. This poses an issue in ICL due to LLM input size limitations. To address this, Agrawal et al. (2023) proposed R-BM25. R-BM25 employs a recall-based n-gram overlap (Agrawal et al., 2023) to extract word n-grams and their numbers from the test source and BM25 retrieved examples.

Fine-tuning mBART-50: Different ICL methodologies, including our own, are assessed in comparison to the process of fine-tuning a pre-trained multilingual MT model, specifically mBART-50. The selection of mBART-50 is based on its alignment with the language specifications of the experiment and its proven track record of achieving success in MT tasks through the utilization of pre-trained models (Yuan et al., 2022; Pham et al., 2022). The fine-tuning of mBART-50 is carried out using the training data outlined in Section 3.4.

[6]https://github.com/dorianbrown/rank_bm25

[7]https://github.com/lfwa/carbontracker

3.7 Computational Costs

We monitored and reported the computational costs of the models utilized in our experiments using the *carbontracker* package.[7] This involved calculating the carbon footprint (CO_2eq) emissions, time to prediction (TTP), and electricity consumption (kWh) associated with our experiments. Our experiments were conducted using NVIDIA A40 GPUs.

The script for running our experiments is publicly available at `anynomous.com`.

4 Experiments Results

This section presents the results of our experiments. To ensure a fair comparison, we conducted a statistical analysis test (t-test) to determine if our models significantly outperformed the baseline.

Comparing to previous work, the results shown in Table 1, indicate that R-BM25 with 16 ICEs outperforms other methods. It is notable that there is a positive correlation between the number of examples and evaluation scores (consistent through all methods – Random, Task-level, BM25, and R-BM25), although at the expense of prediction time (i.e., TTP). Employing 16 examples significantly improved performance compared to using only one example in the random approach.

Analyzing the performance of our methods in Mode 1 (referred to as "M 1", with P = 3, 8, or 16 in Table 1), we observe that our proposed methodology with different patience thresholds consistently outperforms all previous methods, including the baseline. This trend holds for both the COMET and BLEU metrics across all the methods. Specifically, our method exhibits a minimum improvement of 0.52 points in the BLEU score (from 45.20 to 45.72) with patience threshold of 3 and a maximum improvement of 1.58 points in the BLEU score (from 45.20 to 46.78) with a patience threshold of 16 compared to R-BM25 with 16 examples.

Method	$p+q$	BLEU	COMET	TTP (hh:mm)	CO2 (kg)	GPU (kWh)
Random	1 + 0	10.38	0.6895	01:51	00.13	00.39
Random	16 + 0	31.65	0.7844	02:20	00.19	00.58
Task-level	1 + 0	29.17	0.7586	62:50	09.83	29.10
Task-level	16 + 0	32.88	0.8083	78:30	12.80	35.91
BM25	0 + 1	39.24	0.7833	00:56	00.06	00.19
BM25	0 + 16	44.50	0.8120	00:58	00.07	00.19
R-BM25	0 + 1	40.88	0.7990	01:01	00.06	00.21
R-BM25	0 + 16	**45.20**	**0.8218**	01:04	00.07	00.21
M 1, P = 3	0 + 16	45.72	0.8395	01:49	00.22	00.67
M 1, P = 8	0 + 16	**46.43**	**0.8501**	03:48	00.50	01.51
M 1, P = 16	0 + 16	**46.78**	**0.8554**	05:11	00.68	02.05
M 2, P = 3	0 + 16	46.05	0.8400	01:30	00.21	00.64
M 2, P = 8	0 + 16	**46.59**	**0.8518**	03:52	00.51	01.52
M 2, P = 16	0 + 16	**46.52**	**0.8564**	05:00	00.66	02.01
M 3, P = 3	0 + 16	49.89	0.8532	01:36	00.22	00.66
M 3, P = 8	0 + 16	**52.63**	**0.8725**	03:14	00.45	01.40
M 3, P = 16	0 + 16	**53.50**	**0.8791**	04:08	00.55	01.65
mBART-50	N/A	42.76	0.8659	11:20	01.88	04.82

Table 1: **Method Performance in BLEU and COMET Scores.** M 1 to 3 denotes Mode 1 to 3; P is the patience value; p and q are as defined in Section 3.5. "N/A" (not applicable) indicates that fine-tuning does not use ICEs. Bold font represents the highest translation performance. Two numbers are in bold if they are statistically similar (t-test, $p\_value = 0.05$).

Consequently, our methods in Mode 1 are ranked based on their performance, with patience 3 being the least effective model, followed by patience 8, and finally patience 16, representing the most effective method. This ranking indicates that increasing the patience threshold can significantly enhance the translation performance. However, the improvement with patience 16 is not statistically significant compared to patience 8, suggesting that more ICEs do not necessarily enhance translation performance. Similarly, while more substantial contextual improvement (as indicated by the COMET) is observed at the maximum patience threshold (16), it is not statistically significant compared to patience 8.

The Mode 2 results demonstrate that all three patience thresholds surpass the methods in the literature. However, this improvement is not statistically significant when compared with the respective experiments in Mode 1. This suggests that ordering the examples according to n-gram (unigram) similarity does not enhance the translation performance in our methodology.

When it comes to Mode 3, we should stress that this is an unrealistic scenario, but used as the highest bound. The results indicate that with a patience of 3, the BLEU score is 4.17 points lower (49.89-45.72). With a patience of 8, this gap increases to 6.2 points (52.63-46.43), and with a patience of 16, it widens further to 6.72 points (53.50-46.78). These differences arise from the QE model estimations in our experiment compared to the scenario where reference labels are available to the search algorithm.

4.1 Time to Prediction (TTP)

Among the methods examined, task-level execution required the most time, with approximately 62 hours for one example and 78 hours for 16 examples. Our method (Mode 1) with a patience value of 16 is relatively time-intensive, taking approximately 5 hours, while a patience value of 3 is comparable to the baseline method, differing by only around 50 minutes. Mode 2 is nearly equivalent to Mode 1 in terms of TTP, whereas Mode 3, where the reference labels are accessed, requires less time than Modes 1 and 2. In addition, the search algorithm incorporates a termination condition, and given that QE estimation rarely triggers this condition, numerous ICEs are left unattempted, resulting in significant time savings.

It is also important to note the time required to train the QE models used in the prediction process. As provided in Appendix 3, the training time for the generic QE model is $+/-$ 5 hours and 55 minutes, while the specific QE model takes about $+/-$ 6 hours and 54 minutes. Although these training times are significant, it is crucial to recognize that QE models, similar to MT models, can be reused for the same language pair and domain, thereby amortizing the initial training cost over multiple predictions.

The last row of Table 1 shows the scores of the translations obtained with the mBART-50 model fine-tuned on the same training set as in ICL. Despite mBART-50 being tailored for MT across 50 languages, it did not outperform the R-BM25 method with 16 examples (best from the existing methods); it was better only than Random, Task-level, BM25, and R-BM25, each with only 1 example. However, when considering translation performance from a contextual perspective, the COMET results indicate that fine-tuning mBART-50 leads to superior performance compared with lexical overlap. Nevertheless, fine-tuning took significantly longer than identifying ICEs and obtaining inferences from the XGLM.

Compared to our methodology, especially when considering the least performing method (M 1, P = 3), it is significantly worse – 6.47% (42.76 to 45.72). This highlights the substantial efficacy of ICL compared to fine-tuning. Nonetheless, it is noteworthy that various factors might contribute to this observation: e.g., the model's size might be a critical factor, especially during deployment, where larger models like XGLM could pose challenges.

5 Analysis

Output analysis Pre-trained LLMs often exhibit over-generation, i.e., the generation of a larger number of tokens than expected by a human (in comparison to a reference), necessitating extensive post-processing (e.g., post-editing) (Bawden and Yvon, 2023). Figure 1 shows the tokenized output lengths (translations) for our model (Mode 1, patience 8),[8] alongside the R-BM25 with 16 examples. The analysis shows that the length distributions for both models align with the reference distribution, suggesting that the models do not over-generate.

To quantitatively compare these distributions to the reference, we employed the Kolmogorov-Smirnov (KS) test (Kolmogorov, 1933). The results indicate that for R-BM25 versus the reference, the KS statistic is relatively high (0.0749), reflecting a significant difference between the translation lengths of R-BM25 and the reference distribution. The extremely low p-value (2.39×10^{-5}) further confirms this significant discrepancy. Conversely, for Mode 1 with P=8 versus the reference, the KS statistic is considerably lower (0.0232), indicating a much smaller difference in translation lengths. The higher p-value (0.6451) suggests no significant difference, implying that the distribution of Mode 1, P=8 is similar to the reference distribution.

These findings suggest that our proposed methodology could yield translations closer in length to the reference, potentially reducing the need for labor-intensive post-processing efforts and enhancing computational efficiency.

[8]Our other models in Mode 1 exhibited similar distributions.

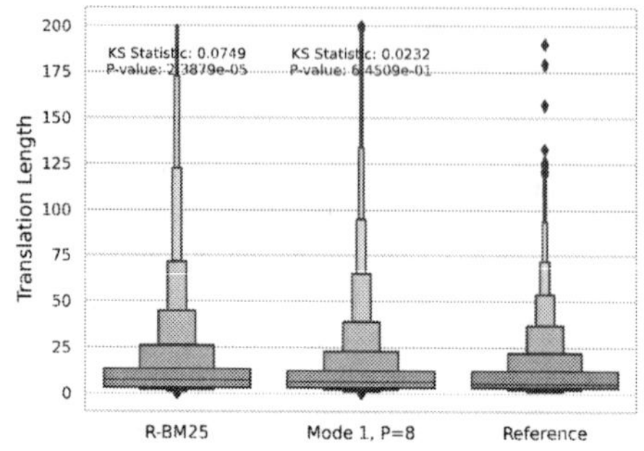

Figure 1: **Tokenized Translation Lengths** comparison between R-BM25, our Mode 1, P=8, and the reference. "KS" denotes the Kolmogorov-Smirnov test, with the p-value indicating significance.

ICE Number Analysis The number of selected ICEs holds a significant importance within the ICL algorithm, as it directly impacts the token processing time and the capacity of LLMs to handle additional ICE instances. We analyzed the number of ICEs that our algorithm selected across all three modes. The results (Table 2) show that the minimum number of ICEs selected is 1, while the maximum is: 12 for Mode 1, 16 for Mode 2, and 16 for Mode 3. The average (mean) number of ICEs is found to be lowest in Mode 3 and highest in Mode 1. In addition, Mode 2 results in a reduction in the number of ICEs within our proposed algorithm. The notably lower average number of ICE instances in Mode 3 can be attributed to its access to the test set, allowing for the selection of optimal ICE combinations based on test set performance and activating an early stopping condition if the score exceeds 100. Contrarily, while Mode 1 exhibits similarities to Mode 3, its relatively higher average can be linked to inaccuracies in QE estimation. Moreover, our analysis shows that QE estimations rarely reach a score of 100, thus rendering the early stopping condition inactive.

Mode	Min	Mean	Max
#1	[1, 1, 1]	[2.25, 3.76, 4.84]	[12, 16, 16]
#2	[1, 1, 1]	[2.20, 3.70, 4.74]	[12, 16, 16]
#3	[1, 1, 1]	[2.15, 3.47, 4.47]	[12, 16, 16]

Table 2: **Number of ICEs selected for each mode at different patience thresholds.** Labels [x, y, z] correspond to patience values 3, 8, and 16.

CO_2 Emissions Our analysis reveals that using XGLM for translation yields lower CO_2 emissions than fine-tuning mBART-50, making it a more environmentally sustainable choice. In Mode 1 of our proposed methodology, with patience 16, XGLM emitted 0.68 KG of CO_2, while fine-tuning mBART-50 emitted 1.88 KG. Interestingly, the task-level method with 16 ICEs emitted the highest amount of CO_2, totaling 12.80 KG. Our proposed approach leads to higher CO_2 emissions than R-BM25.

6 Related Work

ICL for MT. ICL[9] represents a relatively new paradigm in natural language understanding. Unlike traditional fine-tuning approaches, where a PLM undergoes parameter updates using a specific dataset, ICL typically directly generates the output without any modification to its parameters (Radford et al., 2019; Brown et al., 2020). This is achieved by solely providing the model with a few examples, known as ICEs, which prime the PLM to enhance its performance for the given task (Jiang et al., 2020).

As shown by Vilar et al. (2023), the quality of translation is directly proportionate to the quality of ICEs, where quality refers to ICEs being relevant, clear, accurate, and domain-specific. However, considering all ICEs during processing is computationally demanding (Alves et al., 2023). Hence, it is crucial to selectively choose ICEs that can enhance MT quality. Goyal et al. (2022) conducted a study where ICEs were randomly selected. Despite finding that this random selection of ICEs resulted in good translation performance, the neglect of their order, which was identified as important (Liu et al., 2022; Lu et al., 2022), was a drawback in this approach. To address this, methodologies such as (Agrawal et al., 2023) introduced a re-ranking technique (R-BM25). However, their methodology relies solely on n-grams to order examples, which can enhance fluency but may overlook contextual factors. In our approach, we investigated the unigram order of initial ICEs provided by the BM25 algorithm. We leave the in-depth analysis of ICE order for future work. Additionally, Kumar et al. (2023) highlighted the advantages of using multiple features in ICE selection to improve translation quality, while our QE-based approach simplifies ICE selection without needing to generate additional features, ensuring efficiency.

QE in MT Evaluation. QE models offer a quick solution to the assessment of the overall usefulness of translated text. These models do not rely on reference translations, thereby reducing the human effort required for quality evaluation (Tamchyna, 2021; Murgolo et al., 2022; Zerva et al., 2022; Blain et al., 2023). Similar to MT models, previous studies highlight the importance of domain-specific QE for accurately estimating translation quality across diverse domains (Lee, 2020; Sharami et al., 2023). This is why, in our work, we employed a domain-specific QE model instead of a generic one to enhance the selection of ICEs.

Integrating QE into ICL offers significant, yet largely unexplored, potential. QE can also better capture out-of-domain gender and word-sense-disambiguation errors (Dinh and Niehues, 2023). Additionally, integrating QE can mitigate reference bias, a significant challenge in accurately estimating the output quality of LLMs (Goyal et al., 2023; Raunak et al., 2023b). The introduction of COMET-QE (Raunak et al., 2023a) exemplifies this pursuit, providing a metric tailored to evaluate the quality of perturbed prompts provided to GPT-3 (Brown et al., 2020), aiming to mitigate reference bias. While in our approach, we employ domain-specific QE to guide the selection of ICEs, this underscores the potential of QE in refining LLM inputs (i.e., ICEs).

7 Conclusion

We propose a novel in-context learning (ICL) methodology for enhancing the translation capabilities of large language models (LLMs) while optimizing computational resources. Our approach leverages domain-specific quality estimation (QE) to guide in-context selection, particularly focusing on determining the suboptimal number and the combinations of in-context examples (ICEs). This novel strategy moves beyond the conventional reliance solely on translation references from development sets seen in prior methods.

We evaluated our approach across different modes and early stopping patience values on the German-to-English IT dataset. Our experiments consistently showed the superior performance of our methodology, surpassing all prior works across both

[9] Also referred to as the prompt retrieval method

BLEU and COMET metrics. Our method consistently improves BLEU scores, although this comes at the cost of increased computation time. We also investigated the impact of ordering the ICEs based on their unigram overlap with the source text and found it to be not statistically significant. Furthermore, our experiments highlighted the value of ICL compared to fine-tuning a pre-trained large model, namely mBART-50. We also highlighted that our method leads to less carbon emissions while achieving better translation performance.

In the future, we would like to conduct further research on the impact of our proposed methodology across different language pairs, domains and LLMs. Also, we aim to explore alternative metrics beyond BLEU to tailor the selection process, as well as additional features such as bigram, type/token ratio, and length when ordering examples prior to their input into LLMs.

8 Acknowledgments

We would like to thank the anonymous reviewers for their helpful comments.

References

Agrawal, S., Zhou, C., Lewis, M., Zettlemoyer, L., and Ghazvininejad, M. (2023). In-context examples selection for machine translation. In Rogers, A., Boyd-Graber, J., and Okazaki, N., editors, *Findings of the Association for Computational Linguistics: ACL 2023*, pages 8857–8873, Toronto, Canada. Association for Computational Linguistics.

Aharoni, R. and Goldberg, Y. (2020). Unsupervised domain clusters in pretrained language models. In *Proceedings of the 58th Annual Meeting of the Association for Computational Linguistics (Volume 1: Long Papers)*. Association for Computational Linguistics.

Alves, D., Guerreiro, N., Alves, J., Pombal, J., Rei, R., de Souza, J., Colombo, P., and Martins, A. (2023). Steering large language models for machine translation with finetuning and in-context learning. In Bouamor, H., Pino, J., and Bali, K., editors, *Findings of the Association for Computational Linguistics: EMNLP 2023*, pages 11127–11148, Singapore. Association for Computational Linguistics.

Bawden, R. and Yvon, F. (2023). Investigating the translation performance of a large multilingual language model: the case of BLOOM. In Nurminen, M., Brenner, J., Koponen, M., Latomaa, S., Mikhailov, M., Schierl, F., Ranasinghe, T., Vanmassenhove, E., Vidal, S. A., Aranberri, N., Nunziatini, M., Escartín, C. P., Forcada, M., Popovic, M., Scarton, C., and Moniz, H., editors, *Proceedings of the 24th Annual Conference of the European Association for Machine Translation*, pages 157–170, Tampere, Finland. European Association for Machine Translation.

Blain, F., Zerva, C., Rei, R., Guerreiro, N. M., Kanojia, D., C. de Souza, J. G., Silva, B., Vaz, T., Jingxuan, Y., Azadi, F., Orasan, C., and Martins, A. (2023). Findings of the WMT 2023 shared task on quality estimation. In Koehn, P., Haddow, B., Kocmi, T., and Monz, C., editors, *Proceedings of the Eighth Conference on Machine Translation*, pages 629–653, Singapore. Association for Computational Linguistics.

Brown, T., Mann, B., Ryder, N., Subbiah, M., Kaplan, J. D., Dhariwal, P., Neelakantan, A., Shyam, P., Sastry, G., Askell, A., Agarwal, S., Herbert-Voss, A., Krueger, G., Henighan, T., Child, R., Ramesh, A., Ziegler, D., Wu, J., Winter, C., Hesse, C., Chen, M., Sigler, E., Litwin, M., Gray, S., Chess, B., Clark, J., Berner, C., McCandlish, S., Radford, A., Sutskever, I., and Amodei, D. (2020). Language models are few-shot learners. In Larochelle, H., Ranzato, M., Hadsell, R., Balcan, M., and Lin, H., editors, *Advances in Neural Information Processing Systems*, volume 33, pages 1877–1901. Curran Associates, Inc.

Dinh, T. A. and Niehues, J. (2023). Perturbation-based QE: An explainable, unsupervised word-level quality estimation method for blackbox machine translation. In Utiyama, M. and Wang, R., editors, *Proceedings of Machine Translation Summit XIX, Vol. 1: Research Track*, pages 59–71, Macau SAR, China. Asia-Pacific Association for Machine Translation.

Goyal, N., Gao, C., Chaudhary, V., Chen, P.-J., Wenzek, G., Ju, D., Krishnan, S., Ranzato, M., Guzmán, F., and Fan, A. (2022). The Flores-101 evaluation benchmark for low-resource and multilingual machine translation. *Transactions of the Association for Computational Linguistics*, 10:522–538.

Goyal, T., Li, J. J., and Durrett, G. (2023). News summarization and evaluation in the era of gpt-3.

Jiang, Z., Xu, F. F., Araki, J., and Neubig, G. (2020). How Can We Know What Language Models Know? *Trans-*

actions of the Association for Computational Linguistics, 8:423–438.

Koehn, P., Hoang, H., Birch, A., Callison-Burch, C., Federico, M., Bertoldi, N., Cowan, B., Shen, W., Moran, C., Zens, R., Dyer, C., Bojar, O., Constantin, A., and Herbst, E. (2007). Moses: Open source toolkit for statistical machine translation. In Ananiadou, S., editor, *Proceedings of the 45th Annual Meeting of the Association for Computational Linguistics Companion Volume Proceedings of the Demo and Poster Sessions*, pages 177–180, Prague, Czech Republic. Association for Computational Linguistics.

Koehn, P. and Knowles, R. (2017). Six challenges for neural machine translation. In Luong, T., Birch, A., Neubig, G., and Finch, A., editors, *Proceedings of the First Workshop on Neural Machine Translation*, pages 28–39, Vancouver. Association for Computational Linguistics.

Kolmogorov, A. N. (1933). Sulla determinazione empirica di una legge di distribuzione. *Giornale dell'Istituto Italiano degli Attuari*, 4:83–91.

Kumar, A., Puduppully, R., Dabre, R., and Kunchukuttan, A. (2023). CTQScorer: Combining multiple features for in-context example selection for machine translation. In Bouamor, H., Pino, J., and Bali, K., editors, *Findings of the Association for Computational Linguistics: EMNLP 2023*, pages 7736–7752, Singapore. Association for Computational Linguistics.

Lee, D. (2020). Two-phase cross-lingual language model fine-tuning for machine translation quality estimation. In Barrault, L., Bojar, O., Bougares, F., Chatterjee, R., Costa-jussà, M. R., Federmann, C., Fishel, M., Fraser, A., Graham, Y., Guzman, P., Haddow, B., Huck, M., Yepes, A. J., Koehn, P., Martins, A., Morishita, M., Monz, C., Nagata, M., Nakazawa, T., and Negri, M., editors, *Proceedings of the Fifth Conference on Machine Translation*, pages 1024–1028, Online. Association for Computational Linguistics.

Lin, X. V., Mihaylov, T., Artetxe, M., Wang, T., Chen, S., Simig, D., Ott, M., Goyal, N., Bhosale, S., Du, J., Pasunuru, R., Shleifer, S., Koura, P. S., Chaudhary, V., O'Horo, B., Wang, J., Zettlemoyer, L., Kozareva, Z., Diab, M., Stoyanov, V., and Li, X. (2022). Few-shot learning with multilingual generative language models. In Goldberg, Y., Kozareva, Z., and Zhang, Y., editors, *Proceedings of the 2022 Conference on Empirical Methods in Natural Language Processing*, pages 9019–9052, Abu Dhabi, United Arab Emirates. Association for Computational Linguistics.

Liu, J., Shen, D., Zhang, Y., Dolan, B., Carin, L., and Chen, W. (2022). What makes good in-context examples for GPT-3? In Agirre, E., Apidianaki, M., and Vulić, I., editors, *Proceedings of Deep Learning Inside Out (DeeLIO 2022): The 3rd Workshop on Knowledge Extraction and Integration for Deep Learning Architectures*, pages 100–114, Dublin, Ireland and Online. Association for Computational Linguistics.

Lu, Y., Bartolo, M., Moore, A., Riedel, S., and Stenetorp, P. (2022). Fantastically ordered prompts and where to find them: Overcoming few-shot prompt order sensitivity. In Muresan, S., Nakov, P., and Villavicencio, A., editors, *Proceedings of the 60th Annual Meeting of the Association for Computational Linguistics (Volume 1: Long Papers)*, pages 8086–8098, Dublin, Ireland. Association for Computational Linguistics.

Luo, M., Xu, X., Dai, Z., Pasupat, P., Kazemi, M., Baral, C., Imbrasaite, V., and Zhao, V. Y. (2023). Dr.icl: Demonstration-retrieved in-context learning.

Murgolo, E., Sharami, J. P. R., and Shterionov, D. (2022). A quality estimation and quality evaluation tool for the translation industry. In *Proceedings of the 23rd Annual Conference of the European Association for Machine Translation*, pages 307–308, Ghent, Belgium. European Association for Machine Translation.

Negri, M., Turchi, M., Chatterjee, R., and Bertoldi, N. (2018). ESCAPE: a large-scale synthetic corpus for automatic post-editing. In *Proceedings of the Eleventh International Conference on Language Resources and Evaluation (LREC 2018)*, Miyazaki, Japan. European Language Resources Association (ELRA).

Petrov, A., Malfa, E. L., Torr, P. H. S., and Bibi, A. (2023). Language model tokenizers introduce unfairness between languages.

Pham, N.-Q., Nguyen, T. N., Nguyen, T.-B., Liu, D., Mullov, C., Niehues, J., and Waibel, A. (2022). Effective combination of pretrained models - KIT@IWSLT2022. In Salesky, E., Federico, M., and Costa-jussà, M., editors, *Proceedings of the 19th International Conference on Spoken Language Translation (IWSLT 2022)*, pages 190–197, Dublin, Ireland (in-person and online). Association for Computational Linguistics.

Post, M. (2018). A call for clarity in reporting BLEU scores. In *Proceedings of the Third Conference on Machine Translation: Research Papers*, pages 186–191, Belgium, Brussels. Association for Computational Linguistics.

Radford, A., Wu, J., Child, R., Luan, D., Amodei, D., and Sutskever, I. (2019). Language models are unsupervised multitask learners.

Ranasinghe, T., Orasan, C., and Mitkov, R. (2020). TransQuest: Translation quality estimation with cross-lingual transformers. In Scott, D., Bel, N., and Zong, C., editors, *Proceedings of the 28th International Conference on Computational Linguistics*, pages 5070–5081, Barcelona, Spain (Online). International Committee on Computational Linguistics.

Raunak, V., Menezes, A., and Awadalla, H. (2023a). Dissecting in-context learning of translations in GPT-3. In Bouamor, H., Pino, J., and Bali, K., editors, *Findings of the Association for Computational Linguistics: EMNLP 2023*, pages 866–872, Singapore. Association for Computational Linguistics.

Raunak, V., Menezes, A., Post, M., and Hassan, H. (2023b). Do GPTs produce less literal translations? In Rogers, A., Boyd-Graber, J., and Okazaki, N., editors, *Proceedings of the 61st Annual Meeting of the Association for Computational Linguistics (Volume 2: Short Papers)*, pages 1041–1050, Toronto, Canada. Association for Computational Linguistics.

Rei, R., Stewart, C., Farinha, A. C., and Lavie, A. (2020). COMET: A neural framework for MT evaluation. In Webber, B., Cohn, T., He, Y., and Liu, Y., editors, *Proceedings of the 2020 Conference on Empirical Methods in Natural Language Processing (EMNLP)*, pages 2685–2702, Online. Association for Computational Linguistics.

Robertson, S. and Zaragoza, H. (2009). The probabilistic relevance framework: Bm25 and beyond. *Found. Trends Inf. Retr.*, 3(4):333–389.

Ruder, S. (2016). On word embeddings - Part 2: Approximating the Softmax. `http://ruder.io/word-embeddings-softmax`.

Sharami, J. P. R., Shterionov, D., Blain, F., Vanmassenhove, E., Sisto, M. D., Emmery, C., and Spronck, P. (2023). Tailoring domain adaptation for machine translation quality estimation. In Nurminen, M., Brenner, J., Koponen, M., Latomaa, S., Mikhailov, M., Schierl, F., Ranasinghe, T., Vanmassenhove, E., Vidal, S. A., Aranberri, N., Nunziatini, M., Escartín, C. P., Forcada, M., Popovic, M., Scarton, C., and Moniz, H., editors, *Proceedings of the 24th Annual Conference of the European Association for Machine Translation*, pages 9–20, Tampere, Finland. European Association for Machine Translation.

Sia, S. and Duh, K. (2023). In-context learning as maintaining coherency: A study of on-the-fly machine translation using large language models. In Utiyama, M. and Wang, R., editors, *Proceedings of Machine Translation Summit XIX, Vol. 1: Research Track*, pages 173–185, Macau SAR, China. Asia-Pacific Association for Machine Translation.

Specia, L. and Farzindar, A. (2010). Estimating machine translation post-editing effort with HTER. In Zhechev, V., editor, *Proceedings of the Second Joint EM+/CNGL Workshop: Bringing MT to the User: Research on Integrating MT in the Translation Industry*, pages 33–43, Denver, Colorado, USA. Association for Machine Translation in the Americas.

Tamchyna, A. (2021). Deploying MT quality estimation on a large scale: Lessons learned and open questions. In *Proceedings of Machine Translation Summit XVIII: Users and Providers Track*, pages 291–305, Virtual. Association for Machine Translation in the Americas.

Tang, Y., Tran, C., Li, X., Chen, P.-J., Goyal, N., Chaudhary, V., Gu, J., and Fan, A. (2020). Multilingual translation with extensible multilingual pretraining and finetuning.

Tiedemann, J. (2012). Parallel data, tools and interfaces in OPUS. In Calzolari, N., Choukri, K., Declerck, T., Doğan, M. U., Maegaard, B., Mariani, J., Moreno, A., Odijk, J., and Piperidis, S., editors, *Proceedings of the Eighth International Conference on Language Resources and Evaluation (LREC'12)*, pages 2214–2218, Istanbul, Turkey. European Language Resources Association (ELRA).

Trotman, A., Puurula, A., and Burgess, B. (2014). Improvements to bm25 and language models examined. In *Proceedings of the 19th Australasian Document Computing Symposium*, ADCS '14, page 58–65, New York, NY, USA. Association for Computing Machinery.

Vilar, D., Freitag, M., Cherry, C., Luo, J., Ratnakar, V., and Foster, G. (2023). Prompting PaLM for translation: Assessing strategies and performance. In Rogers, A., Boyd-Graber, J., and Okazaki, N., editors, *Proceedings of the 61st Annual Meeting of the Association for Computational Linguistics (Volume 1: Long Papers)*, pages 15406–15427, Toronto, Canada. Association for Computational Linguistics.

Xu, H., Kim, Y. J., Sharaf, A., and Awadalla, H. H. (2024). A paradigm shift in machine translation: Boosting translation performance of large language models.

Ye, N. and Li, J. (2023). A k-nearest neighbor approach for domain-specific translation quality estimation. In Feng, Y. and Feng, C., editors, *Machine Translation*, pages 69–80, Singapore. Springer Nature Singapore.

Yuan, B., Li, Y., Chen, K., Lu, H., Yang, M., and Cao, H. (2022). An improved multi-task approach to pre-trained model based mt quality estimation. In *CCMT*.

Zerva, C., Blain, F., Rei, R., Lertvittayakumjorn, P., C. De Souza, J. G., Eger, S., Kanojia, D., Alves, D., Orăsan, C., Fomicheva, M., Martins, A. F. T., and Specia, L. (2022). Findings of the WMT 2022 shared task on quality estimation. In *Proceedings of the Seventh Conference on Machine Translation (WMT)*, pages 69–99, Abu Dhabi, United Arab Emirates (Hybrid). Association for Computational Linguistics.

Zhu, W., Liu, H., Dong, Q., Xu, J., Huang, S., Kong, L., Chen, J., and Li, L. (2023). Multilingual machine translation with large language models: Empirical results and analysis.

Appendices

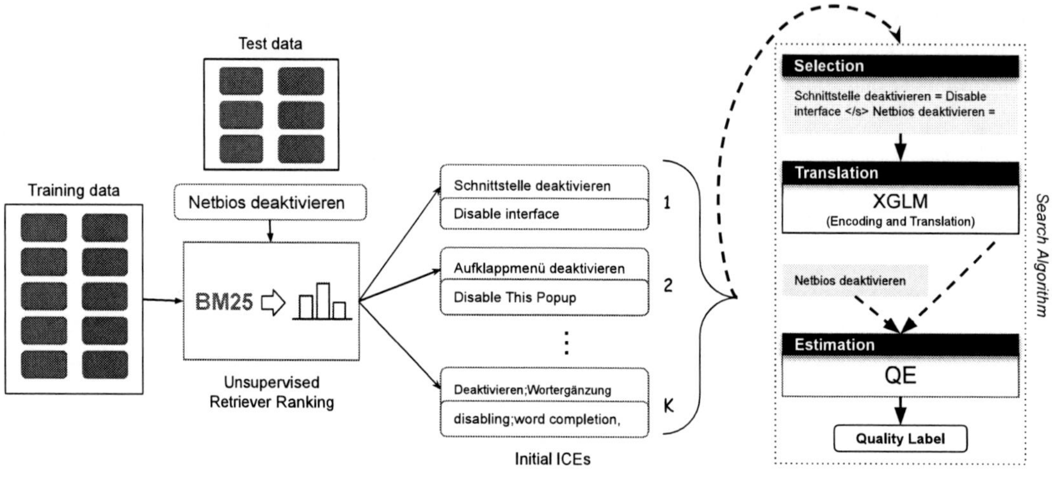

Figure 2: **Overview illustration showing an iteration of our proposed methodology.**

Metric	Generic Model	Specific Model
Training Time (hh:mm)	05:55	06:54
CO_2 Emissions (kg)	1.41	1.46
Electricity Consumption (kWh)	3.63	3.76

Table 3: **Training Time, CO_2 Emissions, and Electricity Consumption for QE Models.**

ICEs: Die Sockets, die im except Array aufgelistet sind, werden auf Ausnahmen überwacht. = The sockets listed in the except array will be watched for exceptions. $</s>$ Geben Sie den Namen der Variablen ein, deren Wert überwacht werden soll. = Enter the name of the variable whose value is to be monitored. $</s>$ Nur erlaubt bei Sockets für lokale Displays und den globalen Socket. = Permitted only on sockets of local displays and the global socket. $</s>$ Legt fest, ob Scandaten-Information, die in den MPEG2-Videoströmen enthalten sind, aktualisiert werden sollen. = This controls whether to update the scan data information contained in the MPEG-2 video streams. $</s>$ Die Sockets, die im write Array aufgelistet sind, werden daraufhin überwacht, ob ein Schreibvorgang den Socket blockiert. =
Translation: The sockets listed in the write array will be watched for whether a write operation blocks the socket.
Reference Label: The sockets listed in the write array will be watched to see if a write will not block.
QE: 67.59, **BLEU score (using reference label):** 52.89

Table 4: **An example of selected ICEs** for a source text, its corresponding translation, reference label, and QE estimation compared to the BLEU score computed based on the reference label.

```
function SEARCH(...)
    temp ← [("", 0.0, "")]
    prompt ← ""
    itr ← 0
    best_qe_score ← 0.0
    patience_counter ← 0
    while itr < iteration and patience_counter < early_stop_patience do
        available_Prompts ← GENERATEAVAILABLEPROMPTS(...)                ▷ Initial ICEs
        if available_prompts is not empty then
            selected_prompt_index ← itr mod k                        ▷ Phase 1: Selection
            selected_prompt ← available_prompts[selected_prompt_index]
            prompt ← CONSTRUCTFULLPROMPT(...)(see 3.3)
            input_ids[0] ← ENCODEPROMPT(...)                        ▷ Phase 2: Translation
            if length(input_ids) > LLM_max_length then
                return temp
            end if
            output ← GENERATEOUTPUT(...)
            final_output ← DECODEOUTPUT(...)
            qe_input ← PREPAREQEINPUT(source, final_output)         ▷ Phase 3: Estimation
            qe_score ← ESTIMATEQUALITY(qe_input, model_QE)
            temp.append((prompt, current_qe_score, final_output))
            if current_bleu_score ≥ 100 then
                return temp
            end if
            temp ← SORTTEMP(...)
            if qe_score ≤ best_qe_score then
                patience_counter ← patience_counter + 1
            else
                patience_counter ← 0
            end if
            best_qe_score ← temp[0][1]
        end if
        itr ← itr + 1
    end while
    return temp
end function
```

Algorithm 1: **Pseudocode outlining the proposed Search Algorithm.** Each phase of the methodology is annotated alongside the relevant code. Function arguments are omitted for simplicity. The first element of the returning list (*temp*) includes the selected prompt, its associated QE score, and the translated text.

Some Tradeoffs in Continual Learning for Parliamentary Neural Machine Translation Systems

Rebecca Knowles Rebecca.Knowles@nrc-cnrc.gc.ca
Samuel Larkin Samuel.Larkin@nrc-cnrc.gc.ca
Michel Simard Michel.Simard@nrc-cnrc.gc.ca
Marc Tessier Marc.Tessier@nrc-cnrc.gc.ca
Gabriel Bernier-Colborne Gabriel.Bernier-Colborne@nrc-cnrc.gc.ca
Cyril Goutte Cyril.Goutte@nrc-cnrc.gc.ca
Chi-kiu Lo 羅致翹 ChiKiu.Lo@nrc-cnrc.gc.ca
National Research Council Canada

Abstract

In long-term translation projects, like Parliamentary text, there is a desire to build machine translation systems that can adapt to changes over time. We implement and examine a simple approach to continual learning for neural machine translation, exploring tradeoffs between consistency, the model's ability to learn from incoming data, and the time a client would need to wait to obtain a newly trained translation system.

1 Introduction

There are many translation use cases in which translation is ongoing, i.e., new translations are being produced by translators. We experiment with approaches to using the flow of new data produced by translators to continually update neural machine translation (NMT) systems indefinitely. The intuition behind this is a desire to keep the system(s) up-to-date and optimal for the task of translation over time. This could include new topics that are being discussed, changes to terminology, use of spelling variants, or changes in translator/translation preferences; we specifically highlight terminology in this work due to the ease of measurement.

Our planned continual learning approach is to build a BASELINE-INITIAL system (trained on all data up to a fixed point in time) and iteratively finetune (continue training) it on chunks of new data, which we refer to as *stages*. This simulates the real-life scenario in which new translations are produced and then the goal is to use them to improve the quality of the existing initial translation system.

We use the term "continual learning" in this work, though we note that a number of different terms have been used more or less interchangeably to refer to this concept in the machine translation (MT) and machine learning literature.[1] In the context of MT, they refer to the idea of using the flow of new data to continue to train an MT system indefinitely, producing systems that are always up-to-date: that learn new terms, phrases and formulations, new concepts, changing translations (of old terms—interestingly, this suggests that while most old knowledge should be retained, some of it should be forgotten/overwritten), etc., as they appear. Within this work we will refer to these approaches as *continual learning* (hereafter CL).

The research question we address is whether a simple approach of regularly finetuning a base model works successfully as a CL approach to NMT, especially in a Parliamentary setting, where the domain may evolve over time, but is not expected to suddenly change completely. We describe proof-

[1] Those include "continuous learning", "lifelong learning", "translation project adaptation", as well as the related concepts of "online learning" and "incremental learning" or "incremental updating".

of-concept experiments, in an idealized setting, but with real data, where we compare with several baselines. While our work examines a realistic use case, it is limited by our focus on one language pair (English–French) and one domain (parliamentary text). We examine tradeoffs with respect to questions of various measures of model performance, and note areas where more study is needed to determine the usefulness of these approaches. We also provide a brief discussion of the technical infrastructure that would be required to implement these approaches in practice, with considerations around feasibility and potential costs and risks.

2 Related Work

We provide a brief overview of related CL literature from machine learning (more broadly) and machine translation (more specifically).

2.1 CL for Natural Language Processing

In their survey on CL techniques in natural language processing (NLP), Biesialska et al. (2020, p. 6524) define CL as "a machine learning paradigm, whose objective is to adaptively learn across time by leveraging previously learned tasks to improve generalization for future tasks." Language usage and topics of interest change over time due to various linguistic and social processes and, as a result, machine learning models at the heart of NLP applications tend to become less accurate or stale. Periodically training new models, using data that better reflects the changing distribution of data, is an effective but often highly inefficient and costly solution. This motivates the need to find ways to "continue" the training of NLP models as new data becomes available. In practice, however, existing models often struggle to adapt to new information while simultaneously retaining previously learned knowledge, a problem which can eventually lead to *catastrophic forgetting*, where the improvement on a new task or new data set simultaneously results in a dramatic degradation in quality on the original training task or data (Goodfellow et al., 2014). This gives rise to the *stability-plasticity dilemma* discussed in Biesialska et al. (2020): the main challenge in CL is to strike a balance between the model's *stability* (its ability to retain prior knowledge) and its *plasticity* (its ability to adapt to new knowledge). That survey highlights three major approaches to this challenge: *rehearsal* approaches, where older training samples are kept for each task and periodically revisited while updating a model; *regularization* approaches, which modify the learning objective to aid knowledge consolidation while learning subsequent tasks, for example by slowing down the learning of parameters deemed important for previous tasks; and *architectural* approaches, where changes are made to a model's architecture, making it possible to introduce task-specific parameters and isolate or better control their effects.

2.2 CL for Machine Translation

In machine translation and computer-aided translation, updating MT models based on new translation data has been a recurring topic. This differs from the broader definition of CL, where the task itself may change: here the task of translation remains the same but the data distribution changes in potentially unpredictable ways. One type of data that is of particular interest is professional translator feedback in the form of post-edited MT output. Cettolo et al. (2014)—in the phrase-based statistical MT paradigm—proposed an approach that they call "translation project adaptation." In their setting, a translator performed post-editing, and this post-edited data was then used to adapt the MT system for the future, iteratively improving the accuracy of translations. This concept was later adapted to the neural machine translation (NMT) setting by numerous researchers. For example, Álvaro Peris and Casacuberta (2019) perform updates by finetuning the parameters of a NMT model with every new post-edited sentence (in simulation), yielding better quality translations than the base model and reducing the human effort required to correct the system's output. Kothur et al. (2018) and Knowles (2019) find similar results in simulations of finetuning on individual sentences and document-specific dictionaries. As in other applications of CL, catastrophic forgetting is a major concern.

The three major approaches to CL have also been applied to MT by researchers, including rehearsal approaches (Chu et al., 2017; Zhang et al., 2019; Bengio et al., 2009, i.a.), regularization approaches (Khayrallah et al., 2018; Kirkpatrick et al., 2017; Cao et al., 2021, i.a.), and architectural approaches (Freitag and Al-Onaizan, 2016; Gu and Feng, 2020; Gu et al., 2022; Li et al., 2020; Bapna and Firat, 2019; Wang et al., 2022, i.a.).

In this paper, we do not explore any of these specifically proposed solutions to the catastrophic forgetting problem; instead we simply aim to be alert to the risks (by measuring performance on new data and held-out original data). Since we examine a scenario where we do expect gradual change over time, there are likely some things that *should* be forgotten over time as others are learned (e.g., new preferred terminology or translations).

3 Data Setup

The general data setup for our experiments is designed to mimic in a controlled fashion a real-world scenario in which there exists a backlog of professional translations, and an incoming sequence of additional new translation pairs that are generated each day by translators. Translations are collected regularly and used to incrementally update the MT model, which is then used to produce future translations. We call each such collection period a "stage".

All experiments are based on English–French or French–English data from the proceedings of the debates (a.k.a. "Hansard") in the Canadian House of Commons, one of the two chambers of the Canadian Parliament. This data ranges in time from 2006-04-03 to 2023-09-29, is segmented into sentences, and is timestamped so it can be ordered sequentially, with 5-minute precision.[2] We explain here how we use this data for both hyperparameter-tuning experiments and full data experiments where we train and test the continual learning approach and several baselines: (1) a BASELINE-INITIAL system (trained in a standard, non-CL, manner on all data up to an initial stopping point in time); (2) a BASELINE-FINAL system (trained in a standard, non-CL, manner on all data up to a final stopping point in time); (3) a BASELINE-RECENCY model (a stronger BASELINE, specially finetuned on the CL data).

3.1 Full Experiment Data

The bottom portion of Fig. 1 shows how we have set up the data for our full experiments, while the top portion shows how the subset of data used for the hyperparameter tuning described in this work overlaps with the full data. For building the BASELINE-INITIAL system, we use all Hansard data from 2006-04-03 until (but excluding) 2021-11-22 ($A + B$ in Fig. 1); this last date coincides with the beginning of Canada's 44th Parliament. It is partitioned into training (A), development, and test splits (*baseline-initial-dev* and *baseline-initial-test*, sampled from B). Development and test splits for this model are 2000 sentences randomly sampled from the most recent 40000 pairs of sentences (B in Fig. 1); whatever remains is added to the training data. The *baseline-initial-test* data is also used for examining the stability of the CL systems.

All data that falls between 2021-11-22 and 2022-10-24 (inclusive; $C + D$ in Fig. 1) is divided into CL "stages". We picked a fixed stage size of 3000 sentences, close to the average number of sentences per day in the Hansard (2904).[3] Due to the small size of the stages, we choose a CL approach where we do not use a development set for early stopping; instead we use a fixed learning rate and number of epochs for all stage training. These 3000-sentence stages are used iteratively as test and then training data in CL; once a stage has been trained on, it is never again used as test.

Data for the BASELINE-FINAL system is built analogously to the BASELINE-INITIAL system, using all data from 2006-04-03 until 2022-10-24 ($A + B + C + D$ in Fig. 1), including part of the data from 2022-10-24. Again, we partition this $A+B+C+D$ data into *baseline-final-train*, *baseline-final-dev* and *baseline-final-test* by uniformly sampling 2000 sentences each for the latter two from the most recent 40000 sentences (D in Fig. 1).

The rest of the data from 2022-10-24—i.e., that which is not in set D—is included in the *epilogue* (E in Fig. 1). In practice, for the remainder of this paper, when we refer to *epilogue-test* data we only use the first 40000 lines of the *epilogue* data.

See Table 1 and Appendix A for more information on data set sizes.

3.2 Hyperparameter Tuning Data

Before experimenting on the full data set, we need to select hyperparameters. We use fixed values for

[2]Re. duplicates: in order to evaluate system performance in a realistic usage scenario, duplicates or sentences that appear in training are not removed from test and tuning sets (Appendix A). This allows us to monitor the "translation memory effects" in our systems.

[3]In this simplified, idealized setting, one day's text may spreads across multiple stages, and a stage may include several days. Future work may experiment with training on varying stage sizes.

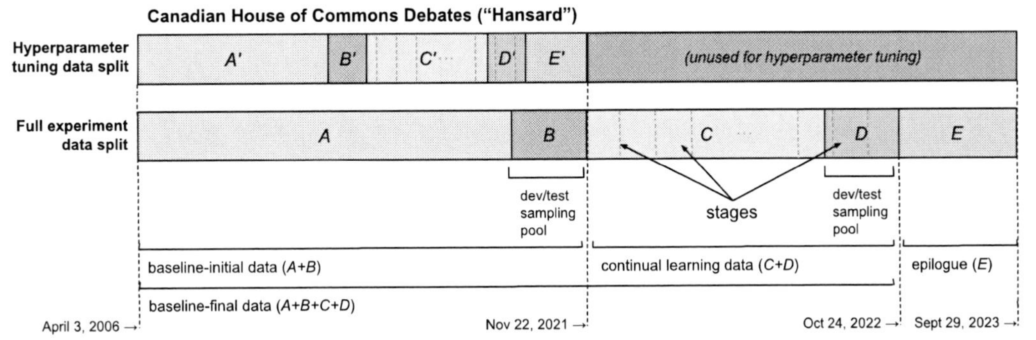

Figure 1: Data splits for hyperparameter tuning and full experiments. In the Full experiment data split, the BASELINE-INITIAL system is trained on parts A and B; the BASELINE-FINAL system is trained on parts A, B, C and D, but excluding *baseline-initial-test*. For both these BASELINE systems, tuning and test sets (2000 sentence pairs each) are sampled from parts B and D respectively; all remaining data from each set is used for training. Starting from the BASELINE-INITIAL system, CL systems are trained by iteratively fine-tuning on data "stages"; each stage is used entirely for training or testing (with no held-out tuning set). The *epilogue* (part E) is used for testing only. The Hyperparameter (HP) Tuning Split (at the top) is structured similarly.

the learning rate and number of epochs during CL, but in order to properly choose these hyperparameters without train/test set contamination, the hyperparameter tuning data must be separate from the data we use for our final CL experiments. For this, we create a second data split, with the same structure as described above, but using data entirely contained within that set's *baseline-initial* data ($A + B$ in Fig. 1). We call this the *Hyperparameter Tuning* data set: HP data for short. In the HP data, the CL portion begins with the second session of the 43rd Parliament, on 2020-09-23 , and contains only 16 stages of 3000 sentences, ending on 2020-10-22. The HP data is shown in the top portion of Fig. 1. Parts $A', \ldots, E'$ in that data serve analogous functions to $A, \ldots, E$ in the full data.

The *HP-epilogue-test* set consists of 4000 sentences sampled from the 40000 sentences (approximately 14 days between 2020-10-22 and 2020-11-06) immediately following the HP CL data, rather than simply the sentences immediately following the end of the CL data as is done in our full experiments.

4 Performance Evaluation

We are interested in three main types of performance evaluation: plasticity (improvement on new data), stability (maintaining high performance on past data), and volatility (whether the translations change dramatically or incrementally between models). The goal for CL is high plasticity, high stability (i.e., no catastrophic forgetting), and low volatility.

We study plasticity on two data sets: the *epilogue-test* test set (used only for testing and never in training or parameter setting) and the sequence of intermediate test set stages. On the *epilogue-test*, we measure translation quality (using automatic metrics) of the output produced by the BASELINE-INITIAL system, each incremental CL system, and the BASELINE-FINAL or BASELINE-RECENCY system. We can compare these scores directly.

We also consider a *stage-wise evaluation* representative of real-life applications. For this evaluation, a stage is initially used as a test set, and then the CL system trains on it, testing on the subsequent stage, until reaching the *epilogue*; a stage is never again used for testing after it has been trained on. While we can compare the CL system with each of the BASELINES on each stage, we cannot directly compare the scores of the *stages* to one another (they are different test sets and most automatic metrics are not directly comparable across test sets). Instead, we compare the *difference* in metric score between the BASELINE-INITIAL system and any systems of interest. We draw an idealized line between 0 at the start of CL to the difference between BASELINE-FINAL and BASELINE-INITIAL (measured on the

Data for:	Hyperparameter Tuning Train	Tune	Test	Full Experiments Train	Tune	Test
Baseline systems						
BASELINE-INITIAL	4494960	2000	2000	4880109	2000	2000
BASELINE-FINAL	4540960	2000	2000	5262109	2000	2000
Continual learning						
CL initial	*(same data as* BASELINE-INITIAL*)*			*(same data as* BASELINE-INITIAL*)*		
per stage	3000	–	3000 *("next" stage)*	3000	–	3000 *("next" stage)*
CL total	48000 *(16 stages)*	–	45000	384000 *(128 stages)*	–	381000
***epilogue-test* set**	–	–	4000	–	–	367653

Table 1: Number of sentence pairs in hyperparameter tuning and full data sets.

epilogue-test) at the end of CL.

To measure stability (and whether catastrophic forgetting occurs), we use the held-out *baseline-initial-test* data set. If catastrophic forgetting occurs, we might expect to see major decreases in quality on this test, whereas if the CL approach is successful, we might expect maintained quality (or small variation; there may be changes in terminology or other such domain evolution features). This measurement will also be done with automatic MT metrics.

We examine volatility during our HP search experiments using the *HP-epilogue-test* set. A highly volatile system would see major changes from system to system; a less volatile system would likely see most translations remain similar to one another.

5 Hyperparameter Tuning Experiments

Even using the simple CL approach we have selected, we need to set some hyperparameters. We limit these to the learning rate (LR) and the number of epochs. In this section we describe the setup of our hyperparameter tuning experiments. We describe BASELINE models built specifically for HP tuning in Section 5.1, the tuning procedure in Section 5.2, performance over time in Section 5.3, and volatility in Section 5.4. We note that for our HP tuning data set, we are considering a smaller range in time than in our full data set.

5.1 Baseline Models

We train the HP-BASELINE-INITIAL model on the *HP-baseline-initial-train* data, with early stopping done using the *HP-baseline-initial-dev* set. The HP-BASELINE-FINAL is trained using the same settings as the HP-BASELINE-INITIAL, using the relevant HP data described in Fig. 1. We build a stronger BASELINE with a recency bias, an oracle finetuned model: HP-BASELINE-RECENCY. This model is the HP-BASELINE-INITIAL finetuned on all CL data, selected from a grid search of hyperparameters based on oracle performance (BLEU score) on the *HP-epilogue*.

All models were trained using Sockeye (Hieber et al., 2022), on 4 `Tesla V100-SXM2-32GB` GPUs. Appendix B describes training in more detail.

5.2 Hyperparameter Tuning

Using the HP CL data set, we experiment with 6 different LRs between 1×10^{-6} and 3×10^{-4}, and 8 values for the number of epochs, from 1 to 2^7. For each experiment, these are fixed to avoid the risk of using a validation set (e.g., for early-stopping) that is too small to draw accurate conclusions from. When training on a stage is complete, the resulting model is used for translation of the test sets and as the starting model parameters for finetuning using the subsequent stage's data. For each setting, we run experiments on the sixteen stages, then compute BLEU score[4] gain at each stage, i.e., the difference between

[4]BLEU scores (Papineni et al., 2002) are computed using `sacrebleu` (Post, 2018) with a signature of `nrefs:1|case:mixed|eff:no|tok:13a|smooth:exp|version:2.3.2`.

the scores obtained with the CL system and the HP-BASELINE-INITIAL system. For a CL system fine-tuned on stage n, it can be tested on the held-out HP-BASELINE-INITIAL test data, stage $n + 1$, and the held-out *epilogue-test* data. Whenever we compare scores of two or more systems, we compare them on the same test set.

Rather than a single stand-out pair of hyperparameters from our grid search, we found a cluster of similarly-performing ones. From this, we chose a high-performing (high median BLEU score gain over stages, relatively low standard deviation) set of HPs with a low number of epochs (to decrease training time and cost).[5] We selected the following HPs for our full experiments: for EN-FR, LR=1.0×10^{-5} and 8 epochs, and for FR-EN, LR=3.0×10^{-6} and 8 epochs. We will perform our initial analyses using these parameters. We later also compare against other settings. See Appendix C for additional details on HP selection.

5.3 Performance Over Time

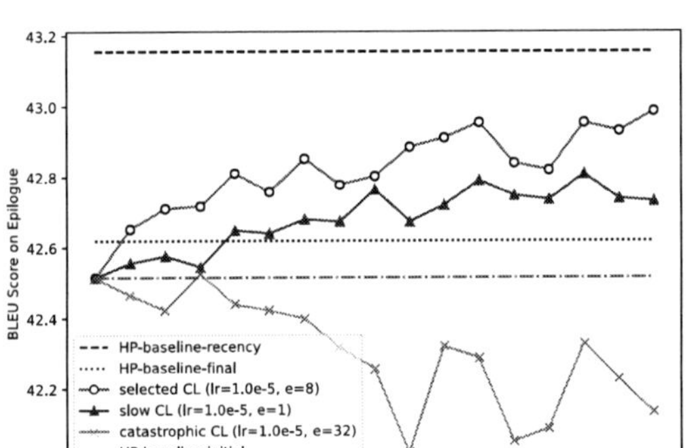

Figure 2: Empirical incremental (EN-FR) evaluation on *HP-epilogue-test* set after training on each stage.

Fig. 2 shows incremental evaluation on the *HP-epilogue-test* set. The "selected CL" HPs were selected as described above. For the "slow CL" and "catastrophic CL" we chose a fixed LR with different numbers of epochs. For the sake of readability, we do not show the *worst* catastrophic forgetting model, as it drops off very quickly and would dominate the plot. The catastrophic forgetting scenario did occur, as expected, when the combination of LR and epochs was too high, presumably leading to overfitting on the stage training data. Both our "selected" and "slow" CL models outperform the HP-BASELINE-FINAL model but do not reach the score of the HP-BASELINE-RECENCY.

5.4 Volatility

We also want to know whether the translations are changing substantially after each stage of training, or whether they remain generally consistent while capturing useful changes. This is likely relevant to the translator experience; highly volatile systems, where the translations of similar texts differ greatly from day to day, may reasonably lose the trust of translators or otherwise cause frustration. We examine this using the 4000-line *HP-epilogue-test* set.

Using the "selected" CL hyperparameter settings for EN-FR, we look at pairs of outputs in sequence to check how many translations change. For example, comparing the HP-BASELINE-INITIAL model to the model trained on the first stage, 1244 lines differ in their translations, while 2756 remain identical. Of all the pairs of models we examine, this is the greatest number of differing lines; most range between 1000 and 1100. Next we compute BLEU scores between the pairs of models, on the sets of sentences whose output translations differ. We treat the earlier model's output as the "reference" and the newer model's output as the hypothesis. These BLEU scores range from 79.5 to 82.4, indicating very high overlap between these sentences, and a visual inspection confirms this; the CL models exhibit low volatility. Performing the same tests using the "catastrophic" settings from Fig. 2 (which were not even the worst case we observed), the number of sentences that differ between adjacent models ranges from 1812 to 2056, and the BLEU scores range from 76.3 to 79.0, indicating higher volatility. If we consider the worst "catastrophic" CL (LR of 3.0×10^{-4} and 128 epochs), this is even more extreme: 3754 to 3892 lines of output differ (meaning only 246 to 108 lines remain the same) and the BLEU scores between them drop to between 30.8 and 43.7.

Thus we find that with a strong set of HPs, we observe relatively low levels of volatility, supporting our decision to focus more on other aspects in

[5]There are a number of different ways one could choose between these, this heuristic is only one possible approach.

selecting the HPs. However, it would still be useful to verify through user studies that translators using the system find this behaviour satisfactory.

6 Full Data Experiments

Using the full experimental data set allows us to examine CL performance over a longer timespan and to see whether it remains consistent,[6] and whether we need to build in additional safeguards, e.g. the ability to roll back to an earlier model if a particular update degrades quality. We also examine the various measures of plasticity, stability, and volatility over a larger timespan.

We build BASELINE models using the same configurations as the HP-BASELINES, but using the larger data set. For the BASELINE-RECENCY model, we finetuned the BASELINE-INITIAL model on all but the last stage of the CL data, using a lower initial LR and using the last stage of CL as a validation set for early stopping rather than an oracle.

We begin with the same preliminary experiments that we produced for HP selection, which we describe in Section 6.1. We then examine questions of novel vocabulary in Section 6.2.

6.1 General Analysis

We examine the results obtained with the HPs we selected for EN-FR: LR=1.0×10^{-5} and 8 epochs; finding that our heuristics seem to have led us to select hyperparameters that are too aggressive, we examine a lower LR version as well: LR=3.0×10^{-6} and 8 epochs.[7] As we see in Figs. 3a (original HPs) and 3b (lower LR), only the lower LR HP successfully outperforms the BASELINE-FINAL model on the *epilogue-test* data and has a clear upward trajectory; neither outperform the BASELINE-RECENCY model, though both outperform BASELINE-INITIAL. In Fig. 3c, the stage-wise evaluation, we see the relative performance bouncing up and down, sometimes dipping below the BASELINE-INITIAL. In contrast, with the lower LR, Fig. 3d shows an upward trend and less severe drops below the BASELINE.[8] The lower LR also shows better stability performance (see Appendix D.2). This suggests that the lower LR set of HPs is better, on the basis of our earlier goals. However, there is a tradeoff: this system is slower to learn translations of new terms (see Section 6.2).

6.2 New Terminology

As Kothur et al. (2018) suggest finetuning NMT on new revised translations as an effective way of incorporating new vocabulary, an interesting case for CL is the appearance of new words or phrases that appear in the CL data but that did not appear in the BASELINE-INITIAL system's training data ("out-of-vocabulary" or OOV). We examined a number of such terms (see examples in Table 2), both single words and multi-word terms that appeared for the first time in parliamentary proceedings between November 2021 and October 2022. Where terms have multiple forms (e.g., plurals, inflected forms), we manually clustered these together as appropriate. We then assessed to what degree the BASELINE-INITIAL and CL systems produced the correct translations, as found either in *Termium Plus*[9] or in the Parliament translators' "Aide-mémoire" (tip sheet), where translators consign recommendations for commonly encountered translation problems.

In Fig. 4, we show a visual representation of terms and their translations over time. This allows us to see how it often takes repeated instances of a term and its translation appearing in training stages before it starts to appear in the CL output. Additionally, this highlights the difference between the two CL models, as we see that the one with the lower LR is slower to adapt to these new terms (this is the broader trend across terms examined).

NMT systems are sometimes capable of handling OOV proper names correctly, insofar as they are written similarly in the source and target languages. However, casing differences can be a prob-

[6] We do note that there is an upper limit on performance; i.e., we cannot expect BLEU scores or BLEU score differences to continue increasing forever, as they range from 0-100. Additionally, natural variation in language means that a "perfect" BLEU score of 100 is not generally a desired or achievable goal. The same is generally true of other reference-based automatic metrics.

[7] Results in the FR-EN direction show similar trends given the same lower LR HP settings; we include these figures in Appendix D.1.

[8] We see a similar pair of trends when measuring with COMET (Rei et al., 2022) – version `unbabel-comet==2.2.2` with model `Unbabel/wmt22-comet-da` – instead of BLEU or chrF, with our initially selected hyperparameter settings even drifting below the baseline, while the lower LR shows a positive upward trend; see Fig. 10 in Appendix D.

[9] Termium Plus is the Government of Canada's terminology and linguistic data bank: `https://www.btb.termiumplus.gc.ca` (Bernier-Colborne et al., 2017).

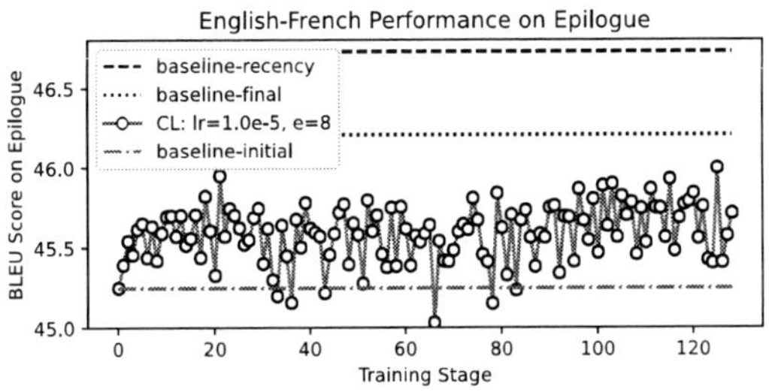

(a) 1.0×10^{-5} LR and 8 epochs

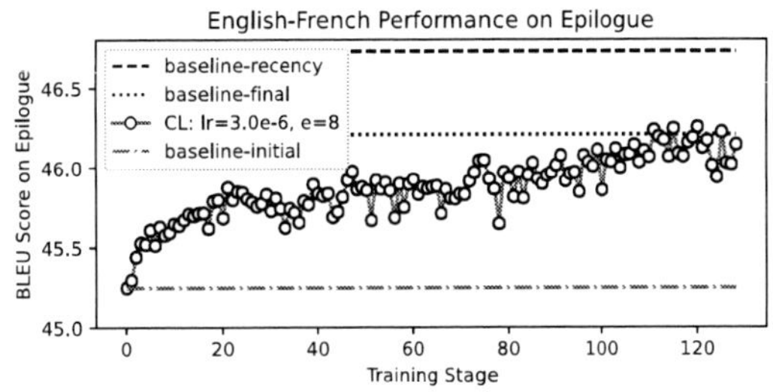

(b) 3.0×10^{-6} LR and 8 epochs

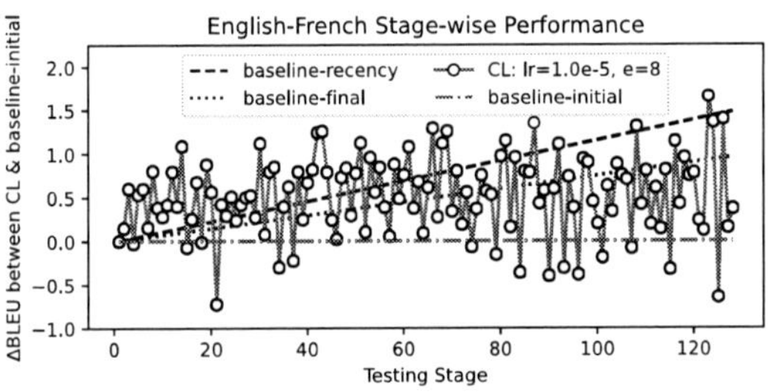

(c) 1.0×10^{-5} LR and 8 epochs

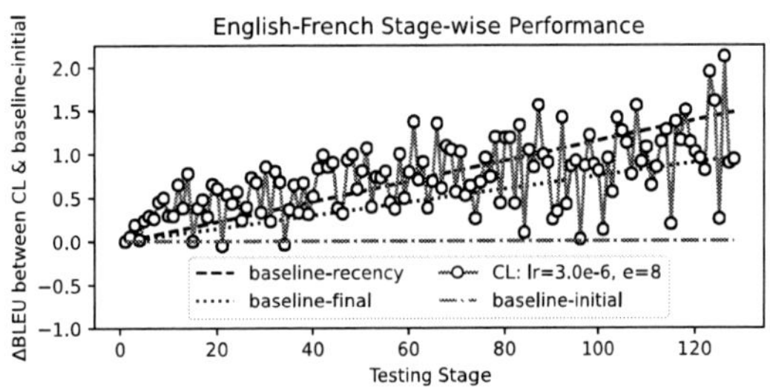

(d) 3.0×10^{-6} LR and 8 epochs

Figure 3: **Top:** EN-FR incremental evaluation on the *epilogue-test* set after training on each stage of data, compared against BASELINES, for two LRs. **Bottom:** EN-FR stage-wise evaluation showing relative performance (ΔBLEU between CL model and BASELINE-INITIAL model) on individual CL stages.

EN Term	FR Term	EN matches seg.	EN matches stg.	FR reference consistency	FR MT Accuracy base.-init.	FR MT Accuracy CL	"CL Priming" seg.	"CL Priming" stg.
advergames	publidivertissements ♡	9	1	100%	0%	0%	–	–
crypto(-)asset	crypto(-)actif ♡	54	4	100%	0%	4%	52	2
divisive	clivant(e)(s)	193	64	11%	0%	1%	166	48
freedom convoy	convoi pour la liberté ♠	80	33	75%	0%	61%	10	6
greedflation	cupidiflation ♡♠	43	11	72%	0%	0%	–	–
omicron	Omicron ♠	355	64	98%	3%	55%	50	8
vaccine passport(s)	passeport(s) vaccin(al,aux) ♡	61	36	100%	64%	93%	0	0

Table 2: Examples of English terms encountered in CL data, along with the recommended translation in French. Translations marked ♡ are those prescribed by Termium Plus; those marked ♠ are those prescribed in the Parliament translators' "Aide-mémoire". *Reference consistency* is the percentage of English term occurrences for which the corresponding French term appears in the reference translation. *MT Accuracy* is computed over the full CL data, as the percentage of the time that the MT system (either BASELINE-INITIAL or the CL system with hyperparameters 1.0×10^{-5} LR and 8 epochs) produces correct output for a given source term. "CL Priming" refers to the amount of exposure of the CL system to a new term before it produces a first correct translation for that term; it is reported in number of segments and number of stages (when the system never successfully translates a term, this is indicated by "–").

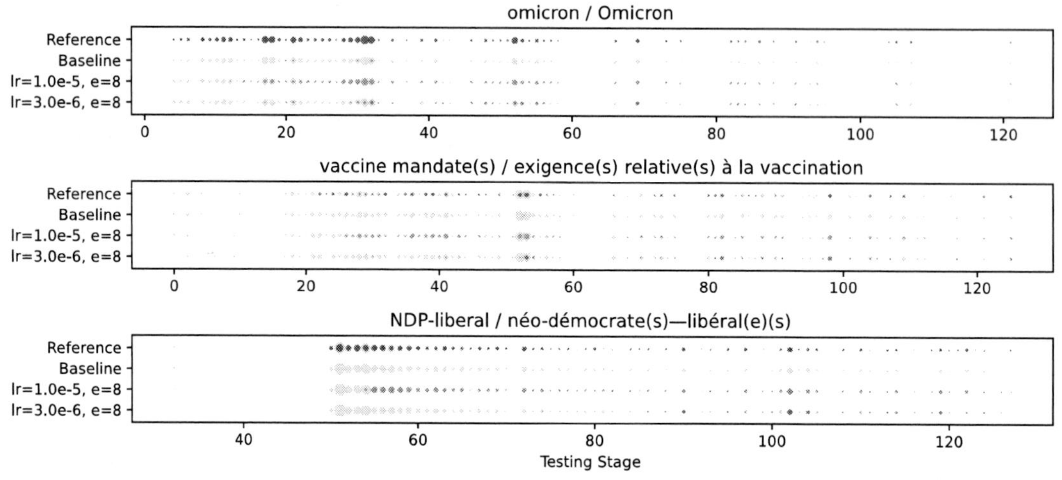

Figure 4: Terminology learning over time. The area of each outer grey circle represents the number of times the source term appeared in a stage; the darker overlapping inner circle represents the number of times its translation appeared in the reference, BASELINE system, and two CL systems (tested stage-wise), respectively. Each horizontal axis ranges from the first occurrence of the given term in the CL data to the last.

lem for the BASELINE-INITIAL system, as in the COVID variant *omicron*, which must be written with an initial capital in French. The CL system eventually catches this difference after 8 stages, containing 50 occurrences. In some cases, if multiple occurrences of a new term appear in the first few stages, CL can respond more quickly. For example, it appears to learn the translation of *cryptoasset* after just two stages, containing 51 occurrences of the term. When all occurrences of a new term occur within the same stage (e.g., *advergames*), the CL system may learn the proposed translation, but never gets the chance to demonstrate this. CL treatment of a new term can be affected if its translation is not consistent across all stages. For example, even though the term *greedflation* appears 43 times in 11 stages, CL fails to capture its proposed translation (*cupidiflation*), possibly because this is not used systematically in the reference (72%).[10]

For multi-word terms, the effectiveness of the BASELINE-INITIAL and CL systems depends in part on the term's degree of lexicalization (or fixedness, or more generally termhood). For example, for *vaccine passport* or *vaccine passports*, the BASELINE-INITIAL system does produce the correct translation (*passeport vaccinal* or *passeports vaccinaux*) 64% of the time. But it also produces various alternatives, such as *passeport de vaccins*, *passeports pour les vaccins*, etc. In contrast, the CL system gets it right 93% of the time. In another instance, the BASELINE-INITIAL system systematically fails to translate *freedom convoy* as *convoi pour la liberté*, preferring *convoi de la liberté*. CL picks up the correct form after six stages, containing 10 occurrences, and from there produces the prescribed translation for 70% of the remaining occurrences (61% global accuracy). Other terms with a relatively complex translation, for example *rent-to-own programs – programmes de location avec option d'achat* and *housing accelerator fund – fonds pour accélérer la construction de logements* are particularly difficult for the baseline-initial system; in this case, CL eventually produces the correct translation, sometimes quite rapidly (after just two stages for *rent-to-own programs*), sometimes more slowly (after eight stages for *housing accelerator fund*).

[10]Regarding the consistency of reference translations, it should be noted that in these experiments, systems were trained and tested without regard for the original language in which texts were initially produced. Therefore, some apparently inconsistent translations may instead be reflective of usage variations in the source language.

7 Implementation and Future Work

All of these experiments were performed in simulation, and there are a number of additional factors that would need to be taken into account in order to implement and run CL in a practical setting. These include data collection (live rather than after full publication), monitoring (automatically or manually monitoring performance over time), roll-back (to earlier versions before restarting CL), and integration into computer-aided translation tools.

All of these considerations come with costs and risks. There are financial costs in terms of hardware (e.g., GPU purchases or cloud costs) as well as the maintenance and monitoring of the system. There are risks in terms of volatility, instability, and the possibility for catastrophic forgetting. Though our setup has aimed to mitigate some of those risks, a live system would need to incorporate monitoring and failsafes for them. Finally, these costs and risks would need to be weighed against the level of improvements observed by translators in using the tool: that is, are the benefits significant enough to warrant that investment in hardware, system development, and maintenance, as compared to other less-dynamic approaches. This requires validation through user studies, which will enable us to better understand whether the desired goals are being achieved, such as improving translations of novel terms or learning from translator corrections, in addition to maintaining high translation quality. In particular, it will be important to examine whether the changes we observe using automatic metrics are actually significant to users of the tool, and whether they find them to be beneficial or not. We will be interested to explore the impacts of plasticity, stability, and volatility on translator satisfaction.

As we noted, our initial hyperparameter selection heuristics did not result in ideal performance. Future work could more closely examine how to select the hyperparameters. Ideally this would be done in consultation with the intended users of the system, to ensure that we focus on the preferred properties of the system (whether that be consistency, rapid adaptation to new terminology, or other factors). For terminology, it may also be worth comparing against dictionary-based methods, though (Knowles et al., 2023) also note some challenges to that approach, focusing on this same domain.

8 Conclusion

In conclusion, we have demonstrated in simulation that a simple approach to CL can be effectively applied to Parliamentary machine translation systems. We find that choosing a good set of hyperparameters enables us to build models with high levels of plasticity and stability, with low levels of volatility. However, we also demonstrate tradeoffs: time, plasticity, and performance. Our approach provides incremental improvements over time, but a client who is willing to wait longer for a better system may prefer to opt for finetuning on a larger amount of recent data rather than these incremental improvements. Similarly, we see a tradeoff between rapidly learning new vocabulary and the overall performance. While we have measured the success of our models using automatic metrics, future work will also be needed to have human translators provide evaluation and feedback.

Acknowledgments

We wish to thank the parliamentary translation team and all our partners at the Canadian government's Translation Bureau, without whom this work would not have been possible.

References

Bapna, A. and Firat, O. (2019). Non-parametric adaptation for neural machine translation. In Burstein, J., Doran, C., and Solorio, T., editors, *Proceedings of the 2019 Conference of the North American Chapter of the Association for Computational Linguistics: Human Language Technologies, Volume 1 (Long and Short Papers)*, pages 1921–1931, Minneapolis, Minnesota. Association for Computational Linguistics.

Bengio, Y., Louradour, J., Collobert, R., and Weston, J. (2009). Curriculum learning. In *Proceedings of the 26th annual international conference on machine learning*, pages 41–48.

Bernier-Colborne, G., Barrière, C., and Ménard, P. A. (2017). Fine-grained domain classification of text using TERMIUM plus. In Frontini, F., Grčić Simeunović, L., Vintar, Š., Khan, A. F., and Parvisi, A., editors, *Proceedings of Language, Ontology, Terminology and Knowledge Structures Workshop (LOTKS 2017)*, Montpellier, France. Association for Computational Linguistics.

Biesialska, M., Biesialska, K., and Costa-jussà, M. R. (2020). Continual lifelong learning in natural language processing: A survey. In Scott, D., Bel, N., and Zong, C., editors, *Proceedings of the 28th International Conference on Computational Linguistics*, pages 6523–6541, Barcelona, Spain (Online). International Committee on Computational Linguistics.

Cao, Y., Wei, H.-R., Chen, B., and Wan, X. (2021). Continual learning for neural machine translation. In Toutanova, K., Rumshisky, A., Zettlemoyer, L., Hakkani-Tur, D., Beltagy, I., Bethard, S., Cotterell, R., Chakraborty, T., and Zhou, Y., editors, *Proceedings of the 2021 Conference of the North American Chapter of the Association for Computational Linguistics: Human Language Technologies*, pages 3964–3974, Online. Association for Computational Linguistics.

Cettolo, M., Bertoldi, N., Federico, M., Schwenk, H., Barrault, L., and Servan, C. (2014). Translation project adaptation for mt-enhanced computer assisted translation. *Machine Translation*, 28(2):127–150.

Chu, C., Dabre, R., and Kurohashi, S. (2017). An empirical comparison of domain adaptation methods for neural machine translation. In Barzilay, R. and Kan, M.-Y., editors, *Proceedings of the 55th Annual Meeting of the Association for Computational Linguistics (Volume 2: Short Papers)*, pages 385–391, Vancouver, Canada. Association for Computational Linguistics.

Freitag, M. and Al-Onaizan, Y. (2016). Fast domain adaptation for neural machine translation. *ArXiv*, abs/1612.06897.

Goodfellow, I. J., Mirza, M., Xiao, D., Courville, A. C., and Bengio, Y. (2014). An empirical investigation of catastrophic forgeting in gradient-based neural networks. In Bengio, Y. and LeCun, Y., editors, *2nd International Conference on Learning Representations, ICLR 2014, Banff, AB, Canada, April 14-16, 2014, Conference Track Proceedings*.

Gu, S. and Feng, Y. (2020). Investigating catastrophic forgetting during continual training for neural machine translation. In Scott, D., Bel, N., and Zong, C., editors, *Proceedings of the 28th International Conference on Computational Linguistics*, pages 4315–4326, Barcelona, Spain (Online). International Committee on Computational Linguistics.

Gu, S., Hu, B., and Feng, Y. (2022). Continual learning of neural machine translation within low forgetting risk regions. In Goldberg, Y., Kozareva, Z., and Zhang, Y., editors, *Proceedings of the 2022 Conference on Empirical Methods in Natural Language Processing*, pages 1707–1718, Abu Dhabi, United Arab Emirates. Association for Computational Linguistics.

Hieber, F., Denkowski, M., Domhan, T., Barros, B. D., Ye, C. D., Niu, X., Hoang, C., Tran, K., Hsu, B., Nadejde, M., Lakew, S., Mathur, P., Currey, A., and Federico, M. (2022). Sockeye 3: Fast neural machine translation with pytorch. *arXiv*, abs/2207.05851.

Hunter, J. D. (2007). Matplotlib: A 2d graphics environment. *Computing in Science & Engineering*, 9(3):90–95.

Khayrallah, H., Thompson, B., Duh, K., and Koehn, P. (2018). Regularized training objective for continued training for domain adaptation in neural machine translation. In Birch, A., Finch, A., Luong, T., Neubig, G., and Oda, Y., editors, *Proceedings of the 2nd Workshop on Neural Machine Translation and Generation*, pages 36–44, Melbourne, Australia. Association for Computational Linguistics.

Kirkpatrick, J., Pascanu, R., Rabinowitz, N., Veness, J., Desjardins, G., Rusu, A. A., Milan, K., Quan, J., Ramalho, T., Grabska-Barwinska, A., Hassabis, D., Clopath, C., Kumaran, D., and Hadsell, R. (2017). Overcoming catastrophic forgetting in neural networks. *Proceedings of the National Academy of Sciences*, 114(13):3521–3526.

Knowles, R. (2019). *Interactive and Adaptive Neural Machine Translation*. PhD thesis, The Johns Hopkins University, Baltimore, Maryland, USA.

Knowles, R., Larkin, S., Tessier, M., and Simard, M. (2023). Terminology in neural machine translation: A case study of the Canadian Hansard. In Nurminen, M., Brenner, J., Koponen, M., Latomaa, S., Mikhailov, M., Schierl, F., Ranasinghe, T., Vanmassenhove, E., Vidal, S. A., Aranberri, N., Nunziatini, M., Escartín, C. P., Forcada, M., Popovic, M., Scarton, C., and Moniz, H., editors, *Proceedings of the 24th Annual Conference of the European Association for Machine Translation*, pages 481–488, Tampere, Finland. European Association for Machine Translation.

Kothur, S. S. R., Knowles, R., and Koehn, P. (2018). Document-level adaptation for neural machine translation. In Birch, A., Finch, A., Luong, T., Neubig, G., and Oda, Y., editors, *Proceedings of the 2nd Workshop on Neural Machine Translation and Generation*, pages 64–73, Melbourne, Australia. Association for Computational Linguistics.

Larkin, S., Joanis, E., Stewart, D., Simard, M., Foster, G., Ueffing, N., and Tikuisis, A. (2022). Portage Text Processing. https://github.com/nrc-cnrc/PortageTextProcessing.

Li, Y., Zhao, L., Church, K., and Elhoseiny, M. (2020). Compositional language continual learning. In *8th International Conference on Learning Representations (ICLR)*.

Lo, C.-k., Knowles, R., and Goutte, C. (2023). Beyond correlation: Making sense of the score differences of new MT evaluation metrics. In Utiyama, M. and Wang, R., editors, *Proceedings of Machine Translation Summit XIX, Vol. 1: Research Track*, pages 186–199, Macau SAR, China. Asia-Pacific Association for Machine Translation.

Mathur, N., Baldwin, T., and Cohn, T. (2020). Tangled up in BLEU: Reevaluating the evaluation of automatic machine translation evaluation metrics. In Jurafsky, D., Chai, J., Schluter, N., and Tetreault, J., editors, *Proceedings of the 58th Annual Meeting of the Association for Computational Linguistics*, pages 4984–4997, Online. Association for Computational Linguistics.

Moi, A. and Patry, N. (2022). Huggingface's tokenizers. https://github.com/huggingface/tokenizers.

Papineni, K., Roukos, S., Ward, T., and Zhu, W.-J. (2002). Bleu: a method for automatic evaluation of machine translation. In Isabelle, P., Charniak, E., and Lin, D., editors, *Proceedings of the 40th Annual Meeting of the Association for Computational Linguistics*, pages 311–318, Philadelphia, Pennsylvania, USA. Association for Computational Linguistics.

Paszke, A., Gross, S., Massa, F., Lerer, A., Bradbury, J., Chanan, G., Killeen, T., Lin, Z., Gimelshein, N., Antiga, L., Desmaison, A., Kopf, A., Yang, E., DeVito, Z., Raison, M., Tejani, A., Chilamkurthy, S., Steiner, B., Fang, L., Bai, J., and Chintala, S. (2019). Pytorch: An imperative style, high-performance deep learning library. In *Advances in Neural Information Processing Systems 32*, pages 8024–8035. Curran Associates, Inc.

Popović, M. (2015). chrF: character n-gram F-score for automatic MT evaluation. In Bojar, O., Chatterjee, R., Federmann, C., Haddow, B., Hokamp, C., Huck, M., Logacheva, V., and Pecina, P., editors, *Proceedings of the Tenth Workshop on Statistical Machine Translation*, pages 392–395, Lisbon, Portugal. Association for Computational Linguistics.

Post, M. (2018). A call for clarity in reporting BLEU scores. In Bojar, O., Chatterjee, R., Federmann, C., Fishel, M., Graham, Y., Haddow, B., Huck, M., Yepes, A. J., Koehn, P., Monz, C., Negri, M., Névéol, A., Neves, M., Post, M., Specia, L., Turchi, M., and Verspoor, K., editors, *Proceedings of the Third Conference on Machine Translation: Research Papers*, pages 186–191, Brussels, Belgium. Association for Computational Linguistics.

Rei, R., C. de Souza, J. G., Alves, D., Zerva, C., Farinha, A. C., Glushkova, T., Lavie, A., Coheur, L., and Martins, A. F. T. (2022). COMET-22: Unbabel-IST 2022 submission for the metrics shared task. In Koehn, P., Barrault, L., Bojar, O., Bougares, F., Chatterjee, R., Costa-jussà, M. R., Federmann, C., Fishel, M., Fraser, A., Freitag, M., Graham, Y., Grundkiewicz, R., Guzman, P., Haddow, B., Huck, M., Jimeno Yepes, A., Kocmi, T., Martins, A., Morishita, M., Monz, C., Nagata, M., Nakazawa, T., Negri, M., Névéol, A., Neves, M., Popel, M., Turchi, M., and Zampieri, M., editors, *Proceedings of the Seventh Conference on Machine Translation (WMT)*, pages 578–585, Abu Dhabi, United Arab Emirates (Hybrid). Association for Computational Linguistics.

Rei, R., Stewart, C., Farinha, A. C., and Lavie, A. (2020). COMET: A neural framework for MT evaluation. In Webber, B., Cohn, T., He, Y., and Liu, Y., editors, *Proceedings of the 2020 Conference on Empirical Methods in Natural Language Processing (EMNLP)*, pages 2685–2702, Online. Association for Computational Linguistics.

Wang, D., Wei, H., Zhang, Z., Huang, S., Xie, J., and Chen, J. (2022). Non-parametric online learning from human feedback for neural machine translation. *Proceedings of the AAAI Conference on Artificial Intelligence*, 36(10):11431–11439.

Zhang, X., Shapiro, P., Kumar, G., McNamee, P., Carpuat, M., and Duh, K. (2019). Curriculum learning for domain adaptation in neural machine translation. In

Burstein, J., Doran, C., and Solorio, T., editors, *Proceedings of the 2019 Conference of the North American Chapter of the Association for Computational Linguistics: Human Language Technologies, Volume 1 (Long and Short Papers)*, pages 1903–1915, Minneapolis, Minnesota. Association for Computational Linguistics.

Álvaro Peris and Casacuberta, F. (2019). Online learning for effort reduction in interactive neural machine translation. *Computer Speech & Language*, 58:98–126.

A Data

Table 1 shows the sizes of the training, tuning, and test sets for our HP tuning and experiments; we provide some additional notes here.

In order to keep our setup as realistic as possible, we do not deduplicate the data (and the Hansard is known to have repetitive/boilerplate text). Regarding duplicates, within our 2000-sentence test and tuning sets, about 7.5% of sentences (either source or target) also appear in the training set. Looking at pairs of sentences (source and target) instead, this number falls to 4.75%. Internal repetition (sentences that repeat within a test or tuning set) is about 1%. Repeated sentences tend to be short: their average length is 10.3 words, compared to 20.1 words for all test and tuning sets.

B NMT Model Training

We train all models using Sockeye version `3.1.31` (Hieber et al., 2022), commit `13c63be5` with PyTorch `1.13.1` (Paszke et al., 2019). Table 3 lists the parameter settings in our experiments that differ from the Sockeye defaults. Training was performed on 4 `Tesla V100-SXM2-32GB` GPUs.

For data preprocessing, a bilingual `SentencePieceUnigramTokenizer` with a vocabulary of 32k tokens was trained using HuggingFace's tokenizers (Moi and Patry, 2022) library version `0.14.1` on all of the 4498960 French and 4498960 English sentences from HP-BASELINE-INITIAL. The tokenizer also applies a few normalizations done by Portage (Larkin et al., 2022). Our vocabulary is augmented with generic tokens and other domain-specific tokens (unused in these experiments, but intended for future work on domain adaptation); this yields a final vocabulary of 32123 tokens.

Name	Value
amp	*True*
grading clipping type	*abs*
max sequence length	*200:200*
params	*previous model when CL*
batch size	*8192*
batch type	*max-word*
cache last best params	*1*
cache metric	*bleu*
cache strategy	*last*
checkpoint interval	10^7
decode and evaluate	*-1 (entire validation)*
initial learning rate	*see Table 4*
keep last params	*1*
learning rate scheduler type	*None*
max epochs	*see Table 4*
metrics	*perplexity & accuracy*
min epochs	*Same as max epochs*
optimizer	*Adam*
optimizer Betas	*0.9, 0.98*
optimized metric	*BLEU*
update interval	*2*
vocabulary size	*32121*
attention heads	*16:16*
shared vocabulary	*True*
transformer FFN	*4096:4096*
transformer model size	*1024:1024*
weight tying	*True*

Table 3: Differences between Sockeye's default parameters and our HP configuration.

B.1 Baselines

The HP-BASELINE-INITIAL was trained on the *HP-baseline-initial-train* data, with early stopping done using the *HP-baseline-initial-dev* set.

The HP-BASELINE-FINAL was trained using the same settings as the HP-BASELINE-INITIAL, using the relevant HP data described in Fig. 1 (i.e., early stopping based on *HP-baseline-final-dev* data).

To build an even stronger final BASELINE with a recency bias (i.e., recently exposed to all the HP CL data), we implemented an oracle finetuned model which we call HP-BASELINE-RECENCY. Using both the HP-BASELINE-INITIAL and HP-BASELINE-FINAL models as starting points, we finetuned them with the full set of CL data, using as the LR and number of epochs the full set used in the hyperparameter search (described in Section 5.2). We then selected the best finetuned model based on performance on the *HP-epilogue* data (thus making this an oracle BASELINE). For EN-FR this was the one trained with LR=3.0×10^{-5} and 4 epochs starting from the HP-BASELINE-INITIAL model, while for FR-EN this was LR=3.0×10^{-6} and 64 epochs also starting from the HP-BASELINE-INITIAL model.

Using the full data sets, we built BASELINE models by applying the same approach as described for the HP-BASELINE models. All models were trained with the exact same configuration as for the HP experiments but using their respective corpora.

We also note differences in how we trained the BASELINE-RECENCY model for the full data. Using BASELINE-INITIAL's configuration, we lowered its learning rate from 0.06325 to 0.006325 and initialized its weights with those of BASELINE-INITIAL, to finetune BASELINE-INITIAL on recent data. We use all stages except the last one for its training corpus. The last stage was used as a validation corpus to control early stopping.

B.2 Continual Learning

We start CL from the BASELINE-INITIAL model (either HP-BASELINE-INITIAL or BASELINE-INITIAL). For our realistic CL setup, we choose not to use a validation set and do not perform early stopping; that is, we set a fixed number of epochs (training iterations over the full stage of data) and train until those epochs have been completed. We also keep the learning rate fixed throughout the training, rather than using a variable learning rate. When the training on a stage is complete, we select the last saved model checkpoint (produced at the end of training) to use for translation of the test sets and to use as the starting model parameters for finetuning on the subsequent stage's data. The choice not to use a validation set enables us to use the full stage data (which is already fairly small) for training. By doing this hyperparameter setting, we aim to pick a learning rate and number of epochs that are at low risk of overfitting to the data, while also providing desired improvements, thus aiming to achieve the same desired end goal as using a validation set. Also, this avoids the risk of using a validation set that is too small to draw accurate conclusions from.

C Effects of Hyperparameters

Table 4 shows the set of learning rates and epochs used for our hyperparameter grid search.

Parameter	Values
initial learning rate	*3e-4, 1e-4, 3e-5, 1e-5, 3e-6, 1e-6*
max epochs	*1, 2, 4, 8, 16, 32, 64, 128*

Table 4: Grid search values for HP tuning.

In Fig. 5 (EN-FR), we can see how the combination of learning rate and number of epochs impacts performance.[11] The subplots show the minimum BLEU gain (with negative values indicating a degradation in BLEU), the median BLEU gain, and the maximum BLEU gain observed for a given set of hyperparameters as measured across stages 2-16 after training on stages 1-15, respectively.

The first notable result from these plots is that—as expected—we do see catastrophic forgetting if the learning rate, number of epochs, or both are too high. This is apparent in the lower right corner of all plots, where we see increasingly large drops in BLEU scores from the HP-BASELINE-INITIAL model to the CONTINUAL LEARNING models trained on various stages. A brief examination of a sample of the output for the high learning rate and large number of epochs suggests that the systems still retain the ability to generate output that is generally fluent, but that there are substitutions (likely due to overfitting on the previous stage) that can heavily impact adequacy.

The second notable result is that we find similar patterns between BLEU and chrF. Both are surface-level automatic evaluation metrics, so it is not a surprise to see this correlation, particularly for this well-studied language pair. Nevertheless, this replication of similar results across metrics can make us more confident that the observed patterns are real. This is particularly important because the BLEU and chrF differences are relatively small, and it is known that such small differences may not always correspond to perceivable significant differences if we were to perform human judgments (Mathur et al., 2020; Lo et al., 2023, i.a.). However, we do note that in this particular case, where the model may

[11] We also examined this in the FR-EN direction and with chrF Popović (2015) implemented in sacrebleu Post (2018) with signatures BLEU: `nrefs:1|case:mixed|eff:no|tok:13a|smooth:exp|version:2.3.2` and chrF: `nrefs:1|case:mixed|eff:yes|nc:6|nw:0|space:no|version:2.3.2`, but found similar results.

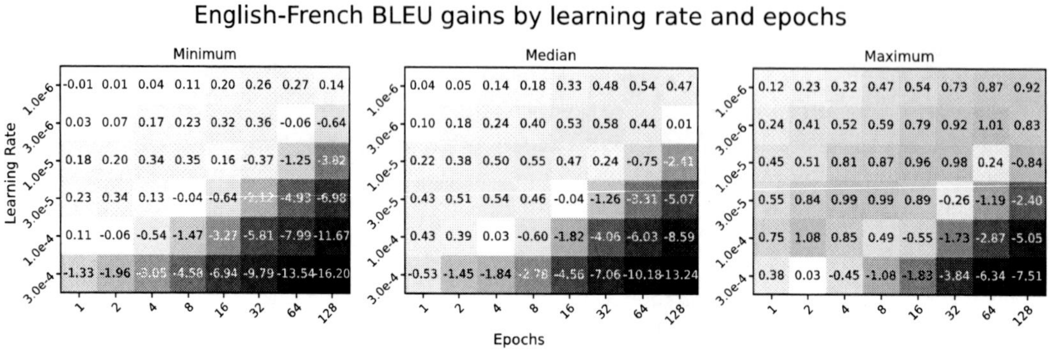

Figure 5: EN-FR results for BLEU score gains from CL (over HP-BASELINE-INITIAL model) as measured over HP stages 2-16 (after finetuning on stages 1-15 respectively).

primarily be learning a new name or new term and otherwise leaving the output fairly similar to previous output, there may be reason to expect that these BLEU and chrF scores may capture genuine signal. We explored this question of volatility in Section 5.4 and the question of new terminology in Section 6.2.

Finally, we observe that there is a cluster of pairs of learning rates and number of epochs that show similar performance. Given the concerns about making decisions based on such small automatic score metric differences, we may instead choose to select from the pool of top systems on some other basis, such as training time required.

C.1 Selection of HPs

Our experimental setup is designed to let us explore the performance of different hyperparameter settings without any test set contamination. However, our main goal is to actually perform this CL in the longer-term, more realistic setting. To do this, we want to be able to select hyperparameters based on the results on the data used for our hyperparameter search; then we wish to see how these perform on the realistic data. We later run additional experiments on the full data for comparison, but we would like the initial run to be as realistic as possible: selecting just one set of parameters.

In order to do this, we need to decide on an approach to hyperparameter selection. We have a cluster of pairs of hyperparameters that perform similarly, with very small differences in automatic metric scores. For example, given a high-performing pair of hyperparameters, we may also find that a slightly larger number of epochs paired with a slightly lower learning rate will perform similarly (or vice versa). So how should we choose between these? At first glance, we may wish to maximize the minimum of some automatic metric over the stages in our hyperparameter search; this, however, has the downside of overemphasizing the impact of a single stage (potentially problematic if one or more of the stages are unusual in some way that impacts automatic metric scores). Alternatively we may aim for consistency, selecting hyperparameters that exhibit a low standard deviation in automatic metric score differences; of course, this is no guarantee of strong performance, as a very low-performing system could also have a low standard deviation. And a high median on its own also fails to tell the whole story.

We are seeking to balance various interests in our selection of hyperparameters. These include plasticity (ability to learn from new data), stability (maintaining high performance on past data), low volatility (no dramatic changes from stage to stage), and cost (i.e., time, compute resources, or both). We also need to balance risk and reward, i.e., whether we want a model that reaches the highest scores but may also exhibit greater inconsistency or variance, or a model that may not obtain the highest automatic metric scores but is also fairly consistent in terms of overall performance.

As was evident from the heatmaps (Fig. 5), we have a number of different hyperparameter settings that perform quite similarly, clustered along the diagonal. When we examine their distributions over the hyperparameter tuning experiment stages via the boxplots in Fig. 6, the large overlaps in interquartile range hammer home that these top performing hyperparameters are not significantly different from one another. Thus, for our initial experiment, we choose a high-performing (high median BLEU score, relatively low standard deviation) set of hyperparameters with a low number of epochs (in order to decrease training time and cost, particularly since not all users of these tools may have access to GPUs). For EN-FR this is 1.0×10^{-5} LR and 8 epochs. For FR-EN this is 3.0×10^{-6} LR and 8 epochs. We then also compare this against another HP setting. As noted earlier, there are a number of different ways one could choose between these, this heuristic is only one possible approach.

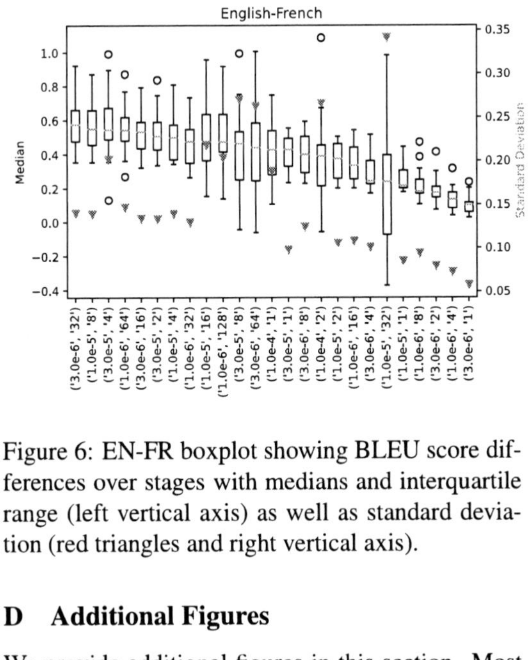

Figure 6: EN-FR boxplot showing BLEU score differences over stages with medians and interquartile range (left vertical axis) as well as standard deviation (red triangles and right vertical axis).

D Additional Figures

We provide additional figures in this section. Most scalable figures in this paper are produced using Matplotlib (Hunter, 2007), version 3.7.1.

D.1 French–English Figures

The results for FR-EN are similar to those from the lower learning rate for EN-FR, as we observe in Figs. 7 and 8.

D.2 Stability Figures

Fig. 9 shows the stability of CL models. Ideally, performance would remain relatively constant. With our initially selected learning rate performance eventually begins to drop. This is not overly concerning in and of itself: as new data comes in, this may change preferred translations, potentially causing mismatches with the original reference data which would be viewed as improvements by the users on later data. With the lower learning rate we observe that, as expected, stability is improved and performance even increases slightly.

D.3 English–French COMET Figures

Figs. 10a and 10b use COMET (Rei et al., 2020) version `unbabel-comet==2.2.2` with model `Unbabel/wmt22-comet-da` to measure performance on the *epilogue-test*. They correspond to the BLEU score Figs. 3a and 3b, respectively.

Overall, we see similar trends between COMET and the BLEU scores used in the rest of the paper; if we had used COMET rather than BLEU for our hyperparamter selection, we still would have been choosing between a very similar set of top hyperparameters.

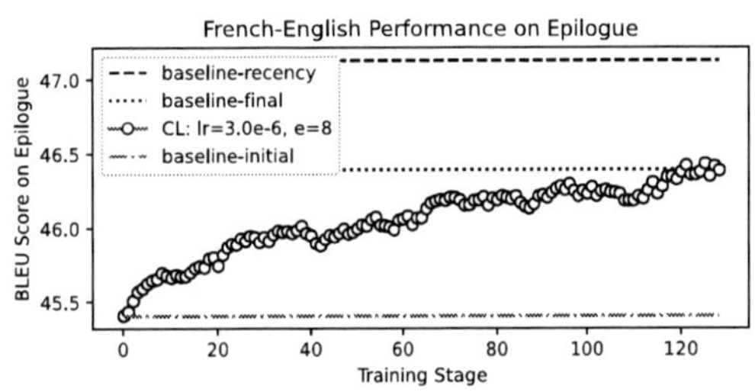

Figure 7: FR-EN incremental evaluation on the *epilogue-test* set after training on each stage of data, compared against BASELINES.

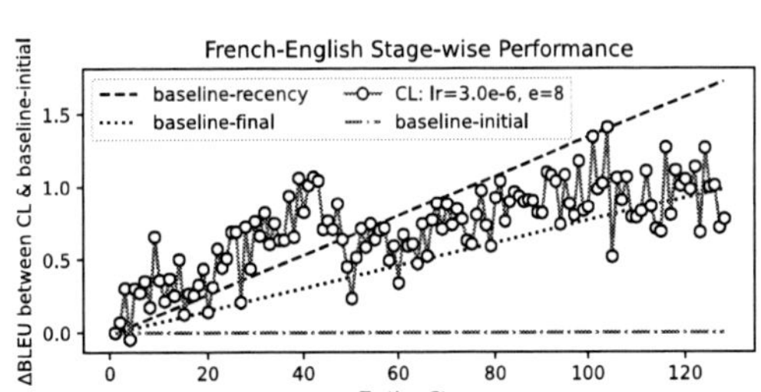

Figure 8: FR-EN stage-wise evaluation showing relative performance (ΔBLEU between CL model and BASELINE-INITIAL model) on individual CL stages.

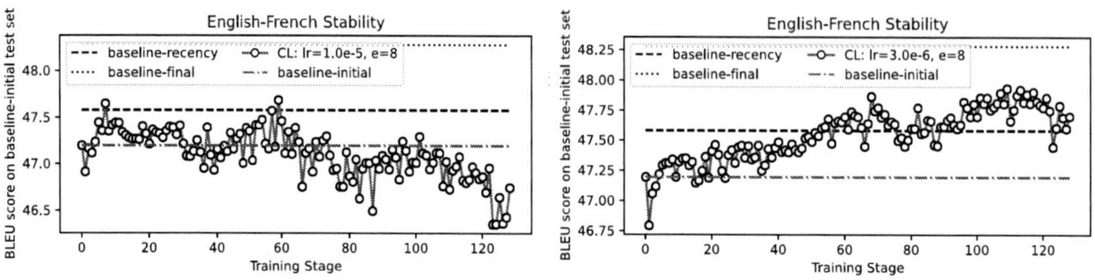

(a) 1.0×10^{-5} LR and 8 epochs

(b) 3.0×10^{-6} LR and 8 epochs

Figure 9: EN-FR stability over CL stages, tested on held-out *baseline-initial-test* data.

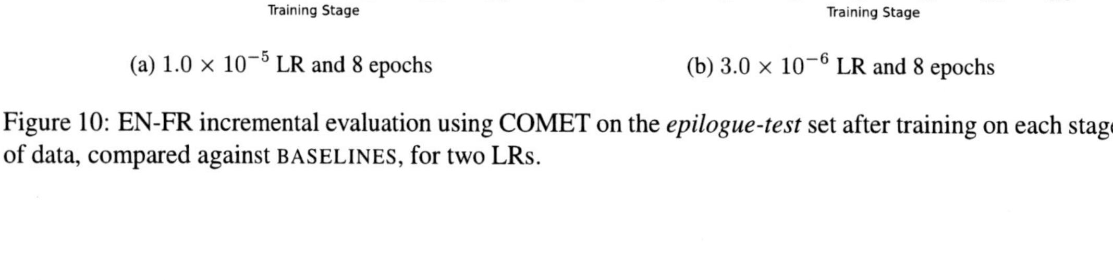

(a) 1.0×10^{-5} LR and 8 epochs

(b) 3.0×10^{-6} LR and 8 epochs

Figure 10: EN-FR incremental evaluation using COMET on the *epilogue-test* set after training on each stage of data, compared against BASELINES, for two LRs.

Position Paper: Should Machine Translation be Labelled as AI-Generated Content?

Michel Simard
National Research Council Canada
michel.simard@nrc-cnrc.gc.ca

Abstract

In September 2023, the Government of Canada issued a *Guide on the Use of Generative AI* with recommendations for Canadian government institutions and their employees. As other similar documents published by various organizations in recent years, this document makes recommendations regarding transparency, stating that whenever generative AI is used to produce content, the reader should be informed that "*messages addressed to them are generated by AI*". While this guide does not address specifically the case of machine translation, it does mention translation as a potential application of generative AI. Therefore, one question that naturally arises is: Should machine-translated texts be explicitly labelled as AI-generated content wherever they are used? In this position paper, we examine this question in detail, with the goal of proposing clear guidelines specifically regarding MT, not only for government institutions, but for anyone using MT technology. Our main conclusion is that machine-translated text is indeed AI-generated content. As such, it should be explicitly marked everywhere it is used. We make recommendations as to what form this labelling might take. We also examine under what conditions MT labelling can be removed or omitted.

1 Introduction

In September 2023, the Government of Canada issued a *Guide on the Use of Generative AI*[1], providing "*preliminary guidance to federal institutions on their use of generative AI tools*". Among other things, this document makes recommendations regarding transparency, stating that whenever generative AI is used by Canadian government institutions, the users should be informed that "*messages addressed to them are generated by AI*" (Government of Canada, 2023).

While the recommendations in this guide are very general and do not target any one specific application of generative AI, the authors explicitly mention language translation as a potential use of these technologies. But they don't go as far as identifying machine-translated text as AI-generated content. Of course, machine translation and artificial intelligence are very tightly linked, both historically and technologically. Therefore, one question that naturally arises is: **Should machine-translated text be explicitly labelled as AI-generated content wherever it is used?**

In this position paper, we examine this question in detail, with the goal of proposing clear guidelines specifically regarding machine translation, not only for government institutions, but for anyone using MT technology to produce versions of a text in a language other than the one in which it was initially written. We present the wider context in which this question arises in Section 2, then address our fundamental question, as well as several others in Section 3. We wrap up with a summary of recommendations in Section 4.

Our main conclusion is that machine-translated text is indeed AI-generated content. As such, it should be explicitly marked everywhere it is used. We make recommendations as to what form this labelling might take. We also examine under what conditions MT labelling can be removed or omitted.

[1] https://www.canada.ca/en/government/system/digital-government/digital-government-innovations...

2 The Wider Context: Labelling of AI-generated Content

In its recommendations to Canadian federal institutions on the use of generative AI technologies, the *Guide on the Use of Generate AI* includes guidelines on transparency: "*To maintain public trust and ensure the responsible use of generative AI tools, federal institutions should [...] identify content that has been produced using generative AI [and] notify users that they are interacting with an AI tool*". In particular, the guide contains a section about "*[d]istinguishing humans from machines*", with specific recommendations to "*[i]nform users when messages addressed to them are generated by AI*" or to "*use watermarks so that users can identify content generated by AI*" (Government of Canada, 2023).

These recommendations from the Government of Canada are not an isolated case. Increasingly, there has been pressure on Big Tech and media to label AI-generated content (abbreviated *AIGC* henceforth). The UNESCO's 2022 *Recommendation on the Ethics of Artificial Intelligence* (UNESCO, 2022), which was adopted by all 193 member states in November 2021, includes a clause about identifying AIGC:

> 127. Member States should ensure that users can easily identify whether they are interacting with a living being, or with an AI system imitating human or animal characteristics [...]

This principle is gradually taking the form of laws and regulations in various places. For example, the European Commission (EC) added labelling requirements to its *Code of Practice on Online Disinformation* (European Commission, 2022), a voluntary framework of industry self-regulation to fight disinformation, to which most AI actors have already agreed (one notable exception is X, formerly Twitter, which pulled out during the summer of 2023). The EC's Digital Services Act (DSA) (European Commission, 2024) includes provisions requiring large online platforms to label "*manipulated audio and images*" (O'Carroll, 2023; Zakrzewski and Lima-Strong, 2023).

The United States, Canada and other countries are expected to adopt similar rules shortly. The United States government has recently convened the major players in AI to adhere to a set of guidelines aimed at ensuring safe, secure, and trustworthy AI. These guidelines specifically include provisions to "*[d]evelop and deploy mechanisms that enable users to understand if audio or visual content is AI-generated, including robust provenance, watermarking, or both, for AI-generated audio or visual content.*"[2] A similar Code of Conduct (Innovation, Science and Economic Development Canada, 2023) was unveiled in Canada in September 2023, instructing companies to "*[d]evelop and implement reliable and freely available methods to detect content generated by their systems (e.g., watermarking)*" and to "*[e]nsure that systems that could be mistaken for humans are clearly and prominently identified as AI systems*" (Thompson, 2023; Pisano, 2023).

While legislation and recommendations have mostly focused on audio and video content, it is clear that textual content should not be an exception. Generative AI tools based on Large Language Models (LLMs) have rapidly been identified by analysts as a potential risk for the massive increase of dis- and misinformation. This topic was specifically addressed during a workshop organized by OpenAI, Georgetown University's Center for Security and Emerging Technology and the Stanford Internet Observatory in October 2021.[3] During this workshop, the question of Digital Provenance Standards was specifically discussed (Goldstein et al., 2023).

The primary goal of AIGC labelling is to fight dis- and misinformation, but there is a more general intention to inform users and create a more healthy and transparent social environment where trust can flourish, reflecting the ethical imperative "*to not blur the distinction between the categories of human and machine*" (Grinbaum and Adomaitis, 2022).

3 The Case of Machine Translation

In this document, we ask whether machine-translated texts should be labelled as AI-generated content wherever they are used. But before we can address this question, we first need to clarify whether MT *is* AIGC. Then, assuming it is, whether it is appropriate to label it, and if so, where and how. We address each of these questions (and more) be-

[2] `https://www.whitehouse.gov/briefing-room/statements-releases/2023/07/21/fact-sheet-biden-harris-...`

[3] `https://openai.com/research/forecasting-misuse`

low.

3.1 Is Machine Translated Text "AI-generated Content"?

TL;DR: Yes.
The Canadian Federal Government's *Guide on the Use of Generative AI*, as other similar documents, cites language translation as an example of tasks that generative AI can be used to perform or support. But it doesn't go as far as saying that machine-translated text is AI-generated content. We examine this question here.

When asked this precise question, it is surprising to see how many MT researchers and practitioners are hesitant or even reluctant to answer unequivocally. In practice, many of these people don't see themselves as "doing AI". They typically view their activity or area of expertise as either computational linguistics, natural language processing, machine learning, etc., but not AI. When pressed, many will highlight that AI is a badly defined concept to start with (more on this below), that it is a catch-all term or worst, just a buzzword. It is open for debate whether this tendency to dissociate with the "AI" label is the result of a conscious decision or just the self-preservation instinct of those who have survived a couple of AI winters!

Researchers have been studying the problem of automatic language translation for more than 60 years. But since the beginning, MT research was not only an end in itself: over time, it proved a fertile ground for the development and testing of some of the central ideas and methods of the artificial intelligence landscape: language analysis, understanding and generation, knowledge representation, pattern recognition, machine learning and, more recently, neural networks and deep learning, to name just a few. Today, the methods used for most text-generation AI applications are increasingly similar to those used for MT: the Transformer neural networks used in the vast majority of LLMs were first developed for translation (Vaswani et al., 2017). In some cases the tools (models, etc.) are literally the same: conversational AI systems are now increasingly used to translate text between many languages (Jiao et al., 2023; Hendy et al., 2023).

But does that make MT "artificial intelligence"? To answer this question, we also need to ask: What is Artificial Intelligence? In their classic AI textbook, Russell et al. (2010) cite no less than eight definitions of AI, among which the two following:

- *"The art of creating machines that perform functions that require intelligence when performed by people."* (Kurzweil et al., 1990)
- *"The study of how to make computers do things at which, at the moment, people are better."* (Rich and Knight, 1990)

Britannica, the web version of the well-known encyclopedia, describes AI as: *"the ability of a digital computer or computer-controlled robot to perform tasks commonly associated with intelligent beings."*[4] And more recently, Coursera, the online learning platform, talks about *"the theory and development of computer systems capable of performing tasks that historically required human intelligence"*.[5]

Admittedly, these are very broad and vague definitions. Yet it seems fairly uncontroversial to claim that translation is a task *"that historically required human intelligence"*, that is *"commonly associated with intelligent beings"*, at which *"at the moment, people are better"* or that *"require[s] intelligence when performed by people."*

To sum up: whether we look at it from a historical, technological or theoretical perspective, MT is AI, and therefore MT text is AI-generated content.

3.2 Should MT be labelled as AI-generated content?

TL;DR: Yes.
If MT text is AIGC, then it follows that any policy for AIGC should apply to MT as well. In the eyes of many, however, not all AI is made equal. For example, most would agree that a picture that was "enhanced" using a cell phone's AI-based photo improvement app doesn't quite fall into the same category as a photo-realistic image generated from a text prompt by a deep learning, text-to-image model.[6] In the case of machine translation, the text is generated from an input text which we assume was itself written by a human. Because the translation aims at

[4] https://www.britannica.com/technology/artificial-intelligence

[5] https://www.coursera.org/articles/what-is-artificial-intelligence

[6] Interestingly, we can ask whether photo-realistic image generation *is* AI, by any of the definitions in Section 3.1.

rendering the meaning of the source text in the target language as accurately as possible, it is tempting to see MT as merely an intermediary in the communication, a kind of "filter".

However, as argued earlier, the methods used for MT and those used for other text-generation applications are increasingly similar, when they are not altogether the same. Therefore, the risks inherent to the use of machine translation are essentially the same as those typically associated with chatbots and other conversational generative AI applications. There is a growing body of reported cases of MT errors with potentially grave consequences for people. Of course, there is the infamous example of the man who was arrested by the police in 2016, after Facebook's MT translated his "Good Morning" post to "hurt them" in English and "attack them" in Hebrew (Hern, 2017). But much more recently, Meta's MT was reported to add the word "terrorist" to some Palestinian users' Instagram profiles (Taylor, 2023). Again, in recent news, there were numerous reports of asylum applications being mishandled by United States immigration as a result of their over-reliance on MT (Liebling et al., 2020; Bhuiyan, 2023; Deck, 2023). MT systems routinely used by medical doctors in the United States when interacting with patients who don't speak English (Mehandru et al., 2022) have been shown to produce errors in medical documents, some of which can cause harm to patients (Khoong et al., 2019; Mehandru et al., 2023).

In summary, there is no good reason to believe that the nature of the risks inherent to MT are substantially different from that of those feared in other AIGC applications. Therefore, we recommend that MT should be labelled as AI-generated content.

3.3 Should there be a specific "MT" label?

TL;DR: Yes.

One of the purposes of labelling AIGC is, as UNESCO puts it, to "*ensure that users can easily identify whether they are interacting with a living being, or with an AI system imitating human or animal characteristics*". In the case of MT, however, there are additional reasons to do that.

Even though the quality of translations produced by MT has greatly improved over the past few years, systems are still known to produce errors. In general, MT quality is highly dependent on text domain and genre, but more importantly on the specific language pair involved (Hendy et al., 2023). Even for well-resourced language pairs such as English-German, accuracy errors (word or phrase mistranslations) make up the majority of problems and are still more than three times more likely to appear in state-of-the-art MT output than in translations produced by professional translators (Freitag et al., 2021). As pointed out by Vieira (2020): "*MT has great potential to facilitate and promote multilingualism, but its speed and usefulness may also prompt end-users to underestimate the complexities of translation while overestimating the capabilities of the technology, which in turn may lead to its misuse.*" This has prompted the need for a new type of digital literacy, what has been called *MT literacy*: "*Using machine translation is easy; using it critically requires some thought. When faced with free, online machine translation, the important question is not how to but rather whether, when, and why to use this technology.*" (Bowker, 2019b; Bowker and Ciro, 2019)

But MT literacy itself is useless if users are unaware that a particular piece of text is machine-translated. Therefore, for users to develop and make use of their judgement when dealing with MT output, it must be explicitly marked as such.

3.4 What should an "MT label" look like?

Obviously, an MT label should state that a given text is a translation and that the translation was performed by a machine. But any additional information that can help the user better assess the risks associated with MT can be useful. For example, an MT label might include:

- The source language. Knowing the source language may alert the user to specific kinds of errors, and therefore help them better assess the risk.
- The source text or, more conveniently, a pointer to the source version of the text. The user may be fluent enough in the source language that they prefer reading the original. Or they might know someone who does and who might be willing to verify the translation. Or they might have other tools at their disposal to help them assess the quality of the translation.
- The name of the MT system that generated it (possibly a detailed signature). Knowing what

system was used might help the user better assess the risks.

- A timestamp indicating when the translation was generated. Knowing that a translation was produced a (relatively) long time ago may inform the user about the expected quality.
- A full disclaimer or warning, informing the user of the potential risks associated with the technology, and/or pointing to resources on MT literacy.

Putting all this information inside a label might be cumbersome. A better approach would be to have a short text advising that "This text was translated from ⟨SourceLanguage⟩ by AI", followed by a link or reference to a document with more detailed information. The label should be written in the same language as the text itself. However, a link or reference to a version of the disclaimer in the document's source language could also be useful.

For organizations with large publication bases, it might be relevant to design a standard logo to accompany the label, thus making the texts (and their associated risks) easier and quicker to recognize by users.

3.5 Labelling vs. Watermarking

TL;DR: Labelling.

In the conversation about transparency and AIGC, there sometimes appears to be some confusion between *labelling* and *watermarking*. It is important to distinguish between the two.

According to Wikipedia: "*A label (as distinct from signage) is a piece of paper, plastic film, cloth, metal, or other material affixed to a container or product, on which is written or printed information or symbols about the product or item. Information printed directly on a container or article can also be considered labelling. [...] Labels may be used for any combination of identification, information, warning, instructions for use, environmental advice or advertising.*"[7] Disregarding the physical medium on which labels are said to be printed ("...*a piece of paper, plastic film, cloth*...") this definition fits nicely with what most people have in mind when talking about labels for AIGC.

Watermarking is quite a different beast. Initially, the term *watermark* referred to a recognizable image or pattern in paper used to determine authenticity. The concept was ported to the digital world in the form of "digital watermarks", i.e. markers covertly embedded in digital content. Digital watermarks have been used for a wide range of applications, such as copyright protection, source tracking, ID card security, fraud and tamper detection, etc.

While this sort of digital watermarking has been more commonly applied to audio, video or image data, techniques also exist for the watermarking of AI-generated text. For example, as early as 2011, Venugopal et al. (2011) proposed a watermarking method for statistical MT that operated by biasing the text generation towards a given portion of the lexicon, i.e. by favouring certain words over others. Text generated in this fashion could then be identified with high accuracy using a statistical test that "knew" the details of the bias. Similar methods have now been proposed for general neural text-generation applications (Kamaruddin et al., 2018; Kirchenbauer et al., 2023). Alternatively, some are advocating for "*AI to have its own alphabet*" (Croll, 2023): under such a scheme, MT systems would naturally produce text using a dedicated character encoding that would uniquely identify its synthetic origin.

For technology provider, the main purpose of watermarking is to be able to detect AI-generated text, especially content that was generated using their own technology, to avoid the model degradation that comes from training on synthetic data (Alemohammad et al., 2024; Shumailov et al., 2024). Because of the requirements of this application, the watermarking techniques developed for MT and other text-generation are typically designed to be resistant to later transformations to the text, such as revisions or post-editing, at least up to a certain point. As a result, a technique such as that of Venugopal et al. (2011) makes it possible to recognize MT text even if the text has been manually edited, for example by a translator. While this is an advantage for excluding MT data from future training sets and test data, it is problematic if the marking is required to be *reversible*, i.e. if we need to be able to "unmark" or "unlabel" text at will, as is the case here (see Section 3.8).

Another important requirement for the application we are interested in here is *perceptibility*: What-

[7] https://en.wikipedia.org/wiki/Label

ever form the labelling takes, the user must be able to see it (or hear it, sense it, etc.) somehow. While both types of watermarking above (encoding-based and lexical) can be detected using computer functions, they are not inherently perceptible.

A final problem with such watermarking is that it either disappears or becomes very difficult to detect as soon as the text is printed on a "hard" medium, such as a (paper) book, a restaurant menu, a road sign, etc. Similarly, watermarking may be lost to someone accessing the information through a screen reader, an audio recording, a braille reader or some other assistive technology.

In the end, for the purposes of informing the end user that a text was machine-translated, a textual label appears to be the simplest and most effective solution. This is what we recommend. However, depending on the intended use of the text, nothing precludes MT text to be both labelled *and* watermarked.

3.6 How do we know it's MT in the first place?

TL;DR: We don't, and so we must rely on voluntary identification.

3.6.1 Automatic Detection

Regulators (the EU, etc.) emphasize the responsibility of technology providers in developing ways to automatically detect AIGC. But most actors in the field recognize that building (and maintaining) such technology is a huge challenge, if not a losing battle altogether (Jovanović et al., 2024; Sadasivan et al., 2024; Krishna et al., 2023; Heikkilä, 2022). Some have recently proposed that any organisation developing a foundation model intended for public use (such as a LLM) should be required by law to demonstrate a reliable detection mechanism for the content generated by the model, as a condition of its public release, and make that detection mechanism freely available to users (Knott et al., 2023). While technology exists to do just that (see Section 3.5), no such legislation has appeared anywhere yet.

For MT, some people have looked at the problem of automatic detection in the past (see for example Bhardwaj et al. (2020)), and there are possibly some specific situations where it can be done reliably. For example, detection may be straightforward if watermarking has been used and the corresponding detection algorithm is available or when the challenge is to find out whether a specific MT system has been used, using methods similar to those developed for plagiarism detection (van der Werff et al., 2022). But for the general case, automatic detection of MT is probably not a viable approach.

3.6.2 Voluntary Labelling

Regarding general AIGC, early actions on the publishing side of Big Tech (social media, etc.) have focused on voluntary labelling by content producers (Suciu, 2023). For example, TikTok is encouraging users to label their AI-generated content as such (Sato, 2023), and Google and Meta require disclosure of AI content in political ads (Duffy, 2023; Isaac, 2023). At the AIGC-producing end, OpenAI puts restrictions on what can and cannot be done with their products. Their Usage Policies have requirements of transparency for some specific usages, encouraging users to "*disclose to people that they are interacting with AI*".[8]

Regarding MT, some MT providers (for example, Systran[9]) offer the possibility of including some form of labelling or watermarking in their system's output. But very often, MT is just one component within a larger application, and the MT system is not the one ultimately responsible for the display of its output.

Therefore, it should be the responsibility of whoever is disseminating (publishing, sending, posting, etc.) a machine translated text to propagate the label for that text if it already exists, or to create one if it doesn't.

It should be noted that this has implications for language service providers (LSPs): organizations who outsource the translation of their content to public or private-sector services will want to know whether their translation providers are using MT as a "productivity tool", and if so, whether all translated content has been manually verified and edited as required (see Section 3.8). Therefore, there should be a requirement for LSPs to appropriately label the texts they return to their clients.

But in the end, our recommendations apply to *all*: anyone disseminating machine translated texts or using MT to create content is responsible for labelling their content as appropriate.

[8] https://openai.com/policies/usage-policies/

[9] https://docs.systran.net/translate/en/user-guide/translation-tools/file-translation...

3.7 Where should MT be labelled?

TL;DR: Everywhere.

Should MT text be labelled everywhere it is used? Or should it be limited to institutional websites and other high-visibility communication channels with users? Should it apply only to contents with long shelf-life or should it also be used for punctual communication such as social media posts and institutional or commercial emails? What about institution-internal and personal communication: email, instant messaging, forms, software user interfaces, etc.?

There are clearly downsides to systematic, wall-to-wall labelling. Text is first and foremost a means of communication, and effective communication as is required from public and private institutions should be clear, precise and to the point. Labels may conflict with other visual requirements of the text, get in the way of communication and affect the user experience in unwanted ways. One extreme example that comes to mind is MT for software localization, where textual content often takes the form of individual words or phrases in buttons, menus, etc. Another example is column or row headers in tables or short captions in figures of automatically generated web pages. When these text items are machine-translated, it is not obvious how to label them clearly, especially if they are mixed with other, non-MT'd elements and if the labels should carry all the relevant information (see Section 3.4).

But then, how does one decide what to label and when? On the related topic of when and how MT text should be post-edited by professional translators, it has been suggested that the level of human intervention should relate to the purpose, value and shelf-life of the content (Way, 2013). Following this logic, labelling would be more appropriate for texts that are expected to have a longer shelf-life or are deemed to be more valuable or serve a more important purpose. But how do we measure value or purpose? And, perhaps more importantly, how do we measure the effect of translation errors on users? We have seen earlier how some errors can have serious consequences for users, even in short-lived, casual settings (see Section 3.2). It has also been observed that small errors, inconsequential in appearance, if they are recurring, may have just as serious effects on users as more critical errors, by gradually eroding the confidence of users over time. Research in the field of User Experience suggests that it may be useful to consider interactions with MT not only as static and isolated events but as part of a communicative process in the short and long term (Guerberof-Arenas and Moorkens, 2023).

Risks in translation (either human or computer) are a somewhat understudied area. In one of the few studies on the subject, Canfora and Ottmann (2018) hypothesize that in the realm of translations, as in areas where risks have been studied more systematically (healthcare, aviation, chemical industry, etc.), severe accidents are likely not caused by one single error but are the result of several failures, each of which would individually lead to only uncritical incidents. Furthermore, they suggest that all incidents, regardless of their severity, have the same root causes and that near misses are nothing but hazardous situations that only by chance did not turn into major accidents. One important implication of this observation is that we can effectively reduce the probability of severe accidents by reducing the number of near misses and minor incidents.

This suggests that the right way to go is to systematically label MT everywhere it is used. If the purpose of labelling is "*to not blur the distinction between the categories of human and machine*" (Grinbaum and Adomaitis, 2022), then this is the logical approach. For users who are knowledgeable about the limitations of MT, this will have the effect of "raising the right flags". And for those who are not, it will foster MT literacy by exposing users to "positive" and "negative" examples in various types of communication settings.

For situations where systematic and precise labelling might interfere with effective communication or with user experience, the best solution may be to have a general disclaimer at the top or bottom of the display (web page, document, form, etc.) stating that "some elements of this page may have been generated by MT", with a link or a reference to resources where the user may find more information. At the other end of the spectrum, for a very long machine-translated document, it may be necessary to repeat this disclaimer periodically.

3.8 What if the MT text was post-edited or verified by a human?

TL;DR: The label can be removed or omitted.

The question of transparency for AIGC is in large part one of responsibility and liability: If a person, either natural or juridical, is willing to stand behind a given content, i.e. certify or guarantee that this content is accurate, adequate, well-formed and fit-for-purpose, then in principle, this should suffice for that content to be viewed as "human-equivalent". And from there, remove any AIGC label that may have initially been affixed to that content, i.e. "unlabel" it.

In the case of MT, this "approval" amounts to certifying that the content is an accurate and well-formed ("fit-for-purpose") version in the target language of the source text of which it is a translation (Bowker, 2019a). In an ideal world, such verification would always be done by a professional translator, but in many practical settings, it can be performed by a competent, bilingual individual with a good knowledge of the original text domain, target audience and communicative intent of the translation.

"Responsibility" is the key word here: by removing an MT label or omitting to label MT-generated text, one is effectively taking personal responsibility for the validity and quality of that content (or, conversely, for any translation error that it may contain).

3.9 What if the source text that was machine-translated is itself AIGC?

TL;DR: It should be labelled as AIGC *and* MT.

This case is simple: any content naturally inherits characteristics of every step or processing it went through. So a text that was originally generated by an AI system (say, ChatGPT, as a response to a prompt or question) and then machine translated (either by the same system or a different one) remains fundamentally AI-generated. In principle, this kind of text would carry both labels: AIGC and MT. And to remove both labels, one would have to validate for each separately, i.e. make sure that the source text is factually accurate, grammatically correct, etc. and then make sure that its translation is adequate, grammatically correct, etc.

4 Summary of Recommendations

Machine translation is AI-generated content. As such, it is subject to the same recommendations as other AIGC. Our recommendation is that machine-translated text be systematically labelled everywhere it is used. The label should explicitly say that the content was machine-translated and specify the language from which it was translated; if possible, the label should also provide a link or reference to the original text, as well as pointers to general resources about MT literacy.

The only condition under which such a label could be omitted or removed is if the entirety of the affected text has been verified and certified fit-for-purpose, ideally by a professional translator, otherwise by a competent bilingual who accepts full responsibility for the quality and appropriateness of the translation.

Acknowledgements

This work has greatly benefited from conversations with and comments from many people. I wish to express special thanks to (in alphabetical order) Gabriel Bernier-Colborne, Lynne Bowker, Atsushi Fujita, Cyril Goutte, Rebecca Knowles, Samuel Larkin, Chi-kiu Lo, Alan Melby and Joss Moorkens.

References

Alemohammad, S., Casco-Rodriguez, J., Luzi, L., Humayun, A. I., Babaei, H., LeJeune, D., Siahkoohi, A., and Baraniuk, R. (2024). Self-Consuming Generative Models Go MAD. In *The Twelfth International Conference on Learning Representations*.

Bhardwaj, S., Alfonso Hermelo, D., Langlais, P., Bernier-Colborne, G., Goutte, C., and Simard, M. (2020). Human or Neural Translation? In Scott, D., Bel, N., and Zong, C., editors, *Proceedings of the 28th International Conference on Computational Linguistics*, pages 6553–6564, Barcelona, Spain (Online). International Committee on Computational Linguistics.

Bhuiyan, J. (2023). Lost in AI translation: growing reliance on language apps jeopardizes some asylum applications. *The Guardian*. Thu 7 Sep 2023.

Bowker, L. (2019a). Fit-for-purpose translation. In *The Routledge handbook of translation and technology*, pages 453–468. Routledge.

Bowker, L. (2019b). Machine translation literacy as a social responsibility. In Adda, G., Choukri, K., Kasinskaite-Buddeberg, I., Mariani, J., Mazo, H., and Sakriani, S., editors, *Proceedings of the 1st international conference on Language Technologies for All*

(LT4All), pages 104–107, Paris, France. European Language Resources Association.

Bowker, L. and Ciro, J. B. (2019). *Machine translation and global research: towards improved machine translation literacy in the scholarly community*. Emerald Publishing, Bingley, first edition edition. OCLC: on1075580986.

Canfora, C. and Ottmann, A. (2018). Of ostriches, pyramids, and Swiss cheese: Risks in safety-critical translations. *Translation Spaces*, 7(2):167–201.

Croll, A. (2023). To Watermark AI, It Needs Its Own Alphabet. *Wired*. July 27, 2023.

Deck, A. (2023). AI translation is jeopardizing Afghan asylum claims. *Rest of World*. 19 April 2023.

Duffy, C. (2023). Google to require disclosures of AI content in political ads. *CNN*. Fri September 8, 2023.

European Commission (2022). The 2022 Code of Practice on Disinformation | Shaping Europe's digital future.

European Commission (2024). The Digital Services Act package | Shaping Europe's digital future.

Freitag, M., Foster, G., Grangier, D., Ratnakar, V., Tan, Q., and Macherey, W. (2021). Experts, Errors, and Context: A Large-Scale Study of Human Evaluation for Machine Translation. *Transactions of the Association for Computational Linguistics*, 9:1460–1474.

Goldstein, J. A., Sastry, G., Musser, M., DiResta, R., Gentzel, M., and Sedova, K. (2023). Generative language models and automated influence operations: Emerging threats and potential mitigations. arXiv:2301.04246 [cs].

Government of Canada (2023). Guide on the use of generative AI.

Grinbaum, A. and Adomaitis, L. (2022). The ethical need for watermarks in machine-generated language. arXiv:2209.03118 [cs].

Guerberof-Arenas, A. and Moorkens, J. (2023). Ethics and Machine Translation: The End User Perspective. In Moniz, H. and Parra Escartín, C., editors, *Towards Responsible Machine Translation: Ethical and Legal Considerations in Machine Translation*, pages 113–133. Springer International Publishing, Cham.

Heikkilä, M. (2022). How to spot AI-generated text. *MIT Technology Review*. 19 December 2022.

Hendy, A., Abdelrehim, M., Sharaf, A., Raunak, V., Gabr, M., Matsushita, H., Kim, Y. J., Afify, M., and Awadalla, H. H. (2023). How Good Are GPT Models at Machine Translation? A Comprehensive Evaluation. arXiv:2302.09210 [cs].

Hern, A. (2017). Facebook translates 'good morning' into 'attack them', leading to arrest. *The Guardian*. Tue 24 October 2017.

Innovation, Science and Economic Development Canada (2023). Voluntary Code of Conduct on the Responsible Development and Management of Advanced Generative AI Systems.

Isaac, M. (2023). Meta to Require Political Advertisers to Disclose Use of A.I. *The New York Times*. 8 November 2023.

Jiao, W., Wang, W., Huang, J.-t., Wang, X., Shi, S., and Tu, Z. (2023). Is ChatGPT A Good Translator? Yes With GPT-4 As The Engine. arXiv:2301.08745 [cs].

Jovanović, N., Staab, R., and Vechev, M. (2024). Watermark Stealing in Large Language Models. In Salakhutdinov, R., Kolter, Z., Heller, K., Weller, A., Oliver, N., Scarlett, J., and Berkenkamp, F., editors, *Proceedings of the 41st International Conference on Machine Learning*, volume 235 of *Proceedings of Machine Learning Research*, pages 22570–22593. PMLR.

Kamaruddin, N. S., Kamsin, A., Por, L. Y., and Rahman, H. (2018). A Review of Text Watermarking: Theory, Methods, and Applications. *IEEE Access*, 6:8011–8028.

Khoong, E. C., Steinbrook, E., Brown, C., and Fernandez, A. (2019). Assessing the Use of Google Translate for Spanish and Chinese Translations of Emergency Department Discharge Instructions. *JAMA Internal Medicine*, 179(4):580.

Kirchenbauer, J., Geiping, J., Wen, Y., Katz, J., Miers, I., and Goldstein, T. (2023). A Watermark for Large Language Models. In Krause, A., Brunskill, E., Cho, K., Engelhardt, B., Sabato, S., and Scarlett, J., editors, *Proceedings of the 40th International Conference on Machine Learning*, volume 202 of *Proceedings of Machine Learning Research*, pages 17061–17084. PMLR.

Knott, A., Pedreschi, D., Chatila, R., Chakraborti, T., Leavy, S., Baeza-Yates, R., Eyers, D., Trotman, A., Teal, P. D., Biecek, P., Russell, S., and Bengio, Y. (2023). Generative AI models should include detection mechanisms as a condition for public release. *Ethics and Information Technology*, 25(4):55.

Krishna, K., Song, Y., Karpinska, M., Wieting, J., and Iyyer, M. (2023). Paraphrasing evades detectors of AI-generated text, but retrieval is an effective defense. In Oh, A., Naumann, T., Globerson, A., Saenko, K., Hardt, M., and Levine, S., editors, *Advances in Neural Information Processing Systems*, volume 36, pages 27469–27500. Curran Associates, Inc.

Kurzweil, R., Richter, R., Kurzweil, R., and Schneider, M. L. (1990). *The age of intelligent machines*, volume 580. MIT press Cambridge.

Liebling, D. J., Lahav, M., Evans, A., Donsbach, A., Holbrook, J., Smus, B., and Boran, L. (2020). Unmet Needs and Opportunities for Mobile Translation AI. In *Proceedings of the 2020 CHI Conference on Human Factors in Computing Systems*, pages 1–13, Honolulu HI USA. ACM.

Mehandru, N., Agrawal, S., Xiao, Y., Gao, G., Khoong, E., Carpuat, M., and Salehi, N. (2023). Physician Detection of Clinical Harm in Machine Translation: Quality Estimation Aids in Reliance and Backtranslation Identifies Critical Errors. In Bouamor, H., Pino, J., and Bali, K., editors, *Proceedings of the 2023 Conference on Empirical Methods in Natural Language Processing*, pages 11633–11647, Singapore. Association for Computational Linguistics.

Mehandru, N., Robertson, S., and Salehi, N. (2022). Reliable and safe use of machine translation in medical settings. In *Proceedings of the 2022 ACM Conference on Fairness, Accountability, and Transparency*, pages 2016–2025.

O'Carroll, L. (2023). Google and Facebook urged by EU to label AI-generated content. *The Guardian*. 5 June 2023.

Pisano, V. (2023). How can we tell whether content is made by AI or a human? Label it. *Macleans.ca*. 29 May 2023.

Rich, E. and Knight, K. (1990). *Artificial intelligence Subsequent Edition [M]*. McGraw-Hill College, second edition.

Russell, S. J., Norvig, P., and Davis, E. (2010). *Artificial intelligence: a modern approach*. Prentice Hall series in artificial intelligence. Prentice Hall, Upper Saddle River, 3rd edition.

Sadasivan, V. S., Kumar, A., Balasubramanian, S., Wang, W., and Feizi, S. (2024). Can AI-Generated Text be Reliably Detected? arXiv:2303.11156 [cs].

Sato, M. (2023). TikTok introduces a way to label AI-generated content. *The Verge*. 19 September 2023.

Shumailov, I., Shumaylov, Z., Zhao, Y., Papernot, N., Anderson, R., and Gal, Y. (2024). AI models collapse when trained on recursively generated data. *Nature*, 631(8022):755–759.

Suciu, P. (2023). 'Created By AI' Warning Labels Are Coming To Social Media. *Forbes*. 2 August 2023.

Taylor, J. (2023). Instagram apologises for adding 'terrorist' to some Palestinian user profiles. *The Guardian*. 20 October 2023.

Thompson, E. (2023). Ottawa unveils new AI code of conduct for Canadian companies. *CBC News*. 27 September 2023.

UNESCO (2022). Recommendation on the Ethics of Artificial Intelligence.

van der Werff, T., van Noord, R., and Toral, A. (2022). Automatic Discrimination of Human and Neural Machine Translation: A Study with Multiple Pre-Trained Models and Longer Context. In Moniz, H., Macken, L., Rufener, A., Barrault, L., Costa-jussà, M. R., Declercq, C., Koponen, M., Kemp, E., Pilos, S., Forcada, M. L., Scarton, C., Van den Bogaert, J., Daems, J., Tezcan, A., Vanroy, B., and Fonteyne, M., editors, *Proceedings of the 23rd Annual Conference of the European Association for Machine Translation*, pages 161–170, Ghent, Belgium. European Association for Machine Translation.

Vaswani, A., Shazeer, N., Parmar, N., Uszkoreit, J., Jones, L., Gomez, A. N., Kaiser, L., and Polosukhin, I. (2017). Attention is all you need. In *Proceedings of the 31st International Conference on Neural Information Processing Systems*, NIPS'17, page 6000–6010, Red Hook, NY, USA. Curran Associates Inc.

Venugopal, A., Uszkoreit, J., Talbot, D., Och, F., and Ganitkevitch, J. (2011). Watermarking the Outputs of Structured Prediction with an application in Statistical Machine Translation. In Barzilay, R. and Johnson, M., editors, *Proceedings of the 2011 Conference on Empirical Methods in Natural Language Processing*, pages 1363–1372, Edinburgh, Scotland, UK. Association for Computational Linguistics.

Vieira, L. N. (2020). Machine translation in the news: A framing analysis of the written press. *Translation Spaces*, 9(1):98–122.

Way, A. (2013). Emerging use-cases for machine translation. In *Proceedings of Translating and the Computer 35*, London, UK. Aslib.

Zakrzewski, C. and Lima-Strong, C. (2023). Europe moves ahead on AI regulation, challenging tech giants' power. *Washington Post*. 14 June 2023.

Best Practices of Successive Halving on Neural Machine Translation and Large Language Models

Xuan Zhang xuanzhang@jhu.edu
Kevin Duh kevinduh@cs.jhu.edu
Department of Computer Science, Johns Hopkins University, Baltimore, Maryland, 21218, USA

Abstract

Hyperparameter optimization (HPO) enhances neural machine translation (NMT) models but demands substantial computational resources. Successive halving, a multi-fidelity HPO method, mitigates this by early stopping unpromising models and allocating more resources to promising ones. This method is particularly relevant for NMT and large language models, which are computationally intensive. However, successive halving relies on a noisy estimation of model performance and assumes that early performance is highly correlated with final performance. We introduce a table lookup benchmark dataset to study the reliability of successive halving and propose best practices for its application in NMT and large language models.

1 Introduction

Hyperparameter optimization (HPO) is crucial yet resource-intensive for transformer-based neural machine translation (NMT) models. Hyperparameters such as learning rate, optimizer, batch size, and the number of nodes in each layer significantly influence the achievement of a state-of-the-art (SOTA) system. According to the ARR Responsible NLP Research guidelines, presenting extensive tables of hyperparameters and the best-found values is essential in research publications. [1]

Recently, with the rise of large language models (LLMs), NMT built upon LLMs has shown promising results (Hendy et al., 2023; Zhu et al., 2023; Sia and Duh, 2023; Zhang et al., 2023b). Adapting LLMs to NMT tasks typically involves in-context learning and supervised fine-tuning. Given the abundance of parallel data, fine-tuning has proven to be more effective than in-context learning (Zhang et al., 2023b). Parameter efficient fine-tuning (PEFT), such as Low-Rank Adapter (LoRA, Hu et al., 2021), is often favored over full fine-tuning due to its efficiencyfewer parameters are trained while achieving comparable or superior performance. Despite the fixed architecture of LLMs during PEFT, new hyperparameters are introduced, including the LoRA rank and the specific parameters to tune, alongside traditional hyperparameters like batch size and learning rate.

NMT models, whether trained from scratch or fine-tuned from LLMs, require extensive computational time, often taking days or weeks to converge. This makes hyperparameter searches over a reasonable space challenging. For instance, if an NMT model takes 2 GPU days to train, tuning 5 hyperparameters with 3 different values each would result in a total of $3^5 * 2 = 486$ GPU days! Practitioners with limited computational resources are thus often forced to resort to manual tuning or random search instead of more systematic methods like grid search or advanced HPO algorithms, increasing the risk of unfair comparisons between systems.

Successive halving (Karnin et al., 2013; Jamieson and Talwalkar, 2016) accelerates HPO by terminating unpromising models early in a set of models trained in parallel, saving more resources with more aggressive early stopping strategies. It has shown effectiveness in computer vision (Li et al., 2018) and NLP tasks (Dodge et al., 2020).

[1] https://aclrollingreview.org/responsibleNLPresearch/

However, its effectiveness for training NMT models or adapting LLMs for NMT tasks remains unclear.

The termination decision in successive halving is heuristic, based on the ranking of model performance up to the current timestamp. It assumes that early performance is highly correlated with late performance, which may not always be true. This raises the question: Does this assumption hold for NMT? If not, can we make it more reliable without relying solely on this assumption?

This paper focuses on the effectiveness of successive halving for HPO in NMT models, whether trained from scratch or fine-tuned from an LLM. Our main contributions are summarized as follows:

- **Dataset:** We build a benchmark dataset, ***NMTLC***[2], to facilitate NMT HPO research. This dataset contains models trained from scratch and fine-tuned from LLMs, with recorded learning curves for various hyperparameter settings. In total, it comprises 2469 models trained on 9 different corpora, costing approximately 2519 GPU days. This is the first HPO benchmark dataset that contains NMT learning curves and features models fine-tuned from LLMs.
- **Evaluation:** We evaluate the effectiveness of successive halving for NMT HPO under different experimental setups.
- **Model:** We introduce a novel model for learning curve extrapolation, built upon the LCRankNet introduced in Wistuba and Pedapati (2020), and name it ***LCRankNet-v2***[3]. We aim to determine whether "looking into the predicted future" enhances the reliability of successive halving compared to "looking back to the completed past."

Our findings indicate that the initial assumption of successive halving-that early performance predicts late performancegenerally holds true for NMT HPO with appropriate setups.

2 Related work

2.1 Hyperparameter optimization

Hyperparameter optimization (HPO) aims to find the optimal hyperparameter configuration with minimal evaluations. HPO methods can be broadly classified into sequential and parallel approaches. Sequential methods, such as Bayesian optimization (Brochu et al., 2010; Shahriari et al., 2015; Frazier, 2018), evaluate one configuration at a time, using the results to inform subsequent evaluations. Parallel methods evaluate multiple configurations simultaneously; examples include population-based training (Jaderberg et al., 2017), CMA-ES, and successive halving (Karnin et al., 2013; Jamieson and Talwalkar, 2016). While most HPO methods are black-box approaches that treat the model training process as opaque, successive halving is a multi-fidelity method that leverages approximations. It uses smaller subsets of data or limits training time to obtain noisy measurements, thereby accelerating the search for optimal configurations.

2.2 Hyperparameter search for NMT

Research on HPO for NMT is limited. Qin et al. (2017) propose an evolution strategy-based HPO method for NMT. Zhang and Duh (2020) release a benchmark dataset (Section 4.1) for comparing HPO methods on NMT, focusing on models trained from scratch. Deb et al. (2022) use a glass-box method to analyze how hyperparameters influence NMT performance, highlighting its connection with HPO. Zhang et al. (2023a) present an HPO toolkit for NMT, implemented as a wrapper on top of the open-source Sockeye NMT software. This toolkit implements the Asynchronous Successive Halving Algorithm (Li et al., 2020), promoting configurations as soon as they are guaranteed to be in the top half, thus running successive halving asynchronously and effectively utilizing computational resources.

2.3 Learning curve extrapolation

Learning curve extrapolation aims to predict model performance later in training based on early checkpoints. Kolachina et al. (2012) model learning curves for statistical machine translation systems by fitting them to various power-law family functions. Domhan et al. (2015) use a weighted combination of parametric model families to model learning curves. Klein et al. (2022) build a Bayesian neural network, while Chandrashekaran and Lane (2017) propose an ensemble method, and Baker et al. (2017)

[2]NMTLC dataset: https://github.com/Este lle/hpo_nmt

[3]LCRankNet-v2 code: https://github.com/Este lle/hpo_nmt

use frequentist regression models for learning curve extrapolation. Adriaensen et al. (2024) propose a transformer pretrained on data generated from a prior, performing approximate Bayesian inference. Wistuba and Pedapati (2020) introduce LCRankNet, which encodes hyperparameters, dataset IDs, model architectures, and partial learning curves for performance prediction.

3 Successive halving

The goal of successive halving (Karnin et al., 2013; Jamieson and Talwalkar, 2016) is to efficiently find the optimal hyperparameter configuration within a given search space. Suppose we have N configurations to explore. We begin by training all N models, and at every c checkpoints, we continue training only the top $\frac{1}{p}$ configurations based on their performance up to that point, discarding the rest. This process is repeated until only one configuration remains, which is then trained to convergence.

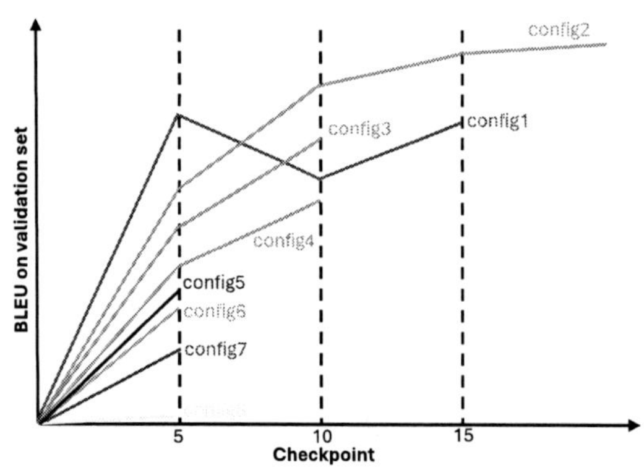

Figure 1: An example of successive halving, where $N = 10, c = 5, p = 2$.

As shown in Figure 1, we start with $N = 10$ configurations and halve ($p = 2$) the number of configurations every $c = 5$ checkpoint. Each cut is based on the best performance of the configurations up to the current checkpoint. For example, at checkpoint 10, when comparing config1 and config3, we compare config1's performance at checkpoint 5 with config3's performance at checkpoint 10.

In this example, assuming it takes one GPU day (20 checkpoints) for each model to converge, successive halving can reduce the total time for hyperparameter search from 10 days to 3.75 days. The aggressiveness of successive halving can be adjusted by changing the values of p and c. For instance, if $p = 3$ and $c = 2$, the total time could be further reduced to 1.3 days. However, a more aggressive strategy increases the risk of discarding good configurations too early. In the case of $p = 3$ and $c = 2$, config1 might be chosen over config2, even if config2 could have performed better in the long run.

4 NMTLC benchmark datasets

To evaluate successive halving on NMT HPO, extensive model training until convergence is required to determine if good models are prematurely discarded. This process is resource-intensive, as each new configuration sampled for successive halving necessitates training a new NMT system from scratch. To facilitate this study, we have created a benchmark dataset that supports a table-lookup framework. We pre-train a large set of NMT systems and record their configurations and learning curves in a table. This allows for efficient evaluation of successive halving by looking up the table as needed, without training each model from scratch, significantly speeding up the experimental process.

Our dataset includes 2469 models trained on 9 different corpora, encompassing both models trained from scratch and those fine-tuned from LLMs, with a total computational cost of approximately 2519 GPU days. This is the first HPO benchmark dataset to contain NMT learning curves, enabling detailed studies on learning curves. It is also the first to include models fine-tuned from LLMs, facilitating HPO research on this emerging task.

method	domain[4]	lang	train	dev	#cfg
scratch	IARPA	sw-en	24k	2675	767
	IARPA	so-en	24k	2675	604
	TED Talks	zh-en	170k	1,958	118
	TED Talks	ru-en	170k	1,958	176
	WMT19	ja-en	4M	5,405	150
	WMT19	en-ja	4M	5,405	168
FT	WMT23	fr-en	404k	289	162
	WMT23	zh-en	421k	2139	162
	WMT23	de-en	435k	2342	162

Table 1: Data used for training NMT systems.

[4]IAPRA: IARPA MATERIAL; TED Talks: Duh (2018); WMT19: Li et al. (2019); WMT23: Neves et al. (2023).

dataset	bpe (1k)	#layers	#embed	#hidden	#att_heads	init_lr (10^{-4})
zh, ru, ja, en	10, 30, 50	2, 4	256, 512, 1024	1024, 2048	8, 16	3, 6, 10
sw	1, 2, 4, 8, 16, 32	1, 2, 4, 6	256, 512, 1024	1024, 2048	8, 16	3, 6, 10
so	1, 2, 4, 8, 16, 32	1, 2, 4	256, 512, 1024	1024, 2048	8, 16	3, 6, 10

Table 2: Hyperparameter search space for trained-from-scratch NMT systems.

4.1 Data & setup for training from scratch

Zhang and Duh (2020) provided a HPO benchmark for NMT tasks, where models are trained from scratch without incorporating learning curves, primarily focusing on evaluating black-box HPO methods such as Bayesian optimization. From their data, we extracted hyperparameter configurations, evaluation results, and learning curves with perplexity on the development set for 1983 NMT models. Table 1 summarizes the 6 MT corpora used for training the systems. The data cover five language pairs and three domains with varying resource levels, from low to high. Table 2 presents the hyperparameter search space for different language pairs.

4.2 Data & setup for fine-tuning from LLMs

LLMs excel in most NLP tasks (Yang et al., 2024). Recently, fine-tuning LLMs for machine translation has shown promising results (Zhang et al., 2023b; Moslem et al., 2023; Zhu et al., 2024). Learning curves from fine-tuned models are rarely studied in the context of HPO and learning curve extrapolation, particularly for fine-tuned LLMs in machine translation. To address this gap, we include fine-tuned LLMs in our NMTLC benchmark datasets.

MT Data: We explore 3 language pairs as shown in Table 1. For fr-en, the input format is as follows:

> Translate French to English: French: [fr sent] English: [en sent] <eos>

A special <eos> token is added for post-processing.

Hyperparameters: We consider four hyperparameters to define the search space:

- **LLM (6):** BLOOMZ 560m, 1b7, and 3b, XGLM 564M, 1.7B, and 2.9B. BLOOMZ is a multilingual model fine-tuned with the xP3 dataset (Muennighoff et al., 2022). XGLM is a multilingual model trained on 30 diverse languages. We treat the choice of LLM as a hyperparameter since in practice the choice of the base model affects final MT accuracy. Various versions affect model size, feed-forward size, number of layers, and vocabulary size.
- **LoRA rank (3):** 2, 16, and 64.
- **Batch size (3):** 16, 32, and 64.
- **Learning rate (3):** $2e-5$, $1e-4$, and $2e-4$.

Fine-tuning Setup: We utilize QLoRA (Dettmers et al., 2023) for parameter-efficient fine-tuning. We set the LoRA scaling factor to 32, limit trainable parameters to the self-attention layers, and apply a dropout rate of 0.05 in the LoRA layer. The model weights are quantized to 4-bit precision, and mixed-precision training (using float16 and float32) is enabled to accelerate the process. We use the Adam optimizer, evaluating performance every 1000 steps, and consider the model converged when performance does not improve for 12 checkpoints. Models are trained on a single NVIDIA RTX GPU with 24GB of memory.

Samples: Each sample in the benchmark dataset includes:

1. Hyperparameter configuration.
2. Meta-information about the MT dataset (size, language pairs, domain).
3. Learning curve: a list of evaluation results (perplexity, BLEU[5]) on the development set throughout training until convergence.
4. Optimal performance: the best point on the learning curve.

For de-en, we provide perplexity learning curves. For fr-en and zh-en, we include both perplexity and BLEU learning curves to study the correlation between these metrics.

4.3 Statistics

We present the statistics of samples in the NMTLC benchmark dataset in this section.

BLEU distribution Figure 2 illustrates the performance variance of NMT models trained with differ-

[5] Obtained by greedy search.

ent hyperparameter configurations in the NMTLC dataset, measured by the BLEU score. Models trained from scratch (*scratch*) and those fine-tuned from LLMs (*ft*) exhibit distinct BLEU score distributions. The BLEU scores of the *scratch* models generally follow a left-skewed distribution, indicating that most configurations result in good performance. In contrast, the BLEU scores of the *ft* models display a multimodal distribution, suggesting a wide variation in performance, with many configurations yielding either very good or poor results. For instance, in *ft_fr-en*, the BLEU scores range widely, with differences up to 30 points between the best and worst models. Additionally, some configurations in almost all tasks (except *scratch_ja-en*) produce nearly zero BLEU scores, underscoring the importance of extensive hyperparameter search. This highlights the necessity of successive halving in efficiently exploring a large search space to find optimal hyperparameter configurations.

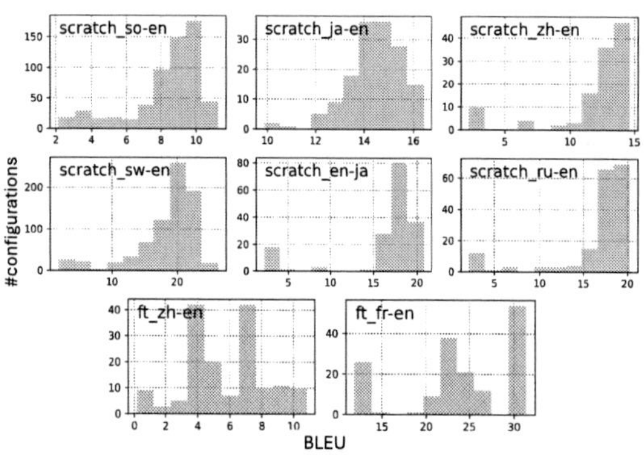

Figure 2: BLEU distribution on the hyperparameter search space.

Length distribution Figure 3 shows the distribution of the lengths of the learning curves in the NMTLC dataset, where longer curves indicate models that take more time to converge. The length distribution reveals that in most tasks, a small number of models have extended training times, resulting in a long right tail in the distribution. In these cases, successive halving can be particularly beneficial, as it can terminate unpromising models early in the training process, thereby saving substantial computational resources. Additionally, the length distributions vary across different tasks. While *scratch_ja-en*, *scratch_en-ja*, and *ft_zh-en* exhibit distributions similar to a normal distribution, other tasks display more left-skewed distributions. This variability further underscores the importance of using successive halving to efficiently navigate the diverse convergence behaviors and optimize hyperparameter configurations.

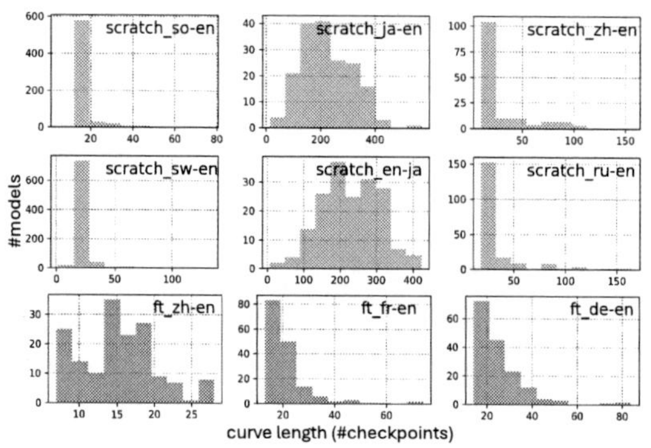

Figure 3: Learning curve length distribution on the hyperparameter search space.

5 On the reliability of successive halving on neural machine translation

To evaluate the reliability of successive halving in NMT, we begin by identifying an appropriate evaluation metric (perplexity vs. BLEU) for termination decisions (Section 5.1). We then investigate whether halving consistently retains the best-performing half of configurations at different learning curve lengths (Section 5.2.1). Finally, we conduct extensive successive halving runs on random subsets of the configuration search space to assess its ability to consistently select the best configuration (Section 5.2.2).

5.1 BLEU vs. perplexity

During training, models can be evaluated on the development set using either BLEU or perplexity. BLEU is more aligned with the ultimate goal of NMT, as BLEU scores are commonly reported for system comparison on development and test sets. However, perplexity is more closely aligned with the training objective and is significantly more efficient to compute. In our experiments, calculating perplexity is approximately 1000 times faster than BLEU on a single sentence, which means obtaining a BLEU score for an evaluation set can take hours. For HPO, we aim to select a configuration quickly while ensuring it achieves the best BLEU score. This raises the question: can we use perplexity instead of BLEU for selection and termination decisions in successive halving to accelerate HPO?

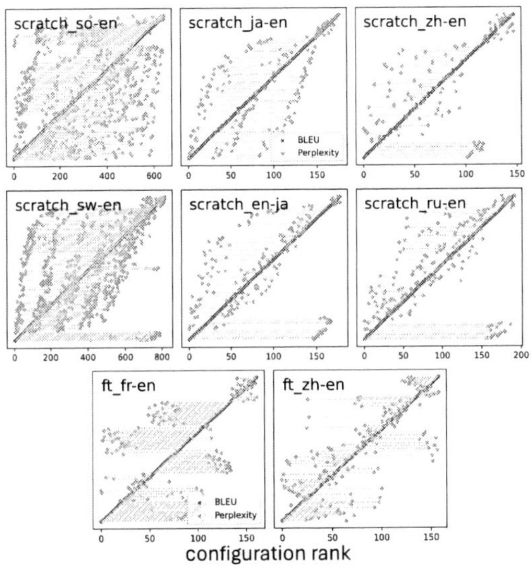

Figure 4: Configurations ranked by perplexity and BLEU. Configurations are ranked by their lowest perplexity on the development set and highest BLEU score, respectively.

Figure 4 shows the ranking of configurations by their best BLEU and perplexity scores on the development set. The results indicate that perplexity does not consistently align with BLEU across all datasets. For example, in *scratch_sw-en*, *scratch_en-ja*, and *scratch_ja-en*, configurations with the best BLEU scores (lower left) often have the worst perplexity. This suggests that perplexity may not be a suitable alternative to BLEU for model selection and early stopping in HPO for NMT tasks.

5.2 Successive halving on NMT

In this section, we evaluate the reliability of successive halving on NMT tasks.

5.2.1 Binary rank

In successive halving, at each checkpoint, the bottom half of the configurations are discarded based on their performance up to that point. To understand how the ranking of partial learning curves correlates with the full curves, we calculate Spearman's rank correlation coefficient (ρ) on the binary ranks of configurations at each checkpoint (Figure 5).

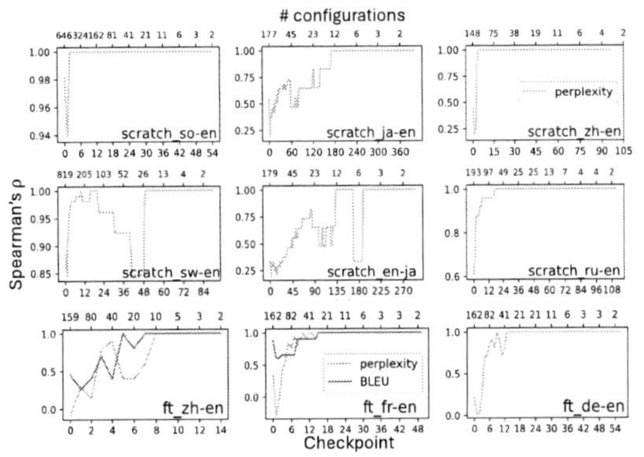

Figure 5: Spearman's rank correlation coefficient ρ on binary ranks of learning curves at each checkpoint. At each checkpoint, learning curves are ranked based on their best performance (perplexity or BLEU on the development set) up to that point. Curves are assigned a rank of 0 if they are in the top half and 1 if they are in the bottom half. There are fewer longer learning curves, as shown in the figure, as the checkpoint number increases, the number of models (upper x-axis) decreases.

Generally, as the number of checkpoints increases, the correlation between the rankings of partial and full learning curves improves. This trend holds true for both perplexity and BLEU. Some datasets, such as *scratch_so-en*, *scratch_zh-en*, and *scratch_ru-en* for perplexity, and *ft_fr-en* for BLEU, achieve high correlation early in training.

5.2.2 Evaluation results

We run successive halving 100 times on randomly sampled subsets of hyperparameter configurations, varying p and c as shown in Table 3. The reliability of successive halving is measured by whether the best configuration is selected at the end (**acc**) and when the best configuration is discarded (**dif**).

Most runs achieve either perfect **acc** or a **dif** of around 1, indicating that the best configuration is usually selected, and if not, it is discarded near the final stage. Increasing the discarding aggressiveness by increasing p and decreasing c reduces reliability (lower **acc** and higher **dif**) unevenly across datasets– *fr-en(ft)* is significantly affected, while *so-en(st)* and *zh-en(st)* remain stable.

	average	p=2,c=10 acc	dif	p=2,c=5 acc	dif	p=4,c=10 acc	dif
st	sw-en	99	0	97	0	95	0
	so-en	100	0	100	0	100	0
	zh-en	100	0	100	0	100	0
	ru-en	100	0	96	0	100	0
	ja-en	69	0.2	67	0.1	68	0.1
	en-ja	77	0.1	69	0.2	70	0.1
ft	fr-en	69	1.2	11	3.6	54	0.9
	zh-en	100	0	83	0.7	100	0
	de-en	100	0	61	1.6	57	0.8

Table 3: Successive halving evaluation results. Each dataset runs successive halving 100 times on randomly selected 40 configurations. The discarding ratio $\frac{p-1}{p}$ and frequency c checkpoints are varied. **Acc** indicates the percentage of runs where the best configuration is selected, and **dif** represents the average difference between total stages and the stage that discards the best configuration. A **dif** of 1 means the best configuration was discarded at the last stage.

6 Learning curve extrapolation

Successive halving uses the best performance observed so far (*BSF*) to rank configurations at each checkpoint, assuming early performance correlates with final performance. However, as shown in Figure 5, this correlation can be low when learning curves are short. To improve on the heuristic BSF, we explore "looking forward into the predicted future" by extrapolating the optimal performance of a configuration based on partial learning curves. This predicted optimal accuracy can then be used to rank configurations more effectively in successive halving.

6.1 LCRankNet-v2

Our learning curve extrapolation model, LCRankNet-v2, is a variation of LCRankNet (Wistuba and Pedapati, 2020). It takes three inputs: partial learning curves, hyperparameter configurations, and task meta-information (including dataset ID, task type, source and target language, and base model). The architecture is shown in Figure 6. We removed the architecture embedding component from LCRankNet since it is defined in the hyperparameter configuration in our settings. The experimental setup and configurations for LCRankNet-v2 are detailed in Appendix A.

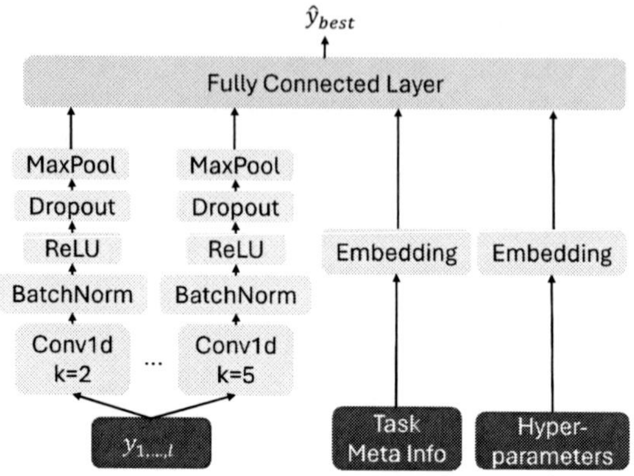

Figure 6: Architecture of LCRankNet-v2. Partial learning curves $(y_{1,\cdots,l})$ are processed through convolutional layers with kernel sizes ranging from 2 to 5. Task meta-information and hyperparameter configurations are embedded and then combined with the curve features. The concatenated features are fed into fully connected layers to predict the best performance of the configuration ($\hat{y}_{best}$).

6.2 Training objectives

LCRankNet-v2 is trained using two loss functions: reconstruction loss $\mathcal{L}_{rec}$ and rank loss $\mathcal{L}_{rank}$. Given the true best performance y^i_{best} and the prediction $\hat{y}^i_{best}$ for learning curve i, the reconstruction loss is:

$$\mathcal{L}_{rec} = \sum_i (y^i_{best} - \hat{y}^i_{best})^2. \tag{1}$$

The probability that configuration i outperforms configuration j is defined as:

$$p_{i>j} = \begin{cases} 1 & \text{if } y^i_{best} > y^j_{best} \\ 0.5 & \text{if } y^i_{best} = y^j_{best} \\ 0 & \text{if } y^i_{best} < y^j_{best} \end{cases} \tag{2}$$

The corresponding prediction is:

$$\hat{p}_{i>j} = \frac{e^{\hat{y}^i_{best} - \hat{y}^j_{best}}}{1 + e^{\hat{y}^i_{best} - \hat{y}^j_{best}}}. \tag{3}$$

The rank loss is a binary cross-entropy loss:

$$\mathcal{L}_{rank} = \sum_{i,j} -p_{i>j} \log \hat{p}_{i>j} - (1 - p_{i>j}) \log(1 - \hat{p}_{i>j}) \tag{4}$$

To ensure fair comparisons, we always compare partial learning curves of the same length when computing $\mathcal{L}_{rank}$. To handle curves of different lengths, we include multiple truncated versions of each full learning curve in the training set. The total loss is:

$$\mathcal{L}_0 = w_{rec}\mathcal{L}_{rec} + w_{rank}\mathcal{L}_{rank}. \quad (5)$$

Additionally, we consider the *BSF* when ranking configurations. If the model predicts that performance will not improve beyond *BSF*, we set $\hat{y}_{best}$ to BSF. The probability of improvement p^{imp} over BSF is defined similarly to $pi > j$, and the improvement loss $\mathcal{L}_{imp}$ is:

$$\mathcal{L}_{imp} = \sum_i -p_i^{imp} \log \hat{p}_i^{imp} - (1-p_i^{imp}) \log(1-\hat{p}_i^{imp}). \quad (6)$$

The updated total loss is:

$$\mathcal{L}_1 = \mathcal{L}_0 + w_{imp}\mathcal{L}_{imp}. \quad (7)$$

During training, we set w_{rec} to 1, w_{rank} to 1000, and w_{imp} to 100. At inference, if $\hat{p}_i^{imp} > 0.5$, we set $\hat{y}_{best}$ to *BSF*.

6.3 Experiment results

We conduct experiments to evaluate whether learning curve extrapolation improves the reliability of successive halving. Specifically, we compare the accuracy of ranking configurations on perplexity using LCRankNet-v2's predictions versus the heuristic *BSF*. LCRankNet-v2 was trained using a leave-one-out strategy, excluding the target dataset from the training data and warming up the network with 20 examples from the target dataset, as suggested by Wistuba and Pedapati (2020).

In Table 4, we compare the performance of the heuristic *BSF* and LCRankNet-v2 trained to minimize $\mathcal{L}_0$ in predicting the rank between two configurations given partial learning curves, where we consider all the possible pairs with the same length. There are four cases: both methods rank correctly (**B◯P◯**), both methods rank incorrectly (**B✕P✕**), or one is correct and the other is incorrect (**B✕P◯** or **B◯P✕**). On 7 out of 9 datasets, **B✕P◯** is less than **B◯P✕**, indicating that while LCRankNet-v2 can sometimes correct *BSF*'s mistakes, overall, *BSF* performs better.

When trained to minimize $\mathcal{L}_1$, LCRankNet-v2 converges to *BSF* on all datasets, resulting in **B✕P◯** = **B◯P✕** = 0, and **B◯** = **P◯**. Therefore, LCRankNet-v2 does not outperform the heuristic *BSF* in most of our settings.

	acc	B◯P◯	B✕P◯	B◯P✕	B✕P✕
sw-en	99.78%	95.30%	0.04%	4.48%	0.18%
so-en	99.76%	93.79%	0.19%	5.97%	0.05%
zh-en	75.73%	63.07%	17.61%	12.66%	6.63%
ru-en	99.63%	83.35%	0.12%	16.28%	0.24%
ja-en	95.86%	73.19%	2.35%	22.67%	2.08%
en-ja	94.73%	64.64%	4.73%	30.09%	0.56%
fr-en	84.43%	57.69%	6.94%	26.64%	8.73%
zh-en	75.73%	63.07%	17.61%	12.66%	6.63%
de-en	85.94%	35.20%	5.32%	50.74%	8.74%

Table 4: Performance of LCRankNet-v2 trained with $\mathcal{L}_0$. **Acc** (or **B◯**) indicates the accuracy of ranking configuration pairs based on *BSF*. *B* represents ranking by *BSF* (vanilla successive halving), while *P* represents ranking by LCRankNet-v2's prediction. If **B✕P◯** > **B◯P✕**, successive halving is more reliable with LCRankNet-v2's prediction.

Is learning curve extrapolation necessary for successive halving on NMT? Not really. In Table 4, **P** generally underperforms compared to **B** in ranking configurations. This suggests that incorporating learning curve extrapolation is unlikely to significantly alter the results of successive halving.

7 Conclusions

Successive halving is both efficient and effective for hyperparameter search in NMT tasks, significantly reducing computational resources and reliably selecting the best model with appropriate setups. However, its reliability depends on the target task and the choices of the cutting ratio (p) and cutting frequency (c). Based on the studies conducted in this paper, we propose the following **best practices for successive halving in NMT and LLMs**:

1. Rank configurations at each checkpoint based on BLEU rather than perplexity.
2. Before running an extensive hyperparameter search with successive halving, train several configurations to convergence to estimate training time and learning curve trends, which helps in determining appropriate values for p and c.
3. Instead of keeping only one configuration at the end, increase the number of configurations that are trained to convergence (two might be sufficient, as our experiments suggest) to reduce the risk of discarding the best one at the last stage.

Acknowledgements

This work is supported in part by an Amazon Initiative for Artificial Intelligence (AI2AI) Fellowship for Ph.D. students.

References

Adriaensen, S., Rakotoarison, H., Müller, S., and Hutter, F. (2024). Efficient bayesian learning curve extrapolation using prior-data fitted networks. *Advances in Neural Information Processing Systems*, 36.

Baker, B., Gupta, O., Raskar, R., and Naik, N. (2017). Accelerating neural architecture search using performance prediction. *arXiv preprint arXiv:1705.10823*.

Brochu, E., Cora, V. M., and De Freitas, N. (2010). A tutorial on bayesian optimization of expensive cost functions, with application to active user modeling and hierarchical reinforcement learning. *arXiv preprint arXiv:1012.2599*.

Chandrashekaran, A. and Lane, I. R. (2017). Speeding up hyper-parameter optimization by extrapolation of learning curves using previous builds. In *Machine Learning and Knowledge Discovery in Databases: European Conference, ECML PKDD 2017, Skopje, Macedonia, September 18–22, 2017, Proceedings, Part I 10*, pages 477–492. Springer.

Deb, K., Zhang, X., and Duh, K. (2022). Post-hoc interpretation of transformer hyperparameters with explainable boosting machines. In *Proceedings of the Fifth BlackboxNLP Workshop on Analyzing and Interpreting Neural Networks for NLP*, pages 51–61, Abu Dhabi, United Arab Emirates (Hybrid). Association for Computational Linguistics.

Dettmers, T., Pagnoni, A., Holtzman, A., and Zettlemoyer, L. (2023). Qlora: Efficient finetuning of quantized llms. *arXiv preprint arXiv:2305.14314*.

Dodge, J., Ilharco, G., Schwartz, R., Farhadi, A., Hajishirzi, H., and Smith, N. (2020). Fine-tuning pretrained language models: Weight initializations, data orders, and early stopping. *arXiv preprint arXiv:2002.06305*.

Domhan, T., Springenberg, J. T., and Hutter, F. (2015). Speeding up automatic hyperparameter optimization of deep neural networks by extrapolation of learning curves. In *Twenty-fourth international joint conference on artificial intelligence*.

Duh, K. (2018). The multitarget ted talks task. `http://www.cs.jhu.edu/~kevinduh/a/multitarget-tedtalks/`.

Frazier, P. I. (2018). A tutorial on bayesian optimization. *arXiv preprint arXiv:1807.02811*.

Hendy, A., Abdelrehim, M., Sharaf, A., Raunak, V., Gabr, M., Matsushita, H., Kim, Y. J., Afify, M., and Awadalla, H. H. (2023). How good are gpt models at machine translation? a comprehensive evaluation. *arXiv preprint arXiv:2302.09210*.

Hu, E. J., Shen, Y., Wallis, P., Allen-Zhu, Z., Li, Y., Wang, S., Wang, L., and Chen, W. (2021). Lora: Low-rank adaptation of large language models. *arXiv preprint arXiv:2106.09685*.

Jaderberg, M., Dalibard, V., Osindero, S., Czarnecki, W. M., Donahue, J., Razavi, A., Vinyals, O., Green, T., Dunning, I., Simonyan, K., et al. (2017). Population based training of neural networks. *arXiv preprint arXiv:1711.09846*.

Jamieson, K. and Talwalkar, A. (2016). Non-stochastic best arm identification and hyperparameter optimization. In *Artificial intelligence and statistics*, pages 240–248. PMLR.

Karnin, Z., Koren, T., and Somekh, O. (2013). Almost optimal exploration in multi-armed bandits. In *International conference on machine learning*, pages 1238–1246. PMLR.

Klein, A., Falkner, S., Springenberg, J. T., and Hutter, F. (2022). Learning curve prediction with bayesian neural networks. In *International conference on learning representations*.

Kolachina, P., Cancedda, N., Dymetman, M., and Venkatapathy, S. (2012). Prediction of learning curves in machine translation. In *Proceedings of the 50th Annual Meeting of the Association for Computational Linguistics (Volume 1: Long Papers)*, pages 22–30.

Li, L., Jamieson, K., DeSalvo, G., Rostamizadeh, A., and Talwalkar, A. (2018). Hyperband: A novel bandit-based approach to hyperparameter optimization. *Journal of Machine Learning Research*, 18(185):1–52.

Li, L., Jamieson, K., Rostamizadeh, A., Gonina, E., Ben-Tzur, J., Hardt, M., Recht, B., and Talwalkar, A. (2020).

A system for massively parallel hyperparameter tuning. *Proceedings of Machine Learning and Systems*, 2:230–246.

Li, X., Michel, P., Anastasopoulos, A., Belinkov, Y., Durrani, N., Firat, O., Koehn, P., Neubig, G., Pino, J., and Sajjad, H. (2019). Findings of the first shared task on machine translation robustness. In *Proceedings of the Fourth Conference on Machine Translation*.

Moslem, Y., Haque, R., and Way, A. (2023). Fine-tuning large language models for adaptive machine translation. *arXiv preprint arXiv:2312.12740*.

Muennighoff, N., Wang, T., Sutawika, L., Roberts, A., Biderman, S., Scao, T. L., Bari, M. S., Shen, S., Yong, Z.-X., Schoelkopf, H., et al. (2022). Crosslingual generalization through multitask finetuning. *arXiv preprint arXiv:2211.01786*.

Neves, M., Jimeno Yepes, A., NÃľvÃľol, A., Bawden, R., Di Nunzio, G. M., Roller, R., Thomas, P., Vezzani, F., Vicente Navarro, M., Yeganova, L., Wiemann, D., and Grozea, C. (2023). Findings of the wmt 2023 biomedical translation shared task: Evaluation of chatgpt 3.5 as a comparison system. In *Proceedings of the Eighth Conference on Machine Translation*, pages 43–54, Singapore. Association for Computational Linguistics.

Qin, H., Shinozaki, T., and Duh, K. (2017). Evolution strategy based automatic tuning of neural machine translation systems. In *Proceedings of the 14th International Workshop on Spoken Language Translation*.

Shahriari, B., Swersky, K., Wang, Z., Adams, R. P., and De Freitas, N. (2015). Taking the human out of the loop: A review of bayesian optimization. *Proceedings of the IEEE*, 104(1):148–175.

Sia, S. and Duh, K. (2023). In-context learning as maintaining coherency: A study of on-the-fly machine translation using large language models. In *Proceedings of Machine Translation Summit XIV (Volume 1: Research Track)*.

Wistuba, M. and Pedapati, T. (2020). Learning to rank learning curves. In *International Conference on Machine Learning*, pages 10303–10312. PMLR.

Yang, J., Jin, H., Tang, R., Han, X., Feng, Q., Jiang, H., Zhong, S., Yin, B., and Hu, X. (2024). Harnessing the power of llms in practice: A survey on chatgpt and beyond. *ACM Transactions on Knowledge Discovery from Data*, 18(6):1–32.

Zhang, X. and Duh, K. (2020). Reproducible and efficient benchmarks for hyperparameter optimization of neural machine translation systems.

Zhang, X., Duh, K., and McNamee, P. (2023a). A hyperparameter optimization toolkit for neural machine translation research. In *Proceedings of the 61st Annual Meeting of the Association for Computational Linguistics (Volume 3: System Demonstrations)*, pages 161–168, Toronto, Canada. Association for Computational Linguistics.

Zhang, X., Rajabi, N., Duh, K., and Koehn, P. (2023b). Machine translation with large language models: Prompting, few-shot learning, and fine-tuning with qlora. In *Proceedings of the Eighth Conference on Machine Translation*, pages 468–481, Singapore. Association for Computational Linguistics.

Zhu, D., Chen, P., Zhang, M., Haddow, B., Shen, X., and Klakow, D. (2024). Fine-tuning large language models to translate: Will a touch of noisy data in misaligned languages suffice? *arXiv preprint arXiv:2404.14122*.

Zhu, W., Liu, H., Dong, Q., Xu, J., Kong, L., Chen, J., Li, L., and Huang, S. (2023). Multilingual machine translation with large language models: Empirical results and analysis. *arXiv preprint arXiv:2304.04675*.

A LCRankNet-v2 Training Setup

We pad partial learning curves to a length of 450. The convolutional layers have an output channel size of 128. Each hyperparameter and task meta-information is embedded with a size of 2. The feed-forward layer size is set to 128. For regularization, we use a dropout rate of 0.1 and a weight decay of 10^{-3}. The initial learning rate is set to 10^{-4}, with Adam as the optimizer and cosine annealing as the learning rate scheduler. The minimum learning rate (η_{min}) is set to 10^{-7}, and $T_{\max}$ is set to 10,000. Validation occurs every 1000 steps, and the batch size is 64. Training runs for 5 epochs.

Entropy– and Distance-Regularized Attention Improves Low-Resource Neural Machine Translation

Ali Araabi a.araabi@uva.nl
Vlad Niculae v.niculae@uva.nl
Christof Monz c.monz@uva.nl
Informatics Institute, University of Amsterdam, Amsterdam, The Netherlands

Abstract

Transformer-based models in Neural Machine Translation (NMT) rely heavily on multi-head attention for capturing dependencies within and across source and target sequences. In Transformers, attention mechanisms dynamically determine which parts of the sentence to focus on in the encoder and decoder through self-attention and cross-attention. Our experiments show that high-resource NMT systems often exhibit a specific peaked attention distribution, indicating a focus on key elements. However, in low-resource NMT, attention tends to be dispersed throughout the sentence, lacking the focus demonstrated by high-resource models. To tackle this issue, we present EaDRA (Entropy– and Distance-Regularized Attention), which introduces an inductive bias to prioritize essential elements and guide the attention mechanism accordingly. Extensive experiments using EaDRA on diverse low-resource language pairs demonstrate significant improvements in translation quality, while incurring negligible computational cost.

1 Introduction

Neural networks have revolutionized Machine Translation (MT), as evidenced by the significant progress made in recent years (Sutskever et al., 2014). The Transformer architecture (Vaswani et al., 2017) has garnered substantial attention and achieved remarkable advancements across various downstream tasks (Devlin et al., 2019; Liu et al., 2020; Brown et al., 2020), including its application to Neural Machine Translation (NMT). However, the performance of the Transformer architecture heavily relies on the effectiveness and reliability of its attention mechanism.

Our observations from well-performing models suggest that attention should prioritize important elements, resulting in a peaked distribution of attention weights. By emphasizing crucial information, the attention mechanism enables more accurate predictions. This selective attention allows the model to effectively capture and utilize relevant information, leading to improved performance. Therefore, optimizing the attention mechanism is critical for harnessing the full potential of the Transformer architecture and enhancing its performance across tasks, including NMT. However, achieving focused attention behavior poses a significant challenge for NMT systems Raganato et al. (2020), especially in low-resource settings. Our preliminary experiments show that as the amount of available training data decreases, NMT systems tend to exhibit a lack of the desired focused attention behavior. In such low-resource scenarios, where training data is limited, the attention distribution becomes more dispersed and less selective. Consequently, the model's ability to effectively capture and utilize crucial information is hindered, leading to reduced translation performance. Therefore, as the amount of available data diminishes, it becomes crucial to develop techniques that can guide the attention mechanism towards relevant and informative elements of the source sentence. In order to address this issue, prior research has suggested hard-coded or fixed attention patterns for self-attention heads to improve translation quality (Raganato et al., 2020; You et al., 2020). However, the complexity and diversity of language necessitate the consideration of varied attention patterns for different sentences in the context of translation. By constraining the attention weights to fixed values, the model may encounter difficulties in accommodating diverse sentence structures and capturing long-range dependencies with accuracy.

Consequently, this constraint may result in diminished performance (You et al., 2020), particularly for sentences that do not align harmoniously with the predetermined attention patterns.

In this paper, after identifying a significant difference in the entropies of attention heads between high-resource and low-resource trained models (Section 5.1), we introduce an inductive bias through the proposition of entropy and distance regularization (Section 3.3). Our approach aims to induce selective attention by regularizing the distance and entropy in the distribution of attention heads. Specifically, we introduce a novel term into the loss function to guide the learning process, which encourages the low-resource NMT model to emulate the patterns observed in the attention of higher-resource models. This additional bias is incorporated to improve the low-resource NMT model's capability to capture intricate language patterns and enhance translation performance. Experimental results demonstrate the effectiveness of our approach and underscore the importance of inductive bias in narrowing the performance disparity between low– and high-resource NMT systems.

2 Related work

Prior work has explored various approaches to improve low-resource performance by leveraging high-resource language pairs. This includes initializing model parameters from a large-scale trained model (Zoph et al., 2016), as well as techniques such as Multilingual Neural Machine Translation (Aharoni et al., 2019), cross-lingual knowledge distillation (Tan et al., 2019; Saleh et al., 2020) and large pre-trained models that aim for universal language understanding (Liu et al., 2020; Tang et al., 2020; Brown et al., 2020; Touvron et al., 2023). While these methods have significantly improved low-resource NMT, they rely on the availability of a large amount of additional data. However, it is crucial to explore techniques that facilitate the more efficient utilization of the model. Inductive bias plays a fundamental role in machine learning as it allows for the incorporation of prior knowledge or assumptions into learning systems (Mitchell, 1980). Different regularization techniques and architectural choices can introduce specific biases to shape the behavior of models. For example, regularization biases models towards relying less on a few influential features, Convolutional Neural Networks bias models to capture local relationships between input, and attention mechanisms (Bahdanau et al., 2015; Vaswani et al., 2017) bias models to capture long-range dependencies. Additionally, in the context of attention mechanisms, specific biases can be introduced to shape the behavior of models and improve their performance. Lin et al. (2018) encourage the attention to pay more focus on the content words rather than functions words. In the context of summarization, Aralikatte et al. (2021) propose an attention mechanism that proactively generates tokens in the decoder that are similar or topical to the input. Niculae and Blondel (2017) introduce an attention mechanism that is encouraged to assign similar attention weights to consecutive words. Structured attention networks (Kim et al., 2017) incorporate graphical models to generalize simple attention, while the training time significantly (5×) increases. More similar to our motivation, LP-SparseMAP (Niculae and Martins, 2020) models attention distance between consecutive words for a classification task by introducing trainable parameters, but its scalability to large-scale experiments is limited. In contrast, our approach, based on applying a regularizer, is faster, less complex, and can be efficiently executed on GPUs, making it scalable for large-scale training and fine-tuning setups.

The closest work to our method is Fixed-attention (Raganato et al., 2020), which enforces fixed (untrainable) attention patterns. However, they focus solely on encoder self-attention, overlooking the importance of cross-attention heads in neural machine translation (Voita et al., 2019; You et al., 2020). Similarly, You et al. (2020) introduce Hard-Coded Gaussian Attention that replaces the attention distribution computation, i.e., scaled dot product of queries and keys, with a fixed Gaussian distribution, leading to a negative impact on translation quality. Given the concept of entropy that has been used in machine translation (Montahaei et al., 2019), in the next section, we propose our method that can be applied to all different attention components, i.e., encoder self-attention, decoder self-attention, and encoder-decoder (cross) attention, while consistently yielding significant improvements across various experimental setups.

3 Methodology

3.1 Entropy

Entropy, a fundamental concept in information theory, has found various applications in the field of NLP (Pimentel et al., 2021; Vanmassenhove et al., 2021). One prominent area where the concept of entropy has been utilized is in language modeling and generation (Han et al., 2018; Meister et al., 2020). By quantifying the degree of uncertainty or unpredictability of a language model's output, entropy serves as a measure of the model's confidence or information content (Shannon, 1948). Given a probability vector $\boldsymbol{a} \in \mathbb{R}^n$, i.e., whose entries are non-negative and sum to 1, the Shannon entropy is defined as:

$$H(\boldsymbol{a}) := -\sum_{i=1}^{n} a_i \log_2(a_i) \tag{1}$$

In order to capture the shape of attention distributions (more peaked versus more flat) we use the Shannon entropy, defined in Equation 1. For a discrete distribution of dimension n, Shannon entropy takes values between 0 and $\log_2 n$, with $H(\boldsymbol{a}) = 0$ when $\boldsymbol{a}$ is a peaked one-hot vector, and $H(\boldsymbol{a}) = \log_2 n$ when $\boldsymbol{a} = (1/n, \dots, 1/n)$. where we define the length-normalized entropy:

$$H_N(\boldsymbol{a}) := \frac{1}{\log_2 n} H(\boldsymbol{a}) \tag{2}$$

in order to remove unwanted effects induced by varying sentence lengths, by ensuring the output of H_N falls within the range of 0 to 1.

3.2 Entropy penalties

We propose a method to replicate the desirable behavior observed in higher-resource models by introducing an inductive bias to the attention mechanism in lower-resource models, encouraging a focused behavior to guide the attention mechanism towards more important information. In Transformers, there are multiple attention heads that allow the model to capture diverse and fine-grained relationships within the input sequence: enc (self-attention in the encoder), dec (self-attention in the decoder), and x (encoder-decoder or cross attention). Each attention mechanism computes the attention distribution for each word in the input sentence x. More specifically, when translating a sentence pair x, y, the attention heads of a Transformer model compute several attention distributions:

$$\text{Attention}(x, h, t) = \sum_{i=1}^{n} \boldsymbol{a}_{i,h,t} \cdot V_{i,h,t} \tag{3}$$

where $V_{i,h,t}$ is the value matrix and $\boldsymbol{a}_{i,h,t}$ is the attention distribution at word i calculated at head h, for attention type $t \in \{\text{enc}, \text{dec}, \text{x}\}$. $\boldsymbol{a}_{i,h,t}$ is a probability vector of length n_{src} when $t \in \{\text{enc}, \text{x}\}$ and of length n_{tgt} when $t = \text{dec}$.

To encourage peaked attention and nudge attention heads toward selecting the important information, we apply an entropy-minimizing penalty on all attention distributions:

$$R_{\text{peak}} := \sum_{i,h,t} H_N(\boldsymbol{a}_{i,h,t}), \tag{4}$$

By itself, this regularizer can force attention heads to trivial solutions, e.g., where all mass is concentrated on a token in a sentence. To mitigate this we invoke another inductive bias based on a desirable property observed in high-performing models: even though individual attention heads are peaked, the attention distribution averaged over the entire sentence:

$$\bar{\boldsymbol{a}}_{h,t} = \frac{1}{n} \sum_{i=1}^{n} \boldsymbol{a}_{i,h,t} \tag{5}$$

should be flat. We therefore propose an additional sentence-level entropy-maximizing penalty:

$$R_{\text{sent}} := -\sum_{h,t} H_N(\bar{\boldsymbol{a}}_{h,t}) \tag{6}$$

3.3 EaDRA (Entropy- and Distance-Regularized Attention)

In this section, we propose a distance-based method that goes beyond simply minimizing attention entropies. This method not only reduces entropy and enhances attention concentration, but also induces a preference for attending to adjacent tokens, motivated by the significance of proximity-based attention in NMT tasks (Raganato et al., 2020).

To develop the intuition, we focus on a single attention head (hence temporarily dropping the h, t

indices). Imagine for a moment our attention was a hard selection mechanism, e.g., $(\boldsymbol{e}_i)_{j_i} = 1$, indicating that attention at token i selects only token j_i. If neighboring words and contiguous phrases are highly relevant to each other, we would expect the total distance between consecutive selections

$$R_{\text{dist}} \cong \sum_{i=1}^{n-1} d(j_i, j_{i+1}) \tag{7}$$

to be rather small, where d is a discrete, one-dimensional distance function,[1] and $\cong$ is used since this is just an intuition and not yet a usable definition: since our attention is soft and not hard, we cannot directly measure this total distance suggested by Equation 7. Instead, we relax the definition by considering expectation over j_i and j_{i+1}, interpreted as random variables with marginal distributions $\boldsymbol{a}_i$, respectively $\boldsymbol{a}_{i+1}$. We can then penalize the total *expected distance*:

$$\begin{aligned} R_{\text{dist}} &:= \sum_{i=1}^{n-1} \mathbb{E}_{j_i}\mathbb{E}_{j_{i+1}}[d(j_i, j_{i+1})] \\ &= \sum_{i-1}^{n-1} \boldsymbol{a}_i^\top \boldsymbol{D} \boldsymbol{a}_{i+1}, \end{aligned} \tag{8}$$

where $\boldsymbol{D}$ is the distance matrix defined by $(\boldsymbol{D})_{st} = d(s,t)$ for our chosen distance function d. This matrix can be precomputed and the quadratic form in Equation 8 is fast to evaluate on GPUs, although we remark, since d is symmetric, that $\boldsymbol{D}$ is a Toeplitz matrix and therefore R_{dist} could be computed via fast discrete Fourier transform.

Putting together all terms, our objective for a given training sentence pair (x, y) minimizes:

$$\begin{aligned} L(x,y) = &\sum_{i=1}^{n} -\log p(y_i \mid x, y_{1:i-1}) \\ &+ \alpha_{\text{peak}} R_{\text{peak}} + \alpha_{\text{sent}} R_{\text{sent}} + \alpha_{\text{dist}} R_{\text{dist}}. \end{aligned} \tag{9}$$

Here, α parameters control the relative impact of the various penalties. We call this method EaDRA (Entropy- and Distance-Regularized Attention), the distance-based and entropy-based regularizers. Unlike fixed diagonal patterns in attention, EaDRA allows for more flexibility in achieving a peaky attention distribution.

4 Experimental setup

4.1 Data setup

In our preliminary experiments, we use a dataset comprising 4 million German-English training samples from WMT14, which includes Europarl, Common Crawl, and News Commentary.

Code	Dataset	#Sents
Ex. LR		
Be-En	TED Qi et al. (2018)	4.5k
Gl-En	TED Qi et al. (2018)	10k
De-En	WMT14	50k
Sk-En	TED Qi et al. (2018)	55k
LR		
Ko-En	Jungyeul Park et al. (2016)	90k
Kk-En	WMT19	91k
En-De	WMT14	100k
Vi-En	IWSLT15 (Cettolo et al., 2012)	133k
En-De	IWSLT14 (Cettolo et al., 2012)	160k
Tr-En	WMT17	207k
Ja-En	IWSLT17 (Cettolo et al., 2012)	223k
En-De	WMT14	250k

Table 1: Details of extremely low-resource (Ex. LR) and low-resource (LR) datasets in our experiments.

To simulate the low-resource scenario in a controlled setting, we randomly choose subsets of 50k, 100k, 250k and 1m samples. We evaluate on the newstest2014 test set. Additionally, we conduct experiments on two sets of language pairs (Table 1), one representing low-resource scenarios and the other representing extremely low-resource scenarios.

All datasets, except Japanese-English, are preprocessed by applying punctuation normalization, tokenization (Koehn et al., 2007), limiting the length of the sentences to 200 tokens and removing sentence pairs with a source/target length ratio exceeding 1.5, following previous work (Ng et al., 2019). Then, we use BPE (Sennrich et al., 2016) to split the data with BPE parameter selection with respect to the data size (Araabi and Monz, 2020).

For the Japanese-English language pair, we use SentencePiece with a shared vocabulary size of 16k, as it has been widely recognized for its effectiveness in handling Japanese text (Kudo and Richardson,

[1] We use the absolute distance, $d(s,t) = |s - t|$, but arbitrary functions may be used instead.

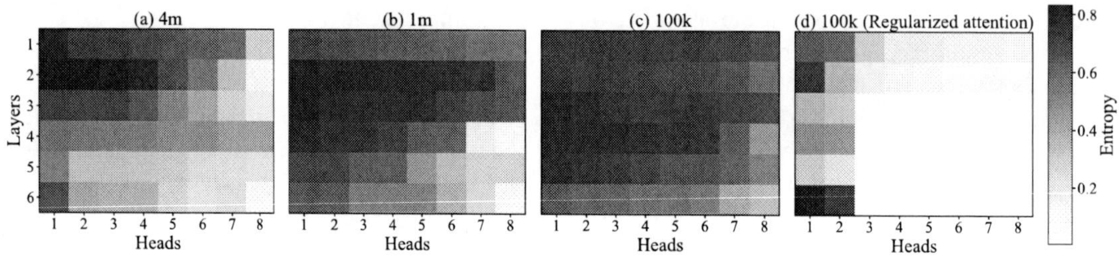

Figure 1: Entropy distribution of the encoder self-attention in a Transformer with 6 layers and 8 attention heads. (a), (b), and (c) are models trained on 4m, 1m, and 100k samples, respectively. (d) is the model trained on 100k samples after applying EaDRA. All training sets are random samples from WMT14 En-De. Entropy values are sorted within each layer to highlight the contrasting patterns.

2018). In order to evaluate the models, for Belarusian (Be), Galician (Gl), Slovak (Sk), Korean (Ko), [1] Kazakh (Kk), WMT German (De), Vietnamese (Vi), Turkish (Tr), and Japanese (Ja) we use their own official test sets. For IWSLT German (De), following (Raganato et al., 2020) we use the concatenation of the IWLST 2014 dev sets (tst2010–2012, dev2010, dev2012).

Model	#sent	min	ave	max	BLEU
T.base	4m	0.08	0.42	0.83	28.1
	1m	0.04	0.58	0.79	24.1
	100k	0.34	0.66	0.77	13.5
$\text{EaDRA}_{\text{enc+dec}}$	100k	0.01	0.18	0.82	16.2

Table 2: Statistics of entropy values over all encoder self-attention heads of models with different sample sizes from WMT14 English-German, trained on Transformer-base. $\text{EaDRA}_{\text{enc+dec}}$ denotes EaDRA applied on the self-attention in the encoder and decoder of Transfomer.

4.2 Model Configuration

We adopt the Transformer-base (denoted by T.base) architecture with its original hyperparameters (Vaswani et al., 2017) as our baseline model, upon which our proposed modifications are built. In addition, we consider the Fixed-attention method (Raganato et al., 2020) as the most closely related baseline approach. Our experiments are conducted using the Fairseq library (Ott et al., 2019). We evaluate the translation quality using sacreBLEU (Post, 2018) as evaluation metric.[2] All experiments can be completed within a few hours using a single GPU with the model parameters ranging from 49m to 65m.

5 Results

In this section, we start with a comprehensive analysis of multi-head attention entropy across various data setups. Subsequently, we demonstrate the striking effectiveness of EaDRA when compared to both the Transformer model and the most closely related approach, Fixed Attention. Additionally, we delve into the influence of EaDRA's hyperparameters. Moreover, we present results involving large pre-trained fine-tuning, a method widely recognized as a strong baseline.

5.1 Analysis of entropy in multi-head attention

The limitations in low-resource NMT performance can be attributed to the inherent difficulties associated with training models using limited data (Koehn and Knowles, 2017). However, the impact of this data scarcity on the multi-head attention mechanism remains unclear. Building on the observation of dispersion of weights in attentions (Voita et al., 2019; Correia et al., 2019), in this section we aim to analyze and compare the weight distribution of multi-head attention in NMT models across different data regimes. For this purpose, entropy serves as a useful measure by providing valuable insights into the

[1] https://github.com/jungyeul/korean-parallel-corpora/tree/master/korean-english-news-v1

[2] sacreBLEU signature:
nrefs:1—case:lc—eff:no—tok:13a—smooth:exp—version:2.0.0

peakedness of the attention distribution. We conduct preliminary experiments to investigate the entropy of attention heads and gain insights into their behavior. Figure 1 (a-c) illustrates the entropy of encoder self-attention heads for models trained on different sample sizes: 4m, 1m, and 100k. A clear trend is observed where the entropy of attentions decreases as the amount of training data increases. Therefore, the models trained with smaller data sizes face challenges in learning focused attention distributions. Based on this observation, we hypothesize that this trend of decreasing entropy with larger training samples will continue, and with a substantial amount of data, ideally, the entropy will approach zero. Figure 1 (d) illustrates the entropies of the encoder self-attention after the application of our method, showing a significant decrease in entropy. This decrease indicates a higher level of peakedness or concentration in the attention distribution. In order to compare EaDRA's entropy patterns with those of Fixed-attn, it is essential to note that Fixed-attn primarily utilizes attention heads characterized by fixed diagonal or tridiagonal-like patterns. As a result, the entropy for three of these heads reaches zero, while the remaining heads consistently maintain an entropy close to zero, forming a consistent value irrespective of the dataset size or input characteristics.

Table 2 presents the statistics of Figure 1. We observe a substantial difference in the average and minimum entropy values across all attention heads between the higher-resource models and low-resource one. Therefore, EaDRA results in a significant decrease in entropy of attention weights, resulting in a more peaked distribution of attention weights similar to what can be achieved with a large amount of training data. However, it is crucial to contextualize these findings by considering that a fair comparison, as exemplified by the performance of EaDRA compared to the T.base trained on 100k samples, demonstrates the efficacy of our approach under more controlled conditions, where both are trained on a similar number of sentences. Additionally, it is worth noting that the improvement observed in row 4 is a direct consequence of our precise parameter tuning for EaDRA.

5.2 EaDRA in multi-head attention components

While Raganato et al. (2020) only focus on the encoder self-attention, EaDRA is applicable to all attention components. We empirically demonstrate this through our experiments, which involve the encoder self-attention, decoder self-attention, and cross-attention. The performance of EaDRA on various components and their combinations is presented in Table 3. The results demonstrate that EaDRA consistently leads to substantial improvements across all cases, with the encoder and decoder combination (enc+dec) yielding the highest performance on lower-resource setups.

model	50k	100k	250k	1m
T.base	6.2	13.5	19.9	24.1
Fixed-attn	9.3	13.1	19.0	20.4
$\text{EaDRA}_{\text{enc}}$	9.4	15.2	20.2	24.4
$\text{EaDRA}_{\text{dec}}$	8.1	15.2	20.0	24.4
EaDRA_{x}	8.2	14.1	20.0	24.5
$\text{EaDRA}_{\text{dec+x}}$	8.2	14.8	20.0	24.4
$\text{EaDRA}_{\text{enc+x}}$	9.0	15.6	**20.6**	24.6
$\text{EaDRA}_{\text{enc+dec}}$	**9.7**	**16.2**	20.2	24.1
$\text{EaDRA}_{\text{enc+dec+x}}$	9.6	16.1	20.4	**24.7**

Table 3: Results of applying EaDRA to encoder self-attention (enc), decoder self-attention (dec), and cross-attention (x) on 50k, 100k, 250k, and 1m random samples from WMT14 English-German. BLEU scores are reported on newstest2014. Fixed-attn refers to our reimplementation of the Fixed-attention method (Raganato et al., 2020)

However, the cross-attention component does not benefit substantially from EaDRA, compared to the other components and combinations. We speculate that this observation may be attributed to the inherent differences in word ordering between the source and target languages, where EaDRA might discourage some specific reorderings. Moreover, EaDRA consistently outperforms Fixed-attention in all experimental settings and Fixed-attention fails to exhibit any improvement over the vanilla Transformer, except for the smallest training set with 50k samples. Notably, as the amount of training data decreases, the degree of performance degradation in Fixed-attention also diminishes. In addition, we conduct experiments with applying Fixed-attention to other attention components (decoder self-attention and cross-attention) and their combination, observing a notable decline in translation quality. This observation aligns with the results of hard-coded attention (You et al., 2020), which revealed that hard-coded encoder and decoder attention adversely affect translation quality, and hard-coded cross-attention leads to a more significant decrease in BLEU score, potentially due to its higher importance in the translation process (Voita et al., 2019; Gheini et al., 2021). Nevertheless, due to EaDRA's focus on biasing attentions without imposing strict constraints, it exhibits flexibility that allows for improvements even in case of cross-attention.

To further explore the impact of EaDRA in achieving focused attention, we perform a set of experiments in low-resource settings across various translation tasks. The results are summarized in Table 4, clearly demonstrating the significant improvements achieved by EaDRA. Specifically, our analysis focus on individual attention components as well as the combined encoder and decoder attention components ($\text{EaDRA}_{\text{enc+dec}}$), which consistently outperformed other combinations in smaller samples from WMT14 En-De, as shown in Table 3.

Interesting observations arise in the context of extremely low-resource scenarios, specifically for Belarusian and Galician datasets, with training sample sizes of only 4.5k and 10k, respectively. Surprisingly, in these cases, Fixed-attention outperforms EaDRA. We suspect that this superiority of fixed attention patterns in extreme scenarios can be attributed to the model's limited capacity to effectively learn attention distributions with such a small amount of training data, even when biased towards selective attention. The fact that the performance degradation is mitigated as the training size decreases and Fixed-attention only exhibits improvement on the smallest dataset, see Table 3, further supports this hypothesis. Also, this observation aligns with the findings of Araabi and Monz (2020) in extremely low-resource settings, which demonstrate that in the presence of limited data, having more than two attention heads leads to a significant performance drop, potentially as the model struggles to learn attention patterns.

[1]For more details, see Appendix A.

5.3 Hyper-Parameters

We tune the hyperparameters (α_{peak}, α_{sent}, and α_{dist}) for every attention components separately, such that once the optimal value of a hyper-parameter has been determined, it remains fixed and we sweep over the next one. [1] We conducted additional experiments to investigate the influence of the number of attention heads used in EaDRA. Figure 2 depicts the relationship between the BLEU score and the number of attention heads employed in EaDRA (enc), showing that around 6 attention heads appear to be an optimal choice. This pattern was consistent across the experiments conducted for decoder self-attention and cross-attention, indicating that 6 heads yield favorable results for all attention components.

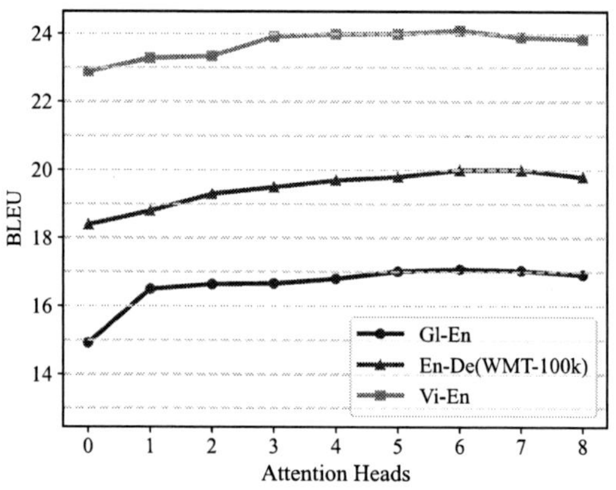

Figure 2: Effect of EaDRA with involving different number of encoder attention heads on validation BLEU score. Similar patterns are observed for other language pairs and attention components.

Initially, we conducted hyperparameter tuning on a subset of the data, specifically 100k training samples from the WMT14 English-German dataset. This process resulted in a substantial improvement of +3.1 BLEU points over Fixed-attention. Encouraged by these promising results, we proceeded to apply the same hyperparameter settings to the 50k, 250k, and 1m datasets, which led to substantial improvements across all scenarios. These findings demonstrate the effectiveness of the optimized hyperparameter values across different tasks, eliminating the need for fine-tuning on each individual task.

model	Be-En 4.5k	Gl-En 10k	Sk-En 55k	Ko-En 90k	Vi-En 133k	De-En 160K	Tr-En 207k	Ja-En 223k
T.base	5.0	13.1	22.8	6.5	25.6	32.0	16.2	10.6
Fixed-attn	5.5	**18.8**	25.4	8.1	25.3	32.4	17.0	11.7
$\text{EaDRA}_{\text{enc}}$	5.2	15.3	**26.3**	7.8	27.3	32.8	17.4	**11.8**
$\text{EaDRA}_{\text{dec}}$	5.2	16.1	25.9	**8.3**	**27.6**	**33.0**	**17.6**	11.0
EaDRA_{x}	5.3	15.6	25.7	7.6	26.7	32.7	16.6	11.1
$\text{EaDRA}_{\text{enc+dec}}$	**5.8**	16.7	25.3	8.1	27.3	32.9	17.3	11.3

Table 4: Comparing EaDRA applied to single attention components and also combination of encoder and decoder self-attention with Fixed-attention and Transformer-base for low-resource language pairs.

However, it is important to note that a more thorough hyperparameter sweep for each language pair in Table 4 produced slightly different optimal parameter values, which resulted in slight further improvements.

5.4 Large pre-trained fine-tuning

Large pre-trained models, such as mBART (Liu et al., 2020), have become an integral part of many natural language processing tasks, as they capture a vast amount of knowledge from extensive training on massive datasets. Modifying or fine-tuning such models while preserving their learned representations is a challenging task, requiring careful consideration of the model's complex architecture, attention mechanisms, and overall behavior. Therefore, it is imperative to develop methods that can leverage the existing strengths of pre-trained models while pushing for further improvements.

model	Ko-En 90k	Kk-En 91k	Vi-En 133k	Tr-En 207k	Ja-En 223k
mBART-FT	**16.0**	17.2	36.0	22.8	16.3
Fixed-attn	15.1	16.8	35.2	21.9	15.7
$\text{EaDRA}_{\text{enc}}$	**16.0**	**18.1**	**36.4**	**23.0**	**16.5**
$\text{EaDRA}_{\text{enc+dec}}$	15.6	17.9	36.1	21.0	16.2

Table 5: Comparison of Fine-tuning mBART using Fixed-attention (Raganato et al., 2020) and EaDRA applied to encoder self-attention and also encoder and decoder self-attention components.

Table 5 shows the effectiveness of applying EaDRA on top of mBART across all language pairs except Ko-En. We use the same hyper-parameter values that were tuned for 100k samples from the WMT14 En-De dataset. However, interestingly, we found that involving only two attention heads in EaDRA yields slightly higher performance. This observation can be attributed to the fact that the attention heads in mBART already exhibit a significant degree of peakedness—perhaps thanks to the pretraining—and further regularization through EaDRA does not yield additional improvements. We observe a consistent degradation of mBART when using the Fixed-attention method. One possible explanation is that applying fixed attention patterns on top of mBART introduces limitations or constraints that hinder the model's ability to fully leverage its capacity, ultimately leading to performance degradation. This suggests that the flexibility and adaptability of mBART's attention mechanisms play a crucial role in its overall performance. Furthermore, our experiments with the two most importance fixed patterns, namely the previous and next tokens (Raganato et al., 2020), also resulted in performance degradation.

6 Discussion

By introducing regularization techniques that target distance and entropy in attention heads, we achieve substantial improvements over various language pairs. Extensive experiments demonstrate the effectiveness of these methods in low-resource NMT scenarios. The flexibility offered by EaDRA enables the NMT model to selectively allocate attention during training. Conversely, fixed and unlearnable attention patterns prove to be more beneficial in the case of extremely low-resource languages with fewer than 50k training samples. In such scenarios, fixing the attention mechanism provides a more reliable approach, as the model's capacity to learn from a small dataset is limited.

7 Conclusion

In this work, we mitigate the challenge of improving low-resource NMT by introducing a form of regularized attentions. We introduce EaDRA, which promotes focused attention by prioritizing key elements. Extensive experiments on diverse low-resource language pairs demonstrate significant improvements in translation quality, validating the effectiveness of EaDRA. Our findings highlight the importance of attention regularization techniques in enhancing NMT performance, particularly in low-resource settings. EaDRA offers a practical and scalable solution with negligible computational overhead and a few lines of code.

8 Limitations

We only focus on improving low-resource NMT. However, higher-resource settings might also gain from regularized attentions facilitated by EaDRA and it may contribute to faster convergence as well. Additionally, we demonstrate the effectiveness of our proposed method using multiple low-resource language pairs, whereas there are many other language pairs with limited data. Furthermore, the encouragement of focused attention rather than dispersed attention through EaDRA leads us to hypothesize that our method may exhibit higher generalizability to sentence perturbations. This, in turn, could result in less volatile behavior of the NMT system (Fadaee and Monz, 2020). We leave these investigations to future work.

References

Aharoni, R., Johnson, M., and Firat, O. (2019). Massively multilingual neural machine translation. In Burstein, J., Doran, C., and Solorio, T., editors, *Proceedings of the 2019 Conference of the North American Chapter of the Association for Computational Linguistics: Human Language Technologies, NAACL-HLT 2019, Minneapolis, MN, USA, June 2-7, 2019, Volume 1 (Long and Short Papers)*, pages 3874–3884. Association for Computational Linguistics.

Araabi, A. and Monz, C. (2020). Optimizing transformer for low-resource neural machine translation. In Scott, D., Bel, N., and Zong, C., editors, *Proceedings of the 28th International Conference on Computational Linguistics, COLING 2020, Barcelona, Spain (Online), December 8-13, 2020*, pages 3429–3435. International Committee on Computational Linguistics.

Aralikatte, R., Narayan, S., Maynez, J., Rothe, S., and McDonald, R. T. (2021). Focus attention: Promoting faithfulness and diversity in summarization. In Zong, C., Xia, F., Li, W., and Navigli, R., editors, *Proceedings of the 59th Annual Meeting of the Association for Computational Linguistics and the 11th International Joint Conference on Natural Language Processing, ACL/IJCNLP 2021, (Volume 1: Long Papers), Virtual Event, August 1-6, 2021*, pages 6078–6095. Association for Computational Linguistics.

Bahdanau, D., Cho, K., and Bengio, Y. (2015). Neural machine translation by jointly learning to align and translate. In Bengio, Y. and LeCun, Y., editors, *3rd International Conference on Learning Representations, ICLR 2015, San Diego, CA, USA, May 7-9, 2015, Conference Track Proceedings*.

Brown, T. B., Mann, B., Ryder, N., Subbiah, M., Kaplan, J., Dhariwal, P., Neelakantan, A., Shyam, P., Sastry, G., Askell, A., Agarwal, S., Herbert-Voss, A., Krueger, G., Henighan, T., Child, R., Ramesh, A., Ziegler, D. M., Wu, J., Winter, C., Hesse, C., Chen, M., Sigler, E., Litwin, M., Gray, S., Chess, B., Clark, J., Berner, C., McCandlish, S., Radford, A., Sutskever, I., and Amodei, D. (2020). Language models are few-shot learners. In Larochelle, H., Ranzato, M., Hadsell, R., Balcan, M., and Lin, H., editors, *Advances in Neural Information Processing Systems 33: Annual Conference on Neural Information Processing Systems 2020, NeurIPS 2020, December 6-12, 2020, virtual*.

Cettolo, M., Girardi, C., and Federico, M. (2012). Wit3: Web inventory of transcribed and translated talks. In *Conference of European Association for Machine Translation*, pages 261–268.

Correia, G. M., Niculae, V., and Martins, A. F. T. (2019). Adaptively sparse transformers. In Inui, K., Jiang, J., Ng, V., and Wan, X., editors, *Proceedings of the 2019 Conference on Empirical Methods in Natural Language Processing and the 9th International Joint Conference on Natural Language Processing, EMNLP-IJCNLP 2019, Hong Kong, China, November 3-7, 2019*, pages 2174–2184. Association for Computational Linguistics.

Devlin, J., Chang, M., Lee, K., and Toutanova, K. (2019). BERT: pre-training of deep bidirectional transformers for language understanding. In Burstein, J., Doran, C., and Solorio, T., editors, *Proceedings of the 2019 Conference of the North American Chapter of the Association for Computational Linguistics: Human Language Technologies, NAACL-HLT 2019, Minneapolis, MN, USA, June 2-7, 2019, Volume 1 (Long and Short Papers)*, pages 4171–4186. Association for Computational Linguistics.

Fadaee, M. and Monz, C. (2020). The unreasonable volatility of neural machine translation models. In Birch, A., Finch, A. M., Hayashi, H., Heafield, K., Junczys-Dowmunt, M., Konstas, I., Li, X., Neubig, G., and Oda, Y., editors, *Proceedings of the Fourth Workshop on Neural Generation and Translation, NGT@ACL 2020, Online, July 5-10, 2020*, pages 88–96. Association for Computational Linguistics.

Gheini, M., Ren, X., and May, J. (2021). Cross-attention is all you need: Adapting pretrained transformers for machine translation. In Moens, M., Huang, X., Specia, L., and Yih, S. W., editors, *Proceedings of the 2021 Conference on Empirical Methods in Natural Language Processing, EMNLP 2021, Virtual Event / Punta Cana, Dominican Republic, 7-11 November, 2021*, pages 1754–1765. Association for Computational Linguistics.

Han, Y., Jiao, J., Lee, C., Weissman, T., Wu, Y., and Yu, T. (2018). Entropy rate estimation for markov chains with large state space. In Bengio, S., Wallach, H. M., Larochelle, H., Grauman, K., Cesa-Bianchi, N., and Garnett, R., editors, *Advances in Neural Information Processing Systems 31: Annual Conference on Neural Information Processing Systems 2018, NeurIPS 2018, December 3-8, 2018, Montréal, Canada*, pages 9803–9814.

Kim, Y., Denton, C., Hoang, L., and Rush, A. M. (2017). Structured attention networks. In *5th International Conference on Learning Representations, ICLR 2017, Toulon, France, April 24-26, 2017, Conference Track Proceedings*. OpenReview.net.

Koehn, P., Hoang, H., Birch, A., Callison-Burch, C., Federico, M., Bertoldi, N., Cowan, B., Shen, W., Moran, C., Zens, R., Dyer, C., Bojar, O., Constantin, A., and Herbst, E. (2007). Moses: Open source toolkit for statistical machine translation. In Carroll, J. A., van den Bosch, A., and Zaenen, A., editors, *ACL 2007, Proceedings of the 45th Annual Meeting of the Association for Computational Linguistics, June 23-30, 2007, Prague, Czech Republic*. The Association for Computational Linguistics.

Koehn, P. and Knowles, R. (2017). Six challenges for neural machine translation. In Luong, T., Birch, A., Neubig, G., and Finch, A. M., editors, *Proceedings of the First Workshop on Neural Machine Translation, NMT@ACL 2017, Vancouver, Canada, August 4, 2017*, pages 28–39. Association for Computational Linguistics.

Kudo, T. and Richardson, J. (2018). Sentencepiece: A simple and language independent subword tokenizer and detokenizer for neural text processing. In Blanco, E. and Lu, W., editors, *Proceedings of the 2018 Conference on Empirical Methods in Natural Language Processing, EMNLP 2018: System Demonstrations, Brussels, Belgium, October 31 - November 4, 2018*, pages 66–71. Association for Computational Linguistics.

Lin, J., Sun, X., Ren, X., Li, M., and Su, Q. (2018). Learning when to concentrate or divert attention: Self-adaptive attention temperature for neural machine translation. In Riloff, E., Chiang, D., Hockenmaier, J., and Tsujii, J., editors, *Proceedings of the 2018 Conference on Empirical Methods in Natural Language Processing, Brussels, Belgium, October 31 - November 4, 2018*, pages 2985–2990. Association for Computational Linguistics.

Liu, Y., Gu, J., Goyal, N., Li, X., Edunov, S., Ghazvininejad, M., Lewis, M., and Zettlemoyer, L. (2020). Multilingual denoising pre-training for neural machine translation. *Trans. Assoc. Comput. Linguistics*, 8:726–742.

Meister, C., Salesky, E., and Cotterell, R. (2020). Generalized entropy regularization or: There's nothing special about label smoothing. In Jurafsky, D., Chai, J., Schluter, N., and Tetreault, J. R., editors, *Proceedings of the 58th Annual Meeting of the Association for Computational Linguistics, ACL 2020, Online, July 5-10, 2020*, pages 6870–6886. Association for Computational Linguistics.

Mitchell, T. M. (1980). *The need for biases in learning generalizations*. Citeseer.

Montahaei, E., Alihosseini, D., and Baghshah, M. S. (2019). Jointly measuring diversity and quality in text generation models. *CoRR*, abs/1904.03971.

Ng, N., Yee, K., Baevski, A., Ott, M., Auli, M., and Edunov, S. (2019). Facebook fair's WMT19 news translation task submission. In Bojar, O., Chatterjee, R., Federmann, C., Fishel, M., Graham, Y., Haddow, B., Huck, M., Jimeno-Yepes, A., Koehn, P., Martins, A., Monz, C., Negri, M., Névéol, A., Neves, M. L., Post, M., Turchi, M., and Verspoor, K., editors, *Proceedings of the Fourth Conference on Machine Translation, WMT 2019, Florence, Italy, August 1-2, 2019 - Volume 2: Shared Task Papers, Day 1*, pages 314–319. Association for Computational Linguistics.

Niculae, V. and Blondel, M. (2017). A regularized framework for sparse and structured neural attention. In Guyon, I., von Luxburg, U., Bengio, S., Wallach, H. M., Fergus, R., Vishwanathan, S. V. N., and Garnett, R., editors, *Advances in Neural Information Processing Systems 30: Annual Conference on Neural Information Processing Systems 2017, December 4-9, 2017, Long Beach, CA, USA*, pages 3338–3348.

Niculae, V. and Martins, A. F. T. (2020). Lp-sparsemap: Differentiable relaxed optimization for sparse structured prediction. In *Proceedings of the 37th International Conference on Machine Learning, ICML 2020, 13-18 July 2020, Virtual Event*, volume 119 of *Proceedings of Machine Learning Research*, pages 7348–7359. PMLR.

Ott, M., Edunov, S., Baevski, A., Fan, A., Gross, S., Ng, N., Grangier, D., and Auli, M. (2019). Fairseq: A fast, extensible toolkit for sequence modeling. In *Proceedings of the 2019 Conference of the North American Chapter of the Association for Computational Linguistics: Human Language Technologies, NAACL-HLT 2019*, pages 48–53.

Park, J., Hong, J., and Cha, J. (2016). Korean language resources for everyone. In Park, J. C. and Chung, J., editors, *Proceedings of the 30th Pacific Asia Conference on Language, Information and Computation, PACLIC 30, Seoul, Korea, October 28 - October 30, 2016*. ACL.

Pimentel, T., Meister, C., Teufel, S., and Cotterell, R. (2021). On homophony and rényi entropy. In Moens, M., Huang, X., Specia, L., and Yih, S. W., editors, *Proceedings of the 2021 Conference on Empirical Methods in Natural Language Processing, EMNLP 2021, Virtual Event / Punta Cana, Dominican Republic, 7-11 November, 2021*, pages 8284–8293. Association for Computational Linguistics.

Post, M. (2018). A call for clarity in reporting BLEU scores. In *Proceedings of the Third Conference on Machine Translation: Research Papers, WMT 2018, Belgium, Brussels, October 31 - November 1, 2018*, pages 186–191.

Qi, Y., Sachan, D. S., Felix, M., Padmanabhan, S., and Neubig, G. (2018). When and why are pre-trained word embeddings useful for neural machine translation? In *Proceedings of the 2018 Conference of the North American Chapter of the Association for Computational Linguistics: Human Language Technologies, NAACL-HLT*, pages 529–535.

Raganato, A., Scherrer, Y., and Tiedemann, J. (2020). Fixed encoder self-attention patterns in transformer-based machine translation. In Cohn, T., He, Y., and Liu, Y., editors, *Findings of the Association for Computational Linguistics: EMNLP 2020, Online Event, 16-20 November 2020*, volume EMNLP 2020 of *Findings of ACL*, pages 556–568. Association for Computational Linguistics.

Saleh, F., Buntine, W. L., and Haffari, G. (2020). Collective wisdom: Improving low-resource neural machine translation using adaptive knowledge distillation. In Scott, D., Bel, N., and Zong, C., editors, *Proceedings of the 28th International Conference on Computational Linguistics, COLING 2020, Barcelona, Spain (Online), December 8-13, 2020*, pages 3413–3421. International Committee on Computational Linguistics.

Sennrich, R., Haddow, B., and Birch, A. (2016). Neural machine translation of rare words with subword units. In *Proceedings of the 54th Annual Meeting of the Association for Computational Linguistics, ACL 2016, August 7-12, 2016, Berlin, Germany, Volume 1: Long Papers*. The Association for Computer Linguistics.

Shannon, C. E. (1948). A mathematical theory of communication. *Bell Syst. Tech. J.*, 27(3):379–423.

Sutskever, I., Vinyals, O., and Le, Q. V. (2014). Sequence to sequence learning with neural networks. In Ghahramani, Z., Welling, M., Cortes, C., Lawrence, N. D., and Weinberger, K. Q., editors, *Advances in Neural Information Processing Systems 27: Annual Conference on Neural Information Processing Systems 2014, December 8-13 2014, Montreal, Quebec, Canada*, pages 3104–3112.

Tan, X., Ren, Y., He, D., Qin, T., Zhao, Z., and Liu, T. (2019). Multilingual neural machine translation with knowledge distillation. In *7th International Conference on Learning Representations, ICLR 2019, New Orleans, LA, USA, May 6-9, 2019*. OpenReview.net.

Tang, Y., Tran, C., Li, X., Chen, P., Goyal, N., Chaudhary, V., Gu, J., and Fan, A. (2020). Multilingual translation with extensible multilingual pretraining and finetuning. *CoRR*, abs/2008.00401.

Touvron, H., Lavril, T., Izacard, G., Martinet, X., Lachaux, M., Lacroix, T., Rozière, B., Goyal, N., Hambro, E., Azhar, F., Rodriguez, A., Joulin, A., Grave, E., and Lample, G. (2023). Llama: Open and efficient foundation language models. *CoRR*, abs/2302.13971.

Vanmassenhove, E., Shterionov, D. S., and Gwilliam, M. (2021). Machine translationese: Effects of algorithmic bias on linguistic complexity in machine translation. In Merlo, P., Tiedemann, J., and Tsarfaty, R., editors, *Proceedings of the 16th Conference of the European Chapter of the Association for Computational Linguistics: Main Volume, EACL 2021, Online, April 19 - 23, 2021*, pages 2203–2213. Association for Computational Linguistics.

Vaswani, A., Shazeer, N., Parmar, N., Uszkoreit, J., Jones, L., Gomez, A. N., Kaiser, L., and Polosukhin, I. (2017). Attention is all you need. In Guyon, I., von Luxburg, U., Bengio, S., Wallach, H. M., Fergus, R., Vishwanathan, S. V. N., and Garnett, R., editors, *Advances in Neural Information Processing Systems 30: Annual Conference on Neural Information Processing Systems 2017, December 4-9, 2017, Long Beach, CA, USA*, pages 5998–6008.

Voita, E., Talbot, D., Moiseev, F., Sennrich, R., and Titov, I. (2019). Analyzing multi-head self-attention: Specialized heads do the heavy lifting, the rest can be pruned. In Korhonen, A., Traum, D. R., and Màrquez, L., editors, *Proceedings of the 57th Conference of the Association for Computational Linguistics, ACL 2019, Florence, Italy, July 28- August 2, 2019, Volume 1: Long Papers*, pages 5797–5808. Association for Computational Linguistics.

You, W., Sun, S., and Iyyer, M. (2020). Hard-coded gaussian attention for neural machine translation. In Jurafsky, D., Chai, J., Schluter, N., and Tetreault, J. R., editors, *Proceedings of the 58th Annual Meeting of the Association for Computational Linguistics, ACL 2020, Online, July 5-10, 2020*, pages 7689–7700. Association for Computational Linguistics.

Zoph, B., Yuret, D., May, J., and Knight, K. (2016). Transfer learning for low-resource neural machine translation. In Su, J., Carreras, X., and Duh, K., editors, *Proceedings of the 2016 Conference on Empirical Methods in Natural Language Processing, EMNLP 2016, Austin, Texas, USA, November 1-4, 2016*, pages 1568–1575. The Association for Computational Linguistics.

9 Appendices

A Optimal hyperparameter values

The optimal values for the hyperparameters of several models discussed in the paper are presented in Table 6. Interestingly, our preliminary experiments indicate that α_{dist} appears to render α_{peak} redundant. As for the remaining models not listed in the table, we adopt the same hyperparameter values as those used for WMT En-De (100k) experiments. Furthermore, for experiments with applying EaDRA to combinations of attention heads, we do not perform additional hyperparameter tuning.

Dataset	α_{dist}	α_{sent}
	$\text{EaDRA}_{\text{enc}}$	
WMT En-De (100k)	0.02	0.8
Be-En	0.02	1.2
Gl-En	0.02	0.8
Sk-En	0.02	0.8
Ko-En	0.01	0.4
Vi-En	0.02	0.6
Tr-En	0.04	1.2
Ja-En	0.02	0.8
	EaDRA_{x}	
WMT En-De (100k)	0.1	8
Be-En	0.1	8
Gl-En	0.15	5
Sk-En	0.1	8
Ko-En	0.05	8
Vi-En	0.2	8
Tr-En	0.1	10
Ja-En	0.1	10
	$\text{EaDRA}_{\text{dec}}$	
WMT En-De (100k)	2	0.8
Be-En	1	0.9
Gl-En	1	0.8
Sk-En	2	0.8
Ko-En	0.5	0.8
Vi-En	4	1
Tr-En	3	1.5
Ja-En	2	0.8

Table 6: Hyperparameters of $\text{EaDRA}_{\text{enc}}$, EaDRA_{x}, and $\text{EaDRA}_{\text{dec}}$ for the models presented in the paper.

B Ablation study

To gain deeper insights into the individual contributions of the proposed regularization terms, we conducted an ablation study focusing on the English-German language pair, utilizing a training set of 100k samples from WMT. The study specifically aimed to isolate the effects of the distance and sentence regularization terms. Table 7 demonstrates that employing only the distance regularization term resulted in attention heads converging to trivial solutions, leading to a concentration of attention on a single token within a sentence. While this induced a reduction in entropy, it adversely impacted overall performance. Conversely, exclusive reliance on the sentence regularization term led to an overly uniform attention distribution, manifesting as a diagonal attention pattern across the sentence.

These findings emphasize the necessity of striking a balance between the two regularization terms. The combination of both distance and sentence regularization proves instrumental in achieving the desired focused attention distribution, thus reinforcing the efficacy of our proposed approach in low-resource NMT scenarios. It is worth noting that while $\text{EaDRA}_{\text{enc+dec}}$ was used for this ablation study, it is conceivable that alternative configurations would have produced similar results.

Method	α_{dist}	α_{sent}	BLEU
T.base	0.00	0.00	13.5
EaDRA	0.02	0.80	16.2
EaDRA w/o α_{dist}	0.00	0.80	15.2
EaDRA w/o α_{dist}	0.02	0.00	0.7

Table 7: Ablation study results for English-German task with 100k training samples from WMT14. $\text{EaDRA}_{\text{enc+dec}}$ is used for this experiment.

C Convergence Speed Analysis

Given that EaDRA introduces a term into the loss function, it is imperative to assess its convergence speed. In Figure 3, we present the validation scores for two systems trained with 100k English-German samples from WMT14 on the same GPU.

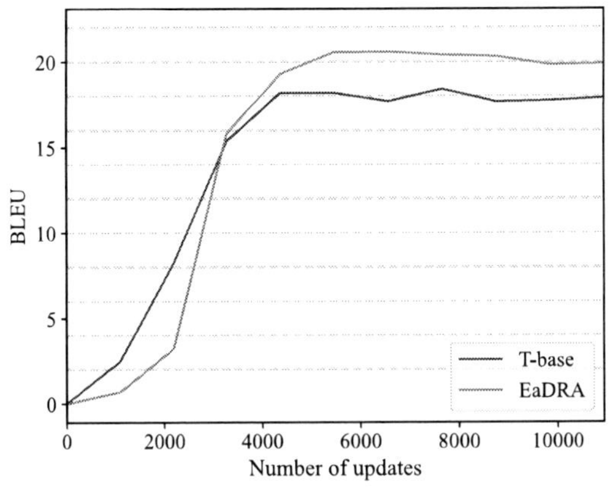

Figure 3: Convergence speed comparison on validation scores of EaDRA and T-base models trained on 100k English-German samples from WMT14.

The results demonstrate that EaDRA sustains a convergence speed comparable to the baseline. This observation underscores the efficiency of EaDRA in terms of convergence, further solidifying its viability in practical applications. This suggests that the incorporation of EaDRA does not come at the cost of prolonged training times, making it a practical choice for low-resource NMT tasks

Enhancing Translation Quality by Leveraging Semantic Diversity in Multimodal Machine Translation

Ali Hatami
Insight SFI Research Centre for Data Analytics,
Data Science Institute, University of Galway, Ireland
ali.hatami@insight-centre.org

Mihael Arcan
Lua Health, Galway, Ireland
mihael@luahealth.io

Paul Buitelaar
Insight SFI Research Centre for Data Analytics,
Data Science Institute, University of Galway, Ireland
paul.buitelaar@insight-centre.org

Abstract

Despite advancements in neural machine translation, word sense disambiguation remains challenging, particularly with limited textual context. Multimodal Machine Translation enhances text-only models by integrating visual information, but its impact varies across translations. This study focuses on ambiguous sentences to investigate the effectiveness of utilizing visual information. By prioritizing these sentences, which benefit from visual cues, we aim to enhance hybrid multimodal and text-only translation approaches. We utilize Latent Semantic Analysis and Sentence-BERT to extract context vectors from the British National Corpus, enabling the assessment of semantic diversity. Our approach enhances translation quality for English-German and English-French on Multi30k, assessed through metrics including BLEU, chrF2, and TER.

1 Introduction

Neural Machine Translation (NMT) has significantly improved translation quality with transformer-based models (Cho et al., 2014; Vaswani et al., 2018), integrating cross-attention for better semantic understanding (Vaswani et al., 2017). Despite focusing on the broader context in the text-only translation model, resolving word ambiguity persists as a challenge. In natural language, lexical ambiguity (Gonzales et al., 2017) refers to the occurrence where a single word possesses multiple meanings or interpretations, thereby complicating comprehension of the text. For example, in the domain of finance and economy, the word "*bank*" almost always refers to a financial institution rather than the side of a river.

Multimodal Machine Translation (MMT), a subset of NMT, incorporates visual information to enhance translations. Recent studies highlight the potential of leveraging both textual and visual data to improve accuracy and contextuality (Yao and Wan, 2020; Zhao et al., 2022; Wang and Xiong, 2021; Hatami et al., 2023). MMT utilises visual cues to disambiguate input words and select appropriate translations, particularly beneficial for ambiguous sentences or when visual context provides crucial details not explicit in the text. Despite the benefits of integrating visual information into MMT, this can sometimes result in degraded translation quality, particularly when there is insufficient data, including parallel visual and textual data, to adequately train the model. For sentences with unambiguous interpretations, textual context alone might suffice for accurate translation. Unlike NMT, MMT can be susceptible to noise or irrelevant information in the visual data, which may introduce errors or distractions, leading to inaccurate translations.

This paper aims to explore the correlation between sentence ambiguity and translation quality, focusing on effectively integrating visual cues into the translation process to enhance overall quality. We assess sentence ambiguity using semantic diversity in Latent Semantic Analysis (LSA) and Sentence-BERT (S-BERT) vector embedding spaces, investigating the impact of visual information across varying levels of ambiguity. By experimenting with different ambiguity scores, we determine the optimal value where visual cues enhance translation quality, comparing outcomes with text-only and multimodal models. For sentences with low ambiguity, we employ a text-only approach, while for those with higher ambiguity, we utilize a multimodal approach.

2 Related Work

Lexical ambiguity presents a major hurdle in machine translation, making it challenging to discern the correct word meaning and translation due to multiple senses and contextual variations. While Multimodal Machine Translation (MMT) leverages visual cues to aid disambiguation, the efficacy of visual features varies, particularly when textual context is sufficient. Despite the potential of visual cues to improve accuracy, their impact may be constrained when textual information is already rich. This underscores the importance of seamlessly integrating visual and textual data for optimal translation outcomes (Caglayan et al., 2016, 2019).

Various methodologies have been proposed to enhance the quality of the visual modality in MMT. For example, Yao and Wan (2020) introduced a multimodal transformer-based self-attention mechanism to encode relevant image information. To capture diverse relationships, Yin et al. (2020) proposed a graph-based multimodal fusion encoder. Ive et al. (2019) devised a translate-and-refine mechanism, employing images in a second-stage decoder to refine text-only NMT models for ambiguous words. Additionally, Calixto et al. (2019) utilised a latent variable model to extract multimodal relationships between images and text. Recent methods aim to mitigate visual information noise and select relevant visual features correlated with text. For instance, Wang and Xiong (2021) employed object-level visual modeling to mask irrelevant objects and specific words in the source text, facilitating visual feature analysis. Similarly, Zhao et al. (2022) integrated object detection into the image encoder to extract visual features of object regions and applied them to a doubly-attentive decoder model.

The Multimodal Lexical Translation (MLT) approach aims to accurately translate ambiguous words within both visual and textual contexts. Introduced with the MLT dataset, which includes 4-tuples of ambiguous words, visual and textual contexts, and translations aligned with both, this resource facilitates the evaluation of lexical disambiguation within Multimodal Machine Translation (MMT) (Lala and Specia, 2018). The study by Lala et al. (2018) examines the effectiveness of multimodal re-ranking methods in improving a standard sequence-to-sequence attention-based Neural Machine Translation (NMT) system. By integrating cross-lingual word sense disambiguation and data augmentation techniques, the authors aim to enhance translation quality and develop an image-based, cross-lingual approach for accurately predicting translation candidates for ambiguous words in the source sentence.

The translate-and-refine approach (Ive et al., 2019), introduced to improve upon previous MMT model, employs images in a second-stage decoder to refine translation drafts by incorporating both textual and visual contexts. This method achieves state-of-the-art results, demonstrating superior performance over text-only models, especially in complex linguistic scenarios, by refining translations only when necessary through deliberation networks. In their analysis, Tang et al. (2018) examine how encoder-decoder attention mechanisms in Neural Machine Translation (NMT) models handle ambiguous nouns during word sense disambiguation (WSD). Contrary to expectations, attention tends to focus more on the ambiguous noun itself rather than surrounding context tokens, suggesting that contextual information for WSD is primarily encoded in the encoder's hidden states. This study sheds light on the challenges of WSD in NMT models, particularly due to data sparsity, and offers insights into the learning process of attention mechanisms in Transformers.

In addressing ambiguity in Multimodal Machine Translation (MMT), Futeral et al. (2023) propose a novel approach incorporating neural adapters, guided self-attention mechanisms, and a visually conditioned masked language modeling objective.

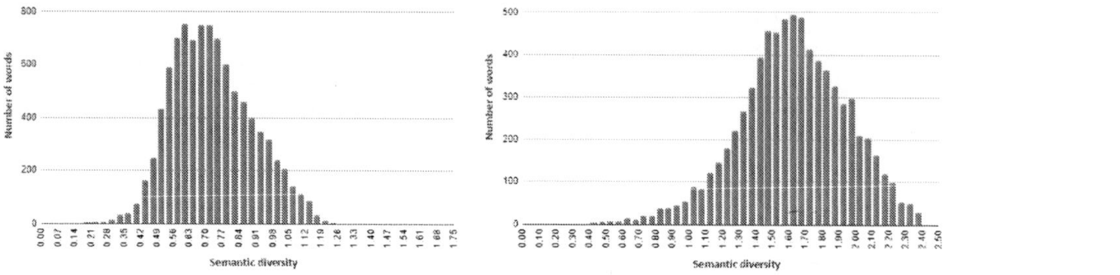

Figure 1: Histogram showing the distribution of lexical ambiguity scores across words in BNC (left: S-BERT and right: LSA)

Their study underscores the importance of using image context to improve translation quality, introducing the CoMMuTE dataset as a tool to evaluate and enhance multimodal translation. The dataset includes 155 English sentences with two possible translations in French, German, and Czech, facilitating assessment of MMT models in leveraging visuals for accurate translations, especially with ambiguous content. In Bowen et al. (2024), techniques for identifying visually and contextually relevant tokens in Multimodal Machine Translation (MMT) systems are explored, employing natural language processing (NLP), object detection, and deterministic selection strategies. The study, conducted using the GRAM MMT architecture (Vijayan et al., 2024), reveals performance improvements over baseline models by training on synthetically collated datasets of masked sentences and images, emphasizing the importance of visual context in enhancing translation accuracy within MMT systems. In Hatami et al. (2022), an approach utilizing *WordNet* synsets to gauge sentence ambiguity was proposed to evaluate the effect of incorporating visual information in translation models, demonstrating the potential of visual cues to improve translation accuracy, especially in challenging tasks like English-German translation, as observed in the analysis of the Multi30k dataset.

This paper investigates how integrating visual elements affects translation quality by examining the relationship between sentence ambiguity and accuracy, using semantic diversity in sentence vector spaces to quantify ambiguity and assessing the impact of visual information on translation quality across different levels of ambiguity scores.

3 Methodology

This section details the methodology for enhancing translation quality in MMT by utilizing semantic diversity. It involves computing lexical ambiguity scores for nouns, extending to sentence-level ambiguity, and exploring sentence ambiguity to optimize translation scores for text-only and MMT models.

3.1 Lexical Ambiguity Score

We computed the lexical ambiguity score for all words in the British National Corpus (BNC) by tokenizing sentences from the Multi30k dataset training set, resulting in a word list with 10,105 unique words, including morphological variants to capture potential differences in ambiguity scores based on their roles in sentences. Utilizing Latent Semantic Analysis (Landauer and Dumais, 1997) and S-BERT (Reimers and Gurevych, 2019), we derived lexical ambiguity scores based on distributional semantics (Harris, 1954), which infer word meanings from contextual usage, considering that words appearing in the same context likely share the same meaning, while differing contexts may lead to varied interpretations.

In adopting LSA based on Hoffman's work (Hoffman et al., 2012), we segmented the BNC corpus into 1,000-word texts to construct a co-occurrence matrix, applying singular value decomposition (SVD) to reveal latent semantic structures and word associations. Concurrently, for S-BERT, we segmented the BNC into sentences, preprocess them for quality, and utilized the pre-trained S-BERT model[1] to generate 768-dimensional sentence embeddings, capturing semantic information comprehensively. To compute lexical ambiguity, we as-

[1]https://www.sbert.net/

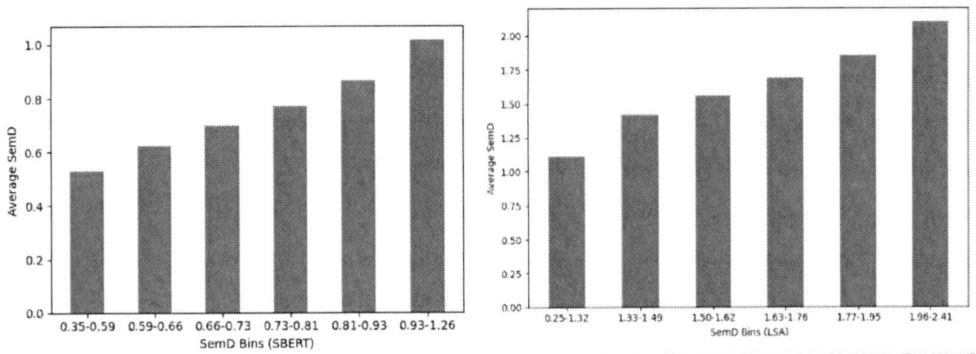

buoy	soldiers	penalties	inverted	playing	using
scuffle	gutter	spice	advertised	signal	with
chops	steam	brook	vacant	tiny	from
fog	naked	army	peers	align	either
bread	tongs	innocent	scramble	march	on

Top 5 words for each bin

computers	stripes	dressed	admits	things	also
camping	ornate	rained	dotted	abound	which
beverage	corks	brutality	measuring	saying	from
bathroom	wool	sprinkled	specialize	reaches	further
arcs	hut	annoyed	travel	fashioned	as

Top 5 words for each bin

Figure 2: Average Semantic Diversity (SemD) across different bins, displaying the top 5 words in each bin from BNC (left: S-BERT and right: LSA)

sessed textual similarity through LSA and S-BERT, leveraging Semantic Diversity (*SemD*) scores to represent ambiguity. By measuring cosine similarity between vectors, we determined ambiguity levels, with higher similarity indicating lower ambiguity and vice versa, enabling precise ambiguity scoring for individual words. To do this, we first calculated the mean of the similarity of all pairwise combinations of texts or sentences including the word (*w*). Then we took the logarithm of this mean and reversed the sign to obtain the *SemD* value of the word (*w*). The equation for *SemD* of word w is:

$$SemD_w = -log(\frac{\sum_{i,j \,\epsilon\, V_w} cos\_sim(v_i, v_j)}{n})$$

where V_w is the set of all context vectors for word *w*, and $v_i, v_j \,\epsilon\, V_w$.

The histograms in Figure 1 compare the distribution of words across different ambiguity score ranges for LSA and S-BERT. S-BERT shows a positively skewed distribution, with most words having lower ambiguity scores, while LSA displays a negatively skewed distribution, indicating a higher prevalence of words with higher ambiguity scores.

Figure 2 illustrates the average SemD across 6 bins, showcasing the lexical ambiguity scores along with the top 5 words in each bin. These results, derived from the BNC, compare S-BERT and LSA in assigning SemD to each word.

3.2 Sentence Ambiguity Score

After computing *SemD* values for all words in the vocabulary, we utilize these values to derive ambiguity scores for sentences in the test set, focusing solely on nouns, which carry specific semantic content and are extracted using *SpaCy*[2].

To compute the ambiguity score at the sentence level, two mathematical functions, the arithmetic mean (*Mean*) and the geometric mean (*G-Mean*), are utilized. The arithmetic mean aggregates and divides the lexical ambiguity scores of all nouns in a sentence by the total number of content words, giving equal weight to each score, while the geometric mean calculates the *n-th* root of the product of lexical ambiguity scores, assigning less weight to larger values and mitigating the influence of outliers. These methods enable the quantification of ambiguity within sentences, facilitating comparisons based on their ambiguity scores.

The histograms in Figure 3 display sentence ambiguity scores calculated using *Mean* and *G-Mean* for LSA and S-BERT. LSA exhibits a normal distribution of scores between 1.13 and 2.18, while S-BERT shows a positively skewed distribution be-

[2]https://spacy.io/usage/linguistic-features

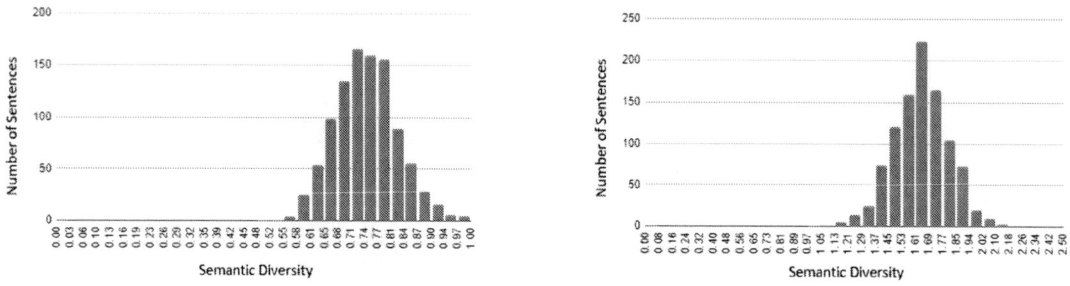

(a) S-BERT (G-Mean) (b) LSA (G-Mean)

Figure 3: Histograms showing the distribution of sentence ambiguity scores across sentences in Multi30k

tween 0.55 and 1.00, indicating lower ambiguity. These ambiguity scores are used to sort sentences in the test set in ascending order and then apply a hybrid approach to translate the sentences. In Section 3.3, we explain the details of this approach.

3.3 Translation Quality Measure

Despite the benefits of incorporating visual data into multimodal machine translation (MMT), its use can sometimes lead to reduced translation quality compared to text-only approaches. This decline may occur due to the presence of noise or irrelevant visual information, which could introduce errors or distractions, ultimately resulting in inaccurate translations (see Figure 4).

We utilize sentence ambiguity scores based on *SemD* to decide between using Text-only or Multimodal models for translation. By adopting a hybrid approach, we determine whether visual information enhances translation quality, leveraging the ambiguity score to select the most suitable model for sentences in a specific ambiguity range. After computing ambiguity scores for all sentences in the test set, we ranked the sentences based on the sentence ambiguity score calculated using *Mean* and *G-Mean* for both LSA and S-BERT. Then we divided the test set into 20 sets, each including 50 sentences. The first set in the sorted sentence list has the lowest ambiguity score, and the last set has the highest ambiguity score. The hybrid approach aims to employ the Text-only MT model for sentence sets with lower ambiguity and utilize Multimodal models for those with higher ambiguity. By using a Hybrid model, we explore the effectiveness of visual information in translating sentences with higher ambiguity scores, thereby evaluating translation quality to determine the optimal range of ambiguity for leveraging visual information.

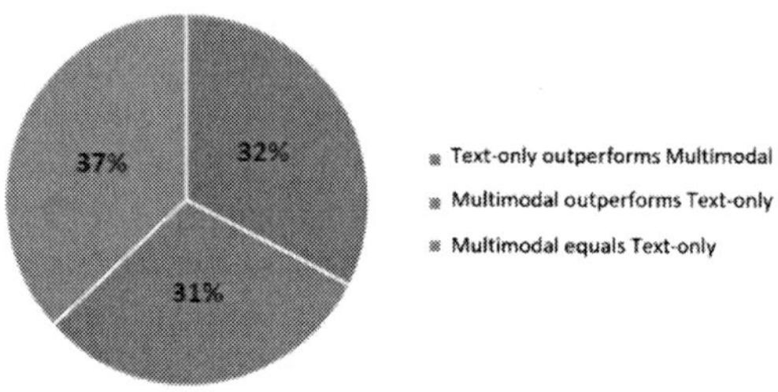

Figure 4: Comparing sentence-level BLEU scores of Text-only and Multimodal MT models for English to German translation on the Multi30k 2016 test set.

4 Experimental Setup

This section provides insights into the dataset used in this work, neural architectures involving text-only and multimodal models, and context vector embedding methods: LSA and S-BERT, and the translation evaluation metrics BLEU, ChrF2 and TER.

4.1 Dataset

During our experiment, we employed two datasets: the British National Corpus (BNC) and Multi30k. The BNC facilitated the extraction of sentence vectors for computing lexical ambiguity, while the Multi30k dataset served for training and evaluating our translation models.

4.1.1 British National Corpus (BNC)

The British National Corpus (BNC) (Aston and Burnard, 1998) is a vast collection comprising 100 million words of both written and spoken British English texts, designed to represent the language comprehensively. It encompasses diverse sources such as newspapers, periodicals, academic books, fiction, letters, and spoken conversations, offering insights into contemporary British English usage across various contexts. As a rich repository of language patterns and expressions, the BNC serves as a valuable resource for linguistic research and language analysis, facilitating a deeper understanding of British English in its diverse forms.

4.1.2 Multi30k Dataset

Multi30K (Elliott et al., 2016) is an extension of the Flickr30K Entities dataset that consists of 29,000 images paired with descriptions in English, along with translated sentences in German, French, and Czech (Elliott et al., 2017). The dataset is specifically designed for evaluating MMT systems, where both textual and visual information are utilised for translation tasks. Multi30K provides validation and test sets, each containing 1,000 images aligned with the descriptions.

4.2 Semantic Representation Techniques

In this section, we explain two techniques for extracting semantic representation vectors from given contexts: Latent Semantic Analysis and S-BERT. These approaches offer sophisticated methods to capture the underlying semantic meanings embedded within texts, which can be used to determine the similarity between them.

4.2.1 Latent Semantic Analysis (LSA)

LSA is a technique that leverages patterns of word co-occurrence to construct high-dimensional semantic spaces. To implement LSA, the BNC is divided into text samples, each representing a different context. A co-occurrence matrix is generated, tracking which words appear in each context. Each word is represented as a vector, with elements corresponding to its frequency in a context. Using singular value decomposition (SVD), LSA extracts the underlying structure in the co-occurrence matrix, revealing higher-order relationships between words based on their co-occurrence patterns. SVD reduces the dimensionality of the word vectors (to 300 dimensions), with the similarity structure of these vectors approximating the original matrix. Consequently, word representations can be interpreted as points in a high-dimensional space, where proximity indicates similarity in meaning based on context. Additionally, LSA places individual contexts in the same semantic space, enabling comparisons between contexts based on their content similarity.

4.2.2 S-BERT

S-BERT extends the capabilities of the BERT model by focusing on generating high-quality sentence embeddings. Unlike traditional BERT models, which are primarily trained on word-level tasks like next-sentence prediction and masked language modeling, S-BERT fine-tunes the BERT architecture to produce embeddings at the sentence level. It was trained on a combination of two Natural Language Inference (NLI) datasets: the Stanford NLI (SNLI) dataset and the Multi-Genre NLI (MultiNLI) dataset. S-BERT typically employs Siamese or triplet network architectures during fine-tuning, enabling it to capture contextual information and nuances in meaning. By considering the surrounding context, S-BERT generates embeddings that are suitable for tasks such as semantic textual similarity. Cosine similarity between associated sentence vectors indicates the similarity between word meanings in different sentences, with higher similarity indicating lower ambiguity in word meaning.

4.3 Neural Machine Translation

4.3.1 Text-only Machine Translation

A text-only transformer model serves as the baseline in our experiment, utilizing solely the textual captions of images for translation. Trained using the OpenNMT toolkit (Klein et al., 2018) on the Multi30k dataset for English to German, French, and Czech translations, the model comprises a 6-layer transformer architecture with attention mechanisms in both encoder and decoder stages, trained for 50K steps. Sentencepiece (Kudo and Richardson, 2018) is employed to segment words into subword units, offering a language-independent approach to tokenization without necessitating pre-processing steps, thus enhancing the model's adaptability and versatility in handling raw text.

4.3.2 Multimodal Machine Translation

In the MMT model, we adopt the Gated Fusion MMT model Wu et al. (2021), which fuses visual and text representations by employing a gate mechanism. Gated Fusion is a mechanism used to integrate visual information from images with textual

En → De	Test 2016						Test 2017					
	LSA			S-BERT			LSA			S-BERT		
	BLEU ↑	chrF2 ↑	TER ↓	BLEU ↑	chrF2 ↑	TER ↓	BLEU ↑	chrF2 ↑	TER ↓	BLEU ↑	chrF2 ↑	TER ↓
Baseline (MMT)	40.1	64.6	40.6	40.1	64.6	40.6	31.9	59.8	49.6	31.9	59.8	49.6
Hybrid (50)	40.7	**65.0**	39.9	40.7	**65.0**	39.8*	**32.6**	**60.6***	**48.5***	**32.6**	60.5*	**48.5***
Hybrid (100)	40.8	**65.0**	**39.7***	**40.9**	**65.0**	**39.7***	32.5	60.4*	48.6*	**32.6**	60.5*	48.6*
Hybrid (150)	40.8	**65.0***	39.9*	**40.9**	**65.0**	39.8*	32.4	60.3	48.8*	32.4	60.4*	48.8*
Hybrid (200)	40.6	**65.0**	40.1	40.7	64.9	39.9	32.4	60.3	48.6*	32.3	60.4*	48.8*
Hybrid (250)	40.6	64.9	40.2	40.5	64.9	40.1	32.2	60.2	48.8*	32.1	60.3	49.0
Hybrid (300)	40.6	**65.0**	40.2	40.5	64.8	40.1	32.0	60.1	49.0*	32.1	60.1	49.0
Hybrid (350)	40.5	64.8	40.3	40.4	64.7	40.1	32.1	60.1	48.9*	32.0	59.9	49.1
Hybrid (400)	40.5	64.8	40.2	40.5	64.8	40.0	32.3	60.1	48.8*	31.9	59.9	49.1
Hybrid (450)	40.4	64.7	40.3	40.5	64.8	40.0	32.1	59.9	49.0*	32.0	60.0	49.0*
Hybrid (500)	40.4	64.7	40.3	40.5	64.7	40.2	32.2	60.0	49.0*	32.1	60.0	49.0*
Hybrid (550)	40.3	64.7	40.4	40.4	64.8	40.1	32.2	59.9	49.0*	32.0	59.9	49.1*
Hybrid (600)	40.2	64.6	40.5	40.4	64.7	40.1	32.1	59.8	49.2	31.9	59.9	49.2
Hybrid (650)	40.3	64.7	40.4	40.3	64.6	40.1*	32.0	59.8	49.2	32.2	59.9	49.1*
Hybrid (700)	40.3	64.7	40.3	40.2	64.5	40.4	32.2	59.8	49.3	32.1	59.8	49.2*
Hybrid (750)	40.3	64.7	40.3	40.2	64.6	40.3	32.3	59.9	49.3	32.2	59.9	49.3
Hybrid (800)	40.3	64.7	40.4	40.2	64.7	40.3	32.3	59.9	49.3	32.2	59.8	49.4
Hybrid (850)	40.1	64.6	40.4	40.3	64.7	40.2*	32.2	59.9	49.5	32.4*	59.9	49.4
Hybrid (900)	40.1	64.5	40.5	40.3	64.7	40.2*	32.1	59.9	49.6	32.2*	59.9	49.5
Hybrid (950)	40.2	64.7	40.5	40.2	64.7	40.4	31.9	59.8	49.7	32.0	59.8	49.6

En → Fr	Test 2016						Test 2017					
	LSA			S-BERT			LSA			S-BERT		
	BLEU ↑	chrF2 ↑	TER ↓	BLEU ↑	chrF2 ↑	TER ↓	BLEU ↑	chrF2 ↑	TER ↓	BLEU ↑	chrF2 ↑	TER ↓
Baseline (MMT)	**62.3**	75.3	25.5	**62.3**	75.3	25.5	55.6	70.7	30.9	55.6	70.7	30.9
Hybrid (50)	62.1	75.4	25.2	62.2	**75.5**	**25.1**	55.9	71.0	30.8	55.9	**71.1**	30.8
Hybrid (100)	62.0	75.3	25.3	62.2	**75.5**	25.2	55.9	**71.1**	30.7	**56.0**	**71.1**	30.7
Hybrid (150)	61.8	75.2	25.4	62.1	75.4	25.3	55.9	71.0	30.7	55.8	71.0	30.9
Hybrid (200)	61.7	75.2	25.3	62.0	75.3	25.4	55.9	**71.1**	**30.6**	55.9	**71.1***	30.7
Hybrid (250)	61.8	75.2	25.4	61.9	75.2	25.4	55.7	70.9	30.7	55.9	**71.1***	30.7
Hybrid (300)	61.8	75.2	25.4	61.9	75.2	25.5	55.5	70.9	30.8	55.7	70.9	30.7
Hybrid (350)	61.7*	75.1	25.6	61.7	75.1	25.5	55.5	70.8	30.9	55.8	71.0	30.7
Hybrid (400)	61.7*	75.1	25.6	61.6*	75.0	25.7	55.6	70.8	30.8	55.9	**71.1***	30.7
Hybrid (450)	61.7*	75.1	25.6	61.7*	75.0	25.8	55.5	70.8	30.8	55.9	71.0	30.7
Hybrid (500)	61.6*	75.1	25.7	61.7*	75.0	25.7	55.5	70.7	31.0	55.8	70.9	30.7
Hybrid (550)	61.8*	75.1	25.6	61.8*	75.0	25.8	55.3	70.6	31.0	55.7	70.8	30.9
Hybrid (600)	61.9	75.1	25.6	61.9	75.1	25.7	55.3	70.6	31.0	55.5	70.7	31.0
Hybrid (650)	62.0	75.2	25.6	62.0	75.2	25.5	55.5	70.6	31.0	55.5	70.7	31.0
Hybrid (700)	62.1	75.3	25.5	62.1	75.2	25.5	55.4	70.6	31.1	55.5	70.7	31.1
Hybrid (750)	62.0	75.2	25.7	62.0	75.2	25.6	55.5	70.7	31.0	55.4	70.7	31.1
Hybrid (800)	62.0*	75.1*	25.7	62.1	75.2	25.6	55.5	70.6	31.0	55.3	70.6	31.1
Hybrid (850)	62.0*	75.1*	25.6	62.1	75.2	25.6	55.6	70.7	31.0	55.5	70.7	31.1
Hybrid (900)	62.1	75.2	25.6	62.2	75.2	25.6	55.6	70.7	30.9	55.6	70.7	31.0
Hybrid (950)	**62.3**	75.3	25.5	62.1	75.2*	25.7*	55.6	70.7	31.0	55.6	70.7	31.0

Table 1: BLEU, chrF2, and TER scores for baseline and Hybrid models for English-to-German and English-to-French translations. Numbers in parentheses show sentences where the model uses visual information (e.g., Hybrid (50) refers to the top 50 ambiguous sentences using Multimodal, while the remaining 950 use a text-only model). * indicates a statistically significant result compared to the baseline multimodal at a significance level of $p < 0.05$. Bold numbers indicate the best results in each test dataset for each score.

information from source sentences during the translation process. The main idea behind Gated Fusion is to control the amount of visual information that is blended into the textual representation using a gating matrix. The source sentence x is fed into a vanilla Transformer encoder to obtain a textual representation H_{text} of dimension T×d. The image z is processed using a pre-trained ResNet-50 CNN which has been trained on the ImageNet dataset (Russakovsky et al., 2015) to extract a 2048-dimensional average-pooled visual representation, denoted as $Embed_{image}(z)$. The visual representation $Embed_{image}(z)$ is projected to the same dimension as H_{text} using a weight matrix W_z. A gating matrix of dimension T×d is generated to control the fusion of the textual and visual representations. The gating matrix is computed as:

$$\Lambda = \text{sigmoid}(W_\Lambda \text{Embed}_{\text{image}}(z) + U_\Lambda H_{\text{text}})$$

where W and U are model parameters.

4.4 Evaluation Metrics

We use three evaluation metrics: BLEU (Papineni et al., 2002), ChrF2 (Popović, 2015), and TER (Snover et al., 2006). BLEU assesses translation precision by comparing candidate translations to reference translations based on *n-grams*. ChrF2 evaluates the similarity between character *n-grams* in machine-generated and reference translations, particularly beneficial for languages with complex writing systems. TER quantifies the number of edits needed to align machine translations with human-generated references. We conduct statistical significance testing using the *sacrebleu*[3] toolbox.

5 Results

In this section, we analyze the results of our experiments. We present the findings for both LSA and S-BERT approaches on the 2016 and 2017 Multi30k test sets for English to German and English to French translations. Table 1 provides a comprehensive comparison of different models' performance in terms of BLEU, chrF2, and TER metrics, offering insights into the effectiveness of integrating sentence ambiguity scores with a multimodal setting in English to German and French translations. We report translation scores for the baseline multimodal and the Hybrid models for LSA and S-BERT using *G-Mean*[4].

Table 1 presents the translation performance of baseline and Hybrid models for English-to-German (En $\rightarrow$ De) and English-to-French (En $\rightarrow$ Fr) across different test datasets and Hybrid configurations. The table highlights metrics including BLEU score (higher is better), chrF2 score (higher is better), and TER score (lower is better). Each Hybrid model variant is indicated by the number of sentences (in parentheses) where visual information aids translation, with the remainder utilizing a text-only model[5]. Statistically significant improvements over the baseline multimodal model at $p<0.05$ are marked with *, while the best-performing scores in each dataset are indicated in bold.

The results indicate that the sentence ambiguity score plays an important role in determining the importance of using visual information in English-to-German translation compared with English-to-French translation. In English-to-German translation for Test 2016, the baseline multimodal model achieves a performance with a BLEU score of 40.1, a chrF2 score of 64.6, and a TER of 40.6 using LSA and S-BERT. In contrast, the Hybrid models show improvements over the baseline. In LSA, Hybrid (50) achieves a BLEU score of 40.7, a chrF2 score of 65.0, and a TER of 39.9. Hybrid (100) and Hybrid (150) continue to outperform the baseline across all metrics. In S-BERT, similar to LSA, Hybrid (100) and Hybrid (150) achieved a BLEU score of 40.9, a chrF2 score of 65.0, and notably reduced the TER to 39.7. For both LSA and S-BERT, Hybrid (50) to Hybrid (150) achieve statistically significant improvements in chrF2 and TER in some configurations. By increasing the number of sentences that the Hybrid model uses visual information for, the results get close to the baseline multimodal model (see Hybrid (950)). For Test 2017, the performance of the Hybrid models remains consistent with Test 2016, indicating stability in the proposed approach for English-to-German translation. For this test set, Hybrid (50) maintains improvements over the baseline with a BLEU score of 32.6, a chrF2 score of 60.6, and a TER of 48.5, representing a statisti-

[3]https://github.com/mjpost/sacrebleu

[4]Based on our experiments, *G-Mean* shows better results compared with *Mean*. Therefore, due to limited space, we reported the results for *G-Mean*.

[5]The total number of sentences in the test sets is 1,000.

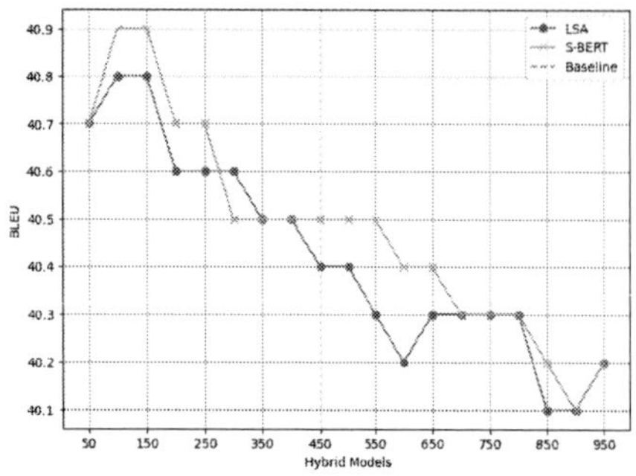

(a) En → De, Test 2016

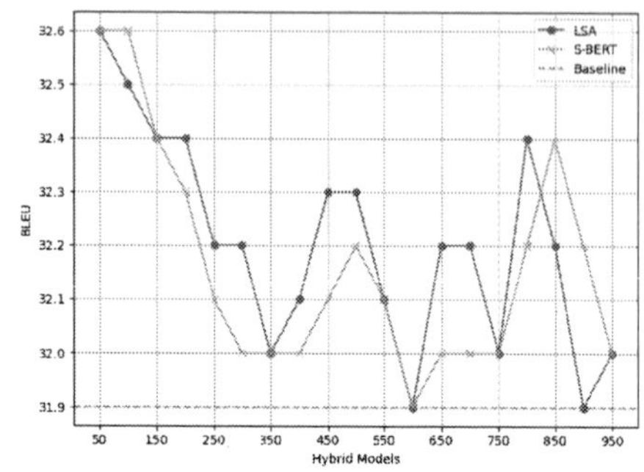

(b) En → De, Test 2017

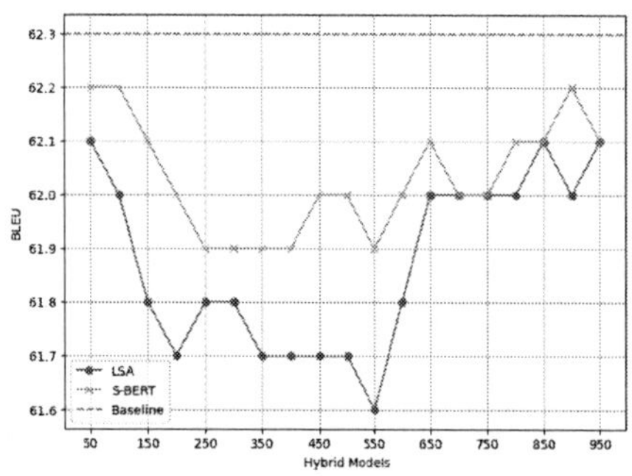

(c) En → Fr, Test 2016

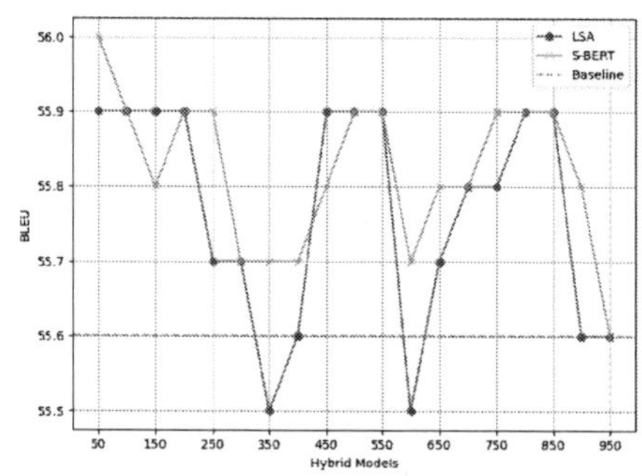

(d) En → Fr, Test 2017

Figure 5: The charts display BLEU scores across various Hybrid models in English to German and French for the 2016 and 2017 test sets. Solid lines represent BLEU scores for S-BERT and LSA, while dashed lines indicate the overall performance for multimodal MT models.

cally significant improvement over the baseline. Hybrid (100) and Hybrid (150) consistently outperform the baseline, with results showing statistical significance.

In English-to-French translation, the Hybrid models show slight improvement over the baseline multimodal model. In Test 2016, the baseline model has a higher BLEU score compared with the Hybrid models. The Hybrid model of 50 slightly improves the chrF2 and TER scores, but they are not statistically significant. Similar to Test 2016, Test 2017 does not represent notable improvements regarding BLEU, chrF2, and TER scores. This indicates that the idea of using ambiguity scores to evaluate the importance of using visual information is less effective for English-to-French translation.

To better analyze the role of a sentence ambiguity score in the proposed Hybrid models, the BLEU scores for LSA and S-BERT for *G-Mean* are presented in Figure 5. In each subgraph, the red dashed line shows the overall BLEU scores for the baseline multimodal model for each language pair in the 2016 and 2017 test sets. The orange and blue lines show the BLEU scores in different Hybrid models. For both language combinations, LSA and S-BERT follow the same pattern. In English-to-German translation, by increasing the number of sentences in the Hybrid model, the BLEU scores started from 40.9 and 32.6 for Test 2016 and Test 2017, respectively, and reached the baseline multimodal models. This indicates that visual information is useful in translating around 150 sentences with higher ambiguity scores. However, using visual information for the remaining sentences with lower ambiguity ranking sharply drops translation performance. In contrast, for English-to-French translation, we do not see the same pattern. In Test 2016, all Hybrid models have BLEU scores lower than the baseline multimodal model, showing the effectiveness of using visual information in most sentences. In Test

- **Src.:** Two boys play soccer against each other.
- **Ref.:** Zwei Jungen spielen gegeneinander Fußball.
- **Text-only:** zwei jungen spielen gegeneinander fußball.
- **Multimodal:** zwei jungen spielen fußball gegen einander.

- **Src.:** Two people riding bikes through a mountainous region.
- **Ref.:** Zwei Personen Fahren auf Fahrrädern durch eine Gebirgslandschaft.
- **Text-only:** zwei menschen fahren mit fahrrädern durch eine bergigen gegend.
- **Multimodal:** zwei personen fahren auf fahrrädern durch eine gebirgslandschaft.

Figure 6: Examples from Multi30k illustrate the effectiveness of using images based on the ambiguity level of the source sentence. The top image shows a source sentence with a low ambiguity score (1.46), which was translated more accurately using the Text-only model. The bottom image shows a source sentence with a high ambiguity score (1.81), where the Multimodal model provided a better translation.

2017, there are consistent fluctuations by changing the number of sentences, but it remains above the baseline model except in a few cases.

Figure 6 shows examples from the Multi30k dataset to illustrate the impact of sentence ambiguity on the effectiveness of translation models. The top image presents a source sentence with a low ambiguity score of 1.46, where the Text-only model outperformed the Multimodal model according to automatic evaluation metrics like the BLEU score. However, interestingly, human analysis revealed that the translation provided by the Multimodal model not only better explained the image but was also more readable than even the reference sentence. Conversely, the bottom image presents a source sentence with a higher ambiguity score of 1.81, where the Multimodal model produced a superior translation compared to the Text-only model. While various factors can influence the performance of multimodal translation models, these findings suggest that the sentence ambiguity score can serve as a valuable parameter in determining when visual information enhances translation quality.

6 Conclusion

This study contributes to the ongoing discussion on the effective utilisation of visual cues in translation tasks and provides insights into optimizing multimodal translation systems. In this paper, we investigate the impact of integrating visual elements into the translation process on overall translation quality. Through an analysis of the relationship between sentence ambiguity and translation quality, we aimed to determine the circumstances under which visual information enhances translation quality. By establishing ambiguity scores for individual sentences using semantic diversity within sentence vector embedding spaces, we investigated how visual information influences translation quality across different ranges of sentence ambiguity scores. Our research highlights the importance of discerning the contextual relevance of visual information in multimodal tasks, suggesting semantic diversity as a valuable metric for determining the significance of visual cues in multimodal machine translation models. We plan to look at clustering approaches to cluster meanings or usages of words based on their semantic similarities. This can be used to assign ambiguity scores to each word based on the number of clusters.

Acknowledgements

We thank the anonymous reviewers for their insights on this work. This publication has emanated from research conducted with the financial support of Science Foundation Ireland (SFI) under Grant Number SFI/12/RC/2289_P2 (Insight), co-funded by the European Regional Development Fund. For the purpose of Open Access, the author has applied a CC BY public copyright licence to any Author Accepted Manuscript version arising from this submission.

References

Aston, G. and Burnard, L. (1998). *The BNC Handbook: Exploring the British National Corpus with SARA*. Edinburgh textbooks in empirical linguistics. Edinburgh University Press.

Bowen, B., Vijayan, V., Grigsby, S., Anderson, T., and Gwinnup, J. (2024). Detecting concrete visual tokens for multimodal machine translation.

Caglayan, O., Aransa, W., Wang, Y., Masana, M., García-Martínez, M., Bougares, F., Barrault, L., and van de Weijer, J. (2016). Does multimodality help human and machine for translation and image captioning? In *Proceedings of the First Conference on Machine Translation: Volume 2, Shared Task Papers*, pages 627–633, Berlin, Germany. Association for Computational Linguistics.

Caglayan, O., Madhyastha, P., Specia, L., and Barrault, L. (2019). Probing the need for visual context in multimodal machine translation. In *Proceedings of the 2019 Conference of the North American Chapter of the Association for Computational Linguistics: Human Language Technologies, Volume 1 (Long and Short Papers)*, pages 4159–4170, Minneapolis, Minnesota. Association for Computational Linguistics.

Calixto, I., Rios, M., and Aziz, W. (2019). Latent variable model for multi-modal translation. In *Proceedings of the 57th Annual Meeting of the Association for Computational Linguistics*, pages 6392–6405, Florence, Italy. Association for Computational Linguistics.

Cho, K., van Merriënboer, B., Bahdanau, D., and Bengio, Y. (2014). On the properties of neural machine translation: Encoder–decoder approaches. In Wu, D., Carpuat, M., Carreras, X., and Vecchi, E. M., editors, *Proceedings of SSST-8, Eighth Workshop on Syntax, Semantics and Structure in Statistical Translation*, pages 103–111, Doha, Qatar. Association for Computational Linguistics.

Elliott, D., Frank, S., Barrault, L., Bougares, F., and Specia, L. (2017). Findings of the Second Shared Task on Multimodal Machine Translation and Multilingual Image Description. In *Proceedings of the Second Conference on Machine Translation*, Copenhagen, Denmark.

Elliott, D., Frank, S., Sima'an, K., and Specia, L. (2016). Multi30K: Multilingual English-German image descriptions. In *Proceedings of the 5th Workshop on Vision and Language*, pages 70–74, Berlin, Germany. Association for Computational Linguistics.

Futeral, M., Schmid, C., Laptev, I., Sagot, B., and Bawden, R. (2023). Tackling ambiguity with images: Improved multimodal machine translation and contrastive evaluation. In Rogers, A., Boyd-Graber, J., and Okazaki, N., editors, *Proceedings of the 61st Annual Meeting of the Association for Computational Linguistics (Volume 1: Long Papers)*, pages 5394–5413, Toronto, Canada. Association for Computational Linguistics.

Gonzales, A. R., Mascarell, L., and Sennrich, R. (2017). Improving word sense disambiguation in neural machine translation with sense embeddings. In *Conference on Machine Translation*.

Harris, Z. S. (1954). Distributional structure. *WORD*, 10(2-3):146–162.

Hatami, A., Buitelaar, P., and Arcan, M. (2022). Analysing the correlation between lexical ambiguity and translation quality in a multimodal setting using WordNet. In Ippolito, D., Li, L. H., Pacheco, M. L., Chen, D., and Xue, N., editors, *Proceedings of the 2022 Conference of the North American Chapter of the Association for Computational Linguistics: Human Language Technologies: Student Research Workshop*, pages 89–95, Hybrid: Seattle, Washington + Online. Association for Computational Linguistics.

Hatami, A., Buitelaar, P., and Arcan, M. (2023). A filtering approach to object region detection in multimodal machine translation. In Utiyama, M. and Wang, R., editors, *Proceedings of Machine Translation Summit XIX, Vol. 1: Research Track*, pages 393–405, Macau SAR, China. Asia-Pacific Association for Machine Translation.

Hoffman, P., Ralph, M., and Rogers, T. (2012). Semantic diversity: A measure of semantic ambiguity based on variability in the contextual usage of words. *Behavior research methods*, 45.

Ive, J., Madhyastha, P., and Specia, L. (2019). Distilling translations with visual awareness. In *Proceedings of the 57th Annual Meeting of the Association for Computational Linguistics*, pages 6525–6538, Florence, Italy. Association for Computational Linguistics.

Klein, G., Kim, Y., Deng, Y., Nguyen, V., Senellart, J., and Rush, A. (2018). OpenNMT: Neural machine translation toolkit. In *Proceedings of the 13th Conference of the Association for Machine Translation in the Americas (Volume 1: Research Track)*, pages 177–184, Boston, MA. Association for Machine Translation in the Americas.

Kudo, T. and Richardson, J. (2018). SentencePiece: A simple and language independent subword tokenizer and detokenizer for neural text processing. In *Proceedings of the 2018 Conference on Empirical Methods in Natural Language Processing: System Demonstrations*, pages 66–71, Brussels, Belgium. Association for Computational Linguistics.

Lala, C., Madhyastha, P. S., Scarton, C., and Specia, L. (2018). Sheffield submissions for WMT18 multimodal translation shared task. In *Proceedings of the Third Conference on Machine Translation: Shared Task Papers*, pages 624–631, Belgium, Brussels. Association for Computational Linguistics.

Lala, C. and Specia, L. (2018). Multimodal lexical translation. In *Proceedings of the Eleventh International Conference on Language Resources and Evaluation (LREC 2018)*, Miyazaki, Japan. European Language Resources Association (ELRA).

Landauer, T. K. and Dumais, S. T. (1997). A solution to plato's problem: The latent semantic analysis theory of acquisition, induction, and representation of knowledge. *Psychological Review*, 104:211–240.

Papineni, K., Roukos, S., Ward, T., and Zhu, W.-J. (2002). Bleu: a method for automatic evaluation of machine translation. In *Proceedings of the 40th Annual Meeting of the Association for Computational Linguistics*, pages 311–318, Philadelphia, Pennsylvania, USA. Association for Computational Linguistics.

Popović, M. (2015). chrF: character n-gram F-score for automatic MT evaluation. In *Proceedings of the Tenth Workshop on Statistical Machine Translation*, pages 392–395, Lisbon, Portugal. Association for Computational Linguistics.

Reimers, N. and Gurevych, I. (2019). Sentence-bert: Sentence embeddings using siamese bert-networks. In *Proceedings of the 2019 Conference on Empirical Methods in Natural Language Processing*. Association for Computational Linguistics.

Snover, M., Dorr, B., Schwartz, R., Micciulla, L., and Makhoul, J. (2006). A study of translation edit rate with targeted human annotation. In *Proceedings of the 7th Conference of the Association for Machine Translation in the Americas: Technical Papers*, pages 223–231, Cambridge, Massachusetts, USA. Association for Machine Translation in the Americas.

Tang, G., Sennrich, R., and Nivre, J. (2018). An analysis of attention mechanisms: The case of word sense disambiguation in neural machine translation. In Bojar, O., Chatterjee, R., Federmann, C., Fishel, M., Graham, Y., Haddow, B., Huck, M., Yepes, A. J., Koehn, P., Monz, C., Negri, M., Névéol, A., Neves, M., Post, M., Specia, L., Turchi, M., and Verspoor, K., editors, *Proceedings of the Third Conference on Machine Translation: Research Papers*, pages 26–35, Brussels, Belgium. Association for Computational Linguistics.

Vaswani, A., Bengio, S., Brevdo, E., Chollet, F., Gomez, A. N., Gouws, S., Jones, L., Kaiser, L., Kalchbrenner, N., Parmar, N., Sepassi, R., Shazeer, N., and Uszkoreit, J. (2018). Tensor2tensor for neural machine translation. *Computing Research Repository (CoRR)*, abs/1803.07416.

Vaswani, A., Shazeer, N., Parmar, N., Uszkoreit, J., Jones, L., Gomez, A. N., Kaiser, L., and Polosukhin, I. (2017). Attention is all you need. *Computing Research Repository (CoRR)*, abs/1706.03762.

Vijayan, V., Bowen, B., Grigsby, S., Anderson, T., and Gwinnup, J. (2024). Adding multimodal capabilities to a text-only translation model.

Wang, D. and Xiong, D. (2021). Efficient object-level visual context modeling for multimodal machine translation: Masking irrelevant objects helps grounding. In *Thirty-Fifth AAAI Conference on Artificial Intelligence, AAAI 2021, Thirty-Third Conference on Innovative Applications of Artificial Intelligence, IAAI 2021, The Eleventh Symposium on Educational Advances in Artificial Intelligence, EAAI 2021, Virtual Event, February 2-9, 2021*, pages 2720–2728. AAAI Press.

Wu, Z., Kong, L., Bi, W., Li, X., and Kao, B. (2021). Good for misconceived reasons: An empirical revisiting on the need for visual context in multimodal machine translation. *CoRR*, abs/2105.14462.

Yao, S. and Wan, X. (2020). Multimodal transformer for multimodal machine translation. In *Proceedings of the 58th Annual Meeting of the Association for Computational Linguistics*, pages 4346–4350, Online. Association for Computational Linguistics.

Yin, Y., Meng, F., Su, J., Zhou, C., Yang, Z., Zhou, J., and Luo, J. (2020). A novel graph-based multi-modal fusion encoder for neural machine translation. In *Annual Meeting of the Association for Computational Linguistics*.

Zhao, Y., Komachi, M., Kajiwara, T., and Chu, C. (2022). Region-attentive multimodal neural machine translation. *Neurocomputing*, 476:1–13.

Can Synthetic Speech Improve End-to-End Conversational Speech Translation?

Bismarck Bamfo Odoom[1] bodoom1@jhu.edu
Nathaniel R. Robinson[1] nrobin38@jhu.edu
Elijah Rippeth[2] erip@cs.umd.edu
Luis Tavarez-Arce[3] ltavare1@jhu.edu
Kenton Murray[1] kenton@jhu.edu
Matthew Wiesner[1] wiesner@jhu.edu
Paul McNamee[1] mcnamee@jhu.edu
Philipp Koehn[1] phi@jhu.edu
Kevin Duh[1] kevinduh@cs.jhu.edu
[1] Johns Hopkins University, Baltimore, MD, USA
[2] University of Maryland, College Park, MD, USA
[3] SCALE 2023 Workshop Participant

Abstract

Conversational speech translation is an important technology that fosters communication among people of different language backgrounds. Three-way parallel data in the form of source speech, source transcript, and target translation is usually required to train end-to-end systems. However, such datasets are not readily available and are expensive to create as this involves multiple annotation stages. In this paper, we investigate the use of synthetic data from generative models, namely machine translation and text-to-speech synthesis, for training conversational speech translation systems. We show that adding synthetic data to the training recipe increasingly improves end-to-end training performance, especially when limited real data is available. However, when no real data is available, no amount of synthetic data helps.

1 Introduction

The growing globalization of our society requires effective technologies that foster communication among individuals of varying language backgrounds. Speech translation is an important technology that fosters everyday communication among individuals from different language backgrounds, bridging cultural and linguistic barriers. The technology has improved dramatically in recent years thanks to deep learning, but most gains have been demonstrated on formal settings such as parliamentary speeches, prepared monologues, and university lectures. Informal conversations pose significant challenges due to the lack of training data. Conversations deviate from formal written language and include informal expressions, slang, overlapping speech, incomplete sentences, varying intonation, pace, and emotion, which are typically not present in standard speech translation datasets. To capture these nuances, conversational datasets are essential for training models to understand and translate real-life spoken language accurately. However, creating this type of data usually involves individuals talking on the telephone for hours about various topics, followed by multiple annotation stages involving segmenting the long-form speech into chunks, transcribing the various chunks, and then translating them into the target language. Executing these tasks is tedious, time-consuming, and expensive.

This motivates a new approach of utilizing synthetic data from generative models. Generative

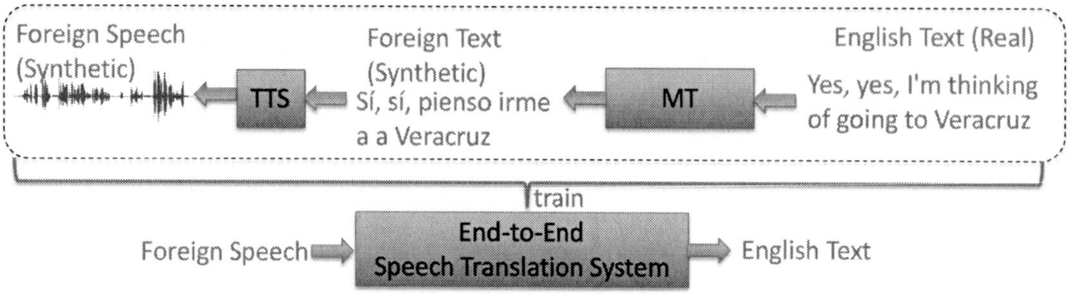

Figure 1: Overview of approach in generating three-way parallel data (foreign speech, foreign text, english text) for training end-to-end conversational speech translation systems.

models present an attractive solution by being able to produce large amounts of synthetic conversational speech quickly in a flexible and cost-effective manner. When used as a data augmentation technique, this synthetic data can potentially improve the performance of speech translation systems in conversational speech domains.

Over the years, machine translation has seen significant advances. Machine translation (MT) models utilizing the transformer architecture when trained on large data sets across multiple languages generalize better and can generate adequate and fluent translations in near real-time. In addition, text-to-speech synthesis (TTS) has attained significant strides resulting in high-quality synthesized voices that closely mimic human speech. In this study, we leverage the advances from MT and TTS to show that a synthetic conversational speech dataset that is easier and cheaper to create can be used for the task of conversational end-to-end speech translation. To do this, we create a dataset of synthetic speech by back-translating monolingual text from the target language to the source language, and then generating the speech in the source language speech from the back-translated text using a TTS system (Figure 1).

We seek to answer the following questions:

1. Does incorporating synthetic data into the training recipe help end-to-end training for conversational speech translation?
2. How do we use synthetic data effectively for end-to-end conversational speech translation?
3. Can synthetic data be used in place of real data for conversational end-to-end speech translation?

2 Background and Related Work

Synthetic Data The use of synthetic data has been extensively studied for text-based machine translation. Sennrich et al. (2016a) shows that generating synthetic source sentences from target monolingual data through back-translation helps boost neural machine translation performance. Amin et al. (2021) investigate the use of synthetic data for training RNN-T ASR models via a multi-stage training pipeline with continual learning. Rossenbach et al. (2020) show that training attention-based ASR systems on synthetic data leads to huge improvements in word-error-rate (WER). Rossenbach et al. (2021) compare the benefits of training with synthetic data for four ASR architectures, namely - attention encoder-decoder (AED), hybrid ASR, CTC, and monotic RNN-T. Fang and Feng (2023) train a target-to-unit model to map the target text to source speech units (Lee et al., 2022). They then utilize a unit vocoder to map the source units into a waveform. Robinson et al. (2022); Karakasidis et al. (2023) expand these augmentation methods to low-resource and accented ASR, respectively.

Text-to-Speech Synthesis The task of text-to-speech synthesis (TTS) is to generate an output speech corresponding to an input transcript. Early techniques such as formant synthesis used the source-filter model for intelligibility but lacked naturalness. Modern neural synthesis methods, such as Tacotron2 (Shen et al., 2018), TransformerTTS (Li et al., 2019), FastSpeech (Ren et al., 2019) and VITS (Kim et al., 2021) simplify the pipeline and deliver high-quality voice output by leveraging deep learning. Tacotron2 employs an autoregressive decoder with attention mechanisms, while TransformerTTS replaces RNNs with Transformers for faster training. FastSpeech optimizes the process by using non-autoregressive methods, addressing the speed limitations of previous models. VITS employs a conditional variational autoencoder augmented with normalizing flows and an adversarial training process which enhances the quality of synthesized speech.

Speech Translation Speech translation research has seen a revival in recent years. For example, the IWSLT 2023 campaign showcased a variety of tasks, including multilingual speech translation, speech-to-speech translation, low-resource speech translation, automatic dubbing or subtitling, and simultaneous speech translation (Agarwal et al., 2023). Both cascaded systems consisting of speech recognition and machine translation components as well as end-to-end direct speech translation systems have been explored. End-to-end systems can be trained with a combination (Babu et al., 2022) of 2-fold parallel data or via multi-task learning (Radford et al., 2023). In the majority of cases, the training data for these systems come from TED talks, university lectures, conference presentations, European parliamentary speeches. These are prepared, public talks which exhibit different characteristics from the informal multiparty conversations of interest here.

3 Data Creation Methods

We use the term three-way parallel data to refer to the aligned source speech, source transcript, and target translation that is necessary for end-to-end speech translation model training. We first describe the manually-created 3-way parallel data (referred to as **Real** in subsequent sections) used for baseline models. We then explain the synthetically generated 3-way parallel data (which we refer to as **Synth** in subsequent sections) used for data augmentation.

3.1 Real 3-way Parallel Data

We use the Fisher-Callhome Spanish-English dataset (Post et al., 2013), a three-way conversational telephone speech dataset consisting of Spanish speech, Spanish transcript, and English text translation for our experiments. While we argue that there is a lack of manually-created conversational data, this dataset is a rare exception: it is an immensely large dataset by academic research standards, created by crowdsourcing translations of an existing transcribed speech recognition dataset. The reason we chose this dataset is that is enables us to perform data ablation experiments to understand how much real data is needed in a data augmentation setup.

For preprocessing, we resample the audio to 16kHz and apply speed perturbation (0.9, 1.0, 1.1). The audio is transformed into a 80 dimensional log-filterbank and we apply specaugment (Park et al., 2019) with bi-cubic time-warping. We use byte-pair-encoding (BPE) tokenization (Sennrich et al., 2016b) with a vocabulary of size 4000.

3.2 Synthetic 3-way Parallel Data

To create the synthetic speech-text pairs, we use over 500,000 lines of conversational-style text in English. This text was collected from the English translations of various conversational speech datasets (Ansari et al., 2020; Song et al., 2014). We back-translate (Sennrich et al., 2016a) this text using the `nllb-200-1.3B`[1] multilingual machine translation model (Team et al., 2022) into Spanish. Spanish speech is synthesized by feeding the back-translated text into the VITS [2] text-to-speech system. Specifically, we use the VITS model trained on CSS10 Spanish (Park and Mulc, 2019) then apply voice conversion using freevc24[3]. The target speakers used for voice conversion are the speakers for the original files; future work is to explore more diversity in speakers by sampling in speaker embedding space (Jia et al., 2019).

To illustrate the whole pipeline with a concrete example, we begin with a Callhome Chinese file spoken by speaker A: First, we translate the English text portion to Spanish text. Second, we synthesize a generic Spanish voice using VITS. Finally, we apply voice conversion with speaker A as the target speaker, generating a Spanish voice that sounds like the original Chinese speaker A. This

[1] `https://huggingface.co/facebook/nllb-200-1.3B`
[2] `https://github.com/coqui-ai/TTS`
[3] `https://github.com/OlaWod/FreeVC`

Corpus	**Lang**	**#Hours**		
		Train	**Dev**	**Test**
Real: Spanish Fisher/Callhome	Sp-En	170	9.3	4.5/1.8
Synth: backtranslation + TTS	Sp-En	520	-	-

Table 1: Dataset statistics showing the number of hours of both real and synthetic speech. We use both the Fisher and the Callhome test sets.

procedure is repeated independently for each file that we wish to add to the augmentation dataset. This process yielded about 520 hours of synthetic speech in Spanish. The resulting dataset consists of synthetic speech in Spanish, back-translated text in Spanish (transcript), and the English text (translation). We apply the same preprocessing techniques in Section 3.1 and refer to this dataset as **Synth** in subsequent sections.

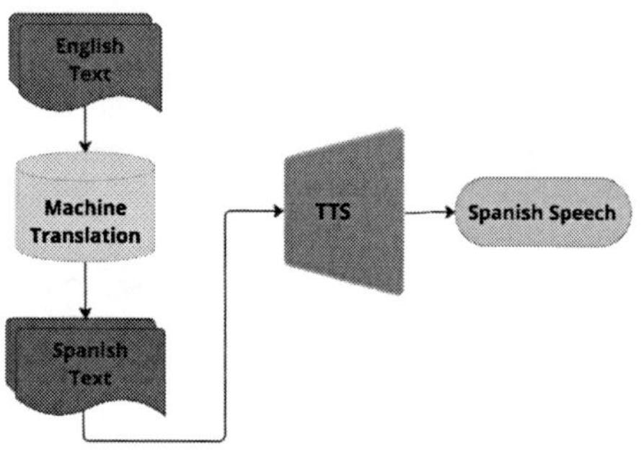

Figure 2: The synthetic data generation pipeline. We collect over 500,000 lines of English conversational style text and translate them into Spanish. We pass the back-translated text into a text-to-speech synthesis (TTS) system to synthesize Spanish speech from the transcript.

3.2.1 Quality of Synthetic Speech

We use the NISQA model (Mittag et al., 2021) to analyze the speech quality. The model consists of a convolutional neural network with a self-attention and attention-pooling block. The model predicts the mean opinion score which is a common metric used to measure the quality of TTS generated speech. The model predicts a mean opinion score of 4.29 out of 5 signifying that the synthesized speech is of high quality. Text references are not available to measure the translation quality (e.g. BLEU) of the synthetic text used to generate the synthetic speech. However, we know that NLLB is generally a strong model for this language pair; while domain differences may degrade text translation, a manual check of a small subset of translations reveals that they mostly preserve the semantics.

4 Speech Translation Model

4.1 Model Architecture

The speech encoder is based on the conformer architecture (Gulati et al., 2020), which combines the strengths of convolutional neural networks (CNNs) and Transformer models to handle the speech input efficiently. We use 8 conformer blocks with 16 attention heads within its multi-head self-attention modules, enabling the model to focus on different segments of the input sequence concurrently. Each Conformer block contains feed-forward networks with 2048 linear units. We use relative positional encodings and relative self-attention mechanisms, the swish activation function is used, and dropout of 0.1.

The text decoder is a Transformer model (Vaswani et al., 2017) featuring 8 blocks with 2048 linear units each. The ReLU activation function is used and a dropout rate of 0.1. The total number of trainable parameters is 38.7M. We initialize all models from scratch and train on 2 NVIDIA V100 32GB GPUs. All models are trained for 50 epochs with batch size of 64.

4.2 Data Augmentation Scheme

We perform a simple data augmentation scheme: concatenating the **Real** data in Section 3.1 and the **Synth** data as one training set. The training objective treats samples from both datasets in the same way, with no specific up-sampling or down-sampling. More advanced methods are conceivable, such as pre-training on **Synth** and fine-tuning **Real** and modifying the training objective to treat real and synthetic data differently. In this work, we focused on the simple data concatenation, with experiments focusing on different data proportions, to more easily study the impact of synthetic data.

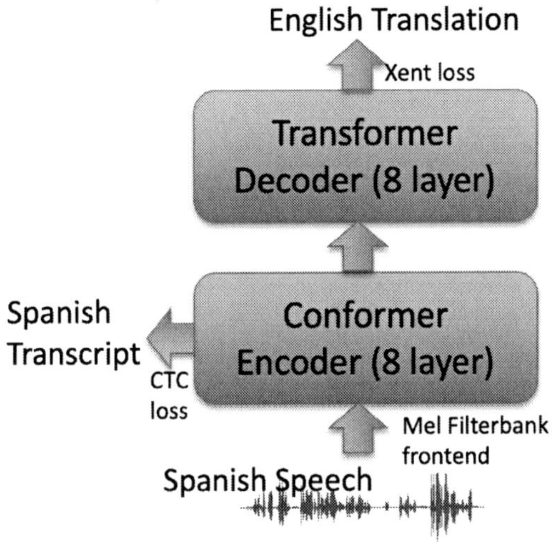

Figure 3: Model architecture. The frontend extracts log-mel filterbank features from the speech. The encoder consists of 8 conformer blocks and the decoder is a transformer decoder featuring 8 transformer blocks.

5 Experiments and Results

This section outlines the various experiments and results of this study. We use the ESPnet (Watanabe et al., 2018) toolkit for all experiments. We evaluate all systems with BLEU (Papineni et al., 2002), as implemented by SacreBLEU[4] (Post, 2018).

5.1 Training on only real data

Firstly, we train multiple systems on only real speech. These systems are treated as baselines. We train with 5, 10, 20, 50, 100, and 170 hours of **Real** speech. As shown in Table 2, the performance continues to improve as we scale the size of the dataset.

5.2 Training with both real and synthetic data

Here, we investigate whether incorporating **Synth** data into our training recipe helps end-to-end training. We do this by training the same system end-to-end on a dataset comprising both real and synthetic speech.

5.2.1 Fixing amount of real speech and varying amount of synthetic speech

In many circumstances, due to the expensive nature of collecting conversational speech data, practitioners have a fixed budget of data to train models on. We mimic this situation by fixing the amount of real speech in the training recipe and then progressively increasing the amount of synthetic data in the training recipe. We simulate the low data resource case where we have less than 10 hours of real speech, the mid-data resource case, where we have about 50 hours of real speech, and the relatively high resource data case where we have over a hundred hours of real speech. As shown in Table 2, there is a consistent improvement in model performance with increased synthetic speech when the amount of real speech remains fixed. This suggests that given a fixed amount of real training speech, including synthetic speech improves performance. Robinson et al. (2022) corroborated this trend for ASR.

5.2.2 How much improvement do we get?

We observe that when there is a small amount of real speech, including a large amount of synthetic speech can lead to substantial improvements in model performance as compared to when there is a higher amount of real speech. This is particularly useful for low-data resource scenarios.

From Table 2, we observe the cases where there are 5 and 170 hours of **Real** and **Synth** data, respectively. Adding these 170 hours of **Synth** results in +9.1 and +9.0 BLEU over the baseline trained on only real speech for Fisher and CallHome test sets, respectively. Increasing the amount of synthetic speech in the training recipe to 340 hours results in +10.7 and +9.7 BLEU compared to the baseline. Further increasing the amount of synthetic speech to 520 hours results in +14.7 and +11.8 BLEU. For the high-resource case with 170 hours of real speech, adding 170 hours of synthetic speech results in +1.4 and +2.3 BLEU on Fisher and CallHome test sets, respectively. Doubling the amount of synthetic speech results in +1.1 and +2.0 BLEU, and increasing to 520 hours gives +1.5 and +2.0 BLEU. This suggests that when there is already a large amount of real speech in training, including more synthetic speech does not provide significant additional benefits. The real data likely captures most relevant vari-

[4]Signature:BLEU+case:mixed+nrefs:1+tok:13a+smooth:exp+version:2.3.1

Training data (hours)		BLEU	
Real	**Synth**	**Fisher ↑**	**Callhome ↑**
0	0	0	0
	170	0	0
	340	0	0
	520	0	0
5	0	0.6	0.7
	170	9.7	9.7
	340	11.3	10.4
	520	**15.3**	**12.5**
10	0	0.7	1.1
	170	12.2	12.5
	340	13.9	13.4
	520	**17.0**	**14.9**
20	0	5.8	5.6
	170	16.7	15.3
	340	17.6	16.0
	520	**19.3**	**16.4**
50	0	14.3	12.3
	170	21.9	17.6
	340	22.1	18.2
	520	**22.9**	**19.0**
100	0	21.7	17.0
	170	24.5	20.3
	340	25.1	20.0
	520	**24.9**	**20.2**
170	0	25.3	20.1
	170	26.7	**22.4**
	340	26.4	22.1
	520	**26.8**	22.1

Table 2: BLEU scores of systems trained on varying amounts of the Real and Synth. When Synth is 0 the system was trained on only Real. When real is 0, the system was trained on only Synth.

ations, and the synthetic data may not add much new information.

5.3 Training on only synthetic data

To explore an extreme scenario, we conducted experiments where no real speech was included in the training setup. Instead, models were trained only on **Synth**. This approach of relying solely on synthetic data for training poses domain adaptation challenges. The models must generalize from the synthetic training environment, which may not fully capture the nuances and variations present in real speech. Consequently, we observed performance discrepancies when these models, trained only on synthetic data, were applied to real speech.

5.3.1 Does training on only synthetic data work?

When evaluated on the **Real** test set, the model obtains a BLEU score of 0, signifying a complete lack of generalizability due to the absence of real-world data during training. However, we obtain up to 30 BLEU on our best system when we evaluate on **Synth-Fisher** and **Synth-CallHome**, which are versions of the real test set where the input speech is synthesized using the same TTS system. (See Table 6.) This shows that the systems trained on only synthetic data do not generalize outside the synthetic data domain (though it suggests speech translation models trained only on synthetic data could theoretically be paired with voice conversion to accomplish speech translation, by converting real voices to synthetic voices before inference). See §5.3.3 for more on this analysis on this trend.

5.3.2 Bridging the generalization gap

Our experiments show that this generalization gap is mitigated by incorporating a small amount of real data into the training recipe. This helps the model generalize beyond the synthetic domain. When trained on only the synthetic data, the system cannot model the noisy channel effects introduced, as

Spanish Trancript	English Translation	Synth-170 Translation	Synth-170-Real-5 Translation
Sí, eso es para eso, de seguro. No importa.	Yes, that's what's for, sure. It doesn't matter.	Uh uh	Yes, it's for Suhur, it's not matter
Y qué estudia, mama, qué están estudiando.	And what's she studying, mom, what career.	Uh uh	And that's all, mom, who's studying
mmm sí eso pasa aquí en Estados Unidos acá pa- casi demandan a la empresa	hmmm, if that happens here in the United States, they, they would sue the company	Uh uh	And if that happens here is a company in Canada

Table 3: Example translations to show how adding a small amount of real data to a synthetic training recipe helps the model generalize beyond the synthetic domain. Synth-170 is the system trained on 170 hours of synthetic data. Synth-170-Real-5 is the system trained on 170 hours of **Synth** data and 5 hours of **Real**

Spanish Trancript	English Translation	Synth-340 Translation	Synth-340-Real-5 Translation
Sí, eso es para eso, de seguro. No importa.	Yes, that's what's for, sure. It doesn't matter.	ah ah	yes, for that, of course, it doesn't matter
Y qué estudia, mama, qué están estudiando.	And what's she studying, mom, what career.	no no	and what was my mom? What are you studying?
mmm sí eso pasa aquí en Estados Unidos acá pa- casi demandan a la empresa	hmmm, if that happens here in the United States, they, they would sue the company	ah no	and that happens here in the United States, send me a company

Table 4: Example translations to show how adding a small amount of real data to a synthetic training recipe helps the model generalize beyond the synthetic domain. Synth-340 is the system trained on 340 hours of synthetic data. Synth-340-Real-5 is the system trained on 340 hours of **Synth** data and 5 hours of **Real**

Spanish Trancript	English Translation	Synth-520 Translation	Synth-520-Real-5 Translation
Sí, eso es para eso, de seguro. No importa.	Yes, that's what's for, sure. It doesn't matter.	And, and	yes, that's for sure, they don't matter
Y qué estudia, mama, qué están estudiando.	And what's she studying, mom, what career.	in, in, in, in	And that's it, mom, what's she studying?
mmm sí eso pasa aquí en Estados Unidos acá pa- casi demandan a la empresa	hmmm, if that happens here in the United States, they, they would sue the company	Right, right, In	hmmm, that happens here in the United States, they would sue the company

Table 5: Example translations to show how adding a small amount of real data to a synthetic training recipe helps the model generalize beyond the synthetic domain. Synth-520 is the system trained on 520 hours of synthetic data. Synth-530-Real-5 is the system trained on 520 hours of **Synth** data and 5 hours of **Real**

Dataset	Hours	Synth-Fisher ↑	Synth-CallHome ↑
Synth	5	0.0	0.0
	10	0.1	0.4
	20	0.2	0.3
	50	4.5	5.5
	100	2.3	1.6
	170	5.8	6.9
	340	11.4	8.5
	520	**30.7**	**26.0**

Table 6: BLEU scores for training on varying hours of only synthetic speech and testing on synthetic speech testsets

the data was collected from telephone conversations. Introducing a small amount of real data likely helps the system model the acoustic mismatch. The performance increases further if the amount of synthetic data is increased. For example, in Table 2, given **Synth** amounts 170, 340, and 520 hours, when we add 5 hours of **Real** data to each, the 520-hour recipe does best. We display example outputs for these systems compared with those trained on no **Real** data in Tables 3, 4, and 5.

5.3.3 Inference on Synthetic Data

As mentioned in §5.3.1, models trained on only synthetic speech do not generalize to real speech. We look deeper by evaluating the performance of the models on **Synth-CallHome** and **Synth-Fisher**, the synthetic versions of the real test sets. We use this as a proxy to examine the claim that training on only synthetic data may not generalize to real test sets. As shown in Table 6, models trained on only synthetic data perform well on synthetic test sets (inputs that match the acoustic conditions of their training data), though they cannot perform at all for real test sets.

6 Takeaways

We summarize our findings here: (1) When there is a small amount of real speech available, including a large amount of synthetic speech leads to higher performance gains in end-to-end training; (2) When there is a large amount of real data available, including synthetic data leads to minimal performance gains; (3) Training only on synthetic speech data does not generalize outside of the synthetic domain; (4) To generalize outside the synthetic data domain, some amount of real speech has to be present in the training recipe (5) When there is no real data present, no amount of synthetic data helps.

7 Conclusion

We investigated whether using synthetic data generated from backtranslation and text-to-speech synthesis for end-to-end conversational speech translation improves performance. Incorporating synthetic data into a conversation speech translation training recipe helps improve the overall system's performance especially when there is limited real speech available. When models are trained on only synthetic data, we find that models do not generalize beyond their training domain. This mismatch between the synthetic training data and real-world data leads to suboptimal performance when models trained on only synthetic data are applied to real speech. This highlights the importance of incorporating at least some real speech data during training to bridge the domain gap effectively. In the case where no real speech is available, no amount of synthetic data helps.

There are several open questions worth examining as future work:

- What happens if a self-supervised pre-trained speech encoder like wav2vec (Baevski et al., 2020) is incorporated into the model? Would it be more or less robust to synthetic data?
- What happens if TTS quality is much lower, which is likely in lower-resource languages? (For example, it would be instructive to repeat the experiments with other languages.)
- Would the conclusions change if we examine more advanced augmentation besides simple concatenation of **Real** and **Synth**?
- Could a model trained only on synthetic speech be paired with voice conversion to accomplish speech translation?

References

Agarwal, M., Agrawal, S., Anastasopoulos, A., Bentivogli, L., Bojar, O., Borg, C., Carpuat, M., Cattoni, R., Cettolo, M., Chen, M., Chen, W., Choukri, K., Chronopoulou, A., Currey, A., Declerck, T., Dong, Q., Duh, K., Estève, Y., Federico, M., Gahbiche, S., Haddow, B., Hsu, B., Mon Htut, P., Inaguma, H., Javorský, D., Judge, J., Kano, Y., Ko, T., Kumar, R., Li, P., Ma, X., Mathur, P., Matusov, E., McNamee, P., P. McCrae, J., Murray, K., Nadejde, M., Nakamura, S., Negri, M., Nguyen, H., Niehues, J., Niu, X., Kr. Ojha, A., E. Ortega, J., Pal, P., Pino, J., van der Plas, L., Polák, P., Rippeth, E., Salesky, E., Shi, J., Sperber, M., Stüker, S., Sudoh, K., Tang, Y., Thompson, B., Tran, K., Turchi, M., Waibel, A., Wang, M., Watanabe, S., and Zevallos, R. (2023). FINDINGS OF THE IWSLT 2023 EVALUATION CAMPAIGN. In Salesky, E., Federico, M., and Carpuat, M., editors, *Proceedings of the 20th International Conference on Spoken Language Translation (IWSLT 2023)*, pages 1–61, Toronto, Canada (in-person and online). Association for Computational Linguistics.

Amin, F., Yang, W., Liu, Y., Barra-Chicote, R., Meng, Y., Maas, R., and Droppo, J. (2021). Synthasr: Unlocking synthetic data for speech recognition. *arXiv preprint arXiv:2106.07803*.

Ansari, E., Axelrod, A., Bach, N., Bojar, O., Cattoni, R., Dalvi, F., Durrani, N., Federico, M., Federmann, C., Gu, J., Huang, F., Knight, K., Ma, X., Nagesh, A., Negri, M., Niehues, J., Pino, J., Salesky, E., Shi, X., Stüker, S., Turchi, M., Waibel, A., and Wang, C. (2020). FINDINGS OF THE IWSLT 2020 EVALUATION CAMPAIGN. In *Proceedings of the 17th International Conference on Spoken Language Translation*, pages 1–34.

Babu, A., Wang, C., Tjandra, A., Lakhotia, K., Xu, Q., Goyal, N., Singh, K., von Platen, P., Saraf, Y., Pino, J., Baevski, A., Conneau, A., and Auli, M. (2022). XLS-R: Self-supervised Cross-lingual Speech Representation Learning at Scale. In *Proc. Interspeech 2022*, pages 2278–2282.

Baevski, A., Zhou, H., Mohamed, A., and Auli, M. (2020). wav2vec 2.0: A framework for self-supervised learning of speech representations.

Edunov, S., Ott, M., Auli, M., and Grangier, D. (2018). Understanding back-translation at scale. In *Proceedings of the 2018 Conference on Empirical Methods in Natural Language Processing*, pages 489–500, Brussels, Belgium. Association for Computational Linguistics.

Fang, Q. and Feng, Y. (2023). Back translation for speech-to-text translation without transcripts. In Rogers, A., Boyd-Graber, J., and Okazaki, N., editors, *Proceedings of the 61st Annual Meeting of the Association for Computational Linguistics (Volume 1: Long Papers)*, pages 4567–4587, Toronto, Canada. Association for Computational Linguistics.

Gulati, A., Qin, J., Chiu, C.-C., Parmar, N., Zhang, Y., Yu, J., Han, W., Wang, S., Zhang, Z., Wu, Y., and Pang, R. (2020). Conformer: Convolution-augmented transformer for speech recognition. *arXiv preprint arXiv:2005.08100*.

Hu, T.-Y., Armandpour, M., Shrivastava, A., Chang, J.-H. R., Koppula, H., and Tuzel, O. (2021). Synt++: Utilizing imperfect synthetic data to improve speech recognition. *arXiv preprint arXiv:2110.11479*.

Jia, Y., Johnson, M., Macherey, W., Weiss, R. J., Cao, Y., Chiu, C.-C., Ari, N., Laurenzo, S., and Wu, Y. (2019). Leveraging weakly supervised data to improve end-to-end speech-to-text translation. In *ICASSP 2019 - 2019 IEEE International Conference on Acoustics, Speech and Signal Processing (ICASSP)*, pages 7180–7184.

Karakasidis, G., Robinson, N., Getman, Y., Ogayo, A., Al-Ghezi, R., Ayasi, A., Watanabe, S., Mortensen, D. R., and Kurimo, M. (2023). Multilingual tts accent impressions for accented asr. In *International Conference on Text, Speech, and Dialogue*, pages 317–327. Springer.

Kim, J., Kong, J., and Son, J. (2021). Conditional variational autoencoder with adversarial learning for end-to-end text-to-speech. *arXiv preprint arXiv 2106.06103*.

Kong, J., Kim, J., and Bae, J. (2020). Hifi-gan: Generative adversarial networks for efficient and high fidelity speech synthesis. In *Advances in Neural Information Processing Systems*, pages 17022–17033.

Lee, A., Chen, P.-J., Wang, C., Gu, J., Popuri, S., Ma, X., Polyak, A., Adi, Y., He, Q., Tang, Y., Pino, J., and Hsu, W.-N. (2022). Direct speech-to-speech translation with discrete units. In Muresan, S., Nakov, P., and

Villavicencio, A., editors, *Proceedings of the 60th Annual Meeting of the Association for Computational Linguistics (Volume 1: Long Papers)*, pages 3327–3339, Dublin, Ireland. Association for Computational Linguistics.

Li, N., Liu, S., Liu, Y., Zhao, S., and Liu, M. (2019). Neural speech synthesis with transformer network. *Proceedings of the AAAI Conference on Artificial Intelligence*, 33:6706–6713.

Li, Y. A., Han, C., Raghavan, V. S., Mischler, G., and Mesgarani, N. (2023). Styletts 2: Towards human-level text-to-speech through style diffusion and adversarial training with large speech language models.

Mittag, G., Naderi, B., Chehadi, A., and Möller, S. (2021). Nisqa: A deep cnn-self-attention model for multidimensional speech quality prediction with crowdsourced datasets. In *Interspeech 2021*. ISCA.

Papineni, K., Roukos, S., Ward, T., and Zhu, W.-J. (2002). Bleu: a method for automatic evaluation of machine translation. In *Proceedings of the 40th Annual Meeting of the Association for Computational Linguistics*, pages 311–318, Philadelphia, Pennsylvania, USA. Association for Computational Linguistics.

Park, D. S., Chan, W., Zhang, Y., Chiu, C.-C., Zoph, B., Cubuk, E. D., and Le, Q. V. (2019). Specaugment: A simple data augmentation method for automatic speech recognition. In *Interspeech 2019*. ISCA.

Park, K. and Mulc, T. (2019). Css10: A collection of single speaker speech datasets for 10 languages. *Interspeech*.

Post, M. (2018). A call for clarity in reporting BLEU scores. In *Proceedings of the Third Conference on Machine Translation: Research Papers*, pages 186–191, Belgium, Brussels. Association for Computational Linguistics.

Post, M., Kumar, G., Lopez, A., Karakos, D., Callison-Burch, C., and Khudanpur, S. (2013). Improved speech-to-text translation with the fisher and callhome Spanish-English speech translation corpus. In *Proceedings of the 10th International Workshop on Spoken Language Translation: Papers*.

Radford, A., Kim, J. W., Xu, T., Brockman, G., Mcleavey, C., and Sutskever, I. (2023). Robust speech recognition via large-scale weak supervision. In Krause, A., Brunskill, E., Cho, K., Engelhardt, B., Sabato, S., and Scarlett, J., editors, *Proceedings of the 40th International Conference on Machine Learning*, volume 202 of *Proceedings of Machine Learning Research*, pages 28492–28518. PMLR.

Ren, Y., Ruan, Y., Tan, X., Qin, T., Zhao, S., Zhao, Z., and Liu, T.-Y. (2019). Fastspeech: Fast, robust and controllable text to speech. In *Advances in Neural Information Processing Systems*.

Robinson, N., Ogayo, P., Gangu, S., Mortensen, D. R., and Watanabe, S. (2022). When is tts augmentation through a pivot language useful? In *Proceedings of the Annual Conference of the International Speech Communication Association, INTERSPEECH*, volume 2022, pages 3538–3542.

Rossenbach, N., Zeineldeen, M., Hilmes, B., Schlüter, R., and Ney, H. (2021). Comparing the benefit of synthetic training data for various automatic speech recognition architectures. In *2021 IEEE Automatic Speech Recognition and Understanding Workshop (ASRU)*, pages 788–795.

Rossenbach, N., Zeyer, A., Schlüter, R., and Ney, H. (2020). Generating synthetic audio data for attention-based speech recognition systems. In *ICASSP 2020 - 2020 IEEE International Conference on Acoustics, Speech and Signal Processing (ICASSP)*, pages 7069–7073.

Sennrich, R., Haddow, B., and Birch, A. (2016a). Improving neural machine translation models with monolingual data. In Erk, K. and Smith, N. A., editors, *Proceedings of the 54th Annual Meeting of the Association for Computational Linguistics (Volume 1: Long Papers)*, pages 86–96, Berlin, Germany. Association for Computational Linguistics.

Sennrich, R., Haddow, B., and Birch, A. (2016b). Neural machine translation of rare words with subword units. In Erk, K. and Smith, N. A., editors, *Proceedings of the 54th Annual Meeting of the Association for Computational Linguistics (Volume 1: Long Papers)*, pages 1715–1725, Berlin, Germany. Association for Computational Linguistics.

Shen, J., Pang, R., Weiss, R. J., Schuster, M., Jaitly, N., Yang, Z., Chen, Z., Zhang, Y., Wang, Y., Skerrv-Ryan, R., Saurous, R. A., Agiomvrgiannakis, Y., and Wu, Y. (2018). Natural tts synthesis by conditioning wavenet on mel spectrogram predictions. In *2018 IEEE International Conference on Acoustics, Speech and Signal Processing (ICASSP)*, pages 4779–4783.

Song, Z., Strassel, S., Lee, H., Walker, K., Wright, J., Garland, J., Fore, D., Gainor, B., Cabe, P., Thomas, T., Callahan, B., and Sawyer, A. (2014). Collecting natural SMS and chat conversations in multiple languages: The BOLT phase 2 corpus. In *Proceedings of the Ninth International Conference on Language Resources and Evaluation (LREC'14)*, pages 1699–1704, Reykjavik, Iceland. European Language Resources Association (ELRA).

Team, N., Costa-jussà, M. R., Cross, J., Çelebi, O., Elbayad, M., Heafield, K., Heffernan, K., Kalbassi, E., Lam, J., Licht, D., Maillard, J., Sun, A., Wang, S., Wenzek, G., Youngblood, A., Akula, B., Barrault, L., Gonzalez, G. M., Hansanti, P., Hoffman, J., Jarrett, S., Sadagopan, K. R., Rowe, D., Spruit, S., Tran, C., Andrews, P., Ayan, N. F., Bhosale, S., Edunov, S., Fan, A., Gao, C., Goswami, V., Guzmán, F., Koehn, P., Mourachko, A., Ropers, C., Saleem, S., Schwenk, H., and Wang, J. (2022). No language left behind: Scaling human-centered machine translation. *arXiv preprint arXiv:2207.04672*.

van den Oord, A., Dieleman, S., Zen, H., Simonyan, K., Vinyals, O., Graves, A., Kalchbrenner, N., Senior, A., and Kavukcuoglu, K. (2016). Wavenet: A generative model for raw audio. *arXiv preprint arXiv:1609.03499*.

Vaswani, A., Shazeer, N., Parmar, N., Uszkoreit, J., Jones, L., Gomez, A. N., Kaiser, L. u., and Polosukhin, I. (2017). Advances in neural information processing systems. volume 30.

Watanabe, S., Hori, T., Karita, S., Hayashi, T., Nishitoba, J., Unno, Y., Enrique Yalta Soplin, N., Heymann, J., Wiesner, M., Chen, N., Renduchintala, A., and Ochiai, T. (2018). ESPnet: End-to-end speech processing toolkit. In *Proceedings of Interspeech*, pages 2207–2211.

The Translator's Canvas: Using LLMs to Enhance Poetry Translation

Natalia Resende resenden@tcd.ie
Trinity Centre for Literary and Cultural Translation, School of Languages, Literatures and Cultural Studies, Trinity College Dublin, D02 CH22, Ireland
James Hadley hadleyj@tcd.ie
Trinity Centre for Literary and Cultural Translation, School of Languages, Literatures and Cultural Studies, Trinity College Dublin, D02 CH22, Ireland

Abstract

We explore the potential of LLMs to enhance the translation process of rhymed and non-rhymed poetry. We examine LLMs' performance (ChatGPT-3.5, ChatGPT-4, Google Gemini) in terms of lexical variety, lexical density, and sentence length compared to human translations (HT). We also examine the models' abilities to translate sonnets while preserving the rhyme scheme of the source text. Our findings suggest that LLMs can serve as valuable tools for literary translators, assisting with the creative process and suggesting solutions to problems that may not otherwise have been considered. However, if the paradigm is flipped, such that instead of the systems being as tools by human translators, humans are used to post-edit the outputs to a standard comparable to the published translations, the amount of work required to complete the post-editing stage may outweigh any benefits associated with using machine translation in the first place.

1 Introduction

The translation of poetry has long been a contentious issue in the field of literary translation (Jones, 1986). The debate stems from the challenges inherent to translating poetry, which, depending on the specific poetic form in evidence, may require a delicate balancing act of content, style, tone, various types of phonetic devices, such as rhyme. Differences in language and poetic tradition may necessitate compromises and creative solutions with many competing constraints making the translation of poetry a highly complex activity. Literary translation has historically been regarded as the "last bastion of human translation" (Toral and Way, 2014), and poetry translation could be thought of as the most extreme example of this phenomenon. However, recent advances in the widespread availability of Large Language Models (LLMs) have shifted the conversation to ask in what ways human translators might make use of electronic tools in the negotiating of literary translation's stylistic and technical complexities.

Much of this work to date has focused entirely on prose, and while advancements have been substantial in this respect, much less attention has fallen onto poetry in general, and formal poetry in particular. Thus, formal poetry, simultaneously combining as it does many of the stylistic features that are known to complicate machine translation, remains an extreme challenge. Nonetheless, the emergence of web-based LLMs offers new opportunities. These models, such as ChatGPT and Google Gemini, enable the customisation of translated outputs through prompt engineering (Amatriain, 2024), whereby users can specify in detail aspects of a text to focus on, change or omit. This capacity sets LLMs apart from the web-based Neural Machine Translation (NMT) systems which have been the mainstay of the machine translation systems (MT) widely available to literary translators for the past decade or so. Generally speaking, such NMTs are limited to one or a small number of similar outputs for any given input, with little or no functionality to tailor the translation process around, for example, register, addressee, style, or tone. When it comes to complex operations such as rhyming or counting syllables, specialised systems would be required.

The focus in this discussion falls predominantly on web-based systems which are either free to use or financially accessible, because the funding associated with any given literary translation project is so limited (des Associations de Traducteurs Littéraires , CEATL). Thus, it is unrealistic to imagine literary translators being in a position to invest in expensive bespoke tools which may require training for the facilitation of their work, and therefore, the most realistic use cases when it comes to literary translation centre on systems which are easily and cheaply accessible.

For these reasons, the widespread emergence of LLMs such as ChatGPT and Google Gemini, with their free entry points, represents a significant opportunity for analysing whether such systems might be useful tools for literary translators. Here there is an important distinction to be made between Literary Machine Translation (LMT) and Computer-Assisted Literary Translation (CALT). On the one hand, LMT conceptualises the machine at the centre of the process of producing translated outputs, generally with one or more human beings supporting its work through pre-editing or post-editing. In this view, quality assessment reaches for the ultimate goal of producing outputs of the same standard as human translators (Koponen, 2016). On the other hand, CALT conceptualises the human translator as the primary agent, who makes use of the machine as a tool. In this view, the human translators may use the machine to translate only individual or isolated parts of the text, may use iteration to produce multiple versions of the same passage, and may wholly disregard the outputs of the machine if a better solution is found elsewhere.

The focus of each perspective is reversed. In LMT, the goal is to maximise the quality of the output to minimise editing work by the human. In CALT, the goal is to support human translators in their own idiosyncratic workflows, identifying and trailing possible solutions to translation challenges, and further stimulating human translators' creativity. Thus, whereas in an LMT workflow, producing multiple outputs of the same text, may be perceived as wasteful, because this would imply that each output would also need to be post-edited, in the context of CALT, producing multiple outputs of the same text or text fragment could perceivable be useful for a human translator who may use the machine's outputs more as inspiration than as something approaching a product to be refined.

While there is evidence supporting LLMs in the translation of prose works, especially novels (Karpinska and Iyyer, 2023), their impact on poetry translation remains under-explored. Thus, it is unclear how machine translations produced with the help of LLMs compare stylistically to human translations. Asking about these comparisons is fundamental to assessing whether and how LLMs might be made useful by practising translators of literature, and especially poetry.

To address this question, our initial step involves extracting and examining linguistic features at both the syntactic and lexical level from poems, as well as from translations of them produced by humans and by LLMs in Portuguese and Spanish.

2 Related work

The methodological approach used here is one which analyses and compares the stylistic features of translated text using Natural Language Processing (NLP) techniques. In each case, the candidate translations by each of the LLMs is compared side by side with previously published human translations of the same text. This approach is grounded in a body of literature that has developed since the 1980s to explore the distinctive stylistic characteristics of translated texts primarily on statistical terms. This literature is theoretically rooted in Toury's translation norms (Toury, 1980) which posits that translation is a culturally-bound phenomenon which functions different in different human contexts, and Baker's translation universals (Baker, 1996), which identify aspects of texts which anecdotal experience can allow us to identify translated from non-translated work. The approach responds to these two somewhat subjective theoretical constructs with corpus linguistics and NLP methods, which allow for the results to be statistics-based, and repeatable (Ilise et al., 2010; Ilisei and Inkpen, 2011; Pastor et al., 2008). The research conducted with these methods, has consistently shown that translated text does indeed tend to exhibit simpler syntax and less varied vocabulary than non-translated text (Laviosa, 2002;

Baroni and Bernardini, 2006; Pastor et al., 2008; Volansky et al., 2013a). This phenomenon, often referred to as *translationese* in the literature, is frequently associated with lower quality text, characterized by foreign-sounding and awkward wording and structure (Volansky et al., 2013b; Kunilovskaya and Lapshinova-Koltunski, 2019).

With the advent of MT systems, attention has shifted towards the stylistic features of machine-translated and post-edited texts (Daems et al., 2017; Toral, 2019; Castilho et al., 2019; Castilho and Resende, 2022). This research has gone on to show significant differences in style and content richness between human-translated text and machine-translated text, especially that produced by NMT systems (Castilho et al., 2019; Castilho and Resende, 2022).

Recent research has begun evaluating the translation capabilities of large language models (LLMs) in both literary and technical texts, often in comparison with NMT systems (Peng et al., 2023; Hendy et al., 2023; Karpinska and Iyyer, 2023). Preliminary studies (Cruys, 2023; Roos, 2023) have explored LLMs' ability to preserve the rhyme schemes in poetry translation, focusing on qualitative analysis of a single poem. However, there is a lack of research on how the range of stylistic features which come together to embody poetic texts are managed by LLMs, and how or whether LLMs might be made useful to practising human translators of poetry. This study represents an initial attempt to address this gap in the literature. Given the exploratory nature of the present study, the focus is on a limited corpus to provide a preliminary assessment of the the place these tools could have in a poetry translation workflow, setting the stage for more extensive research in the future.

2.1 Methodology

This analysis conducts a statistics-based stylistic comparison of features extracted from source poems, existing translations of the same poems produced by humans, and newly produced translations by three LLMs. The extracted features are both lexical and syntactic in nature, and designed to assess aspects of the formal qualities of the poems which a reader may not necessarily be consciously aware of when reading the texts, but which have an overall effect on the texts' literary qualities (Pynte et al., 2008). The specific questions addressed are:

1. How do the syntactic and lexical stylistic patterns of LLM-translated poetry compare to those of human-translated poetry?
2. How do these stylistic patterns vary between LLMs? Are there identifiable trends and/or deviations unique to each language model?
3. How do these qualities compare between formally constrained poems and free verse poems?

2.1.1 Corpus

In order to address these questions, this study draws on a small corpus of four published poems. Two of the poems are written in Spanish and two are written in Portuguese. Two of the poems are sonnets and two are free verse poems. A digital version of each poem was either collected from an online resource or was created by digitising a printed version. The choice to include two source languages allows for the comparison of similar features from different sources. The choice to include sonnets and free verse poems allows for the analysis of formal features both under the heavy formal constraint of a complex rhyme scheme, as found in the sonnet form, and under less constrained circumstances in the case of free verse. Before conducting the experiments, at least one published human translation into English of each poem was identified which was also collected in the same way as the source texts. To adhere to copyright laws and ethical standards, only texts not protected by copyright at the time of writing were included in the corpus. Table 1 shows the poems included in the corpus, along with each poem's short name, used in these experiments:

2.1.2 Examining the stylistic features

The poems in the corpus were translated using three large language models (LLMs) accessible online: ChatGPT-3.5, ChatGPT-4, and Google Gemini. A zero-shot approach was employed, instructing the models to translate the source poems into English without any prior training or fine-tuning. This method aimed to evaluate how the models perform in a realistic setting, assuming that most practising literary translators would not rely on advanced prompt engineering techniques. The following prompt was used with all the models under analysis, and with each of the poems in question:

Poem	Author	Year of Composition	Type	Language	Short Name
José	Carlos Drummond Andrade	1942	Free verse	Portuguese	José
Soneto da Fidelidade	Vinícius de Morais	1939	Sonnet	Portuguese	Fidelidade
Amor constante más allá de la muerte	Francisco de Quevedo	1648	Sonnet	Spanish	Amor
Corazón Coraza	Mario Benedetti	1939	Free verse	Spanish	Corazón

Table 1: Selected poems included in the corpus

Prompt 1:

Translate this poem into English

Next, the stylistic features of the translated output were compared with the versions in the human translations. This approach did not assume the human translations to be the correct, the only possible, or the only viable renditions of the poems in question into the target language. Nor was it assumed that all the features of the source texts were uniformly included in their human-translated versions. Rather, noting the features which were and were not included in the human-translated versions gives a basis of comparison between the versions translated by the various systems with what can be considered the current state of the art, in the form of the human translations. For this analysis the following features were extracted from the translated texts:

- Lexical richness
- Lexical density
- Sentence length in words
- Vocabulary overlap
- Rhyming patterns

The stylistic features were extracted from the texts using custom Python scripts. To assess lexical variety, which reflects the diversity of vocabulary in a text, the type/token ratio was calculated by dividing the total number of unique words (types) by the total number of words in each text (tokens).

$$\text{TTR} = \frac{N_t}{N_w} \tag{1}$$

where:

* N_t represents the number of unique words (types) in the text.

* N_w represents the total number of words (tokens) in the text.

Lexical density is a measure of the informational content within a text. It reflects the proportion of content words, relative to the total number of words. Content words are typically defined as nouns, verbs, adjectives, and adverbs, which carry the core message of a sentence.

Mathematically, the lexical density can be expressed as:

$$\text{LD} = \frac{N_c}{N_w} \tag{2}$$

where:

* N_c represents the number of content words in the text.

* N_w represents the total number of words (tokens) in the text.

Sentence length was calculated by counting the number of words between each set of sentence markers.

For the vocabulary overlap analysis, we identified the words present in the human-translated versions that were absent in the LLM-produced translations. This metric was chosen because, on our view, it provides a clearer, more intuitive understanding of the differences between texts in percentage terms. To complement this approach, we also calculated BLEU scores using the NLTK package (Bird et al., 2009), which provided valuable additional insights into the comparative performance of the translations. Finally, to assess the LLMs' ability to reproduce the rhyme schemes of the two sonnets in the corpus, the outputs in each case were categorised using the standard letter-based notation associated with line-end rhyming patterns. In this notation system, the final phonemes of each line of poetry are assigned an alphabetic value which marks the other lines in the same poem with a rhyming phoneme. An example can be seen in the opening stanza of Wordsworth's 1802 Lyrical poem, *Daffodils*:

> I wandered lonely as a cloud
> That floats on high o'er vales and hills,
> When all at once I saw a crowd,
> A host, of golden daffodils;
> Beside the lake, beneath the trees,
> Fluttering and dancing in the breeze.

The lines can be annotated as: ABABCC, because the first and third lines rhyme phonetically, as do the second and fourth lines, and the fifth and sixth lines. However, it is important to note that as in this example, especially in languages with idiosyncratic orthographic conventions like English, rhyming phonetic values do not always correspond to similar spellings.

The first attempt at translating the sonnets with the straightforward prompt resulted in the rhyme scheme of each poem being ignored by the system. Therefore, the prompt was subsequently refined to target this aspect of the texts' stylistics more specifically. The subsequent prompt used for these tasks was:

> **Prompt 2:**
>
> *Can you improve the translation so that it maintains the same rhyme scheme as the source text?*

A few-shot prompting approach, complete with demonstration examples was also employed to facilitate comparison of the outputs achieved from each prompt technique. This strategy involved explaining the rhyme scheme of each the poems by providing examples of word that rhyme within the poem and also specifying the organisation of rhyming words in the poem flow. The advanced prompts designed for the translation of the sonnets can be found in Appendix A.

2.2 Results

The vocabulary overlap experiment asked: *How many words in the HT are not present in the version translated by the LLMs?* To address this question, the number of words present in the HT and not present in the outputs produced by the LLMs was calculated, shown in Table 2.

These results demonstrate that the proportion of vocabulary in the human translation that diverges from the model is higher in the sonnets than in the free verse poems. This finding is predictable, because of the additional formal constraints imposed by the sonnet form, compared to the free verse form. Key formal constraints in this respect include the need to rhyme and to fit lines into specific lengths. These constraints raise the complexity of the translation task, implying a higher synonym and paraphrase usage than in translation problems where these formal constraints are not present. Thus, it is possible to speculate that the greater variation in word choice observable in the models outputs in the case of the sonnets is linked to this additional layer of complexity.

Table 3 presents the BLEU scores, which are consistent with the findings from the vocabulary overlap experiment. The scores indicate that free verse poems consistently achieve higher BLEU scores than sonnets, suggesting closer lexical alignment observed between machine-translated free verse poems and their human-translated counterparts in contrast with greater vocabulary variation in machine-translated sonnets compared to their human translations. Notably, the GPT-4 model produces translations of free verse poems that are closest to the human versions. Conversely, for sonnets, the GPT-3.5 and Gemini models achieve higher BLEU scores, indicating the least variability in lexical choice relative to their human translations, a result also supported by the vocabulary overlap findings.

In terms of lexical variety, despite differences in word choices, the translations produced by the models is consistently narrower than the human translations. This pattern holds true regardless of the source language, the poetic form, the models provider (OpenAi or Google), or the version number of the LLM, as can be seen in Table 4.

The same pattern is also observable in terms of lexical density. Again, in this respect the human trans-

	chatGPT-3.5 vs HT	**chatGPT-4 vs HT**	**Gemini vs HT**
José (Free verse)	38 (17%)	**31 (14%)**	38 (17%)
Fidelidade (Sonnet)	31 (26%)	32 (27%)	**27 (23%)**
Amor (Sonnet)	48 (41%)	48 (41%)	49 (42%)
Corazón (Free verse)	14 (8%)	11 (6%)	11 (6%)

Table 2: Vocabulary Overlap

Poems	GPT-3.5	GPT-4	Gemini
José (free verse)	0.2637	**0.3461**	0.33
Fidelidade (sonnet)	0.21	0.2768	**0.2886**
Amor (sonnet)	**0.0198**	0.0096	0.0197
Corazón (free verse)	0.3597	**0.4092**	0.3064

Table 3: Bleu scores

Poem	HT	chatGPT-3.5	chatGPT-4	Google Gemini
José (Free verse)	0.5	0.45	0.47	0.45
Fidelidade (Sonnet)	0.68	0.66	0.62	0.6
Amor (Sonnet)	0.75	0.7	0.64	0.68
Corazón (Free verse)	0.4	0.42	0.4	0.4

Table 4: Lexical Variety

Poem	HT	chatGPT-3.5	chatGPT-4	Google Gemini
José (Free verse)	0.51	0.43	0.47	0.47
Fidelidade (Sonnet)	0.43	0.4	0.4	0.4
Amor (Sonnet)	0.4	0.53	0.52	0.54
Corazón (Free verse)	0.54	0.38	0.4	0.45

Table 5: Lexical Density

lations consistently score more highly than the versions produced by the LLMs.

In terms of sentence length, the HT tended to produce longer sentences than the LLMs translations as shown in table 6, the noteworthy exception being the free verse poem, *José*, where the HT translations are shorter than those produced by the LLMs. One explanation for the LLMs' propensity to produce longer texts is found in their tendency to include optional pronouns as standard, whereas the human translator generally did not. This tendency constitutes a form of explicitation (Baker, 1993, 1996), or reducing ambiguities in translations, which inevitably contributes to an increase in sentence lengths.

2.2.1 Rhyme scheme reproduction

Table 7 shows the results obtained for the two sonnets and the few-shot approach used to design the prompts targeting the poems' rhyme schemes. In all but one case (Prompt 2. *Fidelidade*), the ChatGPT models appear to be more successful than Gemini in reproducing the rhyme scheme consistently. However, it is worth noting that the discrepancy, not only between the models' outputs within individual prompts but also across prompts, varies substantially and not always in intuitive ways. For instance, even though the words used in the translations differ, from the perspective of conveying the rhyme scheme, prompt 2, which simply asked the model to replicate the rhyme scheme of the source text; and prompt 4, which went into detail on the nature of that rhyme scheme, appear to have been precisely as successful for *Amor*, having successfully reproduced the rhyme in every line. However, prompt 2 is less successful in the case of *Fidelidade* for GPT-4 (64% of the source rhyme scheme), and much less successful for GPT-3.5 (29% of the source rhyme scheme). It is worth noting that the rhyme schemes of the two poems differ slightly. This implies that the models' ability to reproduce rhyme may be heavily variable, and possibly dependent on the contents of the poem, as well as the extent to which the rhyme schemes in question are represented in the training data. It is also worth considering the source language of the poems under analysis, and the impact this language may have on the results. In this case, *Amor* is written in Spanish, while *Fidelidade* is written in Portuguese. It is worth noting that both the GPT models were highly successful at reproducing the rhyme in the case of the Spanish text, even with a straightforward, zero-shot prompt. On the other hand, the models' success in reproducing rhyme in the Portuguese text was more varied. For the Portuguese sonnet, the GPT models did seem to benefit from the more complex prompts, improving their success rate by 14% (from 29% to 43%) and 15% (from 64% to 79%), respectively. Gemini appears to be much less successful across the board, and its success scores are so low that it is difficult to draw any meaningful conclusions based on this small dataset.

2.3 Discussion and conclusions

It is reasonable to ask whether the rapid emergence of LLMs which are either freely available or available for little cost on the internet for the first time might herald a shift in work practices when it comes to literary translators working with highly form-rich texts, such as poems. The systems clearly have far greater flexibility in terms of output style than the NMT systems which literary translation practitioners, especially those with limited technical expertise, are more likely to encounter. As what might be considered unusual use cases from the perspective of the majority of the work such widely available NMT systems do, addressing textual features such as rhyme or syllable count is seldom part of the systems' functionality. Thus, NMT systems usefulness as tools for human translators working with poetry is limited. In the case of LLMs, however, because prompts can be designed, tailored and used in an iterative fashion, their capacity to be useful in the translation of poetry is comparatively higher.

The experiments conducted here show that when using LLMs to translate both free verse poems and sonnets, the resulting texts differ significantly in terms of lexical variety, lexical density, and average sentence length from their human-translated counterparts. This matches findings from previous studies comparing translated and non-translated texts, as well as human-translated and machine-translated texts. Results show that human-translated texts tend to contain more varied vocabulary than LLM-translated texts and that human translations also tend to contain a higher information load as reflected by higher number of content words, compared to poems translated by LLMs. In addition, the mean sentence length of the human-translated poems is higher than

Poem	HT	chatGPT-3.5	chatGPT-4	Google Gemini
José (Free verse)	3.7	4	3.8	3.6
Fidelidade (Sonnet)	8.6	8.4	8.4	8.6
Amor (Sonnet)	8.4	7.0	8.4	7.7
Corazón (Free verse)	6.5	5.8	6	6

Table 6: Mean Sentence Length

Prompt 2. *Amor*:			
	Rhyme scheme	**Overlap**	**Total count**
Source	ABBA—ABBA—CDC—DCD		
Gemini	ABAB—CDCD—EEE—BFB	1100—0000—000—000	2 (14%)
ChatGPT-3.5	ABBA—ABBA—CD—DCD	1111—1111—111—111	14 (100%)
ChatGPT-4	ABBA—ABBA—CDC —DCD	1111—1111—111—111	14 (100%)
Prompt 2. *Fidelidade*:			
Source	ABBA—ABBA—CDE—DEC		
Gemini	ABAB—ABCA—DED—FEE	1100—1100—000—010	5 (36%)
ChatGPT-3.5	ABAB—CCCC—DDD—EEE	1100—0000—100—010	4 (29%)
ChatGPT-4	ABBA—ABBA—CCD—EFE	1111—1111—100—000	9 (64%)
Prompt 3. *Fidelidade*:			
Source	ABBA—ABBA—CDE—DEC		
Gemini	ABAC—DEFG—HIH—JKL	1100—0000—000—000	2 (14%)
ChatGPT-3.5	ABBA—CDDC—EFE—GEH	1111—0000—001—010	6 (43%)
ChatGPT-4	ABBA—ABBA—CDE—FGH	1111—1111—111—/000	11 (79%)
Prompt 4. *Amor*:			
Source	ABBA—ABBA—CDC—DCD		
Gemini	ABCA—DEFE—GHI—EJA	1100—0000—000—000	2 (14%)
ChatGT-3.5	ABBA—ABBA—CDC—DCD	1111—1111—111—111	14 (100%)
ChatGPT-4	ABBA—ABBA—CDC—DCD	1111—1111—111—111	14 (100%)

Table 7: Generated Rhyme Schemes

the mean sentence length of the poems translated by LLMs, suggesting syntactical differences between human and LLM renditions. (Baker, 1996; Baroni and Bernardini, 2006; Ilise et al., 2010; Ilisei and Inkpen, 2011; Volansky et al., 2013b; Toral, 2019)

When we analyse these results in the context of translationese literature, which posits that higher lexical diversity and density correlate with higher translation quality (Toury, 1980; Gellerstam, 1986; Baker, 1996; Volansky et al., 2013b), they suggest that human translators are more efficient at capturing stylistic nuances and content-based details in translations, whereas the outputs of LLMs tend to exhibit features of simplification as reflected by less varied vocabulary and lower lexical density. This might be because LLMs tend to translate with fewer departures from source text structures. Despite these differences, it can be inferred that the use of LLMs by poetry translators does not necessarily imply a substantial loss of output quality when it comes to lexical variety, lexical density and average sentence length. On the other hand, a reduction in quality could be expected if LLMs are used as part of a post-editing workflow.

In addition, when it comes to rhyme, the experiments here have demonstrated that LLMs can go some way to reflecting complex patterns of word choice based on word-final phonemes in their outputs, in special, GPT models showed a better performance in this specific task as compared to Gemini model. However, it should be noted that the success rate of such rhymed outputs is variable and not entirely predictable. It is likely closely tied to the amount of appropriate training data for the source and target languages that is available to the model (Hoffmann et al., 2024). In this case, "appropriate" does not simply mean material which includes rhyme in general. Instead, as a general principle, the more similar the training data is to the form of the desired output, the more likely the system is to be successful (Sahu et al., 2022). Thus, if the target text is a sonnet, with a complex ABBA-ABBA-CDE-DEC rhyme scheme and the training data includes a wealth of examples of sonnets of the same format, it can be hypothesised that the output, in terms of rhyming, would likely be better than if the training data included a larger amount of poetry, but comparatively less with this specific rhyme scheme. Our experiments also show that prompt engineering can improve the models' ability to reproduce rhyme schemes, thus revealing the potential benefits for translators in receiving training in prompt engineering. This skill could be valuable not only for this specific translation task but also for addressing other translation challenges.

It is important to note that LLMs offer a new approach to choosing words, which differs from unassisted human translation, especially for poetic text types with strict forms, such as sonnets. The vocabulary overlap experiment here shows that LLMs often make different word choices from their human counterparts, which could be used by human translators for inspiration. LLMs' functionality also offers opportunities for facilitating the production of rhymed translation candidates, again, not with the goal of replacing the human translators, but for increasing the speed at which possible rhymed translations candidates can be suggested to the otherwise unaided human translator.

Indeed, follow-on research could investigate the creative potential associated with LLMs in terms of outputting a range of translation candidates for any given input and how or whether this affects the human translator's work. Thus, it may be that there is potential in LLMs for human translators working as part of a CALT (Computer-Assisted Literary Translation) workflow, in encouraging and developing creative outputs. In particular, the systems have the capacity to assist and speed the resolution of complex challenges, such as searching for rhyming pairs of specific lengths that encapsulate specific meanings. By contrast, the usefulness of the systems as the primary actors in poetry translation projects, coupled with human post-editing, is likely heavily limited, as seen in the results of the experiments here on lexical variety, lexical density, average sentence length, and especially, rhyme. Based on the findings gained from this small number of experiments, it appears likely that the post-editing work required to bring the systems' outputs to the standard observable in the published human translations would be so substantial and pervasive as to negate the benefits associated with using the models in the first place.

References

Amatriain, X. (2024). Prompt design and engineering: Introduction and advanced methods.

Baker, M. (1993). Corpus linguistics and translation studies: Implications and applications. In Francis, G. and Tognini-Bonelli, E., editors, *Text and Technology: In Honour of John Sinclair*, pages 233–252. John Benjamins Publishing Company, Netherlands.

Baker, M. (1996). chapter corpus-based translation studies: The challenges that lie ahead. In *Terminology, LSP and Translation: Studies in Language Engineering, in Honour of Juan C. Sager*, page 175–186, Amsterdam: John Benjamins Publishing Company.

Baroni, M. and Bernardini, S. (2006). A new approach to the study of translationese: machine-learning the difference between original and translated text. *Literary and Linguistic Computing*, 21(3):259–274.

Bird, S., Klein, E., and Loper, E. (2009). *Natural Language Processing with Python*. O'Reilly Media Inc.

Castilho, S. and Resende, N. (2022). Post-editese in literary translations. *Information*, 13(2):66.

Castilho, S., Resende, N., and Mitkov, R. (2019). What influences the features of post-editese? a preliminary study. In *Proceedings of the Second Workshop on Human-Informed Translation and Interpreting Technology (HiT-IT 2019)*, Varna, Bulgaria.

Cruys, T. (2023). Up and about, or betwixt and between? In *Computer-Assisted Literary Translation*, pages 158–172. Routledge, New York.

Daems, J., De Clercq, O., and Macken, L. (2017). Translationese and post-editese: How comparable is comparable quality? *Linguistica Antverpiensia New Series - Themes in Translation Studies*, 16:89–103.

des Associations de Traducteurs Littéraires (CEATL), C. E. (2022). Survey on working conditions 2020. Accessed: 2024-06-10.

Gellerstam, M. (1986). Translationese in swedish novels translated from english. In *In Wollin, L. and Lindquist, H. Translation Studies in Scandinavia*, volume 4, pages 88–95, CWK Gleerup, Lund.

Hendy, A., Abdelrehim, M., Sharaf, A., Raunak, V., Gabr, M., Matsushita, H., Kim, Y. J., Afify, M., and Awadalla, H. H. (2023). How good are gpt models at machine translation? a comprehensive evaluation.

Hoffmann, J., Borgeaud, S., Mensch, A., Buchatskaya, E., Cai, T., Rutherford, E., de Las Casas, D., Hendricks, L. A., Welbl, J., Clark, A., Hennigan, T., Noland, E., Millican, K., van den Driessche, G., Damoc, B., Guy, A., Osindero, S., Simonyan, K., Elsen, E., Rae, J. W., Vinyals, O., and Sifre, L. (2024). Training compute-optimal large language models. *arXiv preprint arXiv:2203.15556.*

Ilise, I., Inkpen, D., Pastor, G. C., and Mitkov, R. (2010). Identification of translationese: a machine learning approach. In *In Gelbukh, A. F. (ed.), Proceedings of CICLing-2010: 11th International Conference on Computational Linguistics and Intelligent Text Processing, volume 6008 of Lecture Notes in Computer Science.*, pages 503–511.

Ilisei, I. and Inkpen, D. (2011). Translationese traits in romanian newspapers: a machine learning approach. *International Journal of Computational Linguistics and Applications*, 2(1–2).

Jones, J. (1986). *My First Book this Year*. John Doe.

Karpinska, M. and Iyyer, M. (2023). Large language models effectively leverage document-level context for literary translation, but critical errors persist. In Koehn, P., Haddow, B., Kocmi, T., and Monz, C., editors, *Proceedings of the Eighth Conference on Machine Translation*, pages 419–451, Singapore. Association for Computational Linguistics.

Koponen, M. (2016). Is machine translation post-editing worth the effort?: A survey of research into post-editing and effort.

Kunilovskaya, M. and Lapshinova-Koltunski, E. (2019). Translationese features as indicators of quality in English-Russian human translation. In *Proceedings of the Human-Informed Translation and Interpreting Technology Workshop (HiT-IT 2019)*, pages 47–56, Varna, Bulgaria. Incoma Ltd., Shoumen, Bulgaria.

Laviosa, S. (2002). Corpus-based translation studies: Theory, findings, applications. In *Approaches to translation studies*, Amsterdam & New York: Rodopi.

Pastor, G. C., Mitkov, R., and Pekar, V. (2008). V.: Translation universals: Do they exist? a corpus-based nlp study of convergence and simplification. In *In: Proceedings of the AMTA*.

Peng, K., Ding, L., Zhong, Q., Shen, L., Liu, X., Zhang, M., Ouyang, Y., and Tao, D. (2023). Towards making the most of chatgpt for machine translation.

Pynte, J., New, B., and Kennedy, A. (2008). A multiple regression analysis of syntactic and semantic influences in reading normal text. *Journal of Eye Movement Research*, 2(1).

Roos, A. (2023). The experiment. In *Computer-Assisted Literary Translation*, pages 237–257. Routledge, New York.

Sahu, G., Rodriguez, P., Laradji, I. H., Atighehchian, P., Vazquez, D., and Bahdanau, D. (2022). Data augmentation for intent classification with off-the-shelf large language models.

Toral, A. (2019). Post-editese: an exacerbated translationese. In *Proceedings of Machine TRanslation Summit*, Dublin, Ireland.

Toral, A. and Way, A. (2014). Is machine translation ready for literature. In *Proceedings of Translating and the Computer 36*, London, UK. AsLing.

Toury, G. (1980). *In Search of a Theory of Translation.* The Porter Institute for Poetics and Semiotics. Tel Aviv University, Tel Aviv, Israel.

Volansky, V., Ordan, N., and Wintner, S. (2013a). On the features of translationese. *Digital Scholarship in the Humanities*, 30(1):98–118.

Volansky, V., Ordan, N., and Wintner, S. (2013b). On the features of translationese. *Digital Scholarship in the Humanities*, 30(1):98–118.

A Advanced Prompts

Prompt 3:
The rhyme scheme of the poem Soneto da Fidelidade is ABBA ABBA CDE DEC. Translate this poem into English reproducing the rhyme scheme of the source poem.
In this rhyme scheme:
example 1) A represents words ending in -ento: atento/pensamento
example 2) B represents words ending in -anto: encanto/tanto
example 3) C presents words ending -ure: procure/dure
example 4) D represents words ending in -ive: tive/vive
example 5) E represents words that ends in -ama: chama/ama

Soneto da Fidelidade

De tudo, ao meu amor serei atento (A)
Antes, e com tal zelo, e sempre, e tanto (B)
Que mesmo em face do maior encanto (B)
Dele se encante mais meu pensamento. (A)
Quero vivê-lo em cada vão momento (A)
E em louvor hei de espalhar meu canto (B)
E rir meu riso e derramar meu pranto (B)
Ao seu pesar ou seu contentamento. (A)
E assim, quando mais tarde me procure (C)
Quem sabe a morte, angústia de quem vive (D)
Quem sabe a solidão, fim de quem ama (E)
Eu possa me dizer do amor que tive (D)
Que não seja imortal, posto que é chama (E)
Mas que seja infinito enquanto dure. (C)

Prompt 4:
The rhyme scheme of the poem
Amor constante más allá de la muerte is
ABBA ABBA CDC DCD. Translate this poem into English reproducing the rhyme scheme
of the source poem.
In this rhyme scheme:
example 1) A represents words ending in -era: postrera/lisonjera
example 2) B represents words ending in -ia: dia/mia
example 3) C presents words ending -ido: sido/ardido
example 4) D represents words ending in -ado:

dado/enamorado

Amor constante más allá de la muerte

Cerrar podrá mis ojos la postrera (A)
Sombra que me llevare el blanco día, (B)
Y podrá desatar esta alma mía, (B)
Hora a su afán ansioso lisonjera; (A)
Mas no de esotra parte en la ribera (A)
Dejará la memoria, en donde ardía: (B
Nadar sabra mi llama el agua fría, (B
Y perder el respeto a ley severa. (A)
Alma, a quien todo un dios prisión ha sido, (C)
Venas, que humor a tanto fuego han dado,(D)
Médulas, que han gloriosamente ardido, (C)
Su cuerpo dejará, no su cuidado; (D)
Serán ceniza, mas tendrá sentido; (C)
Polvo serán, mas polvo enamorado. (D)

Evaluation Briefs: Drawing on Translation Studies for Human Evaluation of MT

Ting Liu 劉婷 [a, b] tliu109@uOttawa.ca
Chi-kiu Lo 羅致翹 [b] ChiKiu.Lo@nrc-cnrc.gc.ca
Elizabeth Marshman [a] Elizabeth.Marshman@uOttawa.ca
Rebecca Knowles [b] Rebecca.Knowles@nrc-cnrc.gc.ca
[a]School of Translation and Interpretation, University of Ottawa
[b]National Research Council Canada

Abstract

In this position paper, we examine ways in which researchers in machine translation and translation studies have approached the problem of evaluating the output of machine translation systems and, more broadly, the questions of what it means to define translation quality. We explore their similarities and differences, highlighting the role that the purpose and context of translation plays in translation studies approaches. We argue that evaluation of machine translation (e.g., in shared tasks) would benefit from additional insights from translation studies, and we suggest the introduction of an "evaluation brief" (analogous to the "translation brief") which could help set out useful context for annotators tasked with evaluating machine translation.

1 Introduction

The evaluation of translation quality remains a challenge in the fields of machine translation (MT) and translation studies (TS). Evaluation methods relying on human judgement have changed and developed alongside advances in machine translation technology. In MT, the longstanding goal of these evaluation approaches has been to provide a standardized and possibly even "objective" evaluation process. In this work, we will draw on complementary perspectives from MT and TS.[1] We will show that there are similarities and connections between the fields' views on evaluation, as well as areas where insights from TS could be used to inform and improve approaches to human evaluation of MT.

Controversies resulting from claims that MT quality has reached "parity" with humans (Hassan et al., 2018) as well as problems with human evaluation campaigns at the Workshop on Machine Translation (WMT) have led to MT researchers shining a spotlight on evaluation protocols and their challenges (Toral et al., 2018; Läubli et al., 2018; Knowles, 2021; Castilho and Knowles, 2024, i.a.)—this has also piqued the interest of researchers in TS (e.g., Krüger, 2022).

While many previous works in the MT literature on problems in human MT evaluation have examined questions like how to set up the evaluation process, how to incorporate context, and how to standardize annotator scores, it is rarer for them to focus specifically on the definition at the core of this process: what *is* translation quality?

In this paper, we investigate how perspectives on that question differ between researchers in the fields of MT and TS. We begin with MT researchers' perspectives on current methodologies in human evaluation, focusing on what attributes of quality these evaluations prioritize. We then present a view of theoretical and practical dimensions of translation quality assessment (TQA) within TS in academia and industry. We explore TQA

[1]This paper stems from ongoing research conversations about translation quality and its evaluation between researchers in MT and TS, with this work primarily aimed at an audience familiar with the MT literature.

models in academia such as House's TQA model, Williams' argumentation-centered approach, Colina's approach, and industry-driven approaches like Multidimensional Quality Metrics (MQM). Following a comparative analysis of these methodologies, we highlight one particular facet of quality evaluation that is present in the TQA models but frequently absent from the MT research approaches: an acknowledgement of the purpose of a given translation and the context in which it is produced and expected to be used.

We take the position that MT research could benefit from incorporating these TS perspectives, and we conclude this work by considering how this could be done in practice. Translators are sometimes given a "translation brief" describing the goals of the translation, the intended audience of the translation, and other important contextual information; we propose an analogous "evaluation brief" to serve a similar role in human evaluation of translation. We then discuss how this additional context could be implemented in practice in MT evaluation, including the importance of being aware of how the annotator population differs or is similar to the expected end users of the MT system being evaluated (e.g., in terms of subject area knowledge, dialect, context, etc.), as problems in evaluation could arise due to a mismatch.

2 MT Researcher Perspectives

Since early MT experiments, human evaluation has been positioned as the ideal form of evaluation, with automatic metrics seen as a necessary stand-in. Even BLEU ("bilingual evaluation understudy"), in its name, considers automatic metrics an "understudy" to human evaluators (Papineni et al., 2002). How those human evaluations should be produced has been an open question, with a rotating cast of proposed methodologies and definitions of quality. The methodologies, procedures, and interfaces used for collecting evaluations include sliders with a continuous scale, discrete scales, ranking, annotations of the text, among others. These are often discussed in conjunction with the aspects of quality being considered (e.g., discrete scales for adequacy and fluency[2]), with terminology surrounding methodologies and interfaces blurring the line between the interface itself and the questions that annotators are being asked about quality. But in practice these are orthogonal concerns; various interfaces could be paired with any number of questions about different aspects of quality. This paper categorizes human evaluation methodologies used in MT evaluation into three broad (and sometimes overlapping) groups: manual scoring, semi-automatic (or, from another perspective, this could be viewed as semi-manual), and task-based. We also touch on how these groups of evaluation methodologies typically address questions of quality, and which aspects of quality are regularly considered in MT human evaluation.

We define "manual scoring" evaluations as evaluations in which an annotator directly provides a score or ranking to one or more systems. Early evaluations at shared tasks asked annotators to judge adequacy and fluency on 5- or 7-point scales (LDC, 2002; Koehn and Monz, 2006; Callison-Burch et al., 2007, i.a.) and this approach is frequently revisited in other proposed variants, such as the rating of semantic faithfulness to source text in Licht et al. (2022). In later system ranking tasks (Vilar et al., 2007; Callison-Burch et al., 2007, 2008, 2009, i.a.), annotators were asked "to rank the translations from best to worst (ties are allowed)" (Bojar et al., 2016), without specific guidance about what aspects would make one translation better or worse than another. Recent WMT annotation campaigns have used direct assessment (DA; Graham et al., 2013a, 2014, 2016), where annotators provide a score from 0-100 on a sliding scale. These began with asking for adequacy-oriented human judgements, but were gradually replaced with questions including both meaning and grammar (Kocmi et al., 2023).[3] We include some of the exact questions for human annotators in WMT evaluation campaigns for refer-

[2]Adequacy is defined in terms of the amount of meaning carried over from the source sentence to the translation, while fluency focuses on whether the target language text is grammatical or natural-sounding regardless of semantic content. At times these have been referred to by other terms as well. In earlier stages of MT development, adequacy and fluency were found to be highly correlated, and evaluations shifted to focus only on adequacy (Callison-Burch et al., 2007). More recent research argues that "accuracy and fluency are positively correlated at the level of the corpus but trade off at the level of individual source segments" (Lim et al., 2024).

[3]Notably, the most recent scale design in Kocmi et al. (2022, 2023, 2024) violates best practices in measurement theory and questionnaire design by incorporating these two distinct aspects into a single rating scale (Fowler, 2013, p. 81-82).

ence in Appendix A. In addition to their similarity in terms of annotators directly providing some sort of score for a translation, these approaches have all been challenged at various points due to issues relating to inter- and intra-annotator consistency.

We define our second category of "semi-automatic" evaluations as ones in which an annotator provides some sort of annotation (or transformation like post-editing) to the text, and then a score for the MT is computed (automatically) based on the annotations. This includes approaches such as Human-targeted Translation Edit Rate (HTER; Snover et al., 2006), where the edit rate (an automatic measure of the number of changes/difference) of MT output is measured against the (human) post-edited version, rather than a generic reference, with the expectation that that MT output with higher translation quality requires fewer edits in order to produce an acceptable post-edited translation. Other approaches involve the annotation of errors using an error typology (e.g., Multilingual Quality Metrics, MQM; Burchardt, 2013) followed by computing a score based on the number and severity of errors. Similar approaches, such as HMEANT (Lo and Wu, 2011) and HUME (Birch et al., 2016), involve annotating the shallow semantic structures/units and translation correctness of each semantic unit in the MT output, followed by aggregating these correctness annotations into a score for the translation quality at sentence level. Semi-automatic approaches tend to have more well-defined instructions for annotators. However, even these may have ambiguities in the interpretations of the evaluation task. Al Sharou and Specia (2022) described challenges in consistency of annotating critical errors using an error typology, noting the importance of annotator training while also acknowledging that ambiguities and confusion may nevertheless persist. Lo and Wu (2014) and Birch et al. (2016) both showed that there are compounding disagreements between annotators at the end of the evaluation task using HMEANT and HUME.

The third group consists of task-based evaluations. In this type of extrinsic evaluation, annotators are asked to use MT output to perform a task, e.g., template filling in Laoudi et al. (2006), question answering in Jones et al. (2007), semantic parsing in Moghe et al. (2023), etc.; the performance on the downstream task is scored. These scores are interpreted as the usefulness of the MT output for the downstream task and used to form a score or ranking of the translation quality of the underlying MT system. These task-based approaches typically do not ask annotators to directly judge aspects of MT quality. Instead, they emphasize the utility/usefulness aspect of the translation and implicitly ask "Is the quality of the MT good enough for the annotator to perform the requested task?", "Does one MT system better enable annotators to complete the task than another MT system?", or similar questions.

As far as we can tell, the specific form of the questions posed/directions given to annotators are (with a few exceptions) rarely studied by MT researchers in order to ensure their validity or reliability. In general, despite its goals of producing "objective" scores, human evaluation in MT research has tended to focus either on high-level and potentially undefined or underspecified aspects like generic "quality", divided quality into adequacy and fluency, defined MT performance based on downstream task performance, or used error typologies. Graham et al. (2012) raised the question of whether identifying the "components" of quality that annotators used in their decisions could help to improve the reliability and validity of future evaluations.

3 Translation Studies (TS) Perspectives

We now explore perspectives on translation quality and translation quality assessment (TQA)[4] from TS academia and industry. Academic research in TS often explores theoretical frameworks, pedagogical implications, and methodological innovations (Jakobsen, 2017; Carl, 2021, i.a.), and the translation industry tends to focus on operational efficiency, quality assurance, and client satisfaction, frequently employing quantitative measures and standardized processes to ensure consistency and reliability in translation outputs (Williams, 2004; Pym, 2019; Bowker, 2019, i.a.). Drugan (2013) and Castilho et al. (2018) note the challenges of TQA in practical settings, with an eye toward real-world applicability, often within the constraints of tight timelines and specific client needs. Although there is a significant body of research within TS

[4]TQA is a branch of translation criticism (Holmes, 1988, p. 78), concerning "how to tell whether a translation is good or bad" (House, 2015).

that is process-oriented (Dimitrova, 2010; Saldanha and O'Brien, 2014, i.a.), in this paper we focus on product-oriented aspects of translation, as these align more with the areas of MT evaluation research that we also examine.

3.1 Definitions of Translation Quality

In TS, quality has been conceptualized through diverse contexts and perspectives and has been the subject of many debates. Koby et al. (2014) characterized translation quality in terms of two major senses: narrow and broad. In the narrow sense, translation is text-centric, requiring a full transfer of the source text's message to the target language with correct grammar and cultural appropriateness. Early understandings focused on linguistic fidelity and equivalence, such as textual equivalence (Catford, 1965). This line of work emphasized accurate replication of meaning and structure from source text to target text to ensure the translation closely mirrored the original. Building on this, House (1997) conceives of translation as a double-constrained text, bound to both the source text and the target audience's communicative conditions. Translating involves substituting one language's text with another language's equivalent that serves the same purpose. This functional equivalence is significantly affected by two empirically established categories of translation: overt and covert translation (House, 1997). In an overt translation, the original text's cultural context and linguistic features are preserved so the target audience can experience the original cultural nuances (House, 2001). For example, translating ancient Greek poetry while maintaining references to Greek mythology and cultural practices is a type of overt translation. However, covert translation seeks to create an equivalent text that functions seamlessly in the target culture as if it were an original. Translations with a "cultural filter" adapt the content to the target audience's expectations and cultural norms, creating a text that appears to have been written in the target language originally. Translations of marketing and advertising materials typically fall into this category. This often involves adapting idiomatic expressions, cultural references and humour to align with local tastes and expectations. Thus, translating overtly or covertly depends on the text's nature, the purpose of the translation, and the intended audience.

The broad sense of quality described by Koby et al. (2014) encompasses the narrow sense but adds compliance with negotiated specifications and consideration of end-user needs, ensuring translations meet measurable standards and fit their purpose. This broader perspective first aligns with functionalist approaches which define translation quality as whether a translated text fulfills its intended purpose for the target audience in the given circumstances, ensuring linguistic accuracy and appropriateness in context. Vermeer (1978, 2021) introduced Skopos theory, which argued that linguistic solutions, such as lexical choices and syntactical adjustments, cannot address all translation issues, including maintaining the original text's intent and adapting to cultural differences. Skopos theory considers translation as a purposeful action based on the source text, where the translator must consider the intent of the original text and adapt it to the target culture.

Building on Skopos theory and the process by which translations are commissioned (Vermeer, 1978, 2021), Nord (1997a, p. 46-48) introduced the translation brief or "Übersetzungsauftrag". A translation brief typically includes "the target-text addressee(s), the prospective time and place of text reception, the medium over which the text will be transmitted, and the motive for the production or reception of the text" (Nord, 1997a). ISO (2015) listed 22 key and supplementary elements in a translation brief, which included information about the source content, source and target languages, linguistic specifications (e.g., language variants), audience, purpose, style guide, locale conventions, reference materials, etc., on top of some project management specifications. Similarly, Esselink (2003) introduced a translation kit (or localization kit) as a package of files that includes all necessary information to meet the client's quality standards. More recently, Calvo (2018) used the term "specifications" to reflect the complexity of modern translation projects. Here, "Skopos", "brief", and "specifications" determine the communicative function and quality of the translation.

Chesterman and Wagner (2002, p. 80-84) added a view on quality from an industrial context. Here, translation quality is viewed from different perspectives: as a product judged by end quality, as a process dependent on correct execution, as a service measured by customer satisfaction, and as a copy to be assessed by accuracy and faithfulness to the original text. The view of translation quality as customer/end-user satisfaction is also discussed by Pym (2019, p. 437-452).

Another view on the definition of translation quality stems from the management quality framework in Garvin (1984), which encompasses five perspectives: transcendent, product-based, user-based, manufacturing-based, and value-based. Fields et al. (2014) introduced this framework to the translation industry to increase overall translation effectiveness and satisfaction by balancing stakeholder expectations and addressing diverse quality dimensions.

To conclude, the understanding of quality in TS has evolved significantly from early emphases on linguistic fidelity to a more inclusive understanding that considers functionalist, industrial, and management perspectives. This inclusive view acknowledges that translation quality is multifaceted, considering both linguistic accuracy and the fulfillment of the translation's intended purpose for its end users. This does not cover the full range of definitions of translation quality; the ones we selected for discussion here are especially pertinent.

3.2 Concepts of Translation Quality Assessment (TQA)

Bowker (2000, p. 183) described TQA as "the most problematic area of translation," citing descriptions like "a great stumbling block" (Bassnett-McGuire, 1991), "a complex challenge" (Mahn, 1987), "a most wretched question" (Malmkjær, 1998), and "a thorny problem" (Snell-Hornby, 1992). Historically, TS has favoured "translation criticism over empirical measurement" (Moorkens et al., 2018, p. 12), with a particular emphasis on literary works.

Equivalence is a cornerstone of early TQA (House, 2015, p. 21-22). The concept of equivalence in TS describes the relationship between the source text (ST) and the target text (TT), in which the TT aims to match the ST in terms of meaning, function, and effect. However, equivalence at all levels is often impossible due to linguistic and cultural differences. The concept has evolved through various scholars, from Vinay and Darbelnet (1958) focusing on the stylistic impact, to linguistic categorization by Jakobson (1959), and Nida and Taber (1969) distinguishing between formal and dynamic equivalence. Early TQA models focused on achieving textual and formal equivalence between source and target texts (Lauscher, 2000). However, equivalence-based TQA approaches have often been criticized for being too rigid and not accommodating the diverse functions translations can serve. For a more in-depth overview of the concept, see Appendix B.

Compared to the concept of equivalence, functionalism in translation (Vermeer, 1978; Honig, 1997) emphasizes the purpose and function of translations within their specific contexts over strict equivalence to the source text (Lauscher, 2000). For example, under Skopos theory, translation quality is assessed by how well translations achieve their intended purpose. In doing so, assessments will consider the cultural and situational appropriateness of the translation to ensure it resonates with the target audience and serves its intended function.

The introduction of translation technologies to the translation industry, such as MT and computer-aided translation (CAT) tools, further impact the assessment of translation quality. Bowker (2019, p. 453-468) emphasizes evaluating translations based on their suitability for their intended purpose rather than adhering to a one-size-fits-all notion of quality. This perspective helps translators navigate the "Triple Constraint" of quality, cost, and time, ensuring that translations meet specific end-user needs. By informing clients about the significance of defining the translation's purpose and agreeing on specifications, translators ensure that their work focuses on both linguistic merit and overall effectiveness in fulfilling intended purposes.

3.3 Modern TQA Models and Methodologies

Modern TQA methods can be categorized into quantitative and qualitative dimensions. Quantitative TQA models aim to provide measurable standards and numeric descriptions of translation quality. Qualitative TQA models look at how well the translation conveys the original message, fits within the cultural and contextual setting, and meets the needs of its intended audience. Quantitative TQA models, during the assessment, may break down the translation work into smaller units, e.g., paragraphs, sentences, or even phrases (an approach that is also common in MT); qualitative TQA models usually look at the complete work of the translation as a whole. We begin with a brief discussion of quantitative approaches, as those more closely resemble the MT-style evaluations, before examining qualitative approaches.

Many quantitative models are based on error typologies. Canadian Language Quality Measurement System (Sical) and the Canadian Translators, Terminologists and Interpreters Council (CTTIC) certification exam (CTTIC, 2021) emphasize a structured, numerical approach to quality evaluation. The CTTIC's error-based assessment has a "Marking Scale" that differentiates between major "Translation" errors, like significant misinterpretations (-10 points), and minor "Language" inaccuracies (-5 points). We should note, though, that the CTTIC exam is arguably an evaluation/grading of a *translator*, rather than an evaluation of translation or translated texts more generally.

Other types of error typologies have grown from the intersections of technology and translation. MQM introduces over 100 issue types, arranged in a hierarchical structure (Lommel et al., 2014). They use five main branches: Fluency, Accuracy, Verity, Design, and Internationalization and evaluate translations according to specific project requirements and communicative purposes by selecting relevant issue types. MQM supports multiple levels of granularity and includes tools for calculating quality metrics and is used for both human and machine translation evaluations.

Another type is introduced in ISO (2024), which focuses on segment-based comparisons and detailed error typology to promote objective and reliable quality assessment. The error categories cover points such as: terminology (e.g., inconsistent use of terms), accuracy (e.g., mistranslation, omissions), linguistic conventions (e.g., grammar, spelling), style (e.g., register, unidiomatic style), locale conventions (e.g., formats of dates and currencies), audience appropriateness (e.g., cultural references), and design and markup (e.g., character formatting, layout). Error annotations are made based on the relevant translation project specifications and translation evaluation specifications. To further assist users in analyzing their evaluation needs, that document contains appendices with guiding questions to help users determine their evaluation needs and think about how to best implement an evaluation setup for their situation, covering translation use cases, evaluation purposes, and constraints.

Many modern qualitative TQA models draw on linguistic and functionalist approaches. The model in House (1977, 1997, 2015) is rooted in functional pragmatics. It employs a register analysis (an analysis of the variety of language used in a particular situation/for a particular purpose) to assess how well the source and target text match in terms of these dimensions. In particular, the model analyzes field, tenor, and mode (Halliday, 1973; Halliday and Hasan, 1989)—roughly domain, relationship between the translation participants, and medium of communication—as well as genre.[5]

The functionalist/componential (i.e., breaking quality down into components) approach, described in Colina (2008), evaluates various components of translation quality separately based on their functions or purposes. The evaluation tool—similar to a grading or evaluation rubric—includes descriptive statements for different categories such as linguistic form, functional adequacy, meaning, and specialized content. Raters select descriptors that best match the text's quality in each category, which are then converted into numerical scores for analysis. By separating the evaluation into distinct, well-defined components, the componential nature of the tool likely contributed to the better inter-rater agreement observed in this study, reducing ambiguity and subjectivity. Another aspect of this study was that all raters were given training and an explanation of the methodology before participating, which may have contributed to their confidence and high levels of agreement.

Qualitative TQA models also draw on an end-user-focused approach to complement error typologies. Bowker (2009) used recipient evaluation—surveying the target audience about how well various translation options meet their needs and expectations—to assess quality. This approach positions the end-users of translation at the centre, examining how different language communities may have different use cases, needs and requirements. Similarly, Saldanha and O'Brien (2014) proposed using diverse research instruments, such as questionnaires and eye-tracking, to make a more flexible and precise TQA method to adapt to genre, text function, and translation briefs. Han (2020) also highlighted this integration of various methods to enhance reliability, validity, and practicality to emphasize the

[5] See Appendix C for more details.

need for robust and pragmatic assessment methods to address challenges in evaluating translation quality.

There are also models, such as the argumentation-centred TQA from Williams (2004), which combine both qualitative and quantitative methods. This model focuses on assessing instrumental translations[6] by evaluating how well reasoning and arguments are transferred. It uses two main components: argument schema, including elements like claims, grounds, and rebuttals, and rhetorical topology, which encompasses organizational relations, propositions, and narrative strategies. This model employs a detailed framework for deconstructing arguments to ensure the factual content and the persuasive force are accurately conveyed. It also assigns numerical values to various parameters, including core and field-specific elements like terminology and formatting, to provide a comprehensive quality assessment.

To conclude, TQA is complex in both the academic and industry sectors of translation and localization (Castilho et al., 2018). The lack of a universally agreed-upon measurement standard for quality underscores a broader debate on TQA methodologies, particularly with the increasing integration of MT and human translation in various contexts. As a whole, TQA models in TS advocate for a holistic and context-sensitive evaluation of translation quality, acknowledging that different contexts and purposes require different quality standards, but they differ in how to assess and evaluate these.

4 Overlaps and Differences in MT and TS

The fields of MT and TS do have points of commonality when it comes to human evaluation and assessment of MT quality, while the areas where they differ may have their origins in the underlying objectives and methodologies of the fields. This is noted in Castilho et al. (2018), who point out that many researchers in TS "have argued that evaluation is directly associated with the underlying translation theory that one subscribes to," citing in particular the quote that "different views of translation lead to different concepts of translational quality, and hence different ways of assessing it" (House, 1997). We also note that even within each research community—and in their areas of overlap—there is not a broad consensus on how to define quality or which aspects ought to be considered most important.

There are two main forms of evaluations that overlap between the two fields: error typology-based and task-based evaluations. MQM, developed in the translation industry and TS and recently adopted by MT for some evaluations (Freitag et al., 2021a; Anastasopoulos et al., 2022; Agarwal et al., 2023), breaks MT quality down into a typology of errors. Task-based and recipient evaluations have also been used in both fields. In task-based evaluations, we see the use of MT presented in a particular context, with the users asked to either perform a task or evaluate it from the perspective of their use case. These may come the closest to examining whether or not translations are appropriate for the situations and contexts for which they are intended.

Both fields have recognized the challenge of defining and assessing translation quality, though they have largely taken different approaches in exploring this. At various points in MT evaluation history, we have seen quality broken down into component parts at different levels of granularity (e.g., adequacy and fluency, or error typologies like MQM). Perspectives from TS provide other ways of categorizing the components that come together to make up notions of "quality". These include extra-textual factors that influence quality, as well as borrowing and incorporating understandings of quality from different disciplines, such as functionalism, industry, and management. But in all of these efforts, we see that quality is multidimensional (i.e., made up of various contributing aspects) and situation-dependent; there is not a straightforward simple or

[6]"Instrumental translation" refers to a type of translation where the target text functions independently and serves as an instrument for communication within the target culture (Nord, 1997b). Unlike documentary translation, which focuses on reflecting the source text's original context and form, instrumental translation adapts the source text to meet the communicative needs of the target culture. While this concept bears some resemblance to the distinction between covert and overt translation described in House (1997), the two should not be conflated. Covert translations, like instrumental translations, aim to blend seamlessly into the target culture. However, instrumental translation places a particular emphasis on the functional adaptation of the text to serve the target audience effectively, sometimes requiring significant modifications to the source text. This approach is especially relevant in technical, pragmatic, and other context-sensitive translations where functional equivalence is prioritized.

universal definition.

MT research often seeks a single "objective" metric for MT "quality", which can be used to compute a simple ranking of systems. This is connected to the leaderboard and competition aspects that are common to MT and other areas of machine learning. It also directly relates to the fact that system optimization is a major focus in MT research: optimization towards a single objective is substantially easier than optimization towards multiple (potentially conflicting) objectives. In MT, the response to observing annotator variation in evaluation has often been to modify the evaluation protocols (e.g., changing from a rating scale to ranking to direct assessment) or to seek ways of standardizing annotator scores.

Both MT and TS have considered the question of who should perform annotations. In large-scale MT evaluations, this has often been constrained by the cost of annotation, with interest in crowdsourcing (Callison-Burch, 2009; Denkowski and Lavie, 2010; Bentivogli et al., 2011; Graham et al., 2013b, i.a.) and comparing crowdsourced results against language and translation experts. In TS, Colina (2008) also examines this question of who should perform annotations, finding greater levels of inter-annotator agreement within homogenous groups (e.g., groups of all professional translators or groups of bilinguals who are not translators).

In TS, we see more attention paid to the meaning of quality itself and how best to define that, influenced by definitions and descriptions of quality from different disciplines. TS also tends more towards exploring the notion of subjectivity, with a greater focus on the specific use cases and users of a particular translation and how that translation serves its purpose. This focus on a specific use case can be seen as a difference from MT research, which often purports to aim for a broad or universal use case (see, e.g., the framing of tasks at WMT, such as "News" or "General" translation, without reference to a specific audience for the news/general translations).[7] In TS, there is a significant focus on who the translation is for, what it is intended to do, and the specific circumstances surrounding its creation and use (Bowker, 2009; Chesterman and Wagner, 2002; Colina, 2008, i.a.). This approach ensures that translations are tailored to meet the needs and expectations of their target audience. This contrasts with some MT research proposals of a translation that can be used in any context by anyone. This MT perspective may be tied to underlying assumptions of invertibility as a desired component of MT (since round-trip translation performance has frequently been used as a benchmark of success by MT researchers), a view which is not shared in all of TS.

A recent concept from the MT perspective assumes that a single translation can meet all purposes or that there exists a general-purpose translation, which is often unrealistic given the diversity of language use and cultural contexts.[8] While the concept of a universal translator has long been a goal of some researchers, we note that, over time, MT research has taken various views on how best to approach translation. Early MT successes such as the METEO systems (Chandioux, 1976, i.a.) occurred through focused efforts on limited and specific domains: purpose-built MT. The late 1990s and early 2000s saw the widespread availability of free public online MT systems, such as AltaVista Babel Fish (Yang and Lange, 1998), allowing anyone with an internet connection to (attempt to) translate anything within a limited set of language pairs. MT research has seen both these research tracks—the purpose-built task-specific translation system and the goal of a universal system—pursued in parallel. When researchers or users treat online MT systems, for example, as a box into which any source text can be placed with the expectation of receiving the desired translation, conflict and disappointment are likely to arise. Users of MT technologies are in fact using MT with a purpose, and two users of the same MT system may be using it with two different and

[7]We do note some exceptions to this, such as the specification that the 2024 English–Spanish task is intended to translate into Latin American Spanish, specifically (WMT, 2024), though one could argue that this still covers a wide range of language variants.

[8]For example, we know that it is frequently the case that sentences in isolation may have ambiguities that would require additional context to resolve for translation (Castilho et al., 2020); MT systems that translate at the sentence level will struggle with this. Similarly, if we do not specify language variant well enough, we may produce text that is suitable for one linguistic community that speaks a language but not another (e.g., orthographic, writing system, or vocabulary differences). While most MT evaluations omit such factors as design, layout, formatting, and markup, these factors are more frequently considered in the TS perspective. Consider, for example the task of subtitle or closed-caption translation, which places additional constraints, such as length, on the translation, which we are now also beginning to see addressed in MT.

conflicting purposes. The emphasis on universality that is often present (implicitly or explicitly) in MT research may overlook the specificities that TS scholars deem crucial for high-quality translations. We argue that MTR research should be considering these purposes and specificities when performing evaluations, whether by explicitly highlighting specific use cases, language variants, and so on, or by being clear about how to handle conflicting preferences in translation quality.

5 Evaluation Briefs

In this work, we have looked at how both MT and TS have explored questions of what it means to evaluate the "quality" of a translation. While we have seen that MT has explored some aspects of quality (e.g., adequacy and fluency), TS has enumerated a wider range of aspects that contribute to perceptions and judgments of MT quality; TQA involves decisions that take into account many factors beyond the source and target text, such as the intended target audiences and their linguistic and cultural background, the purpose of translation, and the medium of reception. Without access to these relevant details, human evaluators are reasoning under uncertainty. This leads us to ask: can insights from TS suggest to us aspects that are missing from many of the current implementations of human evaluation of MT from the MT research side?

We argue that the concepts of the purpose and intended audience of a translation are some of the central aspects that have been underexplored in the MT literature. This is also one of the major research areas identified in human-centered MT evaluation by Liebling et al. (2022). Trying to incorporate this into MT evaluation (e.g., of the sorts performed at WMT or other large-scale evaluations) will require MT researchers to first settle on more concrete and well-defined goals for their MT systems. That includes the considerations of the intended use case, the language variants, and the intended audiences.

This is certainly not a new call; Church and Hovy (1993) pointed out that "if the application is not clearly identified (or worse, if the application is poorly chosen), then it is often very difficult to find a satisfying evaluation paradigm." That claim was made in an era of "crummy" MT, but we argue for its continued relevance in an era of improved MT. Among several other goals, Church and Hovy (1993) argued that an appropriate application should "set reasonable expectations" and "should be attractive to the intended users". Now that we have access to much-improved MT for many language pairs and domains, how should we push forward?

We propose being explicit with a "translation brief" (for the use of both the translators producing reference translations and the researchers building MT systems[9]) as well as expanding this to an "evaluation brief". An "evaluation brief" would provide the human evaluators with a wider context and detailed instructions about how to evaluate the translation. This is similar to the "role" or "persona" described in Graham et al. (2012), which annotators are asked to take on when evaluating MT output; that work also highlights the importance of taking great care with the design of such instructions. With the evaluation brief, human evaluators could situate themselves in the use case of the translation and as the intended users of the translation to consider the users' needs and expectations. As for what to include in an evaluation brief, we could draw inspiration from the translation brief: source and target languages (including language variants), relevant information about both the author/speaker and the audience, purpose, style guide, and so on (ISO, 2015).

For example, we can consider two different types of medical texts: medical information that is intended for healthcare workers (domain experts) and medical information in public health announcements that is intended to be accessible to a broad audience (non-experts).[10] An appropriate evaluation

[9]While human translators will make use of the translation brief directly, i.e., deciding on levels of formality, language variants, technical language, and so on to use in their translations, MT researchers are likely to use this more indirectly, such as by selecting which data sources to train on, deciding whether to incorporate model features such as tagging (e.g., for multi-domain or multilingual systems), considering issues such as robustness to input variations, and so on, with the goal of producing a translation system that in turn will follow the translation brief. We could also imagine employing translation briefs when experimenting with large language model-based translation, as part of the instructions provided to the large language model.

[10]We consider here primarily the case in which the expertise level of the audience is held consistent from the source to the target (i.e., translating text for domain experts from a source language into target language text also intended for domain experts); the transformation of text from expert to non-expert (or vice versa) introduces additional challenges.

brief would, at a minimum, indicate which audience and purpose was intended, and perhaps also other relevant concerns like whether there were terminological conventions that should be followed. Importantly, the translation brief (for translators producing reference translations and for MT researchers building systems) and the evaluation brief should generally be in agreement; while there may be some situations (e.g., challenge sets or analyses of MT robustness) where it is appropriate to evaluate MT systems on things outside of the purview of the translation brief, to be fair to the participants of a shared task, the evaluation should match the stated objectives of the task itself.

However, an evaluation brief is likely insufficient on its own; MT researchers also need to think about recruiting human evaluators with skills, knowledge, and cultural expertise appropriate for the specific goals of the translation. In the case of translations that are intended to be acceptable across a wide range of language variants (e.g., dialects, spelling conventions), whether the evaluator pool reflects this diversity would affect the validity of the evaluation results. Similarly, in the case of translations for a highly-technical domain (intended for use by experts), e.g., biomedical translations in (Neves et al., 2023), employing subject matter experts as translation evaluators is necessary for a meaningful evaluation. A lack of such experts may lower evaluation consistency (Freitag et al., 2021b). Importantly, the evaluation brief (and any translation brief) should be reported (e.g., in the appendices of publications), along with relevant information about the annotators (e.g., language skills, expertise, etc.). Current practices often report only high-level information (e.g., whether annotators were translators or non-translator bilinguals); one may wish to consider expanding this to cover a broader range of relevant demographic information about annotators.

6 Conclusion

In this work, we have examined perspectives on both MT quality and how to evaluate MT from the perspectives of MT research and translation studies. We argue that future MT evaluation could benefit from drawing on insights from translation studies. In particular, this includes an increasing focus on the purpose, intended audience, and context of translation. More broadly, we encourage MT researchers to seek collaborations and conversations in TS and beyond. In order to better design the questions that MT researchers ask of evaluators, the field would likely benefit from more interactions with research best practices in measurement theory, survey research methods, human-computer interaction, and more.

Acknowledgments

We thank Malcolm Williams for discussion of his TQA model, and Gabriel Bernier-Colborne for feedback on a draft of this paper.

References

Agarwal, M., Agrawal, S., Anastasopoulos, A., Bentivogli, L., Bojar, O., Borg, C., Carpuat, M., Cattoni, R., Cettolo, M., Chen, M., Chen, W., Choukri, K., Chronopoulou, A., Currey, A., Declerck, T., Dong, Q., Duh, K., Estève, Y., Federico, M., Gahbiche, S., Haddow, B., Hsu, B., Mon Htut, P., Inaguma, H., Javorský, D., Judge, J., Kano, Y., Ko, T., Kumar, R., Li, P., Ma, X., Mathur, P., Matusov, E., McNamee, P., P. McCrae, J., Murray, K., Nadejde, M., Nakamura, S., Negri, M., Nguyen, H., Niehues, J., Niu, X., Kr. Ojha, A., E. Ortega, J., Pal, P., Pino, J., van der Plas, L., Polák, P., Rippeth, E., Salesky, E., Shi, J., Sperber, M., Stüker, S., Sudoh, K., Tang, Y., Thompson, B., Tran, K., Turchi, M., Waibel, A., Wang, M., Watanabe, S., and Zevallos, R. (2023). FINDINGS OF THE IWSLT 2023 EVALUATION CAMPAIGN. In Salesky, E., Federico, M., and Carpuat, M., editors, *Proceedings of the 20th International Conference on Spoken Language Translation (IWSLT 2023)*, pages 1–61, Toronto, Canada (in-person and online). Association for Computational Linguistics.

Al Sharou, K. and Specia, L. (2022). A taxonomy and study of critical errors in machine translation. In Moniz, H., Macken, L., Rufener, A., Barrault, L., Costa-jussà, M. R., Declercq, C., Koponen, M., Kemp, E., Pilos, S., Forcada, M. L., Scarton, C., Van den Bogaert, J., Daems, J., Tezcan, A., Vanroy, B., and Fonteyne, M., editors, *Proceedings of the 23rd Annual Conference of the European Association for Machine Translation*, pages 171–180, Ghent, Belgium. European Association for Machine Translation.

Anastasopoulos, A., Barrault, L., Bentivogli, L., Zanon Boito, M., Bojar, O., Cattoni, R., Currey, A., Dinu, G., Duh, K., Elbayad, M., Emmanuel, C., Estève, Y., Federico, M., Federmann, C., Gahbiche, S., Gong,

H., Grundkiewicz, R., Haddow, B., Hsu, B., Javorský, D., Kloudová, V., Lakew, S., Ma, X., Mathur, P., McNamee, P., Murray, K., Nădejde, M., Nakamura, S., Negri, M., Niehues, J., Niu, X., Ortega, J., Pino, J., Salesky, E., Shi, J., Sperber, M., Stüker, S., Sudoh, K., Turchi, M., Virkar, Y., Waibel, A., Wang, C., and Watanabe, S. (2022). Findings of the IWSLT 2022 evaluation campaign. In Salesky, E., Federico, M., and Costa-jussà, M., editors, *Proceedings of the 19th International Conference on Spoken Language Translation (IWSLT 2022)*, pages 98–157, Dublin, Ireland (in-person and online). Association for Computational Linguistics.

Baker, M. (1992). *In Other Words: A Coursebook on Translation*. Routledge.

Barrault, L., Biesialska, M., Bojar, O., Costa-jussà, M. R., Federmann, C., Graham, Y., Grundkiewicz, R., Haddow, B., Huck, M., Joanis, E., Kocmi, T., Koehn, P., Lo, C.-k., Ljubešić, N., Monz, C., Morishita, M., Nagata, M., Nakazawa, T., Pal, S., Post, M., and Zampieri, M. (2020). Findings of the 2020 conference on machine translation (WMT20). In Barrault, L., Bojar, O., Bougares, F., Chatterjee, R., Costa-jussà, M. R., Federmann, C., Fishel, M., Fraser, A., Graham, Y., Guzman, P., Haddow, B., Huck, M., Yepes, A. J., Koehn, P., Martins, A., Morishita, M., Monz, C., Nagata, M., Nakazawa, T., and Negri, M., editors, *Proceedings of the Fifth Conference on Machine Translation*, pages 1–55, Online. Association for Computational Linguistics.

Barrault, L., Bojar, O., Costa-jussà, M. R., Federmann, C., Fishel, M., Graham, Y., Haddow, B., Huck, M., Koehn, P., Malmasi, S., Monz, C., Müller, M., Pal, S., Post, M., and Zampieri, M. (2019). Findings of the 2019 conference on machine translation (WMT19). In Bojar, O., Chatterjee, R., Federmann, C., Fishel, M., Graham, Y., Haddow, B., Huck, M., Yepes, A. J., Koehn, P., Martins, A., Monz, C., Negri, M., Névéol, A., Neves, M., Post, M., Turchi, M., and Verspoor, K., editors, *Proceedings of the Fourth Conference on Machine Translation (Volume 2: Shared Task Papers, Day 1)*, pages 1–61, Florence, Italy. Association for Computational Linguistics.

Bassnett-McGuire, S. (1991). *Translation Studies*. Routledge, London, revised edition edition.

Bentivogli, L., Federico, M., Moretti, G., and Paul, M. (2011). Getting expert quality from the crowd for machine translation evaluation. In *Proceedings of Machine Translation Summit XIII: Papers*, Xiamen, China.

Birch, A., Abend, O., Bojar, O., and Haddow, B. (2016). HUME: Human UCCA-based evaluation of machine translation. In Su, J., Duh, K., and Carreras, X., editors, *Proceedings of the 2016 Conference on Empirical Methods in Natural Language Processing*, pages 1264–1274, Austin, Texas. Association for Computational Linguistics.

Bojar, O., Chatterjee, R., Federmann, C., Graham, Y., Haddow, B., Huang, S., Huck, M., Koehn, P., Liu, Q., Logacheva, V., Monz, C., Negri, M., Post, M., Rubino, R., Specia, L., and Turchi, M. (2017). Findings of the 2017 conference on machine translation (WMT17). In Bojar, O., Buck, C., Chatterjee, R., Federmann, C., Graham, Y., Haddow, B., Huck, M., Yepes, A. J., Koehn, P., and Kreutzer, J., editors, *Proceedings of the Second Conference on Machine Translation*, pages 169–214, Copenhagen, Denmark. Association for Computational Linguistics.

Bojar, O., Chatterjee, R., Federmann, C., Graham, Y., Haddow, B., Huck, M., Jimeno Yepes, A., Koehn, P., Logacheva, V., Monz, C., Negri, M., Névéol, A., Neves, M., Popel, M., Post, M., Rubino, R., Scarton, C., Specia, L., Turchi, M., Verspoor, K., and Zampieri, M. (2016). Findings of the 2016 conference on machine translation. In Bojar, O., Buck, C., Chatterjee, R., Federmann, C., Guillou, L., Haddow, B., Huck, M., Yepes, A. J., Névéol, A., Neves, M., Pecina, P., Popel, M., Koehn, P., Monz, C., Negri, M., Post, M., Specia, L., Verspoor, K., Tiedemann, J., and Turchi, M., editors, *Proceedings of the First Conference on Machine Translation: Volume 2, Shared Task Papers*, pages 131–198, Berlin, Germany. Association for Computational Linguistics.

Bojar, O., Federmann, C., Fishel, M., Graham, Y., Haddow, B., Huck, M., Koehn, P., and Monz, C. (2018). Findings of the 2018 conference on machine translation (WMT18). In Bojar, O., Chatterjee, R., Federmann, C., Fishel, M., Graham, Y., Haddow, B., Huck, M., Yepes, A. J., Koehn, P., Monz, C., Negri, M., Névéol, A., Neves, M., Post, M., Specia, L., Turchi, M., and Verspoor, K., editors, *Proceedings of the Third Conference on Machine Translation: Shared Task Papers*, pages 272–303, Belgium, Brussels. Association for Computational Linguistics.

Bowker, L. (2000). A corpus-based approach to evaluating student translations. *The Translator*, 6(2):183–210.

Bowker, L. (2009). Can machine translation meet the needs of official language minority communities in Canada? A recipient evaluation. *Linguistica Antverpiensia, New Series – Themes in Translation Studies*, 8:123–155.

Bowker, L. (2019). Fit-for-purpose translation. In O'Hagan, M., editor, *The Routledge Handbook of Translation and Technology*. Routledge.

Burchardt, A. (2013). Multidimensional quality metrics: A flexible system for assessing translation quality. In *Proceedings of Translating and the Computer 35*, London, UK. Aslib.

Callison-Burch, C. (2009). Fast, cheap, and creative: Evaluating translation quality using Amazon's Mechanical Turk. In Koehn, P. and Mihalcea, R., editors, *Proceedings of the 2009 Conference on Empirical Methods in Natural Language Processing*, pages 286–295, Singapore. Association for Computational Linguistics.

Callison-Burch, C., Fordyce, C., Koehn, P., Monz, C., and Schroeder, J. (2007). (Meta-) evaluation of machine translation. In Callison-Burch, C., Koehn, P., Fordyce, C. S., and Monz, C., editors, *Proceedings of the Second Workshop on Statistical Machine Translation*, pages 136–158, Prague, Czech Republic. Association for Computational Linguistics.

Callison-Burch, C., Fordyce, C., Koehn, P., Monz, C., and Schroeder, J. (2008). Further meta-evaluation of machine translation. In Callison-Burch, C., Koehn, P., Monz, C., Schroeder, J., and Fordyce, C. S., editors, *Proceedings of the Third Workshop on Statistical Machine Translation*, pages 70–106, Columbus, Ohio. Association for Computational Linguistics.

Callison-Burch, C., Koehn, P., Monz, C., and Schroeder, J. (2009). Findings of the 2009 Workshop on Statistical Machine Translation. In Callison-Burch, C., Koehn, P., Monz, C., and Schroeder, J., editors, *Proceedings of the Fourth Workshop on Statistical Machine Translation*, pages 1–28, Athens, Greece. Association for Computational Linguistics.

Calvo, E. (2018). From translation briefs to quality standards: Functionalist theories in today's translation processes. *Translation & Interpreting*, 10(1).

Carl, M., editor (2021). *Explorations in Empirical Translation Process Research*. Springer International Publishing.

Castilho, S., Doherty, S., Gaspari, F., and Moorkens, J. (2018). *Approaches to Human and Machine Translation Quality Assessment*, pages 9–38. Volume 1 of Moorkens et al. (2018).

Castilho, S. and Knowles, R. (2024). A survey of context in neural machine translation and its evaluation. *Natural Language Processing*, page 1–31.

Castilho, S., Popović, M., and Way, A. (2020). On context span needed for machine translation evaluation. In Calzolari, N., Béchet, F., Blache, P., Choukri, K., Cieri, C., Declerck, T., Goggi, S., Isahara, H., Maegaard, B., Mariani, J., Mazo, H., Moreno, A., Odijk, J., and Piperidis, S., editors, *Proceedings of the Twelfth Language Resources and Evaluation Conference*, pages 3735–3742, Marseille, France. European Language Resources Association.

Catford, J. (1965). *A Linguistic Theory of Translation: An Essay in Applied Linguistics*. Language and language learning series. Oxford U.P.

Chandioux, J. (1976). METEO, an operational system for the translation of public weather forecasts. In Hays, D. G. and Mathias, J., editors, *Foreign Broadcast Information Service Seminar on Machine Translation*, pages 27–36, Virginia.

Chesterman, A. and Wagner, E. (2002). *Can Theory Help Translators?: A Dialogue Between the Ivory Tower and the Wordface*. Routledge.

Church, K. W. and Hovy, E. H. (1993). Good applications for crummy machine translation. *Machine Translation*, 8(4):239–258.

Colina, S. (2008). Translation quality evaluation: Empirical evidence for a functionalist approach. *The Translator*, 14(1):97–134.

CTTIC (2021). CTTIC translation certification examination marker's guide. Accessed: 2024-06-02.

de Waard, J. and Nida, E. (1986). *From One Language to Another: Functional Equivalence in Bible Translating*. Nelson.

Denkowski, M. and Lavie, A. (2010). Exploring normalization techniques for human judgments of machine translation adequacy collected using Amazon Mechanical Turk. In Callison-Burch, C. and Dredze, M., editors, *Proceedings of the NAACL HLT 2010 Workshop on Creating Speech and Language Data with Amazon's Mechanical Turk*, pages 57–61, Los Angeles. Association for Computational Linguistics.

Dimitrova, B. E. (2010). Translation process. In Gambier, Y. and van Doorslaer, L., editors, *Handbook of Translation Studies*, volume 1, pages 406–411. John Benjamins Publishing Company.

Drugan, J. (2013). *Quality in Professional Translation: Assessment and Improvement*. Bloomsbury.

Esselink, B. (2003). *Localisation and translation*, page 67–86. John Benjamins Publishing Company.

Fields, P., Hague, D., Koby, G., Lommel, A., and Melby, A. (2014). What is quality? A management discipline and the translation industry get acquainted. *Tradumàtica: tecnologies de la traducció*.

Fowler, F. (2013). *Survey Research Methods*. Applied Social Research Methods. SAGE Publications.

Freitag, M., Foster, G., Grangier, D., Ratnakar, V., Tan, Q., and Macherey, W. (2021a). Experts, errors, and context: A large-scale study of human evaluation for machine translation. *Transactions of the Association for Computational Linguistics*, 9:1460–1474.

Freitag, M., Rei, R., Mathur, N., Lo, C.-k., Stewart, C., Foster, G., Lavie, A., and Bojar, O. (2021b). Results of the WMT21 metrics shared task: Evaluating metrics with expert-based human evaluations on TED and news domain. In Barrault, L., Bojar, O., Bougares, F., Chatterjee, R., Costa-jussa, M. R., Federmann, C., Fishel, M., Fraser, A., Freitag, M., Graham, Y., Grundkiewicz, R., Guzman, P., Haddow, B., Huck, M., Yepes, A. J., Koehn, P., Kocmi, T., Martins, A., Morishita, M., and Monz, C., editors, *Proceedings of the Sixth Conference on Machine Translation*, pages 733–774, Online. Association for Computational Linguistics.

Garvin, D. A. (1984). What does "product quality" really mean? *Sloan Management Review*, 26(1):25–43.

Graham, Y., Baldwin, T., Dowling, M., Eskevich, M., Lynn, T., and Tounsi, L. (2016). Is all that glitters in machine translation quality estimation really gold? In Matsumoto, Y. and Prasad, R., editors, *Proceedings of COLING 2016, the 26th International Conference on Computational Linguistics: Technical Papers*, pages 3124–3134, Osaka, Japan. The COLING 2016 Organizing Committee.

Graham, Y., Baldwin, T., Harwood, A., Moffat, A., and Zobel, J. (2012). Measurement of progress in machine translation. In Cook, P. and Nowson, S., editors, *Proceedings of the Australasian Language Technology Association Workshop 2012*, pages 70–78, Dunedin, New Zealand.

Graham, Y., Baldwin, T., Moffat, A., and Zobel, J. (2013a). Continuous measurement scales in human evaluation of machine translation. In Pareja-Lora, A., Liakata, M., and Dipper, S., editors, *Proceedings of the 7th Linguistic Annotation Workshop and Interoperability with Discourse*, pages 33–41, Sofia, Bulgaria. Association for Computational Linguistics.

Graham, Y., Baldwin, T., Moffat, A., and Zobel, J. (2013b). Crowd-sourcing of human judgments of machine translation fluency. In Karimi, S. and Verspoor, K., editors, *Proceedings of the Australasian Language Technology Association Workshop 2013 (ALTA 2013)*, pages 16–24, Brisbane, Australia.

Graham, Y., Baldwin, T., Moffat, A., and Zobel, J. (2014). Is machine translation getting better over time? In Wintner, S., Goldwater, S., and Riezler, S., editors, *Proceedings of the 14th Conference of the European Chapter of the Association for Computational Linguistics*, pages 443–451, Gothenburg, Sweden. Association for Computational Linguistics.

Halliday, M. (1973). *Explorations in the Functions of Language*. Arnold, London.

Halliday, M. and Hasan, R. (1989). *Language, Context and Text: Aspects of Language in a Social Semiotic Perspective*. Oxford University Press, Oxford.

Han, C. (2020). Translation quality assessment: A critical methodological review. *The Translator*, 26(3):257–273.

Hassan, H., Aue, A., Chen, C., Chowdhary, V., Clark, J., Federmann, C., Huang, X., Junczys-Dowmunt, M., Lewis, W., Li, M., Liu, S., Liu, T., Luo, R., Menezes, A., Qin, T., Seide, F., Tan, X., Tian, F., Wu, L., Wu, S., Xia, Y., Zhang, D., Zhang, Z., and Zhou, M. (2018).

Achieving human parity on automatic Chinese to English news translation. *CoRR*, abs/1803.05567.

Holmes, J. S. (1988). *Translated! Papers on Literary Translation and Translation Studies*. Rodopi, Amsterdam.

Honig, H. G. (1997). Positions, power and practice: Functionalist approaches and translation quality assessment. *Current Issues In Language and Society*, 4(1):6–34.

House, J. (1977). *A Model for Translation Quality Assessment*. Narr, Tübingen, 2nd edition.

House, J. (1997). *Translation Quality Assessment: A Model Revisited*. Tübinger Beiträge zur Linguistik. G. Narr.

House, J. (2001). Translation quality assessment: Linguistic description versus social evaluation. *Meta: Journal des traducteurs*, 46(2):243–257.

House, J. (2015). *Translation Quality Assessment: Past and Present*. Routledge.

ISO (2015). *International Standard ISO 17100:2015 Translation services - Requirements for translation services*. International Organization for Standardization.

ISO (2024). *International Standard ISO 5060:2024 Translation services - Evaluation of translation output - General guidance*. International Organization for Standardization.

Jakobsen, A. L. (2017). Translation process research. *The Handbook of Translation and Cognition*, page 19–49.

Jakobson, R. (1959). On linguistic aspects of translation. In *On translation*, pages 232–239. Harvard University Press.

Jones, D., Herzog, M., Ibrahim, H., Jairam, A., Shen, W., Gibson, E., and Emonts, M. (2007). ILR-based MT comprehension test with multi-level questions. In Sidner, C., Schultz, T., Stone, M., and Zhai, C., editors, *Human Language Technologies 2007: The Conference of the North American Chapter of the Association for Computational Linguistics; Companion Volume, Short Papers*, pages 77–80, Rochester, New York. Association for Computational Linguistics.

Knowles, R. (2021). On the stability of system rankings at WMT. In Barrault, L., Bojar, O., Bougares, F., Chatterjee, R., Costa-jussa, M. R., Federmann, C., Fishel, M., Fraser, A., Freitag, M., Graham, Y., Grundkiewicz, R., Guzman, P., Haddow, B., Huck, M., Yepes, A. J., Koehn, P., Kocmi, T., Martins, A., Morishita, M., and Monz, C., editors, *Proceedings of the Sixth Conference on Machine Translation*, pages 464–477, Online. Association for Computational Linguistics.

Koby, G. S., Fields, P., Hague, D., Lommel, A., and Melby, A. (2014). Defining translation quality. *Revista Tradumàtica: tecnologies de la traducció*, 12:404–412.

Kocmi, T., Avramidis, E., Bawden, R., Bojar, O., Dvorkovich, A., Federmann, C., Fishel, M., Freitag, M., Gowda, T., Grundkiewicz, R., Haddow, B., Koehn, P., Marie, B., Monz, C., Morishita, M., Murray, K., Nagata, M., Nakazawa, T., Popel, M., Popović, M., and Shmatova, M. (2023). Findings of the 2023 conference on machine translation (WMT23): LLMs are here but not quite there yet. In Koehn, P., Haddow, B., Kocmi, T., and Monz, C., editors, *Proceedings of the Eighth Conference on Machine Translation*, pages 1–42, Singapore. Association for Computational Linguistics.

Kocmi, T., Bawden, R., Bojar, O., Dvorkovich, A., Federmann, C., Fishel, M., Gowda, T., Graham, Y., Grundkiewicz, R., Haddow, B., Knowles, R., Koehn, P., Monz, C., Morishita, M., Nagata, M., Nakazawa, T., Novák, M., Popel, M., and Popović, M. (2022). Findings of the 2022 conference on machine translation (WMT22). In Koehn, P., Barrault, L., Bojar, O., Bougares, F., Chatterjee, R., Costa-jussà, M. R., Federmann, C., Fishel, M., Fraser, A., Freitag, M., Graham, Y., Grundkiewicz, R., Guzman, P., Haddow, B., Huck, M., Jimeno Yepes, A., Kocmi, T., Martins, A., Morishita, M., Monz, C., Nagata, M., Nakazawa, T., Negri, M., Névéol, A., Neves, M., Popel, M., Turchi, M., and Zampieri, M., editors, *Proceedings of the Seventh Conference on Machine Translation (WMT)*, pages 1–45, Abu Dhabi, United Arab Emirates (Hybrid). Association for Computational Linguistics.

Kocmi, T., Zouhar, V., Avramidis, E., Grundkiewicz, R., Karpinska, M., Popović, M., Sachan, M., and Shmatova, M. (2024). Error span annotation: A balanced approach for human evaluation of machine translation. *arXiv preprint arXiv:2406.11580*.

Koehn, P. and Monz, C. (2006). Manual and automatic evaluation of machine translation between European languages. In Koehn, P. and Monz, C., editors, *Proceedings on the Workshop on Statistical Machine*

Translation, pages 102–121, New York City. Association for Computational Linguistics.

Koller, W. (1979). *Einführung in die Übersetzungswissenschaft*. UTB 819. Quelle & Meyer.

Koller, W. (1989). Equivalence in translation theory. In Chesterman, A., editor, *Readings in translation theory*, pages 99–104. Oy Finn Lectura Ab, Helsinki.

Krüger, R. (2022). Some translation studies informed suggestions for further balancing methodologies for machine translation quality evaluation. *Translation Spaces*, 11(2):213–233.

Laoudi, J., Tate, C. R., and Voss, C. R. (2006). Task-based MT evaluation: From who/when/where extraction to event understanding. In Calzolari, N., Choukri, K., Gangemi, A., Maegaard, B., Mariani, J., Odijk, J., and Tapias, D., editors, *Proceedings of the Fifth International Conference on Language Resources and Evaluation (LREC'06)*, Genoa, Italy. European Language Resources Association (ELRA).

Läubli, S., Sennrich, R., and Volk, M. (2018). Has machine translation achieved human parity? A case for document-level evaluation. In Riloff, E., Chiang, D., Hockenmaier, J., and Tsujii, J., editors, *Proceedings of the 2018 Conference on Empirical Methods in Natural Language Processing*, pages 4791–4796, Brussels, Belgium. Association for Computational Linguistics.

Lauscher, S. (2000). Translation quality assessment: Where can theory and practice meet? *The Translator*, 6(2):149–168.

LDC (2002). Linguistic data annotation specification: Assessment of fluency and adequacy in Arabic-English and Chinese-English translations.

Licht, D., Gao, C., Lam, J., Guzman, F., Diab, M., and Koehn, P. (2022). Consistent human evaluation of machine translation across language pairs. In Duh, K. and Guzmán, F., editors, *Proceedings of the 15th biennial conference of the Association for Machine Translation in the Americas (Volume 1: Research Track)*, pages 309–321, Orlando, USA. Association for Machine Translation in the Americas.

Liebling, D., Heller, K., Robertson, S., and Deng, W. (2022). Opportunities for human-centered evaluation of machine translation systems. In Carpuat, M., de Marneffe, M.-C., and Meza Ruiz, I. V., editors, *Findings of the Association for Computational Linguistics: NAACL 2022*, pages 229–240, Seattle, United States. Association for Computational Linguistics.

Lim, Z. W., Vylomova, E., Cohn, T., and Kemp, C. (2024). Simpson's paradox and the accuracy-fluency tradeoff in translation. *arXiv preprint arXiv:2402.12690*.

Lo, C.-k. and Wu, D. (2011). MEANT: An inexpensive, high-accuracy, semi-automatic metric for evaluating translation utility based on semantic roles. In Lin, D., Matsumoto, Y., and Mihalcea, R., editors, *Proceedings of the 49th Annual Meeting of the Association for Computational Linguistics: Human Language Technologies*, pages 220–229, Portland, Oregon, USA. Association for Computational Linguistics.

Lo, C.-k. and Wu, D. (2014). On the reliability and inter-annotator agreement of human semantic MT evaluation via HMEANT. In Calzolari, N., Choukri, K., Declerck, T., Loftsson, H., Maegaard, B., Mariani, J., Moreno, A., Odijk, J., and Piperidis, S., editors, *Proceedings of the Ninth International Conference on Language Resources and Evaluation (LREC'14)*, pages 602–607, Reykjavik, Iceland. European Language Resources Association (ELRA).

Lommel, A., Uszkoreit, H., and Burchardt, A. (2014). Multidimensional quality metrics (MQM): A framework for declaring and describing translation quality metrics. *Tradumàtica*, 1(12):455–463.

Mahn, G. (1987). Foreign language proficiency criteria in translation. In Rose, M. G., editor, *Translation Excellence: Assessment, Achievement, Maintenance*, pages 44–45. SUNY, Binghamton.

Malmkjær, K. (1998). Linguistics in functionland and through the front door: A response to hans g. hönig. In Schäffner, C., editor, *Translation and Quality*, pages 70–74. Multilingual Matters, Clevedon.

Moghe, N., Sherborne, T., Steedman, M., and Birch, A. (2023). Extrinsic evaluation of machine translation metrics.

Moorkens, J., Castilho, S., Gaspari, F., and Doherty, S. (2018). *Translation Quality Assessment From Principles to Practice*. Springer.

Neves, M., Jimeno Yepes, A., Névéol, A., Bawden, R., Di Nunzio, G. M., Roller, R., Thomas, P., Vezzani, F., Vicente Navarro, M., Yeganova, L., Wiemann, D., and Grozea, C. (2023). Findings of the WMT 2023 biomedical translation shared task: Evaluation of ChatGPT 3.5 as a comparison system. In Koehn, P., Haddow, B., Kocmi, T., and Monz, C., editors, *Proceedings of the Eighth Conference on Machine Translation*, pages 43–54, Singapore. Association for Computational Linguistics.

Nida, E. (1964). *Towards a Science of Translating*. BRILL.

Nida, E. and Taber, C. (1969). *The Theory and Practice of Translation*. Helps for translators. E. J. Brill.

Nord, C. (1997a). Defining translation functions: The translation brief as a guideline for the trainee translator. *Ilha Do Desterro*, 33:39–54.

Nord, C. (1997b). *Translating as a Purposeful Activity: Functionalist Approaches Explained*. St. Jerome.

Papineni, K., Roukos, S., Ward, T., and Zhu, W.-J. (2002). Bleu: a method for automatic evaluation of machine translation. In Isabelle, P., Charniak, E., and Lin, D., editors, *Proceedings of the 40th Annual Meeting of the Association for Computational Linguistics*, pages 311–318, Philadelphia, Pennsylvania, USA. Association for Computational Linguistics.

Pym, A. (2019). Quality. In O'Hagan, M., editor, *The Routledge Handbook of Translation and Technology (1st ed.)*. Routledge.

Pym, A. (2023). *Exploring Translation Theories*. Routledge.

Saldanha, G. and O'Brien, S. (2014). Product-oriented research. In *Research Methodologies in Translation Studies*, pages 50–108. Routledge.

Snell-Hornby, M. (1992). The professional translator of tomorrow: Language specialist or all-round expert? In Dollerup, C. and Loddegaard, A., editors, *Teaching Translation and Interpreting: Training, Talent and Experience*, pages 9–22. John Benjamins, Amsterdam.

Snover, M., Dorr, B., Schwartz, R., Micciulla, L., and Makhoul, J. (2006). A study of translation edit rate with targeted human annotation. In *Proceedings of the 7th Conference of the Association for Machine Translation in the Americas: Technical Papers*, pages 223–231, Cambridge, Massachusetts, USA. Association for Machine Translation in the Americas.

Toral, A., Castilho, S., Hu, K., and Way, A. (2018). Attaining the unattainable? reassessing claims of human parity in neural machine translation. In Bojar, O., Chatterjee, R., Federmann, C., Fishel, M., Graham, Y., Haddow, B., Huck, M., Yepes, A. J., Koehn, P., Monz, C., Negri, M., Névéol, A., Neves, M., Post, M., Specia, L., Turchi, M., and Verspoor, K., editors, *Proceedings of the Third Conference on Machine Translation: Research Papers*, pages 113–123, Brussels, Belgium. Association for Computational Linguistics.

Vandepitte, S. (2017). Translation product quality: A conceptual analysis. In Svoboda, T., Biel, L., and Łoboda, K., editors, *Quality aspects in institutional translation*, pages 15–29. Language Science Press, Berlin.

Vermeer, H. J. (1978). Ein rahmen für eine allgemeine translationstheorie. *Lebende Sprachen*, 23:99–102.

Vermeer, H. J. (2021). Skopos and commission in translational action. In Chesterman, A., editor, *The Translation Studies Reader*. Routledge, 4th edition.

Vilar, D., Leusch, G., Ney, H., and Banchs, R. E. (2007). Human evaluation of machine translation through binary system comparisons. In Callison-Burch, C., Koehn, P., Fordyce, C. S., and Monz, C., editors, *Proceedings of the Second Workshop on Statistical Machine Translation*, pages 96–103, Prague, Czech Republic. Association for Computational Linguistics.

Vinay, J. and Darbelnet, J. (1958). *Stylistique comparée du français et de l'anglais: méthode de traduction*. Bibliothèque de stylistique comparée. Didier.

Williams, M. (2004). *Translation Quality Assessment: An Argumentation-Centred Approach*. University of Ottawa Press.

WMT (2024). Shared task: General machine translation. `https://www2.statmt.org/wmt24/translation-task.html`. Accessed: 2024-08-07.

Yang, J. and Lange, E. D. (1998). SYSTRAN on AltaVista. In Farwell, D., Gerber, L., and Hovy, E., editors, *Proceedings of the Third Conference of the Association for Machine Translation in the Americas: Tech-*

nical Papers, pages 275–285, Langhorne, PA, USA. Springer.

A Questions for DA Annotators in WMT

In the original work of Graham et al. (2013a), annotators were asked questions about fluency using the DA sliding scales. In the Mechanical Turk setup in Bojar et al. (2016, 2017, 2018); Barrault et al. (2019) annotators were asked: "Read the text below. How much do you agree with the following statement:" where the statement was "The black text adequately expresses the meaning of the gray text in English." (*English* was replaced with a different language where appropriate). The Appraise interface used the question "How accurately does the above candidate text convey the original semantics of the reference text? Slider ranges from "Not at all (left) to Perfectly (right)."—though in bilingual assessment, "reference" was replaced with "source" (Bojar et al., 2017, 2018). In Barrault et al. (2019) the Appraise setup asked annotators: "For the pair of sentences below: Read the text and state how much you agree that:" where the statement was "The black text adequately expresses the meaning of the gray text in German (deutsch)." (replaced with a different language where appropriate). Later evaluations with a different interface added clarifications about the location of the two texts (Barrault et al., 2020).

The most recent two WMT shared tasks have used an approach that they call DA+SQM; that interface uses a continuous slider to assign scores on a 7-point (0 to 6) scale, with the 0, 2, 4, and 6 tick marks attached to labels. These labels and their descriptions explicitly include both meaning and grammar, as we see in this example: "4: Most meaning preserved and few grammar mistakes: The translation retains most of the meaning of the source. It may have some grammar mistakes or minor contextual inconsistencies." (Kocmi et al., 2023). This decision to use DA+SQM and these particular labels was supported by "internal preliminary experiments" (Kocmi et al., 2022) that showed that it may produce more stable scores across annotators; the results and supporting data have not been released publicly.

B Translation Equivalence in TS

Table 1 shows different understandings of equivalence in TS, acknowledging that the target text (TT) can never be equivalent to the source text (ST) on all levels (Vandepitte, 2017, p. 151). Vinay and Darbelnet (1958, p.32) suggested that the stylistic impact in translation is critical. Jakobson (1959, p. 233) took a linguistic approach, discussing different types of translation (intralingual, interlingual, and inter-semiotic). Nida (1964); Nida and Taber (1969); de Waard and Nida (1986) drew on Bible Studies and distinguished between formal and functional equivalence, stressing the importance of message over form. Catford (1965, p.27) introduced the concept of "textual equivalent", which refers to a text or section of text in the TT that, in a specific situation, is deemed equivalent to a corresponding text or segment in the ST. This work underscores the challenges of achieving equivalence across languages and the critical role of context in defining linguistic meaning, distinguishing between "textual equivalence" and "formal correspondence" based on their respective roles in translation. House (1997) emphasized functional equivalence between the ST and TT. Koller (1979, 1989) identified five types of equivalence, ranging from denotative to pragmatic. Baker (1992), from a linguistic perspective, elaborated on text-level and pragmatic equivalence. Pym (2023, p. 10-12) framed equivalence as a relationship of 'equal value' between segments of the ST and TT from form to function. While languages and cultures may differ, translations can achieve equivalence by preserving some aspect of value, whether it be in terms of meaning, function, or effect. The work emphasized that equivalence involves "transformation", aiming to preserve or reproduce a certain value from the ST in the TT. This perspective emphasizes the translator's role in navigating cultural differences and making deliberate choices to ensure the translation fulfills its intended purpose, whether that be informing, persuading, or entertaining the target audience.

Exploring these perspectives provides a context for the evolution of TQA approaches. The discussions by Vinay and Darbelnet (1958), Jakobson (1959), Nida and Taber (1969), and others laid the groundwork for what was predominantly a qualitative assessment of translations, rooted in linguistic, functional, and stylistic parameters. This era's

Representative work	Key understandings of equivalence
Vinay and Darbelnet (1958)	Replicate the same message with different wording (p. 32); an emphasis on the stylistic impact in the target text (TT) (p. 256)
Jakobson (1959)	Three kinds of translation: intralingual, interlingual, and inter-semiotic, with interlingual translation as the focus in TS; there is no full equivalence between code-units; translation from one language into another substitutes messages in one language not for separate code-units but for entire messages in some other language (p. 233).
Nida (1964); Nida and Taber (1969); de Waard and Nida (1986)	Two basic types of equivalence: (1) formal equivalence (fidelity to the original text) and; (2) dynamic equivalence; a translation is to seek equivalence of the message rather than conserving the form of the utterance; meaning is given priority over structure; style, though secondary to content, must still be preserved (1986, p. 36)
Catford (1965)	"Translation is an operation performed on language: a process of substituting a text in one language for a text in another. Then, any theory of translation must draw upon a theory of language – a general linguistic theory." (p. 1) Textual equivalence is "any target language text or portion of text which is observed on a particular occasion to be equivalent of a given ST or portion of text" (p. 27) Formal correspondence is "any TL category (unit, class, structure) which can be said to occupy as nearly as possible the same place in the economy of the TT as the ST given category occupied in the ST" (p. 27)
House (1997)	An emphasis on functional equivalence between the ST and the TT.
Koller (1979, 1989)	Five different types of equivalence: denotative (extra-linguistic factors), connotative (verbalized through source text), text-normative (textual and linguistic norms), pragmatic (concerning the receiver of the target text) and formal (the formal-aesthetic qualities of the source text).
Baker (1992)	Word-level equivalence (p. 9-49); grammatical-level equivalence (p. 92-129); textual-level equivalence (cohesion and thematic structure) (p.131-228); pragmatic level equivalence (mainly with implications which refers to the implied not the literal meanings) (p. 230-271).
Pym (2023)	Transformation-based equivalence (p.12)

Table 1: A timeline of understanding "translation equivalence" in TS.

TQA was characterized by its reliance on human expertise, with scholars advocating for various frameworks to grapple with the intangible qualities of a "good translation". These early debates and theories remain influential, offering a point of departure for understanding how the advent of technology has reshaped the methodologies and tools of TQA.

C House's TQA Model (2015)

The House TQA model (House, 2015, p. 127) employs a register analysis derived from the framework in Halliday (1973) and Halliday and Hasan (1989), utilizing the categories of field, tenor, and mode. It includes six parameters:

- **Field**: This refers to the domain of knowledge or social practice that the text relates to and the activities that it refers to. It answers the question of "what is happening" or "what is being talked about." For example, a scientific report on climate change will have a different field than a personal letter, affecting the choice of technical versus everyday language.

- **Tenor**: This includes the participant relationships, the author's provenance, social relationships, social attitudes, and participation. It reflects the social roles and relationships between the participants (e.g., teacher-student, doctor-patient, friend-friend) involved in the communicative event, including the author, the reader, and the translator. Tenor influences aspects of language such as the level of formality, use of pronouns, and the choice of modal verbs expressing obligation, possibility, or permission, reflecting the nature of interpersonal interactions.

- **Mode**: Mode refers to the medium of the text, the channel of communication (spoken or written), and the complexity or simplicity of the language, as well as its connectivity. It refers to how the text is presented and how it establishes a connection with the reader.

- **Register**: This is a central concept that draws together the elements of field, tenor, and mode, to describe the language variety used for a particular purpose. For instance, an academic lecture employs specialized vocabulary and complex structures (field), within a formal relationship between lecturer and students (tenor), delivered through a monologic presentation (mode). Conversely, a casual conversation between friends features everyday topics (field), marked by an informal, equal-status interaction (tenor), in a spontaneous, spoken format (mode).

- **Genre**: Genre is understood in terms of socially ratified forms of texts, like a novel, a legal document, or a poem.

- **Corpus Studies**: This is not traditionally part of House's model but suggests a methodological approach to TQA through the use of corpora to analyze translations in a larger, more empirical context.

House's approach to TQA is functionalist and descriptive. A quality translation is functionally equivalent to the ST, meaning it should enable the reader to understand and do the same things as they would with the ST, taking into account the cultural context and the communicative situation of the TT. The emphasis of the model is on the equivalence of the communicative functions of the texts rather than a word-for-word correspondence.

Word-level Translation Quality Estimation Based on Optimal Transport

Yuto Kuroda[*] kuroda@ai.cs.ehime-u.ac.jp
Graduate School of Science and Engineering, Ehime University,
3 Bunkyo-cho, Matsuyama, Ehime, 790-8577, Japan

Atsushi Fujita atsushi.fujita@nict.go.jp
National Institute of Information and Communications Technology,
3-5 Hikaridai, Seika-cho, Soraku-gun, Kyoto, 619-0289, Japan

Tomoyuki Kajiwara kajiwara@cs.ehime-u.ac.jp
Graduate School of Science and Engineering, Ehime University,
3 Bunkyo-cho, Matsuyama, Ehime, 790-8577, Japan

Abstract

Word-level translation quality estimation (TQE) is the task of identifying erroneous words in a translation with respect to the source. State-of-the-art methods for TQE exploit large quantities of synthetic training data generated from bilingual parallel corpora, where pseudo-quality labels are determined by comparing two independent translations for the same source text, i.e., an output from a machine translation (MT) system and a reference translation in the parallel corpora. However, this process is sorely reliant on the surface forms of words, with acceptable synonyms and interchangeable word orderings regarded as erroneous. This can potentially mislead the pre-training of models. In this paper, we describe a method that integrates a degree of uncertainty in labeling the words in synthetic training data for TQE. To estimate the extent to which each word in the MT output is likely to be correct or erroneous with respect to the reference translation, we propose to use the concept of optimal transport (OT), which exploits contextual word embeddings. Empirical experiments using a public benchmarking dataset for word-level TQE demonstrate that pre-training TQE models with the pseudo-quality labels determined by OT produces better predictions of the word-level quality labels determined by manual post-editing than doing so with surface-based pseudo-quality labels.

1 Introduction

Translation quality estimation (TQE) (Blatz et al., 2004; Specia et al., 2018) is the task of predicting quality labels or scores for a given translation, typically generated by machine translation (MT) systems, with respect to the source text, without referring to a reference translations. Predictions can be made at different levels of granularity, such as sentence and word levels. Sentence-level quality labels help users determine whether to use an MT output as it is or after post-editing (PE). Word-level quality labels better guide post-editors in the translation production process (ISO/TC37, 2017), i.e., identifying words that require revision.

In this paper, we focus on word-level TQE. The data for training and evaluating word-level TQE models consist of tuples of a source text, an MT output, and quality labels for each word in the MT output. In the TQE shared tasks at the Workshop on Machine Translation (WMT) (Specia et al., 2020, 2021; Zerva et al., 2022), binary labels, i.e., {"OK," "BAD"}, are used as the quality labels. As illustrated in the top part of Figure 1, TQE data are pro-

[*]This work was done during an internship of the first author at National Institute of Information and Communications Technology.

duced through manual PE of MT outputs, where revisions indicate that the words in the MT output are erroneous. It is therefore straightforward to determine gold-standard labels using the Translation Edit Rate (TER) toolkit (Snover et al., 2006)[1] by identifying the minimum edit distance between two sequences of words relying on surface-level matching.

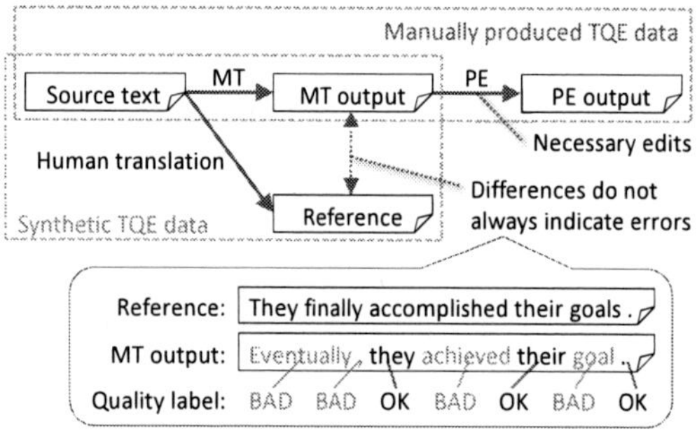

Figure 1: Framework for obtaining TQE data: (a) manual PE and (b) comparison of MT output with a reference translation independently produced by a human translator. An example for the latter exemplifies that the conventional TER-based method regards unessential differences as errors.

To improve the accuracy further, state-of-the-art methods for word-level TQE exploit large quantities of synthetic TQE data for pre-training (Liu et al., 2017; Lee, 2020; Tuan et al., 2021; Rubino et al., 2021; Yang et al., 2023). Figure 1 also shows the typical process of generating synthetic TQE data. First, the source side of a given bilingual parallel corpus is translated with an MT system, and then a pseudo-quality label for each word in the MT output is determined by comparing two independent translations for the same source text: the MT output and the target side of the parallel corpus, i.e., reference translation. Previous work (Liu et al., 2017; Lee, 2020; Tuan et al., 2021; Rubino et al., 2021) has used the TER toolkit for the comparison. However, surface-level differences between independent translations do not necessarily indicate errors. For instance, as shown in Figure 1, they can differ in the use of synonyms, interchangeable word orderings, and so forth, even if the MT output is error-free. Application of the TER toolkit to such pairs inevitably produces incorrect quality labels and consequently misleads the pre-training of TQE models.

In this paper, we describe a method that considers the degree of uncertainty in labeling words in synthetic training data for TQE. To estimate the extent in which each word in the MT output is likely to be correct or erroneous with respect to a reference translation, we propose to use the concept of optimal transport (OT). Given a pair of an MT output and a reference translation, our method first obtains contextual word embeddings. It then determines the optimal alignments between words in the MT output and the reference translation with their likelihood. Following Arase et al. (2023), we expect this approach to identify negligible semantic differences between synonymous expressions and corresponding position-free grammatical elements, and properly label them as "OK." Empirical experiments using a public benchmarking dataset for word-level TQE, i.e., MLQE-PE (Fomicheva et al., 2022), demonstrate that pre-training TQE models with the OT-based quality labels produces better predictions of the word-level quality labels determined by manual PE than models pre-trained on surface-based quality labels determined by TER.

2 Standard Framework

A word-level TQE model is trained on $D_{\text{QE}} = (S_k, T'_k, Y_k)_{k=1}^{N}$, i.e., a set of N triplets of a source text S_k, its machine-translated text T'_k, and a sequence of quality labels Y_k corresponding to the words in T'_k.

2.1 Data for Word-level TQE

Data for word-level TQE can be obtained through post-editing the machine-translated text T'_k into R_k, or annotating errors in T'_k (Freitag et al., 2021). For the former, we can automatically identify the words that have been dropped or revised by comparing T'_k and R_k, typically using the TER toolkit (Snover et al., 2006), and regard them as errors. The post-editing process requires workers who are highly competent in both the source and target languages, and is a laborious task. Therefore, only limited quantities of data are available for a limited number of translation directions and content domains. For instance, the MLQE-PE dataset (Fomicheva et al., 2022) covers only 11 translation directions (see Section 4.1 for details).

[1] http://www.cs.umd.edu/~snover/tercom/

Label type	Problem/Arch.	W_o	$\sigma(\cdot)$	Loss function
Hard	Classification	$\mathbb{R}^{d\times c}$	$\arg\max(softmax(\cdot))$	e.g., Cross-entropy
Soft	Regression	$\mathbb{R}^{d\times 1}$	$sigmoid(\cdot)$	e.g., Mean squared error

Table 1: Architectures and components of word-level TQE models: d indicates the dimension of the contextual word embeddings and c represents the number of possible hard labels ($c = 2$ for {"OK," "BAD"}).

To improve the accuracy, overcoming the data sparseness issue, researchers have exploited synthetic TQE data, which are readily available at a large scale (Liu et al., 2017; Lee, 2020; Tuan et al., 2021; Rubino et al., 2021; Yang et al., 2023). Synthetic TQE data can be generated from a bilingual parallel corpus, $D_{\text{para}} = (S_k, T_k)_{k=1}^N$. The parallel corpus can be filtered with some metrics as exemplified in Section 5.1. Typically, T'_k is first generated by translating each source text S_k with an MT model. Alternatively, T'_k can be obtained by rewriting each target text T_k with a masked language model (Tuan et al., 2021) or translating T_k into another language and translating it back into the target language, i.e., round-trip translation (Ding et al., 2021), which can also be applied to monolingual data of the target language. Then, the pseudo-quality label for each word in T'_k is determined by comparing T'_k with the corresponding human translation in the bilingual parallel corpus, i.e., T_k. Most previous work has employed the TER toolkit for this purpose; however, as exemplified in Figure 1, this results in inaccurate pseudo-quality labels, which would mislead the pre-training of TQE models.

2.2 Training Word-level TQE Models

To train a word-level TQE model, large quantities of synthetic data, such as those obtained by the procedure explained in Section 2.1, are used for pre-training (Liu et al., 2017; Lee, 2020; Tuan et al., 2021; Rubino et al., 2021; Yang et al., 2023). In contrast, small quantities of manually produced data are used for fine-tuning the model.

State-of-the-art approaches for word-level TQE rely on a pre-trained multilingual encoder, such as XLM-RoBERTa (Conneau et al., 2020) and InfoXLM (Chi et al., 2021), to obtain contextual embeddings for the words in the source text S and its machine-translated text T'. To exploit cross-lingual relationships between S and T', previous work (Zerva et al., 2021; Rei et al., 2022) jointly encodes the sequences of words in S and T' with a pre-trained multilingual encoder, and obtains $[h_1, \ldots, h_n]$, i.e., d-dimensional contextual embeddings, for the n words in T'. Then, the label for each word t'_i in T' is predicted as follows:

$$\hat{y}_i = \sigma(W_o L(h_i)), \tag{1}$$

where $L(\cdot)$ denotes additional task-specific transformation layers, W_o is a projection matrix, and $\sigma(\cdot)$ is a normalization function. There are two major options for the labels: (a) a hard label, such as {"OK," "BAD"}, or (b) the degree of badness (or goodness). W_o and $\sigma(\cdot)$ are implemented depending on this choice, as summarized in Table 1. Appropriate loss function is also set according to the label type.

3 Determining Pseudo-Quality Labels with Optimal Transport

This paper describes how better pseudo-quality labels can be assigned to the synthetic TQE data. We assume that the triples $D_{\text{syn}} = (S_k, T'_k, T_k)_{k=1}^N$ are generated from a bilingual parallel corpus, $D_{\text{para}} = (S_k, T_k)_{k=1}^N$, and determine the pseudo-quality label for each word in T'_k by comparing T'_k with the corresponding T_k, as in previous work (Section 2.1).

In the proposed approach, we apply optimal transport (OT), which identifies the optimal way of converting one distribution into another. The application of OT is inspired by its application to monolingual word alignment (Arase et al., 2023). Let $[t'_1, \ldots, t'_n]$ be a sequence of n words in a given machine-translated text T' and $[t_1, \ldots, t_m]$ be a sequence of m words in the corresponding reference translation T. The goal of OT is to identify a matrix $P \in \mathbb{R}_+^{n\times m}$ that best aligns the words in T' and T, where $P_{i,j}$ represents the likelihood of the alignment between t'_i and t_j. To solve our problem with OT, we define the following two concepts:

Mass of each word: this is a probability simplex, i.e., $\sum_l = \{v \in \mathbb{R}_+^l \mid \sum_{i=1}^l v_i = 1\}$. We denote the mass of n words in T' as $a \in \sum_n$ and that of m words in T as $b \in \sum_m$.

Cost for transportation: a cost function for each pair of words, $c(t'_i, t_j) \in \mathbb{R}_+$, can be defined as their dissimilarity. A matrix $C \in \mathbb{R}_+^{n \times m}$, where $C_{i,j} = c(t'_i, t_j)$, represents a summary of the cost for all pairs of words. The cost is typically computed on the basis of contextual word embeddings. In the process of obtaining the embeddings, such as by using a pre-trained multilingual encoder, we can also refer to the source text (see Appendix A), which is an advantage of this method over the TER toolkit.

A matrix $P \in \mathbb{R}_+^{n \times m}$ that minimizes the total cost for transportation is then identified as follows:

$$P = \underset{P' \in U(a,b)}{\arg\min} \sum_{i,j} C_{i,j} P'_{i,j}, \tag{2}$$

where $U(a, b)$ is a set of matrices ($\in \mathbb{R}_+^{n \times m}$) that satisfy a certain constraint. For instance, the following constraint preserves the mass of the source in the target:

$$U(a, b) = \{P \in \mathbb{R}_+^{n \times m} \mid P\mathbb{1}_n = a, P^\top \mathbb{1}_m = b\}, \tag{3}$$

where $\mathbb{1}_l$ is an l-dimensional vector in which all elements are 1. Equation (3) assumes that T' and T can be completely aligned, which conflicts with the motivation of word-level TQE, i.e., the necessity of spotting errors in T'. Therefore, we introduce a constraint that bounds the mass to be transported up to λ_m following the formulation of Partial OT (Figalli, 2010; Caffarelli and McCann, 2010):

$$U(a, b) = \{P \in \mathbb{R}_+^{n \times m} \mid P\mathbb{1}_n \leq a, P^\top \mathbb{1}_m \leq b, \mathbb{1}_n^\top P^\top \mathbb{1}_m = \lambda_m\}. \tag{4}$$

Having obtained the optimal transportation, P, which represents the most plausible alignments between T' and T, we determine the pseudo-quality label for each word t'_i in T'. We consider two variants: soft label ($y_i^{\text{soft}} \in [0, 1]$) and hard label ($y_i^{\text{hard}} \in$ {"OK," "BAD"}).

Soft label is a real number between 0.0 and 1.0, where 0.0 indicates that nothing is transported from the word, strongly suggesting that the word is erroneous, while 1.0 indicates that the word perfectly aligns with a word in T.

$$y_i^{\text{soft}} = \max(P_{i,0}, \ldots, P_{i,m}), \tag{5}$$

$$Y^{\text{soft}} = [y_1^{\text{soft}}, \ldots, y_n^{\text{soft}}]. \tag{6}$$

Hard label is a binary label, {"OK," "BAD"}, which is determined by thresholding the soft label. We introduce this merely for a comparison with the conventional binary labels determined by the TER toolkit.

$$y_i^{\text{hard}} = \begin{cases} \text{“OK”} & y_i^{\text{soft}} > \lambda \\ \text{“BAD”} & \text{otherwise} \end{cases} \tag{7}$$

$$Y^{\text{hard}} = [y_1^{\text{hard}}, \ldots, y_n^{\text{hard}}]. \tag{8}$$

Finally, we obtain two sets of synthetic data for word-level TQE: $D_{\text{QE}}^{\text{soft}} = (S_k, T'_k, Y_k^{\text{soft}})_{k=1}^N$ with the soft labels and $D_{\text{QE}}^{\text{hard}} = (S_k, T'_k, Y_k^{\text{hard}})_{k=1}^N$ with the hard labels.

4 Experiments

To confirm the effectiveness of the proposed method, we conducted experiments using a public dataset for word-level TQE, MLQE-PE (Fomicheva et al., 2022).[2] Following recent shared tasks on word-level TQE (Specia et al., 2020, 2021; Zerva et al., 2022) and Fomicheva et al. (2022), we evaluated TQE models using the Matthews correlation coefficient (MCC) (Matthews, 1975).

4.1 Word-level TQE Dataset

MLQE-PE (Fomicheva et al., 2022) contains test sets for 11 translation directions, each consisting of 1k triplets of source text, an MT output for it, and binary quality labels, i.e., {"OK", "BAD"}, determined by manual PE for the MT output and comparing the result with the raw MT output using the TER toolkit. We used Test20 (`data/post-editing/test`) and Test21 (`data/test21*`) in this repository. For seven[3] translation directions, the MT outputs have been generated by a unidirectional Transformer model (Vaswani et al., 2017) trained

[2] `https://github.com/sheffieldnlp/mlqe-pe`

[3] English-to-German (En→De), English-to-Chinese (En→Zh), Romanian-to-English (Ro→En), Estonian-to-English (Et→En), Nepali-to-English (Ne→En), Sinhalese-to-English (Si→En), and Russian-to-English (Ru→En).

with the fairseq toolkit (Ott et al., 2019);[4,5] training and development data consisting of 7k and 1k triplets, respectively, are also available (`data/post-editing/{train,dev}`). We used the training data for fine-tuning the TQE models and the development data for selecting the hyper-parameters and models, except for Ru→En. We regarded the remaining four translation directions,[6] for which the MT outputs have been generated by mBART50 (Tang et al., 2021), and Ru→En as zero-shot, since we used neither bilingual parallel data nor TQE data for them.[7]

4.2 Synthetic TQE Data

To generate synthetic TQE data, we used the bilingual parallel corpora[8] officially provided by the organizers of WMT21 TQE Task 2 and M2M-100 (Fan et al., 2021).[9] Table 2 summarizes their sizes and our groupings.

Group	Language pair	Bilingual	Synthetic
High	En–De	23,360,441	22,701,552
	En–Zh	20,305,268	16,201,271
Medium	Ro–En	3,901,501	3,027,243
	Et–En	877,769	855,680
Low	Ne–En	498,271	166,893
	Si–En	646,766	570,770

Table 2: Numbers of sentence pairs in the bilingual parallel corpora and the synthetic TQE data.

Before generating machine-translated texts, we fine-tuned M2M-100 for each translation direction on a sample from the bilingual parallel corpora: 1M, 200k, and 50k sentence pairs for the high-, medium-, and low-resource language pairs, respectively; in each pair, both source and target sides were composed of up to 128 sub-word tokens. Fine-tuning of M2M-100 on the sample was carried out with HuggingFace Transformers (Wolf et al., 2020), the AdamW optimizer (Loshchilov and Hutter, 2019) ($\beta_1 = 0.9$, $\beta_2 = 0.999$, $\epsilon = 1 \times 10^{-8}$), batches consisting of 16 sentence pairs, and a learning rate of 3×10^{-5}. This process was terminated after one epoch for each of the high- and medium-resource language pairs and after three epochs for each of the low-resource language pairs. After deduplication, we then decoded the source side of the entire parallel corpora, using beam search with a beam size of 5 and length penalty of 1.0. After decoding, we discarded MT outputs containing more than 128 sub-word tokens together with their corresponding parallel sentences. The numbers of retained sentence pairs are listed in the "Synthetic" column in Table 2.

To determine the pseudo-quality labels, we first obtained the word embeddings using INFOXLM$_{\text{Base}}$ (Chi et al., 2021),[10] inputting a concatenation of MT output T', source text S, and reference translation T in this order with an [SEP] token as the delimiter, and determining the embedding for each word by average pooling of its sub-word embeddings.[11] Then, we determined word alignment by solving OT using OTAlign (Arase et al., 2023);[12] more specifically, we used the entropy-regularized OT (Cuturi, 2013) formulated by Equation (9), which is superior to Equation (2) (Arase et al., 2023).

$$P = \mathop{\arg\min}_{P' \in U(a,b)} \sum_{i,j} C_{i,j} P'_{i,j} - \xi H(P'), \quad (9)$$

where $H(\cdot)$ is the entropy of a candidate matrix, and ξ is a weight for the regularizer, which we set to 0.1. We used a uniform distribution as the mass for each word, i.e., a and b, and took the cosine distance between contextual word embeddings[13] as the cost function, i.e., $C_{i,j}$. In contrast, we optimized the two hyper-parameters of OT for each translation direction through a grid search for λ_m in the range $[0.02, 1.00]$ with a step size of 0.02 and λ in the range $[0.01, 0.99]$ with a step size of 0.01, using the MLQE-PE development data and computing the MCC between the OT-based hard labels and the

[4] https://github.com/pytorch/fairseq

[5] https://github.com/facebookresearch/mlqe/tree/main/nmt_models

[6] English-to-Czech (En→Cs), English-to-Japanese (En→Ja), Khmer-to-English (Km→En), and Pashto-to-English (Ps→En).

[7] Bilingual parallel data for these language pairs could have been used for pre-training the MT models and multilingual encoders.

[8] https://www.statmt.org/wmt21/quality-estimation-task.html

[9] https://huggingface.co/facebook/m2m100_418M

[10] https://huggingface.co/microsoft/infoxlm-base

[11] Some decisions were made through a preliminary experiment. See Appendix A for details.

[12] https://github.com/yukiar/OTAlign

[13] $1 - \cos(h'_i, h_j)$, which has the range $[0.0, 2.0]$, where h'_i and h_j are word embeddings of t'_i and t_j, respectively.

gold-standard labels. Table 3 presents the values for λ_m and λ that achieved the highest MCC.

Translation direction	λ_m	λ	MCC	
			Dev	Syn
En→De	0.02	0.37	0.870	0.805
En→Zh	0.24	0.51	0.833	0.698
Ro→En	0.14	0.33	0.876	0.819
Et→En	0.02	0.35	0.804	0.776
Ne→En	0.14	0.37	0.680	0.777
Si→En	0.02	0.36	0.699	0.849

Table 3: Hyper-parameters that maximize MCC for the MLQE-PE development data (Dev), and MCC between OT-based and TER-based hard labels for the synthetic TQE data (Syn).

Finally, we determined the pseudo-quality labels with the optimal λ_m and λ as explained in Section 3. Table 3 also lists the MCCs between OT-based hard labels in our synthetic TQE data, derived with the optimized hyper-parameters, and TER-based pseudo-quality labels (Section 4.4).

4.3 TQE Model Training

We trained TQE models using OpenKiWi (Kepler et al., 2019) with the necessary modifications for training regression models and using multiple GPUs. As the backbone pre-trained multilingual encoder, we used $\text{INFOXLM}_{\text{Large}}$.[14] For each configuration, we trained a single multi-directional model to deal with all of the test sets, using the training data for six translation directions together: the synthetic TQE data for pre-training (Section 4.2) and manually labeled MLQE-PE training data (Section 4.1) for fine-tuning.

Pre-training was carried out for one epoch with the Adam optimizer ($\beta_1 = 0.9$, $\beta_2 = 0.999$, $\epsilon = 1 \times 10^{-8}$), batches consisting of $2{,}048$ sentence pairs, and a learning rate of 1×10^{-5}. To accommodate the imbalanced distribution of labels, we weighted the "BAD" labels as 3.0 times the "OK" labels when computing the cross-entropy loss for the classification models. When evaluating the regression models, we computed the MCC by thresholding the predicted value at 0.5.

We then fine-tuned the models on the MLQE-PE training data. When fine-tuning a regression model on the manually produced data with the TER-based hard labels, i.e., the MLQE-PE training data, the "BAD" and "OK" labels were casted as 0.0 and 1.0, respectively. We used Adam ($\beta_1 = 0.9$, $\beta_2 = 0.999$, $\epsilon = 1 \times 10^{-8}$), batches consisting of 64 sentence pairs, and a learning rate of 1×10^{-5}. During ten epochs, the model was saved every after 0.5 epochs, and the model that maximized the MCC for the MLQE-PE development data was selected from the 20 checkpoints. For the regression models, we also performed a grid search for the threshold in the range $[0.1, 0.9]$ with a step size of 0.1, using the MLQE-PE development data, and used the results to convert the predictions into binary labels.

4.4 Baseline Methods

We compared our method against the models trained on the synthetic data with pseudo-quality labels determined by the TER toolkit as in MLQE-PE.[15] To re-confirm the impact of pre-training on synthetic TQE data, we also trained classification and regression models only on the MLQE-PE training data.

4.5 Main Results

For each model, we report on the average MCC over three training runs with different random seeds. To confirm the statistical significance of the difference between two sets of predictions, we used paired bootstrap resampling (Koehn, 2004) with $30{,}000$ sub-samples ($10{,}000$ for each random seed) and a significance level of 0.05.

Tables 4 and 5 summarize the MCCs for the non-zero-shot translation directions in Test20 and Test21, respectively, where models #1 and #6 based on TER-based pseudo-quality labels and model #4 based only on manually created training data are the baselines. The upper block presents the results in the pseudo-supervised setting, i.e., models trained only on the synthetic TQE data. The model trained on OT-based soft labels (#3) outperformed those trained on either TER-based (#1) or OT-based hard labels (#2). The lower block shows the results of fine-tuned models, i.e., those directly trained or fine-tuned on the MLQE-PE training data. In this setting, the model pre-trained on OT-based soft la-

[14] `https://huggingface.co/microsoft/infoxlm-large`

[15] `https://github.com/deep-spin/qe-corpus-builder`

ID	Arch.	PT	FT	Test20					
				En→De	En→Zh	Ro→En	Et→En	Ne→En	Si→En
#1	Class.	TER-Hard	—	0.196	0.163	0.240	0.307	0.320	0.372
#2	Class.	OT-Hard	—	0.208	0.154	0.252	0.312	0.344	0.374
#3	Reg.	OT-Soft	—	**0.258**$^{(1)}$	**0.196**$^{(1)}$	**0.301**$^{(1)}$	**0.358**$^{(1)}$	**0.356**	**0.413**$^{(1)}$
#4	Class.	—	TER-Hard	0.449	0.380	0.623	0.552	0.511	0.552
#5	Reg.	—	TER-Hard	0.439	0.373	**0.650**$^{(4)}$	0.537	0.510	0.550
#6	Class.	TER-Hard	TER-Hard	0.485$^{(4)}$	0.398	0.620	**0.577**$^{(4)}$	0.521	**0.571**
#7	Class.	OT-Hard	TER-Hard	0.486$^{(4)}$	0.397	0.615	0.571$^{(4)}$	0.518	0.564
#8	Reg.	OT-Soft	TER-Hard	**0.491**$^{(4)}$	**0.409**$^{(4)}$	0.634	0.569	**0.530**$^{(4)}$	**0.571**

Table 4: MCCs for the non-zero-shot translation directions in Test20: "Arch." indicates the model architecture while "PT" and "FT" denote the type of labels used for pre-training and fine-tuning, respectively. **Bold** signifies the highest value in each block and translation direction. Values with superscripts (~~deleted~~) are statistically significantly higher (lower) than that for the system with the indicated IDs.

ID	Arch.	PT	FT	Test21					
				En→De	En→Zh	Ro→En	Et→En	Ne→En	Si→En
#1	Class.	TER-Hard	—	0.217	0.129	0.248	0.302	0.322	0.348
#2	Class.	OT-Hard	—	0.236$^{(1)}$	0.117	0.258	0.316	0.346	0.355
#3	Reg.	OT-Soft	—	**0.282**$^{(1)}$	**0.151**$^{(1)}$	**0.304**$^{(1)}$	**0.362**$^{(1)}$	**0.366**$^{(1)}$	**0.406**$^{(1)}$
#4	Class.	—	TER-Hard	0.434	0.320	0.636	0.580	0.540	0.558
#5	Reg.	—	TER-Hard	0.406	0.316	**0.657**$^{(4)}$	0.570	0.537	0.554
#6	Class.	TER-Hard	TER-Hard	**0.496**$^{(4)}$	0.329	0.626	**0.605**$^{(4)}$	0.551	**0.586**$^{(4)}$
#7	Class.	OT-Hard	TER-Hard	0.486$^{(4)}$	0.322	0.629	0.591(~~6~~)	0.544	0.571
#8	Reg.	OT-Soft	TER-Hard	0.485$^{(4)}$	**0.332**	0.643$^{(6)}$	0.596	**0.555**	0.582$^{(4)}$

Table 5: MCCs for the non-zero-shot translation directions in Test21.

bels (#8) achieved a higher MCC than the TER-based baseline (#6) for seven out of the 12 test sets. As in previous work (Liu et al., 2017; Lee, 2020; Tuan et al., 2021; Yang et al., 2023), pre-training on the synthetic TQE data brought a consistent improvement over the baseline (#4). However, only for Ro→En, the regression model with the same supervised signals (#5) significantly outperformed the classification-based baseline (#4) and even surpassed all models with pre-training. This suggests some peculiar characteristics of the MLQE-PE training data for this translation direction.

The MCCs for the zero-shot translation directions in Test20 and Test21 are presented in Table 6. There were similar trends as for the non-zero-shot translation directions. The synthetic TQE data with OT-based soft labels (#3) gave the best results in the pseudo-supervised setting. For the settings with fine-tuning, the MCCs for all translation directions benefited from supervised signals for other translation directions. They were further improved by pre-training, especially with OT-based soft labels (#8)

5 Analyses

We investigated the quality of the synthetic TQE data and the potential utility of OT-based labels for manually post-edited data. We used the non-zero-shot translation directions of Test20 because the post-edited texts for the MT outputs are available, enabling contrastive experiments.

5.1 Impact of Quality of Synthetic TQE Data

As mentioned in Section 2.1, bilingual parallel corpora used as the source of synthetic TQE data may include sentence pairs that are less likely to be translations. Pseudo-quality labels derived from seman-

ID	Arch.	PT	FT	Test20	Test21				
				Ru→En	En→Cs	En→Ja	Km→En	Ps→En	Ru→En
#1	Class.	TER-Hard	—	0.132	0.224	0.086	0.177	0.234	0.171
#2	Class.	OT-Hard	—	0.147	0.238	0.101(1)	0.201(1)	0.233	0.172
#3	Reg.	OT-Soft	—	**0.156**(1)	**0.265**(1)	**0.131**(1)	**0.311**(1)	**0.263**(1)	**0.173**
#4	Class.	—	TER-Hard	0.280	0.326	0.148	0.444	0.348	0.313
#5	Reg.	—	TER-Hard	0.286	0.301	0.154	0.451	0.362	0.308
#6	Class.	TER-Hard	TER-Hard	0.282	0.379(4)	0.170	0.469(4)	0.368	**0.340**
#7	Class.	OT-Hard	TER-Hard	**0.289**	**0.381**(4)	0.169	0.473(4)	0.374(4)	0.332
#8	Reg.	OT-Soft	TER-Hard	0.287	0.374(4)	**0.190**(4)	**0.480**(4)	**0.381**(4)	0.334

Table 6: MCCs for the zero-shot translation directions in Test20 and Test21.

tically isolated pairs of machine-translated text and reference translation could mislead the pre-training of models. To gauge the impact of the quality of parallel data, as well as the quality of synthetic TQE data, we conducted a corpus filtering experiment.

For each pair of sentences in the given bilingual parallel corpora, we computed the cosine similarity between their corresponding sentence embeddings determined by LaBSE (Feng et al., 2022),[16] and then filtered out pairs for which the similarity was lower than a pre-determined threshold. Figure 2 depicts the percentages of retained sentence pairs, depending on the threshold. We found that the Ro–En parallel corpus contained lots of noise, with approximately 40% of sentence pairs having a similarity lower than 0.5.

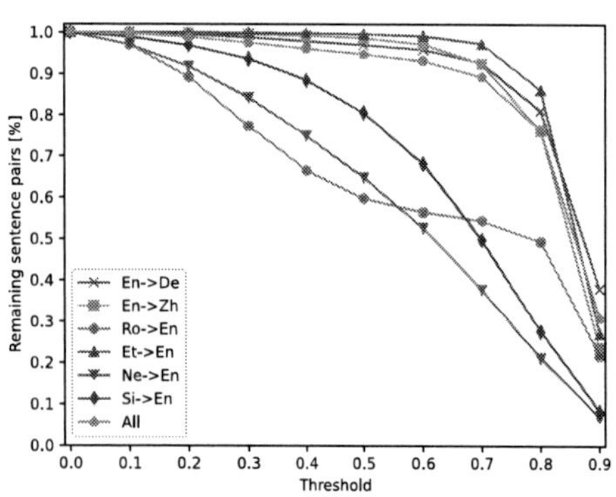

Figure 2: Percentages of remaining sentence pairs after the LaBSE-based filtering.

From the filtered bilingual parallel data, we generated synthetic TQE data and trained TQE models as described in Section 4.3. Finally, we evaluated the model accuracy in terms of MCC, using the non-zero-shot translation directions in Test20.

Table 7 presents the results. In the pseudo-supervised setting, a more aggressive filtering of the parallel corpus produced a higher MCC, suggesting that the quality of synthetic TQE data matters. Among the six translation directions, Ro→En benefited the most; this is to be expected from the statistics shown in Figure 2. In contrast, when fine-tuning was carried out after pre-training, the impact of pre-training, i.e., the gain over the directly supervised model (#5), was often diminished. This implies that the quantity of synthetic TQE data matters when the quality can be guaranteed by fine-tuning on manually produced training data. Besides a slight improvement with corpus filtering, pre-training still had a negative impact on Ro→En, i.e., models #8a and #8b underperformed model #5. In-depth analyses of the MLQE-PE training data of this translation direction is left for future work.

5.2 Fine-tuning on OT-based Labels

Figure 1 illustrated our motivation for obtaining pseudo-labels of better quality, especially for synthetic TQE data. In this section, we examine whether OT also brings some advantages for the authentic data derived through manual PE.

To this end, we first determined the quality labels for the MLQE-PE training data in the same manner as for the synthetic TQE data (Section 4.2). We then fine-tuned the pre-trained models (#2 and

[16] `https://huggingface.co/sentence-transformers/LaBSE`

ID	Arch.	Synthetic Data			FT	Test20					
		Label	Th	Size		En→De	En→Zh	Ro→En	Et→En	Ne→En	Si→En
#3	Reg.	OT-Soft	—	43.5M	—	0.258	0.196	0.301	0.358	0.356	0.413
#3a	Reg.	OT-Soft	0.5	41.2M	—	0.298$^{(3)}$	0.199	0.426$^{(3)}$	0.351	0.379$^{(3)}$	0.414
#3b	Reg.	OT-Soft	0.7	38.8M	—	0.305$^{(3)}$	0.205	0.448$^{(3)}$	0.363	**0.384**$^{(3)}$	**0.425**
#3c	Reg.	OT-Soft	0.9	13.4M	—	**0.316**$^{(3)}$	**0.241**$^{(3)}$	**0.489**$^{(3)}$	**0.392**$^{(3)}$	0.368	0.410
#8	Reg.	OT-Soft	—	43.5M	TER-Hard	**0.491**	0.409	0.634	0.569	**0.530**	**0.571**
#8a	Reg.	OT-Soft	0.5	41.2M	TER-Hard	0.488	0.407	**0.641**	0.571	0.527	**0.571**
#8b	Reg.	OT-Soft	0.7	38.8M	TER-Hard	0.489	**0.410**	**0.641**	**0.573**	0.527	0.568
#8c	Reg.	OT-Soft	0.9	13.4M	TER-Hard	0.484	0.401	0.637	0.565	0.519	0.555
#5	Reg.	—	—	—	TER-Hard	0.439	0.373	0.650	0.537	0.510	0.550

Table 7: MCCs for the non-zero-shot translation directions in Test20 with several threshold values ("Th") for the similarity of parallel sentences: "Size" denotes the number of sentence pairs having a similarity higher than or equal to the threshold.

ID	Arch.	PT	FT	Test20					
				En→De	En→Zh	Ro→En	Et→En	Ne→En	Si→En
#4	Class.	—	TER-Hard	**0.449**	**0.380**	0.623	**0.552**	**0.511**	**0.552**
#5	Reg.	—	TER-Hard	0.439	0.373	**0.650**$^{(4)}$	0.537	0.510	0.550
#4'	Class.	—	OT-Hard	0.431	0.334$^{(4)}$	0.609	0.514$^{(4)}$	0.462$^{(4)}$	0.506$^{(4)}$
#5'	Reg.	—	OT-Soft	0.413$^{(4)}$	0.326$^{(4)}$	0.626	0.484$^{(4)}$	0.443$^{(4)}$	0.482$^{(4)}$
#6	Class.	TER-Hard	TER-Hard	0.485$^{(4)}$	0.398	0.620	**0.577**$^{(4)}$	0.521	**0.571**
#7	Class.	OT Hard	TER-Hard	0.486$^{(4)}$	0.397	0.615	0.571$^{(4)}$	0.518	0.564
#8	Reg.	OT-Soft	TER-Hard	**0.491**$^{(4)}$	**0.409**$^{(4)}$	**0.634**	0.569	**0.530**$^{(4)}$	**0.571**
#7'	Class.	OT-Hard	OT-Hard	0.464	0.350$^{(4,6)}$	0.589$^{(4,6)}$	0.523$^{(4,6)}$	0.467$^{(4,6)}$	0.508$^{(4,6)}$
#8'	Reg.	OT-Soft	OT-Soft	0.444$^{(6)}$	0.344$^{(4,6)}$	0.633	0.503$^{(4,6)}$	0.453$^{(4,6)}$	0.491$^{(4,6)}$

Table 8: MCCs with TER-based hard labels for the non-zero-shot translation directions in Test20.

#3) using these labels, as described in Section 4.3, and directly trained the models on them, as described in Section 4.4.

Table 8 presents the results for Test20. Irrespective of whether the pre-training was carried out, the models trained or fine-tuned on the OT-based pseudo-quality labels (#4' to #8') resulted in lower MCCs than the corresponding models trained on TER-based hard labels (#4 to #8). We consider this result to be natural because the gold-standard labels have been determined by the TER toolkit.

5.3 Predicting OT-based Labels

We also evaluated the predicted results with respect to the OT-based labels for Test20, with the labels determined by OT in the same manner as for the synthetic TQE data (Section 4.2).

The MCCs with OT-based hard labels are summarized in Table 9. Compared with those in Table 8, the MCCs of the TER-based models (#4 to #8) were lower, except for the pseudo-supervised models (#4 and #5) for Et→En, while the MCCs of the OT-based models (#4' to #8') were higher. For all translation directions, except for En→De, the models trained or fine-tuned on OT-based labels scored significantly higher MCCs than those based on TER-based labels. This also revealed that pre-training has little gain for all translation directions, implying that the distributions of OT-based labels for the synthetic TQE data and PE-derived data (see Figure 1) are similar.

We also evaluated the accuracy of the regression models against OT-based soft labels with Pearson's product-moment correlation coefficient (Pear-

ID	Arch.	PT	FT	Test20					
				En→De	En→Zh	Ro→En	Et→En	Ne→En	Si→En
#4	Class.	—	TER-Hard	0.437	0.344	0.589	0.555	0.497	0.521
#5	Reg.	—	TER-Hard	0.431	0.334	0.622$^{(4)}$	0.545	0.503	0.519
#4'	Class.	—	OT-Hard	**0.446**	**0.384**$^{(4)}$	0.647$^{(4)}$	**0.600**$^{(4)}$	**0.599**$^{(4)}$	**0.637**$^{(4)}$
#5'	Reg.	—	OT-Soft	0.430	0.376$^{(4)}$	**0.672**$^{(4)}$	0.577$^{(4)}$	0.587$^{(4)}$	0.623$^{(4)}$
#6	Class.	TER-Hard	TER-Hard	0.454	0.356	0.575	0.562	0.493	0.518
#7	Class.	OT-Hard	TER-Hard	0.472$^{(4)}$	0.367	0.585	0.564	0.501	0.526
#8	Reg.	OT-Soft	TER-Hard	**0.488**$^{(4,6)}$	0.381$^{(4,6)}$	0.603$^{(6)}$	0.565	0.516	0.533
#7'	Class.	OT-Hard	OT-Hard	0.483$^{(4,6)}$	**0.406**$^{(4,6)}$	0.629$^{(4,6)}$	**0.610**$^{(4,6)}$	**0.608**$^{(4,6)}$	**0.643**$^{(4,6)}$
#8'	Reg.	OT-Soft	OT-Soft	0.468	0.401$^{(4,6)}$	**0.679**$^{(4,6)}$	0.594$^{(4,6)}$	0.601$^{(4,6)}$	0.631$^{(4,6)}$

Table 9: MCCs with OT-based hard labels for the non-zero-shot translation directions in Test20.

ID	Arch.	PT	FT	Test20					
				En→De	En→Zh	Ro→En	Et→En	Ne→En	Si→En
#5	Reg.	—	TER-Hard	0.505	0.389	0.697	0.622	0.625	0.651
#5'	Reg.	—	OT-Soft	**0.581**$^{(5)}$	**0.486**$^{(5)}$	**0.773**$^{(5)}$	**0.703**$^{(5)}$	**0.714**$^{(5)}$	**0.751**$^{(5)}$
#8	Reg.	OT-Soft	TER-Hard	0.558	0.444	0.675	0.653	0.647	0.666
#8'	Reg.	OT-Soft	OT-Soft	**0.637**$^{(8)}$	**0.540**$^{(8)}$	**0.779**$^{(8)}$	**0.734**$^{(8)}$	**0.740**$^{(8)}$	**0.766**$^{(8)}$

Table 10: Pearson's r with OT-based soft labels for the non-zero-shot translation directions in Test20.

son's r), performing a statistical significance testing in the same manner as for the MCCs. Table 10 demonstrates that training or fine-tuning on OT-based labels leads to higher correlation. Unlike the results for predicting hard labels, pre-training consistently improved the correlation, irrespective of the types of labels used for fine-tuning, with the exception of "TER-Hard" for Ro→En.

These results confirm that the labels for fine-tuning should be consistent with those to be predicted, as discussed by Yang et al. (2023).

6 Conclusion

This paper has described the application of optimal transport (OT) to determine pseudo-quality labels in synthetic data for word-level TQE. Through experiments, we confirmed that OT-based labels better guide pre-training on large quantities of synthetic TQE data and result in higher accuracy in word-level TQE tasks, as measured by MCC. Our method achieved consistently better results for pseudo-supervised settings and in zero-shot translation directions, encouraging future applications to less-studied translation directions.

In future work, we plan to investigate better and finer-grained specifications of the hyper-parameters for OT. While we determined a single value of λ_m, the upper bound of the mass to be transported, for each translation direction, we consider it should be possible to approximate this value for each sentence pair. We have only evaluated our method for predicting target labels; doing so for source labels is another avenue for extension (Appendix B).

Acknowledgments

We would like to thank the anonymous reviewers, including those for past submissions, for their insightful comments and suggestions on earlier versions of this paper. This work was partly supported by JSPS KAKENHI Grant-in-Aid for Scientific Research (S) 19H05660 and a commissioned research (No. 22501) by National Institute of Information and Communications Technology (NICT), Japan.

References

Arase, Y., Bao, H., and Yokoi, S. (2023). Unbalanced Optimal Transport for Unbalanced Word Alignment. In

Proceedings of the 61st Annual Meeting of the Association for Computational Linguistics (Volume 1: Long Papers), pages 3966–3986.

Blatz, J., Fitzgerald, E., Foster, G., Gandrabur, S., Goutte, C., Kulesza, A., Sanchis, A., and Ueffing, N. (2004). Confidence Estimation for Machine Translation. In *Proceedings of the 20th International Conference on Computational Linguistics*, pages 315–321.

Caffarelli, L. A. and McCann, R. J. (2010). Free Boundaries in Optimal Transport and Monge-Ampère Obstacle Problems. *Annals of Mathematics*, 171(2):673–730.

Chi, Z., Dong, L., Wei, F., Yang, N., Singhal, S., Wang, W., Song, X., Mao, X.-L., Huang, H., and Zhou, M. (2021). InfoXLM: An Information-Theoretic Framework for Cross-Lingual Language Model Pre-Training. In *Proceedings of the 2021 Conference of the North American Chapter of the Association for Computational Linguistics: Human Language Technologies*, pages 3576–3588.

Conneau, A., Khandelwal, K., Goyal, N., Chaudhary, V., Wenzek, G., Guzmán, F., Grave, E., Ott, M., Zettlemoyer, L., and Stoyanov, V. (2020). Unsupervised Cross-lingual Representation Learning at Scale. In *Proceedings of the 58th Annual Meeting of the Association for Computational Linguistics*, pages 8440–8451.

Cuturi, M. (2013). Sinkhorn Distances: Lightspeed Computation of Optimal Transport. In *Proceedings of the 26th Conference on Neural Information Processing Systems*, pages 2292–2300.

Ding, S., Junczys-Dowmunt, M., Post, M., and Koehn, P. (2021). Levenshtein training for word-level quality estimation. In Moens, M.-F., Huang, X., Specia, L., and Yih, S. W.-t., editors, *Proceedings of the 2021 Conference on Empirical Methods in Natural Language Processing*, pages 6724–6733.

Fan, A., Bhosale, S., Schwenk, H., Ma, Z., El-Kishky, A., Goyal, S., Baines, M., Celebi, O., Wenzek, G., Chaudhary, V., Goyal, N., Birch, T., Liptchinsky, V., Edunov, S., Auli, M., and Joulin, A. (2021). Beyond English-Centric Multilingual Machine Translation. *Journal of Machine Learning Research*, 22(107):1–48.

Feng, F., Yang, Y., Cer, D., Arivazhagan, N., and Wang, W. (2022). Language-agnostic BERT Sentence Embedding. In *Proceedings of the 60th Annual Meeting of the Association for Computational Linguistics*, pages 878–891.

Figalli, A. (2010). The Optimal Partial Transport Problem. *Archive for Rational Mechanics and Analysis*, 195:533–560.

Fomicheva, M., Sun, S., Fonseca, E., Zerva, C., Blain, F., Chaudhary, V., Guzmán, F., Lopatina, N., Specia, L., and Martins, A. F. T. (2022). MLQE-PE: A Multilingual Quality Estimation and Post-Editing Dataset. In *Proceedings of the Thirteenth Language Resources and Evaluation Conference*, pages 4963–4974.

Freitag, M., Foster, G., Grangier, D., Ratnakar, V., Tan, Q., and Macherey, W. (2021). Experts, Errors, and Context: A Large-Scale Study of Human Evaluation for Machine Translation. *Transactions of the Association for Computational Linguistics*, 9:1460–1474.

Goyal, N., Du, J., Ott, M., Anantharaman, G., and Conneau, A. (2021). Larger-Scale Transformers for Multilingual Masked Language Modeling. In *Proceedings of the 6th Workshop on Representation Learning for NLP (RepL4NLP-2021)*, pages 29–33.

ISO/TC37 (2017). ISO 18587:2017 Translation Services: Post-editing of Machine Translation Output: Requirements.

ISO/TC37 (2024). ISO 5060:2024 Translation Services: Evaluation of Translation Output: General Guidance.

Kepler, F., Trénous, J., Treviso, M., Vera, M., and Martins, A. F. T. (2019). OpenKiwi: An Open Source Framework for Quality Estimation. In *Proceedings of the 57th Annual Meeting of the Association for Computational Linguistics: System Demonstrations*, pages 117–122.

Koehn, P. (2004). Statistical significance tests for machine translation evaluation. In *Proceedings of the 2004 Conference on Empirical Methods in Natural Language Processing*, pages 388–395, Barcelona, Spain.

Lee, D. (2020). Two-Phase Cross-Lingual Language Model Fine-Tuning for Machine Translation Quality Estimation. In *Proceedings of the Fifth Conference on Machine Translation*, pages 1024–1028.

Liu, L., Fujita, A., Utiyama, M., Finch, A., and Sumita, E. (2017). Translation Quality Estimation Using Only Bilingual Corpora. *IEEE/ACM Transactions on Audio Speech and Language Processing*, 25(9):1762–1772.

Loshchilov, I. and Hutter, F. (2019). Decoupled Weight Decay Regularization. In *Proceedings of the 7th International Conference on Learning Representations*.

Matthews, B. (1975). Comparison of the Predicted and Observed Secondary Structure of T4 Phage Lysozyme. *Biochimica et Biophysica Acta (BBA) - Protein Structure*, 405(2):442–451.

Ott, M., Edunov, S., Baevski, A., Fan, A., Gross, S., Ng, N., Grangier, D., and Auli, M. (2019). fairseq: A Fast, Extensible Toolkit for Sequence Modeling. In *Proceedings of the 2019 Conference of the North American Chapter of the Association for Computational Linguistics (Demonstrations)*, pages 48–53.

Rei, R., Treviso, M., Guerreiro, N. M., Zerva, C., Farinha, A. C., Maroti, C., C. de Souza, J. G., Glushkova, T., Alves, D., Coheur, L., Lavie, A., and Martins, A. F. T. (2022). CometKiwi: IST-Unbabel 2022 Submission for the Quality Estimation Shared Task. In *Proceedings of the Seventh Conference on Machine Translation*, pages 634–645.

Rubino, R., Fujita, A., and Marie, B. (2021). Error Identification for Machine Translation with Metric Embedding and Attention. In *Proceedings of the 2nd Workshop on Evaluation and Comparison of NLP Systems*, pages 146–156.

Snover, M., Dorr, B., Schwartz, R., Micciulla, L., and Makhoul, J. (2006). A Study of Translation Edit Rate with Targeted Human Annotation. In *Proceedings of the 7th Conference of the Association for Machine Translation in the Americas: Technical Papers*, pages 223–231.

Specia, L., Blain, F., Fomicheva, M., Fonseca, E., Chaudhary, V., Guzmán, F., and Martins, A. F. T. (2020). Findings of the WMT 2020 Shared Task on Quality Estimation. In *Proceedings of the Fifth Conference on Machine Translation*, pages 743–764.

Specia, L., Blain, F., Fomicheva, M., Zerva, C., Li, Z., Chaudhary, V., and Martins, A. F. T. (2021). Findings of the WMT 2021 Shared Task on Quality Estimation. In *Proceedings of the Sixth Conference on Machine Translation*, pages 684–725.

Specia, L., Scarton, C., and Paetzold, G. H. (2018). Quality Estimation for Machine Translation. *Synthesis Lectures on Human Language Technologies*, 11(1):1–162.

Tang, Y., Tran, C., Li, X., Chen, P.-J., Goyal, N., Chaudhary, V., Gu, J., and Fan, A. (2021). Multilingual Translation from Denoising Pre-Training. In *Findings of the Association for Computational Linguistics: ACL-IJCNLP 2021*, pages 3450–3466.

Tuan, Y.-L., El-Kishky, A., Renduchintala, A., Chaudhary, V., Guzmán, F., and Specia, L. (2021). Quality Estimation without Human-labeled Data. In *Proceedings of the 16th Conference of the European Chapter of the Association for Computational Linguistics: Main Volume*, pages 619–625.

Vaswani, A., Shazeer, N., Parmar, N., Uszkoreit, J., Jones, L., Gomez, A. N., Kaiser, u., and Polosukhin, I. (2017). Attention is All You Need. In *Proceedings of the 31st Conference on Neural Information Processing Systems*, pages 5998–6008.

Wolf, T., Debut, L., Sanh, V., Chaumond, J., Delangue, C., Moi, A., Cistac, P., Rault, T., Louf, R., Funtowicz, M., Davison, J., Shleifer, S., von Platen, P., Ma, C., Jernite, Y., Plu, J., Xu, C., Le Scao, T., Gugger, S., Drame, M., Lhoest, Q., and Rush, A. (2020). Transformers: State-of-the-Art Natural Language Processing. In *Proceedings of the 2020 Conference on Empirical Methods in Natural Language Processing: System Demonstrations*, pages 38–45.

Yang, Z., Meng, F., Yan, Y., and Zhou, J. (2023). Rethinking the Word-level Quality Estimation for Machine Translation from Human Judgement. In *Findings of the Association for Computational Linguistics: ACL 2023*, pages 2012–2025.

Zerva, C., Blain, F., Rei, R., Lertvittayakumjorn, P., C. de Souza, J. G., Eger, S., Kanojia, D., Alves, D., Orăsan, C., Fomicheva, M., Martins, A. F. T., and Specia, L. (2022). Findings of the WMT 2022 shared task on quality estimation. In *Proceedings of the Seventh Conference on Machine Translation*, pages 69–99.

Zerva, C., van Stigt, D., Rei, R., Farinha, A. C., Ramos, P., C. de Souza, J. G., Glushkova, T., Vera, M., Kepler, F., and Martins, A. F. T. (2021). IST-Unbabel 2021 Submission for the Quality Estimation Shared Task. In *Proceedings of the Sixth Conference on Machine Translation*, pages 961–972.

A Preliminary Investigation

In our preliminary experiment, we first selected a pre-trained multilingual encoder to obtain contextual word embeddings for OT, using the MLQE-PE development data and varying λ_m and λ in the same manner as described in Section 4.2. We also compared two encoding patterns. Table 11 summarizes the MCCs between OT-based hard labels and TER-based labels for the MLQE-PE development data. Among the four candidate encoders, INFOXLM$_{\text{Base}}$ achieved consistently high MCCs across all translation directions. Interestingly, "Large" models consistently underperformed their "Base" counterpart. We also confirmed that referring to the source text leads to higher MCCs in general.

Then, we investigated the ordering of the source text S, its MT output T', and its post-edited version R as the input for INFOXLM$_{\text{Base}}$, even though R must be replaced with an independently produced human reference when generating synthetic TQE data. Table 12 presents the results. Among the six permutations of these three elements, (S, T', R) resulted in the highest MCC in average, but other permutations also achieved comparable MCCs. Assuming that focusing on T' would be effective for synthetic data, we used (T', S, R) in our experiment. This experiment reconfirmed the usefulness of the source text S and revealed that determining pseudo-labels using only the source text and MT output, i.e., (S, T'), is infeasible.

Figure 3 visualizes the sensitivity of the two hyper-parameters λ_m and λ with INFOXLM$_{\text{Base}}$ and the (T', S, R) layout for its input.

Figure 4 depicts that the soft labels determined by OT are highly correlated with the TER-based binary labels. Nevertheless, we consider the continuity of the labels and some discrepancies to improve the prediction; discrepancies include high values with "BAD" label, such as those illustrated in Figure 1, and potentially low values with "OK" label for identical but unrelated word correspondences, such as articles for different nominal elements.

B Label Types to Predict

In the MLQE-PE dataset, word-level quality labels are assigned to both the words and gaps between each pair of adjacent words. The former, the so-called target label, indicates the quality of each word in the MT output, where "BAD" indicates that the word needs to be deleted or substituted with another one. On the other hand, the latter, the so-called gap label, represents whether some words must be inserted in the gap between the adjacent words ("BAD") or not ("OK").

We consider the task of predicting gap labels itself is arguable, because the correct position of a missing word is not necessarily unique: while the positions of missing articles are deterministic, there are multiple possible solutions for inserting untranslated words and phrases. Please refer to ISO/TC37 (2024) and the MQM-based TQE task tackled at WMT since 2022 (Zerva et al., 2022) for further discussion of the inutility of gap labels for translations in the translation production workflow.

C Computation Time

Table 13 summarizes the computation time in GPU hours for each process.

D Limitations

Our experiment covered only 11 translation directions, and our results do not guarantee the same conclusions on other translation directions. As demonstrated by our experiments, the accuracy can be substantially different even for the same translation direction (see Tables 4 and 5). This implies that the difficulty of the task depends on the characteristics of the test data, the MT systems used for generating MT outputs, and human annotators recruited for manual PE.

All experiments were carried out with up to eight NVIDIA Tesla V100 GPUs. If we had a more powerful environment, higher accuracy could be achieved, for instance, by employing larger pre-trained multilingual encoders, such as XLM-RoBERTa$_{\text{XL}}$ and XLM-RoBERTa$_{\text{XXL}}$ (Goyal et al., 2021), larger batch sizes, longer training, and ensembling multiple models.

E Ethics Statement

As shown in our experiments, the predicted labels do not perfectly correlate with the gold-standard labels obtained through manual PE. Therefore, such predicted labels could mislead potential users. This is not specific to our work, but common in the TQE task.

Backbone encoder	Input	En→De	En→Zh	Ro→En	Et→En	Ne→En	Si→En
XLM-RoBERTa$_{\text{Base}}$	(T', R)	0.855	0.802	0.864	0.796	0.671	0.685
XLM-RoBERTa$_{\text{Base}}$	(T', S, R)	0.854	0.771	**0.881**	<u>0.801</u>	**0.687**	<u>0.693</u>
XLM-RoBERTa$_{\text{Large}}$	(T', R)	0.650	0.682	0.655	0.639	0.562	0.579
XLM-RoBERTa$_{\text{Large}}$	(T', S, R)	0.669	0.700	0.702	0.665	0.606	0.610
INFOXLM$_{\text{Base}}$	(T', R)	<u>0.865</u>	<u>0.829</u>	0.869	0.796	0.677	0.689
INFOXLM$_{\text{Base}}$	(T', S, R)	**0.870**	**0.833**	<u>0.876</u>	**0.804**	<u>0.680</u>	**0.699**
INFOXLM$_{\text{Large}}$	(T', R)	0.713	0.710	0.743	0.704	0.628	0.640
INFOXLM$_{\text{Large}}$	(T', S, R)	0.752	0.760	0.772	0.714	0.645	0.654

Table 11: MCCs between OT-based hard labels and TER-based labels for the MLQE-PE development data with different pre-trained multilingual encoders: S, T', and R denote the source text, its MT output, and its post-edited version, respectively. **Bold** and <u>underline</u> indicate the highest and second-highest values, respectively.

Backbone encoder	Input	En→De	En→Zh	Ro→En	Et→En	Ne→En	Si→En
INFOXLM$_{\text{Base}}$	(S, T')	0.052	0.048	0.167	0.042	0.032	0.077
	(T', R)	0.865	0.829	0.869	0.796	0.677	0.689
	(R, T')	0.862	0.826	0.868	0.796	0.680	0.688
	(S, T', R)	0.866	<u>0.838</u>	0.873	<u>0.808</u>	**0.686**	**0.705**
	(S, R, T')	0.866	0.838	<u>0.875</u>	0.805	<u>0.684</u>	<u>0.702</u>
	(T', S, R)	**0.870**	0.833	**0.876**	0.804	0.680	0.699
	(R, S, T')	0.867	0.835	0.874	0.802	0.680	0.697
	(T', R, S)	0.865	**0.839**	0.875	**0.811**	0.679	0.699
	(R, T', S)	<u>0.869</u>	0.835	0.871	0.805	0.682	0.697

Table 12: MCCs for the MLQE-PE development data with different orderings of S, T', and R.

Step	En→De	En→Zh	Ro→En	Et→En	Ne→En	Si→En
Generating synthetic TQE data						
Fine-tuning M2M-100	9	10	2	2	2	2
Translation with M2M-100	963	856	173	31	6	7
OT-based labeling	103	80	15	4	1	2
TQE model training						
Pre-training with TER-based hard labels	372					
Pre-training with OT-based hard labels	372					
Pre-training with OT-based soft labels	366					
Fine-tuning a classification model	5					
Fine-tuning a regression model	5					
Direct training a classification model	5					
Direct training a regression model	5					

Table 13: GPU hours spent for each phase of TQE model training.

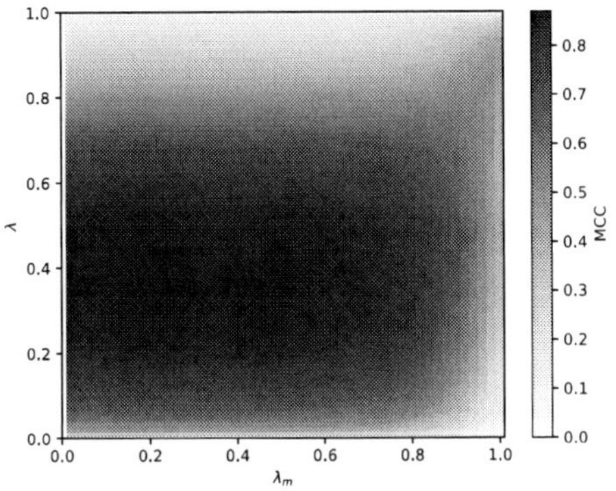

(a) En→De

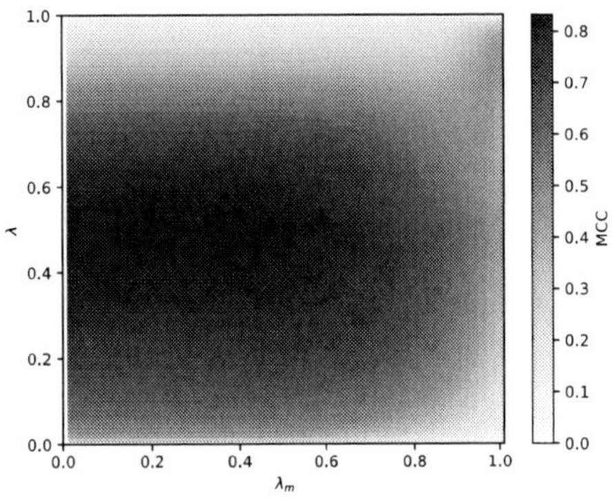

(b) En→Zh

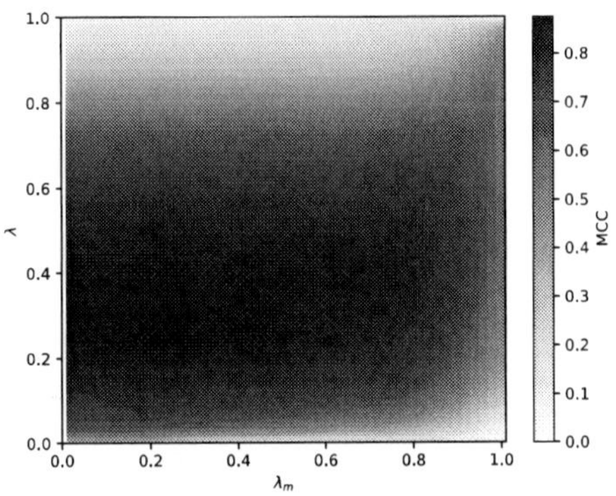

(c) Ro→En

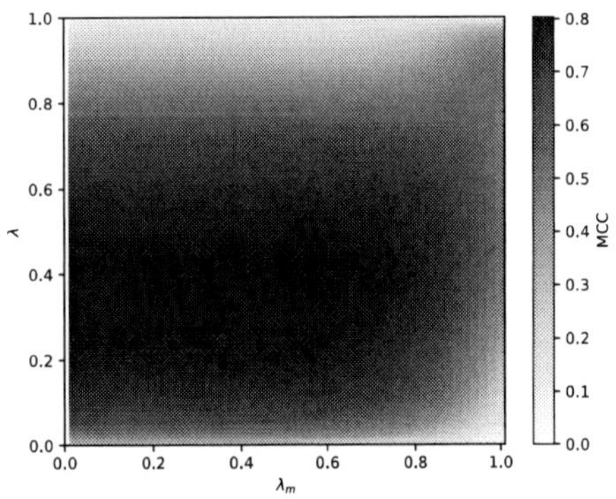

(d) Et→En

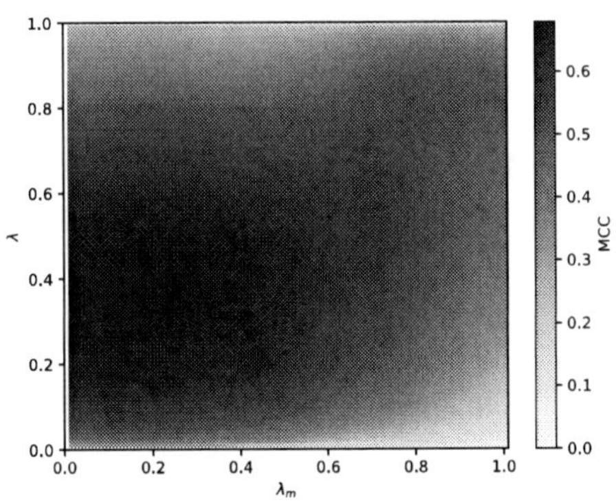

(e) Ne→En

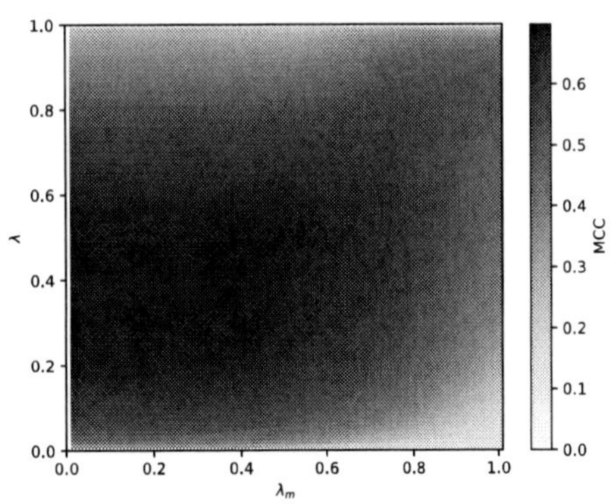

(f) Si→En

Figure 3: MCC for the MLQE-PE development data with different values for λ_m and λ.

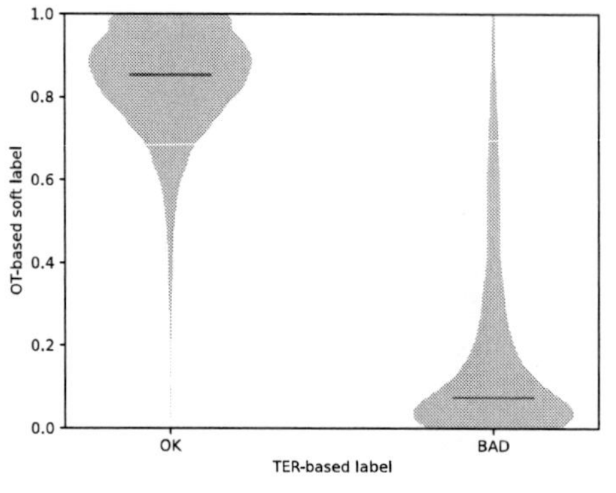

(a) En→De

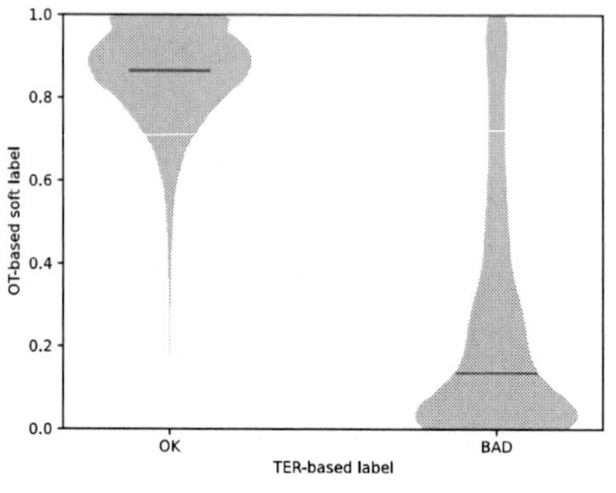

(b) En→Zh

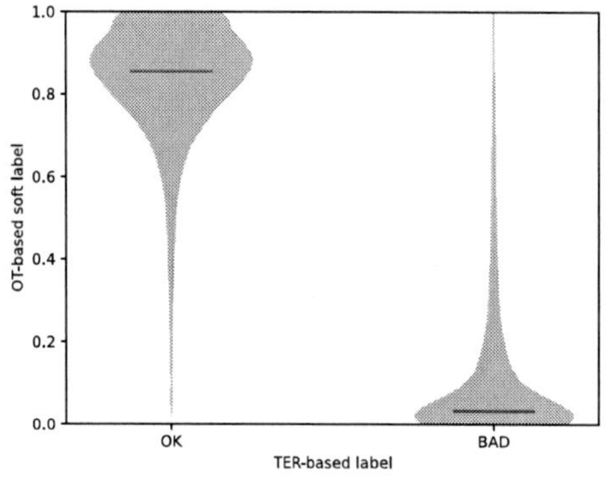

(c) Ro→En

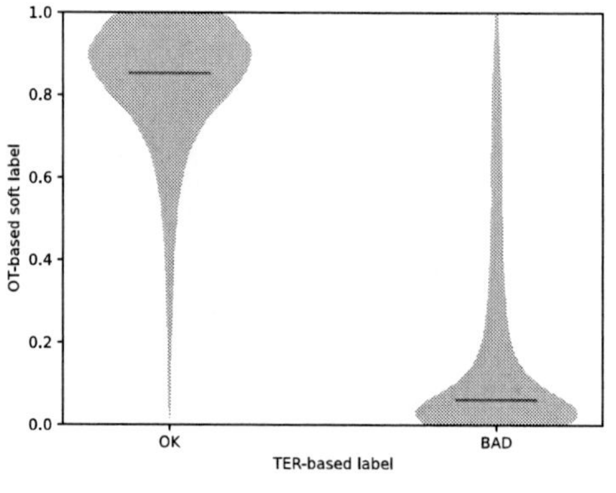

(d) Et→En

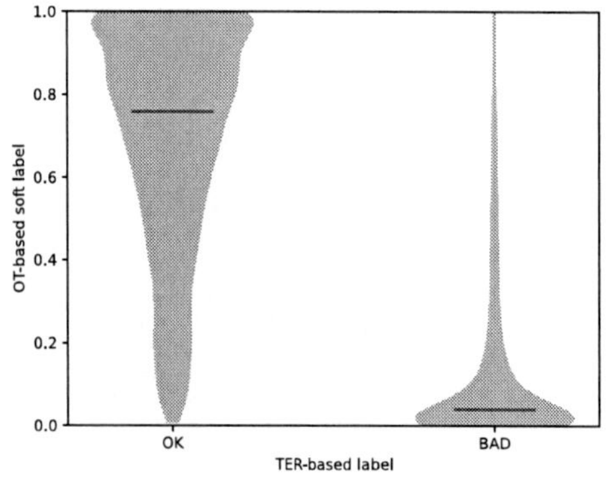

(e) Ne→En

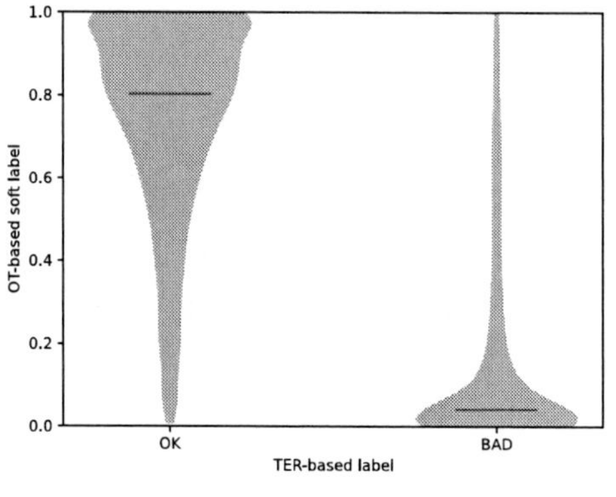

(f) Si→En

Figure 4: Distribution of OT-based soft labels for each of the {"OK," "BAD"} labels in the MLQE-PE development data, determined by the optimal λ_m in Table 3: the dark bar indicates the median.

Improving Rare Word Translation With Dictionaries and Attention Masking

Kenneth J. Sible ksible@nd.edu
David Chiang dchiang@nd.edu
Department of Computer Science and Engineering, University of Notre Dame, Notre Dame, 46556, United States

Abstract

In machine translation, rare words continue to be a problem for the dominant encoder-decoder architecture, especially in low-resource and out-of-domain translation settings. Human translators solve this problem with monolingual or bilingual dictionaries. In this paper, we propose appending definitions from a bilingual dictionary to source sentences and using *attention masking* to link together rare words with their definitions. We find that including definitions for rare words improves performance by up to 1.0 BLEU and 1.6 MacroF1.

1 Introduction

The current state-of-the-art for machine translation (MT) is still the transformer encoder-decoder architecture (Kocmi et al., 2023). While large language models such as LLaMA and GPT-4 have achieved great success on various NLP tasks, they still fall behind dedicated encoder-decoders for MT (Xu et al., 2024). A major drawback of encoder-decoder models, however, is that they continue to struggle with rare word translation (Minh-Cong et al., 2022).

Dictionaries, both monolingual and bilingual, are an indispensable resource for human translators, and in pre-neural statistical MT systems, it was common to use bilingual dictionaries to improve translation of rare words (Tan et al., 2015). However, the use of dictionaries in neural MT is not straightforward, as there is a strong dependence on the surrounding context and word frequency in the training data (Wu et al., 2021). In this paper, we explore a new approach for incorporating dictionaries into neural MT systems. We hypothesize that dictionaries could be useful both for low-resource translation, where the target language has limited training data, and out-of-domain translation, where the testing domain differs significantly from the training domain(s). In addition, dictionaries could facilitate continual learning by enabling zero-shot adaptation of MT systems.

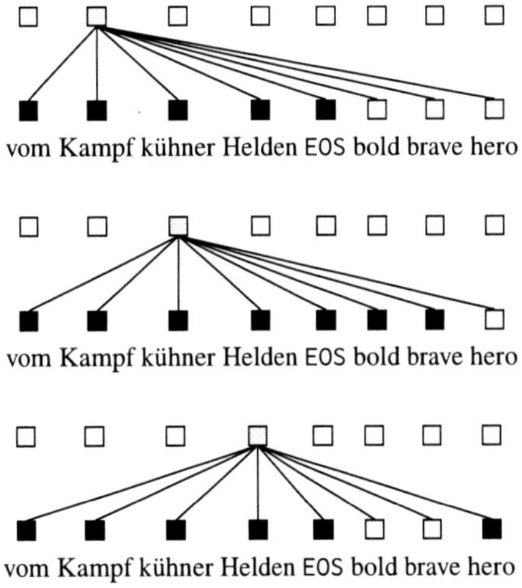

Figure 1: We append definitions of *kühn* 'bold, brave' and *Held* 'hero' to a sentence, and use an attention mask (with learnable strength) to inform the model which definitions correspond to which words. In each picture, the query vectors are above, with one query vector shaded yellow, and the key/value vectors are below, shaded to indicate the strength of the attention mask (black = not masked, white = masked).

However, the morphology of both the source and target language poses a major challenge for the use of dictionaries with MT compared to other NLP tasks that incorporate methods of retrieval-augmented generation (Niehues, 2021). MT systems that incorporate dictionaries must be capable of inflecting definitions for the target language and the context in which those definitions must appear, as dictionary entries and their definitions are often base forms. In Figure 1, we see the adjective *kühner* is declined for the genitive case, but only the lemma *kühn* would be in a German dictionary. Moreover, if the target language has adjective declension, then the MT system must also decline the dictionary form of the definition.

Our approach is to retrieve dictionary definitions for low-frequency words, append the definitions to source sentences containing rare words, and use attention masking to link together rare words with their definitions. We find that appending definitions for rare words improves MT performance by up to 1.0 BLEU and 1.6 MacroF1.

2 Related Work

Previous work on dictionaries for neural MT can be divided into two broad categories, which we call *dictionaries-as-translators* and *dictionaries-as-text*. In the dictionaries-as-translators approach, the dictionary is assumed to contain high-quality translations of words, and the technical challenge is to get the MT system to use the dictionary's translations when appropriate. In the dictionaries-as-text approach, dictionary entries are added somehow to the source sentence, and it is up to the MT system to learn how to use them. In this approach, the dictionary can contain definitions that are not necessarily translations (e.g., one definition for German *halt* is: "Indicating that something is generally known, or cannot be changed, or the like; often untranslatable"). This approach could, in principle, use other resources like monolingual dictionaries, grammars, and so on.

2.1 Dictionaries as translators

In the dictionaries-as-translators category, Zhang et al. (2021) propose a model with three steps: (1) identify source words that can be translated using a dictionary, (2) select one of several translation candidates (*i.e.*, definitions), and (3) copy the selected translation into the output sequence. Similarly, other previous work in this category uses constrained decoding with a translation lexicon: Zhang and Zong (2016), Arthur et al. (2016), Fadaee et al. (2017), Chatterjee et al. (2017), Hasler et al. (2018), Post and Vilar (2018), Thompson et al. (2019), Dinu et al. (2019).

A translation lexicon is a mapping of words from the source language to the target language, whereas a bilingual dictionary provides several possible translations for a given source word in addition to including definitions for untranslatable words such as particles. To incorporate a translation lexicon, we must constrain the output of the MT system, but that approach assumes the correct translation given the source context is contained within the lexicon. However, it quite often is the case that there are several valid translations with some being more appropriate than others for the given context.

2.2 Dictionaries as text

In the dictionaries-as-text category are approaches in which dictionary definitions are added to source sentences so that the model can learn how to use them. Two further questions arise: (1) How do we decide which definitions to include (especially in morphologically-rich languages, where a word in context does not in general match a dictionary headword)? (2) How do we represent the nonlinear structure of the input, which includes both a source sentence and associated definitions?

Niehues (2021) lemmatizes each rare word and retrieves the matching bilingual definition, if any. The definition is inserted into the sentence immediately after the rare word, delimited by #. He uses a combination of subword and character tokenization to improve handling of rare inflected forms.

Zhong and Chiang (2022) use a combination of Levenshtein distance and locality-sensitive hashing to find the closest dictionary headword for each, potentially inflected, rare word. They append the definitions to the end of the source sentence, and they inform the model about the structure of the input using position encodings (PEs). Each definition word's vector has contributions from both its own (sinusoidal) PE as well as the (learnable) PE of the defined word. They use BPE subword segmentation for all words; instead of the PE of the defined word, they choose the PE of its first subword. In contrast to Niehues (2021), Zhong and Chiang (2022) find that the model with BPE can inflect dictionary definitions without switching to character-level tokenization.

3 Methodology

Our approach falls squarely into the dictionaries-as-text category: given a source sentence, we retrieve relevant entries from a bilingual dictionary and include them in the source sentence. To decide which entries to include, we use a source-language lemmatizer, which should be more reliable and faster than fuzzy matching. To represent the input, we use *attention masking* instead of positional encodings since we suspect that attention is a more natural mechanism by which an encoder-decoder model can associate definitions (keys) with rare words (queries).

In this section, we break down our approach for using a bilingual dictionary for machine translation with a transformer-based, encoder-decoder model into the following steps: (1) headword selection, (2) definition retrieval, and (3) attention masking.

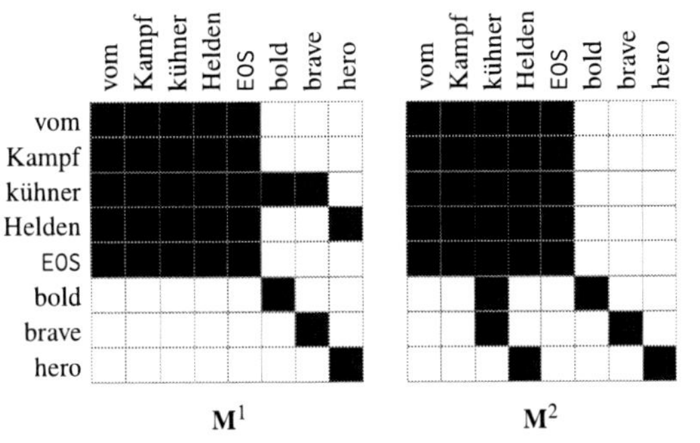

Figure 2: Our system uses two attention masks with learnable strengths. Rows are queries; columns are keys/values. Black = not masked; white = masked. Mask $\mathbf{M}^1$ allows each source word to attend to its definitions (if any). Mask $\mathbf{M}^2$ allows each definition word to attend to the word it defines.

3.1 Headword Selection

In order to classify a source word as *rare*, we compare the number of occurrences in the training data against a frequency threshold that we choose from a hyperparameter search. For a given source word, we say that a word w is *rare* if (a) it has both a frequency below the threshold and an entry in the dictionary, or (b) if w does not meet either of the above criteria, but its lemmatized form meets both.

3.2 Definition Retrieval

If a rare/unknown word is present in the dictionary, we retrieve its definition(s). Otherwise, we first use a lemmatizer and check if the dictionary contains the lemma for the rare/unknown word. Then, we append the definition(s) to the source sentence following the end-of-sentence token <EOS>.

3.3 Attention Masking

The input now contains a source sentence augmented with dictionary definitions, both segmented into subwords using BPE. To inform the model about the structure of the input, we use attention masking (Shen et al., 2018).

Let n be the input length (source subwords plus definition subwords), and let d be the dimensionality of the model's hidden vectors. In standard attention, we compute, for each head h, a matrix of attention weights $\alpha_h \in \mathbb{R}^{n \times n}$:

$$\alpha_h = \text{softmax}\left(\frac{\mathbf{Q}_h \mathbf{K}_h^T}{\sqrt{d}}\right)$$

where $\mathbf{Q}_h, \mathbf{K}_h \in \mathbb{R}^{n \times d}$ are the query and key matrices, respectively, for head h.

We construct two masks (see Figure 2). Both masks allow all source subwords to attend to all source subwords, and all definition subwords to attend to all subwords in the same definition. Note that *kühner* has two definitions, which cannot attend to each other. Mask $\mathbf{M}^1$ allows each source subword to attend to its definitions (if any). Mask $\mathbf{M}^2$ allows each definition subword to attend to the word it defines. Mathematically, we represent each mask as a matrix $\mathbf{M}^k \in \{0, 1\}^{n \times n}$, where $\mathbf{M}^k_{ij} = 1$ means that subword i cannot attend to subword j.

The attention masks are applied softly, with learnable weights. We combine the masks as follows:

$$\alpha_h = \text{softmax}\left(\frac{\mathbf{Q}_h \mathbf{K}_h^T}{\sqrt{d}} - \sum_{k=1}^{m} \exp\left(s_{k,h}\right) \mathbf{M}^k\right)$$

where $m = 2$ is the number of masks and $s_{k,h} \in \mathbb{R}$ is the learnable strength for mask k and head h. We apply the exponential function component-wise to each $s_{k,h}$ to ensure that every element of the summation is positive. The aggregate attention mask is then subtracted from the standard dot-product attention. In this way, the model can decide if and/or when the dictionary definitions are useful and adjust the strengths of the attention masks accordingly (McDonald and Chiang, 2021).

4 Experiments

In this section, we describe our translation model, the source-side lemmatizer, and the bilingual dictionary used hereafter throughout the paper.

4.1 Translation Model

To experiment with the internal architecture, we implement an encoder-decoder model from scratch using PyTorch (Paszke et al., 2019).[1] For the encoder/decoder, we use a transformer model (Vaswani et al., 2017). Hidden vectors have $d = d_{\text{model}} = 512$ dimensions, and feed-forward networks have $d_{\text{FFN}} = 2048$ dimensions. The encoder and decoder each have 6 layers, each with 8 attention heads. We apply dropout to all embedding, feed-forward, and attention layers with a probability of 0.1. Instead of layer normalization, we use FixNorm and ScaleNorm, which have been shown to improve translations in the low-resource setting (Nguyen and Salazar, 2019).

All models are trained on NVIDIA A10 GPUs. We use negative log-likelihood for training with a batch size of 4096, a label smoothing value of 0.1, and an initial learning rate of $3 \cdot 10^{-4}$, which we decay by a factor of 0.8 with a patience of 3 and a minimum learning rate of $5 \cdot 10^{-5}$. In addition, we do early stopping if our model trains for 20 epochs without improvement or exceeds a maximum of 250 epochs. Finally, we filter through the training data by removing empty translations, duplicate sentence pairs, sentences longer than a maximum length of 256, and sentence pairs with a source:target length ratio greater than 1.3. We also normalize the punctuation in both the source and target languages.

4.2 Training/Evaluation Data

For German to English translation, we use data from the WMT22 shared task: Europarl v10 for training (Koehn, 2005), newstest2019 for validation, and newstest2022 for testing. For tokenization, we use sacremoses,[2] an implementation of Moses (Koehn et al., 2007), at the word-level and subword-nmt,[3] an implementation of BPE, at the subword-level. For evaluation, we use a fork of sacrebleu (Post, 2018) for BLEU (Papineni et al., 2002) and MacroF1 (Gowda et al., 2021).[4]

The Europarl corpus for German to English has 1,778,520 sentences, with 1,379,973 remaining after cleaning. We apply BPE with 32,000 merge operations and a dropout probability of 0.1 to obtain a shared vocabulary size of 32,469. The newstest2019 validation set and newstest2022 test set contain 2,000 and 1,984 sentences, respectively. To measure translation performance in a low-resource setting, we limit the Europarl corpus to the first 250,000 sentences. The smaller training set has 190,686 sentences remaining after cleaning. We apply BPE with 8,000 merge operations and a dropout probability of 0.1 to obtain a shared vocabulary size of 8,348.

Regarding the difficulty of finding and/or curating extensive dictionaries for low-resource languages, the available Uyghur-English data for the DARPA LORELEI Year 1 evaluation (Hermjakob et al., 2018), for example, consisted of 99k sentences of parallel text and 240k dictionary entries, so there are cases where the amount of dictionary data available is extensive compared to the amount of parallel text available. Given the lack of available training data for low-resource languages, we would argue that hiring linguists to construct bilingual dictionaries offers a greater overall benefit to the community of native speakers and those wishing to document/preserve/revitalize the language than simply hiring translators to expand the available corpora, as the usefulness of dictionaries extends beyond NLP applications (Garrette and Baldridge, 2013).

To evaluate the performance of our model on out-of-domain translation, we combine the Medline test sets from the WMT20 (Bawden et al., 2020), WMT21 (Yeganova et al., 2021), and WMT22 (Neves et al., 2022) biomedical tasks, removing any duplicate sentence pairs. However, the parallel text is misaligned, so we use the provided alignment files to construct the test set, filtering out all sentence pairs not labeled as OK. The final test set has 1,073 sentences. Table 3 shows an example sentence from the biomedical test set along with the reference translation.

[1] https://github.com/kennethsible/dictionary-attention

[2] https://github.com/hplt-project/sacremoses

[3] https://github.com/rsennrich/subword-nmt

[4] https://github.com/isi-nlp/sacrebleu

Training Corpus	Model	News BLEU	News MacroF1	Biomedical BLEU	Biomedical MacroF1
Europarl (Limited)	Baseline	22.1	18.1	18.2	18.5
	Parallel	22.3	18.2	18.2	18.4
	DPE	22.4	18.4	18.3	18.6
	Masking	**23.4**	**20.0**	**19.1**	**19.9**
Europarl (Full)	Baseline	30.4	25.4	23.8	25.8
	Parallel	30.5	25.4	24.0	25.9
	DPE	31.1	26.3	24.3	26.5
	Masking	**31.2**	**26.8**	**24.4**	**26.9**

Table 1: Baseline refers to the translation model without any dictionaries, Parallel includes a bilingual dictionary as parallel text, DPE appends dictionary definitions and uses positional encodings (Zhong and Chiang, 2022), and Masking (ours) appends dictionary definitions and uses attention masking. To construct Europarl (Limited), we only use the first 250,000 sentences (<10%) of the 1.8 million in Europarl (Full).

4.3 Lemmatizer and Dictionary

For the German lemmatizer, we used the spaCy model `de_core_news_sm`[5] with only the tok2vec, tagger, and lemmatizer enabled in the NLP pipeline. For the bilingual dictionary, we used the most recent development version of the German to English bilingual dictionary provided by TU Chemnitz.[6] To prepare the data for our model, we filtered out:

- All dictionary headwords labeled non-alphabetic in Python, excluding hyphenated compound (*e.g.*, `im eigenen Tempo`).
- All dictionary metadata contained in grouping symbols, such as part-of-speech and gender (*e.g.*, masculine noun `{m}`, transitive verb `{vt}`, biological term `[biol.]`, Austrian dialect `[Ös.]`).
- All dictionary abbreviations used for nominative, accusative, dative, and genitive objects (*e.g.*, `jdm.`, `jdn.`, `jds.`, and `etw.`).
- All German prepositional phrases of the form: preposition + abbreviation (*e.g.*, `bei jdm./etw.`).
- The German reflexive pronoun *sich* whenever preceding a headword (*e.g.*, `sich anschließen`).

The German to English dictionary, after cleaning and applying the filters, has 302,061 entries.

[5] https://spacy.io/models/de

[6] https://ftp.tu-chemnitz.de/pub/Local/urz/ding/de-en-devel/

4.4 Experimental Setup

In addition to our model (Masking), we trained three baseline models: a translation model without any dictionaries (Baseline), a model that includes a bilingual dictionary as parallel text (Parallel), and a model that uses dictionary positional encodings (DPE) (Zhong and Chiang, 2022). For DPE and Masking, we append dictionary definitions to source sentences containing rare words. All models were trained on two datasets: Europarl (Limited) and Europarl (Full).

4.5 Hyperparameter Search

By appending dictionary definitions, we introduce two hyperparameters in the model: the frequency threshold for rare words and the number of definitions (or word senses) appended for each rare word. In our experiments, we used frequency thresholds of 5, 10, 15, 25, and 50, and restricted the number of definitions appended to 1, 5, 10, and unbounded.

5 Results

In this section, we report and analyze the results of our experiments described in the previous section. We found that appending definitions for rare words and using attention masking (Masking) improved translation performance over the baseline models: Baseline, Parallel, and DPE.

Furthermore, we observed that using a lower frequency threshold during training and increasing that threshold during inference resulted in the largest performance improvement. We speculate that this

Source	Mit seiner **Tarnkappe** **entkam** **Siegfried** dem **kampferprobten** **Ritter**, einem Mit seiner T@@ ar@@ n@@ k@@ app@@ e ent@@ kam Sie@@ g@@ fri@@ ed dem kampf@@ er@@ prob@@ ten R@@ it@@ ter , einem with his invisibility cloak evaded Sigurd the battle-hardened knight a **Todfeind**, und **schlich** sich aus der Burg. To@@ d@@ fein@@ d , und sch@@ lich sich aus der Burg . deadly enemy and crept himself out of the castle **Tarnkappe**: {invisibility cloak}; **entkam**: {evaded, escaped, got away}; **Siegfried**: {Sigurd}; **kampferprobt**: {battle-seasoned, battle-hardened, battle-tested, combat proven}; **Ritter**: {knight, knights, companion of the order of knighthood, chevalier}; **Todfeind**: {deadly enemy, mortal enemy}; **schlich**: {crept, slunk, tiptoed}
Reference	With his invisibility cloak, Siegfried evaded the battle-hardened knight, a deadly foe, and crept out of the castle.
Baseline	With his cap, Siegfried escaped the tried and tested ritter, a death-enemy, and smashed from the castle.
Parallel	With his cap, Siegfried escaped the tried and tested Ritter, a death enemy, and came out of the castle shamefully.
DPE	With his glasscloak, Sigurd escaped the fighter's knight, a deadly enemy, and crept out of the castle.
Masking	With his invisibility cloak, Sigurd escaped the battle-tested knight, a deadly enemy, and crept out of the castle.
Apple	With his camouflage cap, Siegfried escaped the battle-tested knight, a mortal enemy, and crept out of the castle.

Table 2: On a German sentence (Source), our system's output (Masking) is closer to the Reference than the Baseline system's, even when the dictionary is included in the baseline system's training data (Parallel) or dictionary positional encodings (Zhong and Chiang, 2022) are used instead of attention masking (DPE). Even Apple's Translate app translates *Tarnkappe* over-literally as *camouflage cap*. Rare words are written in boldface. The Reference sentence was written by the first author to demonstrate multiple rare words with a variety of parts of speech and inflections, and a native German speaker translated it into the Source sentence.

Source	Typisch für ein **konjunktivales** **Lymphom** ist eine **lachsfarbene** **Schwellung**. Typ@@ isch für ein kon@@ jun@@ ktiv@@ ales L@@ ymp@@ ho@@ m ist eine la@@ chs@@ far@@ bene Schwell@@ ung . typical for a conjunctival lymphoma is a salmon-colored swelling **Lymphom**: {lymphoma}; **lachsfarben**: {salmon, salmon-coloured, salmon-colored}; **Schwellung**: {swelling-up, swelling, puffiness, tumescence, intumescence, intumescentia, tumentia, tumefaction, tumidity, turgescence, turgidity, engorgement}
Reference	A salmon-colored swelling is typical for conjunctival lymphoma.
Baseline	A lax threshold is typical of a lax lymphom in economic terms.
Parallel	A low level threshold is typical of a cyclical lymphom.
DPE	A cyclical lymphom is typically characterised by a lame threshold.
Masking	A salmon-coloured lymphoma is typical of a cyclical lymphoma.
↳ Restricted	A salmon-coloured swelling is typical of a current lymphoma.
↳ Updated	A salmon-coloured swelling is typical of a conjunctival lymphoma.

Table 3: On a German sentence (Source) from the biomedical dataset, our system's output (Masking) is closer to the Reference than the Baseline system's, even when the dictionary is included in the baseline system's training data (Parallel) or dictionary positional encodings (Zhong and Chiang, 2022) are used instead of attention masking (DPE). Rare words are written in boldface. We also edited the input manually for demonstration purposes: For Restricted, the number of definitions appended has been restricted to 3 since *Schwellung* has 12, which causes the model to struggle. For Updated, we restricted the number of definitions appended to 3 and added a definition for *konjunktival* 'conjunctival' to the dictionary (not previously present).

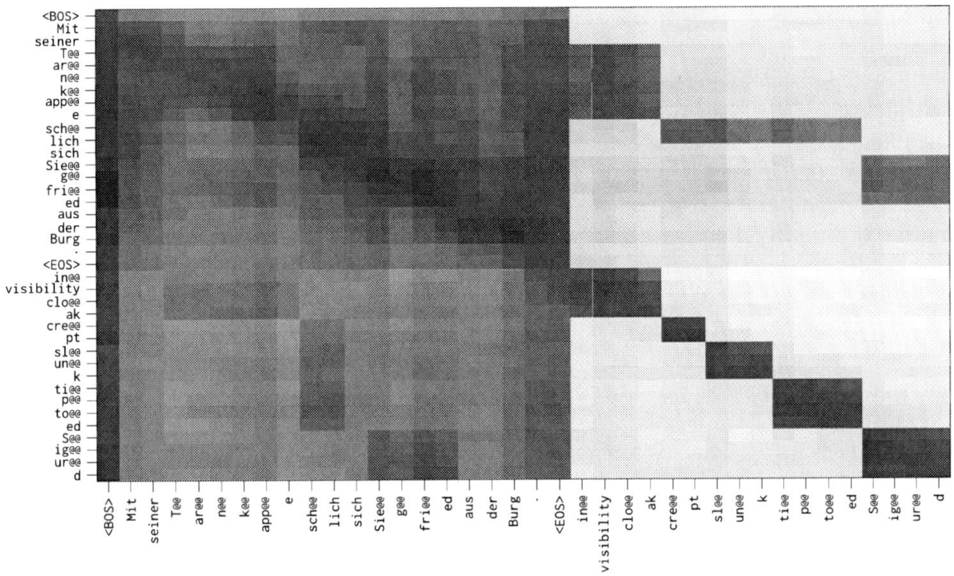

Figure 3: The attention scores of the Masking model for the German sentence: "Mit seiner Tarnkappe schlich sich Siegfried aus der Burg" with the definition string "invisibility cloak crept slunk tiptoed Sigurd." The attention scores are summed for all encoder layers and attention heads. We observe both attention masks being utilized by the model.

behavior is a result of larger thresholds incorrectly classifying unknown compound words (*i.e.*, those not occurring in the training data) as rare when they are already translatable by the baseline models as a result of subword tokenization. If we are attempting to teach the model to use definitions, including them when they are not necessary may actively work against our training objective.

During a hyperparameter search, we found that using 10 for the frequency threshold and 10 for the maximum number of definitions appended yields the largest improvement in translation performance. Table 1 compares our model against the three baseline models for both the general (news) and out-of-domain (biomedical) datasets. All metrics reported in the table were averaged over 5 random restarts and statistical significance was verified with paired t-tests. Masking (our model) outperforms the three baseline models on both metrics and all improvements are statistically significant (p-value < 0.05), except for the BLEU improvement over DPE for Europarl (Full).

In the low-resource setting, DPE struggles to improve over the baseline models, while Masking has the largest BLEU improvement, demonstrating a boost in low-resource translation performance. In the high-resource setting, although DPE and Masking are not significantly different in BLEU, they are significantly different in MacroF1. Since rare words are less frequent in the high-resource setting, the BLEU improvement of DPE and Masking over Baseline and Parallel is not as large. However, Masking has the largest MacroF1 improvement, demonstrating a boost in rare word translation performance.

In Table 2, we compare candidate translations of a German sentence containing rare words against an English reference. The sentence was written in English, and translated by a native German speaker, to demonstrate the capability and robustness of our model in using the dictionary. The German sentence contains seven rare words of varying part-of-speech, including adjective declension and verb conjugation. In the Source row, the English glosses are shown beneath each German word to match the Reference translation along with the corresponding subword tokenization. To reduce the sentence length, the definitions are listed separately instead of appended to the German sentence.

Baseline and Parallel contain several incorrect

translations of rare words. In particular, we observe that *Tarnkappe* and *Todfeind* were translated over-literally, with the first noun in the compound being dropped all together. Even the Apple Translate app translated *Tarnkappe* over-literally as *camouflage cap*. The DPE model, instead of dropping the first noun like Baseline/Parallel, used a seemingly random noun and translated the second over-literally. Only the Masking model correctly translated *Tarnkappe* as *invisibility cloak*. In fact, Masking used at least one definition for every rare word, getting the closest to the Reference.

In Table 3, we compare candidate translations of a German sentence taken directly from the Medline test set. The sentence contains four rare words, but our dictionary has no definition for *konjunktival*. *Lymphom*, despite having a definition, is copied to English sentence by Baseline, Parallel, and DPE. Masking correctly translates *Lymphom* and *lachsfarben*, but all models mistranslate *Schwellung*. We found that Masking often ignores definitions if there are too many appended for a given rare word. To demonstrate, we restricted the number of definitions for *Schwellung* to 3 and see that the model correctly translates the word. We also succeeded in translating *konjunktival* correctly by adding the English definition to the dictionary, demonstrating that the dictionary coverage is a limiting factor.

In Figure 3, we use an attention heat map to visualize the attention scores for a German sentence. The sentence shown is a trimmed version of the example in Table 2. To build the heat map, we summed the attention scores for every encoder layer and every attention head. We see that the attention masks shown in Figure 2 are clearly visible in the heat map. However, the model decided to put more emphasis on the first mask than the second, which is done by adjusting the mask strengths.

6 Discussion

Rare Word Classification As mentioned previously, compound words that do not occur in the training data may still be accurately translated as a result of subword segmentation, suggesting that frequency is not an ideal or reliable metric for classifying rare words. In the future, frequency could be replaced with a source-side estimation of model confidence in the translation of rare words.

Incorrect Lemmatization We could not find an acceptable lemmatizer for the German language since even spaCy would occasionally misidentify the lemma for, *e.g.*, a declined adjective or a past participle. Furthermore, no lemmatizer that we found could correctly identify the infinitive form for separable verbs or *trennbare Verben*, a common class of verbs in the German language. In the future, we could explore more robust lemmatization techniques or the inclusion of inflected forms in the dictionary.

Lemmatization Ambiguities We have identified several cases where lemmatization causes the model to use a definition that is not grammatically correct in the context of the source sentence. For example, if the past tense form of a verb is not present in the dictionary and the definition for the infinitive form is used, the model often avoids inflecting the infinitive form to the correct tense unless the sentence contains, *e.g.*, an auxiliary verb. Similarly, nouns ending in –er in German have no plural ending, which creates an ambiguity as to whether the English definition should be plural. A dictionary that directly contains inflected forms may resolve such ambiguities.

Definition/Word Sense Pruning We appended definitions for each word sense and part-of-speech with the assumption that the model could learn to leverage syntactic or semantic knowledge of the source sentence to select an appropriate translation for the rare words from among those definitions appended. However, we find that the model is often spoiled for choice, in that the model may use an inappropriate definition, or none at all, if there are too many without a clear way to disambiguate. In the future, we could implement a strategy to select the most relevant definitions or limit the number of appended definitions per rare word, such as pruning based on document-level context or prior domain knowledge.

Phrases and Compound Words We appended definitions only for single words, which includes both hyphenated and concatenated compound words in German, but did not consider phrases whose translations may not be directly deducible from the constituent words. Similarly, we did not consider separating compound words into the constituent words and recursively searching for definitions if the compound words are not present in the dictionary themselves since subword segmentation often handles these.

7 Conclusion

In this paper, we proposed using bilingual dictionaries and attention masking to improve translation performance for rare words, a problem that encoder-decoder models continue to struggle with in MT. Our method was to append definitions to source sentences for low-frequency words and use attention masking to associate rare words with their definitions. We found that our method improved MT performance by up to 1.0 BLEU and 1.6 MacroF1. In the future, we are interested in incorporating other external knowledge sources, such as monolingual dictionaries and knowledge graphs, to reduce translation ambiguity and further improve the translation of rare words.

8 Limitations

The following are two limiting factors of our masking approach to including bilingual dictionaries in machine translation: (1) the quality and coverage of the lemmatizer and/or dictionary is a bottleneck to further improvement and (2) appending definitions increases sentence length and therefore runtime.

9 Acknowledgements

This material is based upon work supported by the National Science Foundation under Grant No. IIS-2137396.

References

Arthur, P., Neubig, G., and Nakamura, S. (2016). Incorporating discrete translation lexicons into neural machine translation. In Su, J., Duh, K., and Carreras, X., editors, *Proceedings of the 2016 Conference on Empirical Methods in Natural Language Processing*, pages 1557–1567, Austin, Texas. Association for Computational Linguistics.

Bawden, R., Di Nunzio, G. M., Grozea, C., Jauregi Unanue, I., Jimeno Yepes, A., Mah, N., Martinez, D., Névéol, A., Neves, M., Oronoz, M., Perez-de Viñaspre, O., Piccardi, M., Roller, R., Siu, A., Thomas, P., Vezzani, F., Vicente Navarro, M., Wiemann, D., and Yeganova, L. (2020). Findings of the WMT 2020 biomedical translation shared task: Basque, Italian and Russian as new additional languages. In Barrault, L., Bojar, O., Bougares, F., Chatterjee, R., Costa-jussà, M. R., Federmann, C., Fishel, M., Fraser, A., Graham, Y., Guzman, P., Haddow, B., Huck, M., Yepes, A. J., Koehn, P., Martins, A., Morishita, M., Monz, C., Nagata, M., Nakazawa, T., and Negri, M., editors, *Proceedings of the Fifth Conference on Machine Translation*, pages 660–687, Online. Association for Computational Linguistics.

Chatterjee, R., Negri, M., Turchi, M., Federico, M., Specia, L., and Blain, F. (2017). Guiding neural machine translation decoding with external knowledge. In Bojar, O., Buck, C., Chatterjee, R., Federmann, C., Graham, Y., Haddow, B., Huck, M., Yepes, A. J., Koehn, P., and Kreutzer, J., editors, *Proceedings of the Second Conference on Machine Translation*, pages 157–168, Copenhagen, Denmark. Association for Computational Linguistics.

Dinu, G., Mathur, P., Federico, M., and Al-Onaizan, Y. (2019). Training neural machine translation to apply terminology constraints. In Korhonen, A., Traum, D., and Màrquez, L., editors, *Proceedings of the 57th Annual Meeting of the Association for Computational Linguistics*, pages 3063–3068, Florence, Italy. Association for Computational Linguistics.

Fadaee, M., Bisazza, A., and Monz, C. (2017). Data augmentation for low-resource neural machine translation. In Barzilay, R. and Kan, M.-Y., editors, *Proceedings of the 55th Annual Meeting of the Association for Computational Linguistics (Volume 2: Short Papers)*, pages 567–573, Vancouver, Canada. Association for Computational Linguistics.

Garrette, D. and Baldridge, J. (2013). Learning a part-of-speech tagger from two hours of annotation. In Vanderwende, L., Daumé III, H., and Kirchhoff, K., editors, *Proceedings of the 2013 Conference of the North American Chapter of the Association for Computational Linguistics: Human Language Technologies*, pages 138–147, Atlanta, Georgia. Association for Computational Linguistics.

Gowda, T., You, W., Lignos, C., and May, J. (2021). Macro-average: Rare types are important too. In Toutanova, K., Rumshisky, A., Zettlemoyer, L., Hakkani-Tur, D., Beltagy, I., Bethard, S., Cotterell, R., Chakraborty, T., and Zhou, Y., editors, *Proceedings of the 2021 Conference of the North American Chapter of the Association for Computational Linguistics: Human Language Technologies*, pages 1138–1157, Online. Association for Computational Linguistics.

Hasler, E., de Gispert, A., Iglesias, G., and Byrne, B. (2018). Neural machine translation decoding with terminology constraints. In Walker, M., Ji, H., and Stent, A., editors, *Proceedings of the 2018 Conference of the North American Chapter of the Association for Computational Linguistics: Human Language Technologies, Volume 2 (Short Papers)*, pages 506–512, New Orleans, Louisiana. Association for Computational Linguistics.

Hermjakob, U., Li, Q., Marcu, D., May, J., Mielke, S. J., Pourdamghani, N., Pust, M., Shi, X., Knight, K., Levinboim, T., Murray, K., Chiang, D., Zhang, B., Pan, X., Lu, D., Lin, Y., and Ji, H. (2018). Incident-Driven Machine Translation and Name Tagging for Low-resource Languages. *Machine Translation*, 32(1):59–89.

Kocmi, T., Avramidis, E., Bawden, R., Bojar, O., Dvorkovich, A., Federmann, C., Fishel, M., Freitag, M., Gowda, T., Grundkiewicz, R., Haddow, B., Koehn, P., Marie, B., Monz, C., Morishita, M., Murray, K., Nagata, M., Nakazawa, T., Popel, M., Popović, M., and Shmatova, M. (2023). Findings of the 2023 Conference on Machine Translation (WMT23): LLMs are here but not quite there yet. In Koehn, P., Haddow, B., Kocmi, T., and Monz, C., editors, *Proceedings of the Eighth Conference on Machine Translation*, pages 1–42, Singapore. Association for Computational Linguistics.

Koehn, P. (2005). Europarl: A parallel corpus for statistical machine translation. In *Proceedings of Machine Translation Summit X: Papers*, pages 79–86, Phuket, Thailand.

Koehn, P., Hoang, H., Birch, A., Callison-Burch, C., Federico, M., Bertoldi, N., Cowan, B., Shen, W., Moran, C., Zens, R., Dyer, C., Bojar, O., Constantin, A., and Herbst, E. (2007). Moses: Open source toolkit for statistical machine translation. In Ananiadou, S., editor, *Proceedings of the 45th Annual Meeting of the Association for Computational Linguistics Companion Volume Proceedings of the Demo and Poster Sessions*, pages 177–180, Prague, Czech Republic. Association for Computational Linguistics.

McDonald, C. and Chiang, D. (2021). Syntax-based attention masking for neural machine translation. In Durmus, E., Gupta, V., Liu, N., Peng, N., and Su, Y., editors, *Proceedings of the 2021 Conference of the North American Chapter of the Association for Computational Linguistics: Student Research Workshop*, pages 47–52, Online. Association for Computational Linguistics.

Minh-Cong, N.-H., Ngo, V. T., and Nguyen, V. V. (2022). A simple and fast strategy for handling rare words in neural machine translation. In Hanqi, Y., Zonghan, Y., Ruder, S., and Xiaojun, W., editors, *Proceedings of the 2nd Conference of the Asia-Pacific Chapter of the Association for Computational Linguistics and the 12th International Joint Conference on Natural Language Processing: Student Research Workshop*, pages 40–46, Online. Association for Computational Linguistics.

Neves, M., Jimeno Yepes, A., Siu, A., Roller, R., Thomas, P., Vicente Navarro, M., Yeganova, L., Wiemann, D., Di Nunzio, G. M., Vezzani, F., Gerardin, C., Bawden, R., Estrada, D. J., Lima-Lopez, S., Farre-Maduel, E., Krallinger, M., Grozea, C., and Neveol, A. (2022). Findings of the WMT 2022 biomedical translation shared task: Monolingual clinical case reports. In *Proceedings of the Seventh Conference on Machine Translation*, pages 694–723, Abu Dhabi. Association for Computational Linguistics.

Nguyen, T. Q. and Salazar, J. (2019). Transformers without tears: Improving the normalization of self-attention. In Niehues, J., Cattoni, R., Stüker, S., Negri, M., Turchi, M., Ha, T.-L., Salesky, E., Sanabria, R., Barrault, L., Specia, L., and Federico, M., editors, *Proceedings of the 16th International Conference on Spoken Language Translation*, Hong Kong. Association for Computational Linguistics.

Niehues, J. (2021). Continuous learning in neural machine translation using bilingual dictionaries. In *Proceedings of the 16th Conference of the European Chapter of the Association for Computational Linguistics: Main Volume*, pages 830–840, Online. Association for Computational Linguistics.

Papineni, K., Roukos, S., Ward, T., and Zhu, W.-J. (2002). BLEU: a method for automatic evaluation of machine translation. In *Proceedings of the 40th Annual Meeting on Association for Computational Linguistics*, ACL '02, pages 311–318, USA. Association for Computational Linguistics.

Paszke, A., Gross, S., Massa, F., Lerer, A., Bradbury, J., Chanan, G., Killeen, T., Lin, Z., Gimelshein, N., Antiga, L., Desmaison, A., Köpf, A., Yang, E., DeVito, Z., Raison, M., Tejani, A., Chilamkurthy, S., Steiner, B., Fang, L., Bai, J., and Chintala, S. (2019). PyTorch: an imperative style, high-performance deep learning library. In *Proceedings of the 33rd International Conference on Neural Information Processing Systems*, number 721, pages 8026–8037. Curran Associates Inc., Red Hook, NY, USA.

Post, M. (2018). A call for clarity in reporting BLEU scores. In Bojar, O., Chatterjee, R., Federmann, C., Fishel, M., Graham, Y., Haddow, B., Huck, M., Yepes, A. J., Koehn, P., Monz, C., Negri, M., Névéol, A., Neves, M., Post, M., Specia, L., Turchi, M., and Verspoor, K., editors, *Proceedings of the Third Conference on Machine Translation: Research Papers*, pages 186–191, Brussels, Belgium. Association for Computational Linguistics.

Post, M. and Vilar, D. (2018). Fast lexically constrained decoding with dynamic beam allocation for neural machine translation. In Walker, M., Ji, H., and Stent, A., editors, *Proceedings of the 2018 Conference of the North American Chapter of the Association for Computational Linguistics: Human Language Technologies, Volume 1 (Long Papers)*, pages 1314–1324, New Orleans, Louisiana. Association for Computational Linguistics.

Shen, T., Jiang, J., Zhou, T., Pan, S., Long, G., and Zhang, C. (2018). DiSAN: directional self-attention network for RNN/CNN-free language understanding. In *Proceedings of the Thirty-Second AAAI Conference on Artificial Intelligence and Thirtieth Innovative Applications of Artificial Intelligence Conference and Eighth AAAI Symposium on Educational Advances in Artificial Intelligence*, AAAI'18/IAAI'18/EAAI'18. AAAI Press.

Tan, L., van Genabith, J., and Bond, F. (2015). Passive and pervasive use of bilingual dictionary in statistical machine translation. In Babych, B., Eberle, K., Lambert, P., Rapp, R., Banchs, R. E., and Costa-jussà, M. R., editors, *Proceedings of the Fourth Workshop on Hybrid Approaches to Translation (HyTra)*, pages 30–34, Beijing. Association for Computational Linguistics.

Thompson, B., Knowles, R., Zhang, X., Khayrallah, H., Duh, K., and Koehn, P. (2019). HABLex: Human annotated bilingual lexicons for experiments in machine translation. In Inui, K., Jiang, J., Ng, V., and Wan, X., editors, *Proceedings of the 2019 Conference on Empirical Methods in Natural Language Processing and the 9th International Joint Conference on Natural Language Processing (EMNLP-IJCNLP)*, pages 1382–1387, Hong Kong, China. Association for Computational Linguistics.

Vaswani, A., Shazeer, N., Parmar, N., Uszkoreit, J., Jones, L., Gomez, A. N., Kaiser, Ł., and Polosukhin, I. (2017). Attention is all you need. In Guyon, I., Luxburg, U. V., Bengio, S., Wallach, H., Fergus, R., Vishwanathan, S., and Garnett, R., editors, *Advances in Neural Information Processing Systems*, volume 30. Curran Associates, Inc.

Wu, Q., Xing, C., Li, Y., Ke, G., He, D., and Liu, T.-Y. (2021). Taking notes on the fly helps language pretraining. In *International Conference on Learning Representations*.

Xu, H., Kim, Y. J., Sharaf, A., and Awadalla, H. H. (2024). A paradigm shift in machine translation: Boosting translation performance of large language models. In *Proceedings of the Twelfth International Conference on Learning Representations (ICLR)*.

Yeganova, L., Wiemann, D., Neves, M., Vezzani, F., Siu, A., Jauregi Unanue, I., Oronoz, M., Mah, N., Névéol, A., Martinez, D., Bawden, R., Di Nunzio, G. M., Roller, R., Thomas, P., Grozea, C., Perez-de Viñaspre, O., Vicente Navarro, M., and Jimeno Yepes, A. (2021). Findings of the WMT 2021 biomedical translation shared task: Summaries of animal experiments as new test set. In Barrault, L., Bojar, O., Bougares, F., Chatterjee, R., Costa-jussa, M. R., Federmann, C., Fishel, M., Fraser, A., Freitag, M., Graham, Y., Grundkiewicz, R., Guzman, P., Haddow, B., Huck, M., Yepes, A. J., Koehn, P., Kocmi, T., Martins, A., Morishita, M., and Monz, C., editors, *Proceedings of the Sixth Conference on Machine Translation*, pages 664–683, Online. Association for Computational Linguistics.

Zhang, J. and Zong, C. (2016). Bridging neural machine translation and bilingual dictionaries.

Zhang, T., Zhang, L., Ye, W., Li, B., Sun, J., Zhu, X., Zhao, W., and Zhang, S. (2021). Point, disambiguate and copy: Incorporating bilingual dictionaries for neural machine translation. In Zong, C., Xia, F., Li, W., and Navigli, R., editors, *Proceedings of the 59th Annual Meeting of the Association for Computational Linguistics and the 11th International Joint Conference on Natural Language Processing (Volume 1: Long Papers)*, pages 3970–3979, Online. Association for Computational Linguistics.

Zhong, X. J. and Chiang, D. (2022). Look it up: Bilingual dictionaries improve neural machine translation. arXiv:2010.05997.

How Much Data is Enough Data? Fine-Tuning Large Language Models for In-House Translation: Performance Evaluation Across Multiple Dataset Sizes

Inacio Vieira* inacio@gmail.com
Department of Computing, Dublin City University, Dublin, Ireland & Alpha CRC, Cambridge, UK

Will Allred* william.allred2@mail.dcu.ie
Department of Computing, Dublin City University, Dublin, Ireland

Séamus Lankford seamus.lankford@adaptcentre.ie
Department of Computer Science, Munster Technological University, Cork, Ireland

Sheila Castilho sheila.castilho@adaptcentre.ie
SALIS/ADAPT Centre, Dublin City University, Dublin, Ireland

Andy Way andy.way@adaptcentre.ie
ADAPT Centre, School of Computing, Dublin City University, Dublin, Ireland

Abstract

Decoder-only LLMs have shown impressive performance in MT due to their ability to learn from extensive datasets and generate high-quality translations. However, LLMs often struggle with the nuances and style required for organisation-specific translation. In this study, we explore the effectiveness of fine-tuning Large Language Models (LLMs), particularly Llama 3 8B Instruct, leveraging translation memories (TMs), as a valuable resource to enhance accuracy and efficiency.

We investigate the impact of fine-tuning the Llama 3 model using TMs from an organisation in the software sector. Our experiments cover five translation directions across languages of varying resource levels (English to Brazilian Portuguese, Czech, German, Finnish, and Korean). We analyse diverse sizes of training datasets (1k to 207k segments) to evaluate their influence on translation quality. We fine-tune separate models for each training set and evaluate their performance based on automatic metrics, BLEU, chrF++, TER, and COMET.

Our findings reveal improvement in translation performance with larger datasets across all metrics. On average, BLEU and COMET scores increase by 13 and 25 points, respectively, on the largest training set against the baseline model. Notably, there is a performance deterioration in comparison with the baseline model when fine-tuning on only 1k and 2k examples; however, we observe a substantial improvement as the training dataset size increases. The study highlights the potential of integrating TMs with LLMs to create bespoke translation models tailored to the specific needs of businesses, thus enhancing translation quality and reducing turn-around times. This approach offers a valuable insight for organisations seeking to leverage TMs and LLMs for optimal translation outcomes, especially in narrower domains.

1 Introduction

In recent years, decoder-only large language models (LLMs) have revolutionised the machine translation (MT) field due to their ability to learn from vast amounts of data and generate high-quality translations (Alves et al., 2023a; Moslem et al., 2023a; Mu et al., 2023; Robinson et al., 2023; Zhu et al.,

Datasets	Segments
Aligned Training	1000, 2000, 5000, 10000, 14688
Dev	1837
Test	1353

Table 1: Segment counts for the various aligned training dataset sizes, the development set, and the test set.

2023; Lyu et al., 2024). LLMs, such as Llama 3 8B Instruct,[1] have shown impressive capabilities in adapting to translation tasks, generating human-like accurate output, making them invaluable tools for the sector (Li et al., 2023; Moslem et al., 2023b; Lyu et al., 2024). However, out-of-the-box LLMs do not always capture all the nuances, appropriate tone, and terminology required for specialised or organisation-specific translations (Moslem et al., 2022; Alves et al., 2023b; Zheng et al., 2024). This is where translation memories (TMs) offer a potential solution.

A TM is a database that stores previously human-translated segments and their respective translations. They are particularly useful to language service providers (LSPs) as they deal with repetitive content and organisation-specific style and terminology, enhancing the efficiency and accuracy of translations (Bloodgood and Strauss, 2014; Bulte and Tezcan, 2019; Moslem et al., 2023a). Therefore, the integration of TMs and LLMs can create models that better understand organisational requirements and lead to higher quality outputs and reduced turnaround times. However, this approach depends on several factors, like the amount, quality and specificity of the TMs used as training data for fine-tuning.

Previous work explored fine-tuning of models with TM for translation for specific domains and the benefit that offers to performance (Haque et al., 2020; Moslem et al., 2022). Accordingly, TM provides much value because of its high quality and domain relevance (Bulte and Tezcan, 2019; Xu et al., 2020; Cai et al., 2021; Knowles and Littell, 2022). This research highlights the gains available when leveraging existing TMs during the fine-tuning process of LLMs.

In this paper, we investigate a real-life scenario where we fine-tune Llama 3 8B Instruct (Llama Team, 2024) using TMs from a specific organisation. Additionally, since increasing the fine-tuning data requires dedicating more resources and time, we explore different dataset sizes to evaluate their impact on translation quality and identify the most efficient return on investment. We conduct experiments in five translation directions (from English) on languages of varying resource level (Brazilian Portuguese (PT-BR), Czech (CS), German (DE), Finnish (FI), and Korean (KO)). This approach can lead to bespoke translation models that cater to the unique needs of different companies when compared to generic LLMs.

2 Methodology

2.1 Data

The raw dataset consists of TMs from an anonymous organisation that operates in the software sector. The three datasets employed cover knowledge base, mobile user interface, and mobile reference materials.

The five target languages dataset (PT-BR, CS, DE, FI, and KO) are filtered to remove duplicates, source-copies, and segments over 150 words to ensure none would go over the maximum length set during training. All HTML tags are removed, and double spaces are converted to single spaces. Any rows containing only dates, version numbers, or any programming language are also removed. Rows are then randomly shuffled to mitigate any temporal bias that could arise from the chronological order of the data, ensure the model does not memorise sequences, and prevent the evaluation set from being biased towards a particular section of the data.

The dataset is then transformed into an interlingual aligned dataset for all five target languages where any rows with missing translations for any target languages, are dropped. This results in a

[*]These authors contributed equally to this work

[1]https://huggingface.co/meta-llama/Meta-Llama-3-8B-Instruct

Lang	Full Training Data	Dev Data	Total Segments
Brazilian Portuguese (PT-BR)	217,555	54,389	271,944
Czech (CS)	107,555	26,889	134,804
German (DE)	223,894	55,973	279,867
Finnish (FI)	207,218	51,805	259,023
Korean (KO)	162,360	40,590	202,950

Table 2: Segment counts for the full datasets used during training.

dataset where all source segments have translations available in all five target languages. The dataset is then split into training, development, and test sets, as shown in Table 1.

Further filtering is applied to the test set removing segments that had over 75% similarity with any segments in the training dataset to ensure robust testing and minimal memorisation. We measure similarity as a combination of the Levenshtein distance (Levenshtein, 1965) and a 5-gram-based similarity (Lopez-Gazpio et al., 2019). This reduced the size of the test split from 1837 to 1353. The test split with under 75% similarity was used for all experiments.

In the interest of using all the data available, we also compile all segments in a given language into a dataset for each target language. This includes any segment that would not fit the inter-lingual alignment criteria applied above. This will now be referred to as the 'full dataset'. These larger training sets allow us to train beyond the 14.7k aligned segments and make use of the total volume of available segments in order to explore what impact that would have on results. The full training sets range from 107k (CS) to 223k (DE) examples, as shown in Table 2.

2.2 Model

We use the Llama 3 8B Instruct model and its associated tokenizer (Llama Team, 2024). The decision between the Instruct and the base model is based on an extensive MT evaluation of Llama 3 models (Wu et al., 2024) using the Flores-200[2] dataset (Guzmán et al., 2019; Costa-jussà et al., 2022). Even though Wu (2024) dealt with the opposite language direction (X to English), we consider the close results between Instruct and the base model involving the five languages included in this paper to be a good indicator of proximity in performance between the models. Our baseline consists of the test set metric results obtained from the out-of-the-box Llama 3 8B Instruct model. We use QLoRA (Hu et al., 2021; Dettmers et al., 2023) for efficient fine-tuning with 4-bit quantisation using Hugging Face Transformers. We perform fine-tuning on a high performance cluster with four A100-SXM4-80GB GPUs. From Hugging Face, we leverage the Supervised Fine-Tuning Training (SFTTrainer),[3] which is a wrapper of the Trainer class[4] optimized for fine-tuning language models like Llama. On the largest dataset size, fine-tuning takes approximately 2.3 hours (Appendix A).

2.3 Inference

2.3.1 Prompting

At inference time, we use many of the recommended parameters from previous work (Moslem et al., 2023b) and model documentation to produce translation outputs from the baseline model and the fine-tuned versions (cf. Appendix C). Meta's Llama 3 documentation[5] provides a recommended prompt format and instructions to implement special tokens during inference and training (Llama Team, 2024).

The prompt and the source segment were passed to the model for inference to obtain each translation. This constitutes zero-shot as it did not include examples in the prompt (Zhang et al., 2023). A JSON scheme ({*"translation": "string"*}) was also added to the prompt in order to obtain a structured output (Wu et al., 2024). During training, the

[2]github.com/facebookresearch/flores/blob/main/flores200/README.md

[3]https://huggingface.co/docs/trl/en/sft_trainer

[4]https://huggingface.co/docs/transformers/en/main_classes/trainer

[5]https://llama.meta.com/docs/model-cards-and-prompt-formats/meta-llama-3/

BitsAndBytes Quantisation Configuration	
load_in_4bit	True
bnb_4bit_quant_type	“nf4”
bnb_4bit_use_double_quant	True
bnb_4bit_compute_dtype	torch.bfloat16
PEFT LoRA Configuration	
low-rank matrix dimension (r)	64
scaling factor (lora_alpha)	16
dropout probability (lora_dropout)	0.1
training of bias parameters (bias)	“none”
Training Arguments	
batch size for training and evaluation	32 examples
learning rate	2e-3
lr_scheduler_type	“constant”
bf16	True

Table 3: Fine-tuning hyperparameters.

same format was applied with the addition of the specific EOS token (< |*end_of_text*| >) as recommended by Meta’s documentation (cf. Appendix B).

2.3.2 Translation

In order to obtain higher efficiency, both baseline and fine-tuned models are converted to the CTranslate2[6] (Klein et al., 2020) format (with 8-bit quantisation) and provided with parameters for inference (cf. Appendix C).

2.3.3 Stopping Criteria and Post-processing

In early experiments, we observe frequent instances of overgeneration; an issue recently explored further by Zheng et al. (2024). By using ”}assistant” as a *stop_token* in our *stopping_criteria*, we find much less post-processing is required in order to obtain the pure translation.

Our post-processing consists of extracting the translation by removing the ‘{*“translation”:* “’ prefix and the trailing ‘ ”} ’. The newline characters are replaced by spaces. On some occasions, especially in the models produced by the smaller training datasets (1k and 2k examples), further cleaning is required as the model inadvertently overgenerated some HTML tags like ‘<br>’ and ‘<p>’. This is important to properly assess the translation quality.

2.4 Evaluation

To evaluate the performance of our models, we report BLEU (Papineni et al., 2002), chrF++ (Popović, 2017), TER (Snover et al., 2006) via sacreBLEU,[7] and COMET[8] (Rei et al., 2020). We use multiple metrics to make our experiments more comparable to a wider variety of work and to provide insight into certain aspects of performance.

It is important to note that the experiment aims to show the training efficiency of the PEFT fine-tuning method and its ability to approximate the model’s translating capabilities to the training material. Therefore, we pay special attention to the automatic metrics measuring *n*-gram differences and edits (BLEU, chrF++, TER) whilst still considering the quality estimation aspect of COMET as a means of comparing inter-source languages and other similar research. Our results are compared to those obtained from the baseline model, an out-of-the-box Llama 3 8B Instruct model, and to GPT 3.5. We also ask five professional translators to post-edit 100 translations from the best-performing model into their language pair. They also answer a questionnaire about

[6]https://github.com/OpenNMT/CTranslate2

[7]https://github.com/mjpost/sacrebleu

[8]wmt20-comet-da, https://github.com/Unbabel/COMET

the quality of the automatically translated segments. The questionnaire asks for comments on the quality of the translations.

3 Results and Discussion

The results in Table 4 show an increase in performance across all the languages for all datasets with more than 5k segments compared to the baseline. The fully aligned 14.7k dataset sees a BLEU score increase of 4.8 points or relative increase of 17.42% on average over the baseline, over all target languages, while chrF++ and COMET increases 7.1 and 16.9, respectively. Similarly, TER decreases by 9 points. The 100k+ datasets also demonstrate consistent performance gains with an average increase of 13.7 BLEU, 12.7 chrF++, and 25 COMET, while TER decreases to 15.5.

To provide a point of comparison, we evaluate the performance of GPT-3.5[9] on our test set. While GPT-3.5 outperforms our highest-performing model in BLEU and chrF++ for DE and FI, the 100k+ datasets often surpass GPT-3.5 in other languages and metrics. This demonstrates the effectiveness of creating bespoke models through fine-tuning mid-sized LLMs when leveraging domain-specific data. Targeted fine-tuning can yield competitive or superior results compared to larger, general-purpose models like GPT-3.5.

3.1 Small Dataset Deterioration

Regarding translation quality across different training data sizes, we note a deterioration in quality for models trained on the smaller datasets (1k and 2k) in relation to the baseline. Despite a smooth reduction in both training and evaluation loss during training across all sizes, these smaller datasets still lead to poorer performance on all metrics. This can be due to the fact that the 1k and 2k datasets are insufficient to offer the models a wide enough variety of examples, leading to overfitting where the model performs well on training but poorly on the unseen test data (Barone et al., 2017; Atrio and Popescu-Belis, 2022; Garcia et al., 2023; Ramírez Atrio, 2023).

It is possible that the lack of diversity in the smaller models fails to capture the range of linguistic and translation nuances present in the test data which hinders the model's ability to generalise beyond the specific examples seen during training. Furthermore, the smaller datasets may make the models more susceptible to noise, such as translation errors or inconsistencies, leading to the learning of incorrect patterns and degrading performance on the test data, affecting the automatic metrics results, while the loss continues to drop due to fitting noisy data (Barone et al., 2017; Atrio and Popescu-Belis, 2022; Ramírez Atrio, 2023).

Another possible explanation for the deterioration is a decrease in training data quality in the 1k and 2k dataset sizes. To examine this, we use COMET-Kiwi (Rei et al., 2023), a popular quality estimation metric, to evaluate the quality of the training data. The scores are consistent for each language with variations within a narrow range of 1-2 points (cf. Appendix D). For example, FI has the highest variation with a maximum score of 79.58 (1k and 14.7K) and a minimum score of 78.12 (5k), resulting in a range of only 1.46 points. The minimal variation in score indicates consistent data quality across all dataset sizes for each language. Therefore, the deterioration in performance is unlikely to be due to a decrease in data quality for the 1k and 2k training data sizes.

Hyperparameter fine-tuning could be employed to mitigate this early deterioration in situations where only small datasets are available. This may include dropout or other regularisation techniques to prevent overfitting on small training sets. Adjustment of the learning rate, batch sizes and QLoRA hyperparameters should also be explored to deal with this specific case of deterioration (Barone et al., 2017; Atrio and Popescu-Belis, 2022; Dettmers et al., 2023; Ramírez Atrio, 2023).

Overall, a different approach is required in order to obtain gains when the training data is scarce. Our experiments suggest the need for at least 5k examples to achieve an improvement in metrics under the hyper-specific domain and circumstances we explore.

The issues above seem to be mitigated on the larger sets whilst maintaining the same hyperparameters as previously reported (cf. Table 3). We observe performance recovery on 5k examples, overtaking the baseline model, then consistently improving over all metrics as dataset size increases, and achieving increasingly impressive results across all metrics when training on anything above the 10k

[9]https://chat.openai.com/

Lang	Data Size	BLEU ↑	chrF++ ↑	TER ↓	COMET ↑
	GPT 3.5	56.50	76.33	32.03	86.02
	Baseline	48.25	69.21	39.36	77.28
	1k	48.00	69.34	40.11	78.28
PT-BR	2k	46.04	67.93	44.09	75.70
	5k	49.73	69.92	38.03	80.80
	10k	50.90	70.92	35.96	86.15
	14.7k	53.42	73.07	32.92	89.18
	100k+	**62.45**	**78.57**	**26.20**	**95.98**
	GPT 3.5	31.78	55.02	58.17	72.99
	Baseline	26.25	49.97	63.27	62.43
	1k	26.53	50.15	64.97	64.20
CS	2k	25.23	48.35	68.76	58.28
	5k	27.57	51.35	62.84	66.85
	10k	27.96	52.40	63.26	66.62
	14.7k	31.57	54.75	60.07	73.73
	100k+	**39.72**	**61.45**	**52.00**	**84.22**
	GPT 3.5	**42.41**	**65.88**	50.07	65.31
	Baseline	34.32	59.16	57.60	58.36
	1k	34.58	59.07	58.42	60.86
DE	2k	32.45	57.08	62.93	53.87
	5k	35.31	59.37	56.19	63.66
	10k	37.23	60.58	53.59	66.82
	14.7k	37.88	61.08	52.71	68.50
	100k+	42.27	65.15	**48.59**	**73.01**
	GPT 3.5	**33.80**	**59.18**	**58.29**	83.84
	Baseline	23.97	49.70	70.36	62.64
	1k	24.14	49.48	71.18	65.22
FI	2k	19.07	46.97	83.00	58.34
	5k	22.05	47.32	75.12	60.54
	10k	25.88	50.71	65.99	74.91
	14.7k	26.48	51.32	64.91	73.66
	100k+	31.71	57.13	59.72	**84.71**
	GPT 3.5	33.07	49.72	60.60	63.28
	Baseline	20.81	35.37	77.95	36.45
	1k	20.12	42.16	83.37	35.24
KO	2k	19.25	41.13	82.48	26.03
	5k	28.60	46.84	65.42	54.17
	10k	31.36	52.62	60.86	70.56
	14.7k	28.15	58.88	53.11	76.65
	100k+	**45.80**	**64.81**	**44.73**	**84.30**

Table 4: Evaluation results of fine-tuning Llama 3 8B on datasets of various sizes. **Bold** text indicates the best score. The models trained on the largest dataset (100k+) perform the best. The scores deteriorate from the baseline for 1k and 2k but recover and increase from 5k onward. Underlined text indicates the worst scores.

sets and excelling on the 100k+ sets.

3.2 Resource Level

It is interesting to note that the performance for KO has improved after the 14.7k fine-tuning and becomes comparable to or better than the performance of the other language directions, despite the lower initial baseline score across all metrics. For instance, the COMET score for the KO baseline is 36.5 while the average for all other languages is 57.7. We find that the lower resource languages (KO being the lowest of the target languages explored) have the highest relative gains, turning around a very poor baseline across all metrics. The COMET score for KO increased to 84.3 compared to the average of 84.5 in the 100k+ datasets for PR-BR, DE, FI, and CS, resulting in KO's comparable performance to the high resource languages, i.e. PT-BR and DE.

These results probably relate not only to the resource level of the language but also to the amount of Korean data in the Llama 3 training recipe. According to MetaAI, "over 5% of the Llama 3 pretraining dataset consists of high-quality non-English data that covers over 30 languages" (Meta, 2024). While the Llama Team provides more detail on the training and data mix Llama 3, the exact proportion of Korean data is not discussed (Llama Team, 2024). Our baseline metrics suggest that Korean does not feature highly on that list given that it scores significantly lower than all other languages. This might be attributed to the fact that there were not enough examples to produce a firm understanding of the language but enough to provide a foundation that heavily benefited from fine-tuning. As mentioned, this is an assumption as we lack sufficiently detailed information on the training recipe.

When looking at the target languages, we note that PT-BR shows the best performance at 14.7k and 100k+ dataset. This indicates that, even for a well-resourced language, the foundation model gained a strong understanding of the language during pretraining. However, it did not seem to benefit as much from fine-tuning as KO, a lower resource language. This corroborates the finding that resource level is a strong determiner of LLM MT performance (Robinson et al., 2023).

3.3 Human Evaluation

Regarding the human evaluation, the qualitative comments from the translators reveal that the largest model struggles with ambiguity. Evaluators mention that segments that lacked complete information needed to be completely reworked. For example, the segment, "Get basic, step-by-step instructions to learn" lacks a final object, which impacts the translation. While human translators often face and resolve such ambiguities through research or decision-making with incomplete information, the model processes segments in isolation, unable to access potentially clarifying context from adjacent segments. This limitation provides insight into the model's performance in real-world translation scenarios.

4 Conclusions

Fine-tuning on TMs has been demonstrated to enhance the performance of LLMs in MT tasks. In this paper, we investigate the relationship between automatic metric results and training set sizes to identify the optimal balance where resource investment yields the most significant improvements in translation quality. In our experiments, it has become evident that fine-tuning on training datasets whose size is larger than 5k examples returned increasingly better results in 19 out of the 20 language-training set size combinations explored.

By leveraging TMs, the model becomes more adept at recognising and reproducing previously translated segments, their style, and terminology. Furthermore, fine-tuning on TM data helps the model adapt to specialised fields.

The test and training sets used come from a much narrower corpus of data than in similar experiments that deal with wider domains, i.e. medicine (Moslem et al., 2023b). The hyper-specific nature of the training data employed in our approach may partly explain the promising results. We therefore leverage the advantage that smaller models licensed for business-use offer; they can be adapted several times over for narrow and specific domains, as well as multiple languages with little investment, instead of aiming for a more general purpose or multilingual model. The hyper-specific purpose of our trained model, i.e. one language direction and a narrow domain, suits the size and easiness of training of an 8B parameter mode.

Being a commonly experienced scenario in the localization industry, this is an under-explored approach that organisations could be pursuing in order to make the most out of their access to TMs and LLMs for MT in order to obtain the best possible return on investment when leveraging their previously human-translated material.

Low-resource languages seem to be in a perfect position to benefit from leveraging small business-friendly models, like Llama 3 8B. The gains in automatic metric results for KO are substantially higher for high resource languages, like PT-BR and DE, returning the highest increase in performance compared to the metrics obtained from training on similar set sizes in those languages. KO observes an increase of 130% on COMET from the baseline to the 100k+ dataset, whereas the average increase amongst the other target languages is 46% (cf. Table 4).

It is important to mention that, just as Wu (2024) acknowledges the FLORES-200 dataset leakage into Llama 3, it is possible that some of our test set was also scraped by the Llama 3 models, as parts of the material were published online prior to the Llama 3 family's pre-training. We face the same challenge as the whole AI researching community, forced to either constantly come up with new test sets or simply acknowledge the potential leakage of test data (Xu et al., 2024). We urge large tech companies to disclose at a minimum the test sets that were not ingested by their models for the benefit of the whole community. We acknowledge the Llama Team's leadership in this area (Llama Team, 2024).

5 Future Work

Future work in the area may benefit from the introduction of checkpoints during training and subsequent intermediate evaluation would enable the visualisation of a clearer learning curve, and the identification of potential dips in performance and points of diminishing returns. This approach would facilitate the analysis and allow for a finer and more efficient evaluation process.

In the future, we aim to obtain a bespoke test set directly from the organisation that owns the TMs. This tailored test set would consist of examples specifically designed in-house according to strict guidelines, ensuring they are completely original and reflective of the organisation's unique requirements and style. By using a bespoke and unseen test set, we can more accurately assess the performance of our fine-tuned models in a real-world context.

Finally, further investigation is required with regard to the training hyperparameters across the different dataset sizes in order to obtain better results with smaller training sets under 5k examples. Several strategies can be explored to optimise performance on smaller datasets. Adjustments such as modifying the dropout rates to prevent overfitting, applying regularisation techniques to enhance model generalisation, and fine-tuning the learning rate to ensure efficient convergence can be particularly beneficial in this case.

6 Acknowledgements

This research is supported by Science Foundation Ireland through ADAPT Centre (Grant No. 13/RC/2106) (`www.adaptcentre.ie`) at Dublin City University. We thank Alpha-CRC for their essential collaboration.

References

Alves, D., Guerreiro, N., Alves, J., Pombal, J., Rei, R., de Souza, J., Colombo, P., and Martins, A. (2023a). Steering large language models for machine translation with finetuning and in-context learning. In Bouamor, H., Pino, J., and Bali, K., editors, *Findings of the Association for Computational Linguistics: EMNLP 2023*, pages 11127–11148, Singapore. Association for Computational Linguistics.

Alves, D., Guerreiro, N., Alves, J., Pombal, J., Rei, R., de Souza, J., Colombo, P., and Martins, A. (2023b). Steering Large Language Models for Machine Translation with Finetuning and In-Context Learning. In Bouamor, H., Pino, J., and Bali, K., editors, *Findings of the Association for Computational Linguistics: EMNLP 2023*, pages 11127–11148, Singapore. Association for Computational Linguistics.

Atrio, À. R. and Popescu-Belis, A. (2022). On the Interaction of Regularization Factors in Low-resource Neural Machine Translation. In Moniz, H., Macken, L., Rufener, A., Barrault, L., Costa-jussà, M. R., Declercq, C., Koponen, M., Kemp, E., Pilos, S., Forcada, M. L., Scarton, C., Van den Bogaert, J., Daems, J., Tezcan, A., Vanroy, B., and Fonteyne, M., editors, *Proceedings of the 23rd Annual Conference of the European Association for Machine Translation*, pages 111–120, Ghent, Belgium. European Association for Machine Translation.

Barone, A. V. M., Haddow, B., Germann, U.,

and Sennrich, R. (2017). Regularization techniques for fine-tuning in neural machine translation. arXiv:1707.09920 [cs].

Bloodgood, M. and Strauss, B. (2014). Translation memory retrieval methods. In Wintner, S., Goldwater, S., and Riezler, S., editors, *Proceedings of the 14th Conference of the European Chapter of the Association for Computational Linguistics*, pages 202–210, Gothenburg, Sweden. Association for Computational Linguistics.

Bulte, B. and Tezcan, A. (2019). Neural Fuzzy Repair: Integrating Fuzzy Matches into Neural Machine Translation. In Korhonen, A., Traum, D., and Màrquez, L., editors, *Proceedings of the 57th Annual Meeting of the Association for Computational Linguistics*, pages 1800–1809, Florence, Italy. Association for Computational Linguistics.

Cai, D., Wang, Y., Li, H., Lam, W., and Liu, L. (2021). Neural Machine Translation with Monolingual Translation Memory. In Zong, C., Xia, F., Li, W., and Navigli, R., editors, *Proceedings of the 59th Annual Meeting of the Association for Computational Linguistics and the 11th International Joint Conference on Natural Language Processing (Volume 1: Long Papers)*, pages 7307–7318, Online. Association for Computational Linguistics.

Costa-jussà, M. R., Cross, J., Çelebi, O., Elbayad, M., Heafield, K., Heffernan, K., Kalbassi, E., Lam, J., Licht, D., Maillard, J., Sun, A., Wang, S., Wenzek, G., Youngblood, A., Akula, B., Barrault, L., Gonzalez, G. M., Hansanti, P., Hoffman, J., Jarrett, S., Sadagopan, K. R., Rowe, D., Spruit, S., Tran, C., Andrews, P., Ayan, N. F., Bhosale, S., Edunov, S., Fan, A., Gao, C., Goswami, V., Guzmán, F., Koehn, P., Mourachko, A., Ropers, C., Saleem, S., Schwenk, H., and Wang, J. (2022). No Language Left Behind: Scaling human-centered machine translation.

Dettmers, T., Pagnoni, A., Holtzman, A., and Zettlemoyer, L. (2023). QLoRA: Efficient Finetuning of Quantized LLMs. arXiv:2305.14314 [cs].

Garcia, X., Bansal, Y., Cherry, C., Foster, G., Krikun, M., Johnson, M., and Firat, O. (2023). The Unreasonable Effectiveness of Few-shot Learning for Machine Translation. In *Proceedings of the 40th International Conference on Machine Learning*, pages 10867–10878. PMLR. ISSN: 2640-3498.

Guzmán, F., Chen, P.-J., Ott, M., Pino, J., Lample, G., Koehn, P., Chaudhary, V., and Ranzato, M. (2019). The FLORES evaluation datasets for low-resource machine translation: Nepali–English and Sinhala–English. In Inui, K., Jiang, J., Ng, V., and Wan, X., editors, *Proceedings of the 2019 Conference on Empirical Methods in Natural Language Processing and the 9th International Joint Conference on Natural Language Processing (EMNLP-IJCNLP)*, pages 6098–6111, Hong Kong, China. Association for Computational Linguistics.

Haque, R., Moslem, Y., and Way, A. (2020). Terminology-Aware Sentence Mining for NMT Domain Adaptation: ADAPT's Submission to the Adap-MT 2020 English-to-Hindi AI Translation Shared Task. In *Proceedings of the 17th International Conference on Natural Language Processing (ICON): Adap-MT 2020 Shared Task*, pages 17–23, Patna, India. NLP Association of India (NLPAI).

Hu, E. J., Shen, Y., Wallis, P., Allen-Zhu, Z., Li, Y., Wang, S., Wang, L., and Chen, W. (2021). LoRA: Low-Rank Adaptation of Large Language Models. arXiv:2106.09685 [cs].

Klein, G., Zhang, D., Chouteau, C., Crego, J., and Senellart, J. (2020). Efficient and high-quality neural machine translation with OpenNMT. In *Proceedings of the Fourth Workshop on Neural Generation and Translation*, pages 211–217, Stroudsburg, PA, USA. Association for Computational Linguistics.

Knowles, R. and Littell, P. (2022). Translation Memories as Baselines for Low-Resource Machine Translation. In Calzolari, N., Béchet, F., Blache, P., Choukri, K., Cieri, C., Declerck, T., Goggi, S., Isahara, H., Maegaard, B., Mariani, J., Mazo, H., Odijk, J., and Piperidis, S., editors, *Proceedings of the Thirteenth Language Resources and Evaluation Conference*, pages 6759–6767, Marseille, France. European Language Resources Association.

Levenshtein, V. (1965). Binary codes capable of correcting deletions, insertions, and reversals. *Soviet physics. Doklady*.

Li, J., Zhou, H., Huang, S., Cheng, S., and Chen, J. (2023). Eliciting the Translation Ability of Large Language Models via Multilingual Finetuning with Translation Instructions. arXiv:2305.15083 [cs].

Llama Team (2024). The Llama 3 Herd of Models.

Lopez-Gazpio, I., Maritxalar, M., Lapata, M., and Agirre, E. (2019). Word n-gram attention models for sentence similarity and inference. *Expert Systems with Applications*, 132:1–11.

Lyu, C., Du, Z., Xu, J., Duan, Y., Wu, M., Lynn, T., Aji, A. F., Wong, D. F., and Wang, L. (2024). A Paradigm Shift: The Future of Machine Translation Lies with Large Language Models. In Calzolari, N., Kan, M.-Y., Hoste, V., Lenci, A., Sakti, S., and Xue, N., editors, *Proceedings of the 2024 Joint International Conference on Computational Linguistics, Language Resources and Evaluation (LREC-COLING 2024)*, pages 1339–1352, Torino, Italia. ELRA and ICCL.

Meta (2024). Introducing meta llama 3: The most capable openly available llm to date. https://ai.meta.com/blog/meta-llama-3/.

Moslem, Y., Haque, R., Kelleher, J., and Way, A. (2022). Domain-Specific Text Generation for Machine Translation. In Duh, K. and Guzmán, F., editors, *Proceedings of the 15th biennial conference of the Association for Machine Translation in the Americas (Volume 1: Research Track)*, pages 14–30, Orlando, USA. Association for Machine Translation in the Americas.

Moslem, Y., Haque, R., Kelleher, J. D., and Way, A. (2023a). Adaptive Machine Translation with Large Language Models. In Nurminen, M., Brenner, J., Koponen, M., Latomaa, S., Mikhailov, M., Schierl, F., Ranasinghe, T., Vanmassenhove, E., Vidal, S. A., Aranberri, N., Nunziatini, M., Escartín, C. P., Forcada, M., Popovic, M., Scarton, C., and Moniz, H., editors, *Proceedings of the 24th Annual Conference of the European Association for Machine Translation*, pages 227–237, Tampere, Finland. European Association for Machine Translation.

Moslem, Y., Haque, R., and Way, A. (2023b). Fine-tuning Large Language Models for Adaptive Machine Translation. arXiv:2312.12740 [cs].

Mu, Y., Reheman, A., Cao, Z., Fan, Y., Li, B., Li, Y., Xiao, T., Zhang, C., and Zhu, J. (2023). Augmenting large language model translators via translation memories. In Rogers, A., Boyd-Graber, J., and Okazaki, N., editors, *Findings of the Association for Computational Linguistics: ACL 2023*, pages 10287–10299, Toronto, Canada. Association for Computational Linguistics.

Papineni, K., Roukos, S., Ward, T., and Zhu, W.-J. (2002). Bleu: a Method for Automatic Evaluation of Machine Translation. In *Proceedings of the 40th Annual Meeting of the Association for Computational Linguistics*, pages 311–318, Philadelphia, Pennsylvania, USA. Association for Computational Linguistics.

Popović, M. (2017). chrF++: words helping character n-grams. In *Proceedings of the Second Conference on Machine Translation*, pages 612–618, Copenhagen, Denmark. Association for Computational Linguistics.

Ramírez Atrio, A. (2023). *Regularization Techniques for Low-Resource Machine Translation*. PhD thesis, EPFL, Lausanne.

Rei, R., Guerreiro, N. M., Pombal, J., van Stigt, D., Treviso, M., Coheur, L., C. de Souza, J. G., and Martins, A. (2023). Scaling up CometKiwi: Unbabel-IST 2023 Submission for the Quality Estimation Shared Task. In Koehn, P., Haddow, B., Kocmi, T., and Monz, C., editors, *Proceedings of the Eighth Conference on Machine Translation*, pages 841–848, Singapore. Association for Computational Linguistics.

Rei, R., Stewart, C., Farinha, A. C., and Lavie, A. (2020). COMET: A Neural Framework for MT Evaluation. In *Proceedings of the 2020 Conference on Empirical Methods in Natural Language Processing (EMNLP)*, pages 2685–2702, Online. Association for Computational Linguistics.

Robinson, N., Ogayo, P., Mortensen, D. R., and Neubig, G. (2023). ChatGPT MT: Competitive for high- (but not low-) resource languages. In Koehn, P., Haddow, B., Kocmi, T., and Monz, C., editors, *Proceedings of the Eighth Conference on Machine Translation*, pages 392–418, Singapore. Association for Computational Linguistics.

Snover, M., Dorr, B., Schwartz, R., Micciulla, L., and Makhoul, J. (2006). A Study of Translation Edit Rate with Targeted Human Annotation. In *Proceedings of the 7th Conference of the Association for Machine Translation in the Americas: Technical Papers*, pages 223–231, Cambridge, Massachusetts, USA. Association for Machine Translation in the Americas.

Wu, M. (2024). Evaluating the Machine Translation Capability of Llama-3 Models. Publication Title: GitHub repository.

Wu, M., Vu, T.-T., Qu, L., Foster, G., and Haffari, G. (2024). Adapting large language models for document-level machine translation.

Xu, J., Crego, J., and Senellart, J. (2020). Boosting Neural Machine Translation with Similar Translations. In Jurafsky, D., Chai, J., Schluter, N., and Tetreault, J., editors, *Proceedings of the 58th Annual Meeting of the Association for Computational Linguistics*, pages 1580–1590, Online. Association for Computational Linguistics.

Xu, R., Wang, Z., Fan, R.-Z., and Liu, P. (2024). Benchmarking benchmark leakage in large language models.

Zhang, X., Rajabi, N., Duh, K., and Koehn, P. (2023). Machine Translation with Large Language Models: Prompting, Few-shot Learning, and Fine-tuning with QLoRA. In Koehn, P., Haddow, B., Kocmi, T., and Monz, C., editors, *Proceedings of the Eighth Conference on Machine Translation*, pages 468–481, Singapore. Association for Computational Linguistics.

Zheng, J., Hong, H., Wang, X., Su, J., Liang, Y., and Wu, S. (2024). Fine-tuning Large Language Models for Domain-specific Machine Translation. arXiv:2402.15061 [cs].

Zhu, W., Liu, H., Dong, Q., Xu, J., Huang, S., Kong, L., Chen, J., and Li, L. (2023). Multilingual Machine Translation with Large Language Models: Empirical Results and Analysis. arXiv:2304.04675 [cs].

A Appendix A

Lang	Size	Loss	Dev Loss	Train Runtime
PT-BR	1k	1.4922	1.0706	69
	2k	0.8271	0.8290	120
	5k	0.7506	0.6325	290
	10k	0.4222	0.5337	551
	14.7k	0.4918	0.4714	820
	100k+	0.6031	0.5964	8423
CS	1k	1.5428	1.0795	70
	2k	0.9446	0.8880	124
	5k	0.6643	0.6586	296
	10k	0.6475	0.5880	574
	14.7k	0.5346	0.5169	837
	100k+	0.5600	0.4800	8000*
FI	1k	1.5342	1.1519	71
	2k	0.9631	0.9602	125
	5k	0.5876	0.6286	302
	10k	0.5662	0.5874	589
	14.7k	0.3996	0.5138	866
	100k+	0.5964	0.5867	8241
DE	1k	1.5551	1.1397	69
	2k	0.9591	0.9301	121
	5k	0.4371	0.6426	290
	10k	0.4553	0.5639	550
	14.7k	0.5310	0.5037	819
	100k+	0.6672	0.6603	8000*
KO	1k	1.5851	1.0651	67
	2k	0.7765	0.7733	120
	5k	0.6086	0.6340	270
	10k	0.4662	0.5666	543
	14.7k	0.4167	0.4923	807
	100k+	0.7822	0.7052	5791

Table 5: Training Details by Language. Train Runtime is measured in seconds. Starred numbers are estimates.

B Appendix B

B.1 Special Token Descriptions

< |*begin_of_text*| >: *This is equivalent to the BOS token.*

< |*eot_id*| >: *This signifies the end of the message in a turn.*

< |*start_header_id*| >{*role*}< |*end_header_id*| >: *These tokens enclose the role for a particular message. The possible roles can be: system, user, assistant.*

< |*end_of_text*| >: *This is equivalent to the EOS token.*

B.2 Prompt

< |*begin_of_text*| > < |*start_header_id*| >*system*< |*end_header_id*| >

You are a helpful AI assistant for translation from {*source_language*} *to* {*target_language*}. *You MUST answer with the following JSON scheme:* {*"translation": "string"*} < |*eot_id*| >
< |*start_header_id*| >*user*< |*end_header_id*| >

{*source_sentence*}< |*eot_id*| >< |*start_header_id*| >*assistant*< |*end_header_id*| >

B.3 Training Prompt

< |*begin_of_text*| >< |*start_header_id*| >*system*< |*end_header_id*| >

You are a helpful AI assistant for translation from {*source_language*} *to* {*target_language*}. *You MUST answer with the following JSON scheme:* {*"translation": "string"*} < |*eot_id*| >

< |*start_header_id*| >*user*< |*end_header_id*| > {*source_sentence*}< |*eot_id*| >

< |*start_header_id*| >*assistant*< |*end_header_id*| >***{target_sentence}***< |***end_of_text***| >

C Appendix C

Inference Parameters	
sampling_topk	1
max_batch_size	8096
min_length	1
max_length	double the source length

Table 6: CTranslate2 Inference Parameters.

D Appendix D

Lang	Data Size	Comet-Kiwi ↑
PT-BR	1k	77.95
	2k	77.81
	5k	77.65
	10k	77.77
	14.7k	78.92
CS	1k	79.71
	2k	78.98
	5k	78.57
	10k	78.78
	14.7k	79.71
DE	1k	78.58
	2k	78.22
	5k	78.34
	10k	78.21
	14.7k	78.73
FI	1k	79.58
	2k	78.70
	5k	78.12
	10k	78.54
	14.7k	79.58
KO	1k	81.93
	2k	81.56
	5k	81.20
	10k	81.22
	14.7k	81.55

Table 7: Quality Evaluation results of training datasets of different sizes using Comet-Kiwi metric.

Examining Cognitive Biases in ChatGPT 3.5 and 4 through Human Evaluation and Linguistic Comparison

Giada Pantana giada.pantana@edu.unige.it
Department of Modern Languages and Cultures, University of Genoa, Genoa, IT
Marta Castello marta.castello@creative-words.com
Creative Words, Genoa, IT
Ilaria Torre ilaria.torre@unige.it
Department of Informatics, Bioengineering, Robotics, and Systems Engineering, University of Genoa, Genoa, IT

Abstract

This paper aims to investigate the presence of cognitive biases, more specifically of Availability heuristics, Representativeness heuristics and Framing, in OpenAI's ChatGPT 3.5 and ChatGPT 4, as well as the linguistic dependency of their occurrences in the Large Language Models' (LLMs) outputs. The innovative aspect of this research is conveyed by rephrasing three tasks proposed in Kahneman and Tversky's works and determining whether the LLMs' answers to the tasks are correct or incorrect and human-like or non-human-like. The latter classification is made possible by interviewing a total of 56 native speakers of Italian, English and Spanish, thus introducing a new linguistic comparison of results and forming a "human standard". Our study indicates that GPTs 3.5 and 4 are very frequently subject to the cognitive biases under discussion and their answers are mostly non-human-like. There is minimal but significant discrepancy in the performance of GPT 3.5 and 4, slightly favouring ChatGPT 4 in avoiding biased responses, specifically for Availability heuristics. We also reveal that, while the results for ChatGPT 4 are not significantly language dependent, meaning that the performances in avoiding biases are not affected by the prompting language, their difference with ChatGPT 3.5 is statistically significant.

1 Introduction

In the last years, Large Language Models (LLMs) have been used exponentially thanks to their capabilities to be queried with natural language and to return content- and context-aware responses. They became popular within the general public, and businesses swiftly introduced these models in their workflow aiming at becoming more productive, while reducing employees' workload. Natural language itself is not only our easiest and quickest way to communicate to these language models, but also the main reason why we tend to anthropise these machines (Roberts and al., 2024), making our relationship with them resonate widely and strongly in our everyday life. Nonetheless, "LLMs simply do not have the capacity to distinguish between truth and falsehood and, therefore, without malicious intent, [they] can confidently present fictions as if they were truths" (Roberts and al., 2024, p. 4). For this reason, we have the responsibility to prove if, how and when they are most reliable. Much work has been done in delicate fields such as legal, medical and educational (Schmidgall and al., 2024; Pal and al., 2023; Pal, 2024; Curran and al., 2023; Gutiérrez-Cirlos and al., 2023; Ji and al., 2023b) to analyse how to improve their use in the professionals' decision-making process and to help users make more conscious choices. When only taking the outputs into consideration, the main hindrance to their implementation into businesses and field-specific tasks are hallucinations, defined as "the generated content that is nonsensical or unfaithful to the provided source content" (Ji and al., 2023a, p. 4). Hallucinations are defined as intrinsic, when the output contradicts the source, or extrinsic, when the output cannot be verified from the source (Ji and al., 2023a). Given the potentially harmful and often subtle nature of this phenomenon, researchers have developed various hallucination mitigation techniques. These techniques operate at different levels of the LLM's functioning to help reduce their occurrence. Addressing the issue can involve either prompt engineering or developing models to reduce the elicitation of hallucinations. Specific actions are available for each level of the LLM's functioning (Tonmoy and al., 2024).

Alongside the phenomena that hinder menaces, the utility of LLMs is threatened by the presence of cognitive biases in their outputs. As hallucinations, cognitive biases are concepts mainly used to describe human behaviours and have been adapted to this field to define machines' dysfunctions. Generative Artificial Intelligence (GenAI) can exhibit biases due to various factors. Some of the key causes are that LLMs are trained on human-made data, including historical data. They can be skewed and affected by under/over-representation of certain phenomena. Moreover, biases can be introduced in the process of data annotation and refinement, often based on Reinforced Learning with Human Feedback (RLHF) (Christiano and al., 2023; Chen and al., 2023; Navigli and al., 2023) and propagate into the models. Thus, machines can potentially inherit and enhance human cognitive biases.

The main focus of this article is to verify whether ChatGPT 3.5 and ChatGPT 4 are susceptible to three specific cognitive biases, known in the literature as *Availability heuristics*, *Representativeness heuristics* and *Framing* (Tversky and Kahneman, 1973, 1983, 1981). The Dictionary of Psychology issued by the American Psychological Association defines them as follows. *Availability heuristics* is: "a common strategy for making judgments about likelihood of occurrence in which the individual bases such judgments on the salience of the information held in their memory about the particular type of event"[1]. *Representativeness heuristics* is: "a strategy for making categorical judgments about a given person or target based on how closely the exemplar matches the typical or average member of the category"[2]. Finally, *Framing* is: "the process of defining the context or issues surrounding a question, problem, or event in a way that serves to influence how the context or issues are perceived and evaluated"[3].

A recent trend in Generative Artificial Intelligence literature is "machine psychology" by Thilo Hagendorff, meaning that the LLM is positioned by the researchers as the subject of their psychological tests, initially designed to investigate human misbehaviour (Hagendorff, 2023). According to this approach, LLMs are tested for cognitive biases using their chatbot interfaces. The tools mainly investigated for tracking cognitive biases are Open AI's ChatGPT (version 3.5, 3.5 Turbo and 4), Google's Gemini, Anthropic's Claude in different versions and Llama in different versions (Macmillan-Scott and M., 2024; Azaria, 2023; Chen and al., 2023; Schmidgall and al., 2024). Most studies refer to the tasks proposed by Kahneman and Tversky to test cognitive biases (Macmillan-Scott and M., 2024; Azaria, 2023; Chen and al., 2023; Kliegr and al., 2021) and have unmasked that LLMs are, in fact, victims of these biases, including but not limited to: Confirmation bias (Macmillan-Scott and M., 2024; Chen and al., 2023; Kliegr and al., 2021; Berberette and al., 2024; Ke and al., 2024; Dos Santos and Cury, 2023; Schmidgall and al., 2024), Availability heuristics (Azaria, 2023; Chen and al., 2023; Kliegr and al., 2021; Berberette and al., 2024), Overconfidence (Chen and al., 2023; Kliegr and al., 2021; Schmidgall and al., 2024), Representativeness heuristics (Macmillan-Scott and M., 2024; Chen and al., 2023; Kliegr and al., 2021), Framing (Azaria, 2023; Chen and al., 2023), Recency effect (Berberette and al., 2024; Schmidgall and al., 2024). The primary methodology described in these studies either directly or indirectly refers to the "machine psychology" approach (Hagendorff, 2023).

This paper addresses the following research questions:

1. Do ChatGPT 3.5 and 4 show *Availability heuristics*, *Representativeness heuristics* and *Framing* biases in their outputs?

2. Are there any differences in the performance outcomes of ChatGPT 3.5 and ChatGPT 4?

[1] https://dictionary.apa.org/availability-heuristic, last access: 3/14/2024

[2] https://dictionary.apa.org/representativeness-heuristic, last access: 3/14/2024

[3] https://dictionary.apa.org/framing, last access: 3/14/2024

3. Are the two ChatGPT models language dependent in reporting the aforementioned biases?

Based on the results of previous research, it can be supposed that: - LLMs show biases like *Availability heuristics* (Berberette and al., 2024; Kliegr and al., 2021; Azaria, 2023), *Representativeness heuristics* (Macmillan-Scott and M., 2024; Chen and al., 2023; Kliegr and al., 2021) and *Framing* (Chen and al., 2023; Azaria, 2023) in their outputs;
- there are differences between ChatGPT 3.5 and 4, where 4 should be less subject to biases since it is trained on more data, or at least gives better performances according to OpenAI (OpenAI et al., 2024);
- LLMs should be language dependent since the data with which they are trained differ among languages, causing different performances, or at least their results in Massive Multitask Language Understanding (MMLU) are, despite a minimal difference, better in English than Italian or Spanish (OpenAI et al., 2024).

2 Methodology

In consideration of recent literature, the aim is to analyse the biases of *Availability heuristics*, *Representativeness heuristics* and *Framing* in two LLMs, namely ChatGPT 3.5 and 4[4]. This will be done by introducing a new rephrasing approach to three specific Tversky and Kahneman tests, namely the Judgement of word frequency (Tversky and Kahneman, 1973) to demonstrate *Availability heuristics*, the Linda problem (Tversky and Kahneman, 1983) to demonstrate *Representativeness heuristics* and the Framing of Contingencies (Tversky and Kahneman, 1981) to demonstrate *Framing*.
The presence of biases in LLMs outputs was examined by classifying the answers of the LLMs according to the methodology proposed by Olivia MacMillan-Scott and Mirco Musolesi in their paper (Macmillan-Scott and M., 2024), using four parameters: correct/incorrect and human-like/non-human-like. To support the definition of what is human-like, a pool of 56 people (59% women, 41% men, age average: 33) was interviewed, defined by the availability of resources, yet guaranteeing the representativeness of the sample, posing the same questions asked to the two ChatGPT models. Ethics approval was not obtained since the research did not involve sensitive personal information or interventions that required formal ethical oversight. Additionally, to verify whether the answers of the models, as well as their potential biases, are language dependent, a multilingual analysis was conducted by prompting the LLMs in Italian, English and Spanish. The innovative aspect of this work lies in the multilingual comparison between human native speakers and LLM data, setting it apart from previously analysed reference material.
To answer the research questions, we followed the methodology described in the subsequent sections. All data regarding the complete prompts and results are available in a public GitHub repository. [5]

2.1 LLM tools

Open AI's ChatGPT 3.5 and 4 were chosen for this research paper as they are among the most commonly used LLMs in the literature regarding the testing on cognitive biases (Macmillan-Scott and M., 2024; Azaria, 2023; Chen and al., 2023; Berberette and al., 2024; Ke and al., 2024; Dos Santos and Cury, 2023; Schmidgall and al., 2024). Chat GPT 3.5 was chosen because it is free and therefore widely accessible; Chat GPT 4, expected to have better performance (OpenAI et al., 2024), was analysed to determine if it provides potentially less biased answers than the former model.
The models were not customised or specifically trained. The chatbot interface was used to test the prompts and obtain the answers. Zero-shot prompting (Kojima and al., 2022) was applied to address the LLMs, at times integrated with an iterative approach to elicit a unique and definite answer from the machines. The prompt testing for the LLMs was carried out from 15th March to 10th April 2024. The prompting texts are described below and reported in Table 1 in the Appendix.

2.2 Prompt definition

One prompt was tested for each bias: the Judgement of word frequency for *Availability heuristics*, the Linda problem for *Representativeness heuristics* and the Framing of Contingencies for *Framing*. Each prompt was tested in three languages: Italian, English and Spanish. Below, the methodology for

[4] https://chat.openai.com/auth/login, last access 4/10/2024
[5] https://github.com/CreativeWords/Cognitive_Bias_GPT

defining the three tests and how the same prompt was formulated in the three different languages under scrutiny will be explained.

All the prompts tested were re-elaborated from preexisting psychology tests originally targeting human subjects. This paper focuses on addressing LLMs, instead, following the "machine psychology" approach (Hagendorff, 2023). The tests were rephrased in respect to the originals proposed by Tversky and Kahneman to avoid the risk of them being part of the training data of the LLMs, thus minimizing any potentially compromised performance that would have prevented our detection of real biases. As Thilo Hagendorff explains in his paper (Hagendorff, 2023), it is essential to ensure that the machine has not seen the test before. Given the limited information available on the training dataset, this can be guaranteed by reformulating the questions with new components while preserving the original logical structure. Regarding the languages involved, it necessary to ensure the accuracy and reliability of the translations. To achieve this, the initial drafts of the three prompts were created in Italian by native speakers. Professional translators and native speakers of each language were assigned to translate the prompts into English and Spanish. The three final prompts were subsequently used to query the LLMs. The prompts were submitted 56 times to GPT 3.5 and 56 times to GPT 4, of which 27 times using the Italian prompt, 11 times the English prompt and 18 times the Spanish prompt. This was done to ensure the LLM models were prompted as many times as the human pool (56 people), allowing an effective comparative evaluation. Another reason behind this choice was the need to minimise the chances of randomness (Macmillan-Scott and M., 2024). Each task was prompted in a new, empty chat each time to avoid any occurrence of recency effect[6] (Macmillan-Scott and M., 2024). All prompts are reported in the Appendix in Table 1 following the same logic: name of the test, name of the bias to test, original question by Tversky and Kahneman, and English translation of the prompt. The Italian and Spanish versions are reported in the full repository of data on GitHub. The first prompt in Table 1 was used to test the *Availability heuristics* cognitive bias. Words were tested instead of single letters. "Yes" and "no" were defined as usable words due to their similar frequency of occurrence in all three languages. The deciding factor was supposing that neither people nor machines have enough knowledge or data on words' frequency to consciously give a correct answer, thus requiring to make a decision using System 1, which is a fast, intuitive and emotional decision-making mechanism (Kahneman, 2011).

The second prompt in Table 1 was used to test the *Representativeness heuristics* cognitive bias, starting from the Linda problem. Being the test question extracted from the original paper and dislocated from the task, the square brackets in the original column were added to make the request clearer. Using the same pattern as the original, a different situation was imagined. The various options in the answers are all potential assumptions one can make about Julia based on the initial description given of her. "I don't know" was added to provide respondents with a non-biased option.

The third prompt in Table 1 instead is intended to test the *Framing* bias. In this case, percentages and minor lexical and syntactic changes were used to manipulate the framing of two identical situations. This was built to elicit a preference of one framing of information over another to give an illusion of certainty, defined by Kahneman and Tversky as "pseudocertainy effect" (Tversky and Kahneman, 1981). In the same table, the English question is formulated with a spelling mistake, i.e. "well-todden" instead of "well-trodden". The typo was noticed only after prompting ChatGPT, but the decision was made to replicate the task nonetheless, as the LLM could still properly understand and answer the question.

2.3 Evaluation metric

To catalog the outputs of the LLMs, the scheme by Olivia MacMillan-Scott and Mirco Musolesi (Macmillan-Scott and M., 2024) was applied. They consider "correct" the LLM answer that precisely addresses the question. "Incorrect" is a non-accurate response. In this categorisation, they just refer to the final answer given by the chatbot, without taking into consideration the reasoning behind the answers. For "human-like" and "non-human-like" they refer to the answer a human would have given to the same test. Eventually, they categorise the LLMs' answers in a table, employing this classification: "R: rea-

[6]https://dictionary.apa.org/recency-effect, last access 3/28/2024

soned, IR: incorrect reasoning, H: human-like, NH: non-humanlike, CR: correct reasoning. Both Incorrect (NH) and Incorrect (CR) belong to the incorrect & non-human-like categorisation" (Macmillan-Scott and M., 2024).

Given the rephrasing we did of the Tversky and Kahneman tests, relying on their original responses was not feasible. For this reason, it was necessary to first discern the "correct" (unbiased) and "incorrect" (biased) answers for our tasks. The same questions were then posed to human respondents to establish the "human-like" standard. The methodology for the human testing is reported below in section 2.3.2.

2.3.1 Correct and Incorrect

First, "correct" and "incorrect" answers were identified in all the rephrased tests. To prevent any potential anchoring bias[7], the correct answer was intentionally repositioned. The "correct" and "incorrect" answers for each test are the following: for *Availability heuristics* "No" is correct and "Yes" is incorrect. For *Representativeness heuristics* the correct answer is "I don't know" and the incorrect ones are "A house on the beach. A house on the beach and a motorbike. A house on the beach and a bike". For *Framing* the correct response is "C". "A" and "B" are incorrect.

For *Availability heuristics*, six single-language corpora were checked – two for each language – and it was consistently observed that "No" occurs more frequently than "Yes". The Italian average for "No" is 281.113 occurrences and 158.325 for "Yes". In Spanish, "No" has an average of 36.326.326 occurrences, while "Yes" scores 1.775.599. For English, "No" is more common, with 13.597.439 cases, and only 1.058.347 for "Yes". The links to the corpora can be found on the GitHub space.

Moving on, the correct answer to the *Representativeness Heuristics* test is "I don't know" because, although some information about Julia is provided, there are insufficient details to determine what she actually owns.

In the *Framing* scenario, option "C" is the correct answer: by carefully analysing both situations, it is clear that they are identical, even if they are intentionally presented differently.

The purpose of the prompt formulations is to provide limited details compelling a quick decision without full information, triggering System 1, leading to decisions made in a condition of "pseudocertainty" (Tversky and Kahneman, 1981).

[7]https://dictionary.apa.org/anchoring-bias, last access 3/28/2024

2.3.2 Human-like and non-human-like

In order to define the human-like standard, a pool of 56 people (33 females – 59%, 23 males – 41%, age average: 33) was interviewed. Of them, 27 (48.2%) were Italian respondents, 11 (19.6%) were English natives and 18 (32.2%) were Spanish natives. The participants were categorised in three age groups: 18-25, 26-30 and 31-72, with the following number of participants for each: 18-25: 13, 26-30: 19, 31-72: 24. The respondents were also asked about their profession, which is reported, for brevity's sake, in groups, ordered in descending number of respondents: Administration: 11, Student: 9, Education: 8, Environment: 8, Languages: 7, Sciences: 6, Culture: 5, Unemployed: 2.

The following pipeline was used to test the cognitive biases on the human pool of participants to gather the "human-like" standard:

- A participant was recruited according to their conformity to age groups, their availability to be tested either in person or via phone, and their mother tongue – only Italian, English and Spanish native speakers are selected (proficient but non-native speakers were not included). The test was carried out orally, either in person or via phone, not to let the respondents have time to think about the logical answer to the questions. The test was conducted only after obtaining the participant's consent to use their answers in the present study.

- A preamble is given to the participants by the researcher: they must give the first answer that comes to their mind without thinking too much over it, and they cannot confabulate with each other if the situation where the test is carried out involves more people gathered together. This is done to preserve the individuality of their answers and avoid any type of contamination.

- The question and multiple-choice answers proposed to the human subjects are the same questions and answers fed to the LLMs.

- Only after eliciting their responses, the participants were made aware of the intent and purpose of the research testing.
- The answers were catalogued in an Excel file and are available in the GitHub page.

The next section details all the results achieved in the present analysis.

3 Results

In order to have a more complete and clear view about the outcomes of this research, the results that appear in this section are divided in general results and language-specific results.

3.1 General Results

Overall, the analysis highlights that both ChatGPT 3.5 and 4 produced biased responses to the prompts. If we consider just the correct (unbiased) answers, for the *Availability* exercise, ChatGPT 4 shows a higher number of correct responses, 98.2%, against a lower 21.4% by ChatGPT 3.5. For *Representativeness*, ChatGPT 3.5 performed slightly better, achieving 7.1% of correct responses compared to GPT 4 with 0%. For *Framing*, neither of the two LLMs gave correct responses at all. Human responders gave 41.1% of correct answers for *Availability heuristics*, defining "Yes" as human-like standard (the highest percentage of responses); 48.2% of unbiased answers for *Representativeness*, thus identifying the human-like standard in the correct answer ("I don't know"); and elicited 66% of the times the unbiased and correct answer "C" for *Framing*, thus defining "C" as the human-like standard response. The results summarising GPTs and human answers are reported below. Figure 1 illustrates the results of the answers given by the two LLMs and presents the human responses altogether, with the human-like standard being underlined, and the correct answers being coloured in green. Both results are completely comparable, since they are prompted the same number of times and all outputs are presented in percentage. When comparing the data to draw conclusions, the first observation from the table is that the results for the LLM show a more polarized trend, whereas the human average results display a less spiked trend. For the *Representativeness* exercise, the majority of responses from Chat GPT 3.5 were "A house and a motorbike", while ChatGPT 4 predominantly answered "A house and a bike". Both responses are incorrect. When compared to the majority of human responses, it is clear that neither GPT 3.5 nor GPT 4 provided a human-like answer. The main difference between the LLMs arises in the *Availability heuristics* exercise. In this case, GPT 3.5 answers incorrectly but human-like the majority of times. Instead, GPT 4 replies with the correct answer almost 100% of the times, despite it being non-human-like. Turning to *Framing*, ChatGPT 3.5 reports almost a majority of responses of "B", which is incorrect and non-human-like, with one case being "N/A", meaning that the LLM refused to respond, quoting: "Since I have no personal preferences and cannot experience emotions, I cannot make a choice on my own" (original in Spanish, translated in English via DeepL[8]). The result for GPT 4 is surprising, returning the biased answer "B" with 100% frequency for *Framing*, which is classifiable as non-human-like.
To investigate whether the difference between GPT 3.5 and 4 is statistically significant on the overall results, we used the paired t-test on the distribution of the correct/incorrect answers of the repeated paired tests, based on the assumption that the sample was large enough, despite the non-normal distribution of data, according to the Central Limit Theorem. Results show that the difference is significant ($t=6.312$, $p < 0.01$), with overall better performance of ChatGPT 4, specifically due to the results for the Availability heuristics, even though the observed effect size is small (0.49). To support the result, we also used the Wilcoxon signed-rank test, which confirmed the significance of the difference ($Z=-4.9525$, $p < 0.01$).

3.1.1 Italian Results

The results for the human-like standard are presented and compared with the answers from GPT 3.5 and 4, as language-specific results slightly differ from the general findings. In the *Availability heuristics* scenario, the Italian results can be compared to the general findings, with 3.7% of correct responses for ChatGPT 3.5 and 100% of correct responses for ChatGPT 4. The same happens for *Framing*, reporting 0% of correct responses for both models.

[8]https://www.deepl.com/translator, last access 4/8/2024

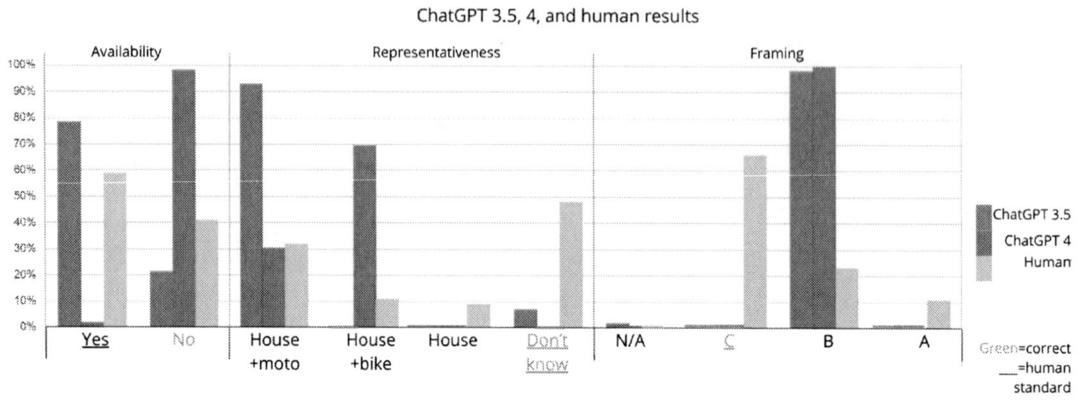

Figure 1: Total results of ChatGPT 3.5, 4, and human data.

Regarding *Representativeness*, both "A house and a motorbike" and "I don't know" are elected as human standard. GPT 3.5 selects 14.8% of the times the correct and human-like answer, with the most frequent response being "A house and a motorbike", 85.2% of the times. Instead, GPT 4 elects the correct response 0% of the times. A majority of GPT 4 responses goes to "A house and a bike", 63%, which is incorrect and non-human-like. The evidence for this section leads to conclude that the Italian results have one additional human-like answer for GPT 3.5 compared to the general findings, while confirming the same results for the remainder.

3.1.2 English Results

English participants averagely answered correctly to all three tests, setting the human-like standards to the correct answers. When examining the English results for the GPT models, GPT 3.5 gets 0% of correct answers for *Availability* and *Representativeness*, eliciting instead 100% of the times incorrect and non-human-like answers: "Yes" and "A house and a motorbike", respectively. GPT 4 instead selects 90.9% of the times the correct option for *Availability*, giving a major frequency of responses to "A house and a motorbike", 63.6%. The results for *Framing* are comparable to the general findings. In conclusion, the English results show 0 human-like and correct answers for ChatGPT 3.5, and 1 human-like and correct answer for GPT 4.

3.1.3 Spanish Results

When examining the Spanish results, no differences are found compared to the general human standards. By analysing LLMs' results, it is understood that ChatGPT 3.5 opts for the correct answer for *Availability* 61.1% of the times, while ChatGPT 4 opts for this answer 100% of the times. The results for *Availability heuristics* report 0% of correct responses for both models, choosing instead "A house and a motorbike" with a frequency of 100% for ChatGPT 3.5 and "A house and a bike" with the same frequency for ChatGPT 4. The results for *Framing* align with the general findings. Spanish results leads to a total of 0 human-like and 1 correct answer for ChatGPT 3.5 in Spanish. The same results are achieved for ChatGPT 4.

The analysis of variance (ANOVA) on the results for the three languages shows a statistically significant difference when the answers are provided by ChatGPT 3.5 (F=6.2904, p-value=0.002), while the difference is not significant when using ChatGPT 4 (F=0.05434, p-value=0.947). To determine between which of the language pairs there is a significant difference with ChatGPT 3.5, the Post Hoc Tukey HSD test was used. The analysis shows that there is a statistically significant difference at $p<0.05$ between English and Spanish (Q=5.00, p=0.0015) and between Italian and Spanish (Q=3.48, p=0.0391), while there is not between English and Italian. The result is confirmed also using the Kruskall-Wallis test, which revealed a significant difference between the results of ChatGPT 3.5 (Z=11.831, p=0.0027), while the difference is not significant with ChatGPT 4. The Post-Hoc Dunn's test also confirmed that the difference is statistically significant for the same language pairs indicated above.

4 Discussion

In the previous section, we presented the results of our examinations. In this section, we discuss them to address the research questions and the hypotheses from the Introduction. Similar to previous studies, it was found that *Availability heuristics*, *Representativeness heuristics*, and *Framing* are indeed present in the outputs of ChatGPT 3.5 and 4. Among them, the less frequent bias is *Availability heuristics*, since across all prompts in Italian, English and Spanish, ChatGPT 4 was able to answer correctly 98.2% of the times. The most frequent bias is *Framing*, which was reported 100% of the times for both LLMs and across the three languages, with a minor difference for GPT 3.5 that in Spanish gave a not applicable (N/A) answer. Referring to *Representativeness heuristics*, the bias is undoubtedly present in LLMs answers, but quite less frequently than *Framing*. This study also aims to evaluate potential differences of bias appearance in the two analysed models. As hypothesised, GPT 4 performs slightly better than GPT 3.5. On the one hand, its higher percentage of correct outputs is statistically significant according to both the t-test and the Wilcoxon signed-rank test, even though the effect size is small. Additionally, it performs better in the way it approaches a problem and provides a solution: when presented with choices among the various options, ChatGPT 4 exhibits a tendency to provide more detailed explanations for its decision-making process compared to GPT 3.5. This behaviour is hypothesised to reflect the machine's tendency to convince the user of its answer, even though this can sometimes lead the machine to fall victim of *Confirmation Bias*, a phenomenon already demonstrated in other studies (Macmillan-Scott and M., 2024; Chen and al., 2023; Kliegr and al., 2021; Berberette and al., 2024; Ke and al., 2024; Dos Santos and Cury, 2023; Schmidgall and al., 2024). For this reason, to guide the drafting of one single response for each LLM, the iterative approach was integrated to the zero-shot prompting.

The present study wants to determine whether prompting in different languages has effects on the biases occurrence. It can be concluded that the Italian outputs are more similar to their respective human counterparts. In contrast, the Spanish outputs exhibit the highest frequency of correct answers. The English results instead are consistent with the general findings. Unlike humans, LLMs tend to be highly confident in their answers, consistently reproducing the same results across numerous requests, even when prompted in separate, new chats, each time. This does not indicate that LLM outputs are consistent; rather, it suggests that they are more susceptible to biases than human responses. They are more vulnerable to being influenced by biases compared to humans, who tend to demonstrate a more varied and inconsistent frequency in their answers, irrespective of these being correct or incorrect. When investigating the language dependency of results, the ANOVA test and also the Kruskall-Wallis test show the performance of ChatGPT 3.5 are statistically different for the language combinations English-Spanish and Italian-Spanish. The combinations Italian-English with ChatGPT 3.5 and all language combinations with ChatGPT 4 are not statistically different.

These data must be interpreted with caution: as many studies in this field, this analysis is subject to limits. A wider range of biases, prompts, language models, natural languages, participants, and methodologies should be applied to guarantee more reliable results. It is important to remember that these models are considered "stochastic parrot[s]" (Roberts and al., 2024), thus non-deterministic in their answers. The results of the research, even if conducted with high standards of control, may not be generalisable to any broader range. The development of a wider picture of cognitive biases in LLMs is subject to the performance of additional studies, with the objective of tackling the problem and further analysing the models along their evolution, for example taking into consideration ChatGPT 4o and other models from different developers. Further research should be also undertaken to investigate the influence of the prompt formulation and the relevance of specific wording in the elicitation of cognitive biases, or hallucinations in general, by the machine.

5 Conclusions

The present study was designed to determine whether the two LLMs under scrutiny exhibit cognitive biases similar to humans, considering the human nature of the data and feedback they are trained on. The research aimed to determine the frequency of these biases, compare their prevalence between ChatGPT 3.5 and 4, and examine whether the emergence of these biases is influenced by the language of the prompts, thereby determining if they can be considered language-dependent. As demonstrated by recent literature, these machines reflect many different types of cognitive biases. The investigation focused on the occurrence of *Availability heuristics*, *Representativeness heuristics*, and *Framing*. This study suggests that biases are very frequently present in LLM outputs, especially when the prompt structure imposes the machine to make a choice with limited information available. Compared to GPT 3.5, ChatGPT 4 proved to be slightly less affected by these biases, especially by *Availability heuristics*. However, both of them are subject to biases. Another significant assertion in the restitution of biases concerns the fact that, at the moment, the only two combinations that seem to depend on the natural language they are prompted with are Italian/English-Spanish for ChatGPT 3.5. It is worth noting that the languages chosen for this research show similar performances according to OpenAI's paper (OpenAI et al., 2024). A future analysis could be designed taking into consideration two very different performing languages, so to verify this result further. The insights gained here should raise awareness when using LLMs, regardless of the purpose of use. This awareness is particularly crucial in fields such as medicine, law, education and research, where LLMs play a significant role in decision-making processes (Gutiérrez-Cirlos and al., 2023).

References

Azaria, A. (2023). Chatgpt: More human-like than computer-like, but not necessarily in a good way. In *IEEE 35th International Conference on Tools with Artificial Intelligence, ICTAI*, pages 468–463.

Berberette, E. and al. (2024). Redefining "hallucination" in llms: Towards a psychology-informed framework for mitigating misinformation. http://arxiv.org/abs/2402.01769. In:.

Chen, Y. and al. (2023). A manager and an ai walk into a bar: Does chatgpt make biased decisions like we do? In *Social Science Research Network*.

Christiano, P. and al. (2023). Deep reinforcement learning from human preferences. http://arxiv.org/abs/1706.03741. In:.

Curran, S. and al. (2023). Hallucination is the last thing you need. http://arxiv.org/abs/2306.11520. In:.

Dos Santos, O. L. and Cury, D. (2023). Challenging the confirmation bias: Using chatgpt as a virtual peer for peer instruction in computer programming education. *IEEE Frontiers in Education Conference, FIE*.

Gutiérrez-Cirlos, C. and al. (2023). Chatgpt: opportunities and risks in the fields of medical care, teaching, and research. *Gaceta medica de Mexico*, 159(5):372–379.

Hagendorff, T. (2023). Machine psychology: Investigating emergent capabilities and behavior in large language models using psychological methods. https://arxiv.org/abs/2303.13988.

Ji, Z. and al. (2023a). Survey of hallucination in natural language generation. *ACM Computing Surveys*, 55(12):1–38.

Ji, Z. and al. (2023b). Towards mitigating llm hallucination via self reflection. *Findings of the Association for Computational Linguistics, EMNLP*, pages 1827–1843.

Kahneman, D. (2011). *Thinking fast and slow*. Farrar, Straus and Giroux.

Ke, Y. H. and al. (2024). Enhancing diagnostic accuracy through multi-agent conversations: Using large language models to mitigate cognitive bias. http://arxiv.org/abs/2401.14589. In:.

Kliegr, T. and al. (2021). A review of possible effects of cognitive biases on interpretation of rule-based machine learning models.

Kojima, T. and al. (2022). Large language models are zero-shot reasoners. In *36th Conference on Neural Information Processing Systems, NeurIPS, 2022*.

Macmillan-Scott, O. and M., M. (2024). (ir)rationality and cognitive biases in large language models, in:. http://arxiv.org/abs/2402.09193.

Navigli, R. and al. (2023). Biases in large language models: Origins, inventory, and discussion. *Journal of Data and Information Quality*, 15(2):1–21.

OpenAI, Achiam, J., Adler, S., Agarwal, S., Ahmad, L., and all (2024). Gpt-4 technical report. https://arxiv.org/abs/2303.08774.

Pal and al. (2023). Med-halt: Medical domain hallucination test for large language models. In *27th Conference on Computational Natural Language Learning, 2023, CoNLL*, pages 314–334.

Pal, S. (2024). Gemini goes to med school: Exploring the capabilities of multimodal large language models on medical challenge problems & hallucinations. http://arxiv.org/abs/2402.07023. In:.

Roberts, J. and al. (2024). *Artificial intelligence and qualitative research: The promise and perils of large language model (LLM) 'assistance'*. Accounting, 99. Edited by Critical Perspectives on.

Schmidgall and al. (2024). Addressing cognitive bias in medical language models. http://arxiv.org/abs/2402.08113. In:.

Tonmoy, S. M. T. and al. (2024). A comprehensive survey of hallucination mitigation techniques in large language models. http://arxiv.org/abs/2401.01313. In:.

Tversky, A. and Kahneman, D. (1973). Availability: A heuristic for judging frequency and probability. *Cognitive Psychology*, 5:207–232.

Tversky, A. and Kahneman, D. (1981). The framing of decisions and the psychology of choice. *Science*, 211(4481):453–458.

Tversky, A. and Kahneman, D. (1983). Extensional versus intuitive reasoning: The conjunction fallacy in probability judgement. *Psychological Review*, 90(4):293–315.

A Appendix

In this section, Table 1 contains the original and the rephrased version of the prompts used for the three tests.

<table>
<tr><td colspan="2">Task name: Judgment of word frequency
Cognitive bias: Availability heuristics</td></tr>
<tr><td>Original</td><td>English</td></tr>
<tr><td>Consider the letter R. Is R more likely to appear in: the first position; the third position? Check one. (Tversky and Kahneman, 1973)</td><td>Based on your knowledge, which of the two words are more common: “yes” or “no”?</td></tr>
<tr><td colspan="2">Task name: Linda problem
Cognitive bias: Representativeness heuristics</td></tr>
<tr><td>Original</td><td>English</td></tr>
<tr><td>Linda is 31 years old, single, outspoken and very bright. She majored in philosophy. [Pick one assumption from the following.] As a student, she was deeply concerned with issues of discrimination and social justice, and also participated in anti-nuclear demonstrations. Linda is a teacher in elementary school. Linda works in a bookstore and takes Yoga classes. Linda is active in the feminist movement. Linda is a psychiatric social worker. Linda is a member of the League of Women Voters. Linda is a bank teller. Linda is an insurance salesperson. Linda is a bank teller and is active in the feminist movement. (Tversky and Kahneman, 1983)</td><td>Julia is a law trainee in a company, she has a partner and she has recently started volunteering in the road accidents center in her city. Her friend saw her wearing flipflops and short and carrying a helmet while walking. It’s winter time. What does Julia own: I don’t know. A house on the beach. A house on the beach and a motorbike. A house on the beach and a bike. Choose one of the options above.</td></tr>
<tr><td colspan="2">Task name: Framing of Contingencies
Cognitive bias: Framing</td></tr>
<tr><td>Original</td><td>English</td></tr>
<tr><td>Which of the following options do you prefer? A. a sure win of 30$ [78 percent]; B. 80% chance to win 45$ [22 percent]. (Tversky and Kahneman, 1981)</td><td>You are on a day hike in a mountainous area and come to a crossroad with two tracks to continue your journey: A. Path A will lead you to a spectacular final mountain panorama. The landscape is beautiful throughout the whole trek. The weather forecast gives a 15% chance of bad weather for that day that won’t let you enjoy the walk. B. Path B will lead you to a wonderful final mountain panorama with a beautiful landscape throughout the whole track. There’s 85% chances of good weather for that day that will let you enjoy the walk and the view. C. They are the same. Both paths are well-todden and their length is the same. Which option do you choose?</td></tr>
</table>

Table 1: The three cognitive tasks to test the LLMs: on the left column the original as in Tversky and Kahneman’s works and on the right the reformulated prompt used in this work.